Research Methods, Statistics, and Applications

Second Edition

Kathrynn A. Adams

Guilford College

Eva K. Lawrence

Guilford College

Los Angeles | London | New Delhi
Singapore | Washington DC | Melbourne

FOR INFORMATION:

SAGE Publications, Inc.
2455 Teller Road
Thousand Oaks, California 91320
E-mail: order@sagepub.com

SAGE Publications Ltd.
1 Oliver's Yard
55 City Road
London, EC1Y 1SP
United Kingdom

SAGE Publications India Pvt. Ltd.
B 1/I 1 Mohan Cooperative Industrial Area
Mathura Road, New Delhi 110 044
India

SAGE Publications Asia-Pacific Pte. Ltd.
3 Church Street
#10–04 Samsung Hub
Singapore 049483

Acquisitions Editor: Leah Fargotstein
Editorial Assistant: Elizabeth Wells
Marketing Manager: Shari Countryman
Production Editor: Veronica Hooper
Copy Editor: Ellen Howard
Typesetter: Hurix Digital
Proofreader: Dennis W. Webb
Indexer: Sheila Bodell
Cover Designer: Glenn Vogel

Printed in the United States of America.

Library of Congress Cataloging-in-Publication Data

Names: Adams, Kathrynn Ann, author. | Lawrence, Eva K., author.
Title: Research methods, statistics, and applications / Kathrynn A. Adams (Guilford College), Eva K. Lawrence (Guilford College).
Description: Second edition. | Thousand Oaks, California : Sage, [2019] | Includes bibliographical references and index.
Identifiers: LCCN 2017046336 | ISBN 9781506350455 (pbk. : alk. paper)
Subjects: LCSH: Research—Statistical methods. | Research—Methodology. | Statistics.
Classification: LCC Q180.55.S7 A33 2019 | DDC 001.4/22—dc23 LC record available at https://lccn.loc.gov/2017046336

This book is printed on acid-free paper.

SFI label applies to text stock

18 19 20 21 22 10 9 8 7 6 5 4 3 2 1

For my departmental colleagues/mentors:
Claire, Richie, and Jerry and my ever-supportive guys—K. A. A.

For my undergraduate research advisor, Grayson Holmbeck,
my graduate advisor, Al Farrell,
and my family—E. K. L.

Sara Miller McCune founded SAGE Publishing in 1965 to support the dissemination of usable knowledge and educate a global community. SAGE publishes more than 1000 journals and over 800 new books each year, spanning a wide range of subject areas. Our growing selection of library products includes archives, data, case studies and video. SAGE remains majority owned by our founder and after her lifetime will become owned by a charitable trust that secures the company's continued independence.

Los Angeles | London | New Delhi | Singapore | Washington DC | Melbourne

Research Methods, Statistics, and Applications

Second Edition

Detailed Contents

Brief Contents

CHAPTER 5 Describing Your Sample — **131**

CHAPTER 14 Focusing on the Individual Case Studies and Single *N* Designs

Companion Site

The SAGE edge companion site for Research Methods, Statistics, and Applications, Second Edition, is available at **edge.sagepub.com/adams2e.**

SAGE edge for Students provides a personalized approach to help students accomplish their coursework goals.

- Mobile-friendly **eFlashcards** strengthen understanding of key terms and concepts

- Mobile-friendly **self-quizzes** allow for independent practice and assessment

- **Multimedia content** includes video and audio links, plus relevant websites for practice and research

- Carefully-selected **SAGE journal articles** tie important research to chapter concepts

- **Datasets** to accompany material in the book are available for download

SAGE edge for Instructors supports teaching by making it easy to integrate quality content and create a rich learning environment.

- Chapter-specific **test banks** provide a diverse range of pre-written multiple-choice, true/false, and short answer/essay questions

- **Sample syllabi** provide suggested course models

- A robust **Instructor's Manual** contains a wealth of resources for each chapter, including **lesson plans, class activities, and homework assignments**

- Editable, chapter-specific **PowerPoint®** slides assist in lecture preparation.

- Author-selected **SAGE journal articles** accompanied by **discussion questions** tie important research to chapter concepts

- **Multimedia content** includes video and audio links, plus relevant websites for practice and research

- **Datasets** to accompany material in the book are available for download

- **Answers** to the end-of-chapter practice exercises help assess student progress

- **Tables and figures** from the book are available to download for use in your course

To students: Many features of this text are designed to support your learning. Rather than simply expecting you to remember what you learned in previous chapters, we provide a "Review of Key Concepts" at key points throughout the text. We also have a strong focus on ethics. We introduce you to some of the basic ethical issues in Chapter 1, and then follow up with "Ethics Tips" in subsequent chapters so that you can understand the need to think critically about ethics throughout the research process. Moreover, we integrate questions and practice opportunities at key points within the chapters to help you engage with and learn the material. And we provide answers to these practice questions in the appendix so that you can immediately check your level of understanding and skill and decide whether you need to revisit material. Finally, at the end of each chapter, you will find resources that allow you to further test how well you understand the material.

We hope you will find this textbook useful, and maybe even a little bit enjoyable. Our goal is to spark your interest in conducting research and increase your ability to critically analyze research.

NEW TO THIS EDITION

We used the first edition in our own research methods and analysis courses for several years and with great success. Our students appreciated the conversational tone of the writing, the practice opportunities, and the applications of key concepts. Other professors who adopted or reviewed the first edition commented positively about the writing style and organization, and the integration of current research. Many mentioned that they found the final "putting it all together" chapter to be a unique and important feature of the text. In writing this second edition, we aimed to build on and strengthen those aspects that students and professors found most useful.

The second edition includes new and more diverse examples from the current research literature. As with the first edition, we refer to research on academic honesty throughout the textbook and provide an APA-style research paper and published manuscript on this topic in the appendix. For this edition, we added recent examples from the research literature in criminal justice, politics, education, and counseling.

Each chapter of the second edition ends with "The Big Picture" to help students take a step back and consider the larger implications of what was covered in the chapter. In chapters that refer to statistical analyses, we included flow charts and tables in this section to guide students' decisions about choosing the most appropriate analysis. In this way, we pulled some of what was helpful in the final "putting it all together" chapter and provided it to students earlier and throughout the book.

The second edition has an updated and more user-friendly companion website. Students and professors can find videos, web resources, and practice datasets on the companion website, including three datasets from actual studies the authors conducted with students. Students will find flash cards and web quizzes to help them solidify their knowledge, and instructors will find resources including in-class activities, lecture slides, homework assignments, answers to end of chapter statistics exercises, and test banks. Visit edge.sagepub.com/adams2e

Preface

Together, we have over 45 years of experience teaching an integrated research methods and statistics course. We have used several different texts over the years, but none had quite the right approach to match our integrated class. Some were too focused on statistics, others too focused on methods. None had enough examples, applications, and review, and we found ourselves supplementing these texts with our own material. We finally decided that we should write a book that would consistently integrate methods and statistics, and include multiple examples and practical application. We also sought to use conversational language to make the material more interesting and to take some of the mystery and anxiety out of learning research methods and statistics.

This textbook is modeled after the Research Methods and Analysis course that we teach at Guilford College, which is designed to provide students with firsthand experience of being a researcher as well as the typical content related to the research process. Each semester, students in the class are actively involved in two lines of research—one that is chosen by the instructors and a topic of students' own choosing. We have found that having multiple opportunities for increasingly complex application improves learning, and the research in teaching and learning supports our experience. Although most students approach our course with trepidation, many end up telling us that the course was their most useful because the content dually prepares them for critical analysis of research as an employee or informed citizen as well as for more advanced research training in graduate programs.

We organized this book so that the first few chapters introduce students to basic issues of design, and we then elaborate on these designs in later chapters, detail the statistics used to analyze the designs, and raise ethical issues that might arise with different designs. The text is designed so that professors can cover topics in a different order than presented in the book. In our own research methods course, we have been able to easily skip over some topics and present topics in a different order than what is presented in the text. The chapters are written to support different content or sequencing choices by inserting a "Review of Key Concepts" segment or referring to an earlier chapter when understanding new concepts or statistics depends on material that is covered previously in the text.

We believe one of the greatest strengths of this text is the consistent integration of research methods and statistics so that students can better understand how the research process requires the combination of these elements. Throughout the text, we remind students of the decision making required to select appropriate designs, which then help to determine the most appropriate statistical analysis. These elements of research methods and statistics are set within the context of multiple examples of both proposed and real studies, which allow students to better understand the entire process. The last chapter helps pull together all that the students have learned by providing a summary of the major questions one should answer when designing and carrying out research.

PUBLISHER'S ACKNOWLEDGMENTS

SAGE wishes to acknowledge the valuable contributions of the following reviewers.

Anne-Marie Armstrong, Colorado Technical University
Eliane M. Boucher, Providence College
Malaika Brown, Citrus College
Derrick M. Bryan, Morehouse College
Isabelle Chang, Temple University
Wendie N. Choudary, University at Albany
Diane L. Cooper, University of Georgia
Erin M. Fekete, Ph.D., University of Indianapolis
John D. Foshay, Central Connecticut State University
Charles Fountaine, University of Minnesota Duluth
Paula M. Frew, Emory University
David Han, University of Texas at San Antonio
John M. Hazy, Youngstown State University
Erin Henshaw, Denison University
C. Ryan Kinlaw, Marist College
Karin Lindstrom Bremer, Minnesota State University, Mankato
Joshua C. Watson, Texas A&M University-Corpus Christi

We extend special thanks to Qingwen Dong of University of the Pacific for the skillful technical proofreading to ensure precision in the text.

NEW STUDENT STUDY GUIDE AND IBM® SPSS® WORKBOOK

The *Student Study Guide and IBM® SPSS® Workbook* is a new companion text for the second edition. Students can use the study guide as a self-guided tool to reinforce and apply concepts from the textbook, it can be used as an in-class or in-lab workbook, or professors may wish to assign exercises as homework. We pilot tested the study guide in our research methods and analysis course and students reported the exercises to be invaluable. We found students were much more prepared for class and asked better questions.

The study guide includes review questions that help students solidify and distinguish key terms as well as application exercises that encourage students to make meaningful connections and require critical thinking and active engagement with the material. Additionally, most chapters of the study guide include a "Your Research" exercise so that students can apply key terms and concepts to their own research projects.

Step-by-step directions for IBM® SPSS® data analysis and interpretation are included in relevant chapters. We also provide guidelines and examples for writing up results in APA style. Practice exercises are provided to help students gain competence using the program as well as interpreting and writing up results. We have used this IBM® SPSS® workbook in our research methods and analysis course for over 12 years, and students tell us that they cannot imagine getting through the course without it. Many students keep the workbook for use as a reference book in future classes and research projects.

ACKNOWLEDGMENTS

We would like to thank our students, who were the inspiration for this book. To all of our former, current, and future students, we appreciate what you have taught and will continue to teach us about how to better present concepts and skills associated with the research process.

We are particularly grateful to two students, Sandi Coon and Tabbie Smith, who read through our entire first draft and gave incredibly useful feedback. They helped remind us that students need examples and repetition when learning new material. Sandi also drew many of the cartoons in the book, and we are grateful for her creativity and artistic skill. Thanks also go to Virginia Ferguson, Phil Hong, Celeste Prose, and Nicole Carter for helping to format tables and graphs.

We were fortunate to have reviewers who took the time to provide thorough and constructive feedback for our first and second editions. We took their feedback seriously as we worked on our revisions, and the final version of the book is much improved because of the incorporation of their thoughtful suggestions.

Finally, we extend special thanks to the editorial staff at SAGE, especially Vicki Knight, the editor of the first edition of this book who helped us get this book off the ground, and Leah Fargotstein, our current editor who helped us make improvements for our second edition and encouraged us to add the *Student Study Guide and IBM® SPSS® Workbook*. It is obvious to us that this book would be little more than an idea without their encouragement, prompt response to our questions, and knowledgeable guidance throughout the process of writing the text and companion materials.

About the Authors

Kathrynn (Kathy) A. Adams earned her PhD in general experimental psychology from the University of Alabama in 1977. She was a Charles A. Dana Professor of Psychology at Guilford College when she retired in 2017 after 37 years of teaching. Her professional interests include gender issues, relationships, and teaching pedagogy. She worked with the Preparing Future Faculty Program for 20 years and helped establish the Early College at Guilford, a nationally ranked high school. In her spare time, she spends as much time as possible outdoors, practices yoga, and bakes chocolate desserts.

Eva K. Lawrence earned her PhD in clinical psychology from Virginia Commonwealth University in 2002. She is a Professor of Psychology at Guilford College, where she has taught since 2003. Her research interests include environmental psychology and computer-mediated communication. Eva enjoys walking, yoga, and bike riding, and she loves to listen to live music.

Thinking Like a Researcher

1

Imagine yourself lying on your back in the grass (or in a lawn chair, if you prefer). Stare up into the sky, let your mind wander, and let some of the myriad questions you have about the world come to you. Do not try to answer them, just focus on the kinds of questions that come to mind.

If you are like most students in the social and behavioral sciences, many of your questions are about culture, politics, education, values, or behavior. For example, you might wonder how people develop certain attitudes, why people or animals behave in certain ways, and what interventions might help change behaviors or attitudes. We expect that these questions came pretty easily to you because we have found that curiosity is a key characteristic of students who have opted to focus their studies on the social and behavioral sciences.

Through your studies, you have begun to develop a knowledge base in your discipline. Perhaps this knowledge inspired some of the questions you just generated, and with some additional thought you might be able to apply your knowledge to help answer some of those questions. Perhaps you know this already, but it is worth pointing out that almost all that knowledge you have gained through your coursework was generated through research.

Now you find yourself taking a Research Methods course within your discipline. Perhaps you signed up out of interest, or maybe the course was required or recommended. You may approach the course with excitement, trepidation, or indifference. Regardless of why you are taking the course or how you feel about it, we bet that this will be one of the most influential courses you ever take.

We would even wager that learning about research methods and statistics will change the way you think about the world. We hope you will continue to nurture your curiosity and occasionally stare up in the sky with a sense of wonder. What will change is that you will come to understand the process by

LEARNING OUTCOMES

In this chapter, you will learn

- The connection between thinking critically and thinking like a researcher

- How to think critically about research ethics, including understanding and applying the ethical principles and standards of your discipline

- How to take a scientific approach and apply the steps in the scientific process

- Basic research terms that we will expound on in later chapters

which we know what we know in the social and behavioral sciences, you will learn to generate more in-depth questions that build on this knowledge, and you will develop the tools to systematically investigate those questions you generate. In other words, you will learn to think like a researcher.

CRITICAL THINKING

Critical thinking is essential to all academic pursuits and is therefore an omnipresent term in higher education. We hesitate to use the term here for fear that you have already heard critical thinking defined so many times that the mere mention of it will cause your eyes to glaze over. Bear with us, because although critical thinking is at the heart of what it means to think like a researcher, it is often misunderstood even by those who tout its importance.

One problem is that critical thinking is often equated with criticism. Criticism can be one of the tools used in critical thinking, but simply being critical is not the same as thinking critically. Another problem is that critical thinking is often equated with critical-thinking skills. Critical-thinking skills are used when thinking critically, and are certainly important, but skills alone do not define critical thinking. Moreover, skills are something you have or gain, while critical thinking is something that you do.

Critical thinking is an action that requires dynamic engagement with information or ideas. It involves carefully analyzing that information based on current knowledge, as opposed to relying on personal opinion or beliefs. Additionally, both the knowledge used and the thinking process itself are carefully scrutinized in order to identify and avoid biases. Thinking critically in any academic pursuit and thinking like a researcher are parallel paths. Where they diverge is that researchers think by doing. That is, researchers think critically as they plan, carry out, and evaluate the results of research studies.

THINKING CRITICALLY ABOUT ETHICS

When researchers plan and carry out their research study, they must carefully consider the ethics of their study. Conducting an ethical research study is more than simply doing the right thing and avoiding doing the wrong thing. Although there are some clear dos and don'ts, ethical decisions are often not that simple. Researchers must consider ethics at every stage of the research process, and consequently we will introduce ethics in this chapter as well as discuss ethical issues throughout the book.

Ethics Codes

An ethics code both guides ethical decision making and delineates the ethical standards that must be followed. Current international and federal ethics codes for human research were created in response to some horrific research conducted in the name of science. Two of the most infamous are the Nazi medical experiments and the Tuskegee syphilis study.

During World War II, the Nazis tortured and murdered an estimated six million Jews along with millions of others who did not fit into the "Aryan race." After the war, a series of military tribunals, called the Nuremberg Trials, were held to try to bring justice to those responsible for carrying out these crimes against humanity. Among those prosecuted were physicians who had conducted medical studies on prisoners of Nazi concentration camps. The prisoners were forced into studies that included amputations, sterilization, and exposure to poison, disease, and hypothermia. In response to such atrocities, the Nuremberg Code was created in 1947 as the first ethical code of conduct for research (Grodin & Annas, 1996; Karigan, 2001). In 1964, the principles of this code were updated and clarified in the Declaration of Helsinki. This declaration has been updated and revised over time and currently serves as the international code of ethics for biomedical research (Karigan, 2001). It states that the rights of the individual must take precedence and that individuals must give their consent, preferably in written form, to participate in biomedical research (World Medical Association, 2008).

Another prime example of unethical research, conducted by the United States Public Health Service, began in 1932 and continued until 1972, even after the enactment of both the Nuremberg Code and Declaration of Helsinki. The Tuskegee syphilis study examined the long-term effects of syphilis without the consent of the patients suffering from the disease. In fact, the men who participated in the study were led to believe they were receiving free health care when instead the syphilis diagnosis and treatment were intentionally withheld. This study went on for 40 years, and stopped due only to public pressure resulting from a newspaper investigation that revealed the true nature of the study (Karigan, 2001). As a result, the Belmont Report was crafted as a guide for the ethical treatment of patients who participate in medical research in the United States. The Belmont Report serves as the basis for the current United States Federal Policy for the Protection of Human Subjects, also known as the "Common Rule" (U.S. Department of Health and Human Services, 2009).

The Nazi and Tuskegee research are extreme examples of what can happen when researchers do not think critically about ethics. Before you assume that all the ethical concerns relate to medical research, consider that some of the most influential social psychology experiments put participants under great emotional duress. Participants in Milgram's (1963) obedience study were told to administer increasingly strong shocks to another person, and were ordered to continue if they hesitated. In reality, the other person was part of the study and not shocked at all, but the participants believed they were inflicting pain on another person and consequently demonstrated great discomfort and emotional stress. Participants in Zimbardo's (1972) Stanford prison experiment were randomly assigned to play the role of guards or prisoners in a mock jail. Within a few days, some of the guards exhibited cruel behaviors toward the prisoners and some of the prisoners became docile or depressed. Zimbardo found himself transformed from an unbiased researcher into the role of prison supervisor. It took an outside observer to point out the cruelty of the experiment and convince Zimbardo to stop it (TED, 2008).

These social science studies contributed greatly to our understanding of social phenomena, but was the negative impact on participants worth it? What about studies that ask participants to disclose intimate details of their personal life, give participants false information, observe participants without their consent, or provide a placebo treatment to participants in need of help? And what about studies with animals?

Some of these questions are more relevant to some fields than to others. Because of these differences, researchers in the social and behavioral sciences follow the ethics code of their specific discipline's professional organization (see Table 1.1 for help finding the ethics code for your discipline). Some disciplines, such as political science, use the Federal Common Rule to guide their research (American Political Science Association, 2008). Psychology, sociology, and anthropology have their own ethics codes for research that are either stricter than the Common Rule or more specific to their discipline. For example, the American Psychological Association (APA; 2010a) and the American Anthropological Association (AAA; 2009) have codes of ethics that address animal research, but this type of research does not occur and thus is not addressed in the ethical guidelines for sociology or political science. The AAA guidelines for animal research are much less detailed than the APA's because anthropology researchers do not conduct medical, physiological, or neurobiological research with animals but psychology researchers might.

We summarize key ethical principles and standards for social and behavioral science research in this chapter, but it is worth your while to familiarize yourself with the full ethics code of your discipline. Not only do these codes address research ethics, but they also provide ethical guidelines for the full range of professional activities relevant to the discipline. You can find your discipline's ethics codes by searching on the national or international association website. The associations and web addresses for several social science disciplines appear in Table 1.1.

Ethical Principles

Ethical principles are moral values and ideals. Table 1.2 lists the ethical principles from several different codes of ethics, and you will notice the common principles espoused by the different organizations. These principles do not explain how to behave, but rather serve as guidelines in ethical decision making. For example, all the organizations listed

TABLE 1.1

Find Your Discipline's Ethics Code

Discipline	Association	Website
Anthropology	American Anthropological Association (AAA)	aaa.net
Criminal Justice	Academy of Criminal Justice Sciences (ACJS)	acjs.org
Education	American Educational Research Association (AERA)	aera.net
Political Science	American Political Science Association (APSA)	apsanet.org
Psychology	American Psychological Association (APA)	apa.org
Social Work	National Association of Social Work (NASW)	socialworkers.org
Sociology	American Sociological Association (ASA)	asanet.org

TABLE 1.2

Comparison of Ethical Principles

Federal Common Rule	Academy of Criminal Justice Sciences (ACJS)	American Psychological Association (APA)	American Sociological Association (ASA)
• Respect • Beneficence • Justice	• Beneficence and nonmaleficence • Respect • Honesty and openness • Competence	• Beneficence and nonmaleficence • Fidelity and responsibility • Integrity • Justice • Respect	• Competence • Integrity • Professional and scientific responsibility • Respect • Social responsibility

in Table 1.2 identify respect as a key ethical principle. From a research perspective, this means that the researcher should respect the dignity, individual rights, and worth of participants by safeguarding their privacy, treating participants and their data with care, and honoring their autonomy.

Beneficence is an ethical principle of the Federal Common rule, the Academy of Criminal Justice Sciences (ACJS), and the American Psychological Association (APA). Beneficence is promoting the well-being of society or individuals, and ACJS and APA also include nonmaleficence, which is avoiding harm to others. Applied to research, this means that researchers must carefully weigh the potential benefits of the study with the potential risk to human participants or animal subjects. Research does not necessarily have to benefit the participants directly, but the question under study should have broader importance to humans or animals. Based on this principle, it is clearly not appropriate to study something just because you find it interesting or because the results may benefit you personally. Moreover, the potential benefits of a study should clearly outweigh the possible harm imposed on human participants or animal subjects. See Practice 1.1 to identify risks and benefits of a study, and consider ways to minimize risks.

Ethical Standards

Ethical standards are specific rules or obligations that promote the ethical principles. The ethical standards for research with human participants address informed consent, the appropriate use of deception and incentives, and confidentiality.

Informed Consent

If we are to treat people with respect, then we typically should not study them without their **informed consent**. There are a few situations when a researcher may dispense

Informed consent: An ethical standard by which potential participants are informed of the topic, procedures, risks, and benefits of participation prior to consenting to participate.

with informed consent, such as when the study involves observations in natural and public situations and the participants cannot later be identified. Once you start manipulating situations, interacting with participants, making audio or visual recordings of participants, or asking them to complete questionnaires, informed consent is almost always necessary.

Informed consent implies that potential participants have a clear understanding of what the study is about, who is conducting the research, what they are being asked to do, how long it will take, and benefits and risks of participation *before* becoming part of a study. If you plan to record the participant, the participant must agree to be recorded and understand how the video or audio recordings will be used. Participants should also know that they can decline or withdraw from the study at any time without negative repercussions.

What if you wanted to study participants who cannot legally give their consent to participate? If a study involves anyone under 18 or otherwise under the legal guardianship of someone else, the legal guardian must give consent for that person to participate. The participants should still be informed of the study and asked to participate, and can refuse even if their guardian gave permission. See Practice 1.1 to apply these concepts.

Informed consent may be given verbally, although it is wise to also obtain written consent. Researchers often craft an informed consent form that potential participants read prior to giving their consent with their signature. The form helps ensure that all participants receive the information necessary for them to make an informed choice to participate or not.

Practice 1.1

THINKING CRITICALLY ABOUT ETHICS

Consider the following research proposal:

Early initiation of sexual activity is a risk factor for teenage pregnancy and sexually transmitted disease, and is also highly correlated with drug use, delinquency, and school failure. This study seeks to understand the sexual experiences of middle school students. A letter will be sent home to the parents outlining the goals and procedures of the study. Parents who do not want their child to participate in the study can sign and return a form. Children of parents who do not return this form will be asked to complete an anonymous survey asking them to rate their frequency of specific sexual activities (kissing, petting, oral sex, sexual intercourse), the age at which they first engaged in each of these activities, and the approximate number of partners they have had for each activity.

1. What are the benefits of this study?

2. What are the potential risks to participation? How can the researcher minimize these risks?

3. What is wrong with the informed consent process? How would you change it?

See Appendix A to check your answers.

An informed consent form should include the following information:

1. The purpose of the research or topic of study

2. What participants will do and how long it will take

3. Possible benefits of participation, including any incentives provided by the researchers

4. Any potential risks to participation, including physical or emotional pain or discomfort as well as any risks to confidentiality

5. Steps that will be taken to safeguard the participants' confidentiality

6. The right to decline to participate and the right to withdraw from the study after it begins

7. Verification that declining or withdrawing will not negatively impact the participants and they will still receive any incentives promised by the researcher

8. The names and contact information of the researchers and supervisors

9. A place for the participant (and legal guardian of the participant, if applicable) to sign and date the form, thus giving their informed consent for participation

An example informed consent form appears in Figure 1.1. Note that this consent form is for a simple and anonymous questionnaire and involves compensating participants with extra credit. An informed consent form should be tailored to the individual study and may contain more or less of the detail provided in the example. In particular, if a study might cause any emotional or physical distress, or involves asking very personal questions that the participant might deem sensitive or intrusive (such as questions about illegal behavior or their sex lives), then more detail about the nature of the study and procedures should be provided so that the participants can make an informed decision about their participation.

What if you wanted to assess participants' natural responses to situations? In some cases, fully disclosing the purpose of a study may lead the participants to respond quite differently than if they did not know the purpose of the study. Likewise, in some cases explaining exactly what the participant will be asked to do may interfere with the research. Thus, researchers must determine how informed the consent must be in order for the study to both be ethical and yield meaningful results.

Deception

During the informed consent process, you do not need to disclose all the details of the study, such as what you expect to find or that some participants will be exposed to different conditions. Most researchers agree that withholding this type of information is not

FIGURE 1.1
Example Informed Consent Form

Informed Consent

The study in which I have been asked to participate is about my views about science education. If I choose to participate, I will be given a brief questionnaire that should take about 10 minutes to complete.

I understand that in order to participate in this study, I must be at least 18 years old.

I understand that I will receive a small number of extra credit points for participating in this study; but beyond that, it is unlikely that I will directly benefit from participation. However, the knowledge gained from the study will help us better understand people's attitudes toward science education.

There are no anticipated risks to participation. I understand that my responses are anonymous in that I will not put my name on the questionnaire. Any results will be reported in aggregate form so that my individual responses will not be identifiable. If I sign this consent form, it will be kept in a secure location that is separate from my completed questionnaire. However, my name will be reported to my professor if I wish to earn extra credit for participation.

I understand that I can withdraw from this study and I can refuse to answer any question in the questionnaire by simply leaving that item blank. If I choose to withdraw completely or not answer certain questions, I will not be penalized and I will still receive the extra credit.

If I have questions about the study or wish to find out the results of the study, I can contact Dr. X in the Department of Psychology at the University of Y: (xxx) xxx-xxxx.

I have read and understood this information, and I agree to participate in the study.

Name (Print) _____

Signature _____

Date _____

considered deception (Hertwig & Ortmann, 2008). But what if you intend to mislead or downright lie to your participants? These actions are clearly deceptive, and their use is a very controversial issue in research.

There are two primary arguments against the use of deception. First, deception may harm participants by embarrassing them, making them feel uncomfortable, or leading them to mistrust others (Baumrind, 1985; Fisher & Fryberg, 1994). Second, deception may harm the field by increasing suspicion of research and decreasing the integrity of the individual researcher and the entire research community (Baumrind, 1985; Kelman, 1967). Moreover, deception may invalidate research results even in studies that do not use deception. In a review of empirical research, Hertwig and Ortmann (2008) found evidence that participants who suspected that a study involved deception responded differently than participants who were not suspicious.

Others argue that deception should be allowed under certain circumstances. It may be essential in creating and studying a rare occurrence (e.g., emergencies) and eliciting genuine responses from participants (Hertwig & Ortmann, 2008). Additionally, some claim that deception has only a negligible effect on participants' well-being and the credibility of the field (e.g., Kimmel, 1998).

The acceptability of deception varies by discipline. The code of ethics for anthropologists states that "anthropologists should never deceive the people they are studying regarding the sponsorship, goals, methods, products, or expected impacts of their work" (AAA, 2009, p. 3). Likewise, researchers in experimental economics have essentially banned the use of deception. On the other hand, deception remains a relatively common practice in social psychology and marketing research (Hertwig & Ortmann, 2008). Even if your discipline allows for the use of deception, the pros and cons of using deception warrant serious consideration. If you decide to use deception, special care must be taken to minimize potential harm to the participants and to the integrity of the field. You may also want to check to see if some of your participants suspected the deception and consider if that suspicion impacted your results (Hertwig & Ortmann, 2008).

The ethics codes for political science (per the Common Rule, U.S. Department of Health and Human Services, 2009), educational research (AERA, 2011), psychology (APA, 2010a), and sociology (ASA, 1999) allow for the use of deception in some situations.

For example, the APA ethics code (2010a) specifies that deception is allowable under the following conditions:

1. The use of deception is necessary and justifiable given the potential benefits of the study.

2. The study is not expected to cause any physical pain or significant emotional distress.

3. The researchers debrief participants as soon as possible regarding the deception.

Debriefing

If the study involves any risk or deception, the researcher should include a **debriefing** in order to reduce or mitigate any longer-term effects on the participants. In most cases, debriefing occurs right after the participant completes the study. This is especially important when participation might result in physical or emotional distress because discussing the study immediately afterwards can help assess and reduce the distress, and the researchers can identify an appropriate follow-up plan for those who may need additional help.

In some situations, debriefing participants on the true nature of the study immediately after their participation may contaminate the study. In cases where the potential participants know each other, those who have completed the study and been debriefed could tell future participants about the deception. In these cases, it is acceptable to wait until all data are collected before debriefing participants (assuming that there was no physical risk and minimal emotional risk. If such risk exists, deception would not be ethical).

Debriefing: Clearing up any misconceptions that the participant might have and addressing any negative effects of the study.

Incentives for Participation

Researchers sometimes offer an incentive for participation in order to recruit participants. This may sound reasonable; after all, the participants are investing a certain amount of time and effort. The challenge is that an incentive can be coercive. For example, if someone offered you $1,000 to complete a 15-minute interview about your sex life, you might feel like you could not pass up that amount of money even if you felt uncomfortable being asked about your sex life.

Incentives can be particularly problematic if the study requires that participants meet certain criteria (e.g., nonsmoker, HIV positive). What if a participant lies about his or her medical history in order to qualify? Such incidents may invalidate the study results and worse, result in serious health complications for the participant (Ripley, 2006). Even though the participant is the deceptive one in these situations, the researcher still has an ethical responsibility because the participant was influenced by the monetary compensation.

At what point does an incentive become coercive? It depends both on who the target population is and the amount of time and effort involved in the study. Paying people a fair wage for their time seems like a reasonable action, although the potential for coercion will depend on the participants' economic and cultural contexts. Additionally, paying participants for their time might lead them to believe that they must complete the study in order to receive payment. Remember that the participants have the right to withdraw from the study at any time, and withdrawing does not mean forfeiture of any incentive promised to them. The incentive is provided to the participants for showing up for the study, not for completing the study.

There are no hard-and-fast rules for incentives, although there are a few helpful guidelines:

1. Researchers should carefully consider who their potential participants are and not offer incentives that they would have a difficult time refusing.

2. The incentive should not be contingent on the participant completing the study.

Confidentiality

Researchers should respect participants' dignity and right to privacy. As such, data and results from research should always be confidential. **Confidentiality** occurs when responses and results from an individual participant are private. Keep in mind that confidentiality does not imply anonymity. **Anonymity** occurs when it is impossible for anyone, including the researcher, to link a participant to his or her data. Anonymity is not feasible when a researcher is planning to test participants at several time points or match

Confidentiality: A participant's responses are kept private although the researcher may be able to link the participant with his or her responses.

Anonymity: No one other than the participant can link the participant to his or her responses.

participants' self-report with other information such as school or court records (with the appropriate consent, of course). Both confidentiality and anonymity require vigilance on the part of the researcher, and we will discuss specific strategies in later chapters.

THE SCIENTIFIC APPROACH

Ethics is one of many considerations when conducting a research study. A researcher must also consider how to design a study that yields meaningful results and decide on the most appropriate analyses given the research questions. Although ethics, research design, and statistical analyses have their unique issues and processes, all of these fit within the broader scientific approach.

The scientific approach is a specific type of critical thinking that involves approaching a topic with a genuine desire to understand it, identifying and minimizing biases that interfere with this understanding, avoiding overly simplistic explanations, and following a systematic method to study the topic.

That sounds easy enough, but taking the scientific approach actually requires a fair bit of risk and willingness to critically evaluate results regardless of our personal beliefs. Several questions arise when considering the scientific approach. Are we willing to subject our personal beliefs to science? Are we open-minded enough to pay attention to evidence that contradicts our belief systems? Can we truly be unbiased about a subject we feel passionately about? What might we lose by taking a scientific approach?

It is much easier to avoid the scientific approach and instead rely solely on personal beliefs and experiences. It does not take a lot of effort or thought to fall back on what an authority figure told you, or to base decisions on a significant event in your life, or to follow the advice of someone you trust. We might even say that these tendencies are our default. And let's face it; people can lead full and happy lives without ever challenging this default. See Figure 1.2 for a humorous perspective on this.

So why would anyone want to take a scientific approach? Not only does the scientific approach necessitate risk—it does not feel good to have our personal beliefs challenged or to be shown that our beliefs are inaccurate—but it also takes more effort: falling back on our defaults is quite easy. In his book *Predictably Irrational: The Hidden Forces That Shape Our Decisions*, Ariely (2009) argues that we often make irrational decisions based on these defaults. Moreover, in their book *New World, New Mind: Moving Toward Conscious Evolution*, Ornstein and Ehrlich (2000) suggest that our nonscientific default served an evolutionary purpose, but that in today's society this default way of thinking and making decisions is insufficient for dealing with modern problems. In fact, they argue that many modern problems are the direct results of relying on our defaults.

The Scientific Approach and Decision Making

One reason we might take a scientific approach is that it can help us make better decisions, both individually and as a society. The social sciences were actually formed to improve human welfare and influence social change. Although that connection has never been as seamless as originally envisioned (Scanzoni, 2005), there are many examples of

FIGURE 1.2

Not Your Scientific Approach

This cartoon depicts "easy street" where no one ever challenges your assumptions. On the other hand, the scientific approach requires us to pay attention to information that may contradict our expectations or beliefs, even though this is not the easy way.

Source: Eva K. Lawrence

how social science has improved public policy and individual decision making. Consider the following:

- The statement "I saw it with my own eyes" can be quite convincing. Yet research shows that such eyewitness testimony can be altered by even slight variations in questioning (Loftus 1975; 1992). In 1998, then U.S. Attorney General Janet Reno responded to this research and compiled a working group to suggest improvements to the criminal justice system. The resulting document was the first uniform set of instructions on how to collect accurate and unbiased eyewitness testimony (U.S. Department of Justice, 1999).

- Hearing conflicting eyewitness reports might lead us to discount those reports or question the honesty of the witnesses. During World War II, when German officers gave locations of where a ship went down that varied by hundreds of miles, the majority opinion was that the eyewitnesses were lying. However, research suggests that memory decay happens in a somewhat predictable way, and two cognitive psychologists applied this research to develop a statistical profile of the contrasting eyewitness accounts. In 2008, the ship was found within three nautical miles of the location pinpointed by the psychologists (Spiegel, 2011).

- Many people believe they can "multitask." In actuality, one might be able to switch tasks rapidly, but a person can pay attention only to one task at a time (Hamilton, 2008). Along these lines, research has consistently demonstrated the dangers of using a cell phone while driving (Caird, Johnston, Willness, Asbridge, & Steel, 2014; Caird, Willness, Steel, & Scialfa, 2008; Ferlazzo, DiNocera, & Sdoia, 2008). Almost every state in the United States has banned texting while driving, and those without an all-out ban have cell phone use restrictions for school bus drivers or new drivers (Governors Highway Safety Association, 2016).

- Although having lots of choices might seem advantageous, research suggests that choice might actually decrease motivation (Iyenger & Lepper, 2000) and deplete self-control (Vohs et al., 2014). During his presidency, President Obama applied this research by limiting minor choices, such as what to eat and what to wear, so that he could focus his energy on more important decisions (Lewis, 2012).

Note that in all of these examples, personal beliefs and majority opinion were misleading. Luckily, the scientific approach was used to overcome the default way of thinking and make better decisions.

The Scientific Approach and Knowledge

Being able to make an informed decision is a good argument for the scientific approach. However, the scientific approach does not always lead directly to a decision. Still, the scientific approach can be used to build our knowledge base, improve or refute theories, and develop new ideas.

Take academic honesty as an example. Academic honesty is of particular importance to anyone involved in education. If a student is discovered to have plagiarized, that student receives consequences that can severely impede his or her college career. It may not matter to the academic system if the student was intentionally dishonest or if the student did not understand the rules of plagiarism, in much the same way that a person who speeds will get a ticket even if she did not notice the posted speed limit sign.

A professor who discovers plagiarism may take a scientific approach in order to better understand the reasons behind academic dishonesty. That professor might dig a little deeper and try to discover knowledge and beliefs that students have about plagiarism, in what situations students are more or less likely to plagiarize, and what strategies are most effective in preventing plagiarism. In this example, the advantage of using the scientific approach is gaining knowledge. The end result for the student who plagiarized may be the same, and the policy itself will likely not change. However, the professor's knowledge of plagiarism has increased.

Scientific investigation that leads to increased knowledge, improved theories, or the development of new ideas might not have an immediate effect; but it may serve as a foundation for future research that has real-life applications. For example, earlier research on plagiarism has suggested that plagiarism is more common than anyone would like to believe (Lim & See, 2001; Roig, 1997, 2001). Because of this initial research, other researchers wanted to find out more about why students might plagiarize and found that sometimes students plagiarize due to a lack of knowledge and skill as opposed to actively trying to be deceitful (Culwin, 2006; Landau, Druen, & Arcuri, 2002). Building on that research, there have been several studies examining educational interventions that are effective in improving students' knowledge and skills (Belter & du Pré, 2009; Estow, Lawrence, & Adams, 2011; Owens & White, 2013; Schuetze, 2004; see Figure 1.3).

FIGURE 1.3

Plagiarism: A Bad Idea!

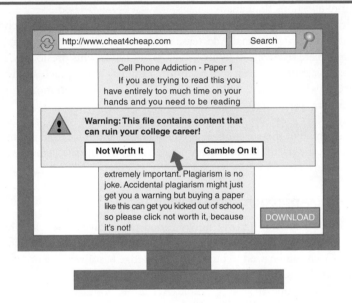

Students who plagiarize—intentionally or unintentionally—risk severe consequences that could damage their college career. Does knowing this make students less likely to plagiarize? What interventions might help improve students' knowledge and skills? Asking questions such as these is the first step in a scientific approach to the topic of plagiarism.

Source: Sandi Coon

The Scientific Method: Defined and Refined

Taking a scientific approach can improve our decision making, and it can help us develop a deeper understanding of a topic. Students often enter the social and behavioral sciences because they are curious about what makes people act in certain ways, or they want to know how best to help others, or they are interested in how our brains work. These are all questions that lend themselves to the scientific approach. In order to investigate these questions scientifically, one must use the scientific method.

Science engenders a sense of certainty among most students. To many, science = hard facts. Some people do not even think of the social and behavioral science disciplines as sciences—or they refer to them as "soft sciences"—because there is so much uncertainty associated with these disciplines. However, science is not about facts. Science is about process. The processes of science are referred to as the scientific method—and *method* is what makes something a science. More specifically, science must include a transparent method that can be evaluated and replicated by others.

You probably remember first learning about the scientific method in your elementary school science courses. Every year young students across our country diligently memorize the steps to the scientific method. Again, the focus on these seemingly hard-and-fast rules of science engenders certainty. If you follow the steps to the scientific method, you get the answer or prove something, right? Well, not exactly. You will rule some things out (or disprove them), you will get some answers, but you will likely generate more questions than answers using the scientific method.

Moreover, the scientific method is not strictly linear, but rather is a cycle. If you complete one step, it may lead you to the next, or it may lead you to rethink an earlier step. And then when it looks like you are finished, the process takes you back to the beginning for you or another researcher to begin again.

To use a physical analogy, when we talk about steps of the scientific method we are not talking about steps in a staircase that we go up once, never backtracking or revisiting previous steps. Rather the steps are more like the ones we experience when we are using a stair-stepping machine such as those found in health clubs. Some of these machines have steps that cycle around and therefore we are constantly revisiting previous steps, just as we do in the scientific method. In the scientific method we might even skip a step and come back to it later (imagine skipping a step on an exercise machine). Keep this in mind as we outline the steps of the scientific method.

Also keep in mind that as we outline the scientific method, we introduce some key concepts that we will expound on in later chapters. We present them here so that you can form a big picture of research from start to finish, and so that you understand the concept within the larger context of the scientific method.

OVERVIEW OF THE RESEARCH PROCESS (A.K.A. THE SCIENTIFIC METHOD)

Step 1: Identify Your Topic

Your professor may simply assign a research topic, but when you have a chance to choose your own topic it is worthwhile to spend some time thinking carefully about a good topic.

What makes a good topic? First, you want to choose a topic that piques your interest. Perhaps you read something interesting for a class, or heard a news story about an unusual event or behavior, or have some personal observations that you want to test. Personal experiences and observations are a good starting point for selecting a topic, but be careful when you choose a topic that interests you. Interest here means something you are interested in finding out more about—not something that you already have an established belief or opinion about that you are not willing to examine in an unbiased manner.

Although finding an interesting topic is a good first step, you want to avoid a few pitfalls. As a student, you probably have limited time and resources. Do not choose a topic that requires participants who you will need special permission to recruit (e.g., children or individuals with psychological disorders) or one that requires equipment that you do not already have. If you are doing the research for a class project and the professor is requiring you to use a certain type of research design (such as an experiment—see step 4), then be sure your research topic is one that lends itself to that type of design.

You need to think ahead a little at this point to consider participants and design; however, you do not want to be too specific with your topic. Have some questions you are interested in examining, but wait until you read past research to develop specific hypotheses or design the specifics of your study.

Throughout this book, we will draw on research from various fields within the social sciences. We will focus on the topic of academic honesty to demonstrate how different research concepts and processes apply within a specific research area. We explain how we choose that research topic in Application 1.1.

Step 2: Find, Read, and Evaluate Past Research

Reading and evaluating past research is one of the most crucial steps in research. You should do it early in the process, but keep in mind that you will likely need to keep going back to the research literature while you design, conduct, and write up your study. In other words, this is not a step you can simply check off and move on. Remember we told

Application 1.1

STEP 1: IDENTIFY A RESEARCH TOPIC—FOCUS ON ACADEMIC HONESTY

As college professors, the authors of this book are keenly aware of and interested in the topic of academic honesty. One situation in particular piqued one of the author's interests in this topic, and helped to narrow the topic from academic honesty to plagiarism. A student copied several sentences from the textbook to answer a question on an assignment. The student did not put quotes around the words she took from the book, but did cite the source. The professor explained to the student that this was plagiarism and rather than reporting the incident to the academic dean asked the student to redo the assignment. The student was quite incensed and believed that her actions did not constitute plagiarism. She was so angry that she went to the dean, who politely told the student that what she had done was indeed an act of plagiarism and recorded this act as part of the student's disciplinary record. This student was so sure that she had not plagiarized that she ended up unintentionally turning herself in for an academic honesty violation.

Although the action clearly constituted plagiarism, the student did not plagiarize intentionally. This raises many questions: What do students believe plagiarism is? How do we raise students' awareness of what plagiarism is and help them avoid it? If a student commits plagiarism, how does that impact our perceptions of the student?

At this point we have a specific topic, but we are just playing around with different research questions. In order to further narrow our topic, we must move on to our second step—to find and read past research on the topic of plagiarism. See Application 1.2 (on p. 26) for more on how we developed a study on this topic.

you these steps were not linear, but rather are steps that you may need to revisit. Reading the research literature on your topic is something you should plan to do throughout the research process. We discuss this in more detail in Chapter 2.

Step 3: Further Refine Your Topic and Develop a Hypothesis or Research Question

The topic you started with might be very different from the one you decide on after you have read past research. Change is a good thing and suggests that you are truly involved in the process of science—process, after all, implies change.

When you have a good handle on what past research has found, you will want to develop a **testable hypothesis** that is based on this research. A common definition of a hypothesis is that it is an educated guess. For our purposes, this means that a hypothesis is a prediction based on past research. A testable hypothesis means that it can be disproven. A belief in true love, angels, or countless other things that cannot be disproven may be very worthwhile on a personal level, but such beliefs are not testable and thus not suitable research questions. On the other hand, we could test the idea that having a belief in true love improves the quality of intimate relationships.

Similarly, as much as we might like the idea that studying research methods will save the world, such a statement is not testable. The only way to disprove a statement such as this would be for the world to end. That is a horrible event on so many levels, and it would be impossible to assess exactly what could have prevented it. With modification, however, we can make this statement testable: Research methods instruction improves decision making. This is not nearly as exciting as our first statement about research methods saving the world, but it is much more focused and testable. Moreover, it meets our standards for a testable hypothesis because it is a prediction based on past research that demonstrates that decision making can be improved with instruction in critical thinking (Helsdingen, van den Bosch, van Gog, & van Merriënboer, 2010).

Testable hypothesis: An educated prediction that can be disproven.

Step 4: Choose a Research Design

You will want to design a study that tests your hypothesis, is feasible for you to carry out given your time and resource constraints, and is ethical. Keep in mind that there is no perfect study and you cannot examine all the factors that interest you in one study. One of the most basic decisions is the type of research design to use.

There are three basic types of research designs: descriptive, correlational, and experimental. A single study may have multiple hypotheses that are tested with one or more of these designs. The type of design depends largely on the goal of the research. Just like it sounds, descriptive research simply describes a sample or a population. Correlational and experimental research designs examine relationships among variables, with experimental research testing a causal relationship. There is also something called a quasi-experimental design in which some, but not all, of the requirements for an experiment are met. We will go into depth on each of these designs in later chapters, but we provide some basic information so that you can begin to familiarize yourself with these designs.

All designs will have variables you measure, manipulate, or control. A **variable** is something that varies in that it has at least two possible values. Gender is a variable because the categories can be male, female, or transgender. On the other hand, male is not a variable because the category does not vary. Similarly, the description of having research knowledge does not vary. To make it a variable, we would need to discuss it in terms of the degree of research methods knowledge, which might be defined as number of social and natural science courses completed, grade in a research methods course, or score on a research knowledge exam.

Descriptive research examines the who, what, when, where, and how, but does not examine relationships among the who, what, when, where, and how. Descriptive research can be exploratory in nature. It is often used to examine phenomena in more depth or to examine an area of research that is either new or needs updating. For example, a descriptive study could be used to better understand what types of science education, such as natural sciences, social sciences, research methods instruction, statistics, and so on, that people find most important. Such a study might examine opinions about how such education should be administered and funded. Moreover, views on science education may change over time and it could be useful to understand attitudinal trends. **Correlational research** examines the relationship between two or more variables but does not test causality. A correlational study tests the degree to which behaviors, events, and feelings co-occur with other behaviors, events, and feelings. For our science education topic, we might want to better understand factors that correlate with attitudes toward science education such as age, academic major, or political views. We might also want to know if science education predicts certain outcomes, such as the ability to distinguish between relevant and irrelevant information when making a decision.

We can use correlational research to predict scores, but we cannot use correlations to explain why the scores occurred. A correlational design cannot determine **causation**, in that it cannot show that one variable caused the effect on another variable. If a correlation exists between two variables, it is possible that one variable caused the change in the other but it is also possible that the relationship exists for other reasons. For example, in a study examining the relationship between research methods instruction and decision-making skills, it might be that taking a research methods class improves decision-making skills.

Variable: A factor in a research study that has two or more possible values.

Descriptive research: Research design in which the primary goal is to describe the variables, but not examine relationships among variables.

Correlational research (or correlational design): Research design in which the relationship among two or more variables is examined, but causality cannot be determined.

Causation: Relationship between cause and effect, in that one variable is shown to have caused the observed change in another variable.

Alternatively, it could be that those who already have good decision-making skills seek out a research methods course. Or perhaps there is a third variable that is impacting results, such as academic major or years of education, and there is actually no direct relationship between research instruction and decision-making skills.

Experimental research examines the relationship between two or more variables and, if properly conducted, can demonstrate causation. An experiment goes beyond prediction to an explanation of a relationship between two variables. At its most basic, an experiment consists of one **independent variable (IV)** and one **dependent variable (DV)**. An **experiment** tests the effect of the IV on the DV.

An experiment requires that:

a. The experimenter systematically manipulates the independent variable (IV).

b. The experimenter randomly assigns participants to receive different levels of the IV.

c. The experimenter measures the effect of the IV manipulation on the dependent variable (DV).

For example, following is a simple experiment to determine if research methods instruction (the independent variable or IV) increases decision-making skills (the dependent variable or DV). We randomly assign participants to one of two IV levels: taking a 1-hour research methods seminar or a 1-hour driver education seminar. To assess our DV, after the seminars we give all the participants scenarios with relevant and irrelevant information and assess their ability to make decisions based only on the relevant information.

In some cases, it is not feasible to conduct an experiment and a quasi-experimental design might be chosen instead. **Quasi-experimental research** includes manipulation of an IV but no random assignment to IV level. For example, we might compare decision-making skills between students in actual driver education and research methods courses. In this case, participants still experience the IV manipulation (research methods vs. driver education) but

---

Experimental research (or experimental design, or experiment): Research design that attempts to determine a causal relationship by manipulating one variable, randomly assigning participants or subjects to different levels of that manipulated variable, and measuring the effect of that manipulation on another variable.

Independent variable (IV): The variable that is manipulated in an experiment.

Dependent variable (DV): The variable that is measured in an experiment and is expected to vary or change based on the IV manipulation.

Quasi-experimental research (or quasi-experimental design, or quasi-experiment): Research design that includes a key characteristic of an experiment, namely, manipulation of a variable. However, it does not have all the requirements for an experiment in that there is no random assignment to the levels of the manipulated variable. Because there is no random assignment, a quasi-experiment cannot demonstrate causation.

they were not randomly assigned. Like a correlational study, a quasi-experiment cannot demonstrate causation. In our example, participants who are in a driver education course might already be very different from those who are in the research methods course, and we therefore cannot be sure that any observed differences in decision-making skills were caused by the research methods course.

Test your understanding of descriptive, correlational, and experimental research designs by completing Practice 1.2. By the way, we realize that you might be tempted to skip over these practice exercises in the chapters or ignore the application boxes. We think taking the extra time will be worth your while, however. We base this on research findings that active repetition of material through practice and application is associated with better learning and retention than simply reading and rereading a text (Fritz, 2011).

Practice 1.2

IDENTIFYING DIFFERENT TYPES OF RESEARCH DESIGNS

1. Why would an experiment not be appropriate to investigate the relationship between ethnicity and health? What would be an appropriate research design?

2. The president of a university wants to understand how the beauty of the campus influenced the incoming class of students' decision to enroll in the university. What would be the most appropriate research design?

3. Briefly outline a study to examine the impact of Facebook on mood. What would be the most appropriate research design?

See Appendix A to check your answers.

Step 5: Plan and Carry Out Your Study

Before you carry out your study, you will need to get approval to do so. Your professor is the first person who will need to OK your study, and he or she will want to make sure you have designed a sound study that conforms to the ethical principles and standards of your discipline. Broadly speaking, your study should not harm others and should maintain the dignity and respect of those involved in the study.

You will want to be sure that the benefits of your study outweigh any harm or inconvenience that your participants might experience. Even doing a quick survey can be harmful to participants if it evokes strong emotions or personal reactions. Moreover, unless you are conducting a naturalistic observation, your study will be intrusive (even if it is only a minor intrusion) and will likely require that the participants take time to help you (even if it is just a few minutes). That is why one of the first criteria that your professor will use in evaluating your study is that it has merit—meaning that the study makes sense, given past research. Asking people to participate in a study that is not based

Kittisak_Taramas

on past research and contributes nothing to our (or your) knowledge base is unethical because the benefits do not outweigh the potential harm that might be done.

In addition to having your professor OK your study, you will likely need to have your study approved by your college or university's **Institutional Review Board (IRB)**. The IRB reviews research conducted by both students and faculty to ensure that the study has merit and therefore the research is justified. The IRB also ensures that the study complies with the ethical standards of the federal Common Rule (introduced earlier in this chapter) or stricter standards set forth by the institution. Remember also that your discipline-specific code of ethics may be stricter or more specific than the Common Rule, and therefore your professor may have required that your study meet the ethical standards of both the IRB and your discipline. Careful planning about selecting and recruiting participants and how exactly you will carry out your study is necessary before you submit a proposal to your professor and the IRB. In some cases, you may want to conduct a pilot or preliminary test for your measures and procedures, and this would also require preapproval by your professor and the IRB.

There are many specific ethical standards to follow; and, as you engage in the approval process for your professor and IRB, it is easy to forget to think critically about why these ethical standards are important. Remember that these standards are not simply tasks to check off in order for you to get approval to complete your project. Instead, the ethical principles behind the standards should guide every step of your research process (see Figure 1.4).

> **Institutional Review Board (IRB):** An established group that evaluates research proposals to ensure that ethical standards are being followed in research that involves human participants.

Who Will You Ask to Participate in Your Study?

One of the key decisions in how you will carry out your study is to determine who your population of interest is. Is your study about males, females, or both? Are you interested only in college students, and if so, does it matter if they are traditional-aged students or not? Once you have determined who your population is, you will need to collect data from a sample of that population. Ideally, the sample should be representative of the population. We will discuss sampling procedures in detail in Chapter 4.

What Are the Procedures for Your Study, and What Materials Will You Use?

After you decide how you will get participants, you need to decide what your participants will actually do or what you will do with or to the participants. Your procedures should be consistent with the research design you chose and your hypothesis. You should consider the impact of your procedure and materials on the participants and avoid any procedures that unduly stress your participants. And, you will want your procedures and materials to be consistent with past research in the topic area.

FIGURE 1.4

Ethical Principles Should Guide the Entire Research Process

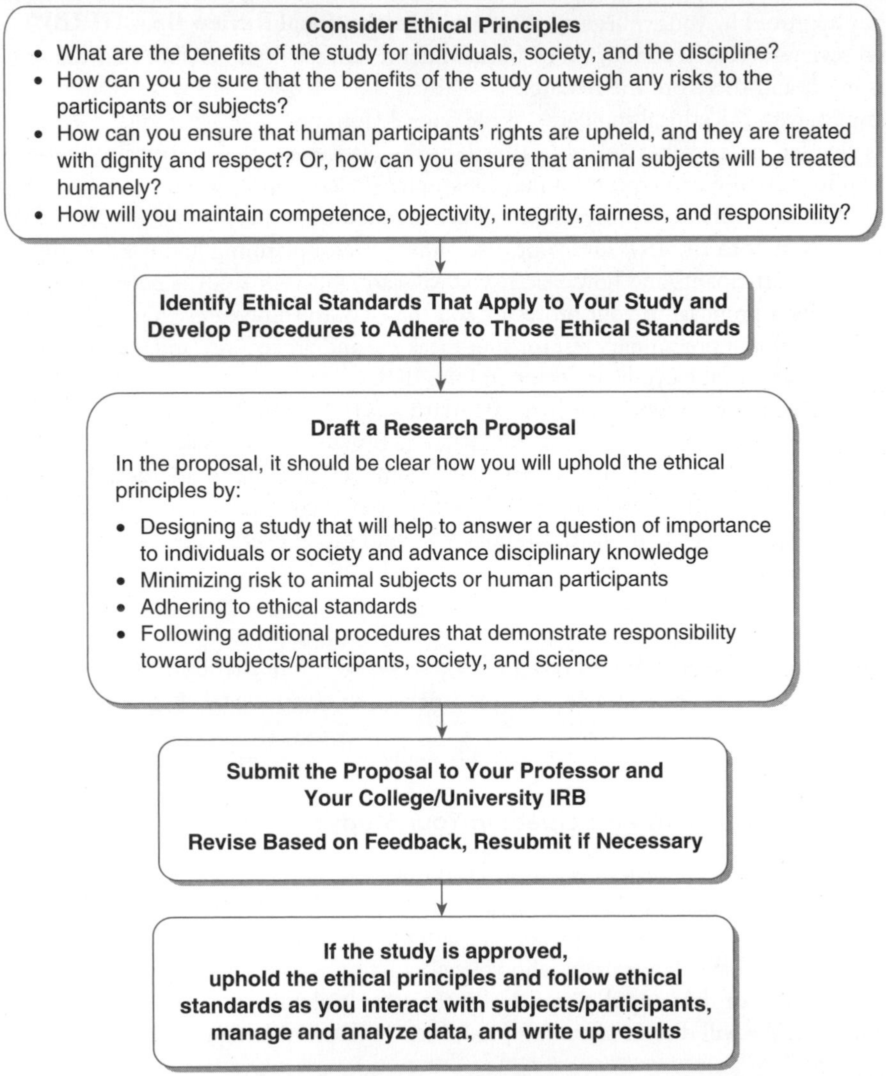

Consider Ethical Principles
- What are the benefits of the study for individuals, society, and the discipline?
- How can you be sure that the benefits of the study outweigh any risks to the participants or subjects?
- How can you ensure that human participants' rights are upheld, and they are treated with dignity and respect? Or, how can you ensure that animal subjects will be treated humanely?
- How will you maintain competence, objectivity, integrity, fairness, and responsibility?

Identify Ethical Standards That Apply to Your Study and Develop Procedures to Adhere to Those Ethical Standards

Draft a Research Proposal

In the proposal, it should be clear how you will uphold the ethical principles by:

- Designing a study that will help to answer a question of importance to individuals or society and advance disciplinary knowledge
- Minimizing risk to animal subjects or human participants
- Adhering to ethical standards
- Following additional procedures that demonstrate responsibility toward subjects/participants, society, and science

Submit the Proposal to Your Professor and Your College/University IRB

Revise Based on Feedback, Resubmit if Necessary

**If the study is approved,
uphold the ethical principles and follow ethical standards as you interact with subjects/participants, manage and analyze data, and write up results**

How you will measure your variables is a key consideration at this point in the planning process. Some of the most common ways to measure your variables are observations, interviews, and questionnaires. Other ways to measure your variables include physical tests such as those for heart rate, skin conductance, and temperature. There are also behavioral measures such as how much money a person spends, how long it takes to complete a task, turning off a light or not, and so on. Finally, you can measure your variables without ever interacting with a person or animal by examining records such as medical or school records, historical documents, or data collected by others.

A measure is a tool that can be used in all the different research designs. Unfortunately, students often assume that certain measures are associated only with certain designs. The most common mistake is that observations, interviews, and questionnaires are only used in descriptive research. Although these are measures commonly used in descriptive research (and we will discuss them in more detail in Chapter 4, which focuses on descriptive designs), these types of measures can be used in all the different research designs.

Step 6: Analyze Your Data

Throughout the course of this book you will learn about different types of analyses to help you test different types of hypotheses and research questions. By the end, you should develop a set of tools that will help you test your hypotheses or provide answers to your research question. Be aware that students sometimes confuse types of research design with types of statistical analyses. It does not help matters that researchers have used "descriptive" and "correlational" to describe both designs and statistics. But try to keep them separate. You may have heard the old adage "correlation does not mean causation," and that refers to correlational design. Causality is a function of research design, not the type of statistics you use to analyze the design.

Ideally, you should choose the best analysis based on your hypothesis or research question. Each analysis is like a tool, and you would not want to use a hammer when a screwdriver is more appropriate for the job. However, beginning researchers will have a limited number of tools, and you might find yourself needing to limit the types of hypotheses you develop in order to run analyses that you know how to do. Even by the end of the course, you will have learned about only a few (albeit key) analyses. It is appropriate for beginning researchers to modify their hypotheses and questions to those that they can actually test, given the tools they have. Just keep in mind that there is a whole world of analyses out there that can answer much more complex questions than you will be able to ask in this beginning Research Methods course.

Step 7: Communicate Results

Once you have carried out and analyzed your data, you will need to consider what the results mean, how they fit or do not fit with past research, what the limitations of your study are, and how a future study might build on yours to address some of these limitations.

Research should be a transparent process, and thus it is important that you make your results public so that others may learn from and build on your study. Remember that a key, ongoing step to the scientific method is reviewing past research. Thus, communicating your results feeds back into the process of science. For a student, this does not necessarily mean that you have to publish your results in a research journal. That is a possibility, but it is more likely you will share your results with your professor and your classmates, and perhaps present your study to other students within and outside your college or university.

Writing a research report is one of the basic ways to communicate your results to others, and we go into more detail on how to do that in Appendix B. When you write a report you have to put the study into context, and you will need to explain your study in your own words. The process of writing and revising the report will help you figure out how to effectively communicate your study and its results to others.

Writing in your own words is critical to your own learning and to others' understanding your work. After all, no one will be able to understand your study if you cannot explain it clearly and concisely yourself. Writing in your own words is also an important ethical issue. If someone plagiarizes the work of others, then they essentially steal someone's ideas and hurt the credibility of the entire field.

You may think you know what plagiarism is and how to avoid it, but plagiarism is more than just passing off someone's entire work as your own. Plagiarism also includes incorrect citation of others' work. You are expected to build on past research, which will require you to summarize and paraphrase the work of others. You should do so in your own words; and whenever you describe others' work, you need to cite the appropriate source. Test your understanding of plagiarism by completing Practice 1.3.

Practice 1.3

IDENTIFYING AND AVOIDING PLAGIARISM

The following was taken directly from Schuetze (2004):

"Increased student confidence in their ability to avoid plagiarism would hypothetically result in an inaccurate perception that they are fully knowledgeable about the complexities involved in proper citations in scientific papers" (p. 259).

Indicate if each of these statements would or would not be considered plagiarism:

a. Increased student confidence in their ability to avoid plagiarism might result in an inaccurate belief that they are fully knowledgeable about the complexities involved in proper citations (Schuetze, 2004).

b. Student confidence in their plagiarism avoidance skills might lead to false perceptions that they understand the intricacies of proper citations.

c. One danger of increasing students' confidence in avoiding plagiarism is that they may overestimate their ability to correctly cite sources (Schuetze, 2004).

d. Increased student confidence in their ability to avoid plagiarism might theoretically result in an incorrect belief that they are completely knowledgeable about the intricacies of proper citations in papers (Schuetze, 2004).

See Appendix A to check your answers.

THE BIG PICTURE: PROOF AND PROGRESS IN SCIENCE

You will sometimes hear people refer to a research study with a statement such as, "This research proves that . . ."; but "proof" is an inaccurate term to describe results of a research study. A single research study examined only a portion of the population and examined the topic in only one very specific way. There can never be complete certainty that the results will generalize to other participants or methods. Not only will a single study not prove something, but neither will an entire body of research. Proof means that there is 100% accuracy, whereas with research there is always some probability of error. It is impossible to study everyone in a population; and, even if that were possible, the measures and methods will never be perfectly accurate. The impossibility of proof will make more sense when you learn more about measurement and statistics in later chapters.

If research does not prove something, then how do we ever know anything in the social and behavioral sciences? How do these disciplines progress? When researchers at the graduate and postgraduate level (and even sometimes undergraduate level) complete a study, they typically submit a research report for publication in a scholarly journal or book, submit their work to present at a conference, or both. Other researchers in the field review and critique the work to help ensure that the study is important enough to be shared publicly and that the methods by which the study was conducted are sound. Once the work is made public, it becomes part of the larger body of knowledge in the field. Future research can then build on this knowledge, and those results will support, refute, or refine the findings of the original study.

Although we never prove something, when research findings consistently demonstrate a certain pattern, we feel confident that the pattern is likely one that will generalize to other samples and methods. For example, psychotherapy outcome research has consistently demonstrated that therapy is effective (e.g., Seligman, 1995; Shapiro & Shapiro, 1982; Smith & Glass, 1977). Research cannot prove that therapy has been or will be effective for everyone, but the body of research supporting the efficacy of therapy suggests that if someone is experiencing psychological distress, there is a good chance that therapy can help.

Once there is sufficient evidence that we feel confident of the validity of a pattern, researchers begin to ask deeper and more complex questions. For example, psychotherapy researchers have moved beyond the basic question of "Does therapy work?" to the more sophisticated questions of "What type of therapy works, for whom, under what conditions, and administered by what type of therapist?" These questions were first posed by Kiesler back in 1971, and therapy outcome research has been chipping away at these questions ever since.

You will get a better sense of how knowledge in a field progresses when you dive into a research topic and start finding and reading research on that topic. Some classic theories and research studies will be cited often, as well as more recent studies that have built on those theories and studies and have helped to refine our knowledge of the area. Current research will pose more in-depth questions, and the results of those studies will inspire additional questions, and the cycle will continue. See Application 1.2 for an example of the research process from start to finish.

Application 1.2

THE SCIENTIFIC METHOD: PLAGIARISM STUDY EXAMPLE

Step 1: Identify a Topic

As educators, we are interested in how we might help students understand and avoid plagiarism.

Step 2: Find, Read, and Evaluate Past Research

We found an article by Schuetze (2004) that demonstrated that a brief homework assignment can help reduce plagiarism.

Step 3: Refine Topic and Develop a Hypothesis

The study by Schuetze (2004) started us thinking about what we already do in our Research Methods and Analysis class. Early in the semester, we give a homework assignment to assess students' knowledge of plagiarism. We then discuss issues of plagiarism in class and also have those students who did not do well on the assignment meet with one of our teaching assistants.

We always choose a research topic for the semester, and students do several studies based on this topic throughout the semester. There is research evidence that such a themed-methods course allows for deeper understanding of material (Marek, Christopher, & Walker, 2004).

Based on this past research, we hypothesized that students who were in a plagiarism-themed research course would demonstrate better knowledge of plagiarism and would have better paraphrasing skills that would help them avoid plagiarism than students who were in a research course with a different theme.

Step 4: Design the Study

Ideally, we would do an experiment to show that the plagiarism-themed course caused improvements in students' knowledge and skills. However, this was not practical or ethical because we cannot randomly assign students to class. Instead, we did a quasi-experiment, which is a design that includes some—but not all—of the procedures for an experiment. We compared students from one semester when we chose plagiarism as our theme to students from another semester when we chose a different theme for the course. We manipulated the theme for the course, but did not randomly assign. Thus, we have some characteristics of an experiment but not all of them.

Step 5: Carry Out the Study

Our participants were students who signed up for the course. All the students received the plagiarism homework at the beginning of the semester, and soon afterwards all the students received instruction and one-on-one feedback as needed. Throughout the semester the students in the plagiarism-themed course did a variety of assignments on the topic of plagiarism, including an article analysis, descriptive study, and experiment. Students in the non-plagiarism-themed course did the same assignments but had gender stereotypes as their course theme. All the students did another plagiarism assignment at the end of the semester.

Step 6: Analyze the Data

We compared the first and second plagiarism homework assignments for those in the plagiarism-themed course with those in the non-plagiarism-themed course. We found that those who were in the plagiarism-themed course showed more improvement on the homework assignment than those in the non-plagiarism-themed course.

Step 7: Communicate Results

We wrote up a report based on our study and submitted it for publication to the journal *Teaching of Psychology*. Several reviewers and the editor of the journal gave us feedback, and we went through many revisions based on this feedback.

The article was accepted for publication and appeared in print in 2011. It is now part of the larger body of research on the topic of plagiarism. Other researchers can integrate the knowledge gained from the study, critique and improve on the method, and build on the findings in their own research studies.

Both an early version and the final publication version of this paper appear in Appendix B.

CHAPTER RESOURCES

Key Terms

Define the following terms using your own words. You can check your answers by reviewing the chapter or by comparing them with the definitions in the glossary—but try to define them on your own first.

Anonymity 10

Causation 18

Confidentiality 10

Correlational research (or correlational design) 18

Debriefing 9

Dependent variable (DV) 19

Descriptive research 18

Experimental research (or experimental design, or experiment) 19

Independent variable (IV) 19

Informed consent 5

Institutional Review Board (IRB) 21

Quasi-experimental research (or quasi-experimental design, or quasi-experiment) 19

Testable hypothesis 17

Variable 18

Do You Understand the Chapter?

Answer these questions on your own, and then review the chapter to check your answers.

1. What is critical thinking, and how does it apply to research?

2. What are ethical principles and ethical standards?

3. Why is informed consent important from an ethical perspective?

4. What are the arguments for and against deception?

5. What are the problems with using incentives, and how might researchers minimize these problems?

6. Why is confidentiality important from an ethical perspective? How is it different from anonymity?

7. What are the risks and benefits of the scientific approach?

8. How does the scientific method relate to the scientific approach?

9. What are factors to consider when choosing a research topic?

10. Why is reading and evaluating past research important in the scientific method?

11. What makes a hypothesis testable?

12. What are the three primary types of research design? What are the similarities and differences among the different designs?

13. What are the ethical issues to consider when choosing a research design, planning a study, and carrying out a study?

14. What is plagiarism?

15. Why is plagiarism an important issue in research and writing?

 **edge.sagepub.com/adams2e**

Sharpen your skills with SAGE edge!
SAGE edge for students provides you with tools to help you study. You'll find mobile-friendly eFlashcards and quizzes, as well as videos, web resources, datasets, and links to SAGE journal articles related to this chapter.

Build a Solid Foundation for Your Study Based on Past Research

2

If you have started to think like a researcher, then likely you will start to see opportunities for research studies everywhere you turn. For example, watching the nightly news might make you imagine a study comparing different types of news media. Or arguing with your significant other might inspire a study idea about communication styles. Or starting a research methods course might make you wonder about what factors impact student success. You may start developing hypotheses or even begin to design and think about how you will carry out your imagined studies.

We certainly do not want to squash your enthusiasm, but as you might recall from Chapter 1, if you went directly from topic to hypothesis development or study design you would be missing one of the most important parts of the research process—finding, reading, and evaluating past research on your topic. As interesting and unique as your ideas may be, it is almost impossible that someone else has not done research on them or a similar topic. Reading and evaluating past research will help you build a solid foundation for your study, and the study you end up designing after a thorough review of the research literature will be much stronger than one designed without this work.

In order to read and evaluate past research, you first need to find it. Time and time again we have students complain that they cannot find any research on their topic. One student even claimed that there had been no research conducted on test anxiety among college students, even though this is an extremely popular topic and there have been hundreds of published studies that have examined this topic in different ways. The student's failure to find relevant research does not mean that he or others who struggle with finding research on a topic are lazy or unintelligent or computer illiterate. On the contrary, the student from this example was intelligent, hard-working, and tech savvy. The problem was that he was using inappropriate

LEARNING OUTCOMES

In this chapter, you will learn

- The difference between a primary and secondary research source
- How to identify scholarly works
- How to find different types of scholarly works
- The parts of a primary research article
- Ways to build on past research to develop your research study
- The basics of APA format

strategies to search for information. The first step in developing an appropriate strategy is to understand the different types of sources available and to discern which ones are most useful. Then you need to find and read past research, and build on and cite that research as you design your own study.

TYPES OF SOURCES

Primary Versus Secondary Sources

Generally speaking, a primary source is the one closest to the original source of information, whereas a secondary source is at least one step removed from the original source of information. What constitutes the original source of information varies by discipline. In the humanities disciplines such as English and history, the information under study is a historical event or creative work. A primary source in these disciplines is a firsthand account of a historical event or an original creative manuscript.

On the other hand, the original source of information in the social and behavioral sciences is a research study. To a social or behavioral scientist, a **primary research source** is a report of a research study in which data were collected and analyzed, and a **secondary research source** is a review or discussion of previous research that does not include a report on an original research study. We will use these more specific social and behavioral scientist definitions of primary and secondary sources in this chapter.

> **Primary research source:** The authors report the results of an original research study that they conducted.
>
> **Secondary research source:** The authors review research but do not report results of an original study.

Scholarly Versus Popular Sources

A **scholarly work** can be a primary or secondary source and must meet all of the following criteria:

- The goal of the work is to advance knowledge and scientific study in the field.
- The author(s) have expertise in the field.
- The work is written for an audience with knowledge in the field, as opposed to the general public.
- The work builds on other sources that meet the above criteria for scholarly works, and these sources are clearly cited.

> **Scholarly works:** Works designed to advance knowledge in a field, written by someone with expertise in that field for others with knowledge of the field, that cite and build upon other scholarly sources.

Scholarly works can also be understood in contrast to popular works. **Popular works** are those that serve to educate or entertain a general audience that includes those without specialized training or expertise in the field. Examples of popular sources include *Wikipedia* and other websites, online blogs, educational pamphlets or fact sheets, some books including textbooks, and articles in newspapers or magazines—including *Psychology Today* and *Scientific American*. Popular works may be written by experts in the field or by journalists or others without specialized knowledge or training in an area. Popular works may refer to and cite scholarly sources, or the work might be the personal opinion of the author. Popular works may even be primary sources when the work includes results of surveys and opinion polls the authors conducted, but the results may be questionable if the goal of the work is to entertain or to support the opinion of the author.

Popular sources can provide basic information on a topic, offer support that a topic is relevant and timely, and give you some ideas for research topics and questions. However, when developing a research study, you will want to build primarily upon scholarly sources.

> **Popular works:** Works designed to entertain or educate and that were written for those who do not necessarily have any knowledge in the topic area.

TYPES OF SCHOLARLY WORKS

In this section, we will outline different types of scholarly work. Understanding these different types of sources will help you further discern the quality and usefulness of different sources. You will then have the opportunity to test your understanding of the distinction between scholarly and popular sources, and evaluate the quality of these different sources by completing Practice 2.1 (see p. 36).

Articles in Academic Journals

There are thousands of journals devoted to publishing scholarly work in the social and behavioral sciences. However, most articles that are submitted for publication in academic journals are not published. There are several reasons for this. First, each academic journal has its own focus or specialty area (e.g., *Cognitive Psychology, American Journal of Sociology, Journal of Teacher Education, Child Development, Law and Human Behavior, Journal of Computer-Mediated Communication*) and editors publish only articles that align with their journal's content and scope. Second, although you might access most of your articles online, the majority of academic journals are also available as bound print media and therefore have limited space. Finally, most journals employ a peer review process in order to ensure that they publish only articles that are of high quality and help to advance scholarship in the field.

Peer Review Process

Remember that scholarly works are written by those who have expertise in the topic area. The **peer review** process, then, involves evaluation of the work by other experts in the field. When a journal editor, who is a leading expert in the field, receives an article, he or she makes an initial decision on whether the article is an appropriate fit for the journal and of high enough quality to warrant further examination. If so, the editor sends the article to at least two other experts to review. These reviewers make recommendations to the editor to accept or reject the article, or as is more likely the case, to withhold the final decision until after the author of the article has made some recommended revisions and resubmitted the article. Almost all the articles that are eventually published have gone through several revisions based on the critique and advice of experts in the field.

> **Peer review:** Process in which scholarly works are evaluated by other experts in the field.

Why is any of this information relevant to you? One reason is it provides some insight into the process and progress of science that we discussed in Chapter 1. The importance of review and revision will also be relevant as you begin writing your own papers (and you might take some solace in the fact that it is not just students whose works are so vigorously critiqued). In more practical and immediate terms, understanding the journal review process can give you one way to evaluate the quality of an article. Generally speaking, articles published in academic journals represent the best work in the field. However, the presence and rigor of the peer review process varies depending on the journal.

As you become more familiar with the academic journals in your discipline, you will realize that some journals are more selective than others. Journals published by a discipline's professional organization (e.g., American Political Science Association [APSA], American Psychological Association [APA], American Sociological Association [ASA]) tend to be the most rigorous. For example, in 2009, 76% of the manuscripts submitted for publication to a journal published by the APA were rejected (APA, 2010b). Online-only journals tend to be less selective, and there are even some journals in which authors pay to have their work published. Information on the publication format and review process for specific journals is provided on the journal's website, and you will likely be able to find the journal's rejection or acceptance rate online as well.

Academic Journals Publish Both Primary and Secondary Sources

Academic journals publish only scholarly work, but you should not assume that an article in an academic journal is a primary source. On the contrary, journal articles can be either primary or secondary sources. In fact, several high-quality journals, such as *Psychological Bulletin,* only publish secondary research articles.

Primary Sources in Academic Journals. Recall that a primary source in the social sciences is a report of an original research study. When such a source is published in an academic journal, it is referred to as a **primary research article** (or empirical journal article). What is sometimes confusing to students is that a primary research article typically provides a summary of past research, just as secondary sources do. The difference is that a primary research article will also include details about the method and results of at least one study that was conducted by the article author(s). Some primary research articles report the method and results of multiple related studies.

Because primary research articles are firsthand accounts of a study that have been reviewed and accepted by experts in the field, they are the best sources of information on a topic. It is therefore important that you know how to identify which articles published in an academic journal are primary research articles. Some ways to determine this is to see if the authors used phrases such as "this study examined" or if they provide some detail about data collection such as how the participants were recruited or the total number of participants. If you cannot find this type of information, it is likely that the article is not a primary source. More information about reading a primary journal article appears later in this chapter.

The types of studies reported in an empirical article vary quite a bit. The design described in a primary research article may be descriptive, correlational, experimental, or a combination of these. The purpose of the study may be to test a theory or expand basic knowledge in an area, or it may be to evaluate the effectiveness of a program or technique, or the purpose may be to describe the development and evaluation of a measurement scale or assessment tool.

Primary research article (or empirical journal article): Report of the method and results of an original research study that is published in an academic journal.

Secondary Sources in Academic Journals. Recall that a secondary source in the social sciences is a review or discussion of previous research that does not include information about a new and original research study. The most common types of secondary sources found in academic journals are literature reviews and meta-analyses.

A **literature review** summarizes the findings of many primary research articles but does not report the method or results of an original study. A **meta-analysis** is a more statistically sophisticated version of a literature review in that a meta-analysis uses the statistical results and sample sizes of past studies to synthesize results. Like a literature review, it does not report the method or results of a new study and is therefore considered a secondary source. Both literature reviews and meta-analyses identify common findings in past research as well as inconsistencies or gaps. As such, reading a recently published literature review or meta-analysis is very useful in helping you understand what research has already been conducted and what research should be conducted in the future. Moreover, they provide an excellent resource to help you identify past research in a topic area.

Literature review: Review of past research without a report of original research.

Meta-analysis: A type of review in which the statistical results of past research are synthesized but no original data were collected or analyzed.

Although useful, the information provided in a review of past research should not be used in lieu of reading the original sources. Whereas a primary research article describes the method and results of a study in anywhere from one page to upwards of 20 pages, a review or meta-analysis will summarize the article in as little as one sentence. The authors of reviews and meta-analyses select only the information that is most relevant to their own article. Consequently, the summary will provide an incomplete, and in some cases even incorrect, picture of the actual study.

Once in a while you will run across a commentary in an academic journal. **Commentaries** are brief responses about a published article that usually involve a critique of a study or review. They can be very interesting to read if you have read the research article that is the topic of commentary. In this case, you might use the commentary as a source for your study or to generate research questions.

> **Commentaries:** Critique or comments about a published research article.

Other Types of Scholarly Work

Conference Papers or Posters

Professional conferences provide a forum for researchers to present their scholarly work (both primary and secondary) in the form of a paper or poster presentation. It can take a year or more for a research article to be published in an academic journal, whereas the works presented at conferences are recent or even in progress. Therefore, these types of scholarly work often represent cutting-edge research. Some professional organizations post the full papers and posters from their conferences online, and some researchers provide the work to conference attendees. More typically, only the titles and summaries are available and you would need to contact the authors directly to obtain the full work. Aside from being relatively hard to come by, the conference review process is not as rigorous as the review process for an academic journal. Consequently, these works should not be the main sources for your study.

Unpublished Manuscripts

Unpublished manuscripts include articles that have been accepted for publication in an academic journal but are not yet published (in press), are currently under review for publication, have not been submitted for publication, or were rejected from an academic journal. It used to be very difficult even to know that such articles existed, but nowadays such manuscripts are often available online. An article that is in press has gone through the review process and can be used and evaluated just as published articles. However, you should be cautious of using other unpublished manuscripts that you find online, paying special attention to the quality of the work.

Scholarly Books

Scholarly books are written by experts in the field and are typically published by professional organizations or universities. One important indicator of a scholarly book is that the content is based on past research that is clearly cited. You should also check to make sure the authors do not make sweeping generalizations based on research evidence and do not seem to use research only when it supports their personal opinion. A book can be a primary source if it also describes a new original research study or program of studies. The time lag from implementation to publication of studies within scholarly books is often lengthy, and you should be aware that more recent work on a topic can probably be found in journal articles.

FIGURE 2.1

Types of Sources

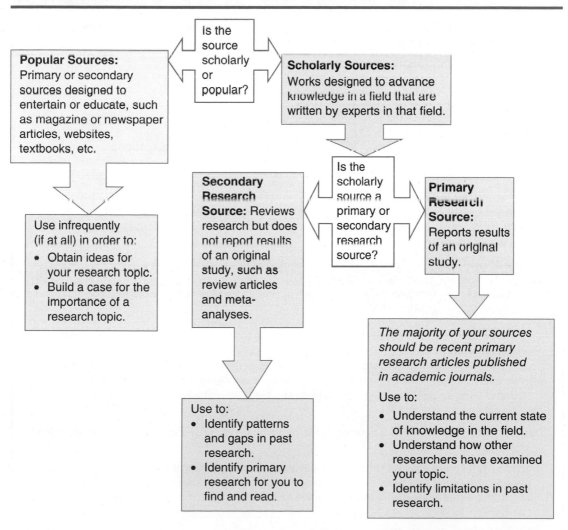

Theses and Dissertations

Theses and dissertations are part of the graduate school requirements for a master's degree and doctorate, respectively. Most often they are original research studies and thus primary sources, but some are reviews or meta-analyses. The full manuscripts are

Kittisak_Taramas

Practice 2.1

ARTICLE COMPARISON

Read excerpts from the following three articles about factors that might impact academic success. As you read each excerpt, consider these questions:

1. Is the article a primary or secondary research source?

2. Is the article a scholarly or popular source?

3. How might the article be useful in taking a scientific approach to the topic?

Article 1

Datu, J. A. D., Yuen, M., & Chen, G. (2016). Grit and determination: A review of literature with implications for theory and research. *Journal of Psychologists and Counsellors in Schools.* Online publication. doi:10.1017/jgc.2016.2

Excerpt: "This article examines the potential benefits of possessing the personality traits of determination and perseverance (often referred to as 'grit') in an academic setting. . . . This article provides a brief review of literature on this topic, reflecting perspectives from various socio-cultural milieus" (p. 1).

Article 2

Hill, P. L., Burrow, A. L., & Bronk, K. C. (2016). Persevering with positivity and purpose: An examination of purpose commitment and positive affect as predictors of grit. *Journal of Happiness Studies, 17,* 257–269. doi:10.1007/s10902-014-9593-5

Excerpt: "Grit, defined as passion and perseverance for one's goals, has been consistently demonstrated as an adaptive resource across multiple domains. Less explored, however, are the correlates of and sources from which grit is derived. The current studies examined two plausible candidates for promoting grit, positive affect and commitment to a purpose, using college student samples from Canada and the United States" (p. 257).

Article 3

Dahl, M. (2015, October 15). In defense of (sometimes) giving up. *New York Magazine.* Retrieved from: http://nymag.com

Excerpt: "[T]here are also times in life when giving up and changing course is the wisest option. These are moments, unfortunately, that grittier individuals may not be so great at spotting, argue researchers from the University of Southern California and Northwestern University" (p. 319).

See Appendix A to check your answers.

book length, and they are available only via interlibrary loan from the library of the university where the work was completed. Consequently, they require time to obtain and read. Although the review process for a thesis or dissertation is usually quite involved (as any graduate student will tell you), in general it is not as rigorous as the journal review process.

Undergraduate Research

There are forums available for undergraduate students to share their original research, including research conferences (e.g., National Conferences of Undergraduate Research [NCUR], Undergraduate Research Conference [URC]) and undergraduate research journals (e.g., *Journal of Undergraduate Research and Scholarly Excellence, URC Undergraduate Research Journal, The Undergraduate Research Journal of Psychology*). The review process for undergraduate research is much less rigorous than for other research, as it should be. Reading these works can give you some great ideas and inspiration, but be judicious in using them as sources for a research study.

Abstracts

Abstracts are one-paragraph summaries of scholarly works. They are not complete works, but rather part of a conference presentation or research article. We mention them here because abstracts are very easy to find online and are very brief. Consequently, students are often tempted to use them as sources. Beware that reading the abstract of a work is not sufficient! Rather, if you find an abstract that interests you, you will need to find and read the full text of the work in order to understand the research the abstract summarizes. Never cite a work when you have read only the abstract.

STRATEGIES TO IDENTIFY AND FIND PAST RESEARCH

Searching Library Databases by Topic

Searching online databases through your college or university library system is the most efficient and effective way to identify past research on a topic. These databases are catalogs of articles published in academic journals, chapters in scholarly books, dissertations, and other scholarly sources. Some databases also catalog some popular sources, such as newspaper articles, so be careful not to assume that all the work you identify through a database is scholarly.

A search of one of the library databases will yield a list of the titles of sources that meet the search criteria and other basic information such as the author(s), source (e.g., name of journal), and year published. By clicking on any of the titles in the list, you can view a more detailed record including a brief summary (the abstract) and a list of keywords associated with the source. Most databases also provide a link to the full text for at least some of the sources listed.

Identify the Appropriate Databases to Search

Choose one or more databases to search based on your discipline, your topic, and whether or not the database is available via your college or university library website.

Table 2.1 lists databases commonly used in the social and behavioral science fields. In psychology, for example, PsycINFO is the most comprehensive database and will help you identify research articles relevant to your topic. It covers psychology as well as related disciplines such as anthropology, education, and sociology. PsycARTICLES is a psychology-specific database that provides the full text of journals published by the American Psychological Association. PsycARTICLES can be useful when you need to narrow your search to only high-quality psychology articles that are available at a click of a button. However, PsycINFO is the preferred database because it covers those articles available in PsycARTICLES as well as many others.

Even if you are studying a particular discipline, you may find the databases for other areas quite useful. For example, a psychology student may end up doing a study related to sports, and therefore might want to use both PsycINFO and SPORTDiscus. Likewise, a student in sociology focusing on health issues might find using both SocINDEX and MEDLINE to be a good way to identify relevant research articles. There are also databases that span a wide range of disciplines, as shown in Table 2.1.

Conducting the Database Search

Keyword Searches. Identifying the appropriate keywords for your database search is a critical step. We recommend that you take some time to brainstorm some words and phrases associated with your topic, try them out, and then make adjustments as necessary to obtain lists of sources relevant to your topic.

Sometimes you will hit on some good keywords right away, other times you will get too few or too many results. Too few hits are obviously a problem, but you do not want too many hits either because it will be too tedious to look through them all in order to identify those that are relevant to your topic. Finding the right keywords is like finding the key that unlocks past research, and sometimes it simply takes trial and error (along with time and patience) to hit on the right words.

Following are some strategies to identify appropriate keywords and phrases:

1. It may sound obvious, but if a keyword yields zero results, check first to be sure you spelled the word correctly. Unlike Google or other online searches, the library database will not ask you if you meant to type something else nor will it automatically complete words or correct errors.

2. If available in the search engine, try the thesaurus function to get keyword ideas. You might also use a print or online thesaurus.

3. If your topic is discussed in one of your textbooks, see what terms they use and try them.

4. If you are able to identify a few relevant sources, check what keywords are listed for them.

5. Try broadening your terms if you are getting too few results. For example, instead of searching for the keywords "social science students' academic success," try just "academic success."

6. Try narrowing your terms if you are getting too many results that are not related to your topic. For example, instead of searching for the keyword "academic success," try "college academic success," "academic motivation," and "academic determination."

TABLE 2.1

Databases Used in the Social and Behavioral Sciences

Database	Field(s)	Is the Full Text Available for the Sources Listed in the Database?
Academic Search Premier	Multidiscipline	Some
AnthroSource	Anthropology	Some
Communication and Mass Media Complete	Communications	Some
Criminal Justice Periodical Index	Criminal Justice	Some
EconLit	Economics	Some
ERIC	Education Studies	Some
JSTOR	Multidiscipline	Some
MasterFILE Premier	Multidiscipline	Some
MEDLINE	Health and Medicine	Some
Project MUSE	Multidiscipline	All
PsycARTICLES	Psychology	All
PsycINFO	Psychology and related fields	Some
Social Sciences Citation Index	Social Sciences	None
Social Sciences Full Text	Social Sciences	All
SocINDEX	Sociology	Some
SPORTDiscus	Sports Studies	Some

Start Broad. When you are just beginning to search for articles on your topic, you will want to keep your search broad. Use keywords associated with your topic, but also search for research on related topics. For example, if you are interested in factors related to academic success for college students who major in the social sciences, do not start with such a specific search. Instead, you might find it helpful to identify research about factors related to academic success for younger students as well as those in other academic disciplines.

There are several reasons why you will want to keep your initial searches broad:

1. To identify the keywords that lead to the results that are most relevant and interesting to you. Once you identify these keywords you can use them as you narrow your search.

2. To give you a sense of the research done in your topic. You will not read all of the research you find during these initial, broad searches, but reading the titles and some of the abstracts will give you an idea of what types of studies are out there. You may also want to file away some studies that are not directly related to your topic but might help you build a broader context for your study.

3. To help you fine-tune your topic. Skimming over the titles and abstracts, you may find that there are other important variables related to your topic that you had not considered before. Or, you might find an interesting article that entices you to veer off in a direction different than you had initially planned. Or, you might realize that there are many studies similar to the way you initially conceptualized your study, and therefore you need to delve a bit deeper in order to create a unique study.

Narrowing Your Search. Next you will want to narrow your search to identify those articles that are most directly related to your revised topic that you will find and read now. For example, you could limit your search to articles that are English only (unless you are bilingual) and published in a peer-reviewed journal. You might also limit your search to only those articles published recently (e.g., within the past 10 years). This does not mean that you can use only new studies to create your study and write your paper. However, the foundation for your study should be recent research, with older studies providing a broader context for your study such as a historical or a theoretical perspective. You certainly do not want to base your study only on old articles, as demonstrated in Figure 2.2.

Other ways to narrow your search are to combine or add keywords. You might use "and" to combine the keywords that led to the most relevant results. You might also try finding a recent review or meta-analysis to provide you with an overview of your topic by using "review" or "meta-analysis" as keywords (e.g., "academic success and review" or "... and meta-analysis"). You might combine your topic keywords with other behaviors and traits associated with your topic (e.g., "academic success and motivation") or with keywords relating to the population you are most interested in examining (e.g., "academic success and social science majors"). If you know you will have to do an experiment on a topic, it is a good idea to read at least one article that describes an experiment, thus you can try using "experiment" as another keyword (e.g., "academic success and experiment"). Keep in mind that this does not mean that all the studies you use must be with

FIGURE 2.2

Focus on Recent Sources

Some older, classic studies may be useful to provide the theoretical or historical context for your research study. However, focus primarily on recent sources.

Source: Eva K. Lawrence

the same type of sample or the same type of study design, but it will be good to find at least a few examples to build on. In Application 2.1, we provide an example of a search on the topic of academic success for social science majors.

More Search Strategies

Use One Source to Find Others

If you have at least one research article related to your topic, you can use the reference section of the article to find additional sources. Many of the library databases will allow you to click on a link that will give you a list of the references. If that is not an option, obtain the full text of the article and manually browse the paper and reference section to identify sources relevant to your topic.

With just one research article, you can also find more recent articles that cited it. This is an especially good strategy because it will show you how others have used the article to build a case for your research. Some databases have a "times cited in this database" link that will take you to a list of all the articles within your chosen database that referenced the article. If that is not an option, you can go to the Social Sciences Citation Index to find articles that cite the work.

If you were to examine the reference sections of several articles on your topic, you might notice that some references are used in most of the articles. These are the influential works in the topic area that you will want to find and read. Paying attention to these works will help identify some classic research on the topic and the older articles (more than 10 years) that still have an impact today—and that you will want to read and cite for your study.

Application 2.1

DATABASE SEARCH FOR FACTORS IMPACTING ACADEMIC SUCCESS IN THE SOCIAL SCIENCES

Initial Searches

First we would list keywords associated with academic success.

Our initial keyword list: academic success, academic achievement, GPA, persistence in college, college success, college achievement

We would conduct databases searches using these keywords to see what types of results we obtain and make modifications if necessary.

For example: If we enter "academic achievement" as a keyword in PsycINFO, we would get over 86,000 results. That's way too many results to wade through, but we can skim through the first few pages of results to help us identify new keywords, such as "motivation" and "self-efficacy" that we might combine with other keywords about college student success and achievement. This very broad search also helps us discover that many of the studies focus on challenges faced by students of color, or those from lower socioeconomic backgrounds.

These initial, broad searches will help us identify the keyword searches that are most successful, identify new keywords, and consider factors we may not have thought of previously (such as the students' background). The results for these searches will likely overlap quite a bit in that we may see some of the same articles again and again.

Narrowing the Search

Once we have identified some of the best keywords and also focused our topic (i.e., how students' backgrounds might impact success), we will want to narrow our database search. First off, we will limit our search to only those articles we will actually be able to read (those in English). We will also limit our search to those published in a peer-reviewed journal during the last 10 years. Then we can use these limits as we further narrow our search by combining effective keywords (e.g., college achievement) with others specific to the students' backgrounds (e.g., social class). We can also conduct keyword searches with "social science" or "research methods course."

At this point we want to find a few of the most recent and relevant articles to read. As we develop our study and write our research paper, we will want to read some of those we found in our broader searches. We will likely need to make additional, more targeted searches when we advance in the process. For now, however, we have accomplished our goal of obtaining some basic ideas of the research literature and identifying those that we want to find and read right now.

Search by Author

As you begin finding relevant articles, you will notice certain authors will be cited in many articles and you may notice several articles on your topic by the same author. Researchers typically develop an area of specialization and author several articles on the same subject. If you find a few names that keep popping up, try doing a library search by the author's name. The author's affiliation, or the institution where he or she worked at the time the article was published, is usually provided by the library database. You could go to the institution's website and search for the author's name to see if he or she provides a list of recent publications. In some cases, it may even be appropriate to e-mail an author and ask for recent publications, and you may even obtain some manuscripts that are in press or under review. At early stages of the search process, contacting the author directly is not worthwhile to you, and may be needlessly burdensome for the author. However, it can be very useful as you fine-tune your study.

Search Relevant Journals

Just as you will notice the same references and authors appearing in your searches, you will find the journals that publish articles on your topic. If you are in the early stages of the research process, it may be worthwhile to do a database search by the journal and limit your search to the last few years. You can scan through the list of titles to see if there are any relevant articles. You might even visit a university library that carries the hard copies of the recent issues of the journal and physically flip through the last year or so of the journal. This is a great way to generate ideas for research at the early phases, and you often come upon articles that strike your interest that you might not have found otherwise.

What About Google Scholar and Other Internet Searches?

Google Scholar (www.scholar.google.com) is not the best tool to use if you are at the beginning stages of research because you will likely get a lot of irrelevant hits, or you may find a lot of unpublished, non-peer reviewed work. However, Google Scholar can be very useful in finding the full text of a specific article you have identified via your library database but that is not available to download through your library. As far as general Internet searches go, we would recommend avoiding them altogether. You are unlikely to find many scholarly sources doing a basic Web search, and you will likely waste a lot of time. Stick with your library databases as your go-to method of identifying relevant research on your topic.

Find the Full Text of a Source

Most databases will provide links to the full text for at least some of the sources they list (see Table 2.1), and the links available will depend on your college or university's library subscription. This is of course the easiest way to find the full text—you do a search in a database and click on the full-text link and poof, like magic, a PDF or HTML document will appear. It is so easy that it is tempting to only use those databases that always provide the full text (such as PsycARTICLES or ProjectMUSE) or to set limits in other databases so that the only results you receive are those that have full-text links. Not surprisingly, these limits will affect your findings, and you may even end up like those students we mentioned at the beginning of the chapter who claimed that there is no research on their topic. For example, at the time of writing this chapter a search in PsycINFO using the search terms "college achievement and social class" yielded 51 results, and 12 of these results were available in full text (which may be higher or lower had the search been made through a different college or university library system). A similar search in PsycARTICLES, however, yielded only 2 results.

What do you do if an article is not available with a click of a button doing a database search? You could try finding the article online by doing a search in Google Scholar or by going to the author's website if he or she has one. If neither applies, you might see if a nearby college or university has the article available and make the trek there. Interlibrary loan is another option, although it can take anywhere from a few days to a few weeks to obtain an article through interlibrary loan. Check with your college or university library about their interlibrary loan policy. If the article is an essential one and you have exhausted all the other means of obtaining the full text, you could contact the author directly to request the article.

READING AND EVALUATING PRIMARY RESEARCH ARTICLES

Format of Unpublished Manuscripts Versus Published Research Articles

Unpublished manuscripts, including student papers, look much different from the articles published in academic journals. When you write your own research papers, your professors will ask you to adhere to a specific style such as APA. Although established by the American Psychological Association, APA style it is not restricted to psychology. In fact, most of the social science disciplines adhere to APA Style. The most recent version of APA Style is detailed in the sixth edition of the *Publication Manual of the American Psychological Association* (2010b), and a condensed APA guide appears in Appendix B. In this appendix, you will see an example of a paper we wrote in its unpublished, manuscript form and in its final, published form.

The primary research articles published in academic journals will vary in length, writing style, the way references are cited, and the headings they use or do not use to organize the article. Many journals use APA format, although others use Modern Language Association (MLA) format or develop their own hybrid format. However, the overall flow and organization of primary research articles will be strikingly similar. Once you understand the basic format, you will know what to expect while reading the article and you will have a good idea of where to look for certain information.

Remember:

- Primary research articles that you read in academic journals will have a very different appearance from the research papers you will write.

- The content and flow of published articles can serve as a model for your own writing, but you should format the paper according to the guidelines of your discipline (such as those outlined in APA's *Publication Manual*).

Organization of Primary Research Articles

Most published primary research articles will be organized in this order: Title, Authors and Affiliation, Abstract, Introduction, Method, Results, Discussion, and References. Depending on the journal, some of these sections may or may not be labeled, some may go by different names, and some sections may be combined. Although most primary research articles will have these (or similar) sections, do not assume that having one or more of these sections ensures that the article is a primary source. A primary research article contains all these sections, but secondary sources may or may not have several or all of these sections. All scholarly works will have a title, list of authors, and a list of references, and most will have an abstract. The excerpts from the two scholarly works back in Practice 2.1 are from the articles' abstracts, but you might recall that only the second article was a primary source. Meta-analyses and some review articles will contain a method section describing the selection criteria for the sources they used, and many will have a discussion or conclusions section. Remember that what makes a primary research article unique is that it describes one or more studies that the authors conducted, and you will need to find evidence that a study was conducted within the article's abstract or method to verify that the article is a primary one.

The following sections describe the key parts of a published primary research article and explain what types of information you will find in each. We also provide some tips for reading and evaluating the sections. The best way to understand how to read and evaluate primary research articles is to have the full text of at least one in front of you. Here, we use examples from an article that we found in PsycINFO using the keywords "college achievement" and "social class":

- *Title:* Closing the Social Class Achievement Gap for First-Generation Students in Undergraduate Biology

- *Authors:* Harackiewicz, Canning, Tibbetts, Giffen, Blair, Rouse, and Hyde (or Harackiewicz et al., with "et al." indicating "and others")

- *Publication year:* 2014

- *Source:* Journal of Educational Psychology

Test your library skills to see if you can find the full text of this article through your college or university library database. To quickly narrow down the results, you can search by the article's title or authors. You should be able to find the reference through either PsycINFO or ERIC, but depending on your library's subscriptions you may or may not be able to pull up the full text. If you do not see a link for the full text, try Google Scholar. But go to your library database first so you get some practice using your library system, which as we mentioned before is the best way to identify relevant sources.

We are serious. Stop reading and go find the full text of the Harackiewicz et al. (2014) article. Doing so will help test your library skills, and furthermore we will use the article in the following sections. Go now.

OK—now that you have the article (You do have it, right?), read on about the different parts of a primary research article. Compare the description of each section to what appears in the Harackiewicz et al. article.

Title

The title is a brief description of the study and will usually include the key variables examined in the study. Most titles are pretty dry and straightforward. Some authors choose to let a little creativity shine through in the title; but if this happens, they also include a more direct description (usually set off by a colon). After scanning through lists and lists of titles from a library database, most students come to appreciate the utilitarian nature of titles. The title should tell you very quickly whether the article is related to your topic. See Application 2.2, which evaluates the title of the article that we asked you to find.

Application 2.2

TITLE OF ARTICLE ABOUT ACADEMIC SUCCESS: CLOSING THE SOCIAL CLASS ACHIEVEMENT GAP FOR FIRST-GENERATION STUDENTS IN UNDERGRADUATE BIOLOGY

Evaluation: This title is quite straightforward and quickly tells us the exact focus of the article. However, just reading this title is not enough to tell us if the authors conducted a study, so we would need to dig a little deeper into the article to find out if this is a primary research article.

Authors

The authors are typically listed right after the title. If there are multiple authors, the author list is usually organized by the degree each contributed, with the first author as the person who was most responsible for the work. This will be important if you decide to use and cite the article. You will want to appropriately credit the authors, and they put some effort in deciding who would be listed first, second, and so on. Therefore do not change the order of authors when you cite the source. See Table 2.2 for guidelines on citing sources in an APA-style paper, and note that these guidelines apply to primary, secondary, scholarly, and popular sources. We provide more detailed guidelines for citations and references in Appendix B.

TABLE 2.2

Guide to APA-Style Citations

Number of Authors	First Citation	Later Citations
One	Dahl (2015) *or* (Dahl, 2015)	Same as first citation
Two	Adams and Lawrence (2018) *or* (Adams & Lawrence, 2018)	Same as first citation
Three to Five	Hill, Burrow, and Bronk (2016) *or* (Hill, Burrow, & Bronk, 2016)	Hill et al. (2016) *or* (Hill et al., 2016)
Six or more	Harackiewicz et al. (2014) *or* (Harackiewicz et al., 2014)	Same as first citation

Paying attention to the authors will also help you identify who the key players are in a certain field. As you delve into a research topic, you will start to notice that many of the authors have published multiple articles on the same topic. As you read further into the article, you may also notice that certain authors are cited by others. You can use this author information to find other relevant articles on your topic.

Abstract

The abstract is a one-paragraph summary of the entire article. In a PDF or print version of a published article, the abstract is often set off from the rest of the paper in a smaller font, centered, or italicized. In an HTML version of the article, the abstract is the first paragraph. Some journals use a heading to identify the abstract, such as "Abstract," "Overview," or "Summary"—but others do not. Like the title, the abstract will help you determine how relevant the article is for your study, but it will provide a little more detail to help you decide if it will be worthwhile to read the full article. Remember that if you cite an article, you must read the full article and not rely solely on the brief information provided in the abstract.

Both primary and secondary sources may include an abstract, and reading the abstract will help you determine whether the source is primary. The abstract of a primary research article will give some indication that the authors conducted an original research study, by indicating the purpose of the study (or studies if multiple ones are described), the method employed, and the key results. In some cases, the abstract of a primary research article will help you determine the type of design used (descriptive, correlational, or experimental). See Application 2.3 for an evaluation of our example article.

Introduction

The Introduction section begins right after the abstract. Published articles usually begin this section without a heading. Some journals have a section labeled "Introduction" followed by a longer section called something like "Literature Review" and then a "Current Study" or "Hypotheses" section, and it might appear that the Introduction ends before

Application 2.3

ABSTRACT FROM HARACKIEWICZ ET AL. (2014)
(BE SURE YOU HAVE THE ARTICLE IN FRONT OF YOU BEFORE YOU READ ON.)

Is it a primary research source?
Yes, the abstract states that an intervention was conducted with 798 students and refers to the results. Identifying the exact number of participants is a good indication that the authors are reporting results from an original research study.
Can we identify research design?
No. There are some hints that this study is an experiment. The authors state that the intervention led to improvements in grades and retention, suggesting that the intervention was a possible independent variable that caused the improvements in grades and retention (possible dependent variables). However, there is no indication in the abstract that participants were randomly assigned to different intervention conditions, and such information would be essential to confirm that the study is indeed an experiment. We will need to read more of the article in order to identify the research design.

the Literature Review section. However, for our purposes and to follow APA format, all these sections represent the introduction.

The purpose of the introduction is to provide the rationale for the study. Reading the introduction will give you insight into the authors' thinking about the topic and the reason they conducted the study. It will also give you a sense of some of the past research in this area.

Introductions range in length and vary in content, but most introductions follow the same general organization. Understanding this organization can help you efficiently read the introduction of a variety of studies. Moreover, you will notice that authors organize their introduction in order to build a case for their study (see Application 2.4). Reading introductions will also serve as a model when you write your own. As you read through introductions for primary research articles, take note of the following:

1. The Introduction section begins by introducing the topic and giving the reader an idea for why the topic is an important one to study.

   - The authors might identify a problem or make an observation, which can be as simple as noting the amount of research already done on the topic.

   - The beginning of the introduction allows the authors a bit more leeway in terms of creativity as well as the types of sources used. We have seen introductions that begin with a nursery rhyme or a quote from a famous person. Popular sources such as Time magazine or CNN may be used to help develop a case that a topic is important, or recent statistics

Application 2.4

HARACKIEWICZ ET AL.'S (2014) INTRODUCTION

1. The Introduction section begins by introducing the topic and explaining why it is important.
In the first paragraph, the authors identify a problem: Students who want to pursue biomedicine may quit because of the challenges they face in introductory biology courses, and this is especially problematic for students of color, women, and first-generation college students. Because their study focused on first-generation college students, the authors spend some time discussing the challenges faced by this group.
2. The majority of the introduction involves a review of past research and theory.
The second paragraph provides a quick review of research linking social class and academic achievement, and suggests that there is an intervention that can help close the social class achievement gap. They then spend the next seven paragraphs detailing the theory and research behind the values affirmation (VA) intervention (all under the heading "Theoretical Framework"). In paragraphs eight and nine (under the heading that begins "Scaling up . . ."), the authors focus more specifically on large introductory undergraduate biology courses because that is the focus of their study. They note limitations of past research, specifically that the VA intervention has not been tested in large introductory courses with multiple instructors. They also note specific challenges with such courses and recommendations for implementation.
3. The introduction ends by focusing on the current study and stating the authors' hypothesis.
In the final paragraph of the introduction (under the heading "Current Study") the authors explain that their study examines the VA intervention in large introductory biology courses with multiple instructors (thus addressing the limitation they identified in the previous paragraphs). They also indicate that they followed the recommendations they noted in the previous paragraph. Lastly, they state their hypothesis.

from website sources may be used to identify trends or emphasize the importance of researching the topic.

2. The review of past research makes up the majority of the introduction.

    • Remember that reviews are secondary sources that can provide you with a brief summary of past research but should not be used in lieu of reading the original, primary source. In other words, do not cite information from the Introduction section of a research article; instead, track down and read the primary source before citing information from it.

    • Some articles begin the review of past research in the first paragraph of the introduction, citing scholarly sources as a way to introduce the importance of a topic. Other authors begin the review of past research in the second or third paragraph. The review of past research may be as little as one paragraph or as long as several pages. The review may be subdivided based on the content of the research reviewed in each subsection.

- As the authors explain the research that has been done that supports their own study, they often make note of the research that is absent, sparse, or inconsistent. In this way, the authors build a case for the need for their own study.

3. The end of the introduction focuses on the study the authors conducted.

- The authors may explicitly state or imply how their research study improves on past research and how their study is unique. For example, they may be using a different method, studying different types of participants, comparing alternative explanations, examining different ways that one variable impacts another, or examining variables that might impact the relationship between variables.

- The hypotheses for the study are typically near or at the very end of the Introduction section. The hypotheses should come as no surprise because all the previous content of the introduction was building a case for these hypotheses. In the case of exploratory research where the authors do not have set hypotheses, the authors may instead state some research questions. Some articles contain both hypotheses and exploratory questions.

Method

The Method section explains the method used to test the hypotheses or to help answer the research questions. The Method section will include information about the participants (or animal subjects), the measures or materials used in the study, and the procedures of the study. Reading the Method section is the best way to identify the research design of the study (see Application 2.5) The authors will usually divide this information among subsections in the Method section, but the exact number, names, and order of these subsections will vary based on the article.

Participants or Subjects. At minimum, you will find information about the total number of human participants or animal subjects in the Method section. Ideally, you will also find information about the characteristics of the participants such as age, gender, and ethnicity. Information about the participants or subjects will help you evaluate the results of the study, and we will discuss some ways to do this later in the chapter.

Measures and Materials. Researchers operationally define their variables by selecting specific measures and materials. Measures can be evaluated in terms of their reliability and measurement validity, and we will discuss both of these in more depth in Chapter 3. Generally speaking, reliability refers to how consistent the measure is. Authors often cite past research that used or developed the measure to support the measure's reliability, or the authors may have evaluated a measure's reliability themselves. However, some authors do not provide any information about reliability of the measures.

Application 2.5

IDENTIFY THE RESEARCH DESIGN OF HARACKIEWICZ ET AL. (2014)

The abstract of the article hinted that this study was an experiment, but did not provide enough detail to confirm that. Recall from Chapter 1 that an experiment requires an independent variable (IV) that is manipulated, random assignment, and measurement of at least one dependent variable (DV), so we will look at the Method section of the article to determine if this study is an experiment or not.

Is there an IV?
Yes, the IV is the intervention. In the first paragraph of "The Intervention" subsection, the authors explain that students were in one of two conditions: the values affirmation condition or a control condition. The rest of this subsection explains exactly what participants in each condition experienced.
Did the researchers randomly assign participants to IV condition?
Yes. In the first paragraph of "The Intervention" subsection, the authors state that participants were randomly assigned to condition.
Is there a DV?
Yes, there are two DVs: grades and continuation to the second biology course. The DVs are detailed in the "Outcome Measures" subsection.

Because all three criteria for an experiment are met, we can therefore conclude that the research design of Harackiewicz et al. is indeed experimental.

The basic definition of measurement validity is the extent to which a measure actually measures what the researcher says it does or the extent to which a manipulation manipulates what the researcher says it does. You can do a simple evaluation of the validity of the measure based on the types of questions or the materials used to measure or manipulate a variable. For example, Harackiewicz et al. (2014) used final grades to evaluate the effectiveness of an intervention. Grades may have decent measurement validity when used to assess academic achievement (which is what these authors did). However, grades would have poor measurement validity for assessing academic motivation or effort.

As you progress in the research process, you will need to find ways to measure and/or manipulate variables in your own study. Reading the Method section will provide you with some ideas on how other researchers operationally define the variables and will cite sources where you can find a measure to use in your study. Some articles will even provide the complete measure or materials such as a script or scenario that you can use or adapt in your study (and appropriately cite the creator of the measure or material, of course).

Procedure and Design. The Procedure section describes the steps the authors followed in the study. A general rule of thumb is that the Procedure section should contain enough information that the reader (you) could replicate the study. You may still have some questions about the details of how the study was conducted, but you should have a good idea about how it was carried out. The description of how the study was conducted is generally listed in the order in which the participant experienced them.

The procedures will help you identify the exact research design (or designs) utilized in the study. In some cases, the authors may include a separate Design section to explain the logic behind the procedures in order to help you understand why the authors did what they did. In all cases, the design of the study should be linked with a specific hypothesis. For example, if the authors hypothesize that one variable will have an effect on (or cause a change to) another variable, then the design utilized to test the hypothesis should be experimental because that is the only design that can test causation.

Results

The Results section is typically the most technical section of the article and the most difficult to understand, especially at first. As you become more comfortable with statistics, Results sections will start to make a lot more sense. However, even if you are reading a research article for the very first time you may be surprised by how much you can understand if you try. By this point in your academic career, you should know some basic statistics such as percentages and means. If you devote some time and energy to reading the results of a study, you will gain familiarity with some of the more advanced statistics and you will see how they are used to test hypotheses, even if you cannot yet decipher what every single number or statistical notation means.

The main focus of the Results section is the results of analyses used to test the hypotheses or help answer the research questions. Take note when the authors state that a result was statistically significant and determine if the results support one of the hypotheses. We will talk more about statistical significance in Chapter 6, but for now simply know that **statistical significance testing** is used to help reduce the likelihood that the results were obtained purely by chance. Researchers do not want to report spurious patterns or relationships, but they do want to be able to identify patterns and relationships in their data that, in fact, exist.

You might also examine the means, percentages, or other numbers associated with the statistically significant result so that you have some understanding of how the authors tested the hypotheses. Tables or graphs can be very useful in summarizing these results, and you should pay special attention to these when they are available.

Statistical significance testing: A process to reduce the likelihood that the results were obtained by chance alone.

Discussion

The Discussion section (also named Conclusions in some journals) will usually begin with an explanation of the results without the technical language. It will also put the results into context—usually first stating if the results support or do not support the hypotheses and then explaining how the results fit or do not fit with past research. The Discussion section will also suggest what the larger implications and applications of the study might be, point out limitations of the study, and offer suggestions for future research that may address limitations and expand on the results of the study.

The Discussion section is a good place to get an overview of the results of the study and to generate ideas for your own research. However, do not rely on it exclusively to understand the results. The discussion is the authors' interpretation of the results, and you may come up with your own explanation based on a thorough reading of the Results section. It would be good practice to read through the results and write out some of the key conclusions, and then compare these to what the authors say. Or you might read the Discussion section first, and then try to figure out how the authors came to their conclusions based on information they provide in the Results section.

Following are three questions to consider when evaluating the results of a study. The authors may address one or more of these in their Discussion section. Even if they do not, you can consider these questions as you evaluate a research study.

1. *Did the study have enough power?* Power refers to the ability to find statistically significant patterns and relationships in the data when they exist. We will discuss power in more detail in Chapter 6, but for now simply know that the stronger the pattern or relationship and the larger the sample, the more power the study has and the greater likelihood of finding statistically significant results.

How do you use this information in evaluating the power of a study? If you have a study that did not find significant results, it is possible that a pattern or relationship does exist but there was not enough power to detect it due to a small sample size or because the way the research measured or manipulated the variables was not strong enough. If you have a study that found significant results with a relatively small sample, the pattern or relationship must have been relatively strong in order for the results to meet the criteria for statistical significance. Likewise, studies with very large samples are able to detect very small patterns or relationships, and the strength of the pattern or relationship should be carefully considered when evaluating the results.

2. *If the authors hypothesized a relationship between variables, did they utilize a design and procedures that helped to demonstrate causation?* If the authors conducted a correlational study, they cannot demonstrate causation and therefore the study cannot help explain why a relationship exists. An experiment helps to demonstrate causation through random assignment, manipulation of an independent variable (IV), and measurement of a dependent variable. These basic requirements of an experiment help improve the study's **internal validity**, or the extent to which one can demonstrate that one variable (the IV) caused a change in another variable (the DV). We will discuss internal validity in more depth in later chapters.

Power: The ability to find statistical significance when in fact a pattern or relationship exists. Sample size and the strength of the relationship between two or more variables are two factors that impact a study's power.

Internal validity: The extent to which you can demonstrate a causal relationship between your IV and DV.

3. *How strong is the external validity of the study?* **External validity** is the extent to which a study's results can be generalized to other samples, settings, or procedures. If the study's authors utilized first-year college students as participants, the external validity could be impacted because the results may not generalize to more advanced students or individuals who are not in college. Similarly, if the authors conducted the study in a controlled laboratory, it is not clear whether or how the results would generalize to a real-world situation. We will discuss external validity in more depth in the next chapter.

> **External validity:** The extent to which the results of a study can be generalized to other samples, settings, or procedures.

References

All the sources cited within the article will be listed in a References section or in footnotes throughout the article. The References section is a good place to look to identify other research on your topic. You will also notice that the number of references listed is quite high given the length of the article. For example, the Harackiewicz et al. (2014) article has 67 references. Most of the references will be cited in the Introduction, and a few new ones may be cited in the Method and Discussion. This demonstrates the importance of building a study on past research, including past methodology, and evaluating the results within the context of past research.

Shape of a Primary Research Article

Once you gain familiarity with the way a primary research article is organized, you will notice that most share a similar shape. This shape is often described as an hourglass in that a primary research article is organized so that it starts broad, moves to the more narrow or specific, and then gets broad again. See Figure 2.3 for a depiction of this organization.

DEVELOP STUDY IDEAS BASED ON PAST RESEARCH

Once you begin to find and read primary research articles on your topic, you might find yourself overwhelmed with information. We recommend that you locate one or two recent articles that you find interesting and that include methodology that you can understand. Carefully evaluate the method and results to identify limitations that you might address or questions that the study raises, and then check the Discussion section for the limitations and future research the authors suggest. Use additional articles to provide background information and help build the rationale for your hypotheses and method (see Application 2.6).

FIGURE 2.3
Shape of a Primary Research Article

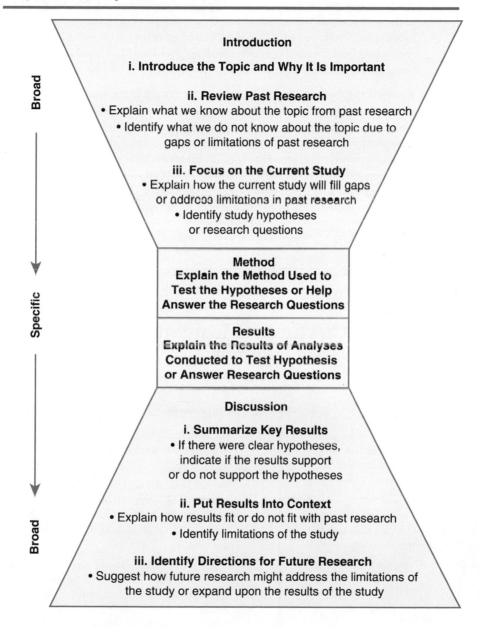

Broad

Introduction

i. Introduce the Topic and Why It Is Important

ii. Review Past Research
- Explain what we know about the topic from past research
- Identify what we do not know about the topic due to gaps or limitations of past research

iii. Focus on the Current Study
- Explain how the current study will fill gaps or address limitations in past research
- Identify study hypotheses or research questions

Specific

Method
Explain the Method Used to Test the Hypotheses or Help Answer the Research Questions

Results
Explain the Results of Analyses Conducted to Test Hypothesis or Answer Research Questions

Discussion

i. Summarize Key Results
- If there were clear hypotheses, indicate if the results support or do not support the hypotheses

ii. Put Results Into Context
- Explain how results fit or do not fit with past research
- Identify limitations of the study

iii. Identify Directions for Future Research
- Suggest how future research might address the limitations of the study or expand upon the results of the study

Broad

Following are some ways to build on a research study:

1. Replicate the study with a different sample, setting, or method. Do this if most of the past research you have read examines one type of sample, setting, or method and you have reason to believe (based on other past research) that the results may be different if conducted with another sample, in another setting, or using another method such as a different measure, manipulation, or procedure.

2. Examine the topic using a different research design. If the study was a quasi- or non-experimental study, conduct an experiment. Do this if causation has not been consistently established by past research, or it has not been consistently established with the population you are examining. Be sure that it is both possible and ethical to conduct an experiment to help establish causation among the variables. Or, if the study is an experiment, you might follow up with a quasi- or non-experimental study to examine some of the findings in more depth, or to test out real-world applications.

3. Conduct a similar study with a different outcome or dependent variable. Do this if you find research evidence supporting the new relationship you plan to examine.

4. Examine how another variable might impact results. Do this if you have research evidence to suggest that results may depend on another variable.

Ethics Tip: Give Credit to Your Sources and Avoid Plagiarism

Marvid

Accuracy

- Just because information appears in an article, it does not mean that that article is the original (primary) source for that information—be sure you accurately cite the original source.

- Take time to understand the findings of a research study or other source so that you can accurately summarize them.

Avoid Plagiarism

- Be sure you know what plagiarism is (see Chapter 1 for a refresher).

- As you take notes, summarize and paraphrase the article in your own words. This takes more time, but it helps ensure that you understand the information before you write it down in your notes.

- If you must directly quote an article as a short cut for taking notes, be sure the direct quotes are in quotation marks along with the authors' names and page numbers from the original source—that way you will not look back at your notes and assume the words are your own.

Application 2.6

DEVELOP STUDY IDEAS BASED ON HARACKIEWICZ ET AL. (2014)

1. *Replicate the study with a different sample, setting, or method.*

Harackiewicz et al. (2014) focused on undergraduate students in an introductory biology course in the United States. We might conduct a similar study with students in a social science research methods course, or we might examine how the intervention works in a non-U.S. setting, or both of these.

Harackiewicz compared the values affirmation (VA) intervention to a control. Other research (some of which is briefly summarized in Practice 2.1) suggests that grit, or determination and passion for one's goals, can aid in student success. We might therefore compare the VA intervention to one that aims to increase grit.

Finally, the authors indicate that they followed strict procedures to ensure that student participants saw the assignment (VA or control) as part of the class but knew that their professors would not evaluate, or even see, their responses. In the discussion, they note "future research might explore which of these conditions are essential" (p. 387), and we could examine a study to test out different procedures. For example, we might conduct a study in which professors do see the students' responses to determine if that leads to different results.

2. *Examine the topic using a different research design.*

Harackiewicz et al. employed an experimental design, and they note in their Discussion section that "it will be important to identify the specific mechanisms underlying underperformance of different groups" (p. 386). We might conduct a descriptive or correlational study to follow up on this suggestion. For example, we might conduct a descriptive study to better understand academic motivation, parental support, and peer support among first generation students.

3. *Conduct a similar study with a different outcome or dependent variable.*

Harackiewicz et al.'s dependent variables were final grades and whether students enrolled in the second-level biology course, but they note that they were not able to identify the mechanisms by which the VA intervention impacted these dependent variables. They identify some potential mechanisms, including sense of belonging in college, concerns about stereotypes, and concordance of the students' personal goals with the institution. We could conduct an experiment examining one or more of these as dependent variables.

4. *Examine how another variable might impact results.*

Harackiewicz et al. found that the VA intervention was effective for improving academic achievement of first-generation students but did not impact continuing-generation students. We might examine other factors that enhance or diminish the effectiveness of the VA intervention. For example, does the VA intervention help or hinder those students high in grit?

APA FORMAT FOR REFERENCES

Because giving proper credit is so critical to avoiding plagiarism, we will briefly describe how to format references at the end of your paper. A more detailed APA format guide appears in Appendix B, and for the most accurate and detailed information you should of course go to the original source—the sixth edition of the *Publication Manual of the American Psychological Association* (2010b).

If you are like many students who struggle with getting the details of APA formatting just right, you might wonder why APA format matters at all. The main rationale for adhering to APA format, or any formatting style, is that the consistency helps readers quickly identify the information they need. As you get more comfortable reading primary research articles, you will come to appreciate that you can find information such as the hypotheses, method, and results in the same place within most articles. Likewise, when you want to read more about a study cited in an article, the consistency in the reference list will help you quickly identify the information you need to find the article using your library's databases.

What to include in a reference for a journal article:

- Author(s) names (last name followed by comma, initial[s] followed by period[s]; comma between individual author's names)

- Year of publication, in parentheses

- Article title

- Journal title and volume

- Do not include issue number unless the journal begins numbering each issue with page 1.

- Page numbers of article

- doi number, if available

Formatting the reference:

- Do not indent the first line of the reference, but indent all subsequent lines of that reference (this is called a "hanging indent").

- For articles with multiple authors: Keep the order of authors the same as it appears in the article, include the last name of each author followed by his/her initial(s), separate the authors by commas, and use both a comma and an ampersand (&) before the last author.

- Put the year of publication in parentheses, followed by a period.

- For the article title, capitalize only the first letter of the first word, the first word after a colon or other punctuation, or proper names.

- Put a period after the title.

- For the journal title, capitalize the first letter of all the main words (e.g., not "of" or "and").

- Italicize the journal title and the volume number, but not the page numbers.

- Use a comma to separate the title, volume, and page numbers.

- Put a period after the page numbers.

- If there is a doi number, type doi in all lowercase letters, then a colon, then the number.

- Do not put a period after the doi number.

- Put a space after any punctuation, except following the colon after "doi").

Look at Figure 2.4 for an example reference, with key points noted. Then practice writing a reference using APA format by completing Practice 2.2.

FIGURE 2.4

Example APA-Formatted Reference With Notation

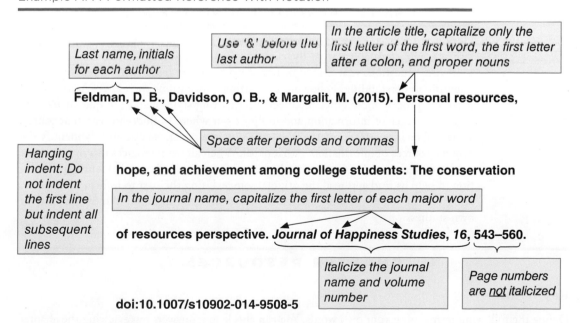

Practice 2.2

WRITE A REFERENCE USING APA FORMAT

Put the following information into an APA-style reference:

- *Article title:* Closing the Social Class Achievement Gap for First-Generation Students in Undergraduate Biology

- *Journal title:* Journal of Educational Psychology

- *Authors:* Judith M. Harackiewicz, Elizabeth A. Canning, Yoi Tibbetts, Cynthia J. Giffen, Seth S. Blair, Douglas I. Rouse, and Janet S. Hyde

- *Date:* 2014

- *Volume:* 106

- *Page numbers:* 375 to 389

- *doi number:* 10.1037/a0034679

See Appendix A to check your answer.

THE BIG PICTURE:
USE THE PAST TO INFORM THE PRESENT

Honoring the past is an integral part of research. Finding, reading, and evaluating past research helps to identify what the current state of knowledge is in an area, and helps to identify questions that should be examined by future research in order to progress scientific understanding. Following formatting conventions such as APA style helps make the process more efficient. Specific formatting styles help us to quickly identify original sources of information and to figure out where to find and read that source. When all citations are formatted the same way in a paper, we can quickly identify the original sources of information in that paper. When all the references in a reference list are formatted the same way, we can look up the citation and quickly identify information to help us find and read the original source. Using the past to inform the present, and crediting sources appropriately, is how researchers build a solid foundation for their own studies.

CHAPTER RESOURCES

Key Terms

Define the following terms using your own words. You can check your answers by reviewing the chapter or by comparing them with the definitions in the glossary—but try to define them on your own first.

Do You Understand the Chapter?

Answer these questions on your own, and then review the chapter to check your answers.

1. What is the difference between a primary and secondary source?

2. What is the difference between scholarly and popular works?

3. Why is the peer review process important?

4. Describe the different types of articles that can be found in academic journals.

5. How can you tell if a journal article is a primary source?

6. Describe scholarly sources that are not found in academic journals.

7. How would you find conference papers or posters, dissertations, or unpublished manuscripts? What are the pros and cons of these types of sources?

8. What databases are most applicable to your discipline and topic?

9. Explain how you would conduct a keyword search on your topic.

10. How else might you find relevant research on your topic?

11. List and briefly describe the purpose of each section in a primary research article.

 **edge.sagepub.com/adams2e**

Sharpen your skills with SAGE edge!
SAGE edge for students provides you with tools to help you study. You'll find mobile-friendly eFlashcards and quizzes, as well as videos, web resources, datasets, and links to SAGE journal articles related to this chapter.

The Cornerstones of Good Research

RELIABILITY AND VALIDITY

C onsider the following scenario:

Twins Chris and Pat both want to lose weight and agree to begin a weight loss program, URN CHRG. They intend to stay on the diet for 6 weeks and agree that whoever loses the most weight will win from the other twin a month's membership at a local athletic club. The twins each purchase inexpensive scales to monitor their weight at their individual apartments. They agree to weigh every 5 days and to record the weight. Pat finds that his weight seems to go up and down, sometimes showing weight loss and sometimes showing weight gain, even though he reports that he is diligently following URN CHRG's weight loss program. In contrast, Chris's recorded weight continuously decreases. At the end of the 6 weeks, they meet at the doctor's office for an official weigh-in. Although they both expect that Chris will weigh less, the doctor's scale shows that in fact Pat weighs less than Chris. The figure on the next page reflects the results of the weigh-ins by the twins.

How could this happen when according to the home scales, Pat weighed more?

If you think the answer may be related to the "cheap" scales they bought, then you would be correct. Yet, psychologists want to know more than just that the weight on the cheap scales is different from the doctor's scale. And as diligent psychology students who understand the research process, Chris and Pat want to investigate exactly what the problem is with their scales. They each bring their scale to the doctor's office and Pat finds that each time he steps on his scale to compare the number to the doctor's scale, the weight varies as much as 10 pounds. Chris finds that he consistently weighs 5 pounds less on his scale than on the doctor's scale. The issues of consistency and accuracy are what we refer to as *reliability* and *validity*.

LEARNING OUTCOMES

In this chapter, you will learn

- The definition of reliability and validity
- How to operationally define constructs with qualitative and quantitative measures
- How to identify different scales of measurement
- Different types of measures, including questionnaires, unobtrusive, and physiological measures
- How to assess the reliability and validity of measures
- How to evaluate the reliability and validity of a study

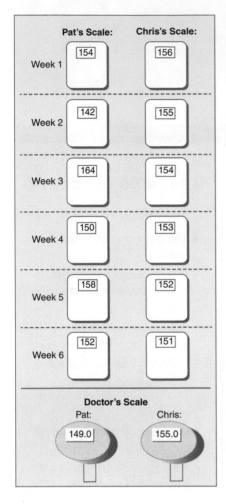

RELIABILITY AND VALIDITY BROADLY DEFINED

Reliability means consistency, and **validity** means accuracy. Both reliability and validity are critical factors in research. You can see from the everyday example at the beginning of the chapter why we need reliable and valid measures in order to accurately describe variables and show results. If we do not have reliable and valid measures, the results of our research will not be meaningful or useful in describing behavior or the factors that influence behavior. As the title of this chapter states, validity and reliability are the foundation of good research.

We typically consider reliability and validity from two perspectives: (1) how we measure specific variables (measure level) and (2) the results of the whole study (study level). We will consider each of these perspectives in detail.

> **Reliability:** Consistency of findings or measures.
>
> **Validity:** Accuracy of findings or measures.

RELIABILITY AND VALIDITY OF MEASUREMENT

Recall that in the scenario at the beginning of this chapter Chris and Pat each had problems with their scales and therefore could not accurately assess their weight. One of these scales suffered from poor measurement reliability, and the other had poor measurement validity.

Measurement reliability concerns the consistency of measurement—in this case, a scale should register the same weight for the same person, especially when one steps on the scale again within a few minutes' time. Pat's scale registered his weight as heavier and lighter within a few minutes, causing us to question the consistency or reliability of his scale in assessing weight.

Measurement validity concerns the ability of an instrument or factor to accurately measure (or assess) what it is supposed to measure. Even though Chris's scale seemed to

> **Measurement reliability:** Consistency of a measure.
>
> **Measurement validity:** Measurement is accurate in that it measures what it purports to measure.

Remember:

- A measure *cannot* be valid unless it is reliable.
- A measure *can* be reliable but not valid.

show a consistent weight loss, the weight shown was not valid, as it was 5 pounds lighter than Chris's real weight as reflected on the doctor's scale. This example demonstrates how a measure can be reliable or consistent (Chris's weight was shown as 5 pounds lighter each time) without being valid.

Sometimes we question validity because we are not sure that the measure in fact represents the variable we are studying. For example, suppose Chris decided to measure his weight loss by how loose his jeans felt. Instead of weighing on a scale, he decided to try on the same pair of jeans every 5 days and found that over 6 weeks' time, the jeans became looser. His jeans may feel less tight with each successive wear, but he may not be measuring weight loss. Instead, he may be measuring the stretch of the jean fabric. Thus, his "measure" of weight (fit of jeans) is not a valid one. In order to be valid, a measure must both be reliable and accurately reflect the variable in question.

CONSTRUCTS AND OPERATIONAL DEFINITIONS

In order to assess the reliability and validity of any measurement instrument, we must clearly define the measures we are using. Although in the social and behavioral sciences we sometimes measure variables that are concrete and well defined, such as weight, time, or cost, we are often examining **constructs** that are more abstract, such as personal opinions, achievement, community support, attention, or self-efficacy. Constructs are variables that cannot be directly observed, nor do we have physical tests that directly assess them. As researchers we have to develop ways to define and measure these abstract constructs. For example, plagiarism as a construct can be broadly defined as claiming ownership for another's ideas, written material, or work. But this definition is not specific enough because there are multiple ways in which one could measure plagiarism according to this definition.

We use **operational definitions** to explicitly define abstract constructs for a specific study. For example, Schuetze (2004) used citation errors to assess plagiarism. Other researchers have focused on paraphrasing in addition to proper citation (Belter & du Pré, 2009; Estow et al., 2011). Most people would agree both improper citation and

Construct: A concept that cannot be directly observed or measured.

Operational definition: The explicit explanation of a variable in terms of how it is measured or manipulated.

paraphrasing constitute plagiarism, but they can also think of other ways one might measure plagiarism (verbally taking credit for another's idea, or cutting and pasting or copying material from another source). In research we must always provide clear definitions of the variables in our studies, and we must be able to defend or explain the rationale for the operational definitions we use. Sometimes the major criticism of a study is the operational definition of variables.

Deciding How to Measure Your Constructs

As a researcher you have many options in terms of operationally defining, or measuring, constructs. One of your first global decisions regarding constructs involves deciding whether to use **qualitative** or **quantitative measures**.

Qualitative measure: Nonnumerical assessment.

Quantitative measure: Numerical measure.

Qualitative Measures

Qualitative measures are nonnumerical, while quantitative measures are numerical. For instance, suppose you are interested in the construct of frustration and decide to observe people's response to having someone get in front of them while they are waiting in line to vote. You could operationally define frustration as a frown, an opening of the mouth and raising of eyebrows, a downturn of the mouth, or a verbal comment to the person who broke in line. In order to get a qualitative measure of frustration, you could have two observers write down the different responses they saw the participant make immediately following the breaking-in-line incident. Many times, the written descriptions by the two observers would then be coded or examined for trends in order to see whether the observers recorded similar responses to breaking in line and whether there are similarities across the participants' responses. In order to evaluate the descriptions, we would read the observers' descriptions of their observations of all the participants. We would look for similar terms or similar behaviors that were described. We might even find that there is a consistent pattern of responses that begins with a raising of the eyebrows and circle of the mouth, then a wrinkled brow followed by staring at the "line breaker," and a downturn of the mouth. We could use numbers (1 = *raising of eyebrows*) or letter codes (F = *frown*) for each of these behaviors and determine how many and in what order they appeared in the observers' descriptions.

Quantitative Measures

Alternatively, you could quantitatively measure frustration by having the two observers rate from 1 to 5 (1 = *no response;* 5 = *very frustrated*) how frustrated the participant was following the breaking-in-line incident. You can see that both measures require some interpretation of the participant's behavior by the observers. However, the qualitative measurement will result in a lot of text to be interpreted, and judgments will be required as responses by different participants are compared. The quantitative measurement will produce a numerical value for each participant that can be averaged without needing interpretation.

We sometimes mistakenly believe that numerical data is "better" or more valid than narrative information because numbers have an agreed-on meaning (e.g., a quantity of 1 has a specific value such that 2 is larger than 1 and smaller than 3 by the same amount). We forget that interpretation can be required in the measurement of numerical data, such as occurred in our example above when the observers rated frustration on a 5-point scale. Even when we rate our own behavior on a numerical scale, we are required to interpret what a value, say 3, means according to our behavior, attitude, or emotion.

Some quantitative measures do not require as much interpretation as our example of rating frustration. A good example is when we operationally define dependence on one's cell phone as the number of minutes spent on the cell phone during the last month (as indicated on the cell phone bill). Regardless of the variables we are studying in research, we most often rely on quantitative measures because of the ease of understanding and analyzing numerical data. We should always remember, however, that some interpretation is often involved in obtaining the numbers we analyze (see Figure 3.1).

FIGURE 3.1
Quantitative Measures

Researchers often require that participants quantify their feelings, attitudes, or behaviors by assigning a number to a variable rather than providing a verbal description of it. Can you name a few advantages and disadvantages of this tendency to use quantitative rather than qualitative data?

Source: Sandi Coon

Scales of Measurement

Data are also measured according to four scales of measurement that vary by four attributes, which determine the preciseness of the scale of measurement. **Identity** means that each number is unique. **Order** reflects that numbers have a sequence and can be identified as occurring before or after other numbers in the sequence. Numbers that have **equal intervals** have the same quantity or interval between each number. Finally, a

Identity: Each number has a unique meaning.

Order: Numbers on a scale are ordered in sequence.

Equal intervals: The distance between numbers on a scale is equal.

true zero exists when a variable has a real rather than an arbitrary zero point. The four scales of measurement are described below from least to most precise.

> **True zero (or absolute zero):** The score of zero on a scale is a fixed point.

Social and behavioral science research employs the four scales of measurement with varying frequencies. The type of statistical analyses employed depends on the type of measurement scales to be analyzed. Thus, it is important that you are able to identify and understand the differences between the scales of measurement.

Nominal Scales

Nominal scales represent categories. Although numbers are used to represent categories within a nominal scale, the numbers have no numerical value. If you were to assign a numerical value to a category, a higher score would not necessarily mean that there was more of some quality. Therefore, nominal scales have only identity, but do not have order or any of the other scale properties.

> **Nominal scale:** A scale of measurement where numbers represent categories and have no numerical value.

Demographic data, such as gender, ethnicity, and marital status, each represent a nominal scale. For example, you may code different types of marital status using numbers, such as 1 = *single,* 2 = *married,* 3 = *divorced,* but the numbers have no value or order. In this case, 1 representing "single" is not greater or less than 2 representing "married." You can count the frequency within each category but you do not perform mathematical operations on the numbers—you may have a larger number (or frequency) of single than married or divorced participants in a study, but there is no average marital status, for example. Another example of a measurement using a nominal scale is political affiliation where 1 = *Democrat,* 2 = *Republican,* 3 = *Green Party,* 4 = *Independent.* A question that is answered with Yes/No or True/False is also an example of a nominal scale.

Ordinal Scales

Ordinal scales represent rankings. This scale of measurement includes numbers that have order so that each number is greater or less than other numbers. However, the interval between the numbers in an ordinal scale is not equal.

> **Ordinal scale:** A scale of measurement with numbers that have order so that each number is greater or less than other numbers but the interval between the numbers is not equal; also called rankings.

Track and field races are scored on an ordinal scale. Think of the results of a 50-yard dash with 12 runners. The runners will cross the finish line in such a manner that we can identify who came in first, who came in second, who came in third, all the way until the 12th or last-place finisher. In this case, each runner's finish (first, second, third, etc.) is represented by a number (1, 2, 3, etc.) that tells us the order of the runners. What we do not know is the time or interval between each of the runner's placement. For example, the runner who came in first may have been far ahead of the second and third runners, who came in very close to one another. Like nominal data, ordinal data cannot be manipulated mathematically because there are no fixed intervals between scores.

TABLE 3.1

Scales of Measurement

Measurement Scale	Used to Measure ...	Properties				Example
		Identity?	Order?	Equal Intervals?	True Zero?	
Nominal	Categories	✓				Types of cars
Ordinal	Rankings	✓	✓			Rankings of football teams
Interval	Ratings	✓	✓	✓		7-point Likert-type scale (*strongly disagree* to *strongly agree*) assessing agreement with the law banning texting while driving
Ratio	Quantity	✓	✓	✓	✓	Amount of time studying for your last Research Methods test

EXAMPLE 3.1

Nominal Scale of Measurement

Circle which party best represents your views.

Democratic

Republican

Green Party

Independent

Source: Democratic and Republican Party logos: © Can Stock Photo Inc./gknec; Green Party logo: Scott McLarty, mclarty@greens.org; Independent Party logo: independenceforever@live.com

Interval Scales

Interval scales are ratings that have both order and equal intervals between values on the scale. The limiting factor for interval scales is that they do not have a true zero. We make assumptions that the interval scale begins at one (or zero sometimes) and represents one extreme of the construct we are measuring, but there is no true point that represents that there is absolutely zero of the quality measured, or an absence of the concept. Interval scales can have as few as 3 values and as many as more than 100.

Temperature is a good example to illustrate the lack of a true zero. On the Fahrenheit scale, 32 degrees is freezing while on the Celsius scale, 0 represents freezing. We have 0 degrees (it's cold!) on both scales, but it is an arbitrary value that has a different meaning on each of the two scales. In addition, even though both scales have a zero point, there is still temperature at 0, so the scales lack a "true" zero where there is an absence of the variable.

> **Interval scale:** A scale of measurement that has both order and equal intervals between values on the scale.

EXAMPLE 3.2
Ordinal Scale of Measurement

Rank order your preference for the following foods, from 1 = *most preferred* to 4 = *least preferred.*

Dessert

Fruit

Meat

Salad

Sources: Dessert: © Getty Images/Jupiterimage; Fruit: Pink Sherbet Photography; Meat: PDPhoto.org; Salad: © Getty Images/ Medioimages/Photodisc

Most of you have probably taken a questionnaire where you were asked to rate how satisfied you were with some service or product that you had recently used or bought. The possibilities may have ranged from 1 = *Very dissatisfied* to 5 = *Very satisfied,* and you could have chosen any value between 1 and 5 to represent your satisfaction from very low to very high. This type of scale is used frequently in the social and behavioral sciences. It is called a **Likert-type scale** named after the psychologist, Rensis Likert, who invented the scale. A Likert-type scale is a type of interval scale if we assume that the interval between each of the values (one) is the same, so that the distance between 2 and 3 is considered the same as the distance between 4 and 5. This quality allows us to perform mathematical operations and statistical analysis on the values from an interval scale, and therefore many (but not all) researchers assume equal intervals for Likert-type scales.

EXAMPLE 3.3
Interval Scale of Measurement

0	1	2	3	4	5
No Hurt	**Hurts Little Bit**	**Hurts Little More**	**Hurts Even More**	**Hurts Whole Lot**	**Hurts Worst**

Source: © 1983 Wong-Baker FACES Foundation. www.WongBakerFACES.org. Used with permission. Originally published in Whaley & Wong's Nursing Care of Infants and Children. © Elsevier Inc.

> **Likert-type scale:** A commonly used type of interval scale response in which items are rated on a range of numbers (usually between 5 and 7 response options) that are assumed to have equal intervals.

Ratio Scales

Ratio scales measure quantity. This scale of measurement has the qualities of an interval scale (order and equal intervals) plus it has a true zero. Traditional quantitative measures such as distance, time, and weight are ratio scales. We do not need to develop a measurement scale to assess these variables as there are already well-established mechanisms for them (e.g., clocks, scales). Our example at the beginning of the chapter of the use of a scale to measure weight demonstrates a ratio scale (as well as the importance of reliability and validity of our measures!). We use ratio scales to measure reaction time, such as how quickly a person responds to a text on her cell phone. We may also operationally define a variable using a ratio scale. For example, we may define cell phone dependence by how long

EXAMPLE 3.4
An Everyday Example of Ratio Scale of Measurement

Source: © Can Stock Photo Inc./forestpath

it is between texts (made or received) during a one-hour period. Although ratio is the most precise scale of the four scales of measurement, we use interval scales more frequently to measure social science concepts.

> **Ratio scale:** A scale of measurement where values measure quantity and have order, equal intervals, and a true zero.

Practice 3.1

IDENTIFYING SCALES OF MEASUREMENT

Assume that you want to examine plagiarism among college students.
Can you identify the four scales of measurement among the items below?

1. I believe plagiarism is a serious problem among college students.

1	2	3	4	5
Strongly Disagree		*Neither Disagree nor Agree*		*Strongly Agree*

2. Have you ever plagiarized?   Yes_____   No _____

3. Rank the seriousness of the following problems among college students

    (1 = *most serious*, 8 = *least serious*).

    ___Alcohol consumption   ___Use of illegal drugs

    ___Stress from school   ___Financial problems

    ___Plagiarism   ___Stress from family

    ___Depression   ___Learning problems

4. How many times have you observed cheating during a test while at college? _____

5. Please provide the following information:

    Gender:_____ Age:_____ Ethnicity:_____

6. Academic Year in School (circle one):

    First year   Sophomore   Junior   Senior

More Practice: Can you think of examples of each scale of measurement using "academic achievement" as your variable?

See Appendix A to check your answers.

TYPES OF MEASURES

Regardless of the scale of measurement used, researchers have many choices in terms of how they will collect data in their study.

Questionnaires

A common method is to use what we call a **questionnaire**. This measure is exactly what you might assume: Participants respond to a question or questions regarding a particular topic, variable, trait, attitude, and so on. Each question, or item, on a questionnaire consists of a stem and a response. The stem can be a statement, question, or single word that describes or lists an attitude, belief, behavior, emotion, or characteristic. Those completing the measure are asked to provide a response to each stem.

A single item can be used to represent a construct, such as one question that assesses education level, for instance. Alternatively, multiple items can be grouped around a particular theme such as opinions about a topic (recycling) or self-assessment of a trait (optimism) and a **scale score** computed based on the items. Many constructs are multidimensional (think about recycling), and the scale measuring them may be composed of different subscales, each of which has several items related to them. In terms of a scale assessing recycling, there may be items that focus on attitudes toward recycling, items that focus on behavior, and items that focus on knowledge. All items on the scale are related to recycling, but there are subscales assessing attitudes, behavior, and knowledge.

The **response format** for questionnaires can be broken into two general types of formats, **open-ended** and **closed-ended response formats**. An open-ended response format allows respondents to provide their own answers, and because it is nonnumerical

Questionnaire: A document, presented in hard copy or on a computer, tablet, or phone, consisting of items that assess one or more constructs.

Scale score: The score that is computed from items assessing a particular construct, most commonly a sum or average of the numbers representing responses to individual items in the document.

Response format: The type of response, either participant generated or choice from among listed options, required by items on a questionnaire.

Open-ended response format: Item on a scale that requires the respondents to generate their own answers.

Closed-ended response format: Item that provides a limited number of choices from which respondents must select.

it is a type of qualitative measure. Closed-ended response formats are typically quantitative measures that provide options the respondents select from and that can vary from dichotomous options (two choices such as Yes/No or True/False), to multiple choice, to Likert-type rating scales. Dichotomous options are always in the **forced-choice response format** in that there is no neutral response. Rating scales may or may not be forced-choice depending on whether there is a middle, or neutral, response option. For example, a Likert-type scale with the four response options of *strongly disagree, disagree, agree,* and *strongly agree* is a forced-choice response format in that it requires the respondent to either disagree or agree to some degree, while a Likert-type scale with five response options of *strongly disagree, disagree, neutral, agree,* and *strongly agree* allows the respondent the option to maintain a neutral stance.

Each type of response has advantages and disadvantages. Open-ended responses must be categorized, and thus the interpretation of such responses can be time-consuming and complicated. In addition, it can be difficult to compare the unique responses of each person. The benefit of open-ended responses, however, is that respondents can provide their own thoughts or ideas rather than having them limited to what the scale lists. Open-ended response formats are commonly used in interviews or pilot studies where we want to solicit people's spontaneous responses and look for similarities among them. Closed-ended responses provide specific and limited answers about an attitude, characteristic, or situation, so compiling frequencies or scores for each respondent can be done quickly. The listed responses, however, may not represent the respondents' thoughts or may lead them to an answer that they would not have provided on their own. Because of the ease of scoring and clarity of responses, most questionnaires use closed-ended response formats.

> **Forced-choice response format:** Response format in which there is no neutral, or middle, option.

Many questionnaires have been developed to assess various constructs (e.g., intelligence, self-esteem, depression, locus of control, liking, loving, attachment style, instructor humor). Next, we describe four scales that have been used in social science research that demonstrate different response formats.

Examples of Different Response Formats for Questionnaires

The Client Perception of Therapy (CPT) uses an open-ended response format for 9 of the 10 items in the scale (Singer, 2013; see Table 3.2a). The scale was developed to assess clients' perspective about and satisfaction with therapy specifically what is helpful or positive. The client responds in writing to the items with the goal of collaborating with their therapist in the treatment process.

A second scale, called the Rotter Internal-External (I-E) Locus of Control Scale, uses a dichotomous response format and assesses whether people hold an internal or an external perspective (Rotter, 1966; see Table 3.2b). Those with an internal perspective are more likely to consider themselves responsible for events and consequences while those with an external perspective believe that their environment or others control events and

Table 3.2a

EXAMPLE OF QUESTIONNAIRE WITH OPEN-ENDED RESPONSE FORMAT

The Client Perception of Therapy Questionnaire—We welcome your participation. One thing we try to do here is provide good care and we would like to learn from your point of view what you think is important about the conversations you have in therapy . . . (p. 164).

What ideas do you have about what needs to happen for improvement to occur?

How well do you feel you related to the therapist? How well did the therapist relate to you?

Did you feel heard, understood, and respected?

Source: Singer, M. (2013). Client perception of therapy (CPT). In K. Corcoran, & J. Fischer (Eds.), *Measures for clinical practice and research: A sourcebook* (5th ed., Vol. 2, pp. 163–164). Oxford, England: Oxford University Press.

Table 3.2b

EXAMPLE OF QUESTIONNAIRE WITH FORCED-CHOICE RESPONSE FORMAT

Rotter's Internal-External (I-E) Locus of Control Scale—*Please circle the a or b statement in each pair that best represents your view of the world. There are no right or wrong answers; we are just interested in your view of the world.*

1. a. Children get into trouble because their parents punish them too much.

   b. The trouble with most children nowadays is that their parents are too easy with them.

2. a. Many of the unhappy things in people's lives are partly due to bad luck.

   b. People's misfortunes result from the mistakes they make.

Source: Rotter, J. (1966). Generalized expectancies for internal versus external control of reinforcement. *Psychological Monographs: General and Applied, 80,* 1–28.

consequences. Each item on the I-E scale consists of a pair of statements, one that represents an internal view and one that represents an external view. Respondents are required to select one statement from the pair that better reflects their view. This response format is referred to as a "forced choice." The full measure has 23 items (plus 6 filler items), and a scale score is computed by adding up the number of external responses so that scores on the scale can range from 0–23, with higher scores reflecting more external views.

The Short Grit Scale (Grit-S) assesses the trait of grit or dedication to one's goals (Duckworth & Quinn, 2009) and employs the commonly used Likert-type response format. The scale consists of eight statements that are rated by respondents on a 5-point scale according to how much a statement is like them (1 = *not at all like me,* 10 = *very much like me*). The eight items are divided into two subscales, Persistence of Effort (4 items) and Consistency of Interest (4 items). Subscales are determined by a statistical analysis, called factor analysis, which examines those items that are responded to similarly or seem interdependent. Once items are identified as related, the researcher decides on a descriptive name for each subscale. In this case, four of the items seemed to describe a willingness to work toward one's goals regardless of any obstacles, and hence the name Persistence of Effort was used for that subscale; while the four items in the Consistency of Interest subscale suggest a commitment to one's particular goals. The Grit-S is short and was found to have only two subscales, but longer questionnaires may have as many as five or six subscales. Other scales or questionnaires used in research may represent a construct as a whole such as Rotter's I-E Locus of Control Scale, which was described above. Occasionally, researchers use only one subscale of a measure because that subscale seems more relevant to their research question than the entire scale.

Table 3.2c

EXAMPLE OF QUESTIONNAIRE WITH LIKERT-TYPE RESPONSE FORMAT

Short Grit Scale (Grit-S)—Mark the number below each item that best describes you.

1. I finish whatever I begin.

1	2	3	4	5
Not at all like me			Very much like me	

2. Setbacks don't discourage me.

1	2	3	4	5
Not at all like me			Very much like me	

3. I often set a goal but later choose to pursue a different one.

1	2	3	4	5
Not at all like me			Very much like me	

Source: Duckworth, A. L., & Quinn, P. D. (2009). Development and validation of the Short Grit Scale (Grit-S). *Journal of Personality Assessment, 91,* 166–174.

Scales sometimes contain items that are worded in opposite ways in order to increase the probability that the respondent is paying attention to the actual content of each item. For example, high scores on the Grit-S scale represent greater grit. Four of the eight items on the scale are written to represent a lack of grit, such as the third item in Table 3.2c, "I often set a goal but later choose to pursue a different one," where a high rating represents low grit. The remaining four items are written to represent grit, such as the first and second items in Table 3.2c, "I finish whatever I begin" and "Setbacks don't discourage me." In order to have the Grit-S scale scored so that higher scores represent more grit, the four items that represent lack of grit are *recoded* so that each "1" becomes a "5," each "2" becomes a "4" and so on. After recoding, all lower ratings reflect low grit and all higher ratings represent high grit.

Observational and Unobtrusive Measures

A second global category of measures is called **observational** and **unobtrusive measures**. We often assess these measures outside the laboratory, although they also can be used in lab studies. Observational measures are just what they imply; we observe an overt behavior, gesture, or facial expression of a person. The people being observed may or may not be aware that they are being observed. Observational measures are different from questionnaires in that the people do not report their behavior, attitude, or emotion; these measures are observed and recorded by others or equipment. The variable to be measured must be operationally defined so that it is explicit enough for observers to determine its presence/absence or level of intensity. The observers who record the behavior should be trained so that their observations are valid (measure the behavior as it is operationally defined) and consistent (reliable) across the observers.

> **Observational measure:** A measure that is rated by observers and sometimes made without the awareness of the person performing the behavior.
>
> **Unobtrusive measure:** A measure that is made of behaviors or situations without disturbing the naturally occurring behavior or situation in order to reduce changes that might occur if there was awareness of measurement.

Unobtrusive measures sometimes are taken in order to make objective judgments about behavior that people may not accurately report, either deliberately or because they are unaware of their behavior. People are unaware of the measurement at the time it is taken and usually are unaware that they have participated in a study. The rationale for unobtrusive measures is not to deceive people but to obtain a valid measure of some factor that people may not report accurately due to concerns about the acceptability of the behavior or due to their lack of attention to their behavior. Webb, Campbell, Schwartz, and Sechrest (1966) wrote a book, *Unobtrusive Measures: Nonreactive Research in the Social Sciences,* documenting the usefulness of such measures as a supplement to questionnaires and surveys that rely on self-report and arguing for their advantages in many situations. They noted such measures as examining carpet wear (how often the carpet needed cleaning or replacing) in front of museum exhibits in order to determine the most popular exhibit and examining the number of empty beer, wine, or liquor bottles in people's trash in order to determine the amount of alcohol consumed at home. In the first case, people may not pay attention to or remember every exhibit they visit and so asking them about their favorite exhibit may not accurately reflect their actual visitation pattern. In the second case, people may underreport the amount of alcohol they drink (for obvious reasons) and so the number of empty bottles may better reflect the amount of alcohol consumed in their home. A selection of different days and different homes could provide a valid measure of alcohol consumed in a particular area or neighborhood. In addition, sampling at least some of the same houses twice could provide a measure of reliability of the measure. Although Webb et al.'s book was written many years ago, unobtrusive measures are still used by researchers today. For example, Clapp, Reed, Martel, Gonzalez, and Ruderman (2014) estimated drinking behavior among low-income residents in a senior center by counting the number of bottles of alcohol in their recycling bins. They found that the number of bottles increased when social security checks were received.

Physiological Measures

Physiological measures assess physical reactions and body functioning. The measure can be very simple in terms of equipment such as temperature taken with a thermometer or more complicated such as brain activity recorded by fMRI. Other measures include skin conductance, heart rate, facial muscle activity, pupil diameter, and EEG. As with any type of measure, interpretation is required. For example, does an increased heart rate imply fear or excitement? Many researchers, however, have found that physiological measures are a useful addition to data collected using traditional self-report and observational techniques. For example, Gibson et al. (2014) studied the engagement of a disabled youth during activities and found that skin temperature, heart rate, and respiration supplemented information gained from questionnaire, interview, and observational measures. They concluded that physiological measures may be particularly appropriate for participants who (because of age, ability, etc.) may be less able or unable to verbally describe their responses or as a more objective measure of constructs. Aldao and De Los Reyes (2016) advocated for including physiological measures as part of assessment and treatment of mental disorders of all ages. They described studies using heart rate and vocal pitch to differentiate those with disorders from controls. Physiological measures may require equipment that is not available or personnel trained on how to use the equipment and/or interpret the output, so this type of measure may not be an available to those just learning how to conduct research. Check with your professor if you are interested in learning more about this type of measure to see if your institution has faculty who are conducting research that involves physiological measures.

> **Physiological measure:** A measure that assesses physical reactions or bodily functioning.

ASSESSING RELIABILITY OF MEASURES

Remember from the discussion of weight at the beginning of the chapter that we want our measure to produce consistent scores given consistent circumstances. Correlation is the statistic that is used to assess reliability—you probably learned about correlation in your introductory course when the methods of your discipline were covered, and learned that a perfect positive correlation equals 1.0 and means that the scores increase or decrease together in a totally consistent pattern. In testing reliability, the closer the correlation is to 1.0, the more reliable the scores on the scale are. There are different types of reliability that can be assessed and are relevant, depending on the situation. You will learn more about when and how to compute correlations in Chapter 8.

Assessing Reliability

Internal Consistency

Internal consistency is used to assess the reliability of scales or subscales. Internal consistency applies only to scales (also called measures) that have multiple items that are meant to be combined into a single score (or subscale scores). Internal consistency means that there is consistency in the way that the participant or observer responded to the multiple items on the scale. We would not want items included in the scale score that do not assess the same variable or that are responded to differently than the other items on a scale.

One common way to compute the internal consistency of a scale is **Cronbach's alpha (α)**, which computes the correlation between responses to all of the items in a scale. In the Grit S (see Table 3.2c, p. 76), we would expect that people would respond similarly (although not necessarily identically) to, "I finish whatever I begin" and "Setbacks don't discourage me." So if a person rated the first item as very much like them, we would expect them to also rate the second item as very much like them. Cronbach's alpha checks for this consistency among all items in a scale. In order for a scale to be considered internally consistent, an alpha of .70 or higher ($\alpha \geq .70$) is desired, although slightly below that is usually considered acceptable.

Cronbach's alpha analysis can tell us the intercorrelations among items and also how alpha would be affected (increased or decreased) if we delete an item. This latter information is important because when alpha is less than .70, we can sometimes delete one or two items in a scale to reach the .70 standard. The two subscales and total scale scores of the Grit-S, mentioned above, were found to be reliable. In a study including 1,554 respondents, the alphas were .77 for Consistency of Interest, .70 for Persistence of Effort, and .82 for the total Grit-S (Duckworth & Quinn, 2009).

Split-half reliability also assesses the internal consistency of the scale. The split-half reliability is a simple correlation of the sum of the scores of half the items to the sum of the other half of the items. However, do not be fooled by the name "split-half" and assume that simply correlating the first and second half of the items is sufficient.

Internal consistency: The consistency of participant responses to all the items in a scale.

Cronbach's alpha (α): Test used to assess the internal consistency of a scale by computing the intercorrelations among responses to scale items; values of .70 or higher are interpreted as acceptable internal consistency.

Split-half reliability: Correlations between the responses to half the items on a scale to the other half (usually even-numbered items correlated with odd-numbered items); values of .70 or higher are considered to denote acceptable reliability.

Sometimes items become more difficult or respondents become fatigued or bored or change in other ways from the beginning to the end of a scale. Such changes would decrease the correlation between the first and second halves of the scale, so in order to check the consistency of answers throughout the scale researchers typically correlate responses to the even and odd items. Like Cronbach's alpha, a correlation of .70 or higher is the accepted standard for split-half reliability.

Test-Retest Reliability

We are sometimes concerned with the consistency of scale scores over time, and in these cases we compute the **test-retest reliability**. People take the measure, wait some period of time, and retake the measure. The total scores for each person for each administration of the scale are then correlated. This type of reliability is particularly relevant for the Self-Control Scale (Tangney, Baumeister, & Boone, 2004), as it was intended to measure the trait of self-control, which should be stable over time. When the scale was first being developed, a sample of college students took the Self-Control Scale a second time approximately three weeks after they completed it the first time. The test-retest reliability was quite high, $r = .89$, showing that the students scored very similarly on the scale both times they completed it. The Grit-S scale is also meant to measure a trait, and adequate reliability ($r = .68$) was found for a sample of middle and high school students who took the scale the second time a year later. (It is unusual to wait such a long time between the two measurements, and the sample was an age group experiencing many developmental changes.) Test-retest reliability is the only type of reliability that can be assessed for a single item that is used to measure a variable. For example, I might ask a class of college students to rate their average self-esteem one day and then to rate it again a week later. Although self-esteem may vary somewhat over time, we would expect that those with high self-esteem would rate themselves higher on both occasions than those with low self-esteem.

Test-retest reliability: A measure of the stability of scores on a scale over time.

Alternate Forms Reliability

Alternate forms reliability is similar to test-retest reliability in that the respondent takes a measure twice. In the case of alternate forms, however, there is more than one form of the measure and the forms are considered to be equal in their ability to measure a construct. Using alternate forms of a scale is one way to avoid practice effects that can occur when one uses the same test or scale to establish reliability. When students take a test such as the SAT more than once, they do not take the exact same test but an alternate form. Each version of the SAT is considered equal in terms of its difficulty and accuracy in measuring the students' mastery of knowledge. One would expect a high positive correlation between two forms of the SAT for a sample of high school seniors.

Alternate forms reliability: The relationship between scores on two different forms of a scale.

Interrater Reliability

Interrater reliability is used when at least two different observers or raters make independent judgments, meaning that they do not know each other's codes or scores. Interrater* reliability is computed by correlating the different raters' scores. We expect to obtain a very* high correlation or agreement (.90 or higher) in order to establish the reliability of the observation measure. In one study (Cramer, Mayer, & Ryan, 2007), trained graduate student observers recorded information about cars leaving a parking structure. Among the information recorded was the gender of the driver, whether the driver was using a cell phone, and whether passengers were present. Interrater reliability was assessed by having pairs of observers make the first 50 observations together. There was very high agreement between the pairs of observers on all three measures: 95.9% agreement about the gender of the driver, 98.9% agreement between observers about the use of a cell phone by a specific driver, and 99% agreement about whether passengers were present.

> **Interrater reliability:** A measure of agreement between different raters' scores.

FIGURE 3.2
Types of Reliability of Individual Measures

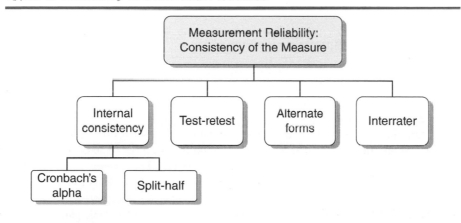

USING DATA ANALYSIS PROGRAMS: MEASUREMENT RELIABILITY

Once you collect data, you can use some type of software to organize the data and to check the reliability of your scale or measure. In our text, we will provide examples from the *Statistical Package for the Social Sciences* (IBM SPSS Statistics 24), which is widely used by social scientists to analyze data. Although the commands and the output for the software used in your course may differ from that shown for SPSS,* the formulas and interpretation of statistical output are the same.

---

*IBM® SPSS® Statistics / SPSS is a registered trademark of International Business Machines Corporation.

Entering Data

All statistical programs have a specific format to follow in entering data. Be sure that you follow the format for the program you are using.

1. Find out how your statistical program treats missing data. Do you leave blank the space when an item was not answered, or is there a particular code for missing data, such as M or 0?

2. It is unethical to eliminate any piece of data because it is not what you expected or does not fit your hypothesis. You should discuss with your professor the possibility of eliminating data that seems to suggest the participant misunderstood what was being asked or did not take the study seriously.

3. Decide on codes for nonnumeric data; for instance, code females as "1," males as "2."

4. Be careful to enter your data accurately, as a mistake in data entry will affect the outcome (even if just a little) of any statistical analysis using those data and can affect the meaning of your results. It is always a good idea to check the accuracy of the entire data file once you have completed entering all the data.

Computing Scale Scores

Many measures in research require that you add or in some way manipulate the individual responses in a scale before computing a total score.

Do you need to recode? One of the most common manipulations we have to perform on data items is to recode some of the items on a scale. Before recoding you must understand how total scores are interpreted for your scale—what do high or low scores imply? You will need to identify whether or which items on the scale do not fit (seem to imply an opposite direction) the stated interpretation. These items will need to be recoded before you can add all the items for a total score on the scale. For example, high scores on the Self-Control Scale (Tangney et al., 2004) are interpreted as signifying high self-control. The scale consists of 36 items that are rated by participants in terms of how much they are like them (1 = *not at all* and 5 = *very much*). Eleven of the items are worded so that a "5" means high self-control ("I refuse things that are bad for me"), while 23 of the items are worded so that a "5" means low self-control ("I am lazy"). The 23 items will then need to be recoded. Follow the directions for your statistical package, which will tell you how to change a response of "1" to "5," a response of "2" to "4," leave "3" as "3," change a response of "4" to "2" and a response of "5" to "1."

Add the scores for a total score: After recoding, you are now ready to compute a total score by adding all of the original items that did not need to be recoded and those that were recoded. Be sure that you include each item (either the original or the recoded score) only once. In our example of the Self-Control Scale, you will sum 11 unaltered ratings from items that did not need to be recoded and 13 recoded ratings to obtain the total self-control score.

Computing Internal Consistency

In many statistical software packages, the internal consistency of multi-item scales can be easily computed using Cronbach's alpha. Remember that Cronbach's alpha examines the consistency of responses within the scale, so that you will use the items that fit the interpretation of the scale (those items that do not need recoding) and the recoded items rather than all of the original items. So computing the internal consistency uses the same values as computing the total scale score. The difference is that one operation (computing the total score) adds the items and the other operation (computing the internal consistency) calculates the correlation among items.

The internal consistency for your sample should be reported when you describe a scale in the Materials or Apparatus section within the Method section in your report.

ASSESSING VALIDITY OF MEASURES

In addition to showing reliability, we also expect scales assessing constructs to be valid or to accurately measure what we say they are measuring. Remember that scales can be reliable without being valid, so it is important to test both reliability and validity. Like reliability, there are different types of validity.

Assessing Validity

Face Validity

The public commonly uses **face validity** to judge whether something measures what it is supposed to measure. For example, someone may tell us that movie *A* is more popular than other movies because the number of tickets sold for movie *A* at their local theater is greater than the number of tickets sold for other movies. The number of tickets sold may be a valid measure of movie popularity; or we may find out that all local high school students were required to see movie *A*, or that a local person stars in movie *A* and everyone wanted to see her in the movie rather than the movie itself. Researchers are suspicious of face validity because it is untested and sometimes based on only one person's opinion or view.

Construct Validity

Construct validity concerns whether a measure is reflective of the hypothetical construct of a variable. It is a general sense of what the variable means. So self-control must be defined in a way that reflects the attitudes, behaviors, and emotions associated with the construct. Several types of validity help us to determine whether our scale has construct validity.

> **Face validity:** Whether a particular measure seems to be appropriate as a way to assess a construct.
>
> **Construct validity:** Whether a measure mirrors the characteristics of a hypothetical construct; can be assessed in multiple ways.

Content validity is related to the items that make up a scale. Do the items in the scale accurately reflect the construct we are attempting to measure? Are all aspects of the construct represented among our items? Researchers may consult with experts in the field, or use a theory that is related to the construct, or examine past research on the construct to develop items to measure a particular construct. The SMS Problem Use Diagnostic Questionnaire (SMS-PUDQ) assesses the problematic or overuse of SMS, otherwise known as text messaging (Rutland, Sheets, & Young, 2007). In developing the SMS-PUDQ the researchers began with a model of addiction (Griffiths, 2005), which included several characteristics of addiction such as withdrawal, tolerance, relapse, mood modification, and compulsivity. They also reviewed past research on the development of the Mobile Phone Problematic Use Scale (MPPUS), which used the same addiction model but focused on cell phone use rather than texting. Finally, they studied research that had examined other types of technology addiction (Internet, for example). Based on all of this information, they developed items for their scale that were meant to assess problematic text messaging. For instance, the item "I use SMS longer than originally intended" was meant to represent compulsivity, which is part of Griffiths's addiction model and fit with the past research on problematic use of cell phones and other technologies. In developing the items for their Self-Control Scale, Tangney et al. (2004) examined existing scales that measured self-control and past research on the construct. Their scale included items assessing the factors related to self-control as identified by past research (e.g., achievement, impulse control, interpersonal relationships). There is no statistical test to assess content validity, but experts or those scrutinizing scales may criticize or praise a scale for its coverage of the construct the scale is intended to measure.

Convergent validity assesses the relationship of a scale to an existing measure of the same or a similar construct that has already shown adequate validity. Convergent refers to the fact that we expect the new scale to be positively correlated to the existing measures or to accepted measures. For example, Rutland et al. (2007) found that scores on the SMS-PUDQ were significantly related to self-reported minutes spent in a week sending and receiving text messages as well as scores on the MPPUS. Likewise, the convergent validity of the Self-Control Scale was established by finding that college students' scores on the scale positively correlated with the factors identified in past research as related to self-control, including higher grades, fewer eating and alcohol problems, and more positive interpersonal relationships (Tangney et al., 2004). The Grit-S was shown to be positively related to Conscientiousness on the Big Five

---

Content validity: Inclusion of all aspects of a construct by items on a scale or measure.

Convergent validity: Positive relationship between two scales measuring the same or similar constructs.

Inventory, education achievement, and ratings of a person's grit by a family member and close friend (Duckworth & Quinn, 2009), suggesting this scale also demonstrates convergent validity.

Not only do we expect our scale to positively correlate with related behaviors or scales, but we also expect scale scores to negatively correlate or have no correlation with scales assessing unrelated or different constructs. This type of validity is called **divergent validity**. For example, the scores for adults on the Grit-S were negatively correlated with a measure of neuroticism and number of career changes (Duckworth & Quinn, 2009). We might also expect that scores on the Self Control Scale would be inversely related to scores on the SMS-PUDQ as it reflects problems with controlling one's texting frequency. We sometimes include such correlations in order to demonstrate the distinctiveness of a scale (divergent validity) or to show that a scale does not measure a different construct (convergent validity).

The final type of construct validity we might measure is **criterion validity**, which relates scores from a scale to a behavior that represents the construct measured by the scale. There are two types of criterion validity: **concurrent validity** and **predictive validity**. These two types of validity differ only in timing of the behavior. Concurrent validity establishes a relationship between a scale and a current behavior, while predictive validity establishes a relationship between a scale score and a future behavior. For instance, SAT scores from the fall could be correlated to seniors' high school cumulative GPA to show concurrent validity of the SAT. The same SAT scores could be correlated to seniors' first-year college GPA to establish predictive validity. Scores on the Grit-S were related to high school students' GPA a year later and to the retention of Military cadets over their first summer at the academy (Duckworth & Quinn, 2009). Using the SMS-PUDQ, we could correlate scores with minutes texting the same day to establish concurrent validity or texting minutes reported on their phone bill the next month to establish predictive validity. We would expect that those who have problems of overuse according to the SMS-PUDQ would have texted more at both times (at the current time and next month) than those who scored lower on the SMS-PUDQ.

Divergent validity: Negative or no relationship between two scales measuring different constructs.

Criterion validity: Positive correlation between scale scores and a behavioral measure.

Concurrent validity: Positive correlation between scale scores and a current behavior that is related to the construct assessed by the scale.

Predictive validity: Positive relationship between scale scores and a future behavior that is related to the construct assessed by the scale.

FIGURE 3.3
Types of Validity of Individual Measures

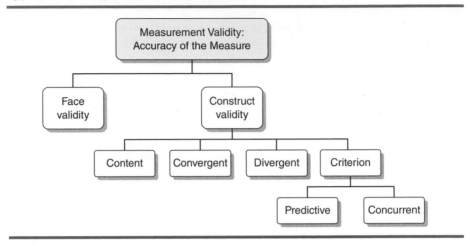

Ethics Tip: Using Appropriate Measures to Get Meaningful Results

According to ethical guidelines, all studies should be designed to increase our knowledge about behaviors, situations, or theories. This means that researchers have a responsibility to use only those measures or procedures that will produce meaningful results. If you (or anyone) conduct research that includes unreliable or invalid measures or employs procedures full of confounds so that you cannot generalize the results or even make sense of them, you have violated the ethical standards for research. You would be wasting participants' time if you collect data with an unreliable measure or one that is not explicitly defined and valid. Likewise, you have wasted participants' time if you cannot make judgments about the results of your study because there are multiple likely explanations for your findings.

Researchers depend on the good will of society in terms of providing willing participants and in supporting legitimate research. Studies that cause suspicion about the usefulness or benefits of social and behavioral studies harm more than just the researcher conducting the meaningless research. Carefully selecting valid and reliable measures is a first step in fulfilling your ethical responsibilities as a researcher.

Practice 3.2

EXAMPLES FROM THE LITERATURE

Review the following excerpts from journal articles. As you do so, consider the following questions:

- What is the purpose of the described scale?
- What do I learn about the development and format of the scale/questionnaire?

- What do I learn about the reliability of the scale?

- What do I learn about the validity of the scale?

Article 1

Levett-Hooper, G., Komarraju, M., Weston, R., & Dollinger, S. (2007). Is plagiarism a forerunner of other deviance? Imagined futures of academically dishonest students. *Ethics and Behavior, 17,* 323–336.

> Academic Dishonesty Student Survey (McCabe, 1992). The Academic Dishonesty Student Survey is a widely used measure to assess academic dishonesty. It measures the frequency of 19 specific student behaviors . . . that are rated on a 4-point scale ranging 1 (*never*), 2 (*once*), 3 (*more than once*), and 4 (*not relevant*). For this study, 18 items from McCabe's scale and 2 additional items ("Cheating in a class taught by an instructor you do not like" and "Cheating in a class taught by an instructor you like") were included in the measure of Academic Dishonesty. . . . Responses of 4 (*not relevant*) were treated as missing data. A high score signifies more dishonest behavior. With a sample of 11,818 participants, McCabe (1992) reported a Cronbach's alpha coefficient of .87 for the total scale score. In the current study, the alpha value for the entire scale was .93. (pp. 326 327)
>
> There was a clear pattern of significant positive correlations between all the three subscales of the Academic Dishonesty Scale and Norm/Rule Violations, suggesting that those who show a lack of academic integrity in college may be more likely to violate norms and rules of society or the workplace in the future. Because one of the Norm/Rule items referred to cheating on an important future test, these results were examined with the critical item removed. Again, the three factors correlated significantly with imagined future norm/rule violations (*r*s = .43, .49, and .43, respectively). (p. 330)

Article 2

Castilho, P., Pinto-Gouveia, J., & Duarte, J. (2015). Evaluating the multifactor structure of the long and short versions of the Self-Compassion Scale in a clinical sample. *Journal of Clinical Psychology, 71,* 856-870.

> Drawing on several Buddhist readings (e.g., Bennett-Goleman, 2001; Brach, 2003; Goldstein & Kornfield, 1987; Salzberg, 1997), Neff (2003a, b) has proposed a definition of self-compassion based on three main components: self-kindness, common humanity, and mindfulness. (p. 857)
>
> The SCS-LF (Self Compassion Scale-Long Form) is a 26-item self-report questionnaire that measures six components of self-compassion: self-kindness . . . ; self-judgment . . . ; common humanity . . . ; mindfulness; and overidentification. . . . Items are rated on a 5-point Likert scale ranging from 1 (*almost never*) to 5 (*almost always*). Research indicates that the SCS-LF demonstrates concurrent validity, convergent validity, discriminate validity, test-retest reliability, and good internal consistency (α = .92; Neff, 2003a). . . .
>
> In the present study, Cronbach's alphas for the total scale in the clinical and nonclinical samples were .92 and .94, respectively, and ranged between .70 and .88 for the subscales. (p. 859-860)

See Appendix A to check your answers.

RELIABILITY AND VALIDITY AT THE STUDY LEVEL

Study Reliability

The **reliability of a study** refers to the expectation that we will find similar results when we repeat a study. In research we are seeking to identify general patterns of behavior. If similar studies find different results, this suggests that we have not found a pattern in which we can have confidence. **Replication,** or repeating a study, is one way to test the reliability of a finding from a study and can be literal or conceptual. A literal replication occurs when we repeat a study in an identical manner, using the same variables and procedure and a similar sample. Most of the time we do not re-do a study in exactly the same form. Makel, Plucker, and Hegarty (2012) examined top psychology journals and found a replication rate of only slightly higher than 1%. Researchers instead are more likely to conduct a conceptual replication by examining the same patterns or relationships in a slightly different way or by including additional variables. Makel et al. argue that disciplines would better understand when findings are "true" if we conducted more literal replications by authors different from those conducting the original study.

> **Reliability of a study:** How consistent the results are across similar studies.
>
> **Replication:** Conducting the same study with new participants (literal replication) or conducting a study examining the same patterns or relationships but with different methods (conceptual replication).

For example, in studying how to reduce plagiarism, researchers have found that hands-on experience is more effective than providing explanations or resources about academic dishonesty (Belter & du Pré, 2009; Culwin, 2006; Estow et al., 2011; Owens & White, 2013; Schuetze, 2004). Of the research we just cited, Schuetze (2004) completed the earliest study with a single homework assignment; Belter and du Pré (2009) required students to show 100% mastery on a quiz about plagiarism, proper citation, and penalties for violations. Students in Culwin's (2006) study completed an essay assignment that was assessed for non-originality; students then received feedback about the violations and discussed academic integrity. Estow et al. (2011) examined the effect of using plagiarism as a research topic for an entire course. They included among the many student assignments a survey of attitudes toward and knowledge about plagiarism and an experiment that examined the effect of student plagiarism and intent on ratings of severity of punishment and mood of professor. Over a five-year period, Owens and White (2013) examined the use of multiple plagiarism-reducing techniques in first year psychology classes. They began with a plagiarism detection software and added in subsequent years in-class online essays with feedback about plagiarism; online graded quizzes covering the definition of plagiarism; appropriate rephrasing, citations, and referencing format; and an in-class tutorial that included peer feedback about students' plagiarism. Each successive year included the techniques from previous years in addition to a new plagiarism exercise.

Although each of the studies examined a different type of "hands-on experience," they all found similar results—that plagiarism was better understood and avoided following the hands-on experience, and thus the conceptual replications were successful in demonstrating reliability of the findings of Schuetze's (2004) study. In other words, the hands-on experience had a reliable effect on reducing plagiarism. This is the reliability that we seek from studies, that the results can be replicated or repeated in future studies.

In contrast to the studies cited above that constitute conceptual replications, a literal replication could have been conducted with college students using Schuetze's procedure of a single homework assignment and assessing its effect on reducing plagiarism among students.

If the studies examining hands-on experience had not found the same results, we would question the reliability of the Schuetze study and would then be skeptical of her results. However, just because we find consistent or reliable results across several studies does not guarantee that those results are accurate.

Note that:

- Results of a study *cannot* be valid unless they are reliable.
- Results of a study *can* be reliable but not valid.

In other words, reliability is a prerequisite for validity but reliability alone is not sufficient to demonstrate validity. The validity of a study refers to how accurate the results are and is examined in two ways: **internal validity** and **external validity**.

> **Internal validity:** The degree to which we can say that we found an accurate relationship among variables, in that changes in one variable (the DV) are caused by changes in another variable (the IV). Relevant only to studies examining causation
>
> **External validity:** The degree to which we can say that the results of a study are accurate for different types of people in different settings assessed with different procedures.

Internal Validity

Internal validity applies when the researchers are interested in examining a causal relationship. If a researcher wants to determine that *A* causes *B*, then he or she must

brown dog studios

REVIEW OF KEY CONCEPTS: INDEPENDENT AND DEPENDENT VARIABLES

1. If A is the variable that is manipulated, and B is the variable that is measured, which is the independent variable (IV) and which is the dependent variable (DV)?

2. What type of research design uses IVs and DVs to demonstrate a causal relationship?

3. What is the other key ingredient of this type of design?

You are correct if you said A is the IV and B is the DV, and that an experiment is the specific type of research design that examines a causal relationship through manipulation of the IV and measurement of the DV. Random assignment to groups is the other key factor in experiments.

manipulate *A*, measure *B*, and control for all the other extraneous variables that could have an effect on *B*.

In reality, it is very difficult to control for every possible extraneous variable in a study. Therefore, internal validity is the extent to which we can say that the result from a study is, in fact, caused or determined by the manipulation of the independent variable rather than some other factor. We want to be confident that our findings are directly related to the independent variable, and this is why researchers examining causality use an experimental design to reduce the chances that something other than the independent variable caused changes in the dependent variable. Internal validity is also why we use control groups to show that when only one factor (the independent variable) is changed, the outcome (the dependent variable) is affected or changed.

Let's apply this information about internal validity to Schuetze's (2004) study. Students in both the experimental and control sections of developmental psychology heard a presentation and received a handout describing plagiarism and how to avoid this academic violation. Students in the experimental group also completed a homework assignment early in the semester that required them to identify statements requiring citations within a brief manuscript. These students received feedback on the assignment and discussed correct citations in class. A comparison of the experimental and control groups on a homework assignment later in the semester that required students to identify where citations belonged showed that the experimental group who had completed a previous assignment performed significantly better than the control group who received similar information but did not complete the earlier assignment. Note that the students were in the same type of class and received similar information about plagiarism. The only difference was the homework assignment, which allowed the experimental group to practice the information they gained from the plagiarism presentation and handout.

We might question the internal validity of the study (that the hands-on experience influenced the skill in correctly citing sources) if the study had included obvious differences between the experimental and control groups other than the citation practice. For example, what if the researcher had obtained participants from two different types of classes, one with more advanced psychology majors and one with first-year students or had used two different assignments to judge the ability to correctly use citations (and thus avoid plagiarism)? In each of these cases a factor besides the additional homework assignment could be responsible for the results. In the former case, the more advanced students will have taken more psychology classes than the first-year students and been exposed to more information about citing sources in psychology papers. In the latter case where two different assignments were used, one of them might be more difficult than the other, which could account for the differences in citation skill. A factor that is not controlled by the researcher and that systematically influences the results is called a **confound**. Confounds or threats to the internal validity of a study come in many forms and will be discussed in detail in Chapter 9.

> **Confound (or confounding variable):** A variable that varies systematically with the variables in a study and is a potential alternative explanation for causality.

External Validity

External validity refers to the ability to generalize the results of a study to other settings, other samples, and other methods. Findings about social situations, attitudes, behaviors, and the factors that impact them are of little use if they apply only to the specific participants in the study. Even if the results are replicated with other participants and produce reliable results, we might question the external validity of the results if all the participants represent a specific group, such as 18-year-old college students taking an introductory psychology course. Additionally, we would wonder about the external validity if studies were conducted primarily within one setting or used one procedure, such as when research is primarily completed with small samples of college students in a laboratory-like setting.

External validity of any particular study is a matter of degree. The more diverse the sample and the more realistic the setting and procedures, the greater the likelihood that the results will generalize beyond the particular people and setting of your study. Limiting your sample to college students or to a laboratory setting does not mean that the study has no external validity. It simply means that we do not know if the results would generalize or not, and that future research is needed to replicate the study with other samples and in other settings. Remember there is no perfect study, and it is not feasible to examine all types of participants in all different settings using all different types of procedures.

For example, we wonder if the homework assignment used by Schuetze (2004) in a developmental psychology course is applicable to other classes within other disciplines (e g , criminal justice, economics, history) or to different age groups (e.g., high school students). Citation skill was measured in the Schuetze study and found to increase with practice. Hopefully other skills related to avoiding plagiarism (paraphrasing, for example) could be increased with hands-on practice. You can see why a researcher might spend her lifetime researching a single topic, as there is much work that can be done to test the external validity of one study.

Practice 3.3 gives you the opportunity to test whether you understand the concepts of validity and reliability at the study level. If you are not able to correctly identify these examples, you may want to review the previous pages.

Balancing Internal and External Validity

Tension always exists between internal and external validity because the greater the internal validity, the harder it is to achieve external validity. Internal validity is established by tightly controlling the experimental situation, which then may decrease the probability that the results will generalize beyond the specific situation defined by the study. However, if the experimental setting and procedure are too uncontrolled in order to better represent circumstances in "real life" where a multitude of factors can vary, the internal validity of the study may be so compromised that one is unable to obtain significant results or is unable to identify which factor or factors have created differences in the dependent variable.

Thus, researchers must find a balance between the internal and external validity so that they are confident that the IV is responsible for the changes in the DV and

Practice 3.3

DISTINGUISHING BETWEEN EXTERNAL VALIDITY, INTERNAL VALIDITY, AND RELIABILITY AT THE STUDY LEVEL

Read the following examples and determine whether they are related to external validity, internal validity, or reliability at the study level.

Cobb, Heaney, Corcoran, and Henderson-Begg (2010) found that student satisfaction in a British University with using texting in class was very high, especially among more timid students. A faculty member at your institution decides to implement a texting system in his classroom to see if he obtains the same results with students at a U.S. university.

Vredeveldt, Tredoux, Nortje, Kempen, Puljević, and Labuschagne (2015) found that during the interview by police, witnesses to serious crimes who were instructed to close their eyes when recalling the crime provided more relevant information than those who kept their eyes open, although the total amount of detail recalled did not differ. Suppose you find that not only did the witnesses who provided more relevant evidence close their eyes but they also were interviewed at the crime site, while the witnesses who kept their eyes open were interviewed at the police station. What aspect of the experiment does this new information call into question?

Estow et al. (2011) examined the topic of plagiarism as a research theme throughout one semester in two different sections of Research Methods. Students completed different assignments that used plagiarism as the focus. The results were the same for both experimental sections in terms of increased understanding of plagiarism and improved paraphrasing skills relative to a control group of students studying research methods but using a different theme.

See Appendix A to check your answers.

that the findings are relevant to other situations and populations. Because of their particular interest, researchers may choose to focus more on one type of validity than the other. For example, if the researcher is examining the effect of a new variable or a new procedure, he may focus on internal validity or increased control within the study in order to increase his chances of finding significant results. Another researcher may be more interested in how well a finding established in one setting generalizes to other settings. For example, there have been studies in the classroom demonstrating cell phones are distracting and they decrease learning (End et al., 2010; Froese et al., 2012; Kuznekoff & Titsworth, 2013; Wood et al., 2012) so a researcher might test if personal cell phone use will decrease productivity in an office setting. This second researcher may focus on external validity by completing the study in a setting that does not allow for the rigid controls that are possible in the laboratory. You should be starting to see how many legitimate possibilities exist for research within a particular area and how each study can add to our knowledge about the effect of an IV on a DV in slightly different and valuable ways.

In Application 3.1, two studies are reviewed in terms of how they balance internal and external validity.

Application 3.1

BALANCING INTERNAL AND EXTERNAL VALIDITY IN RESEARCH

Let's return to two of the studies we described in Chapter 2:

Internal Validity

Harackiewicz et al.'s (2014) study is an experiment, and therefore internal validity is a primary focus. Extensive efforts to maximize internal validity are described in the Method (in The Intervention section), including:

1. The IV condition was the only factor that varied across the groups.

2. Participants were randomly assigned to the IV condition to help ensure that the groups were similar prior to exposure to the IV manipulation (values affirmation or control).

3. The introduction to the study, outward appearance of the writing assignment, and instructions (except for the IV manipulation) were identical. In addition, instructors and lab assistants were unaware of the condition that participants were assigned to—this is called a double blind experiment and will be addressed in later chapters beginning with Chapter 9.

Hill, Burrow, and Bronk's (2016) study of two correlates of grit (positive affect and sense of purpose) is not an experiment, and therefore establishing a causal relationship and having strong internal validity is not a focus.

Even so, maintaining some level of control is important in all studies, not just those that examine causal relationships. Notice that Hill and her colleagues were careful to keep the measures and procedures the same across participants within each of the two studies.

External Validity

Efforts that Harackiewicz et al. took to increase internal validity may reduce the external validity of the study. The sample consisted of students who were participating for credit, in a large introductory biology course with multiple instructors. The study also focused on first-generation students, and the manipulation involved students completing an assignment that their professors would not see. We might wonder how these results would generalize to other samples of students—particularly those in small class situations where they know their professor well and where the professor sees their responses to their essays. Finally, given that the majority of the sample was of traditional college age and White, we might wonder how these results would generalize to adult, non-White college students.

Hill et al. had large samples, but like the Harackiewicz et al. study, the students were undergraduates and the majority of the students were traditional-aged college students, female, and White. One sample was from a Canadian university and another from a U.S. university. We might question how well the results would generalize to different samples of older, non-White, or male undergraduates or to young adults not attending a university.

THE BIG PICTURE: CONSISTENCY AND ACCURACY

Consistency (a.k.a. reliability) and accuracy (a.k.a. validity) are linked in research just as they are in day-to-day life. If you have a friend who consistently shows up on time and another who consistently shows up 15 minutes late, you would say that both of them are reliable. Their reliability allows you to judge the validity, or accuracy, of your meeting time, in that your first friend will set a valid meeting time, and your second friend will not.

In research, measurement reliability suggests that participants are responding to the measure in a consistent way. But just because we have a reliable measure does not mean that it is also valid. We need to take extra steps to determine measurement validity, and we should also consider what type of validity we are assessing. For example, there is a difference between a measure that accurately represents the construct of interest (i.e., content validity) and one that predicts a future outcome (predictive validity). Once we establish reliable and valid measures, we can determine if the results of the study are reliable and valid. If results of a study are replicated and the results are consistent across the replications, we can say that those results are reliable. We then need to consider if the method of the studies allows us to accurately determine causality (internal validity) and if it allows us to accurately generalize the results to other samples, situations, and methods (external validity).

CHAPTER RESOURCES

Key Terms

Define the following terms using your own words. You can check your answers by reviewing the chapter or by comparing them with the definitions in the glossary—but try to define them on your own first.

Alternate forms
   reliability 80
Closed-ended response
   format 73
Concurrent validity 85
Confound (or confounding
   variable) 90
Construct 65
Construct validity 83
Content validity 84
Convergent validity 84
Criterion validity 85
Cronbach's alpha (α) 79
Divergent validity 85
Equal intervals 67
External validity 89
Face validity 83

Forced-choice response
   format 74
Identity 67
Internal consistency 79
Internal validity 89
Interrater reliability 81
Interval scale 70
Likert-type scale 70
Measurement reliability 64
Measurement validity 64
Nominal scale 68
Observational measure 77
Open-ended response format 73
Operational definition 65
Order 67
Ordinal scale 68
Physiological measure 78

Predictive validity 85
Qualitative measure 66
Quantitative measure 66
Questionnaire 73
Ratio scale 71
Reliability 64
Reliability of a study 88
Replication 88
Response format 73
Scale score 73
Split-half reliability 79
Test-retest reliability 80
True zero
   (or absolute zero) 68
Unobtrusive measure 77
Validity 64

Do You Understand the Chapter?

Answer these questions on your own, and then review the chapter to check your answers.

1. What is the difference between internal and external validity? How does each type of validity contribute to the research process?

2. How are operational definitions related to validity and reliability of measures?

3. Distinguish between qualitative and quantitative measures.

4. What are the four scales of measurement, and what qualities distinguish each scale?

5. What scales of measurement are most commonly used in psychological research?

6. What is a questionnaire?

7. What is the difference between open- and closed-ended items? What are the advantages and disadvantages of each type of response?

8. How can we determine if a measure/scale is reliable? Describe the different ways that are possible.

9. What does Cronbach's alpha tell us? What standard/level should alpha achieve?

10. How can we determine if a measure is valid? Distinguish between the different types of validity.

11. What are observational measures?

12. How do we determine if observations are reliable?

13. What are the advantages of unobtrusive measures?

14. Why is it important to identify items that require recoding in a questionnaire?

15. How do confounds influence the validity of a study? Give an example of a possible confound in a study.

16. Explain the balance that must be achieved between the internal and external validity of a study.

Practice Dataset

A researcher conducts an extensive survey on the use of texting. She also collects information about the participants' age and gender. Here is the five-question scale she used to measure attitudes regarding texting with one's romantic partner:

Please rate how much you agree with each statement	Strongly Disagree	Disagree	Neither Agree Nor Disagree	Agree	Strongly Agree
1. Texting allows me to stay in consistent contact with my partner.	1	2	3	4	5
2. Text messages can easily be misunderstood.	1	2	3	4	5
3. Texting is better than talking on the phone because my partner and I can communicate without others hearing any part of our conversation.	1	2	3	4	5

(Continued)

(Continued)

Please rate how much you agree with each statement	Strongly Disagree	Disagree	Neither Agree Nor Disagree	Agree	Strongly Agree
4. Texting decreases face-to-face contact with my partner.	1	2	3	4	5
5. Almost all of my text messages to my partner are positive.	1	2	3	4	5

She collected data from 10 people; here is a summary of the data:

ID	Age	Gender	Texting Questionnaire				
			Q1	Q2	Q3	Q4	Q5
1	31	Female	5	3	2	2	4
2	19	Male	4	4	3	1	5
3	20	Female	4	1	4	1	4
4	55	Male	3	5	2	1	2
5	21	Female	5	1	5	3	5
6	22	Female	5	2	5	1	5
7	18	Male	4	4	5	2	4
8	19	Male	4	3	4	2	4
9	22	Male	4	2	4	1	4
10	24	Female	5	2	2	2	3

1. Enter the data. All variables should be numeric, so be sure to code gender as numbers.

2. Look over the questionnaire. You will want all the questions to indicate more positive views of texting with romantic partners. Right now there are some questions that need to be reverse coded. Recode the questions you identified so that a score of 1 = 5, 2 = 4, 3 = 3, 4 = 2, 5 = 1.

3. Compute the total score on the text-use questionnaire by computing the sum of the five questions. Remember to use the recoded variables here, not the original ones.

4. Compute the internal consistency for the questionnaire by computing Cronbach's alpha. Comment about your results for internal consistency. What could you do to improve the internal consistency of the questionnaire so that it meets the .70 standard?

 **SAGE edge™**   edge.sagepub.com/adams2e

Sharpen your skills with SAGE edge!
SAGE edge for students provides you with tools to help you study. You'll find mobile-friendly eFlashcards and quizzes, as well as videos, web resources, datasets, and links to SAGE journal articles related to this chapter.

Basics of Research Design

DESCRIPTION, MEASUREMENT, AND SAMPLING

How has social media use changed over the years?
What characteristics do people consider important in a leader?
Who values academic honesty?

Descriptive research seeks to answer these types of "who, what, where, when, and how" questions. These questions serve as a way to get more detail about an event or to understand attitudes and behaviors. A descriptive research study is the most basic type of study, and serves as an important first step prior to predicting or explaining events, attitudes, or behaviors. In all research designs, a researcher must also decide what methods of measurement to use and how to obtain a sample.

WHEN IS A DESCRIPTIVE STUDY APPROPRIATE?

Understand Prevalence and Trends

Descriptive research can be used to provide a quick snapshot of the prevalence of a phenomenon. **Prevalence** is the commonness, or frequency, of a behavior, attitude, characteristic, or condition within a specified time period. Such studies are quite common among health researchers who want to know the prevalence of a specific type of risk behavior (e.g., smoking) or disease (e.g., cancer). This descriptive research allows for an assessment of the need for intervention and can also be used to target interventions toward those who seem to be at highest risk.

> **Prevalence:** How common or widespread a behavior, attitude, characteristic, or condition is within a specific time period.

LEARNING OUTCOMES

In this chapter, you will learn

- When a descriptive study is appropriate
- How to evaluate the validity of descriptive research
- Common methods used in research, including surveys, observations, and archives
- How to define a population and obtain a sample using probability and nonprobability sampling techniques

Descriptive research also helps us understand trends. A **trend** is the pattern of change in prevalence over time. To examine trends in behaviors and attitudes, the Pew Research Center has been collecting and sharing information on issues impacting American life since the early 1990s. They poll the public about a variety of subjects including global attitudes and views of the press and public policies. They also track social and demographic trends. This type of descriptive information helps paint a picture of our changing national and political landscape for policy makers, and can prompt further research on how and why behaviors and attitudes change.

> **Trend:** Pattern of change in prevalence over time.

At the beginning of the chapter, we posed the question, *"How has social media use changed over the years?"* Research from the Pew Research Center can help answer this question. Findings from a study comparing social media use from 2012 to 2015 reveal that Facebook continues to be the most popular social media site. Facebook use was steady, with 67% of American adults using this platform in 2012, 71% in 2013 and 2014, and 72% in 2015. Although Instagram and Pinterest are less popular, use of both of these sites more than doubled from 2012 to 2015. Frequency of Instagram use was 13% in 2012 and 28% in 2015, and Pinterest saw a rise from 15% to 31% (Duggan, 2015). Understanding such trends can prompt additional descriptive research. For example, we might want to better understand how individuals use these different sites and what they believe the value of one site might be over another.

Explore a Phenomenon in Depth

Descriptive studies also allow for an in-depth examination of a topic. This type of research can be especially useful for examining a relatively new phenomenon, such as the use of Pinterest. Or, this type of research might be used to gain a better understanding of behaviors and attitudes. For example, at the beginning of the chapter, we raised the question, "What characteristics do people consider important in a leader?" The Pew Research Center asked a question similar to this in 2014 and found that honest, intelligent, and decisive were the top characteristics, followed by organized, compassionate, innovative, and ambitious (Pew Research Center, 2015).

Researchers can also use descriptive research to determine if the patterns they found in their study fit with existing research and theories. If not, they may modify the theories or develop new ones that will be tested with future research. In this way, descriptive research serves as an important first step in the progress of science. Before attempting to predict or explain an event, attitude, or behavior, it must first be accurately described.

Examine a Phenomenon in a Different Population

Just because a phenomenon is described in one population does not necessarily mean that the description will fit a different population. Thus, another reason for conducting a descriptive study might be to consider if patterns and prevalence of behaviors and attitudes that are found in one population are similar in a different population. The rationale for such a study is strengthened if there is research evidence suggesting why the prevalence or pattern might be different. Our final question at the beginning of the chapter was, *"Who values academic honesty?"* Trost (2009) conducted a study to examine the type and frequency of academic dishonesty among Swedish university students. Her rationale for conducting the study was twofold: Past research had suggested that Swedes tend to value honesty and abhor lying to a great degree and that this morality is part of the Swedish identity. Because there had not been any research on academic dishonesty conducted with a Swedish population, she made the case for the need to conduct a descriptive study to document patterns of academic honesty in a different population than had been previously evaluated.

REVIEW OF KEY CONCEPTS: STUDY VALIDITY

Can you recall what type of study validity is under examination when we wonder if results from one study generalize to a different population? More broadly, this type of study validity also deals with questions about whether results from one study will generalize to other participants (or animal subjects), other settings, and other methods.

If you answered "external validity," you are correct! If not, take a minute to review the concepts of validity from Chapter 3. Remember that external validity is not something that a study has or does not have, but instead reminds us to

consider how generalizable the results of one study might be to other participants, settings, or methods. Therefore, when we evaluate the external validity of the Pew Research Center's report on the prevalence of social media use in the United States, we do not say that the results cannot generalize to other countries. Instead, we simply wonder if the results might be similar or different in other countries. In accordance with the process of science, the question of external validity might prompt other researchers to examine this question empirically.

Practice 4.1

WHICH OF THESE QUESTIONS MIGHT BE EXAMINED WITH A DESCRIPTIVE STUDY?

(Hint: There are three questions that could be examined with a descriptive study.)

a. How have the rates of peanut allergies changed over time?

b. Where is most desirable vacation spot?

c. Are men more likely than women to get pulled over for a traffic violation?

d. What is the most popular type of social media site among older adults?

e. Can eating chocolate improve your mood?

See Appendix A to check your answers.

REVIEW OF KEY CONCEPTS: MEASUREMENT VALIDITY AND STUDY VALIDITY

Measurement validity is the extent to which the measures used in a study actually measure what they intend to measure. Types of measurement validity include face validity and construct validity. Construct validity can be further broken down into content, convergent, divergent, and criterion (predictive or concurrent) validity.

Study validity refers to the overall validity of the study and is used to determine the accuracy of the study's conclusions.

Internal validity is the extent to which you can demonstrate a causal link between your variables. External validity is the extent to which results of one study generalize to other samples, settings, and methods.

In order to accurately describe something, the measures used must be valid (see Table 4.1). Recall from Chapter 3 that a measure cannot be valid unless it is reliable. Having all the participants experience the same testing environment can increase reliability of measures in descriptive research as well as having all coders use the same standards. Training any interviewers, observers, or coders and allowing them to practice prior to the start of the study increases validity. Conducting a **pilot study** in which you carry out a study with a smaller sample is a good way to test the measures and work out any kinks prior to conducting the full study.

Pilot study: A preliminary study with a small sample to test measures and procedures.

TABLE 4.1

Validity in Descriptive Studies

Measurement Validity	Study Validity (Internal versus External)
Essential to all studies: Choose measures that are valid in that they accurately measure what they are supposed to measure.	Descriptive study: Focus on external validity in that the results generalize to other samples, settings, and methods.

Measurement reliability is essential to the measurement validity, but reliability alone is not sufficient. To increase the measurement validity, be sure that each question or code assesses only one idea at a time, and adequately represents the construct of interest. Many novice researchers begin designing their study by making up their own questions or codes. After all, this appears to be the best way to ensure that they are worded such that they measure exactly what the researcher wants them to measure. Starting from scratch, however, is not the best way to approach measurement validity. Remember that you will want your study to build on past research, and therefore it is important to find out how others operationally defined their variables. Using measures with established reliability and validity helps your research fit in with past research and also saves time in having to create and test your own measures. If such measures are unavailable or do not seem to actually measure what you want, you can use the measures, questions, and codes from past research as a model or edit them to apply to your own research.

Measurement validity is critical to any type of research study, as is the overall validity of the study. However, the type of study validity that is important varies based on the research design. Descriptive research examines the "who, what, where, when, and how," but it does not examine the "why." In other words, descriptive research does not seek to explain what caused a situation, feeling, or behavior. Purely descriptive studies do not examine the relationship among variables. Because of this, internal validity of the study is not a concern in descriptive research. Instead, external validity of the study is of primary concern in descriptive research. Descriptive studies describe the participants, animals, or archives that were part of the study, but the researcher hopes that the findings will apply beyond the study's sample. The external validity of the study depends on who the population of interest is and how the sample was obtained.

MEASUREMENT METHODS

There are many different measurement methods of descriptive research, but keep in mind that none are exclusively used for descriptive designs alone. We introduce methods commonly used in descriptive research here; but these same methods can be used in correlational research, and some can be used in experimental research as well. Examples of each of these methods can be found in Applications 4.1 and 4.2 (pp. 122, 128), and a comparison of the advantages and disadvantages appears in Table 4.2 (p. 111).

Survey Research

Survey research involves asking people to report on their own attitudes and behaviors. Such self-reports can provide insight into how individuals see themselves and allow the researcher to obtain information about people's thoughts and feelings that cannot be directly observed. The disadvantage is that self-reports may not be accurate, either because people are deceiving themselves or are trying to deceive the researcher.

> **Survey research:** Interviews or questionnaires in which participants report on their attitudes and behaviors.

FIGURE 4.1

Social Desirability Bias

Source: Eva K. Lawrence

In particular, self-reports may be inaccurate due to the **social desirability bias**, meaning that participants may respond based on how they want to be perceived rather than how they actually think or behave. See Figure 4.1 for an example of the social desirability bias. There are ways to minimize or at least measure participants' bias toward social desirability. Anonymity of responses can be helpful, as can neutrally worded questions. Some researchers even include questions or scales designed to test the validity of participants' responses. If participants answer in the affirmative to the question, "I never lie," there is a good chance that they are in fact lying and may be doing so in their other answers.

Many use the term *survey* when referring to questionnaires. However, survey research refers to the method used to collect data, and both interviews and questionnaires are tools used in survey research.

Social desirability bias: Participants may respond based on how they want to be perceived or what is socially acceptable.

Interviews

Interviews are one-on-one conversations directed by a researcher that can take place in person, over the phone, or via e-mail. Anonymity is more difficult with interviews, although the researcher should still carefully guard the participants' confidentiality. Recall from Chapter 1 that *anonymity* means that no one knows the identity of the participant whereas *confidentiality* means that the identities are confidential but may be known to the researcher. A potential lack of anonymity is a clear disadvantage for interviews because it can increase the social desirability bias. Interviews are also subject to **interviewer bias,** in which the interviewer's verbal and nonverbal responses to the participants' answers change how the participants answer subsequent questions. For example, imagine that someone was interviewing you and their eyes got wide and they said, "Wow, that's horrible!" after you provided an honest answer to their question. Their responses would likely impact how you answered the next question. Another disadvantage to interviews is that they are quite time-consuming.

> **Interviewer bias:** The interviewer may provide verbal or nonverbal cues that impact how the participant responds.

Given these considerable disadvantages, you might wonder why anyone would choose to conduct an interview. There are several advantages to interviews, and the decision to conduct an interview necessitates an evaluation of the potential advantages and disadvantages, given the specific focus of the research study. The one-on-one nature of an interview may inspire the participant to take the research more seriously, which may in turn increase the response rate as well as the accuracy of the answers. The interviewer is also privy to additional information that might be missed in other formats. Specifically, the interviewer can take note of not only the participant's response but also the manner in which the participant delivers the response. Face-to-face interviews are especially rich sources for observing nonverbal cues such as facial expressions, hand gestures, pauses, and posture. Finally, interviews can allow for question clarification or follow-up questions, although this depends on how structured the interviews are.

Structured interviews include a standard set of questions that the interviewer asks all participants. The interviewer does not vary the order of questions or the manner in which they are asked. The interviewer also has strict guidelines for how to answer any questions that the participant might have. If the participant asks for clarification of what a question means, the interviewer might be able only to repeat the question and explain that the participant has to use his or her own judgment to interpret the question. The rationale for a structured interview is that it ensures that all participants had similar interview experiences and the exact same questions. It also reduces the potential for interviewer bias. Additionally, a researcher can train novice interviewers to conduct structured interviews.

Semi-structured interviews are much more flexible than structured interviews. The interviewer has a base set of questions or topics that he or she wants

> **Structured interviews:** All questions, follow-up questions, and responses by the interviewer are determined beforehand to ensure that all the participants have a very similar experience.
>
> **Semi-structured interviews:** There is a set of core questions or topics that the interviewer will follow, but the interviewer may prompt for more information, ask follow-up questions, or clarify questions as the interviewer deems necessary.

to cover, but can prompt the participant for more information, add new questions based on the participants' responses, and clarify questions as necessary. The ability to ask additional questions is a great advantage to the semi-structured interview, and the interviewer may be able to discover new information that he or she had not thought to ask about. However, conducting a semi-structured interview requires more training and practice in order to reduce interviewer bias, and a solid knowledge of the research topic in order to formulate neutral follow-up questions during the interview.

Questionnaires

Recall from Chapter 3 that questionnaires require participants to answer questions on paper or online. Questionnaires allow for anonymity and can therefore reduce social desirability bias. Multiple participants can complete the questionnaire at the same time, and thus questionnaires can save a lot of time over interviews. Additionally, administration is easily accomplished by handing out questionnaires in person, sending them through the mail, or e-mailing or posting an online questionnaire. Handing out questionnaires in person is the most work-intensive type of administration, and participants may not believe that their answers are truly anonymous. However, the response rate tends to be higher compared to mailed or e-mailed questionnaires. Additionally, a researcher can help clarify questions if necessary.

Mailed questionnaires were once popular due to the convenience of administration. The response rate for mailed questionnaires, however, is notoriously low and the cost of printing and mailing high. Consequently, most researchers who decide not to hand out questionnaires in person now prefer online administration. The key advantage to online questionnaires over those administered in person is that they allow a researcher to easily and inexpensively reach a large number of people across the world.

Research suggests that online questionnaires often yield results similar to those completed in person, although the utility of online questionnaires may vary based on the topic studied (Krantz, 2011). For example, there is evidence that online questionnaires encourage greater self-disclosure than other methods (Joinson, 1999) and may be particularly useful in mental health research (Stones & Perry, 1997).

At the same time, we cannot assume that an online questionnaire has the same validity as its paper and pencil counterpart, and therefore it is important to test the validity of online questionnaires (Birnbaum, 2004; Buchanan, 2002; Grieve, Witteveen, & Tolan, 2014).

Observational Research

Observational research involves observing and recording the behavior of humans or animals. Observations may stand alone, or they may supplement other research methods. The key advantage of observations in human research is that observations focus on what people actually do, not what they say they do or what they intend to do. One downside to observations is that they are time-consuming.

Another disadvantage is that observations are prone to **observer bias** in which the observers selectively attend to what they expect or hope to see. Fortunately, there are several strategies to reduce observer bias. Having a **blind observer** who does not know what the hypotheses are can greatly reduce observer bias. The term blind here has nothing to do with sight, but rather is a research term indicating that information about a study has been kept secret. It is also wise to have at least two observers. This allows you to compare their observations and test their interrater reliability (see Chapter 3 for a review of interrater reliability). Observers should be carefully trained on what behaviors to attend to and how different behaviors are operationally defined. Ideally, the observers should practice their observations until their interrater reliability is acceptable prior to beginning the actual study. Finally, the more structured the observation, the less room there is for error and bias.

> **Observer bias:** The observers pay closer attention to behaviors that support their expectations or interpret behaviors in ways that support their expectations or lose their focus on the target behavior.
>
> **Blind observer:** Observer who is not informed of the research hypotheses in order to reduce observer bias.

Observers record behaviors on an observer code sheet. At its most flexible, this code sheet is simply a piece of paper on which the observer records a **narrative** account of what the participant did. This can provide a full picture of the participants' behaviors, but the coding for this type of data is most subject to observer bias. A more structured approach is to develop a code sheet ahead of time listing items that operationally define the constructs of most interest to the researcher and that are based on past research. A middle ground would be to have a structured code sheet and to encourage the observer to also narrate any unexpected or noteworthy behavior.

A structured code sheet might include a **checklist** to indicate whether specific behaviors occurred. For example, someone observing spectators at a sporting event might indicate if any of the following behaviors occurred after a score: *cheering, criticisms, standing up*. An observer might also record the timing of a behavior such as how long a behavior lasts (**duration**), how long it takes to complete a task (**task completion time**), how quickly a participant responds to a stimulus (**reaction time**), or the time between two tasks (**latency**).

> **Narrative:** A detailed account of behaviors or responses.
>
> **Checklist:** A list of qualities or behaviors that are checked if present.
>
> **Duration:** How long a behavior lasts.
>
> **Task completion time:** How long it takes to complete a task.
>
> **Reaction time:** How long it takes a participant to respond to a stimulus.
>
> **Latency:** The time between stopping one task and beginning a new task.

REVIEW OF KEY CONCEPTS: SCALES OF MEASUREMENT

Can you recall what scale of measurement is represented by each of the following items:

1. Checklist item: _____Person cheered after the score.

2. Rating: The volume of the cheer was

| 1 | 2 | 3 | 4 | 5 | 6 | 7 |

Not at all loud   *Extremely loud*

3. Duration: The cheering lasted _____ seconds.

Recall that nominal scales are categories that do not have magnitude. Therefore the checklist item represents a nominal scale because the categories are checked or not checked. Interval scales are ratings that have magnitude and equal intervals, but no absolute zero. The rating of the volume is an example of an interval scale. Finally, ratio scales are quantities that have magnitude, equal intervals, and an absolute zero. Duration in seconds is an example of a ratio scale of measurement.

If you had difficulty with this exercise, be sure to review Chapter 3. These scales of measurement will be important when it comes to figuring out how to analyze data.

Finally, the code sheet might also include a **rating scale** to assess the intensity of a behavior. For example, loudness of cheering at a sporting event can be rated on a scale from 1 to 10, with 10 = *extremely loud,* or on a 3-point scale (*soft, moderate, loud*). Recall from Chapter 3 that a Likert-type scale is a specific type of rating scale in which respondents report their intensity of an experience or their level of agreement. A Likert-type scale might ask the observer to report how much they agree that the cheering was loud, rated as 1 = *strongly disagree;* 2 = *disagree;* 3 = *neutral;* 4 = *agree;* 5 = *strongly agree.*

Rating scale: A numerical rating of a particular quality.

Observers may code behaviors that are live or recorded. Recording allows for higher accuracy because the observer can examine the recording many times, and any discrepancy between observers' codes can be investigated by examining the recording. Recording is much more of an invasion of privacy than observing a live situation, and as such has greater ethical implications. The decision to do a live observation or to record the situation also depends on other decisions the researcher makes. Factors that influence the decision are described below.

Covert Versus Overt Observations

In a **covert observation**, the observers do not reveal that they are observing the participants, whereas they do reveal themselves in an **overt observation**. A concern with overt

Covert observation: Observations are made without the participants' awareness.

Overt observation: No attempts are made to hide the observation.

observations is that participants who know they are being observed may change their behavior. This change may be due to the social desirability bias, or it may occur simply because being watched introduces another factor into the situation. Consequently, those who conduct overt observations typically allow the participant some time to acclimate to the situation prior to the start of the study. They may also remove themselves from the situation by watching participants through a one-way mirror, recording the participants, or both.

Covert observations are designed to capture the participants' natural and spontaneous reactions to situations. They can be especially important when observing behaviors that are prone to the social desirability bias. There are ethical considerations with watching someone without their awareness, although less so if the observations take place in a public place. If a covert observation was to happen in a private space, deception would have to be employed. For example, an observer might deceive the participant into believing they are there to observe a child's behavior when in fact the parents' behavior is the focus. As discussed in Chapter 1, the use of deception in research is quite controversial, and the risks and benefits of deception must be carefully weighed. Additionally, recording someone without their consent raises serious ethical concerns especially if the person's face or other identifying feature is recorded.

Naturalistic Versus Contrived Observations

Naturalistic observations occur in the participants' (or animal subjects') natural environment and take place without any interference by the observer or researcher. It might involve observing animals or humans in these settings, or it could instead involve unobtrusive observations as described in Chapter 3. In unobtrusive observations, the observer examines traces of animal or human behavior, such as tracks or garbage.

Contrived observations are those that are set up for research purposes and might include observing participants' reactions to an event or physical stimulus or asking participants to complete a task or engage in an activity. Contrived observations can occur in a laboratory setting where the researcher has the most control over the setting, but they may also occur in a natural environment such as a home, school, or public place.

A naturalistic observation of spectator behavior at a sporting event would require the observer to watch and record participants' reactions during the game. A downside to the naturalistic approach is that the observer has no control over the situation, and a long time may pass before the behavior of interest occurs. Or, the behavior might happen so frequently that it is difficult to capture. If an observer is watching a soccer game to see spectator reactions after goals are scored, the observer might have to wait a long time before either team makes a score; and it is possible that no scores will be made the entire

---

Naturalistic observation: Observation that occurs in a natural environment or situation and does not involve interference by anyone involved in the research.

Contrived observation: The researcher sets up the situation and observes how participants or subjects respond.

game. On the other hand, in basketball, scoring happens quickly and frequently, and it might be difficult to keep track during the game.

A contrived approach could address these issues by creating a situation and then observing people's reactions. A contrived observation of reactions to a sporting event might involve having participants watch a taped or staged game in which the observer knows when a score will occur. Of course, a staged game would not work for a real sporting event and would require quite a bit of coordination to set up. Contrived observations might also employ a **confederate** who appears to be a participant but is actually working with the researcher. In our sporting event example, a confederate may react in a certain way (cheering or booing) after a score is made to see if it impacts how the participant reacts.

> **Confederate:** Someone who pretends to be a participant or uninvolved person, but in actuality is working with the researcher and has been told to behave in a particular way.

Nonparticipant Versus Participant Observations

Nonparticipant observation occurs when the researcher is not directly involved in the situation, whereas **participant observation** involves the active involvement of the researcher in the situation under observation. Participant observation may involve a confederate who interacts with participants in a brief task or situation, or it might involve a deeper infiltration into a social group, either covertly or overtly. The more involved the participant observation, the greater the chance that the participants will exhibit natural and spontaneous behaviors. This is true even if observation is overt because the participants acclimate to the observers' presence and the personal relationships that develop often engender trust and comfort. Greater involvement of the researchers also blurs the line between researcher and participant. The disadvantage of involvement by the researchers is that they may lose their objectivity as they become more entrenched in the group.

Archival Research

Archival research involves the analysis of existing data or records. As with all research, it begins with a careful review of existing research followed by the development of

> **Nonparticipant observation:** The researcher or observer is not directly involved in the situation.
>
> **Participant observation:** The researcher or observer becomes actively involved in the situation.
>
> **Archival research:** Analysis of existing data or records.

a testable hypothesis that builds on past research. The key difference with archival research is that the data have already been collected. Archival research thus has many advantages: A researcher can save time and resources by not collecting data; some archives span a large time frame, and the analysis of those data allows for a systematic examination of historical patterns and trends; and finally, there are fewer ethical considerations with certain types of archives including materials that do not directly involve people or animals, data from a study that has already undergone IRB approval, or public records.

There are also challenges to archival research. Archival research requires that you identify the appropriate archival source and obtain access. Additionally, you must decide how to use the data to test your hypothesis. The biggest disadvantage to archival research is that the data were not collected with your hypothesis in mind, and as such the data available might not represent exactly what you were hoping to analyze.

Secondary Data

One source of archival research is **secondary data**. These are data that were collected for research purposes by some other researcher or organization. Sources of secondary data include governmental agencies, nonprofit organizations, colleges and universities, data repositories, and individual researchers.

> **Secondary data:** Research data that were collected by one researcher or group but analyzed by a different researcher or group.

Some secondary data are relatively easy to access. Data from the Pew Research Center are available for download from the Internet. Data from the National Longitudinal Study of Youth are available on request and have been the source of over 400 research studies (NORC, n.d.). The largest repository of social science data is the Dataverse Network created by the Institute for Quantitative Social Science (IQSS) at Harvard University. Researchers upload their data to the network. Anyone can then search the network, and many datasets are available for download or available with permission of the researcher. Researchers who receive grants from some federal agencies in the United States, including the National Institute of Health (NIH) and National Science Foundation (NSF), are required to share their final research data with other researchers. Sharing data in this way helps to make the process of science as transparent as possible by encouraging replication and verification of research results.

On the other hand, access to other secondary data is limited. Some researchers and institutions prefer not to share their data for fear that the confidentiality of their members or participants might be breached or because they prefer to have control over who analyzes their data and for what purposes.

Additionally, even if you can obtain secondary data, those data may not be coded in such a way that allows you to test your hypothesis. You may instead need to adjust your hypothesis to match the data available. For example, suppose you had originally hypothesized that the use of liquor among adolescents between the ages of 16 and 17 has decreased over the years. However, the secondary dataset you are using categorizes age in larger chunks, such as 15- to 18-year-olds, and had data on alcohol use in general instead of the specific type of alcohol. If you wanted to use that dataset, you would need to adjust your hypotheses based on the data you actually have.

Records and Documents

Other sources of archival research are the countless records and documents that were not created for research purposes. This includes confidential information such as school or medical records that can be accessed only if consent is given by an individual or institution. Other information is publicly available, including websites, newspaper articles, public records, and historical documents. For example, you might examine patterns of what songs or artists made the Billboard music chart; or you might research the statistics of professional athletes or teams; or you might research the history of the United States through records, media, and pictures preserved by the National Archives and Records Administration.

Online social networking, dating, or shopping sites can provide data about users' attitudes, social networks, and behaviors. What individuals or organizations post to online sites is one source of data. For example, you might want to analyze updates or pictures from a social media site such as Facebook. Such information can be easily and ethically obtained from open groups or profiles (such as those from public figures). However, closed groups and personal pages are usually considered private by IRBs. As such, you would need to obtain informed consent to analyze private social media pages (Phillips, 2011). Another source of data may come directly from the online site. For example, Hitsch and colleagues were able to obtain data from a major online dating site in order to analyze browsing behavior and decisions to send an initial email (Hitsch, Hortacsu, & Ariely, 2010). The average student may not have the connections needed to access such data. An alternative source for those with some technical skills is to create or use an application that collects data from online sites. But keep in mind that some sites, including Facebook, explicitly prohibit such automated data collection (Phillips, 2011).

Because archival records and documents were not originally intended for research, they have distinct advantages and disadvantages over other types of data. The advantages are that they allow for the analysis of some behaviors and attitudes that cannot be directly observed, and the records can be used in lieu of a potentially biased self-report or serve as a way to verify self-report. The disadvantage is that the researcher must figure out how to accurately code the data. Not only is this time-consuming, but it also introduces the potential for bias into the coding process if a researcher selectively attends to information that supports the study's hypothesis. This bias can be reduced in ways similar to observational coding: Have people who are blind to the hypothesis code the data, have multiple coders, train the coders well, and check their interrater reliability.

TABLE 4.2

Comparison of Methods

	Advantages	Disadvantages
Survey research (interviews and questionnaires)	Obtain individual's perspective Interviews: obtain detailed responses, participants may pay closer attention to questions, semi-structured interviews allow a researcher to ask follow-up questions Questionnaires: easy to administer, easy to make anonymous, many participants can be surveyed at the same time	Potential social desirability bias Interviews: time-consuming, potential for interviewer bias, difficult to make anonymous, social desirability bias is especially strong (compared to questionnaires) Questionnaires: do not elicit as much in-depth information as can be obtained in an interview, participants might misunderstand or misread questions
Observations	Focus on observable behavior rather than self-report, reducing the social desirability bias	Can be time-consuming to collect and code data Potential observer bias (this can be reduced if observers are well trained and "blind" to hypotheses)
Archival research	No direct data collection necessary Archives may span a larger time frame than would be feasible for a single researcher to collect May have fewer ethical considerations May allow the study of some behaviors and attitudes that cannot be obtained through surveys or observations	Data may be difficult to obtain Data may not fit perfectly with your hypotheses May require a lot of time and effort to code the data

Ethics Tip: Know When to Get Informed Consent

Informed consent is essential under the following situations:

- There is a possibility that participation in the research will cause the participants harm or distress.

- The study is not anonymous.

- The study uses video or audio recordings, and these recordings could be used to identify the participants.

- The study involves observations in nonpublic places.

- The study involves archives that are confidential or that, if revealed, might place participants at risk.

Practice 4.2

EVALUATE METHODS FOR A DESCRIPTIVE STUDY ON ACADEMIC HONESTY

Survey

a. What would be the pros and cons of interviewing students about academic honesty?

b. What would be the pros and cons of administering questionnaires about academic honesty?

Observation

a. Would observations be a viable method to help understand how much students at your college or university value academic honesty? Why or why not?

Archival Research

a. What type of archives might help you understand how much students at your college or university value academic honesty?

b. Do you think it would be possible for you to obtain these archives?

See Appendix A to check your answers.

DEFINING THE POPULATION AND OBTAINING A SAMPLE

Who or What Is the Population of Interest?

A **population** is the group of people, animals, or archives that you are interested in examining. Residency, occupation, gender, age, and time frame are some of the characteristics that might define a population. A **subpopulation** is a portion of the population. Both the population and subpopulations are defined by the researcher. For example, a researcher might define the population as all residents within a certain state, and a subpopulation might be defined as women within that state. If the population of interest is women, a subpopulation might be women between the ages of 18 and 24.

> **Population:** The group that a researcher is interested in examining defined by specific characteristics such as residency, occupation, gender, or age.
>
> **Subpopulation:** A portion or subgroup of the population.

It may seem that the best strategy from an external validity standpoint is to define the population as broadly as possible. If you have human participants, it might be tempting to think of your population as all people. This is a serious mistake, however, because the resources required to create a study that could generalize to all people is greater than any researcher, much less a student researcher, can manage. Consequently, you will want to narrow your population of interest.

The smaller and more clearly defined your population, the easier it is to conduct a study that adequately describes that population. You might define your population as students who are enrolled in your Research Methods class this semester. It is possible to conduct a study that included data from each member of the class, in which case you would expect that the results would adequately describe your population and you could draw conclusions about that narrow population.

On the other hand, if your population is too narrowly defined, you will be severely limited in the conclusions you can draw. It is unlikely that you would be interested only in students enrolled in the class this semester. Instead, you might want your results to generalize to students who have ever taken the course at your college or university, or even to students who have taken a research course at other institutions. Additionally, although it is possible to collect data on every member of a small, clearly defined population, it is also possible that some members of the population will be excluded because they were not present when data were collected, they decided not to participate, or their data were incomplete or contained too many errors.

The problem with collecting data from all members is compounded for larger populations. Take the U.S. census as an example. Every 10 years the U.S. Census Bureau attempts to collect information about how many people are residing in the United States and the residency, ethnicity, and age information of each person. In 2010, the Census Bureau advertised on television, mailed advance letters notifying people of the upcoming census, mailed the census survey itself along with reminders to complete the census, and hand delivered the census to those without postal addresses. Still, 26% of households did not mail back their census forms. Consequently, census workers went door-to-door to reach those nonresponders. In all, the U.S. government hired over 600,000 people and spent $13 billion for the 2010 census (U. S. Census Bureau, 2011).

Given the difficulty and expense of obtaining information from every single person or animal in your population, or obtaining every archive, researchers often choose to obtain a sample from the population. A **sample** is a subset of the population that is meant to represent the full population, and **sampling** is the procedure used to obtain

Sample: A subset of the population from which data are collected.

Sampling: The process by which a sample is selected.

FIGURE 4.2
Sampling

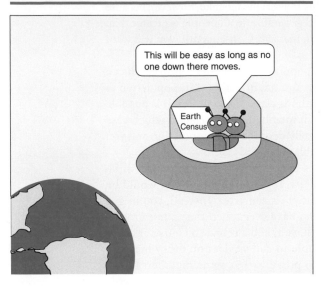

This cartoon illustrates that obtaining information from every participant, subject, or archive in your population is tricky, if not impossible. Consequently, researchers instead obtain a sample of the population.

Source: Eva K. Lawrence

the sample (see Figure 4.2). The extent to which a sample actually represents the population is dependent on the amount of bias in the sampling procedure. **Sampling bias** occurs when the sample does not represent the population, such as when some members of the population are more likely to participate than others and therefore be overrepresented. Sampling bias is of particular concern in descriptive research where the primary goal is to describe the population and maximize the study's external validity. As such, it is important that researchers conducting a descriptive study carefully consider how to obtain a sample that represents the population.

How Will You Obtain a Sample From Your Population?

Probability Sampling

Probability sampling (also called random sampling) is any method of sampling that uses **random selection** in which all members of a particular population or subpopulation have an equal chance of being selected. Probability sampling reduces sampling bias and increases the chance that the sample will be representative of the population.

> **Sampling bias:** The sample does not represent the population.
>
> **Probability sampling (or random sampling):** Sampling procedure that uses random selection.
>
> **Random selection:** A process of selecting a sample in which all members of a population or a subpopulation have an equal chance of being selected.

Random selection is one of the most misunderstood concepts by novice researchers. As such, you should work on remembering the following distinctions:

- Random selection does *not* mean haphazard selection.
  - Random is used in everyday language to mean all sorts of things, including haphazard, careless, pointless, or rambling. Be careful, because random selection is none of these things.

- Random selection requires careful planning to ensure that the sample was chosen only on the basis of membership in a specific population or subset of the population and not other individual characteristics. It also means that each member of the population has an equal chance of being selected.

- Random selection is *not* the same as random assignment.

  - Random selection is a sampling procedure used to ensure a representative population.

  - Random selection can be used in any type of research design, but it is especially important in descriptive research.

  - Random assignment refers to how you assign members of your sample to groups within your study and is used only in experimental designs.

With a small population, random selection might involve writing the names of the members of the population on pieces of paper, putting them in a hat, and then drawing a sample at random. For larger populations, all the names can be listed in a spreadsheet. A computer program such as SPSS can then be used to randomly select a sample, or a researcher might use a random numbers table to select the sample (see Appendix C.1).

Random selection can occur with or without replacement. **Random selection with replacement** means that a selected member of the population is returned to the pool of possible participants and thus may be selected into the sample more than once. **Random selection without replacement** means that once a member of the population is selected, that member is removed from the pool and cannot be selected into the sample again. Random selection with replacement ensures that each selection is completely independent, in that selection of one member does not impact the selection of future members of the sample. This replacement is preferable from a statistical standpoint, but practically speaking most researchers practice random selection without replacement so that a participant is not sampled more than once.

Random selection with replacement: A selected member of the population is returned to the pool of possible participants so that any member may be selected into the sample more than once.

Random selection without replacement: A selected member of the population is removed from the pool of possible participants so that any member may be selected into the sample only once.

Once the sample has been randomly selected, the researcher's work has only just begun. The researcher must now collect data from members of the sample. If someone refuses to participate or if an archive is missing, the researcher cannot simply select a new participant or archive that is more readily available. This would negate the random selection process and introduce sampling bias.

It is rare that any researcher will be able to obtain data from 100% of the selected sample. There are no hard-and-fast rules for what an acceptable response rate is, and it varies based on the standards set by previous research on the topic. A **nonresponse bias** occurs when the researcher is not able to obtain data from members of the sample; and those who responded differ from those who did not, which then limits the external validity of your study. To limit the nonresponse bias, the researcher must attempt to collect data from as many members selected for the sample as possible. This requires perseverance in sending advance notice and reminders to participants, attempting to reach them in various ways (mail, e-mail, telephone, in person), and perhaps offering incentives if ethically appropriate.

Nonresponse bias: The extent to which those who were selected and participated in the study differ from those who were selected but did not participate.

Another strategy is to compare those who responded to those who did not respond to determine if they differ on any key variables (e.g., gender, age, any variable related to the measures collected in the study). This can be done only if you have some data for your nonresponders that you collected from other sources, such as public records. Ideally, the differences between responders and nonresponders will be negligible, and this provides evidence that the nonresponse bias was minimal in the study.

Procedures for Probability Sampling. There are several different ways to achieve probability sampling. These include simple random sampling, stratified random sampling, and cluster sampling.

Simple random sampling is a type of probability sampling in which every single member of the population has an equal chance of being selected for the sample. Table 4.3 outlines the steps for simple random sampling, with an example of each step for a study about academic honesty.

Stratified random sampling is probability sampling that results in the sample representing key subpopulations based on characteristics such as age, gender, and ethnicity. With stratified random sampling, the sample has the same proportion of these groups as are in the population. For example, a researcher might want to stratify her sample based on gender. If the population is 54% female, then the sample will also be 54% female.

Simple random sampling: A type of probability sampling in which every single member of the population has an equal chance of being selected for the sample.

Stratified random sampling: A type of probability sampling that results in the sample representing key subpopulations based on characteristics such as age, gender, and ethnicity.

TABLE 4.3
Simple Random Sampling

Steps in Simple Random Sampling	Example for a Study on Academic Honesty
1. Define the population.	To make sampling manageable, we define the population as the students currently enrolled in one college.
2. Identify all members of the population.	Obtain a list of all the students enrolled in the college from the registrar's office.
3. Randomly select a sample from that population.	Transfer the names to a computer program such as SPSS and then follow the appropriate steps so that the program generates a random sample. Alternatively, use a random numbers table to select the sample.
4. Collect data from that sample. Attempt to both reduce and assess the nonresponse bias.	Approach students who were selected and attempt to collect data from as many of them as possible.
	Continue collecting data, including following up with students using various means and offering incentives for participation, until an appropriate response rate is achieved.
	Compare students who responded to those who did not respond on variables obtained through the registrar's office, such as GPA, year in school, and major.

Stratified random sampling is the standard sampling method for phone interviews conducted by the Pew Research Center. Their sample is stratified based on type of phone, with those with landlines (who may also have a cell phone) sampled at 60% and those who use cell phones exclusively sampled at 40%. This stratification was determined to provide the most diverse sample of adults in respect to age, ethnicity, and socioeconomic status. The landlines are further stratified to ensure proportional representation of different parts of the country, and the cell phone numbers stratified based on both geography and wireless carrier. The sample is selected using random digit dialing (Pew Research Center, n.d.). See Table 4.4 for an outline of the steps in stratified random sampling and an example for a study on academic honesty.

Both simple and stratified random sampling require the researcher to identify all members of the population. For example, if the researcher has defined the population as college students, he or she must first identify all the colleges and universities in the world and then obtain a list of the students enrolled. This is obviously difficult and time-consuming. Consequently, researchers who use one of these two sampling techniques tend to define their population more narrowly. For example, a researcher interested in college students might define her population as college students enrolled in one or a few colleges or universities that will allow the researcher access to student records. Alternatively, a researcher may use cluster sampling when it is impossible or impractical to obtain a list of all members of a specified population.

TABLE 4.4

Stratified Random Sampling

Steps in Stratified Random Sampling	Example for a Study on Academic Honesty
1. Define the population.	We define the population as students currently enrolled in one college.
2. Identify the groups that you want to be proportionately represented in your sample.	For this research, year in school is an important variable because we might assume that beginning students have had less experience with the academic honor code than more advanced students.
3. Identify all the members of the population and to which strata each member belongs.	Obtain a list of all the students enrolled in the college from the registrar's office along with their year in school.
4. Divide the population based on the groups you identified.	Create a database of students for each year: first year, second, third, fourth, fifth, or more.
5. Determine the proportion of the population represented by each group.	Calculate the total number of students in each year and the total number of students in the college. Find the proportion for each year by dividing the total number of students in each year by the total number of students. $$\%_{\text{first year}} = \frac{N_{\text{first year}}}{N_{\text{total students}}}$$
6. Randomly select a sample from each group in proportions equal to those of the population.	Use a computer or random numbers table to randomly select a sample from each year that is equal to the proportion of those in the population. For example, if 25% of the students enrolled in the college are first years, 18% second years, 22% third years, 24% fourth years, and 11% fifth year or beyond, then we will want those same proportions in our sample. For a sample of 100, we would randomly select 25 from the first-year database, 18 from the second-year database, 22 from the third years, 24 from the fourth years, and 11 from the fifth years.
7. Collect data from the samples. Attempt to both reduce and assess the nonresponse bias.	Approach students who were selected, use various strategies to improve the response rate, and continue collecting data until an appropriate response rate is reached for each year in school. Compare students who responded to those who did not respond on year in school as well as other variables obtained from the registrar's office such as GPA and major.

Cluster sampling is a type of probability sampling in which groups, or clusters, are randomly selected instead of individuals. A cluster might be defined as a neighborhood, a school, or a class within a school. See Table 4.5 for the steps in cluster sampling and an example.

> **Cluster sampling:** A type of probability sampling in which groups, or clusters, are randomly selected instead of individuals.

TABLE 4.5

Cluster Sampling

Steps in Cluster Sampling	Example for a Study on Academic Honesty
1. Define the population.	The population is students enrolled in one college.
2. Identify the clusters that will be used for sampling.	Classes would be good clusters for this study, and we would choose a type of class that most students are required to take or choose a popular class time to ensure that our sample contains a variety of students. For example, we might select all classes that meet during the 1 p.m. period on Tuesdays and Thursdays because this is the most popular time period and contains a variety of classes.
3. Identify all of these clusters within the population.	We would write down all the classes that meet on Tuesdays and Thursdays at 1 p.m.
4. Randomly select a sample of clusters.	We would put these classes in a hat and select our sample at random.
5. Collect data from all the individuals within each cluster sample. Attempt to both reduce and assess nonresponse bias.	We would approach the professors who teach the classes we selected and ask if we could conduct a study with the students enrolled in their 1 p.m. class.
	Ideally, we would conduct the study during the class period to help ensure that we would be able to collect data from most of the students in the classes.
	To help ensure that all the professors teaching during the 1 p.m. time slot allow access to their class, we would get administrative support for the study, notify the professors well in advance so that they can plan around the data collection day, and explain the importance of the study.
	We will follow up with any students who were absent the day of the study to help ensure that we obtain data from all the individuals enrolled in the 1 p.m. class periods.
	To assess the possibility of a nonresponse bias, we would compare the types of students who participated to any who did not participate on the type of 1 p.m. class in which they were enrolled and relevant information that the professor of the class or college was willing to provide such as course grade, year in school, or GPA.

How large should your probability sample be? The closer a probability sample comes to including the full population, the more likely that sample will represent the population. Of course, the larger a sample the more time, effort, and expenses are involved. Consequently, it is wise to consider the minimum sample size required in order for the results to represent the population.

To estimate the minimum sample size required for a descriptive study using probability sampling, you must know how large the population is as well as identify both the confidence interval and confidence level. A **confidence interval** is an estimation of the margin of error for your scores, or the range of values within which your scores will fall. Researchers typically aim for a 5% confidence interval. A **confidence level** is a measure of how sure you are that your scores will fall within that confidence interval. Researchers typically choose either a 95% or 99% confidence level.

> **Confidence interval:** An estimation of the range of values within which the scores will fall (margin of error).
>
> **Confidence level:** A measure of how likely the scores will fall within a stated confidence interval.

For example, suppose we conducted our study of academic honesty and found that 15% of students in our sample reported that they have plagiarized. A 5% confidence interval would give us a range of 10–20%. If we had a 95% confidence level, we would be 95% sure that between 10% and 20% of students in the population would report that they plagiarized. Before we can say that, however, we need to determine the sample size necessary to establish that confidence interval and confidence level.

The easiest way to calculate the estimated sample size needed to obtain the desired confidence interval and confidence level is to use an online sample size calculator. Creative Research Systems provides a free sample size calculator at www.surveysystem.com/sscalc.htm. Another option is to use the table provided in Appendix C.2, although this table provides only populations of certain sizes, and you might need to round your sample size up or down. A third option is to calculate the sample size by hand:

Sample size (*ss*) calculation:

$$\text{Step 1}: ss = .25z^2/c^2 \text{ or } \frac{.25z^2}{c^2}$$

$$\text{Step 2}: \text{New } ss = \frac{ss}{1 + \frac{(ss-1)}{\text{pop}}}$$

where z = z score (1.96 for 95% confidence level and 2.576 for 99% confidence level), c = confidence interval expressed as decimal (e.g., .05 = 5% confidence interval), and pop = population.

For example, for a 2.5% confidence interval and 95% confidence level and population of 5,000:

$$\text{Step 1}: ss = \frac{.25(1.96)^2}{(.025)^2} = \frac{.25(3.84)}{.000625} = \frac{.9604}{.000625} = 1536.64$$

$$\text{Step 2}: \text{New } ss = \frac{1536.64}{1 + \frac{(1536 - 1)}{5000}} = \frac{1536.64}{1 + .307128} = 1176$$

Keep in mind a few important points:

- The sample size calculations are only an estimate. The sample size required to best represent the population depends on how homogeneous, or similar, members of the population are. A very homogeneous population requires a smaller sample, whereas a very heterogeneous, or diverse, population requires a larger sample.

- You will likely not obtain 100% of your selected sample. Therefore, you should plan on obtaining a larger sample size to account for this. You can estimate how much larger a sample size you will need based on the response rate of past research. For example, if you expect that you will be unable to collect data from 10% of your selected sample, then you should increase your sample size by 10%.

- The higher your nonresponse rate, the less likely it is that your sample will represent your population.

- Even if you were to obtain 100% of your selected sample, you are never completely sure that the results you obtain from your sample will in fact represent the population. The confidence interval and confidence level demonstrate this point.

Nonprobability Sampling

Nonprobability sampling (also called nonrandom sampling) is any method of sampling that does not rely on random selection. Sampling bias is a serious concern with nonprobability sampling. Unlike probability sampling, there is no set sample size that can be reached that gives us confidence that a nonprobability sample will represent the population. Even if a researcher was able to obtain a sample from the majority of members of a population, it is possible that the sample would not represent the full population. Take the 2010 census as an example. The 26% of those who did not mail

Nonprobability sampling (or nonrandom sampling): Sampling procedure that does not use random selection.

Application 4.1

EXAMPLES OF PROBABILITY SAMPLING

Study A: Archives With Simple Random Sampling

M. McCullough and Holmberg (2005) used Google searches to examine the prevalence of plagiarism in theses completed for a master's degree.

They defined their population as master's theses that were completed during 2003, that were in English, and that were available online via the WorldCat database. The population consisted of 2,600 theses, of which the authors randomly selected a sample of 260 (10%) to examine for evidence of plagiarism. The nonresponse rate was 19% because some of the full texts could not be retrieved.

Study B: Questionnaires With Cluster Sampling

Vowell and Chen (2004) compared how well different sociological theories explained cheating behaviors such as copying or allowing someone else to copy work.

They defined their population as undergraduate students enrolled in one university located in the Southwestern United States. They listed all the 11 a.m. to 12:20 p.m. classes and then randomly selected 42 of those classes. The researchers approached the professors teaching the selected classes and asked them to administer a questionnaire during the selected class. The nonresponse rate was 14% because some professors opted to not include their class in the study.

back their census data likely represent those who are poorer and have less stable living environments than the 74% who did respond.

Even though sampling bias is inherent in nonprobability sampling, a majority of studies actually utilize nonprobability sampling. There are several reasons for this:

1. Nonprobability sampling is easier and much less time-consuming than probability sampling. It does not require identification of all members or clusters in a population. Instead of randomly selecting a sample and then trying to obtain data from each member of a sample, the nonprobability sample is defined simply as anyone (or any animal or archive) contributing data to the study.

2. A truly representative sample is an ideal that a researcher strives for but never fully attains. The representativeness of a probability sample is limited in small samples or by nonresponse and chance error. Additionally, the population defined in probability sampling is typically narrow (e.g., students enrolled in one college) and the question remains if the sample represents a broader population (e.g., all college students).

3. There are methods to examine the representativeness of a sample, including comparisons between the sample characteristics or results obtained in one

study and the average obtained from other studies (we will talk more about this in Chapter 7). Moreover, the external validity of a study can be tested through replication.

The bottom line is that probability sampling is the best choice when your main goal is to describe a population and you are able to identify all the members or clusters in a population, obtain the appropriate sample size, and minimize the nonresponse rate. If these criteria cannot be met, nonprobability sampling is an acceptable alternative in descriptive research. If your primary goal is not to describe a population but rather examine relationships, as in correlational and experimental designs, nonprobability sampling is a perfectly fine and common method of sampling.

Procedures for nonprobability sampling. There are several different ways to achieve nonprobability sampling. These include convenience sampling, quota sampling, maximum variation sampling, and snowball sampling. Like probability sampling, nonprobability sampling requires that you define your population. However, because you will not need to identify every member or cluster in the population, you do not need to be as specific. For our example study of academic honesty, we can simply define the population as U.S. college students.

Convenience sampling is the most basic type of nonprobability sample in which those who were available and willing to provide data make up the sample. See Table 4.6 for the steps for convenience sampling and for an example for a study on academic honesty. Convenience samples may be obtained in a variety of ways, such as advertising for volunteers or asking a group of people in the school cafeteria or outside a grocery store to participate in your study. At the extreme, a convenience sample can be very convenient. You might ask just your friends and family to participate or just those students who attended a school event that you also attended.

> **Convenience sampling:** A type of nonprobability sample made up of those volunteers or others who are readily available and willing to participate.

It is wise, however, to avoid these types of overly convenient samples because they may overrepresent one group in the population. This is particularly problematic if your sample is composed of those who have similar views on the subject you are investigating. Instead, you should make your convenience sampling a bit more inconvenient by obtaining data from various places at various times of day.

You might consider posting an online survey to social media as a method of convenience sampling. There are many advantages to using social media as a data collection tool. It is relatively easy to recruit a large sample, and such a sample is not limited by geographic location. Additionally, social media is used by people from various socioeconomic backgrounds, education levels, and ages; and therefore recruiting via social media can result in a more diverse sample. At the same time, there are some important considerations. First, consider potential ethical implications of posting an online questionnaire. Avoid this type of administration if your study includes feedback that might upset your participants (Buchanan, 2002). Second, you cannot assume that the measures you use will yield similar results when they are presented on social media versus in person (Grieve et al., 2014). You will need to do some additional research to determine whether your measures are appropriate for online administration. And third, if you post only to your personal pages, your sample will likely be limited to those who have views similar to yours. Consider posting to a variety of public pages as well, but keep in mind that some groups or organizations prohibit solicitation of research participants via their social media sites (Phillips, 2011).

Quota sampling is nonprobability sampling that results in the sample representing key subsets of your population, or subpopulations based on characteristics such as age, gender, and ethnicity. The goal is the same as stratified random sampling, but quota sampling is accomplished without random selection. See Table 4.7 for steps in quota sampling and an example.

TABLE 4.6

Convenience Sampling

Steps in Convenience Sampling	Example for a Study on Academic Honesty
1. Define the population.	Because we do not need to identify all members of the population and we believe we can get a range of responses from students across the country, we define our population as U.S. college students.
2. Decide where and when you will be able to find a sample from your population.	We would limit our data collection to college campuses because we will be most likely to find college students there (as opposed to a more general location like a grocery store).
	We will go to several different locations on one college campus at different times of the day to help ensure that our sample contains a variety of types of students. We may also collect data at nearby colleges or even try to recruit from colleges in other states in an attempt at obtaining a diverse sample of students.
3. Collect data. Screen out those who do not belong to your population.	Approach potential participants and first make sure that they are students. Ask students if they are willing to participate in the study.

Maximum variation sampling is a sampling strategy in which the researcher seeks out the full range of extremes in the population. The goal is to achieve a representative

Quota sampling: A type of nonprobability sampling that results in the sample representing key subpopulations based on characteristics such as age, gender, and ethnicity.

Maximum variation sampling: A nonprobability sampling strategy in which the researcher seeks out the full range of extremes in the population.

TABLE 4.7

Quota Sampling

Steps in Quota Sampling	Example for a Study on Academic Honesty
1. Define the population.	The population is U.S. college students.
2. Identify the groups that you want to be proportionately represented in your sample.	We would choose the same groups—year in school—as for our stratified random sample example.
3. Determine the proportion or approximate proportion of the population represented by each group.	Because our population is all U.S. college students, the information from a single college is not sufficient. Instead, we will look to national data that provides averages and approximations on how many college students are in their first, second, third, fourth, and fifth plus year.
4. Decide where and when you will be able to find a sample of the groups you identified.	We would limit data collection to college campuses. We would attempt to find students of various years at the public places on campus, and recruit at other colleges in an attempt to diversify our sample.
5. Collect data from each group in proportions equal to those of the population. When you have reached the quota for one group, you can stop collecting data for that group and focus on completing data collection for the rest of the other group(s).	Approach potential participants and first make sure that they are students. Ask students if they are willing to participate in the study. Be sure that one of the questions we ask, either before or as part of the study, is their year in school. Keep track of how many students of each year we have, and be sure to keep the proportions equal to those in our population. For example, if our population estimate is 25% first-year students then 25% of our sample should also be first-year students. Likewise, the proportion for other years in the population should be matched in our sample. If we are unable to find enough students representing a particular year, we may need to focus our efforts on areas where students of that year typically congregate, advertise for volunteers from that year, or ask friends and professors to help us find participants who are in that year of school.

sample through this purposeful sampling instead of relying on probability. The premise is that the average achieved with maximum variation sampling will approximate the population average. Maximum variation sampling is most commonly used with small samples such as those achieved through interviews. See Table 4.8 for more information about maximum variation sampling.

In **snowball sampling** the participants recruit others into the sample. Snowball sampling is typically used to seek out members of a specific population who are difficult to find or who might be distrustful of a researcher, such as sex workers, undocumented workers, the homeless, those who are HIV positive, or drug dealers. The researcher must first identify at least one member of the population who is willing not only to participate

Snowball sampling: A nonprobability sampling strategy in which participants recruit others into the sample.

TABLE 4.8

Maximum Variation Sampling

Steps in Maximum Variation Sampling	Example for a Study on Academic Honesty
1. Define the population.	Because obtaining a maximum variation sample takes time and focus and is designed for smaller samples, we define the population more narrowly as those students currently enrolled in one college.
2. Identify the extremes in the population.	Given our subject of academic honesty, we will want to have a sample with the following characteristics: One student from each year One who is majoring in each of the disciplines on campus (e.g., social sciences, natural science, humanities) An honors student A student on academic probation A student with an average GPA A student who had violated the academic honor code and one who has not. An international student A student from another state and one from the same state as the college
3. Seek out members of the population who represent various extremes as well as those who represent the average.	Finding these extremes will be challenging. One option is that we can advertise for volunteers or recruit at public places on campus, having this initial group complete a brief questionnaire along with contact information. We can then use this information to screen for those who meet our criteria. We might also ask those who have already agreed to participate if they know anyone who would meet a specific criterion (such as an international student).
4. Collect data.	We will contact those who met our criteria and ask them to participate in our study. If someone refuses, we will simply find a replacement.

in the study but also to help the researcher recruit other participants. If each participant helps recruit several others, the sample will grow exponentially, like a snowball.

Getting your foot in the door to make initial contacts is the first challenge in snowball sampling. It may be that you know someone who could help you, or you may contact someone who already has a relationship with members of the population of interest. For example, if you wanted to conduct a study on the homeless, you might first approach the director of a homeless shelter. The director could then recommend homeless adults who might be willing to talk with you, and could even come with you to the initial meeting. Once you develop the trust of a few initial contacts, they too might personally introduce you to other potential participants.

There are unique considerations when using snowball sampling. Because all the participants know each other or have common associates, they will likely have similar views and experiences. Thus, your sample may represent only that small subset of the already narrowly defined population. There are also ethical implications in asking participants to identify others who might not want to be identified. One way to address this issue is to have the participants give your contact information to others and encourage them to contact you directly. If you have established a good reputation within the population of interest by treating participants with respect and keeping their personal information confidential, it is possible that members of the population will seek you out. Another option is for the participant to obtain permission from others for you to contact them, or even bring potential participants to you with their consent. See Table 4.9 for the steps in snowball sampling and an example.

TABLE 4.9

Snowball Sampling

Steps in Snowball Sampling	Example for a Study on Academic Honesty
1. Define the population.	Snowball sampling would best be used for a smaller, more hard to reach, subset of the college student population. For a study on academic honesty, we will define our population as students who have intentionally cheated on their academic work.
2. Identify strategies for recruiting the initial participants.	We would talk with the judicial board on campus and ask members of that group to help us identify those who were caught cheating, or we might ask professors to refer students who were caught cheating in their class. Since this would be a violation of the students' confidentiality, we would ask the judicial board and professors to contact the students directly and encourage them to contact us or for consent for us to contact them. We might be able to work out an incentive for participation, although we would want to be careful that the incentive was not coercive. We could also hold a focus group on the topic of academic honesty. We would establish the confidential nature of the discussion and ask if there were any students willing to share their own experiences. We would ask those students who revealed that they had cheated for permission to contact them for a follow-up study.
3. Collect data from the initial participants.	We would collect data from our initial participants. We would work on creating a trusting relationship where the participants do not feel judged and feel confident being honest with us. This is important in any research study, but especially so given the topic of our study and our sampling technique.
4. Ask the initial participants to recruit other members from the population, and likewise ask each new participant to help with recruitment.	We would then ask the initial participants to talk with other students who they know have cheated on assignments and either ask them to contact us or get permission for us to contact them. The snowball technique will hopefully give us access not only to those who were caught cheating (who we may have recruited exclusively if we relied on the judicial board or professors to recruit participants) but also to those who were not caught cheating. We would continue this process with each new participant until we had a sample of adequate size, or until we felt that we had reached all the members of the population we were able to reach.

Application 4.2

EXAMPLES OF NONPROBABILITY SAMPLING

Study C: Interviews and Observations With Maximum Variation Sampling

Parameswaran and Devi (2006) examined the prevalence and types of plagiarism that occur within engineering labs, and the attitudes and motivations of students regarding plagiarism.

The researchers conducted individual interviews with mechanical and electrical engineering students and made observations of engineering lab sessions.

The population for the interviews was students enrolled in engineering labs at one university.

Maximum variation sampling was used to select 30 interview participants who represented a range of grade point averages, ethnicities, nationalities, social groups, departments, and years in school.

Study D: Questionnaires With Convenience Sampling

Trost (2009) examined the prevalence of different forms of academic dishonesty among Swedish students.

The population was Swedish university students, and as such the researcher screened out international students. The sample was collected by approaching students at the end of natural sciences, technical sciences, and social science classes at a Swedish university and asking if the students would be willing to complete a questionnaire. A total of 325 were asked to participate, and 3 declined.

Table 4.10 presents a summary of the different sampling techniques we have discussed in this chapter.

TABLE 4.10

Types of Sampling Techniques

Probability (Random) Sampling	Nonprobability (Nonrandom) Sampling
Simple Random Sampling	Convenience Sampling
Stratified Random Sampling	Quota Sampling
Cluster Sampling	Maximum Variation Sampling
	Snowball Sampling

How large should your nonprobability sample be? What is considered a large sample size is relative. A sample of 50 may be considered large if the population itself is very small and homogeneous, whereas a sample of 500 may be considered small if the population it is drawn from is quite large and heterogeneous. The larger the sample size relative to the population size and heterogeneity, the better external validity the study has because it improves your chances that your results will generalize to other samples. However, because probability sampling was not used, there is no guarantee that even a very large sample will be representative of the population.

On the other hand, sample size is still important when conducting certain types of statistics. We will discuss this in more detail in Chapter 6. In the meantime, aim for as large a sample size as is possible, given your resources and time.

THE BIG PICTURE: BEYOND DESCRIPTION

What is beyond description? Correlational and experimental designs, of course! These designs go beyond describing phenomena to examining relationships among phenomena. Describing and examining relationships do not have to be mutually exclusive. Although many social science researchers conduct purely descriptive studies, others choose to use multiple research designs within a single study. In fact, in some disciplines, such as psychology, it is rare for a study to be purely descriptive. It is equally rare that correlational or experimental designs are conducted without first describing the variables of interest.

In particular, descriptive and correlational research often go hand in hand because both of these are nonexperimental designs. Social scientists are incredibly curious. When a researcher collects descriptive information examining several variables, and the data are in a form that allows relationships among the variables to be analyzed, and there is research evidence suggesting that there might be a relationship among the variables, it is too tempting not also to conduct a correlational study.

For example, M. McCullough and Holmberg's (2005) primary goal was descriptive, in that they sought to determine how much plagiarism could be identified using Google searches. However, they also utilized a correlational design to examine the relationship between plagiarism, institution, and subject matter. This allowed the researchers to determine if plagiarism was more common in certain institutions or for certain subjects. Likewise, Trost (2009) examined the prevalence of different types of academically dishonest acts among Swedish students, but she also examined the relationship between gender and academic dishonesty. Both of these examples focused primarily on descriptive research, but they included correlational research as well. We will examine correlational studies in more depth in Chapter 8.

CHAPTER RESOURCES

Key Terms

Define the following terms using your own words. You can check your answers by reviewing the chapter or by comparing them with the definitions in the glossary—but try to define them on your own first.

Do You Understand the Chapter?

Answer these questions on your own, and then review the chapter to check your answers.

1. What are some reasons to conduct a descriptive study?

2. What is survey research? What are some of the pros and cons of interviews and questionnaires?

3. What types of decisions must be made when conducting observational research?

4. What is archival research? What are possible ways to find archives?

5. Evaluate ethical issues, particularly informed consent, with the different descriptive methods.

6. What are the ways to evaluate validity in a descriptive study?

7. How does a researcher define a population and subpopulations?

8. How is probability sampling different from nonprobability sampling?

9. Describe the different types and procedures of probability sampling and of nonprobability sampling.

 **SAGE edge™**   **edge.sagepub.com/adams2e**

Sharpen your skills with SAGE edge!
SAGE edge for students provides you with tools to help you study. You'll find mobile-friendly eFlashcards and quizzes, as well as videos, web resources, datasets, and links to SAGE journal articles related to this chapter.

Describing Your Sample

5

What did you do last night? How would you tell a story about your night to friends who were not with you? No matter the focus of your story, you would need to describe who was there with you. A story about dancing with your peers is quite different from a story about dancing with 10-year-olds or professional football players. If you were to skip that information, surely your friends would interrupt you to inquire about that detail because it would be essential to their understanding of the situation. This would be true if the purpose of your story was to describe an event or if your goal was to predict or explain the relationship between two or more events.

The same is true when you conduct a research study. No matter what type of study you choose to do, you will need to describe your sample in enough detail so that you can paint a clear picture for those who were not with you as you conducted the study. If you skip a key detail about your sample, your audience will have a difficult time understanding and interpreting your results. Likewise, when you read a research article, you will come to expect that the authors will provide you with this basic context. At the same time, you do not need to, nor should you, describe every single detail of your sample, for both ethical and practical reasons.

ETHICAL ISSUES IN DESCRIBING YOUR SAMPLE

When you tell a story to your friends, you may choose to reveal the names of the people involved or you may decide to keep the names of those involved private. As a researcher, however, you are bound by ethical codes of conduct to maintain the dignity and privacy of those who participate in your studies. Consequently, you should never reveal the identities of your participants.

LEARNING OUTCOMES

In this chapter, you will learn

- The ethical and practical considerations of describing your sample

- How to describe your sample using descriptive statistics

- The appropriate statistics and graphs based on the type of data you have

- How to use z scores and percentiles to describe your sample

Giving the names of participants is clearly a violation of their right to confidentiality, but so is revealing identifying information that allows others to guess who the participants are. The book (and movie) *The Help* (Stockett, 2009) helps to illustrate the problem of revealing identifying information about participants. The main character, Skeeter, writes a book about the relationship between African American maids and the White families for whom they work. The maids agreed to participate only after they were assured that their identities would be protected. Skeeter published the book under a pseudonym, changed the name of the town, and changed the names of the maids—all in order to protect the maids' identities. Yet she still provided too many details, so that the maids were eventually found out. In particular, she included a story about a table with a huge crack in it that everyone in town knew belonged to a particular family—which in turn implicated the maid who revealed the story. It did not take long for the women in the town to figure out the identities of the maids who participated, and some of the maids and their family members even lost their jobs because of it.

The Help is fortunately a fictional account, but it demonstrates that even someone with good intentions can make careless mistakes that violate participants' rights to dignity and privacy. Even if the stakes are not so high, it is essential that you maintain the confidentiality of the participants involved by being careful not to reveal information that might identify them.

 ## Ethics Tip: Maintain the Confidentiality of Your Participants

1. Identify participants' data by an ID number, not by names.

2. Keep forms with participants' names and other identifying information separate from their responses.

3. Whenever possible, report data about participants in aggregate form (as a group as opposed to as individuals).

PRACTICAL ISSUES IN DESCRIBING YOUR SAMPLE

Again imagine telling a story to your friends about what you did last night. What details would you include to help paint a clear picture? What details would you choose to omit? Would it be important to tell your friends how many people were there? What about what people were wearing, what color eyes and hair they had, or what they had for breakfast? Some of these details would be essential to help your friends understand the events of your evening. However, including details that are not essential would likely leave your friends bored or confused by your story.

Researchers likewise need to be judicious in the amount of detail they include in their reports. You will need to apply your critical-thinking skills to decide what information is important in order to paint a clear picture of your sample's characteristics, attitudes, or behaviors; what information you should exclude for ethical purposes; and what information is simply not necessary. A good rule of thumb is that you should provide enough information so that another researcher could replicate your study with different participants.

How do we summarize participants' responses or behaviors without giving too much away about who they are? Moreover, how do we describe a sample in a way that is not overly cumbersome, while allowing us to identify the commonalities and differences across different human participants, animal subjects, or archival records? If our goal is to describe the sample (and not make inferences to the population—which we will talk about in the next chapter), we would use descriptive statistics.

DESCRIPTIVE STATISTICS

Descriptive statistics are the numbers used to summarize the characteristics of a sample. They are used when you have data from quantitative measures such as age, heart rate, or responses on a rating scale. Additionally, descriptive statistics can be used to analyze qualitative (nonnumerical) measures if you code the data as numbers. **Coding** is the process of categorizing information, and in **numerical coding** those categories are assigned numbers in order to facilitate quantitative analyses such as descriptive statistics. For example, you might ask the participants to report their ethnicity and then categorize and number each response based on ethnicity categories that either emerged from the data or that you determined beforehand. See Practice 5.1 for directions and practice for numerical coding.

> **Descriptive statistics:** A type of quantitative (numerical) analysis used to summarize the characteristics of a sample.
>
> **Coding:** The process of categorizing information.
>
> **Numerical coding:** The process of categorizing and numbering information for quantitative analyses.

Through the process of numerical coding, you have created a nominal variable. Recall from Chapter 3 that nominal variables have identity but do not have order, magnitude, or an absolute zero. In other words, the numbers are used only to identify the categories, and therefore you can use any numbers to code your data as long as each number is unique to the category (for example, healthy beverages must be identified by a different number than unhealthy beverages).

As you will see in Practice 5.2, the numbers are not necessary for describing nominal variables if you calculate descriptive statistics by hand. The numbers are essential, however, if you were to use a statistical software program such as SPSS or Excel.

Practice 5.1

NUMERICAL CODING

Suppose you observed 10 people at dinner and recorded what type of beverage they drank:

Participant 1: Pepsi

Participant 2: Orange juice

Participant 3: Sprite

Participant 4: Water

Participant 5: Coke

Participant 6: Water

Participant 7: Water

Participant 8: 7-Up

Participant 9: Kool-Aid

Participant 10: Apple juice

If you were to describe what people drank, one option would be to simply list every single type of beverage and how many people drank that beverage. That would be cumbersome, however, and impractical if you had a larger dataset. Instead, you could use numerical coding to organize the data, and later use these codes to describe the data (see Practice 5.2).

1. *Code based on categories that emerge from the data.* First, group the 10 beverages based on similar properties that you identify. Next, name the categories. Finally, for numerical coding, give each category a number.

2. *Code based on pre-determined categories.* Group the 10 beverages into two categories: healthy beverages and unhealthy beverages. For numerical coding, assign healthy beverages a number (e.g., 1) and unhealthy beverages a number (e.g., 2).

See Appendix A to check your answers.

Practice 5.2

DESCRIBE HOW OFTEN SCORES APPEAR IN THE SAMPLE

Suppose you coded your 10 participants from Practice 5.1 as such:

Participant 1: Pepsi (sugary drink)

Participant 2: Orange juice (juice)

Participant 3: Sprite (sugary drink)

Participant 4: Water (water)

Participant 5: Coke (sugary drink)

Participant 6: Water (water)

Participant 7: Water (water)

Participant 8: 7-Up (sugary drink)

Participant 9: Kool-Aid (sugary drink)

Participant 10: Apple juice (juice)

1. Find the frequency of sugary drinks, water, and juice in the sample.

2. What percentage of the sample was observed drinking water with dinner?

Suppose you asked 15 participants how many 8-ounce glasses of plain water they drink per day and obtained the following responses:

Participant 1: 3 glasses   Participant 9: 4 glasses

Participant 2: 1 glass   Participant 10: 12 glasses

Participant 3: none   Participant 11: 5 glasses

Participant 4: 3 glasses   Participant 12: 6 glasses

Participant 5: 5 glasses   Participant 13: 4 glasses

Participant 6: 1 glass   Participant 14: 3 glasses

Participant 7: 7 glasses   Participant 15: 3 glasses

Participant 8: 8 glasses

Calculate the cumulative percentage of 5 to 8 glasses of water per day:

3. Put the data into a frequency table.

4. Find the cumulative frequency for 5 to 8 glasses ($cf_{[5,8]}$).

5. Calculate the cumulative percentage with the following formula, where N = total number of participants: $(cf_{[5,8]}/N)100$.

See Appendix A to check your answers.

There are several types of descriptive statistics, and we have organized some of the most common types according to their main descriptive purpose. Most researchers calculate statistics using SPSS, Excel, STATA, SAS, or another data analysis program. We provide some guidelines for using these data analysis programs later in the chapter. But first we provide the formulas to calculate the descriptive statistics so that you will have a better understanding of these numbers.

Describe How Often a Score Appears in the Sample

Frequency (*f*)

The **frequency** of scores is a simple count of how many times that score occurred in the sample (e.g., there were 45 men in the sample). The statistical notation for frequency is a lowercase and italicized f (statistical notations are always italicized to help them stand out in a paper). As such, you could report: $f_{men} = 45$.

Frequency (*f*): A count of how many times a score appears in the sample.

Percentage

A **percentage** is the proportion of a score within a sample. To calculate percentage, divide the frequency by the total sample size and multiply the result by 100:

$$\text{Percentage} = \frac{f}{N} \times 100$$

where f equals frequency; N equals total sample size.

Whereas frequencies have no fixed end, percentages can range only from 0% to 100%, and as such provide a context for how often a score appears in a sample. For example, if you obtain a frequency of 45 men out of a total sample of 45, then 100% of the sample are men. If you obtain the same frequency of men ($f_{\text{men}} = 45$) from a sample of 1,000, only 4.5% of the sample are men.

Percentage: The proportion of a score within the sample.

Cumulative Percentage

The **cumulative percentage** is the proportion of the sample that falls within a specified interval. You might, for example, want to report the percentage of participants in the sample who were between the ages of 18 and 23.

To calculate the cumulative percentage, you first create a frequency table in order to order your scores. Table 5.1 shows a frequency table for the age of 100 participants. In this sample, there were six participants who were 18, nine who were 19, eight who were 20, and so on.

Once you have your frequency table, determine the interval of scores you are examining. The lowest score in your interval is designated as a and the highest score in your interval is designated as b. You then calculate the cumulative frequency of scores from a to b ($cf_{[a, b]}$) by adding up the frequencies for each of the scores within the interval.

Finally, to find the cumulative percentage, divide the cumulative frequency by the sample size and then multiply by 100 to obtain the percentage.

$$\text{Cumulative Percentage} = \frac{cf_{[a,b]}}{N} \times 100$$

where $cf_{[a, b]}$ equals the cumulative frequency of the scores between a and b interval; N = total sample size.

For our age example, if the age interval we want to examine is 18 to 23, then a is 18 and b is 23. We would add the frequency of all the participants within this interval to calculate the cumulative frequency. In our example, $cf_{[18,23]} = 65$. We would then divide

Cumulative percentage: The proportion of a score that falls within a specified interval.

TABLE 5.1

Frequency Table for the Age of 100 Participants

Age of Participants	f
18	6
19	9
20	8
21	11
22	16
23	15
24	9
25	8
26	4
27	7
28	1
29 to 31	0
32	2
33	2
34	1
35 to 44	0
45	1

the cf by our sample size ($N = 100$) and then multiply by 100 to find the cumulative percentage of 65% (see Table 5.2).

Describe the Central Tendency

Central tendency is a number that represents the central score, around which other scores cluster. There are three types of central tendency that vary in preciseness.

Mode

The **mode** is the most frequent score in the sample. To calculate the mode, identify the frequency of scores in a sample. The score with the highest frequency is the mode. If we have a sample with 45 men and 55 women, women is the modal gender. The mode is not always a unique score, as two or more scores can have the highest frequency. In addition, the mode is not very sensitive as a measure because scores in the sample can change without changing the mode.

Central tendency: A single score that summarizes the center of the distribution.

Mode: The most frequent score in a distribution.

TABLE 5.2

Calculating the Cumulative Frequency (*cf*) and Cumulative Percentage of Participants Between the Ages of 18 and 23

1. Calculate $cf_{[18,23]}$ by adding the frequency (*f*) of participants within the interval of 18 to 23:

Age of Participants	f
18	6
19	9
20	8
21	11
22	16
23	15
24	9
25	8
26	4
27	7
28	1
29 to 31	0
32	2
33	2
34	1
35 to 44	0
45	1

$cf_{[18,23]} = 65$

$N = 100$

2. Calculate the Cumulative Percentage:

$$\frac{cf_{[18,23]}}{N} \times 100$$

$$\frac{65}{100} \times 100 = 65\%$$

Median (*Mdn*)

The **median** is the score that cuts the sample in half so that 50% of the sample will be at or below the median. If we look at the frequency of age in our example, we see that 50% of the participants were 22 years and younger (see Table 5.3). Therefore, 22 is the

Median (*Mdn*): The score that cuts a distribution in half.

median age because it splits the distribution in half. There can be only one median, and thus it is a unique score. The median is also not a very sensitive measure, as the median remains the same even when the particular score values above or below the middle score change. As long as the same number of scores fall at or below the median as fall above it, the median remains the same.

TABLE 5.3

Calculating the Median Age

1. Calculate $cf_{[18,23]}$ by adding the frequency (f) of participants within the interval of 18 to 23:

Age of Participants	f
18	6
19	9
20	8
21	11
22	16
23	15
24	9
25	8
26	4
27	7
28	1
29 to 31	0
32	2
33	2
34	1
35 to 44	0
45	1

50 out of 100 participants (50%) were 22 or younger. $Mdn_{age} = 22$

Mean (M or $\bar{X}$)

The **mean** of a sample is the arithmetic average. There are two acceptable statistical notations for the mean: M or $\bar{X}$. We will use M because it is the preferred notation in published research, although most statisticians prefer $\bar{X}$. To calculate the mean, sum all the scores and then divide by the total number of scores. There is only one mean

Mean (M): The arithmetic average.

in a distribution of scores; the mean is the most sensitive of the three measures of central tendency because it changes every time there is a change in any of the scores in a distribution.

To calculate the mean (*M*):

$$M = \frac{\Sigma X}{N}$$

where Σ equals sum; *X* equals score; *N* equals total sample size.

For example, suppose we ask 15 students to rate how important it is for them to have the newest cell phone model on a scale from 1 to 10, with 10 indicating *extremely important*. The frequency table of their responses is shown in Table 5.4.

First, we would add up all the scores:

$$\Sigma X = 2 + 4 + 4 + 4 + 5 + 5 + 6 + 6 + 6 + 6 + 6 + 7 + 7 + 7 + 7$$

$$\Sigma X = 82$$

Then to calculate the mean, we would divide ΣX by the total number of scores:

$$M = \frac{\Sigma X}{N}$$

$$M = \frac{82}{15}$$

$$M = 5.47 \text{ (rounded to two decimals)}$$

TABLE 5.4

Frequency Table for Responses of 15 Participants

Importance of Owning the Newest Phone	f
1	0
2	1
3	0
4	3
5	2
6	5
7	4
8	0
9	0
10	0

Practice 5.3

CALCULATE THE CENTRAL TENDENCY

1. If 5 participants were observed drinking sugary drinks, 3 water, and 2 juice, what is the modal type of drink?

2. What is the median of the following distribution ($N = 48$):

Glasses of Juice Drank per Week	f
1	1
2	2
3	4
4	4
5	6
6	6
7	12
8	6
9	5
10	1
11–34	0
35	1

3. What is the mean of the following distribution ($N = 15$):

Glasses of Water	f
0	1
1	2
2	0
3	4
4	2
5	2
6	1
7	1
8	1

(Continued)

(Continued)

Glasses of Water	f
9	0
10	0
11	0
12	1

See Appendix A to check your answers.

Describe the Variability of Scores in the Sample

Variability describes how much scores differ in a sample. There are several different ways to measure variability, including minimum and maximum scores, range, and standard deviation.

Minimum and Maximum Scores

The lowest score obtained for a variable in your sample is called the **observed minimum score**, and the highest score obtained is the **observed maximum score**. The observed score is what was actually obtained in the sample and therefore gives the reader a sense of how much scores varied within the sample.

However, the possible scores for a measure could be higher or lower than what was observed. In our example of ratings of importance of having the newest cell phone, the **possible minimum and maximum scores** were from 1 to 10. The observed scores were from 2 to 7 because no one in our sample rated importance as low as 1, or 8 and higher (see Table 5.5).

Range

The **range** is the distance between the minimum score and the maximum score. To calculate the range, subtract the observed minimum from the observed maximum. The range for importance of owning the latest cell phone is 5.

Variability: The degree to which scores differ from each other in the sample.

Observed minimum and maximum scores: The lowest and highest scores on a measure that are obtained in the sample.

Possible minimum and maximum scores: The lowest and highest scores possible for the measurement instrument.

Range: The distance between the observed maximum and minimum scores.

TABLE 5.5

Possible and Observed Minimum and Maximum Scores

	Importance of Owning the Newest Phone	f
Possible Minimum→	1	0
Observed Minimum→	2	1
	3	0
	4	3
	5	2
	6	5
Observed Maximum→	7	4
	8	0
	9	0
Possible Maximum→	10	0

The range provides some information about the variability of scores, but it does not provide enough information by itself. If you were to report that the observed range of ages in our sample was 27, readers would not know how old the youngest or oldest person in your sample was. A range of 27 could describe a sample with an observed minimum of 18 and an observed maximum age of 45, or it could describe a sample with an observed minimum age of 65 and an observed maximum of 92. In both cases, the range of scores is the same but we have two very different representations of age. Consequently, researchers report the range only if they also report the median or mean.

Standard Deviation (SD or S_x)

The **standard deviation** describes how much, in general, the scores in a sample differ from the mean. There are two acceptable statistical notations for the sample standard deviation: SD or S_x. As we did with the mean, we will use the preferred notation in published research, which is SD for the standard deviation. A standard deviation of 0 indicates that every score in the sample is exactly the same as the mean. For example, if all your participants are 18, the mean age is 18 and the standard deviation is 0. As scores become more spread out around the mean, the standard deviation increases. Like the range, the standard deviation is not meant to stand alone in a research report. We report the mean with the standard deviation so that we have a good idea of the midpoint of a distribution and the deviation of the scores around that midpoint.

> **Standard deviation (SD):** A single number that summarizes the degree to which scores differ from the mean.

As with many statistics, the standard deviation can be calculated using a definitional or computational formula. If you are doing most calculations by hand, the computational formula is preferred because there are fewer steps involved. However, the definitional formulas are better suited to aid in your understanding of statistical concepts. Consequently, we provide and discuss definitional formulas in the chapters. Computational formulas are provided in Appendix D if you or your professor prefer them.

The definitional formula for the standard deviation (SD) is:

$$SD = \sqrt{\frac{\Sigma(X-M)^2}{N-1}}$$

where Σ equals sum; X equals score; M equals mean; N equals total sample size.

That formula may seem a bit daunting. If you take a quick peek at Appendix D.1 to view the computational formula for the standard deviation, you might be even more aghast. You might be feeling overwhelmed with the amount of math involved in research, but take heart that most researchers do not do calculations by hand. We will show you calculations in this chapter to aid in your understanding of the concepts, but shortly we will discuss data analysis software that will do these calculations for you. Although you may now be tempted to skip the formulas and calculations, we believe that taking the time to understand how statistics are calculated will give you a better perspective of what the statistic is and how to use and interpret it.

Let's walk through the calculations for the standard deviation using the example data for ratings of how important it is to have the latest cell phone. The first step to calculating a standard deviation is to find the mean of the scores. Recall from the previous section that we already calculated the mean of rating of importance of having the newest phone ($M = 5.47$).

Next, we subtract the mean from each score to find the degree to which each score deviates from the mean. Scores that fall above the mean will have a positive deviation and scores that fall below the mean will have a negative deviation. However, if we added all the positive and negative deviations scores, we would get 0 and that would not represent the overall deviation around the mean. To avoid this problem, we square each deviation, giving us the squared difference $(X–M)^2$ for each score (see Table 5.6).

Now we must find the sum of all the squared differences. We need to take into consideration the frequency of scores in our distribution. For the example in Table 5.6, we multiply each $(X–M)^2$ (the squared difference) from the last column by the frequency (f) shown in the second column of Table 5.6. Adding all these together gives us the sum of the squared differences $[\Sigma(X-M)^2]$.

$\Sigma(X-M)^2 = (12.0409 \times 1) + (2.1609 \times 3) + (0.2209 \times 2) + (0.2809 \times 5) + (2.3409 \times 4)$

$\Sigma(X-M)^2 = 12.0409 + 6.4827 + 0.4418 + 1.4045 + 9.3636$

$\Sigma(X-M)^2 = 29.7335$

We now need to take into account the sample size by dividing our sum of the squared differences $[\Sigma(X-M)^2]$ by one less our sample size ($N-1$). We subtract one from our sample size to mitigate potential error in our sample. Thus, this number is slightly larger than if we had simply divided by the sample size.

TABLE 5.6

Calculating the Squared Difference $(X-M)^2$ for each score

Score (X) of Importance of Owning the Newest Phone	f	$X-M$	$(X-M)^2$
2	1	$2-5.47 = -3.47$	12.0409
4	3	$4-5.47 = -1.47$	2.1609
5	2	$5-5.47 = -0.47$	0.2209
6	5	$6-5.47 = 0.53$	0.2809
7	4	$7-5.47 = 1.53$	2.3409

$$\frac{\Sigma(X-M)^2}{N-1}$$

If we stop here, we have the **variance**. The variance is the average of the squared deviations and by itself is a measure of variability. Variance is a term you might read about in Results sections of articles. One of the most frequently used statistical tests is called Analysis of Variance (ANOVA) that you will learn about in Chapters 10 to 12. Variance, however, is rarely reported as a descriptive statistic due to the fact that the variance is out of proportion in relation to the mean because it is squared. Therefore, we take the square root to calculate the standard deviation (SD), which is a number easier to interpret in relation to the mean. A summary of these steps for our example data are shown below.

$$SD = \sqrt{\frac{\Sigma(X-M)^2}{N-1}}$$

$$SD = \sqrt{\frac{29.7335}{14}}$$

$$SD = \sqrt{2.1238}$$

$$SD = 1.46 \text{ (rounded to two decimal places)}$$

Variance (SD^2): The average of the squared difference between the mean and scores in a distribution, or the standard deviation squared.

CHOOSING THE APPROPRIATE DESCRIPTIVE STATISTICS

What would you think if you read a research report that reported the frequency of men and women in the sample? That sounds reasonable enough, and the frequency would give you adequate information about how gender was distributed in the study's sample.

Practice 5.4

CALCULATING VARIABILITY

Glasses of Water	f
0	1
1	2
2	0
3	4
4	2
5	2
6	1
7	1
8	1
9	0
10	0
11	0
12	1

1. What is the observed minimum and maximum score for how many number of glasses drank per week? How is this different from the possible minimum and maximum scores?

2. What is the range?

3. What is the standard deviation?

    See Appendix A to check your answers.

This description is OK:

The sample consisted of 45 men and 55 women.

But what if the participants' ages were described similarly?

This description is not OK:

There were six participants who were 18 years old; nine who were 19; eight who were 20; 11 who were 21; 16 who were 22; 15 who were 23; nine who were 24; eight who were 25; four who were 26; seven who were 27; one who was 28; none who were 29, 30, or 31; two who were 32; two who were 33; one who was 34; none who were 35, 36, 37, 38, 39, 40, 41, 42, 43, or 44; and one who was 45.

Are you asleep yet? Not only is this description incredibly boring to read, but listing the ages of all the participants is not particularly useful.

Not all descriptive statistics are appropriate for all types of variables. The challenge is to identify the most appropriate statistics to describe the different characteristics of your sample. In order to do this, you will need to determine the type of measurement scale represented by the variable. You should recall from Chapter 3 that there are four different measurement scales, defined by the presence or absence of the properties of identity, magnitude, equal intervals, and a true zero.

REVIEW OF KEY CONCEPTS: SCALES OF MEASUREMENT

- Nominal scales represent categories and have only identity.

- Ordinal scales are rankings that have identity and magnitude.

- Interval scales are ratings that have identity, magnitude, and equal intervals.

- Ratio scales measure quantity and have identity, magnitude, equal intervals, and a true zero.

Also recall from earlier in the chapter that there are three categories of descriptive statistics that you can use to describe:

1. How often a score appears in the sample.

2. The central tendency, which is a single score that summarizes the center of the distribution.

3. The variability of scores in your sample, which is the degree to which scores differ from each other.

The specific descriptive statistics you will use depends on the type of measurement scale. In the next sections, we will explain the appropriate ways to describe variables that are measured on nominal scales, ordinal scales, or interval and ratio scales.

Describing Variables Measured on a Nominal Scale

Descriptive Statistics for Nominal Variables

Because nominal scales represent categories, the numbers themselves are not meaningful. There is no magnitude in that if you were to assign a numerical value to a category, a higher score would not necessarily mean that there was more of some quality. Gender is a nominal scale that is typically described with two categories. For research purposes, we might code males as 1 and females as 2, but this does not indicate that females have more gender than males. We could have just as easily coded females 1 and males as 2, or females as 406 and males as 87. The numbers here serve as a place card for the categories, but they are not to be used for mathematical equations. As such, you are limited to the types of descriptive statistics that you can use for nominal variables. *Do not* calculate a mean, median, or any of the measures of variability for a nominal variable because such calculations are nonsensical.

You can use the following descriptive statistics for nominal variables:

1. Frequencies and/or percentages to describe how often a nominal category appears in the sample

2. The mode as a measure of central tendency

Just because you can use frequencies, percentages, and modes to describe nominal data does not mean that you should report all of these. Choose the descriptive statistics that clearly and concisely describe your data.

- A nominal variable with a few categories might be best described by reporting the frequency or percentage (or both) of each of those categories:

  o There were 4 Independents, 46 Democrats, and 30 Republicans.

  Or

  o Five percent of the sample were Independents, 58% Democrats, and 37% Republicans.

  Or

  o Five percent of the sample were Independents ($n = 4$), 58% Democrats ($n = 46$), and 37% Republicans ($n = 30$).

- On the other hand, it may be too cumbersome to report the exact frequencies if the nominal variable has many categories. In that case, the mode may be sufficient. When reporting the mode, it is good to also report the percentage:

  o Psychology (35%) was the most common major represented in the sample.

- Additionally, you might report the mode as well as the percentages for several of the most common categories:

  o Psychology (35%) was the most common major represented in the sample, followed by sociology (20%) and political science (18%).

Graphing Nominal Data

A graph can be useful in summarizing your descriptive statistics because it provides a quick snapshot. Creating graphs can help you better understand your data, but graphs should be included in a research paper only when the variable depicted is particularly relevant to your study and the graph helps to demonstrate a point or elaborate on information that would be too cumbersome to include in a text. For nominal data, a **bar graph** is useful when there are many categories that you might not want to list in the text of a paper, but it is not particularly helpful to describe a nominal variable with only two or three categories.

Bar graph: Graph used to display nominal or ordinal data in which the frequency of scores is depicted on the y-axis and the categories for nominal data or ranks for ordinal data are depicted on the x-axis. Nonadjacent bars represent the frequency of each category or rank.

When creating a bar graph for a nominal variable, the frequency of scores is on the y-(vertical) axis and the categories are on the x-(horizontal) axis. A bar is used to demonstrate the frequency of each category, and the adjacent bars do not touch because each category is distinct. When graphing nominal data, it usually does not matter what order you place the categories because there is no magnitude. As such, the shape of a bar graph is not meaningful (see Figure 5.1). It is important, however, that you label your graph clearly (see Figure 5.2).

FIGURE 5.1

Bar Graphs

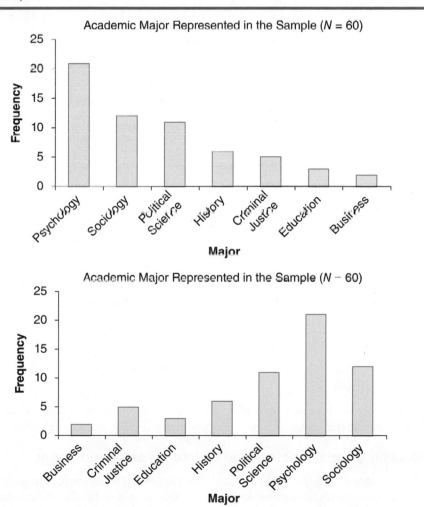

Note: The same nominal data are depicted in these graphs but the categories are listed in different orders. Because nominal variables do not have magnitude, the order of the categories and the shape of the graph are not important.

FIGURE 5.2

Graphing Data

Remember to always label your x- and y-axes, and also title your graphs. Such information is vital for others to accurately interpret your graph. Also note that the graph in this cartoon depicts ratio data (profits) and therefore the shape of the graph is meaningful. Had the graph depicted in this cartoon displayed nominal data, the shape would not matter because nominal data represent categories that can be displayed in different orders.

Source: Eva K. Lawrence

Describing Variables Measured on an Ordinal Scale

Ordinal scales represent rankings that have magnitude, but we do not assume that the intervals between the rankings are equal. Because we do not assume equal intervals with ordinal data, we *do not* calculate the mean and standard deviation.

You can use the following descriptive statistics for ordinal variables:

1. Frequencies and/or percentages to describe the places or rankings in the sample

2. The median as a measure of central tendency

3. The observed minimum and maximum score or the range as a measure of variability

You can use a bar graph to display your ordinal data. Unlike with nominal data, the order of the ranks is important and the *x*-axis should display the ranks in order.

Describing Variables Measured on Interval and Ratio Scales

Interval scales are ratings in which we assume there are equal intervals between scores. Interval scales do not have a true zero, meaning that there is no fixed starting point and a score of zero does not indicate complete absence of a quality. Ratio scales measure quantity and have both equal intervals and a true zero. Although variables measured on interval and ratio scales differ in the absence or presence of a true zero, many of the rules for choosing the appropriate descriptive statistics apply to both scales. Before deciding the best way to describe a variable that is either interval or ratio, we must first determine the type of distribution.

A **normal distribution** is shaped like a bell. It is symmetrical and the majority of the scores center around the middle (the mean), and then taper off at either end. The standard deviation of a normally distributed sample of scores helps us understand how the scores are distributed around the mean. In a normal distribution, about 68% of the scores are between +1 and −1 standard deviation, about 95% are between +2 and −2 standard deviations, and about 99% are within +3 and −3 standard deviations. See Figure 5.3 for an illustration of the normal curve.

> **Normal distribution:** Symmetrical distribution in which scores cluster around the middle and then taper off at the ends.

FIGURE 5.3

The Normal Curve

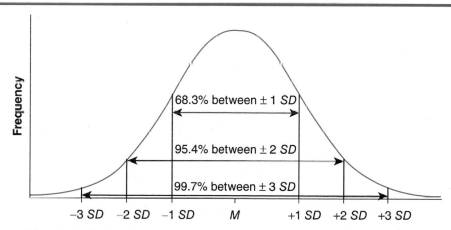

Note: *M* = Mean; *SD* = Standard Deviation.

Descriptive Statistics for Normally Distributed Interval or Ratio Variables

When you have normally distributed interval or ratio data, you should report the following descriptive statistics:

1. The mean as a measure of central tendency

2. The standard deviation as a measure of the variability among scores

If we have a sample that is normally distributed, reporting both the mean and standard deviation would give us an excellent idea of what our scores looked like in our sample.

Example sample 1: $M = 5.20$, $SD = 1.20$.

For this sample, we would expect that about 68% of the scores will fall within 4.00 and 6.40, about 95% will fall within 2.80 and 7.60, and about 99% will fall between 1.60 and 8.80.

Example sample 2: $M = 5.20$, $SD = 0.50$.

For this sample, we would expect that about 68% of the scores will fall within 4.70 and 5.70, about 95% will fall within 4.20 and 6.20, and about 99% will fall between 3.70 and 6.70.

Notice that just reporting the mean does not sufficiently summarize the scores in a sample. Both examples have the same mean, but the standard deviation in the first example is more than twice as large as in the second, which means that there is much more variability in scores (or a much more spread out distribution) in the first example.

For interval data, it is also helpful to provide a context to evaluate the scores. If the examples above were describing scores on a rating scale, we would not know what a mean of 5.20 means—is it a high, moderate, or low score? Some ways of providing the context of normally distributed interval scores are:

1. Percentages for each rating choice

2. Possible and observed minimum and maximum scores

We do not have the same problem of understanding the context of ratio scores. The number 5.20 is meaningful in and of itself if it describes age in years, amount of money, number of errors, or some other variable measured on a ratio scale. However, it may still be useful to provide some context for the range of scores in the sample by reporting the observed minimum and maximum scores or the range.

Deviations From the Normal Curve

In a perfectly normal distribution, the mean, median, and mode are at the same exact point—the middle—of the curve. Like most perfect things, a perfectly normal distribution is quite rare. In fact, Micceri (1989) compared it to a unicorn! Consequently, we do not expect any sample distribution to be perfectly normal. Some minor deviations are to be expected, and researchers consider distributions with such minor deviations to be within the bounds, or meet the criteria, of a normal distribution. One way to determine if your distribution meets the criteria for a normal distribution is to graph the data and evaluate the shape of the distribution.

Using a graph to determine if the distribution is normal. Interval and ratio data can be plotted on a histogram or frequency polygon. A **histogram** is similar to a bar graph in that bars are used to represent the frequency of a score, the frequency is depicted on the *y*-axis, and the scores are depicted on the *x*-axis. The main difference is that the bars are directly adjacent to each other to demonstrate that the scores on an interval and ratio scale are continuous. Scores on a **frequency polygon** are represented with points rather than bars and these points are connected with lines. The score below the observed minimum is included on the *x*-axis, as is the score above the observed maximum. These extreme scores both have a frequency of zero so that the line begins and ends at the *x*-axis, creating a polygon shape.

Histogram: Graph used to display interval or ratio data in which the frequency of scores is depicted on the *y*-axis and the interval ratings or ratio scores are depicted on the *x*-axis. Adjacent bars represent the frequency of each rating or score.

Frequency polygon: Graph used to display interval or ratio data in which the frequency of scores is depicted on the *y*-axis and the scores are depicted on the *x*-axis. Points represent the frequency of each score. The points are connected with straight lines that begin and end on the *x* axis.

An example of a distribution graphed with a histogram and frequency polygon is presented in Table 5.7. Notice that although the distribution is not perfectly normal, it still meets our criteria for a normal curve. The overall shape is symmetrical, with most of the scores clustering around the middle and then tapering off toward the extremes.

TABLE 5.7

Example of a Distribution That Meets the Criteria for the Normal Curve

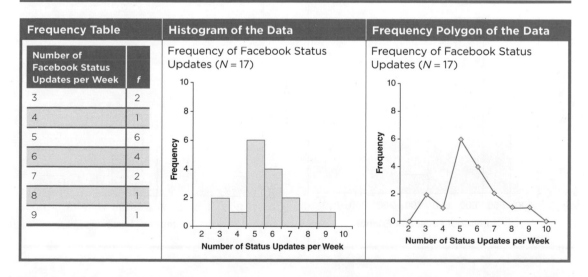

Distributions vary in how peaked they are, and the level of peak is the distribution's **kurtosis**. A normal curve such as the one depicted in Figure 5.3 has a moderate peak, or is a **mesokurtic curve**, in that there is a gradual increase of frequency toward the middle of the curve. If a curve has too much kurtosis, it is no longer considered normal. A distribution that is **leptokurtic** has a high peak because most of the scores are clustered in the middle. A **platykurtic curve** is one in which scores are more spread out and the distribution is flat (see Table 5.8). These deviations from normality are important to consider when interpreting your results; but when describing these distributions, the mean and standard deviation are still the appropriate descriptive statistics.

Kurtosis: The degree of the peak of a normal distribution.

Mesokurtic curve: A normal distribution with a moderate or middle peak.

Leptokurtic curve: A normal distribution with most of the scores in the middle and a sharp peak.

Platykurtic curve: A normal distribution that is relatively spread out and flat.

TABLE 5.8

Leptokurtic and Platykurtic Examples

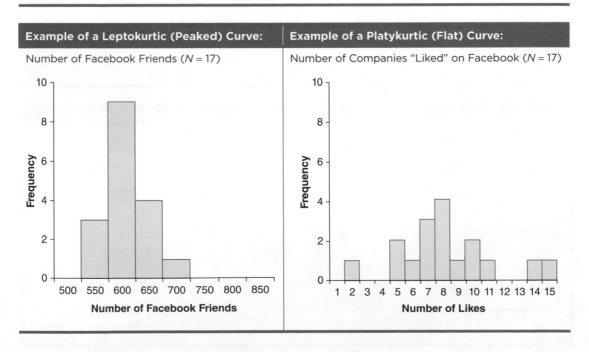

Example of a Leptokurtic (Peaked) Curve:	Example of a Platykurtic (Flat) Curve:
Number of Facebook Friends (*N* = 17)	Number of Companies "Liked" on Facebook (*N* = 17)

A **uniform distribution** violates the criteria for normality because all the ratings or scores have the same frequency. Instead of a curve, the distribution is shaped like a rectangle and as such is also commonly referred to as a rectangular distribution. It is easy to identify a uniform distribution by the unique shape of the histogram or frequency polygon. Although this type of distribution clearly does not meet the criteria for a normal curve, the mean and standard deviation do an adequate job of approximating the central score and variability, respectively. See Table 5.9 for a depiction of a uniform distribution.

A **bimodal distribution** is a non-normal distribution with two distinct peaks and therefore two modes. This type of distribution is easy to detect in a graph (see Table 5.9). In an ideal world, the two modes will represent two distinct groups of participants in your sample (men vs. women). As such, you should split the distribution into two distinct samples and describe each subsample separately using their means and standard deviations. If you cannot identify two distinct subsamples that can help explain the bimodal pattern, you can simply report both modes of the original distribution.

In a **skewed distribution,** most of the scores cluster on one end of the distribution, and there is a long tail at the other end because of one or a few scores (see Table 5.9). You can distinguish between a positively skewed and negatively skewed distribution by looking at the tail of the histogram. The "tail tells the tale" of a skewed distribution: If the tail is on the right (positive side of the distribution) with the majority of scores clustered on the other end of the distribution, the distribution is **positively skewed**; if the tail is on the left (negative side of the distribution) with the cluster of scores on the other end, it is **negatively skewed**. Almost all real-life distributions deviate slightly from the perfect bell-shaped curve we depicted back in Figure 5.3. When we talk about a distribution as skewed, we assume that the skew represents a substantial deviation from normal. See Figure 5.4 for a humorous depiction of normal and skewed distributions.

Uniform distribution: A non-normal distribution in which all scores or ratings have the same frequency.

Bimodal distribution: A non-normal distribution that has two peaks.

Skewed distribution: A non-normal distribution that is asymmetrical, with scores clustering on one side of the distribution and a long tail on the other side.

Positive skew: One or a few positive scores skew the distribution in the positive direction, but most of the scores cluster on the negative end of the scale.

Negative skew: One or a few negative scores skew the distribution in the negative direction, but most of the scores cluster on the positive end of the scale.

TABLE 5.9

Examples of Distributions That Do Not Meet the Criteria for a Normal Distribution

Frequency Table	Histogram	Why Is the Distribution Not Normal?
Rating of Cell Phone Annoyance — **f** 1 — 0 2 — 5 3 — 5 4 — 5 5 — 5	Ratings Frequency of Cell Phone Annoyance ($N = 20$) *Histogram: Frequency (y-axis 0–6) vs. How Annoying Are Cell Phones? (x-axis 1–5)*	This graph is not curved. Instead all the frequencies are exactly the same. This would be considered a **uniform distribution**.
Rating of Addiction to Cell Phone — **f** 1 — 1 2 — 2 3 — 4 4 — 1 5 — 1 6 — 2 7 — 2 8 — 4 9 — 2	Ratings Frequency of Cell Phone Addiction ($N = 19$) *Histogram: Frequency (y-axis 0–5) vs. Level of Cell Phone Addiction (x-axis 1–10)*	This graph does not fit our criteria for a normal curve because the scores cluster around two peaks. This would be considered a **bimodal distribution**.
Number of Text Messages Sent Per Day — **f** 8 — 1 9–19 — 0 20 — 2 21–24 — 0 25 — 5 26 — 7 27 — 3 28 — 1	Frequency of Text Messages Sent per Day ($N = 19$) *Histogram: Frequency (y-axis 0–8) vs. Number of Texts (x-axis 7–29)*	This graph does not fit our criteria for a normal curve because it is asymmetrical. Most of the scores are clustered toward one side of the distribution, with one extreme score on the other side. This would be considered a **skewed distribution**.

FIGURE 5.4
Normal Versus Skewed Distributions

A skewed distribution has scores clustered on one side of the distribution. In this example, the distribution on the right appears to have a strong negative skew.

Sample distributions very rarely fit the ideal normal curve. The distribution on the left is not perfectly normal, but we would likely consider it to meet the criteria of a normal distribution because it only deviates slightly from the normal curve.

Source: E. Lawrence

If your data appear to be skewed, your first strategy should be to examine any **outliers**, or data points that deviate greatly from the main cluster of your distribution. In the skewed distribution depicted in Table 5.9, the one participant who reported sending eight texts per day is an outlier in the sample, and it is that participant's score that is skewing the distribution.

Outliers: Responses or observations that deviate greatly from the rest of the data.

In some cases, an outlier might simply be a data entry mistake, and we would not want to go further without ruling out that possibility. In other cases, a researcher might have reason to believe that the outlier was due to the participant's misunderstanding the question and omit that outlier from further analysis. Omitting data should not be done lightly, and remember that it is unethical to omit data simply because it does not align with your hypothesis. Do not assume an outlier is a mistake unless you have reason to do so. An outlier often represents an actual extreme response that would be important to acknowledge and analyze.

Using statistics to determine skewness. If you have ruled out error as the reason for your skew, you will need to determine if the skew is extreme enough to violate the criteria of normality. It is not always possible to determine this from a graph. Consider our data on the importance of owning the newest phone (rated on a scale from 1 to 10). When the data are graphed with a histogram, there seems to be a slight negative skew. However, it is not clear if that skew is strong enough to violate our criteria for a normal distribution (see Table 5.10).

TABLE 5.10

Example Distribution in Which It Is Not Clear From the Graph if the Distribution Is Normal

Importance of Owning the Newest Phone	f
2	1
3	0
4	3
5	2
6	5
7	4

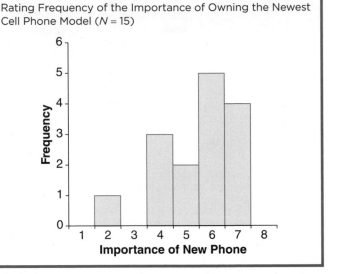

Rating Frequency of the Importance of Owning the Newest Cell Phone Model ($N = 15$)

There are several statistics and tests to help determine if a distribution is substantially skewed. Unfortunately, there is no one clear test that is used by all researchers and statisticians. We will discuss a few commonly used strategies that involve calculating a skewness statistic for the sample (G_1), but keep in mind that your professor may prefer you to use a different standard.

A sample's **skewness statistic (G_1)** indicates the degree of skew in that sample's distribution. This is typically calculated with a data analysis program. If you would like to know how to calculate this statistic by hand, the formula is in Appendix D.2. A skewness statistic of zero indicates that there is no skew, and the degree of skewness increases as the number gets further away from zero. The sign (+ or −) indicates the direction of the skew, with a negative skewness statistic indicating a negative skew and a positive skewness statistic indicating a positive skew. Bulmer (1979) proposed the rule of thumb that a skewness greater than +1 or −1 indicated a distribution with a skew that is a substantial deviation from normal. Some researchers use this criterion, although many use the less stringent parameter of greater than +/−2 to indicate a skew. Still many others take an additional step after calculating the skewness statistic.

Using the skewness statistic alone is generally acceptable if you have a large sample, but with smaller samples the size and variability of the sample can impact the skewness

Skewness statistic (G_1): A number that indicates the degree of skewness in a distribution.

statistic. Consequently, researchers often interpret the skewness statistic in relation to the standard error of the skew (*SES*), which is an estimate of the skewness in the population and can be approximated as $\sqrt{\dfrac{6}{N}}$. Ignoring the sign of the skewness statistic, if it is greater than about twice the standard error of the skew, it is considered outside the normal parameters (Tabachnick & Fidell, 1996).

Consider our example dataset of 15 participants' ratings of the importance of owning the newest cell phone (see Table 5.10). Using a data analysis program or the formula in Appendix D.2, we find the skewness statistic ($G_1 = -0.96$). If we used the quick rule of thumb that a skewness statistic within +/– 2 meets the criteria for normality, we would stop there and conclude that our sample distribution is within normal limits.

We might, however, want to use the criteria that G_1 must be less than twice the standard error of the skew (*SES*) to be considered a normal distribution. In our example, we would calculate the *SES* as: $\sqrt{\dfrac{6}{N}} = \sqrt{\dfrac{6}{15}} = 0.63$. A skewness statistic that was twice this *SES* (or 1.26) would indicate a substantial skew. Recall that in our example, our $G_1 = -.96$. When we ignore the sign, or take the absolute value of our G_1, we find that it is less than 1.26 and we therefore consider the distribution to be within normal limits.

To write up these results, at minimum, we should include the mean and standard deviation because we have normally distributed interval data. Because this is an interval scale, we might want to provide some context for interpreting the scores by including the possible and observed minimum and maximum scores. We do not need to mention skewness because the distribution meets the criteria for normality, and the reader will assume the data are normally distributed unless we tell them otherwise.

Following are two of many possible ways we might write up the results:

Participants' ratings on the importance of owning the newest cell phone model ranged from 2 to 7 out of the possible ratings of 1 to 10, with a higher score indicating greater importance. On average, ratings were in the middle of the scale (*M* = 5.47, *SD* = 1.46), indicating a moderate level of importance.

Or

The mean rating of how important it is to have the newest cell phone model was 5.47 (*SD* = 1.46). The sample mean was in the middle of the 1–10 scale, suggesting a neutral score. In fact, no participants rated importance as lower than 2 or greater than 7.

The skewness statistic provides a clearer indication of skew than simply looking at a graph. Keep in mind, however, that lack of a skew is only one criterion for a normal distribution, and graphing the data can provide key information about your distribution. See Table 5.11 for a comparison of distributions graphed with a histogram and evaluated with a skewness statistic.

Describing a skewed distribution. When you have a distribution with a skew that is a substantial deviation from normal, the mean is not the best measure of central tendency. Generally speaking, the mean will underestimate the central tendency of a negatively skewed distribution because the extreme negative scores pull down the mean.

TABLE 5.11

Comparing Graphs and Skewness Statistics

Histogram	Skewness Statistic (G_1) and Standard Error of the Skew (*SES*)	Interpretation
Frequency of Facebook Status Updates (*N* = 17)	$G_1 = 0.35$ *SES* = 0.59	*The skewness statistic and graph both demonstrate that the distribution meets the criteria for a normal distribution.*
Ratings Frequency of Cell Phone Addiction (*N* = 19)	$G_1 = -0.65$ *SES* = .56	*The skewness statistic demonstrates that the data are not skewed, but just because a distribution is not skewed does not mean that it is normal.* *The skewness statistic will not identify bimodal distributions (as in this example) or uniform distributions.* *Use both a visual inspection of the data (via a histogram or frequency polygon) and the skewness statistic to decide if your distribution is normal.*
Frequency of Text Messages (*N* = 19)	$G_1 = -3.10$ *SES* = .56	*The graph and skewness statistic confirm that the distribution has a substantial negative skew.*

FIGURE 5.5

Comparing the Mean and Median of Skewed Distributions

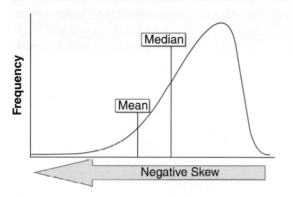

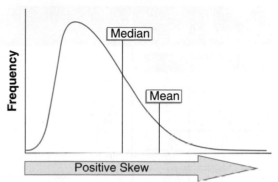

The mean tends to be pulled down by extreme negative scores in a negatively skewed distribution. Consequently, the mean underestimates the central tendency and should not be reported. The median is higher than the mean in a negatively skewed distribution and as such is a better estimate of the central tendency.

The mean tends to be pulled up by extreme positive scores in a positively skewed distribution, overestimating the central tendency. The median is lower than the mean in a positively skewed distribution and as such is a better estimate of the central tendency.

In a positively skewed distribution, the mean will overestimate the central tendency because the extreme positive scores pull up the mean (see Figure 5.5).

Do not report the mean and standard deviation of a skewed distribution. Instead, report:

1. The median as a measure of central tendency

2. The observed minimum and maximum or the range as a measure of the variability among scores

It can also be useful to include:

1. A cumulative percentage for the majority of the distribution

2. The possible minimum and maximum for interval scales

The age distribution example in Table 5.1 on p. 137 is an example of a skewed distribution. Both the skewness statistic and histogram confirm that age in that sample is skewed toward the positive. Therefore, the mean of this distribution ($M = 23.04$) overestimates the central age in the sample, and we should *not* report the mean. Instead, the median ($Mdn = 22$) is a more accurate measure of central tendency (see Table 5.12).

Following are two of many possible ways we might write up a description of the age of our participants. Notice that we mention that the data are skewed, but we do not include the skewness statistic or its standard error. That statistic is calculated only to tell you if you met or did not meet the criteria for a normal distribution; but once that decision is made, you do not need to report the actual skewness statistic.

TABLE 5.12

Example of a Skewed Distribution

Frequency Table		Histogram	Skewness Statistic and Standard Error of the Skew
Age	**f**	Frequency of Age in the Sample (N = 100)	$G_1 = 2.30$
18	6		$SES = 0.24$
19	9		
20	8		
21	11		
22	16		
23	15		
24	9		
25	8		
26	4		
27	7		
28	1		
29 to 31	0		
32	2		
33	2		
34	1		
35 to 44	0		
45	1		

The median age in the sample was 22. Participants ranged in age from 18 to 45, although the data were skewed with more than half the participants (65%) between the ages of 18 to 23.

Or

Participants were between 18 to 45 years old, with a median age of 22. Age was positively skewed because only a few participants ($n = 5$) were over 30.

In summary, not all descriptive statistics are appropriate or useful for all variables. The scale used to measure the variable is one of the first considerations when deciding what descriptive statistics to report. In Table 5.13 you will find information about how to choose the appropriate descriptive statistics.

TABLE 5.13

Choosing the Appropriate Descriptive Statistics Based on the Measurement Scale

Measurement Scale	Appropriate Statistics to . . .		
	Describe How Often a Score Appears in the Sample:	**Describe the Central Tendency:**	**Describe the Variability:**
Nominal	Frequencies and/or percentages	Mode	—
Ordinal	Frequencies and/or percentages	Median	Observed minimum/ maximum or range
Interval or Ratio (Normally Distributed)	Percentages for each score on an interval scale	Mean	Standard deviation
			Possible minimum/ maximum for interval data Observed minimum/ maximum for interval and ratio data
Interval or Ratio (Skewed)	Cumulative percentage	Median	Observed minimum/ maximum or range

Note: Statistics shaded are those that should be reported. Statistics in gray may be useful in certain circumstances.

USING DATA ANALYSIS PROGRAMS: DESCRIPTIVE STATISTICS

We believe it is a useful exercise to try calculating some statistics without the aid of data analysis software so that you have a better understanding and appreciation for how the statistics are generated. However, hand calculations are very time-consuming, are much more prone to error and, frankly, we do not know of any researcher who does not use some sort of statistical software to analyze data. We provide some basic guidelines that can link with a more in-depth manual about your chosen data analysis program. We also provide some specific guidelines for and examples from SPSS.

Calculating Frequencies With a Data Analysis Program

- You should calculate frequencies for all your nominal variables, but it is also a good idea to calculate frequencies for all your variables as a double check of your data entry. A quick scan of the frequency tables can alert you to any scores that are out of the possible range (for example, if you coded males as 1 and females as 2, any score that is not a 1 or 2 is likely due to a data entry error).

- In SPSS, the frequency table will also automatically provide you with the percentages.

- In SPSS, the frequency table will provide you with the cumulative percentages starting from the observed minimum score. Remember that the cumulative percentage is not relevant for nominal data because scores are not ordered by magnitude.

Calculating Central Tendency and Variability With a Data Analysis Program

- It is not necessary to run additional analyses for nominal variables. The mode can be easily discerned by examining the frequency table.

- If you have measurement scales that are composed of several individual variables, be sure to first recode any variables if necessary, check the reliability of the scale, and compute the scale score (see Chapter 3 for more details). Generally speaking, run descriptive statistics only for the full scale, not for all the variables that make up the scale.

- When calculating descriptive statistics for interval and ratio data in SPSS, we recommend you use the frequency command and then select the descriptive statistics you want. For some reason, you cannot calculate the median using the descriptive command in SPSS, and you may need to report that for skewed interval or ratio data.

- In SPSS, the frequency command also provides the option for graphs. We recommend you run a histogram for your interval or ratio scales and single-item variables. This will give you a quick snapshot of your distribution that will help you determine if the distribution is normal or not. You can also request a normal curve with the histogram so that the shape of the distribution is more clearly depicted.

- In SPSS and other statistical software packages, you can run multiple analyses at the same time. We recommend that you calculate all the possible statistics you think you might need. For interval or ratio data, that includes the mean, median, standard deviation, observed minimum and maximum, range, skewness, and histogram. When you write up the results, you will choose the appropriate statistics to report based on the skewness statistic and histogram (see Figure 5.6).

- Data analysis programs can provide you with only the observed minimum and maximum scores, not the possible minimum and maximum. You need to look back at the measure itself in order to identify the possible range of scores.

- In most statistical software packages, you can analyze multiple variables and scales at the same time, but the output may look overwhelming if you are a beginner. As you get more comfortable reading and interpreting output, analyzing multiple variables and scales can save you time.

FIGURE 5.6

Example SPSS Output

Frequencies

Statistics

Importance of New phone

N	Valid	15
	Missing	0
Mean		5.4667
Median		6.0000
Std. Deviation		1.45733
Skewness		−.963
Std. Error of Skewness		.580
Range		5.00
Minimum		2.00
Maximum		7.00

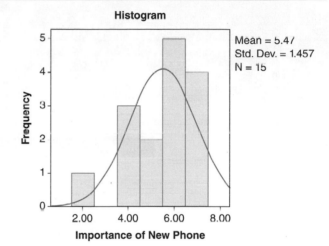

Importance of New Phone

		Frequency	Percent	Valid Percent	Cumulative Percent
Valid	2.00	1	6.7	6.7	6.7
	4.00	3	20.0	20.0	26.7
	5.00	2	13.3	13.3	40.0
	6.00	5	33.3	33.3	73.3
	7.00	4	26.7	26.7	100.0
	Total	15	100.0	100.0	

Note: Notice that more statistics were calculated than will be reported. First, look at the histogram to determine the shape of the curve. Also use the skewness statistic (and compare it to its SES if appropriate) to determine if the distribution is skewed. Then use this information to decide what descriptive statistics to report.

- If the distribution meets the criteria for a normal curve (which it does in this case) or if the distribution is uniform, at minimum you must report the mean and standard deviation. Do not report the median or mode.
- If it is bimodal, either report both modes or split the distribution in two and report the mean and standard deviation of each subsample.
- If it is skewed, report the median and the observed minimum and maximum or the range. *Do not* report the mean and standard deviation or the mode..

Reporting Results in a Research Report

- You do *not* need to, nor should you, report the results of every analysis you ran. Instead, choose the information that is most relevant and paints the clearest picture for your readers.

- You should *not* cut and paste the tables from an output file into your paper. Instead, choose the information you want to present in a table and create the table with a word processing program.

Practice 5.5

IDENTIFYING THE TYPE OF DISTRIBUTION AND CHOOSING THE APPROPRIATE DESCRIPTIVE STATISTICS

1. Consider the data for glasses of water drank per day and answer the questions that follow.

Glasses of Water	f
0	1
1	2
2	0
3	4
4	2
5	2
6	1
7	1
8	1
9	0
10	0
11	0
12	1

a. Graph a histogram and frequency polygon of these data. Remember to label your axes and title the graphs.

b. Calculate a skewness statistic and the standard error of the skewness (either by hand or with a data analysis software program). What do the graphs and skewness statistic tell you about the distribution?

c. What are the best measures of central tendency and variability?

2. Consider the SPSS output about glasses of juice drank per week and answer the questions that follow.

Statistics

juice

N	Valid	48
	Missing	0
Mean		6.6875
Median		7.0000
Std. Deviation		4.68204
Skewness		4.782
Std. Error of Skewness		.343
Range		34.00
Minimum		1.00
Maximum		35.00

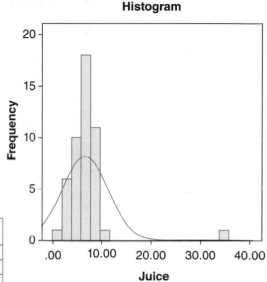

Histogram

juice

	Frequency	Percent	Valid Percent	Cumulative Percent
Valid 1.00	1	2.1	2.1	2.1
2.00	2	4.2	4.2	6.3
3.00	4	8.3	8.3	14.6
4.00	4	8.3	8.3	22.9
5.00	6	12.5	12.5	35.4
6.00	6	12.5	12.5	47.9
7.00	12	25.0	25.0	72.9
8.00	6	12.5	12.5	85.4
9.00	5	10.4	10.4	95.8
10.00	1	2.1	2.1	97.9
35.00	1	2.1	2.1	100.0
Total	48	100.0	100.0	

a. What are the best measures of central tendency and variability? Explain why.

b. Write up the results.

See Appendix A to check your answers.

COMPARING INTERVAL/RATIO SCORES WITH z SCORES AND PERCENTILES

Sometimes we want to know where a score falls within a distribution and not just the central tendency and variability of the entire distribution. One simple way to do this is to see if the score falls above or below the mean. However, that does not provide very much information about how the score compares to the distribution. For example, although you might know that you made above the mean on a Research Methods test, you may want to know exactly where your score places you in terms of the other students taking the test—are you at the 55th percentile or the 85th percentile? Or you may want to know if a psychology major who sent and received 25 text messages yesterday was very unusual (10th percentile) or just somewhat less involved in texting (40th percentile) than the other majors.

If we have the mean and standard deviation of a normal distribution of interval or ratio scores, we can determine how many standard deviations a score falls above or below the mean. Remember that almost all the scores in a normal distribution fall within plus or minus 3 standard deviations from the mean. If we know how many standard deviations a score is from the mean, we know whether it is likely to fall in the extreme top or bottom of the distribution because we have learned that about the middle 68% of the distribution is found between plus or minus 1 standard deviation and about 95% of the distribution is found within plus or minus 2 standard deviations.

z Scores

We may want to know even more specifics about a score's relative position in a distribution. We can find the exact percentile of any score in a normal distribution because statisticians have calculated the percentage of a normal distribution falling between the mean and any score expressed in terms of standard deviations from the mean. Scores that are expressed in terms of standard deviations from the mean are called *z* **scores**.

z **score:** A standardized score based on the standard deviation of the distribution.

To calculate a z score to compare a single score to the sample:

$$z = \frac{X - M}{SD}$$

where *X* equals score; *M* equals mean; *SD* equals standard deviation.

A z score is thus the deviation from the mean divided by the standard deviation. It may be easier to think of a z score as a score expressed in standard deviations from the mean units. If the score we are converting to a z score is above the mean, our z score will be positive. If the score is below the mean, the z score will be negative. So we quickly know from a z score whether the corresponding raw score is above or below the mean of the distribution.

Even if we were given only z scores and did not know the mean and standard deviation of a distribution, a z score immediately tells us if a person scored above or below the mean and how many standard deviations above or below the mean. Thus, both the sign (positive or negative) and the value of the z score are important and help us to better interpret the meaning of a score. With a normal distribution, one can also easily translate z scores to percentiles (see Figure 5.7).

FIGURE 5.7

Normal Distribution With z Scores and Percentiles

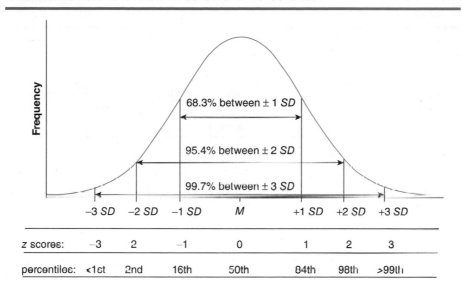

Percentiles

A **percentile** is another way to evaluate a score. A percentile tells you what percentage of a distribution scored below a specific score. The 50th percentile is average. If you scored at the 95th percentile on an exam, that means that you scored better than 95% of the other students who took the exam.

> **Percentile:** The percentage of the distribution that scored below a specific score.

Once we have calculated a z score, we can calculate the percentile. First, we find the percentage of the distribution between our z score and the mean by using the table in Appendix C.3. This table shows the percentage of scores in a normal distribution that lie between the mean and any z score, and an excerpt is shown in Table 5.14.

If the z score is positive, you know the raw score is above the mean and you *add* .50 to the percentage you get from Appendix C.3. We *add* our obtained percentage to .50 because we know that 50% of the distribution falls below the mean, and the table has given us the percentage of the distribution that falls between the mean and our z score (which represents a particular raw score from the distribution).

Example *z* Score and Percentile Calculation

Let's look at a specific example to help you to better understand the calculation of z scores and percentiles. Consider our survey on how important it is to have the newest

TABLE 5.14

Excerpt of Table in Appendix C.3 for the Percentage of Area Under the Curve Between the Mean and a *z* Score

The highlighted number below indicates the percentage from the mean for a *z* score of ±1.05.							
z score to one decimal place	**z score carried to two decimal places**						
	0	**0.01**	**0.02**	**0.03**	**0.04**	**0.05**	**0.06**
0	0	0.0040	0.0080	0.0120	0.0160	0.1099	0.0239
0.1	0.0398	0.0438	0.0478	0.0517	0.0557	0.0596	0.0636
0.2	0.0793	0.0832	0.0871	0.0910	0.0948	0.0987	0.1026
0.3	0.1179	0.1217	0.1255	0.1293	0.1331	0.1368	0.1406
0.4	0.1554	0.1591	0.1620	0.1664	0.1700	0.1736	0.1772
0.5	0.1915	0.195	0.1985	0.2019	0.2054	0.2088	0.2123
0.6	0.2257	0.2291	0.2324	0.2357	0.2389	0.2422	0.2454
0.7	0.258	0.2611	0.2642	0.2673	0.2704	0.2734	0.2764
0.8	0.2881	0.291	0.2939	0.2967	0.2994	0.3023	0.3051
0.9	0.3159	0.3186	0.3212	0.3238	0.3264	0.3289	0.3315
1	0.3413	0.3438	0.3461	0.3485	0.3508	0.3531	0.3554
1.1	0.3643	0.3665	0.3686	0.3708	0.3720	0.3740	0.3776

Source: NIST/SEMATECH e-Handbook of Statistical Methods, http://www.itl.nist.gov/div898/handbook/

cell phone model. We found that the mean for this sample is a rating of 5.47 and the standard deviation is 1.46. Now suppose that we have a participant who we will call "Student A" (because remember if we were reporting these data we would not want to reveal any identifying information). Student A provided a rating of 7. Where does Student A fall in the distribution? First, we would calculate the *z* score using the formula:

$$z = \frac{X - M}{SD} = \frac{7 - 5.47}{1.46} = 1.05$$

Student A's *z* score ($z = 1.05$) tells us not only that her rating is higher than the mean score, but also that her score is 1.05 standard deviations more than the mean. Using Appendix C.3, we find that .3531 (or 35.31%) of the scores lie between the mean and our *z* score of 1.05 (see the highlighted area of Table 5.14, which shows the percentage for $z = +/-1.05$).

To translate the score into a percentile, we *add* .50 (or 50%). We do this because our *z* score was positive (and thus is above the mean) and we know that 50% of the scores in a normal distribution fall below the mean. When we add .50 to the percentage (.3531) between the mean and our z score, we get .8531 or 85.31%. This means that Student A's rating was higher than 85.31% of the rest of the sample.

Practice 5.6

CALCULATING A *z* SCORE AND PERCENTILE

What is the *z* score and percentile for a person who rated importance of having the newest cell phone model as a 4?

See Appendix A to check your answer.

Using Data Analysis Programs for *z* Scores and Percentiles

Data analysis programs allow you to quickly calculate z scores and percentiles for every interval rating or ratio score in your sample. In SPSS, you calculate z scores by using the descriptive command, and you calculate percentiles with the compute command. These commands will create new variables in your dataset, as illustrated in Figure 5.8.

FIGURE 5.8

Example Dataset With *z* Score and Percentile Conversions

Importance	ZImportance	PercentileImp
2.00	-2.37878	.87
4.00	-1.00641	15.71
4.00	-1.00641	15.71
4.00	-1.00641	15.71
5.00	-.32022	37.44
5.00	-.32022	37.44
6.00	.36597	64.28
6.00	.36597	64.28
6.00	.36597	64.28
6.00	.36597	64.28
6.00	.36597	64.28
7.00	1.05215	85.36
7.00	1.05215	85.36
7.00	1.05215	85.36
7.00	1.05215	85.36

Note: The first column is the original score. The second column is the score converted to a *z* score. The third column is the score converted to a percentile.

Application 5.1

EXAMPLE FROM THE RESEARCH LITERATURE

Do you recall the Harackiewicz et al. (2014) article that we had you find and evaluate in Chapter 2? The researchers conducted an experiment to determine if a values affirmation intervention improved academic achievement in an introductory biology course. Although the main goal was to examine a causal relationship, describing the sample is an important component of the study.

- The authors present descriptive statistics to describe the participants. Notice in the following excerpt that no identifying information is provided for individual participants. Instead, the sample is described as an aggregate with frequencies used for gender and identification of first- or continuing-generation student.

  "The final sample comprised 320 men and 478 women, with 644 continuing-generation and 154 first-generation students" (p. 378).

- The authors used percentages to describe what proportion of the students continued onto the next level biology course. In the following excerpt, the authors compare first generation (FG) to continuing generation (CG) in the control and values affirmation (VA) conditions.

  "[I]n the control condition, CG students were more likely to enroll in the second course (77.7%) than FG students (66.2%), but in the VA condition, FG students (85.7%) were more likely to enroll than CG students (74.8%). . ." (p. 380).

- The authors describe other key outcome variables, such as course grade, using means with standard deviations. The table below is an abbreviated version of a table that appears on p. 381 of Harackiewicz et al.'s article. The mean is the first number in each column, followed by the standard deviation in parentheses.

	Continuing-generation		First-generation	
	Control	VA	Control	VA
Course Grade	2.86 (0.69)	2.82 (0.69)	2.38 (0.85)	2.62 (0.78)

THE BIG PICTURE:
KNOW YOUR DATA AND YOUR SAMPLE

For whatever reason, numbers seem to give us a sense of certainty, and this is compounded when you spend a good chunk of time calculating the numbers by hand or with a data analysis program. Once students start coding data and calculating statistics, it is common for them to lose sense of what these numbers actually mean and what they can tell you about your sample. On more than one occasion, we have had a student correctly report results from the SPSS output that made absolutely no sense whatsoever, such as "age ranged from 2 to 32." If prompted, the student would know that there were no 2-year-olds in the sample, but the student had forgotten to think about the data and instead diligently reported numbers that the computer program had spit out.

The saying "garbage in, garbage out" is an important one to remember. You can enter any numbers into a formula or data analysis program and you will get some results. If you do not have quality data, however, those results will be garbage. It is therefore important that you spend time carefully designing your study and deciding on the constructs you will study, choosing reliable and valid instruments to measure those constructs, and then identifying the most appropriate statistics to describe the sample. Even a well-planned study, however, may result in poor data due to participant or coder error or carelessness.

Also keep in mind that descriptive statistics alone will not tell you how well the scores generalize to the population. Recall from Chapter 4 that the ability of your sample to represent the population depends on the type of sampling you used. If your primary goal in describing your sample is to make generalizations to the larger population, you should follow the procedures for probability sampling. Probability sampling increases the representativeness of the sample, but it does not guarantee it. In the next chapter, we will introduce inferential statistics that will help you test how well a sample represents a population or infer conclusions about the relationships among your variables.

CHAPTER RESOURCES

Key Terms

Define the following terms using your own words. You can check your answers by reviewing the chapter or by comparing them with the definitions in the glossary—but try to define them on your own first.

Bar graph 148

Bimodal distribution 155

Central tendency 137

Coding 133

Cumulative percentage 136

Descriptive statistics 133

Frequency *(f)* 135

Frequency polygon 153

Histogram 152

Kurtosis 154

Leptokurtic curve 154

Mean *(M)* 139

Median *(Mdn)* 138

Mesokurtic curve 154

Mode 137

Negative skew 155

Normal distribution 151

Numerical coding 133

Observed minimum and maximum scores 142

Outliers 157

Percentage 136

Percentile 169

Platykurtic curve 154

Positive skew 155

Possible minimum and maximum scores 142

Range 142

Skewed distribution 155

Skewness statistic (G_1) 158

Standard deviation *(SD)* 143

Uniform distribution 155

Variability 142

Variance *(SD²)* 145

z score 168

Do You Understand the Chapter?

Answer these questions on your own and then review the chapter to check your answers.

1. What are the ethical issues involved in describing a sample? What are some ways that you can address these ethical issues?

2. What are the descriptive statistics that describe how often a score appears in a sample?

3. What are the descriptive statistics that describe the central tendency of the sample? When should you use each type of central tendency?

4. What are the descriptive statistics that describe the variability in the sample? When should you use each type of variability?

5. Compare and contrast bar graphs, histograms, and frequency polygons. When would you use each one?

6. What are the characteristics of a normal distribution? What are the best measures of central tendency and variability for normally distributed interval or ratio data?

7. Describe a uniform distribution, bimodal distribution, and skewed distribution. What are the best measures of central tendency and variability for each of these distributions?

8. What is a z score and percentile? Why are these scores useful?

9. What is the difference between a percentage and a percentile?

Practice Dataset and Analyses

1. Use the texting data from the end of Chapter 3 in which you entered data, recoded items from the texting questionnaire, and checked the reliability of the five items using a data analysis program such as SPSS.

2. Compute a total score for attitudes about texting with a romantic partner that has a Cronbach's alpha of at least .70 (see Chapter 3 for a review).

3. Using a data analysis program, calculate descriptive statistics to describe gender.

4. Using a data analysis program, calculate descriptive statistics to describe age and the total score you computed from question 2.

5. Write up your results, reporting only the correct descriptive statistics given the type of measurement scale and the type of distribution of each item or scale.

 **SAGE edge™**   edge.sagepub.com/adams2e

Sharpen your skills with SAGE edge!
SAGE edge for students provides you with tools to help you study. You'll find mobile-friendly eFlashcards and quizzes, as well as videos, web resources, datasets, and links to SAGE journal articles related to this chapter.

Beyond Descriptives

MAKING INFERENCES BASED ON YOUR SAMPLE

When Pokémon GO was released in the summer of 2016, it was immediately a hit, and millions downloaded the game within the first month. Using the camera and GPS on a smart device, players can see Pokémon on their screen as if the creature is in their real location. Many players became totally immersed in the game, and soon there were reports of players running into others, into traffic, or into inappropriate areas in their attempt to capture or battle the Pokémon. Players seemed to pay little attention to their surroundings or indeed to their own safety or the safety of those around them. You and a friend discuss this phenomenon and disagree about whether such behavior while using a digital device is unusual. Your friend believes the reported distraction due to a digital device is a short-lived phenomenon related to the availability of a new game and involving only a few people, while you argue that people are frequently distracted by their devices, sometimes with negative consequences. This issue has implications for more than leisure time. You could also consider classrooms and work locations and whether smart devices distract students or employees from their work. Because you are thinking like a researcher, you decide to examine the question scientifically.

After obtaining permission from school, you and your friend sit at an exit from a large classroom building at school and ask people leaving the building to complete a brief survey if they have just finished taking a class. The survey asks how many times during the just completed class did students use their cell phone, tablet, or computer for a nonclass purpose. You collect data from 10 a.m. to 3 p.m. on a Tuesday.

You find that the mean number of times a digital device was used for a nonclass purpose for your sample is 10.20 ($SD = 2.75$). These statistics tell you about the device use unrelated to a class purpose of your sample of students—the people who took a class on a particular day in a particular building within a particular time. In terms of the discussion between

LEARNING OUTCOMES

In this chapter, you will learn

- About the use of inferential statistics to determine whether the finding of a study is unusual
- The importance of the sampling distribution
- How to carry out the hypothesis testing process
- When to reject or retain a null hypothesis and the types of errors associated with each of these decisions
- The distinction between statistical significance, effect size, confidence intervals, and practical significance

you and your friend, however, you want to know about the non-class use of devices of a larger group (or population) than just those you are able to survey. In this case, you might consider the population from which your sample was drawn as all people who take classes on your campus.

Recall from Chapter 4 that in order to be totally confident that you know about the non-class use of digital devices by all students who take classes on your campus, you would need to survey all of them. Imagine the difficulties of trying to survey the large number of students who are enrolled in classes on a campus at different times and days and at various locations. Even if you restrict your population to those who take classes on Tuesdays in the building you selected, there may be some students who leave the building by a different exit, or who come to the building earlier or later than the survey period, or who for some reason do not attend class the day you collect data. For multiple reasons, it is very unusual for a researcher to be able to collect data from every member of a population.

You might also recall from Chapter 4 that instead of finding every member of the population, researchers take a sample that is meant to be representative of the population. Probability (or random) sampling can improve the representativeness of the sample; but it is work-intensive, and even with probability sampling, there is no 100% guarantee of the representativeness of the sample. And how would you know if your sample is in fact representative of the population?

As an alternative method to learn about your population, you consider obtaining multiple samples of students at your campus in order to make sure that you have information from students who take classes at different buildings or at different times or days. By gathering different samples of students at your school, you would then be able to compare whether your first sample was representative of non-class device use among your other samples of students. It would take a lot of effort and time to gather multiple samples, and you still would not have data from the entire population of students at your campus.

As a new researcher, you might now find yourself frustrated with your options. But what if you had a statistical technique that you could use to test how well your sample represents the campus population? You could also use this statistical technique to examine how your sample's digital device habits compare with the research you read, or to consider if a student's age or gender is an important factor in their digital device habits.

INFERENTIAL STATISTICS

In research we often want to go beyond simply describing our sample using measures of central tendency and variability. Instead, we want to make inferences about the qualities or characteristics of the population that our sample represents. The statistics we use in this process are called **inferential statistics**. When we use inferential statistics, we draw conclusions about a population based on the findings from a single study with a

Inferential statistics: Statistical analysis of data gathered from a sample to draw conclusions about a population from which the sample is drawn.

sample from the population. We do not have to repeatedly conduct the same study with different samples in order to learn about the same population. Of course, replication is not a bad idea, but we want to build information about populations. Inferential statistics allow us to accomplish this goal more quickly than conducting the identical study multiple times with samples from the same population.

Inferential Versus Descriptive Statistics

Inferential	Descriptive
population	sample
parameter	statistic
mu (μ)	mean (M)
sigma (σ)	standard deviation (SD)

brown dogstudios

REVIEW OF KEY CONCEPTS: POPULATION AND SAMPLE

- The population is the group of people, animals, or archives that the researcher has identified as the focus of the study.

- The sample is a subset of the population meant to represent the full population.

- The mean (M) is the average score in the sample and the standard deviation (SD) summarizes how much the scores in the sample distribution vary from the mean.

Do you recall what type of distribution is required in order for the mean and standard deviation to accurately describe the sample?

If you said a "normal distribution," in which the majority of scores cluster around the middle and then taper off toward the ends, then you are correct! If not, take a minute to review the characteristics of a normal distribution described in Chapter 5. The normal distribution is important for inferential statistics. Just as the mean and standard deviation of a sample are used to describe data that meet the criteria for normality, their counterparts in the population (mu and sigma) imply a normally distributed population.

In inferential statistics, we are interested in variables or factors in populations rather than solely in the information we have gathered from the sample we have in our study. The descriptive statistics you are familiar with (means, standard deviations, etc.) are called **parameters** when they are calculated from a population. The mean of a variable for a population is called **mu (μ)**, and the standard deviation is called **sigma (σ)**. We do

Parameters: Statistics from a population.

Mu (μ): Population mean.

Sigma (σ): Population standard deviation.

not often have these exact values (mu or sigma) as we rarely have scores for an entire population. Generally, our population is theoretical and considered to be represented by our sample. Thus, inferential statistics use descriptive statistics from our sample to make assumptions about a particular population from which our sample is drawn. When we use inferential statistics, we ask the question: *Is our sample representative of our population?* In other words, does our sample seem to belong to the population, or is it different enough that it likely represents a totally different population?

So the previous paragraphs do not sound like gobbledygook, let's look at a specific example:

When given the opportunity to do so anonymously, do students at University Anxious (UA) report plagiarism more or less than the national statistics for this measure? This question involves both a sample (students at UA) and a population (national statistics for reports of plagiarism by college students). Suppose the national average for reporting plagiarism is 1%, while the UA students' reporting average is 3%. Would you believe that UA students report plagiarism more frequently than the national average? What if the UA reporting average is 10%? 15%? At what point do you consider the UA average to be different enough from the national average to pay attention to or to believe that the UA students are somehow different from the national population of college students?

What we are asking is, when does a difference in scores make a difference? In other words, when is a difference significant?

Probability Theory

Inferential statistics are based on probability theory, which examines random events such as the roll of dice or toss of a coin. When random events are repeated, they then establish a pattern. For example, we could toss a coin multiple times to see the number of heads and tails that result. We would expect to get heads approximately 50% of the time and tails approximately 50% of the time, especially if we toss the coin a large number of times. In probability theory, each individual random event (in our example, the outcome of one coin toss) is assumed to be independent, which means that the outcome of each coin toss is not affected by the outcome of previous tosses. Another way to say this is that each time we toss a coin, the outcome of our toss is not affected by whether we got a head or a tail on the last or earlier coin tosses. The pattern that results from repeating a set of random events a large number of times is used in statistics to determine whether a particular set or sample of random events (e.g., 8 heads in 10 coin tosses) is typical or unusual.

> "There is a very easy way to return from a casino with a small fortune: Go there with a large one."
>
> —Jack Yelton

Going back to our students at UA and their reporting rate for plagiarism, we use inferential statistics (based on probability theory) to answer the question: *Is there a significant difference between the scores at UA and the national average?* We want to know if an event (the average percentage of UA students reporting plagiarism) is common or is unusual relative to the population (the national average in reporting plagiarism).

We use the results from inferential statistics to make judgments about the meaning of our study. As the quote above about gambling implies, it is important to understand the probability of events occurring—many people who gamble assume that "hitting the jackpot" is a common outcome of gambling, while in reality winning large sums of money is a very rare occurrence. Of course, the success of casinos and lottery systems depends on people believing that they will be that one lucky person in a million or even one in 10 million.

In research, we pay attention to the likelihood of scores or findings occurring, and we use probability theory to help us determine whether a finding is unusual. An easy way to understand how probability theory aids our decision making is to think about the coin toss. If we flip a coin 100 times and we get 45 heads and 55 tails, we usually do not take note of the event. If, however, we flip the coin 100 times and get 10 heads and 90 tails, we begin to wonder if our coin is weighted or different in some way. We expect to get close to the same number of heads and tails (in this case, 50 heads and 50 tails out of 100 tosses) and assume that results that differ a great deal from this expectation may indicate something unusual about the coin. But how different from our expectation do our results need to be for us to believe that there is something unusual about the coin? We may begin to be suspicious if we get 20 heads and 80 tails, but that result could occur even with a "regular" coin.

Probability theory allows us to determine how likely it is that our coin toss results would have occurred in our particular circumstances. In other words, what is the probability that we would get 45 heads and 55 tails if we tossed a coin 100 times? The probability of our results is based on a theoretical distribution where a task (flipping the coin 100 times) is repeated an infinite number of times and the distribution shows how frequently any combination (of heads and tails) occurs in a certain number of repetitions (100 flips of a coin). We find out that we are likely to get 45 or fewer heads 18.4% of the time when a coin is tossed 100 times. (Of course, the same coin would need to be tossed in the same way each time in order for our results to be reliable.)

But if we tossed our coin and got 10 heads and 90 tails, we would learn that we are likely to get 10 or fewer heads only .0000000001% of the time. We then are suspicious that our coin is not typical. We cannot say whether our coin was deliberately weighted or was malformed when it was minted, only that it has a very low probability of being a normal coin. We have to recognize that although 10 heads and 90 tails is a highly unusual result from 100 coin tosses, it is possible to get this result on very, very rare occasions with a normal coin. Thus, while we may decide that our results (10 heads/90 tails) are too unusual for our coin to be normal, we also have to recognize that we may be mistaken and may have obtained very rare results with a normal coin.

All this is to say that researchers make decisions based on the probability of a finding occurring within certain circumstances. So how rare or unusual does a finding have to be in order for us to believe that the finding is significantly different from the comparison distribution (in this case, a distribution produced by tossing a coin 100 times, for an infinite number of times)? In statistics, we have adopted a standard such that we are willing to say that our result does not belong to a distribution, if we find that our result would be likely to occur less than 5% of the time. So if we get a combination of heads and tails that would occur less than 5% of the time with a normal coin, we are willing to say that our coin is significantly different from a normal coin. Our research questions are much more complex than a coin toss, but they are based on examining when a difference is significant. In statistics, we call this process of decision making **hypothesis testing**.

Sampling Distribution Versus Frequency Distribution

In order to decide whether an outcome is unusual, we compare it to a theoretical **sampling distribution**. In Chapter 5, we used the term *frequency of scores* to describe distributions composed of individual scores. In contrast, a sampling distribution is composed of a large number of a specific statistic, such as a mean (*M*), gathered from samples similar to the one in our study.

> **Hypothesis testing:** The process of determining the probability of obtaining a particular result or set of results.
>
> **Sampling distribution:** A distribution of some statistic obtained from multiple samples of the same size drawn from the same population (e.g., a distribution of means from many samples of 30 students).

Let's go back to our previous example where we flipped a coin 100 times and recorded the number of heads and tails. The sampling distribution we compare our results to is composed of scores (# of heads and # of tails) from tossing a coin 100 times and then repeating this exercise an infinite number of times. Each "score" on the distribution represents the findings from tossing a coin 100 times. The coin is tossed many hundreds of times, and a distribution is then built from all these results. Thus, we have a large number of scores from samples of 100 tosses, which give the distribution the name sampling distribution. Of course, no one actually tosses a coin thousands of times—statisticians build the distribution based on probability.

So far, we have been talking about comparing a sample to a population. Many times, however, researchers are interested in comparing two populations. For example, we might want to know if students who major in business text more than students who major in psychology. In this case, our sampling distribution would be created in a multistep process. First, we would ask a sample of business students and a sample of psychology students how frequently they text (say, in a 24-hour period). We would then calculate the mean texting frequency for each sample and subtract one mean from another. We would repeat this process a large number of times and create a distribution of mean differences, which would serve as our sampling distribution. If the difference in texting frequency between the population of psychology students and the population of business students is 5, then we would expect that most of the mean differences we found for our two samples would be close to 5. As we moved farther above

Application 6.1

EXAMPLE OF HYPOTHESIS TESTING

Kuznekoff and Titsworth (2013) investigated the effect of non-class-related cell phone use on student learning. Participants took notes while listening to a brief lecture on communication theories, then had three minutes to review their notes before taking a free recall test, followed by a multiple-choice test. Groups of students were randomly assigned to one of three conditions: (1) a control group that listened to the lecture and took notes as they typically did in class; (2) a low-distraction group that texted or posted to social network sites once each minute while listening to the lecture; or (3) a high-distraction group that texted or posted to social network sites once every 30 seconds while listening to the lecture. Note-taking quality was scored by two coders who evaluated the level of detail at was included in students' notes. Learning was operationalized as the scores on each of the two tests.

We will consider the results for only two of the groups here. As predicted, students who texted/posted every 30 seconds (high-distraction) included significantly less detail in their notes ($M = 15.50$, $SD = 7.06$) than students in the control group ($M = 25.05$, $SD = 11.97$). The high-distraction group also scored significantly lower on the multiple-choice ($M = 8.43$, $SD = 2.24$) and free recall ($M = 6.21$, $SD = 5.06$) tests than did the students in the control group (multiple-choice $M - 10.58$, $SD = 2.43$; free recall $M = 12.84$, $SD = 8.65$).

Why can we say that the means for note-taking detail and test scores are significantly different for the control and high-distraction groups as a function of frequent of texting/posting during a lecture? How can we determine that the differences are not just random or due to chance?

Hypothesis testing is a process that includes the use of inferential statistics and allows us to determine when the differences in note detail and test scores are not likely to be due to chance alone.

or below 5 (as the mean difference), we would expect fewer of our pairs of samples to show these differences.

To sum up this section: *Inferential statistics allow us to determine whether the outcome of our study is typical or unusual in comparison to our sampling distribution.*

HYPOTHESIS TESTING

Now that you understand a bit about probability theory and sampling distributions, we will incorporate this knowledge into the process we use to examine research findings. This process is called hypothesis testing and uses statistics to analyze the data. As a researcher, you should always plan your statistical analysis *before* you conduct your study. If you do not consider how to analyze your data as you design your study, you might collect data that cannot be analyzed or that will not adequately test your hypothesis.

Null and Alternative Hypotheses

After identifying your variable(s) for your study, you should state what you expect to find or your prediction for your study, which is called the **alternative hypothesis (H_a)**. In experimental research this prediction is called the **experimental hypothesis (H_a)** and is always stated in terms of predicting differences between groups. Alternative and experimental hypotheses are both predictions, but they are not the same. All experimental hypotheses are also alternative hypotheses, but many alternative hypotheses are not experimental.

In the simplest case for a study, we compare our sample to some population value. Your alternative hypothesis will predict a difference between your sample and the population on the variable that you measure. For example, we may hypothesize that psychology majors are more likely to text than college students in general. In this case, we would compare the mean texting frequency for a sample of psychology majors and the mean texting frequency for the population of college students.

We contrast the experimental hypothesis with the **null hypothesis (H_0)**, which is stated in terms of no difference or no relationship. The null hypothesis is important to state because that's actually what we test in a study. It sets up the sampling distribution to which we will compare our results. In terms of the example above, the null hypothesis would predict that you would find no difference in texting frequency between your sample of psychology majors and the texting frequency of the population of college students.

A study should *always* be designed to find a difference between treatments, groups, and so on, and thus to reject the null hypothesis. Many novice researchers (usually students just learning about research) will mistakenly design a study to support their null hypothesis, which means that they will try to show that there is no difference between their sample and the population. Such studies will not further our knowledge, because we do not learn anything new about the variable(s) of interest.

> **Alternative hypothesis (H_a):** A prediction of what the researcher expects to find in a study.
>
> **Experimental hypothesis (H_a):** An alternative hypothesis for an experiment stated in terms of differences between groups.
>
> **Null hypothesis (H_0):** A prediction of no difference between groups or no relationship; the hypothesis the researcher expects to reject.

Rejecting the Null Hypothesis

After designing a study and collecting data, we need to make a decision about whether we can reject our null hypothesis, H_0, and support our alternative hypothesis, H_a. In order to decide, we select a statistical test to compare our results (for the variable we have measured) to a theoretical sampling distribution. Remember that our sampling distribution is defined by the null hypothesis. In our study examining the texting behavior of psychology majors, our sampling distribution is created by collecting information

Practice 6.1

NULL AND ALTERNATIVE HYPOTHESES

Go back to Application 6.1 earlier in this chapter and review the study by Kuznekoff and Titsworth (2013).

1. State null and alternative hypotheses for the impact of frequent texting/posting in class on the detail in students' notes.

2. Now develop null and alternative hypotheses that might make sense to examine the impact of where students sit in the classroom on the detail in students' notes. Imagine that you divide students into two groups—those who sit in the front half of the classroom and those who sit in the back half of the class. What might you predict you would find for the two groups in terms of detail in students' notes?

See Appendix A to check your answers.

REVIEW OF KEY CONCEPTS: THE NORMAL DISTRIBUTION

1. What are the characteristics of a normal distribution?

2. What characteristics of a normal distribution allow us to make assumptions about where scores fall or statistics fall in the case of a sampling distribution?

You know your normal distribution facts if you answered bell shaped and symmetrical; the mean, median, and mode are identical; and the range is defined by the mean plus or minus 3 standard deviations. Most scores cluster around the mean, and the frequency of scores decreases as the scores are increasingly higher or lower than the mean.

The area under the curve of a normal distribution is distributed so that 50% of the distribution lies on either side of the mean; approximately 68% of the distribution lies between the mean and plus and minus 1 *SD*, 95% of the distribution lies between the mean and plus and minus 2 *SD*s, and 99% of the distribution lies between the mean and plus and minus 3 *SD*s. As we learned in Chapter 5, we can even determine the exact percentile of any score and thus where it falls in a normal distribution using *z* scores and the *z* table.

about the texting frequency of hundreds of samples of college students and computing a mean texting frequency for each sample. We then have a distribution that is composed of the hundreds of texting frequency means—remember the "scores" in a sampling distribution are always a statistic—in this case our "scores" are the means of texting frequency for each sample of college students.

The sampling distribution shows the values that would occur if our null hypothesis is true—in our example this would occur if the texting frequency of psychology students did not differ from that of all college students. Sampling distributions are normally distributed and have the same characteristics as normally distributed frequency distributions—they are symmetrical and the range is defined by the mean plus or minus 3 standard deviations (*M* +/-3 *SD*). Most scores fall around the mean—you learned in Chapter 5 that the majority of the distribution (approximately 68%) falls within plus or minus 1 standard deviation from the mean. Approximately 95% of a normal distribution is found within 2 standard deviations above and 2 standard deviations below the mean, and approximately 99% of the distribution falls between +/-3 standard deviations from the mean.

Because the normal distribution is symmetrical, the percentage of the distribution on each side of the mean is identical. For example, you know that approximately 95% of a normal distribution is found within +/-2 standard deviations from the mean. That means that 47.5% of the distribution is between the mean and the value representing 2 standard deviations above the mean, and 47.5% of the distribution is found between the mean and the value representing 2 standard deviations below the mean. In addition, we know what percentage of the distribution lies outside of +/-2 standard deviations. If 95% of the distribution is between +/-2 standard deviations, then 5% lies outside this range. Because the distribution is symmetrical, the remaining 5% is split between the top and the bottom of the distribution. So, 2.5% of the distribution falls above the value that represents the mean plus 2 standard deviations, and 2.5% of the distribution falls below the mean minus 2 standard deviations. Figure 6.1 shows a normal distribution and the percentage of the distribution that is found within the range of values represented by 1, 2, and 3 standard deviations from the mean.

In the coin toss example discussed earlier in the chapter, we tossed a coin 100 times and got 45 heads and 55 tails. We can compare these results to a sampling distribution. In the case of the coin toss, we would predict that we would have 50% heads and 50% tails,

FIGURE 6.1

Theoretical Normal Distribution With Percentage of Values From the Mean to 1, 2, and 3 Standard Deviations (Sigma)

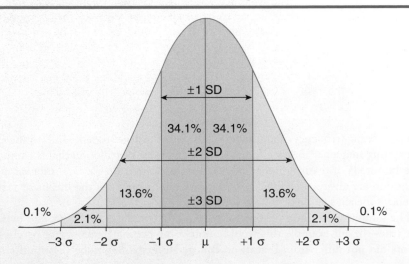

so for 100 tosses we would predict 50 heads and 50 tails. Our sampling distribution would show most instances of 100 tosses would result in close to the 50:50 split of heads and tails, and our result of 45 heads would not be unusual. As results are more and more different from the 50:50 split, however, the frequency of such results would decrease until you find that very few 100 tosses resulted in 90 heads and 10 tails and even fewer tosses resulted in 99 heads and 1 tail. This latter finding (99 heads and 1 tail) would be found in the far tail of the sampling distribution because it would occur very rarely out of 100 tosses.

Let's also consider the texting frequency example with specific values. Suppose the mean texting frequency of college students is 50 times per day and the standard deviation is 10. If we find for our sample of psychology students that their texting mean is 70 times per day, would we consider them to be typical of the population of college students? A mean of 70 would be 2 standard deviations above the mean of 50 and so would belong outside the middle 95% of the distribution. If, however, the psychology students' mean was 45, this sample mean would be .5 standard deviations below the population mean and is within the middle 68% of the distribution. We would consider the first mean (70) to be rare for the population of all college students, while the second mean (45) occurs frequently within a population distribution with a mean of 50 and standard deviation of 10.

A normal distribution (such as a sampling distribution) is a theoretical distribution, and its characteristics can be applied to any M and SD. Thus, the characteristics of the distribution remain the same whether the $M = 55$, $SD = 5$ or the $M = 150$, $SD = 25$. *Test your understanding of the information you have just learned. If the $M = 55$, what range of scores would define 68% of the distribution?* Stop reading now and see if you can figure this out.

Answer: If you added 5 to 55 and subtracted 5 from 55 to get 50–60 as the range, you are correct. You have learned that 68% of a normal distribution is defined by the mean plus and minus 1 standard deviation. In this case, 50 equals the mean minus 1 standard deviation ($55 - 5$) and 60 equals the mean plus 1 standard deviation ($55 + 5$). Now that you know this, calculate the range of scores that defines 68% of the distribution when the $M = 150$, $SD = 25$. Check with your classmates or teacher if you are unsure that you have done this correctly. Now calculate the range of scores representing the middle 95% of the distribution when $M = 55$, $SD = 5$. You should get 45–65. You multiply the SD by 2 and then add and subtract that value to the M [$55 +/- (2 \times 5)$] or $55 \pm 10 = 45$–65.

If a distribution is normal, given any M, SD combination, we can figure out the range of scores expected for that distribution and the percentage of scores lying within specific values. We can then figure out whether we believe that a value is likely to be found within that distribution. For example, if you knew that the $M = 55$, $SD = 5$ for some test and I told you I scored a 60 on the test, would you believe that my score could have come from the $M = 55$, $SD = 5$ distribution? What if I told you I scored 90? In the first example, it is quite likely that I could belong to the $M = 55$, $SD = 5$ distribution as my score of 60 is only 1 SD above the mean. However, if I scored 90, my score would be 7 SD above the mean, and it is very unlikely that I took the test that had $M = 55$, $SD = 5$. This decision-making process reflects the process we use in hypothesis testing.

The area of a sampling distribution that researchers/psychologists usually focus on is 95% of the distribution and the values lying outside this region. We refer to 95%

of the distribution as the **region of acceptance** and the 5% lying outside the region of acceptance as the **region of rejection**. Figure 6.2 provides a pictorial representation of these areas of a distribution. These regions then determine what decision we make about the null hypothesis for our study. If the result from our statistical test is in the region of acceptance, we accept or retain our null hypothesis. This suggests that our statistical finding is likely to occur in a sampling distribution defined by our null hypothesis. (If this statement seems confusing, think of the example above where I had a score of 60 on a test and compared my score to a distribution of test scores with $M = 55, SD = 5$). If our finding is in the region of rejection (in the extreme 5% of the distribution), we reject the null hypothesis. In rejecting the null hypothesis, we are implying that we think that our finding would rarely occur in the sampling distribution by chance alone; in fact, it would occur only 5% or less of the time. Think of the example above where I scored 90, which was also compared to a distribution of test scores where $M = 55, SD = 5$.

If our decision is to reject the null hypothesis, this decision implies that we have supported our alternative or experimental hypothesis. This is the goal we hope to achieve in

Region of acceptance: Area of sampling distribution generally defined by the mean $+/-2$ SD or 95% of the distribution; results falling in this region imply that our sample belongs to the sampling distribution defined by the H_0 and result in the researcher retaining the H_0.

Region of rejection: The extreme 5% (generally) of a sampling distribution; results falling in this area imply that our sample does not belong to the sampling distribution defined by the H_0 and result in the researcher rejecting the H_0 and accepting the H_a.

FIGURE 6.2

Regions of Rejection and Regions of Acceptance for a Two-Tailed Test at $p < .05$

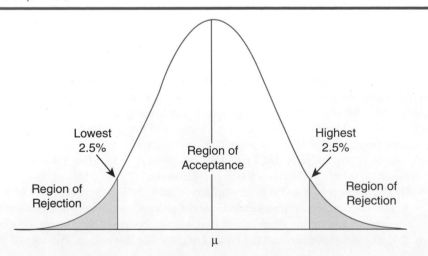

all our studies—to reject the null and to accept the alternative/experimental hypothesis. When our findings fall in the region of rejection and we reject the null hypothesis, we state that we have found **statistical significance** (or a *statistically significant difference*) between the sample and the sampling distribution that we are comparing. If we find significance, we can conclude that our sample must have come from a different distribution than the one defined by our null hypothesis.

The cartoon in Figure 6.3 should help you to see (and remember) that a difference must be in the region of rejection before it is considered statistically significant.

Testing a One- Versus a Two-Tailed Hypothesis

Let's add a few more details to the process of statistical significance testing. Don't worry—these additional details are not difficult to understand, and we will summarize everything once we have covered all the details of hypothesis testing. When we state our hypotheses, we can state them in one of two ways—as a **one-tailed** or a **two-tailed hypothesis**. Thus far, we have considered only two-tailed hypotheses. We have assumed

> **Statistical significance:** When the results of a study fall in the extreme 5% (or 1% if you use a more stringent criterion) of the sampling distribution, suggesting that the obtained findings are not due to chance alone and do not belong to the sampling distribution defined by the H_0.
>
> **Two-tailed hypothesis:** A hypothesis stating that results from a sample will differ from the population or another group but without stating how the results will differ.
>
> **One-tailed hypothesis:** A hypothesis stating the direction (higher or lower) in which a sample statistic will differ from the population or another group.

FIGURE 6.3

Difference Versus Statistical Difference

The hypothesis testing process allows us to go beyond our individual judgment of what is different and determine the probability that our results are significantly different.

Source: Sandi Coon

that we had two regions of rejection, one at the very bottom of the distribution and one at the very top of the distribution (see Figure 6.4, graph a). In a two-tailed hypothesis, we do not care whether our computed value from our study falls in the very bottom or in the very top of our sampling distribution. So our regions of rejection are in both tails of the distribution; hence, the term two-tailed hypothesis. We sometimes refer to a two-tailed hypothesis as a nondirectional hypothesis because we are predicting that our findings will fall in either the very top or very bottom of our sampling distribution.

In a normal distribution, the extreme top or bottom 2.5% of the distribution is defined by 1.96 standard deviations from the mean. This value (±1.96 in a normal distribution) is called the **critical value**, and it defines the region of rejection for a two-tailed test. Results that are more than 1.96 standard deviations above or below the mean in a normal distribution fall in the extreme upper or lower 5% of the distribution (or in the region of rejection). When this happens, we can reject our null hypothesis. Different statistical tests have different critical values to define the region of rejection. You will learn about these values in later chapters.

> **Critical value:** The value of a statistic that defines the extreme 5% of a distribution for a one-tailed hypothesis or the extreme 2.5% of the distribution for a two-tailed test.

In contrast, a one-tailed hypothesis predicts that our computed value will be found in *either* the very top or the very bottom of the sampling distribution. In a one-tailed hypothesis, there is only one region of rejection and hence the term one-tailed hypothesis.* Sometimes we call a one-tailed hypothesis a directional hypothesis because we are predicting the direction (higher *or* lower) of our findings relative to the mean of our sampling distribution.

In a normal distribution, the extreme top or bottom 5% of the distribution is defined as 1.645 standard deviations from the mean. This value (1.645) is the critical value for a one-tailed test that has only one region of rejection. If our results are more than 1.645 standard deviations from the mean, they then fall in the extreme upper or lower 5% of the distribution, and we can reject our one-tailed null hypothesis. Figure 6.4, graph b, depicts the region of rejection for a one-tailed hypothesis.

If we correctly predict the direction of our findings, it is easier to reject our null hypothesis when we use a one-tailed (or directional) hypothesis as the entire region of rejection (5% of the distribution) is in one tail of a normal distribution. If we use a two-tailed test, half of the rejection region is in each tail of the distribution and so our

---

*Kimmel (1957) argued that the use of one-tailed tests should not be based on a mere wish to use a directional hypothesis and thus have a greater chance of rejecting the null. He recommended that one-tailed tests be restricted to situations (a) where theory and previous research predict a specific direction to results and a difference in the unpredicted direction would be meaningless; (b) when a difference in the unpredicted direction would not affect actions any differently than a finding of no difference (as when a new product is tested and assumed to be an improvement over the old product; if results show the new product is significantly worse or no different than the old product, no action will be taken); or (c) if theories other than the one the researcher supports do not predict results in a direction different from the one-tailed hypothesis.

FIGURE 6.4

Regions of Rejection and Regions of Acceptance for One- and Two-Tailed Tests Using a Normal Distribution

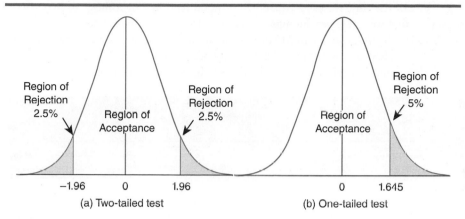

Note: Shaded areas represent regions of rejection for one-tailed and two-tailed tests at the .05 criterion level. Unshaded area under the curve is the region of acceptance for the tests. Critical values define the region of rejection (+/-1.96 for the two-tailed test and +/-1.645 for the one-tailed test).

results must be a more extreme value (in the top or bottom 2.5% of the distribution) in order to reject the null hypothesis. We can see from Figure 6.4, graphs a and b, why it is easier to reject our null hypothesis with a one-tailed than a two-tailed hypothesis. With the one-tailed hypothesis, we need only get a value higher than 1.645 to reject the null, but with a two-tailed hypothesis, we would need a value higher than 1.96 to reject the null hypothesis.

Let's consider an example to illustrate the one- and two-tailed areas of rejection. For a two-tailed area of rejection, we are interested in any scores falling outside the middle 95% of the sampling distribution. Remember that the μ +/- 2 σ defines the middle 95% of the sampling distribution. Note that we are using parameters (μ and σ) because we are considering the population rather than a sample. In terms of the example of texting that we used previously, we found a mean of 50 for the population of college students with a standard deviation of 10. This means that for a two-tailed hypothesis, 50 +/- 2 (10) defines the cutoff values for our region of rejection. Scores below 30 and above 70 fall in the region of rejection.

When we consider a one-tailed test, the region of rejection is the top *or* bottom 95% of the distribution. In this case, the region of rejection is defined by half of the distribution (50%) plus 45% of the other half of the distribution. In a normal distribution, the μ + or -1.64 σ defines the region of rejection depending on whether our region is above or below the mean. Again using μ = 50 and σ = 10, we have 50 + 1.64(10) or 50 − 1.64(10) to define the cutoff value for the region of rejection for a one-tailed test. So if we think our sample of psychology majors texts more than the population of college students, we would use 66.4 (50 + 16.4) as the score defining our region of rejection. If we predict that our sample will text less than the population of college students, we would use 33.6 (50 – 16.4) as the score defining our region of rejection. We can see that the two-tailed test must have a higher (70 vs. 66.4) or lower (30 vs. 33.6) value than the one-tailed test in order for the value to fall in the region of rejection.

Most of the time we use a two-tailed or nondirectional hypothesis in hypothesis testing so that we can reject findings that are rare for our distribution, regardless of the tail in which the findings fall. In addition, as we saw above, we have a more stringent test using a two-tailed test (reducing the probability of a Type I error). Thus, even when we have a directional hypothesis, most researchers still use a two-tailed test.

Practice 6.2

ONE-TAILED AND TWO-TAILED HYPOTHESES

1. Are the following alternative hypotheses directional or nondirectional? One- or two-tailed?

    a. H_a: Students with low verbal ability are more likely to plagiarize than those with high verbal ability.

    b. H_a: Psychology majors will exhibit more interpersonal skills in a new situation than students in other majors.

    c. H_a: Single adults who use online dating services will differ in a measure of shyness than single adults who do not use online dating services.

    d. H_a: Those who report high levels of stress will be more likely to over-eat than those who report low levels of stress.

2. Which alternative hypothesis results in a more stringent test? Explain your answer.

See Appendix A to check your answers.

Setting the Criterion Level (*p*)

In addition to deciding about the type of hypothesis (one- or two-tailed) we wish to test, we have to decide the **criterion level (*p*)** for our region of rejection. Thus far, you have learned about the .05 criterion level, where 5% of the sampling distribution is defined as the region of rejection. As stated earlier, this criterion level is the most common level selected for hypothesis testing. This means that given your sampling distribution, you will reject results that occur less than 5% of the time by chance alone. Another way to say this is that the probability (hence the symbol *p*) is less than 5% that you will get these results by chance alone, given your sampling distribution.

> **Criterion level:** The percentage of a sampling distribution that the researcher selects for the region of rejection; typically, researchers use less than 5% (*p* < .05).

Kittisak_Taramas

Suppose, however, that you want to be more confident that your findings do not belong on the sampling distribution defined by your null hypothesis. Then, you might select the more stringent .01 criterion level, where the region of rejection is composed of only 1% of the sampling distribution. Using the .01 criterion with a two-tailed hypothesis, the lowest .5% (or .005) and the highest .5% of the sampling distribution are defined as the region of rejection. If you use the .01 criterion with a one-tailed hypothesis, then the very bottom 1% *or* the very top 1% of the sampling distribution makes up the region of rejection. Obviously, it is more difficult to reject the null hypothesis using the .01 level, as the region of rejection is much smaller than when one uses the .05 level.

All this is to say that you as the researcher serve as the decision maker in the hypothesis testing process. You determine the null and alternative hypotheses, type of hypothesis (one- vs. two-tailed), and criterion level (.05 vs. .01). Of course, there are some standards to follow. You can't just say that your criterion for significance is 50%. Researchers agree that 5% is an acceptable amount of error, but this number is not set in stone. When results show a significance level between .051 and .10, researchers may describe them as "approaching significance," particularly if there was a very small sample size or the research was a pilot study. Such results can suggest to the researchers that their hypothesis deserves further study. They may then replicate the study with tighter controls or examine their methodology for ways to better measure their variables or to implement their treatment. In any case, researchers should always be aware that the less stringent the criterion level, the more likely they have made an error in deciding to reject the null hypothesis. Researchers must also be aware of the possibility for error if the null hypothesis is not rejected (is retained).

TABLE 6.1

Hypothesis Testing Process

1. State null hypothesis—H_0.
2. State alternative hypothesis—H_a Is it a one-tailed or two-tailed hypothesis?
3. Define sampling distribution and region of rejection criterion level, Are you using $p < .05$ or .01?
4. Collect data and compute appropriate statistical test.
5. Compare results to sampling distribution.
6. Decide whether to reject or retain null hypothesis.
7. Consider the possibility of error in your results.

ERRORS IN HYPOTHESIS TESTING

Once you have named null and alternative hypotheses and your criterion level, you compute a statistical test and compare the finding to the sampling distribution defined by your null hypothesis. If the finding falls in the region of acceptance, you retain the null hypothesis and assume that you do not have support for the alternative hypothesis. If the finding falls in the region of rejection, however, you reject the null hypothesis and accept or support the alternative hypothesis. In the latter case, you can assume that the findings are so different from those predicted by the null hypothesis that they are not part of the sampling distribution defined by the null hypothesis. Although the finding is rare for the sampling distribution (as they are found in the extreme top or bottom of the distribution), they still could occur in the sampling distribution by chance.

Note that in the statistical significance testing process we use the phrases "reject" or "retain" the null hypothesis and "support/accept" or "not support" the alternative hypothesis. We do *not* say that we "proved" the alternative hypothesis because we are working with probability in inferential statistics. We know that even when there is a very high probability that what we find is correct, there is always a small (sometimes a minuscule) chance that we are wrong and that what we have found is in fact a very rare occurrence for a true null hypothesis. Or there is a chance that our finding belongs on a different distribution; but because of this different distribution's overlap with our sampling distribution, it appears that our finding belongs to the sampling distribution. Because there is always a chance for error, we never prove any of our hypotheses but instead support or do not support our hypotheses. Probability and inferential statistics allow us to feel confident that our chance of error is small, but we can never say with absolute finality that we have proven a hypothesis.

Type I and Type II Errors

Think of a class where you usually do very well on assignments, and then for some reason you make a very low and unexpected grade. The low grade does not represent your typical performance in the class, but it is still a grade that will be included in your range of scores for the class. When we reject the null hypothesis, we must understand that our finding could have occurred (just like the low grade), although rarely, within the distribution of scores for our sampling distribution. Thus, there is always the chance that we are making an erroneous decision by rejecting the null hypothesis—this error is called a **Type I error** and is formally defined as incorrectly rejecting a true null hypothesis. The probability of making a Type I error is determined by the criterion level you have used in your hypothesis testing. If you reject the null hypothesis using the .05 criterion level, then the findings are in the extreme 5% of the distribution and the probability of a Type I error is 5%. Similarly, if you reject the null hypothesis using the .01 level, then the probability of making a Type I error is 1%.

If you retain the null hypothesis, there is also a probability of making an error. In this case, although the results fall within the expected middle range of values in the sampling distribution (region of acceptance), they could still belong to a different distribution whose scores overlap with the sampling distribution defined by the H_0. This type of error (incorrectly retaining the null hypothesis) is called a **Type II error**. In this

Type I error: The probability of rejecting a true H_0; defined by the probability of the significance level of your findings.

Type II error: The probability of incorrectly retaining a false H_0.

book, we will not calculate the probability of such an error; it is sufficient that you know when a Type II error may have occurred (hint: whenever you retain the null hypothesis). In hypothesis testing, because you are basing your decision on the probability of a result belonging to a distribution by chance, regardless of the decision you make there is some probability that you have made an error.

In summary, whenever you reject the null hypothesis, there is a probability that you have made a Type I error, and the probability of this error is equal to the p value that you use to reject the null hypothesis. If you reject the null hypothesis at the $p < .05$ level, there is less than a 5% probability that you have made a Type I error. On the other hand, if you retain the null hypothesis, there is the probability that you have made a Type II error. Without additional (and quite complex) calculations, you do not know the exact probability of a Type II error, but you should be aware of the possibility. Because you cannot both reject and retain the null hypothesis at the same time, there is a probability of *either* a Type I or a Type II error based on your decision to reject or retain the null. Therefore, if you reject the null hypothesis, there is the probability of a Type I error but 0% chance of a Type II error. If you retain the null hypothesis, there is a probability of a Type II error but 0% chance of a Type I error.

Table 6.2 illustrates the four possible outcomes of hypothesis testing that we have explained above. The null hypothesis can be either true or false, and you can either retain or reject it. If the null hypothesis is true and you reject it, you have made a Type I error (cell A). Another way to say this is that your findings appear to belong in the region of rejection but actually are a value that, by chance, rarely occurs in the distribution. Figure 6.5 provides an example of a Type I error that may help you distinguish this error. Alternatively, if the null hypothesis is true and you retain it, then you have made a correct decision (cell B). If the null hypothesis is false and you reject it, you have made a correct decision (cell C). If the null hypothesis is false and you fail to reject it, you have made a Type II error (cell D).

In designing and carrying out a study, you make every effort to correctly reject a false null hypothesis (cell C), which is called power, and to avoid making an error in your decision making (cells A and D). There are multiple steps you can take to increase

TABLE 6.2

Four Possible Outcomes in Statistical Significance Testing

		Decision Based on Observed Results	
		Reject	Retain
Reality (not directly observed or tested)	H_0 is True	Type I error A	Correct B
	H_0 is False	Correct C	Type II error D

FIGURE 6.5

A Type I Error

I don't get it. . . The study said eating 4oz of chocolate a day makes you LOSE weight!!?

A humorous example of a potential Type I error you want to avoid . . . assuming (or finding) a difference when there isn't really one.

Source: Sandi Coon

the power of your study, which are described under the section "Reducing the Chance of a Type II Error" (see p. 196).

(see p. 196).

Reducing the Chance of a Type I Error*

When you reject the null hypothesis, the probability of a Type I error is determined by the criterion level, and you can therefore make your study less vulnerable to a Type I error by changing your criterion level. Most of the time social scientists use the $p < .05$ criterion, as they believe that less than 5% probability of making an error is an acceptable risk.

If they are very concerned about the Type I error, they would use a more stringent criterion (such as $p < .01$). The implications of the findings of a study may lead researchers to use a more stringent level. If, for example, you are studying an educational program to prevent plagiarism that is inexpensive and easy to implement, you may feel very comfortable using the .05 criterion. If you inadvertently make a Type I error (incorrectly reject a true null hypothesis), you have not created too much of an expense or bother for those implementing the program and have not harmed the students participating in the program. If, however, your new technique is expensive in terms of dollars and teachers' time, and intrusive in terms of students' confidentiality, you may want to reduce the probability of a Type I error and employ the .01 criterion level.

Another common strategy to reduce Type I error is to use a two-tailed rather than a one-tailed test. Recall that the two-tailed test is a more stringent test because the regions of rejection are split between the two tails of the distribution, and therefore the critical value must be more extreme in order for the results to be considered statistically

---

*Simmons, Nelson, and Simonsohn (2011) criticized current research practice for its focus on finding significant results rather than advancing knowledge. They argue that this focus on statistical significance results in findings that are vulnerable to an unacceptably high probability of Type I errors. They suggest that the flexibility of current research practices increases the probability of Type I errors far beyond 5%. They also contend that these practices stem at least partially from scholarly journals' practice of requiring statistical significance before accepting an article for publication. The authors list several suggestions for modifying the research process and reporting the methods to counteract the increased probability of Type I errors: identify the number of desired participants before conducting a study and include at least 20 participants per condition; list all IVs and DVs in the study and not just the variables in results that showed significance; include analyses for all participants; and include analyses when participants have been excluded.

Application 6.2

APPLYING THE COMPLETE HYPOTHESIS-TESTING PROCESS IN A STUDY

Let's now apply the hypothesis-testing process to the Kuznekoff and Titsworth (2013) study that was briefly described at the beginning of the chapter. We will limit our focus right now to their investigation of the effect of frequent texting/posting on the amount of detail in students' notes. Remember that the researchers had one group of students text/post every 30 seconds during a brief lecture while the control group only listened to the lecture.

A possible null hypothesis would be that there is no difference in the detail in students' notes when text/posting every 30 seconds during a lecture versus when students just listen to the lecture. A nondirectional (two-tailed) alternative hypothesis would state that there will be a difference in students notes when texting/posting every 30 seconds versus only listening, while a directional (one-tailed) hypothesis would state that students who are texting/posting every 30 seconds would have less detail in their notes than the students who are only listening. Either one of these alternative hypotheses is acceptable, but they have different implications for the region of rejection.

If we select a .05 criterion level, then for the nondirectional H_a we will reject the H_0 if the results fall either at the bottom 2.5% or top 2.5% of the distribution defined by the null hypothesis. If we state a directional H_0 then we will reject the H_0 only if our results fall in the direction that we predicted (that students who are texting posting will have less detail in their notes than students who are listening). If we find that those texting/posting had more detail in their notes, we cannot reject our directional H_0 because our results are in the wrong direction from our region of rejection.

Remember that most of the time we use a two-tailed or nondirectional hypothesis in hypothesis testing so that we can reject findings that are rare for our distribution, regardless of the tail in which the findings fall. In addition, a two-tailed hypothesis is a more stringent test than using a directional hypothesis because even when we have correctly predicted the direction of our findings (that the students texting/posting will less detail in their notes than those who are only listening), given a certain criterion level (say .05), our region of rejection in each tail of the distribution is half (2.5%) of what it would be for a one-tailed test (5%) in the predicted tail of the distribution.

The results of the statistical test used by Kuznekoff and Titsworth (2013) fell in the region of rejection (top or bottom 2.5% of the distribution) and allowed them to conclude that they had found statistical significance. They could then reject the null hypothesis and support the alternative hypothesis that students who frequently text/post while listening to a lecture will include fewer details in their notes than students who listen to the lecture. Another way to state the results is to say that the results show that students who text/post during a lecture include significantly less detail in their notes than students who listen to the lecture. We understand that with this decision, there is a 5% chance of having made a Type I error. If, on the other hand, their results had fallen in the region of acceptance, they would have decided to retain the H_0 and concluded that there is no difference in the amount of detail in students' notes of a lecture when they text/post or just listen. In this case, there would have been a probability of a Type II error, but we do not know its exact probability.

Practice 6.3

UNDERSTANDING THE HYPOTHESIS-TESTING PROCESS

Can you enter information from the Kuznekoff *and* Titsworth (2013) *study from Application 6.2 in the different boxes of the flow chart below?*

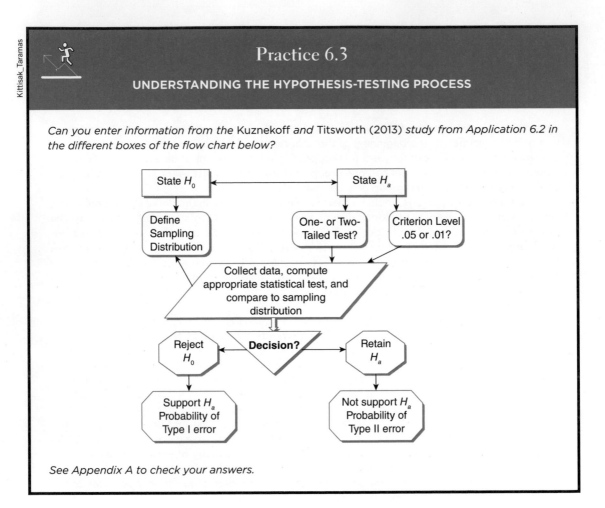

See Appendix A to check your answers.

significant. Although in theory a two-tailed test is used for nondirectional hypotheses, in practice most researchers use two-tailed tests for both directional and nondirectional hypotheses in order to reduce the chance of a Type I error.

Reducing the Chance of a Type II Error

You can avoid a Type II error by choosing a less stringent criterion (such as $p < .06$ or $p < .10$), but then you run the risk of a Type I error. Fortunately, you do not need to play this back-and-forth game because there are better ways to minimize your risk of a Type II error. Consequently, set the criterion level to address Type I error and design a powerful study to address Type II error. **Power** is the ability to detect a statistically

Power: The ability to reject the null hypothesis when it is, in fact, false.

significant result when in fact the result exists in the population. In other words, having enough power in a study allows you to avoid the Type II error of retaining the null when the null is false.

Key factors that impact the power of a study are:

1. Sample size (larger sample size = more power)

2. Amount of error in the research design (less error = more power)

3. Strength of the effect (stronger effect = more power)

Power and Sample Size

In order to have power, you must have enough members of the population represented in your sample for you to feel confident that the results you found in your study are in fact the ones that exist in the population. Thus, one way to increase power is to increase your sample size. The larger the sample size, the more confident we can be that the mean of our sample approaches the mean of the population from which the sample is drawn. Thus, we are more confident that any difference we find according to our statistical test is reliable.

> "It's not about right. It's not about wrong. It's about power."
>
> –From *Buffy the Vampire Slayer* (2002)

Think about the example above about psychology majors' text messaging frequency. Suppose in order to get a sample of psychology majors we ask the 10 students in a Research Methods class how many text messages they sent during the last 24 hours. How well would their data represent all psychology majors at the school if there were 260 majors?

If you answered not very well, you are correct. The class reflects students at a certain level of progress in the major, majors taking a class at a certain time with a particular teacher. The class does not include, for example, majors who are just beginning their study of psychology, those who have completed the Research Methods course, or those who are not sure they want to continue in the major. The class may also be weighted more heavily toward one gender or ethnicity or age that is not reflective of all psychology majors. All of these factors may influence how frequently psychology majors text, and thus the texting frequency of the 10 students may deviate from the texting frequency of all majors.

A larger sample would better reflect all the diversity of characteristics of psychology majors and provide a more reliable and less variable measure of the texting frequency of the majors. When we compare a measure derived from a large sample size to a sampling distribution, we are more likely to detect even a small difference (and significance) between the sample and our sampling distribution because of the increased stability and representativeness of the sample mean. Thus, we have increased confidence in the results of our statistical significance testing. There are formulas to estimate how large a sample you need in order to have enough power to detect a small, medium, or large effect. The formulas vary based on what type of analysis you plan to conduct, and can be quite onerous to complete by hand. Luckily, there are several free online calculators that you can use, such as the one provided by the Columbia University Medical center at biomath.info.

Power and Error in the Research Design

There are many ways to reduce error in your research study and, in doing so, you increase the power of your study. The diversity of your sample can be a source of error. This is called **within-groups variance (or error variance)** and represents the unaccounted-for differences in the sample. In our study about texting among psychology majors, texting frequency is what we are systematically studying and therefore is not considered error. However, all the other individual differences among our sample such as year in school, gender, age, and personal experiences are potential sources of error because these differences may affect the texting frequency of psychology majors. One way to reduce within-groups variance is to increase the **homogeneity of the sample** by limiting the population from which your sample is drawn to only senior psychology majors, or to only women, or to only those who have owned a cell phone for at least five years, and so on. Another way to reduce this type of error is to systematically evaluate potential differences in your sample. For example, you might determine if there is a relationship between year in school and texting, or gender and texting, or if texting is related to how long someone has owned a cell phone. These strategies help you to reduce the within-groups error variance, but you can never eliminate it because some of this error is due to random (unsystematic and unpredictable) differences among individuals, or that which makes each of us unique.

Other ways to reduce error in your study are to select appropriate statistical tests (we will discuss this later in the chapter and in following chapters), reduce sampling bias (see Chapter 4), select reliable and valid measures (see Chapter 3), and choose measures that are sensitive. The **sensitivity** of the measurement instrument determines your ability to detect differences in quality or quantity. We have smoke detectors in our house that we hope are sensitive enough to detect the presence of smoke. Likewise, we choose measurement instruments in a research study that will be sensitive enough to detect differences in the construct we are examining. For example, at minimum we would want a measure of depression to distinguish between someone who is depressed and someone who is not, and a more sensitive measure could further distinguish between different levels of depression (e.g., mild, moderate, extreme).

> **Within-groups variance (or error variance):** The differences in your sample measure that are not accounted for in the study.
>
> **Homogeneity of the sample:** The degree to which the members of a sample have similar characteristics.
>
> **Sensitivity:** The ability of a measurement instrument to detect differences.

Power and the Strength of the Effect

The strength of the effect refers to the magnitude or intensity of a pattern or relationship, and increases the likelihood that the pattern or relationship will be detected. The amount of smoke in your house impacts your ability to observe it, and likewise it is easier to identify strong patterns or relationships in social science constructs. For example, it is easier to detect someone's mood if that person is extremely happy, sad, or angry than if he or she is experiencing more mild or nuanced emotions.

The strength of the effect is something that we measure in research, and as such you do not have as much ability to directly impact it as you do with sample size and error. The extent to which you can increase the strength of the effect depends on the goal of the study and the research design. One strategy is to focus your study on phenomena known through previous research to have a strong pattern or relationship. Another strategy is to conduct an experiment that includes a strong manipulation that you hope will lead to a strong effect. Think of Kuznekoff and Titsworth's (2013) study where they had students text every 30 seconds (a strong manipulation) rather than text every 5 minutes (a weak manipulation) during a lecture.

Practice 6.4

INTERPRETING RESULTS

1. Which of the following results would be considered statistically significant at the $p < .01$ level? Select all that would be statistically significant.

   (a) $p = .05$; (b) $p = .005$; (c) $p = .10$; (d) $p = .001$; (e) $p = .02$; (f) $p = .009$

2. A researcher sets the criterion level at $p < .05$.

   a. If the results revealed $p = .10$:

      i. Are the results statistically significant?

      ii. Would you reject or retain the null hypothesis?

      iii. What type of error might you be making? Name at least two strategies to reduce this error in future research.

   b. If the results revealed $p = .03$:

      i. Are the results statistically significant?

      ii. Would you reject or retain the null hypothesis?

      iii. What type of error might you be making? How might you eliminate this error, and what would the consequences of that be?

3. Without looking at Table 6.2, fill in the blanks for each cell in the table below. Which of the cells indicate power?

		Decision Based on Observed Results	
		Reject	Retain
Reality	H_0 is True		
	H_0 is False		

See Appendix A to check your answers.

EFFECT SIZE, CONFIDENCE INTERVALS, AND PRACTICAL SIGNIFICANCE

Tests of statistical significance do not tell us all that we need to know about the variables we are studying. Three additional measures we can use to interpret the meaning and importance of our findings are the effect size, confidence interval, and practical significance. These standards help us to better understand and interpret the results of a study.

The **effect size** tells you the magnitude or strength of the effect of a variable. One of the easiest types of effect size to understand is the percentage of variability in one variable (the dependent variable), which is accounted for by the independent variable (in the case of experiments) or which is accounted for by the relationship with another variable (in the case of correlations). This effect size, expressed as a percentage, can range from .00 to 1.00. For example, if the effect size equals .10, then 10% of the variability in the dependent variable scores would be accounted for by the independent variable. That would mean that 90% of the variability in the dependent variable is not associated with the independent variable. Thus, in this case, even though you may have found a statistically significant difference in the dependent variable due to the independent variable, the IV does not have very much influence or effect on the dependent variable. On the other hand, if your effect size is .45, then the independent variable accounts for 45% of the variability in the dependent variable. You would interpret this as a strong effect size and want to pursue further the impact of the IV on the DV. In social sciences we study very complex behavior that can be influenced by multiple variables, and it is highly unusual for an independent variable to explain all or most of the variation in the dependent variable scores.

> **Effect size:** Strength or magnitude of the effect of a variable.

The effect size in social science research is more likely to be smaller. In interpreting the proportion of variance accounted for, Cohen (1988) suggested that 1% is considered a small but reasonable effect, 9% is considered a moderate effect, and 25% is considered a large effect. Cohen's recommendations are widely applied in the social sciences. These numbers were never intended to be strict cutoffs but rather to serve as guidelines to enable us to evaluate the strength of relationships between variables.

Cohen's d is another commonly used measure of magnitude of an effect. It is computed by dividing the difference between the means of two groups by their pooled standard deviation.* For example, if the mean for group 1 is 15, the mean for group 2 is 10, and the pooled variance for the two groups is 2.5, then Cohen's $d = 2$ or (15–10)/2.5. The larger the value of Cohen's d, the stronger the effect size. Regardless of the particular measures used or means or standard deviations of groups in studies, the meaning

---

*In their appendix, Fritz et al. (2012) provide formulas for different effect sizes. They note that Cohen's d should be computed using the population standard deviation (sigma or σ) and Hedge's g is computed using the pooled sample standard deviation. Given that sigma is rarely known, they suggest that many who report Cohen's d may actually have computed Hedge's g.

of Cohen's *d* is the same (think of *z* scores). It is a standardized measure of mean differences expressed in standard deviation units, and because of this, some researchers prefer Cohen's *d* instead of the percentage of variability accounted for. See Table 6.3 for guidelines on interpreting effect size, keeping in mind that these guidelines are used to describe the size of the effect and are not designed as cutoff scores. You should always keep in mind the context of your study in interpreting an effect size.

TABLE 6.3

Interpretations of Effect Sizes (Cohen, 1988)

Effect Size		
Proportion of Variability Accounted for	**Cohen's *d***	**Interpretation**
1%	.20	Small/Weak
9%	.50	Medium/Moderate
25%	.80	Large/Strong

Beginning with the publication of the 5th edition of the *APA Publication Manual* (American Psychological Association, 2001), articles in APA format must include the effect size in addition to the results of statistical significance tests. You may find, however, that many of the studies you read do not report effect sizes. Some of them may have been published before 2001 and the publication of the 5th edition of APA's manual. But, reviews of all the articles published in two APA journals in 2009 and 2010 found that fewer than 50% of the results included effect size, regardless of the statistical analyses used (Fritz, Morris, & Richler, 2012).

Similarly, another review of empirical studies published in 14 education and psychology journals found only 49% of the articles reported effect size. In this review, however, the more complicated the analysis, the more likely the reporting of effect size (Sun, Pan, & Wang, 2010). These results suggest that researchers and journals have been slow to adopt the APA guidelines. Regardless of what you find in the articles you read, you should include the effect size test that is appropriate for your analyses. The specific test you employ is determined by both the statistical test you use in your study and your (or your instructor's) preference for describing the effect size. You will learn more about different tests used to determine effect size in later chapters.

The 5th and 6th editions of the publication manual, along with some researchers, recommend that when possible we should focus less on hypothesis testing and *p* values (called null hypothesis statistical testing or NHST) when reporting our results and more on the effect size and **confidence intervals** (CIs) (American Psychological

Confidence interval: Defines the interval that we are confident contains the population μ represented by our sample mean; typically, we compute the 95% confidence interval.

Association, 2001, 2010b; Cumming, Fidler, Kalinowski, & Lai, 2012). Their rationale is that statistical significance sometimes can be found with consistent effects or with large samples even when the effect of a variable or its relationship to another variable is weak and thus not very meaningful. They argue that results are more useful when expressed as the strength of variables (effect size) and the margin of error (confidence interval) for the findings. Some social science journals now require researchers submitting articles to report and focus on these statistics. However, a review of articles in 10 leading psychology journals in 1998, 2003-2004, and 2005-2006 found that while almost all the articles reported the results of NHST, few articles reported and interpreted confidence intervals (Cumming et al., 2012). Still, you should be knowledgeable about the effect size–confidence interval combination.

If we follow this method of reporting results we would report an effect size and also define the interval that we are confident that our computed statistic falls within. For example, if we are considering the mean of a sample of scores, the confidence interval defines the highest mean and the lowest mean (and the values in between) we would expect for a population whose mean (μ) equals the one we found in our study. In APA format, you might see $M = 10.50$ texts, 95% CI [6.25, 14.75], which would be interpreted that we are 95% confident that our mean of 10.50 represents a population mean that falls between 6.25 and 14.75. Remember that the sample for a study is drawn to represent a population so we do not expect the means for all samples from the population to be exactly the population mean (μ). The confidence interval provides us with an estimate about how much error or variability there might be for means of multiple samples drawn to represent the population mean. The formula for the confidence interval includes the standard deviation (*SD*) of the sample and the smaller the *SD* for the scores in a sample, the smaller the range of a confidence interval (or margin of error). As the range for the confidence interval decreases, we can be more confident that a statistic adequately represents the population parameter. If you report confidence intervals, you need not focus on statistical significance.

REVIEW OF KEY CONCEPTS: CONFIDENCE INTERVALS

1. What is a confidence interval?

2. What is a confidence level?

A confidence interval describes the margin of error for a statistic. It tells us the range (or interval) within which we expect our statistic to fall with a certain confidence level. Typically, we use the 95% or 99% confidence level so that we are confident that the "true" value of the statistic we have calculated (a mean, for instance) actually falls within the range of means as determined by our confidence interval either 95% or 99% of the time. (You learned about confidence intervals and confidence levels in Chapter 4 in reference to the minimum sample size needed to represent a population.)

Practical significance refers to the usefulness of our results or findings from our study. In other words: How do the results affect or apply to daily life? Even if we find statistical significance, the difference we find may not be noticeable or noticeably affect people's lives. On the other hand, a study that did not find statistical significance or have a large effect size may still yield important, practical results. A classic example of this is found in the medical literature. Findings from a study comparing heart attacks among those who took aspirin versus a placebo was stopped before completion because preliminary results were so clearly in favor of aspirin's benefits. The effect size was miniscule, with aspirin accounting for only a tenth of a percentage point in the reduction of heart attacks (Rosenthal, 1990). But the difference in outcomes revealed that those who took aspirin were slightly less likely to have a heart attack and much less likely to die from a heart attack, plus there were no clear health problems resulting from aspirin (Steering Committee of the Physicians' Health Study Research Group, 1989). When we are talking about a life and death situation, even a very small difference can be meaningful.

Practical significance: The usefulness or everyday impact of results.

When we conduct studies, we should consider the practical use or implications of our findings. Findings that make a noticeable difference in the world outside the laboratory in addition to being statistically significant are memorable and define areas that are likely to generate additional studies, so practical significance is another aspect of research that we should consider. Of course, some studies further our knowledge of behavior without the practical implications being understood at the time of the study. We often later discover the usefulness of knowledge acquired through basic research. Thus, having practical significance can be beneficial, but practical significance is not required in order for a study to be valued in the social sciences.

Statistical significance, effect sizes, and practical significance vary independently so that you can obtain any combination of the three factors in a study. In one study, you may have statistical significance but find a very small effect size and no practical significance. In another study, you may not find statistical significance but may find a moderate effect size and practical significance. An alternate way to report your results would be to focus on the effect size, confidence interval, and practical significance. These factors can also vary independently so that you could have a strong effect size with a large confidence interval and little practical significance or you could have a weak effect size with a small confidence interval and moderate practical significance. The different combinations of all these factors help us to better interpret our findings.

For example, if you find statistical significance but a very small effect size, the significance may be due to factors such as a large sample size rather than the impact of your variable. On the other hand, if you find a strong effect size but no statistical significance, you may want to revise and replicate your study with more power because the effect size suggests your variable is effective. In addition, if you find a large confidence interval with a strong effect size, you may want to replicate your study with stronger controls in order to reduce the variability in the scores for your variable (which would then reduce the confidence interval).

A few specific examples may help you to understand the different combinations of outcomes from a study. Suppose you find that psychology majors ($M = 42.50$, $SD = 1.24$)

send significantly more text messages than college students in general (M = 39.10, SD = 2.82; p = .03) and that your effect size is 2%, so that the major accounted for only 2% of the variability in texting frequency. The difference between texting 42 times a day versus 39 times a day is minimal in terms of impact on time or attention to one's phone. In this case, you found statistical significance, a small effect size, and very little practical significance in your study.

Consider if, instead, you found that there was no difference (p = .15) in the mean texting frequency for psychology majors (M = 60.5, SD = 4.67) and college students (M = 39.1, SD = 5.82), but the effect size was moderate and the major accounted for 20% of the variability in testing. In this case, the psychology majors sent or received approximately 20 more text messages than their college peers, a difference that might be noticeable and thus have significance in terms of different amounts of time spent on texting, which could influence interactions with others or attention in class.

In yet another study of texting frequency for psychology majors (M = 60.5, SD = 8.67) and college students (M = 42.3, SD = 7.72), you might find that the effect size was 30% but that the confidence interval for the difference in texting frequency is large, and this is due to the variability in texting frequency. This suggests the effect of a psychology major is strong but that we cannot be very confident that our findings represent the "real" or population difference as the range for the interval is so large. The difference in means (18.2) in this study would probably be noticeable, suggesting the results have implications for behavior in class.

Application 6.3

DETERMINING THE EFFECT SIZE, CONFIDENCE INTERVAL, AND PRACTICAL SIGNIFICANCE IN A STUDY

In their study, Kuznekoff and Titsworth (2013) used Cohen's d to compute effect size. In the comparison of the detail in the lecture notes of the control group and the high-distraction group, Cohen's d = .97. This number is interpreted to mean that the means of the two groups varied by almost one standard deviation. As shown in Table 6.3, this difference is interpreted as a large effect size. Kuznekoff and Titsworth (2013) then concluded that there was a strong effect of frequent texting/posting (high distraction) on the detail recorded in students' notes during a lecture. If, however, the effect size (Cohen's d) had been .04, then the means for the control group and high-distraction group would differ by only .04 standard deviation. In this case, Kuznekoff and Titsworth (2013) would then report that the effect of frequent texting/posting on note detail was weak. Remember that researchers recommend that the guidelines for the interpretation of effect sizes should not be taken as rigid standards (Cohen, 1988; Ferguson, 2009). Your interpretation should also take into account the context of the specific study such as the design, sample size, controls, specific measures, and so on.

Although Kuznekoff and Titsworth (2013) did not report the confidence interval, remember that some researchers and APA now recommend including this information. In this case, the authors would have reported the mean difference in details between the high distraction ($M = 15.50$) and no distraction groups ($M = 25.05$) as the statistic $M_{x-x} = 9.55$, 95% CI [lower limit, upper limit]. We do not know these limits but many statistical programs compute them for you. The smaller the difference between the lower and upper limits of the confidence interval, the more confident we would be that our findings represent the population value. So if the limits were 8.00 and 11.10, we could interpret our findings as better representing the population value than if the limits were 4.55 and 14.55. We should also consider the practical significance of the classroom distraction (by texting/posting) study. Students who listened to the lecture and took notes without distractions recorded a mean of 25.05 ($SD = 11.97$) details in their notes, while the students who texted/posted every 30 seconds recorded a mean of 15.50 ($SD = 7.06$) details in their notes.

Because the number of details from the lecture recorded by the highly distracted students was only 60% of the number of details that the control group recorded, the practical implications of these findings seem significant. Students in the high-distraction group would be likely to notice that many details about the lecture were missing when they reviewed their notes or used them to study for an exam. In this case, it appears that the findings have practical significance and may influence students' understanding of the lecture material.

Practice 6.5

INTERPRETING EFFECT SIZE, CONFIDENCE INTERVALS, AND PRACTICAL SIGNIFICANCE

1. After surveying drivers at multiple sites throughout the country, the National Transportation Board reports that drivers report using their cell phones during 60% of their trips in their car. You think that more-educated people will use their cell phones less frequently while driving. You ask 25 of your classmates the percentage of trips in their car (of any duration) that they use their cell phones. Your classmates report a mean of 52%, with a standard deviation of 20. Do your classmates use their cell phones significantly less than the general population when driving?

2. Suppose you find, after comparing your classmates and the general population, the following results. How do you interpret each of these findings?

   a. $p = .08$, Cohen's $d = .30$.

   b. $p = .03$, with 10% of the variance in texting accounted for.

   c. $M = .52$, 95% CI [.45, .59]

   d. What can you say about the practical significance of the findings?

3. An industry report noted that Americans ate an average of 9.5 pounds of chocolate in 2015 (for an average of 12.67 oz. per month). Given the eating habits of your friends, you are sure that the estimate for Americans is low. You ask a sample of 35 adults ranging in

(Continued)

(Continued)

age from 20 to 50 to keep food diaries for a month. They were instructed to keep a record of everything they ate so that they were not aware of your interest in chocolate. You found that the sample reported eating a mean of 18 ounces for the month. This mean was significantly higher than the reported national average, $p = .025$.

a. What other information would be helpful to know in interpreting your results? Explain why.

b. How do you interpret what you do know about the results?

See Appendix A to check your answers.

THE BIG PICTURE: MAKING SENSE OF RESULTS

We hope you can see that attending to all four factors—statistical significance, effect size, confidence intervals, and practical significance—will help you to better understand the meaning of your study's results (see Table 6.4). We also hope that you can see that there are various ways you might report your results. The most common analysis reported today is statistical significance, but the field is changing and more researchers are including the effect size (as required by APA format since 2001). Increasingly, journals are encouraging or requiring researchers to report effect sizes in combination with confidence intervals. Depending on your discipline and even the subspecialty within your discipline, you may see a variety of formats in Results sections of published articles. Check with your instructor to see what format is required for your class.

TABLE 6.4
Four Ways to Evaluate Results

	Statistical Significance	Effect Size	Confidence Interval	Practical Significance
Importance?	Specifies the likelihood that your results are due to chance alone	Provides information on the magnitude of the results	Indicates the margin of error in your results	Encourages you to consider how meaningful or relevant the results are
Simple Example	Is there a statistically significant increase in my mood if I exercise?	How much better do I feel if I exercise?	What is the range of change in my mood if I exercise?	Is any improvement noticeable and meaningful to me or others if I exercise?

CHAPTER RESOURCES

Key Terms

Define the following terms using your own words. You can check your answers by reviewing the chapter or by comparing them with the definitions in the glossary—but try to define them on your own first.

Alternative hypothesis (H_a) 182
Confidence interval 201
Criterion level (p) 190
Critical value 188
Effect size 200
Experimental
 hypothesis (H_a) 182
Homogeneity of the sample 198
Hypothesis testing 180

Inferential statistics 176
Mu (μ) 177
Null hypothesis (H_0) 182
One-tailed hypothesis 187
Parameters 177
Power 196
Practical significance 202
Region of acceptance 186
Region of rejection 186

Sampling distribution 180
Sensitivity 198
Sigma (σ) 177
Statistical significance 187
Two-tailed hypothesis 187
Type I error 192
Type II error 192
Within-groups variance (or error
 variance) 198

Do You Understand the Chapter?

Answer these questions on your own, and then review the chapter to check your answers.

1. Differentiate descriptive and inferential statistics and give an example of the use of each statistic.

2. What does probability theory have to do with hypothesis testing?

3. Explain the process of hypothesis testing as if you were describing it to a friend who is not a social science major. Be sure to cover each step in the process and to define all the terms related to each step.

4. Describe the sampling distribution for the null hypothesis: There is no difference

between the frequency that adolescents text and the frequency that all cell phone users text. Hint: First you need to name the frequency of texting for all users (use any number that seems reasonable).

5. Why can't we "prove" our alternative hypothesis?

6. How can you decrease the probability of Type I and Type II errors in your results?

7. What does the effect size add to the results of statistical significance testing?

8. Why is a large confidence interval less desired than a small confidence interval?

9. Why should you consider the practical significance of a study's findings?

Practice With Statistics

1. Consider the example study in number 4 above comparing the frequency that adolescents text and the frequency that all cell phone users text. Suppose you find that adolescents text ($M = 30.75$, $SD = 6.42$) more than all cell phone users text ($M = 15.35$,

$SD = 5.17$), p = .025. You also find that Cohen's $d = 0.33$.

a. State an alternative hypothesis.

b. Is this a one- or two-tailed hypothesis? Explain.

c. Is this result statistically significant? How do you know?

d. What is the probability of a Type I error? Type II error?

e. How could you reduce the probability of a Type I error?

f. Interpret the effect size in the study.

g. What can you say about the practical significance of your finding?

2. A national sample of adults in the United States reported they spend 35% of their income on housing. Suppose you find that a sample of elderly adults spend 46% of their income on housing, $p = .07$ with age accounting for 20% of the variability in spending.

a. State your null and alternative hypotheses.

b. Can you reject the null hypothesis? Why or why not?

c. What is the probability of a Type I error? Type II error?

d. How might you reduce the probability of a Type II error?

e. Interpret the effect size in the study.

f. Suppose you find $M = .35$ income on housing, 95% CI [.10, .60]. How would you interpret this confidence interval?

g. What can you say about the practical significance of your finding?

 **SAGE edge**™ **edge.sagepub.com/adams2e**

Sharpen your skills with SAGE edge!
SAGE edge for students provides you with tools to help you study. You'll find mobile-friendly eFlashcards and quizzes, as well as videos, web resources, datasets, and links to SAGE journal articles related to this chapter.

Comparing Your Sample to a Known or Expected Score

Is the rate of depression reported among a sample of newly arrived immigrants to the United States different from the national rate of depression reported for adults?

Are students from your institution more likely to be registered to vote than the general college population?

Is the beginning salary for first-generation college graduates from a university different from the beginning salary for all graduates of the university?

Do honors students at a high school spend less time on their cell phones than the average time for all students at the high school?

What is similar about the questions above? If you said that each of the questions compares a sample to a population, you are correct! In Chapter 6, you learned about inferential statistics that allow you to make inferences about a population from your sample. In this chapter, you will learn a type of inferential statistic that allows you to compare your sample to a known or expected score: the one-sample t test. Although we rarely have a population value, it is important to learn about the rationale behind the computation of the simple analyses described in this chapter in order to understand the rationale behind more complicated and commonly used statistics.

CHOOSING THE APPROPRIATE TEST

Chapter 6 described hypothesis testing and the concepts involved in this process. If you are unsure of the steps in the hypothesis testing process, you should review them before reading this chapter.

LEARNING OUTCOMES

In this chapter, you will learn

- How to compare a sample to a known population value when you have interval or ratio data using the one-sample t test
- How to compute the effect size when comparing a sample to a known population
- How to compute the confidence interval when comparing a sample to a known population value

REVIEW OF KEY CONCEPTS: HYPOTHESIS TESTING

What are the steps involved in hypothesis testing?

- State null hypothesis—H_o.

- State alternative hypothesis—H_a. Is it a one-tailed or two-tailed hypothesis?

- Define sampling distribution and region of rejection criterion level. Are you using $p < .05$ or $.01$?

- Collect data and compute appropriate statistical test(s).

- Compare results to sampling distribution.

- Decide whether to reject or retain null hypothesis.

- Consider the possibility of error in your results.

You are now ready to learn about how to compute a specific inferential statistic that is appropriate when we want to compare a sample to a population value. For example, suppose that the rate of depression among the sample of newly arrived immigrants is 12% while the national statistic cited by the Centers for Disease Control and Prevention is 7.2%. Inferential statistics allow you to determine whether the newly arrived immigrants report depression significantly more often than adults across the country.

The specific statistics used for this comparison are dependent on the scale of measurement of the variable that is measured. This is one of the reasons why we have continued to quiz you on the scale of measurement of variables. If you misidentify the scale of measurement, you are likely to compute an inappropriate statistic and obtain results that are meaningless. In this chapter, we will introduce you to the statistical analysis used to compare a sample to a known or expected score when you have interval or ratio data—the **one-sample t test**. (A second type of analysis is used to compare a sample to a known score when you have nominal data—the **chi-square goodness of fit test**. Chapter 13 describes the chi-square goodness of fit test in detail. You can refer to this chapter if you would like to learn more about the chi-square analysis now.)

One-sample t test: An inferential statistic for interval or ratio data that compares a sample mean to a known population mean.

Chi-square goodness of fit: An inferential statistic for nominal data that tests whether the observed frequencies of the categories reflect the expected population frequencies.

In the example questions at the beginning of the chapter, two involve nominal data and two involve ratio data. Can you identify the scale of measurement for each question and the appropriate inferential statistic?

Answers

- Is the rate of depression reported among a sample of newly arrived immigrants to the United States different from the national rate of depression reported for adults? Experiencing depression (or not) is a nominal scale, and therefore the correct inferential statistic is the chi-square goodness of fit.

- Are students from your institution more likely to be registered to vote than the general college population? Being registered to vote (or not) is a nominal scale, and therefore we would use the chi-square goodness of fit.

- Is the beginning salary for first-generation college graduates from a university different from the beginning salary for all graduates of the university? Salary is a ratio scale, and the one-sample t test is the appropriate inferential test.

- Do honors students at a high school spend less time on their cell phones than the average time for all students at the high school? Time on cell phones is a ratio scale, and therefore we would use the one-sample t test.

ONE-SAMPLE t TESTS

We use a one-sample t test to examine the difference between a sample mean and a known population mean when the data are interval or ratio. The one-sample t test is the simplest use of hypothesis testing. Most of the time we do not have scores for all members of a population, but sometimes we have a limited population and collect data from all members of that group, or we collect data from a very large sample that is assumed to reflect the characteristics of a population.

Let's look at a specific example using a one-sample t test. Research has shown that many college students are not knowledgeable about citation format that is required in order to avoid plagiarism (Belter & du Pré, 2009; Culwin, 2006; Landau et al., 2002). Suppose a national study of a large number of first-year students in English classes finds that on a 10-item quiz about citation format, the average number of correct answers is 6.5. We want to know how University Anxious (UA) students' knowledge about citation format compares to that of college students across the nation so we give the citation format quiz to a sample of 25 first-year UA students in an English class. They earn a mean score of 7.50 ($SD = 2.00$). Are the UA students significantly more knowledgeable about citation format than most first-year college students? Another way to say this is: Did UA students score significantly higher on the quiz than did the national group?

We can answer these questions using the one-sample t test. This statistical test is used when we have a small sample (usually 30 or fewer) and a measure that is an interval or ratio scale. Ideally, we would like to have a random sample, but in reality, we usually have a sample of convenience that belongs to the population of interest. We also must have the population mean for the variable of interest (in this case on the quiz given to a large national group of first-year college students). We assume that the population of scores is normally distributed. Using the hypothesis testing format, we begin by stating our null and alternative hypotheses.

Null Hypothesis (H_0)

H_0: There will be no difference in the citation format knowledge quiz scores of UA first-year students and that of a national sample of first-year students.

The null hypothesis predicts that there will be no difference in the mean quiz scores for the sample and population. We might also express the null hypothesis in numerical terms:

$$H_0: M = \mu$$

where M equals the mean of our sample; μ equals the mean of the population. Another way to consider the null hypothesis is as an equation:

$$H_0: \mu - M = 0$$

In other words, if there is no difference between the sample and population means, then subtracting the mean (M) from mu (μ) will equal zero.

Alternative Hypothesis (H_a)

We can express our alternative hypothesis as either a directional (one-tailed) or a nondirectional (two-tailed) hypothesis.

Directional (one-tailed) H_a: First-year UA students will score higher on the citation format knowledge quiz than a national sample of first-year students.

We could also state this directional alternative hypothesis in numerical terms:

$$H_a: M > \mu$$

where M equals the mean of our sample; μ equals the mean of the population.

Nondirectional (two-tailed) H_a: First-year UA students will earn a different mean score on the citation format quiz than the national sample of first-year students.

Or in numerical terms:

$$H_a: M \neq \mu$$

Assumptions of the one-sample t test include:

- Interval or ratio data
- Normally distributed population
- Availability of the population mean (μ)

FORMULAS AND CALCULATIONS: ONE-SAMPLE *t* TEST

Calculating a one-sample *t* test is a very similar process to calculating a *z* score that you learned about in Chapter 5. (As a sample size increases, the distribution of scores more closely approximates a normal distribution, and with very large sample sizes you can use *z*-scores to examine differences between your sample and an expected or known score.) Recall that a *z* score represents the number of standard deviation units a score is from the mean. It is computed by subtracting the mean from a score and dividing that difference by the standard deviation of the sample.

With the one-sample *t* test, we find the difference between the population mean and our sample mean. We then divide that difference by the standard deviation of the sampling distribution of means, which is called the **standard error of the means (σ_x)**. Because σ_x is usually not available, we use the *estimated* **standard error of the means (SD_x)** to calculate the *t*. The subscript *x* denotes that we are estimating the standard deviation of a distribution of means rather than raw scores.

To calculate SD_x, we use the formula:

$$SD_x = \frac{SD}{\sqrt{N}}$$

where *SD* is the sample standard deviation; *N* is the sample size.

Remember in hypothesis testing that we compare our findings to a sampling distribution. In this case the sampling distribution is built by drawing multiple samples of 25 college students and calculating their citation quiz means (*M*). The sampling distribution is made up of means rather than raw scores, and means vary from one another less than individual scores vary from one another. Therefore, the standard deviation of a sampling distribution is smaller than the standard deviation of a sample of raw scores. In order to estimate the standard error of the means (SD_x) for a sampling distribution of our particular sample size, we divide the standard deviation of our sample by the square root of the sample size.

The definitional formula for a one-sample *t* test is:

$$t = \frac{M - \mu}{SD_x} = \frac{M - \mu}{SD / \sqrt{N}}$$

where *M* is the mean of the sample; μ is the population mean; SD_x is the estimated standard error of the means; *SD* is the standard deviation of the sample; and *N* is the sample size.

> **Standard error of the means (σ_x):** Standard deviation of the sampling distribution of means.
>
> **Estimated standard error of the means (SD_x):** Estimated standard deviation of the sampling distribution of means that is used to calculate the *t* test.

In this chapter we are using the definitional formula which follows from our description of the statistical test. If you are hand calculating a one-sample t test, you may find it easier to use the computational formula that is found in Appendix D.3.

If we apply the definitional formula to our example of 25 UA students' scores on a quiz ($M = 7.50$, $SD = 2.00$) and the average found in the research literature ($\mu = 6.50$), we find:

$$t = \frac{M - \mu}{SD\sqrt{N}} = \frac{7.5 - 6.5}{2/\sqrt{25}} = \frac{1.0}{2/5} = \frac{1.0}{.4} = 2.5$$

The calculated $t = 2.5$. How do we know whether this result allows us to reject our null hypothesis and support our alternative hypothesis? In order to make a decision about the significance of our results, we must consider the sampling distribution for our study. We use a chart that was developed for t tests where the critical t value that defines the region of rejection varies as a function of the sample size (see Table 7.1).

TABLE 7.1

Critical t Values for a Particular Probability Level and df

One-tailed	0.10	0.05	0.025	0.01	0.005
Two-tailed		0.10	0.05	0.02	0.01
df					
1	3.078	6.314	12.706	31.821	63.657
2	1.886	2.920	4.303	6.965	9.925
$\wedge\wedge\wedge\wedge\wedge\wedge\wedge\wedge$					
21	1.323	1.721	2.080	2.518	2.831
22	1.321	1.717	2.074	2.508	2.819
23	1.319	1.714	2.069	2.500	2.807
24	1.310	1.711	**2.064**	2.492	2.797
25	1.316	1.708	2.060	2.485	2.787
26	1.315	1.706	2.056	2.479	2.779
27	1.314	1.703	2.052	2.473	2.771
28	1.313	1.701	2.048	2.467	2.763
29	1.311	1.699	2.045	2.462	2.756
30	1.310	1.697	2.042	2.457	2.750
40	1.303	1.684	2.021	2.423	2.704
60	1.296	1.671	2.000	2.390	2.660
120	1.289	1.658	1.980	2.358	2.617
∞	1.282	1.645	1.960	2.326	2.576

We use **degrees of freedom** (*df*) as an estimate of sample size. For a *t* test, *df* is equal to $N - 1$. In the critical *t* value chart, we use *df* to find the value that our calculated *t* value must equal or exceed in order to reject the H_0. Degrees of freedom is formally defined as the number of scores that are free to vary in a sample. For example, if you think of three scores that add up to 10, and the first two scores are 5 and 2, what must the third score be? If you said 3, you are correct. The first two scores could be any value; but in order to add to 10, the third score in our example must be 3. Thus, for our small group of scores, $df = 3 - 1 = 2$. In general, we lose one *df* in any group of scores.

> **Degrees of freedom (*df*):** Determined by the sample size; number of scores free to vary in a sample.

In our example, the one-sample t test was computed from a sample of 25 and our $df = 25 - 1 = 24$. If you look down the .05 column of Table 7.1, you will find that as the sample size and *df* increase, the critical value for *t* at the .05 level comes closer to 1.96 until at infinity (∞) the *t* distribution matches the *z* distribution. This is because, as sample size increases, the *t* distribution becomes more normal and the percentages for the distribution more closely approximate those in the *z* score chart.

To use the *t* table in Table 7.1, look at the far left column and find the *df* for our sample ($df = 24$) and move across that row to the critical level we have selected. Located at the intersection of our *df* and criterion level is the critical value for our study. *Our calculated t value must be equal to or greater than the critical t value that is listed in the table in order for us to reject the null hypothesis.* Remember that in hypothesis testing, we typically use the criterion level of .05 ($p < .05$), which means that the difference between our sample quiz mean and the population quiz mu is likely to occur 5% or less of the time, if our sample belongs to the population of typical first-year college students.

When we use Table 7.1, we must know the degrees of freedom, our selected criterion level, and whether we are using a one- or two-tailed test. For our test, $df = 24$, and we are using a two-tailed test at the .05 level of significance. We look down the left-hand side of Table 7.1 in the *df* column until we reach 24 and move across the row until we get to the .05 column for a two-tailed test. We find the value 2.064 (called the critical value). Our *t* value must be equal to or greater than the value in the table in order to reject our null hypothesis. Our *t* value is 2.5, which is greater than the critical value of 2.064, so we can reject the null hypothesis that there is no difference between the mean of our sample and the population of first-year students. We can accept our alternative hypothesis that there is a significant difference at the .05 level between the population and sample means. We note that the sample mean ($M = 7.5$) is greater than the population mu ($\mu = 6.5$). We may then interpret our findings as showing that UA students demonstrated significantly greater knowledge of citation format in comparison to the typical first-year student in colleges throughout the country. Because we rejected the null hypothesis, there is a probability of a Type I error equal to the *p* level. In this case, we used a .05 criterion level so there is a 5% chance that we have made a Type I error (or that we have incorrectly rejected a true null hypothesis). There is zero probability that we have made a Type II error because we did not retain the null hypothesis.

When you use a *t* table, be sure that you look at the column across the top of the table that matches the criterion level for the type of test (one- or two-tailed test) you are using. Because a one-tailed test has the entire region of rejection in one tail of the distribution (while the region of rejection for a two-tailed test is equally split in either tail of the distribution), for the same critical *t* value, the *p* value for a one-tailed test is twice the *p* value for the two-tailed test. This means that the critical *t* value for the same degrees of freedom is different for one- and two-tailed tests. Let's assume we have a sample of 25 so our *df* would be 24 (*N* − 1). For 24 *df*, a two-tailed test at *p* = .05 lists the critical *t* value of 2.064 (look in Table 7.1), while for a one-tailed test at *p* = .05 the critical value is 1.711. Remember we said in Chapter 6 that the two-tailed test was more conservative; you can see from this example that we must obtain a higher calculated *t* value in order to reject our null hypothesis for the two-tailed test than for the one-tailed test.

Practice 7.1

DETERMINING WHETHER A *t* TEST RESULT IS SIGNIFICANT

Suppose you believe that students from your campus text more than most students. You collect data from 15 students about the number of texts they sent in the last hour and compare it to a national sample of students. After computing your *t* test, you found that *t*(14) = 2.20. Using Table C.4 in Appendix C, name the critical *t* value for each of the four possibilities below and state whether your results would be significant for a:

a.   two-tailed test at the .05 criterion level

b.   two-tailed test at the .01 criterion level

c.   one-tailed test at the .05 level

d.   one-tailed test at the .01 level

See Appendix A to check your answers.

Calculating an Effect Size

Remember that APA format requires that we also calculate the effect size as part of our analysis. With a one-sample *t* test we can use a statistical test called **eta squared (η^2)**, which tells us the percentage of variability in the variable we measured (the quiz grade

Eta squared (η^2): Percentage of variability in a measured variable that is accounted for by the grouping variable.

in our example) accounted for by the group or **Cohen's d (d)**, which is the standardized size of the difference between the two means (in this case the population and sample means).

First, we will calculate eta squared (η^2). The computation formula is:

$$\eta^2 = \frac{t^2}{t^2 + df}$$

where t = our calculated value of t; $df = N–1$.

So for our example we found $t = 2.5$ and entered this value and our df into the formula.

$$\eta^2 = \frac{t^2}{t^2 + df} = \frac{2.5 * 2.5}{(2.5 * 2.5) + (25 - 1)} = \frac{6.25}{6.25 + 24} = \frac{6.25}{30.25} = .21$$

The results of our analysis ($\eta^2 = .21$) show that 21% of the variability in quiz scores of UA students was accounted for by the campus they attended. This particular eta squared (η^2) value is interpreted as a moderate effect size (see Table 6.3, p. 201). So we have found statistical significance ($p < .05$) between the quiz scores of UA students and the national standard, and the school attended had a moderate strength on the quiz scores.

The second type of effect size that we can compute for a one-sample t test is Cohen's d (d), which describes the magnitude of the effect of our group on the measure in standard deviation units.

To compute Cohen's d, we use the computational formula:

$$d = \frac{M - \mu}{SD}$$

where M is the mean of the sample; μ is the population mean; SD is the standard deviation of the sample.

For our example $M = 7.5$, $\mu = 6.5$, and $SD = 2$. We enter these values in the formula:

$$d = \frac{M - \mu}{SD} = \frac{7.5 - 6.5}{2} = \frac{1}{2} = 0.5$$

We use Table 6.3 (p. 201) to interpret our Cohen's $d = 0.5$ and find that we have a moderate effect size for the campus attended on citation knowledge quiz scores. Thus, our two measures of effect size result in the same interpretation. When calculating Cohen's d, if our sample mean is smaller than our population mean, we will obtain a negative Cohen's d value. Because we use the absolute value to interpret Cohen's d, the sign of the computed value does not matter.

Cohen's d (d): The difference between two means expressed in standard deviation units.

Calculating a Confidence Interval

Another way to look at results is to define the interval of mean differences that we are confident that the difference between the population mean and our sample mean falls within. In other words, the **confidence interval** defines the highest mean difference and the lowest mean difference (and the values in between) we would expect for a particular population mean (μ) and the sample mean (M) we found in our study.

For example, if we use $p < .05$, we are defining the interval of mean differences where we can expect 95% of the time the difference between the population mean (μ) and sample mean would fall. We already have all of the values we need to calculate the confidence interval:

$$[(SD_x)\,(-t_{crit})] + (M - \mu) < (M - \mu) < [(SD_x)\,(+t_{crit})] + (M - \mu)$$

For our study, we computed $SD_x = .4$ (in the denominator of the t test formula) and the mean difference $(M - \mu) = 1.0$ (in the numerator of the t test formula). To determine the 95% confidence interval we need to use our df, which was 24, to find the t_{crit} in Table 7.1 for $p < .05$ for a two-tailed test. Looking at the table, we find, $t_{crit} = 2.064$.

If we substitute the values for our study, we have:

$$[(0.4)\,(-2.064)] + 1.0 < 1.0 < [(0.4)\,(+2.064)] + 1.0$$

After multiplying .4 times 2.064, we find:

$$(-0.8256 + 1.0) < 1.0 < (+0.8256 + 1.0)$$

We subtract and add the quotient to our mean difference of 1.0, and we find:

$$0.1744 < 1.0 < 1.8256$$

We interpret these results as meaning we can be 95% confident that our mean difference of 1.00 represents a population whose mean difference falls between 0.17 and 1.83 (our margin of error). In APA format, this confidence interval would be reported as $(M - \mu) = 1.00$, 95% CI [0.17, 1.83]. The confidence interval does not contain zero (0.00), suggesting that there is a difference between the population mean and sample mean. Combined with the moderate effect size found using eta squared (η^2) and Cohen's d, we have evidence that students from UA represent a different population than the national population of first-year college students. The population mean on the citation knowledge quiz was 6.50, and it does not fall within our confidence interval (or the margin of error) for our sample mean. This suggests that UA's mean of 7.50 on the citation knowledge quiz does not belong to the population whose mean on the quiz is 6.50. Combined with the moderate effect size found using eta squared (η^2) and Cohen's d, we have evidence that students from UA represent a different population than other first-year college students.

USING DATA ANALYSIS PROGRAMS: ONE-SAMPLE *t* TEST

Most of the time, of course, you will analyze your data using some statistical package (SPSS, SAS, etc.). In order to use a statistical package, you will need the raw data (individual scores) from your sample and the population value of the variable measured. In our example, we would create a dataset by entering into the statistical program the individual scores for the 25 UA students who took the citation format quiz. See Chapter 3 if you need a review of guidelines for entering data. You should also follow the guidelines for your specific statistical package. To run our one-sample *t* test in SPSS, we would:

- click on Compare Means and select one-sample *t* test, and

- enter the national average of 6.5 as the "test value."

Figure 7.1 shows the output from such a *t* test. The output from the *t* test will show the number of scores (*N*), mean (*M*), and standard deviation (*SD*) for your measure (quiz scores in our example), and the standard error of the means (*SD*) in one box. A second box will show the *t* value, *df, p* value (significance [Sig.]), difference between your sample mean and the population mean (mean difference), and the 95% confidence interval. The confidence interval indicates the margin of error; and in this case, 95% of the time, the mean difference (between our sample and the population mean) is expected to be between .1758 and 1.8242. Note that the output in Figure 7.1 tells you that the significance (*p*) is based on a two-tailed test; and instead of restricting the *p* value to .10, .05, .025, and .01, statistical packages usually provide an exact *p* value. For example,

FIGURE 7.1

Sample Output From a One-Sample *t* Test for 25 Students Comparing Their Scores on a 10-Item Quiz to the National Mean of 6.5 for College Students

T-Test

One-Sample Statistics

	N	Mean	Std. Deviation	Std. Error Mean
QuizGrade	25	7.5000	1.99682	.39936

One-Sample Test

	Test Value = 6.5					
					95% Confidence Interval of the Difference	
	t	df	Sig. (2-tailed)	Mean Difference	Lower	Upper
QuizGrade	2.504	24	.019	1.00000	.1758	1.8242

instead of showing $p < .05$, the SPSS output in Figure 7.1 shows $p = .019$, and that value should be listed when reporting your results. The difference in p values used in our hand calculation and in SPSS creates a difference in the critical t value used in calculating the confidence interval values, which then results in slightly different confidence interval values. Regardless of whether you hand calculate or use SPSS for your analysis, you will need to compute the effect size using the eta squared (η^2) or the Cohen's d formulas that were provided above.

We also should consider the practical implications of the findings. This does not require any additional computations but only a consideration of the statistics we already computed. The UA quiz grades were higher by 1 point (out of a 10-point quiz). When one considers that 1 point is 10% of the grade on the quiz, this improvement may represent a small but noticeable difference in student adherence to required citation format, which may help students avoid committing plagiarism in their work.

Once we have completed all of the appropriate analyses, we would report the findings in a Results section of a report following APA format. The results reported should include descriptive statistics for our variable, the type of statistical tests conducted, and their outcomes. (Remember to check with your instructor to see which statistics he or she would like you to report in your class. If you are submitting an article to a professional journal, you need to review its manuscript guidelines.) In the Discussion section, we would review our major findings, interpret their meaning, discuss possible implications of our results, and suggest future studies. See Application 7.1 for an example.

TABLE 7.2

Checklist of Information in Results and Discussion Sections

Results

- Descriptive statistics for measure(s) (*M*, *SD*)
- Type of statistical test(s)—e.g., one-sample t test, eta squared (η^2), or Cohen's *d*, confidence interval [lower limit, upper limit]
- Outcome for each test

Discussion

- Review major findings.
- Interpret meaning of findings, including how they fit past research.
- Discuss implications/practical significance of findings.
- Note possible limitations of the study.
- Suggest possible future studies.

Application 7.1

SAMPLE RESULTS AND DISCUSSION SECTIONS FOLLOWING APA FORMAT

Results

UA students scored higher ($M = 7.50$, $SD = 2.00$) on the 10-item citation quiz than the national average for first-year college students ($\mu = 6.50$). A one-sample t test found a significant difference between the two groups, $t(24) = 2.50$, $p = .019$, $\eta^2 = .21$. The effect size was moderate, with 21% of the variability in quiz scores of UA students accounted for by the campus they attended.

OR

UA students scored higher ($M - 7.50$, $SD - 2.00$) on the 10-item citation quiz than the national average for first-year college students ($\mu = 6.50$), resulting in a mean difference of 1.00. The confidence interval for these results was ($M - \mu$) = 1.00, 95% CI [0.17, 1.83], and the effect size was moderate with Cohen's $d = 0.50$.

Discussion

If you reported the t *test and effect size in your results*: First-year UA students scored significantly higher on a citation quiz than the national average for first-year college students.

If you reported the confidence interval and effect size in your results: The confidence interval for the mean difference did not include zero, which would indicate no difference between our sample and the national mean, so we have evidence that the UA students' citation quiz scores were higher than that of the national average for first-year college students. In addition the confidence interval is small, suggesting that the study is an accurate reflection of the difference between the national and sample means.

Regardless of the statistics reported: The findings showed a moderate effect of the campus attended. Although the UA students' quiz mean was only 1 point higher, the difference represents 10% of the material on the quiz. Any noticeable improvement in citation knowledge should be helpful to students, as past studies have found that many do not know about the citation format that is required in order to avoid plagiarism (Belter & du Pré, 2009; Culwin, 2006; Landau et al., 2002). More knowledge about citation format may increase student adherence to required citation format, which may then help students avoid committing plagiarism in their work.

There are a couple of possible explanations for the difference in citation knowledge. UA students may enter college having had more instruction during high school about proper citation techniques, or English classes at UA may address citation format early and in more detail than do other schools across the nation. This study included only a small, nonprobability sample of students at UA who completed the citation quiz midway through their first semester. Any of these factors could have influenced our results. Future studies should examine these possible explanations and address these limitations in order to learn more about how to better prepare students to learn about and use proper citation format.

Practice 7.2

WRITING RESULTS AND DISCUSSION SECTIONS

In a survey of a national sample of millennials, they reported that they spend an average of 20.9% of class time using a digital device for non-class-related tasks (McCoy, 2016). You believe that classes at your institution are much too engaging for students to be so inattentive, and you decide to test your belief. You recruit a sample of 20 students who have a class on Tuesday. You ask students to behave as they normally would in the class. After the class, you ask students how much time they spent on any digital device attending to non-class-related tasks. After converting this time to the percentage of class time, you compare their average of non-class-related activity to the national average. The output below resulted.

One-Sample Statistics				
	N	Mean	Std. Deviation	Std. Error Mean
Digital use	20	.1730	.05713	.01278

One-Sample Test						
	Test Value = .209					
					95% Confidence Interval of the Difference	
	t	*df*	Sig. (2-tailed)	Mean Difference	Lower	Upper
Digital use	−2.818	19	.011	−.03600	−.0627	−.0093

In addition, you compute the effect size and find $\eta^2 = .29$ and $d = 0.63$.

1. Write up a Results section following the format your professor expects (e.g., APA).

2. Write up a Discussion section in which you interpret the results; explain how they fit or do not fit with Kuznekoff and Titsworth's (2013) study (review Application 6.1, p. 181); note limitations of the study or alternative explanations for results; and then suggest future research to address the limitations or examine the possible explanations.

See Appendix A to check your answers.

THE BIG PICTURE:
EXAMINING ONE VARIABLE AT A TIME

Congratulations on making some initial steps into the exciting world of data analysis! We realize that at this point some of you may be feeling more overwhelmed than celebratory. Consequently, let's take a step back and think about the key take-home points of this chapter. First, the one-sample t test and the chi-square goodness of fit are used when you are examining one variable at a time in your sample, rather than looking at relationships between variables. Second, they are both inferential statistics that allow you to determine if the score for that one variable you are examining in your sample is significantly different than a population or expected value. Third, the scale of measurement of the variable determines which test to use (see Figure 7.2). And finally, inferential statistics are one way of making sense of your data, but they are not the only way. When interpreting your results, remember to also consider the magnitude of the difference (the effect size), the confidence interval, and the overall context and meaning of the numbers.

FIGURE 7.2

Decision Tree When Examining One Variable in Your Sample

The purpose of the analysis is to . . .

Examine ONE variable in your dataset

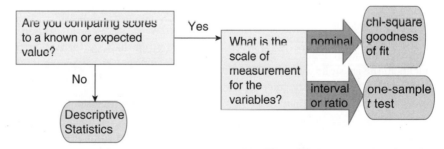

CHAPTER RESOURCES

Key Terms

Define the following terms using your own words. You can check your answers by reviewing the chapter or by comparing them with the definitions in the glossary—but try to define them on your own first.

Chi-square goodness of fit 210

Cohen's d (d) 217

Confidence interval 218

Degrees of freedom (df) 215

Estimated standard error of the
means (SD_x) 213

Eta squared (η^2) 216
One-sample t test 210

Standard error of the means
(σ_x) 213

Do You Understand the Chapter?

Answer these questions on your own, and then review the chapter to check your answers.

1. Name the assumptions that should be met in order to perform a one-sample t test.

2. Give an example of a situation where you would use a one-sample t test.

3. What statistics do you report when you compute a one-sample t test, and what information does each of the statistics provide?

4. What two effect size statistics can be computed with a one-sample t test, and how is each of the statistics interpreted?

5. Why is it important to consider the practical implications of a study analyzed with a one-sample t test?

Practice With Statistics

1. Students in the senior capstone course ($N = 36$) at University Uptight took the Political Science subtest developed by the National Bored Testing Association. The test is a 75-item, multiple-choice test covering all areas of political science. The national norms for the test show a mean of 50. The mean for the students in the capstone was 55, with a standard deviation of 15. Did the students at UU score significantly higher than the national norms?

   a. State your null and alternative hypotheses.

   b. Is this a one- or two-tailed hypothesis? Explain.

   c. Calculate the appropriate statistical test.

   d. Can you reject the null hypothesis? Why or why not?

   e. What is the probability of a Type I error? Type II error?

   f. Write a Results section for your findings. Include the descriptive statistics, type of statistical test and results of the test, and effect size.

   g. Write a Discussion section for your findings. Include the findings, interpretation/explanation/implication of the findings, and possible next studies.

2. According to national surveys by the National Institute of Mental Health, anxiety is one of the most common mental health issues in the United States. You are a social worker working with families living in a high-poverty, high-crime neighborhood; and you decide to study whether anxiety is high for the residents. The Beck Anxiety Inventory (BAI) is a frequently used measure of anxiety for adults and has a lower limit of 19 for moderate anxiety. You recruit a sample of 16 residents who complete the BAI. Their mean on the BAI is 27 ($SD = 16$). Does the

residents' anxiety level differ from moderate anxiety?

a. State your null hypothesis.

b. State a directional *and* a nondirectional alternative hypothesis.

c. Which alternative hypothesis is more appropriate for the problem above? Explain.

d. Calculate the appropriate statistical test.

e. Can you reject the null hypothesis? Why or why not?

f. What is the probability of a Type I error? Type II error?

g. Write a Results section for your findings. Include the descriptive statistics, type of statistical test and results of the test, and effect size.

h. Write a Discussion section for your findings. Include the findings, interpretation/explanation/implication of the findings, and possible next studies.

Practice With SPSS

1. The scores for another sample of 36 University Uptight seniors who took the Political Science subtest described in Practice With Statistics, exercise 1 above, are listed below.

40	68	50	65	39	66
62	50	48	60	54	36
59	42	57	36	41	59
70	52	58	69	55	52
40	52	60	46	52	57
54	48	40	51	63	49

a. Enter the data and compute the appropriate test to determine whether the students at UU scored significantly higher than the national norm of 50.

b. Can you reject the null hypothesis? Why or why not?

c. What is the probability of a Type I error? Type II error?

d. Compute the effect size.

e. Discuss the practical significance of your findings.

f. Write a Results section for your findings. Include the descriptive statistics, type of statistical test and results of the test, and effect size.

g. Write a Discussion section for your findings. Include the findings, interpretation/explanation/implication of the findings, and possible next studies.

2. You decide to sample a larger group of residents in the high-poverty, high-crime neighborhood (from Practice With Statistics, exercise 2) and have them complete the BAI. Their data are below:

15	18	30	45	28
10	34	55	32	20
35	5	25	40	20
40	50	28	48	18
36	46	30	18	51

a. Enter the data and compute the appropriate test to respond to your belief that the residents will score differently than the cutoff norm of 19 for the BAI.

b. Can you support your hypothesis? Why or why not?

c. What is the probability of a Type I error? Type II error?

d. Compute the effect size.

e. Discuss the practical significance of your findings.

f. Write a Results section including all information and in the format required by APA.

g. Write a Discussion section, including all elements required by APA format.

 **edge.sagepub.com/adams2e**

Sharpen your skills with SAGE edge!
SAGE edge for students provides you with tools to help you study. You'll find mobile-friendly eFlashcards and quizzes, as well as videos, web resources, datasets, and links to SAGE journal articles related to this chapter.

Examining Relationships Among Your Variables

CORRELATIONAL DESIGN

8

LEARNING OUTCOMES

In this chapter, you will learn

- The advantages and limits of correlational designs

- How to distinguish between correlational design and correlation as a statistic

- How to compute and interpret the statistics assessing correlations between interval and ratio variables

- How to use a relationship to predict scores of one of the variables in the relationship (regression)

Research can be prompted from an observation a researcher makes or a question she raises because of everyday life events. As a student, you might wonder whether people with particular personality characteristics are more likely to cheat or plagiarize in school. Because studies have found that a large percentage of students anonymously self-report that they have plagiarized or cheated, you could argue that personality is not related to academic integrity. On the other hand, you might argue that students who are more manipulative, cynical, entitled, and likely to engage in different types of misconduct would be more likely to violate academic integrity by cheating or plagiarizing than people who do not possess such characteristics. How could you design a study to investigate whether personality is indeed related to academic dishonesty?

Williams, Nathanson, and Paulhus (2010) designed such a study. They hypothesized that the three constructs (psychopathy, Machiavellianism, narcissism) known as the Dark Triad (Paulhus & Williams, 2002) would be associated with academic dishonesty. Students ($N = 249$) in undergraduate psychology classes completed a take-home packet that included several personality scales and two questions about academic dishonesty. One question asked about turning in work that had been copied from another student, and the second question asked about cheating on tests; both of these questions referred to high school rather than college work in order to elicit honest responses. The results of the study showed that scores on the psychopathy (manipulative, antisocial tendencies, insensitive), Machiavellianism (cynical, drawn to manipulating others), and narcissism (entitled, belief in superiority) inventories were each positively related to the combined responses to the two academic dishonesty items. In other words, they were correlated.

CORRELATIONAL DESIGN

In the study above, the researchers found a significant correlation between certain personality characteristics of college students and self-reported academic dishonesty during high school. What does it mean when we say these variables are correlated? **Correlation** means that we can find a pattern or relationship between variables such that scores on the variables move in an identifiable pattern together. The scores for both variables tend to increase or decrease together, or the scores of one variable tend to increase while the scores of the other variable decrease. Either way, one can identify a pattern between the variables we have measured. In correlation, we examine variables as they already exist. We do not manipulate or control the variables, and we sometimes refer to them as preexisting to denote this fact.

Correlational design is a frequently used type of study in many disciplines and is quite valuable to researchers. **Correlational design** goes beyond the description of a relationship and uses the hypothesis-testing process that we learned about in Chapter 6 to consider whether the relationship we find is significantly different from what we would expect by chance alone. If our finding is significant, this process allows us to generalize beyond our specific sample to the population represented by our sample.

> **Correlation:** A relationship between variables.
>
> **Correlational design:** A type of study that tests the hypothesis that variables are related.

Rationale for Correlational Designs

You may ask why we value correlational studies when they do not control variables and examine only relationships that already exist. There are several reasons why correlational designs are appropriate and may even be the best or only type of design to employ. We discuss these reasons below.

Ethical Issues

We may use a correlational design when a manipulation of variables would be unethical. For example, we might want to study the relationship between accidents and texting while driving. It would be unethical to use an experimental design where we required participants to text while driving to see its impact on accidents. We would not want to encourage such unsafe driving behavior since research has repeatedly found that texting while driving distracts the driver (Drews, Pasupathi, & Strayer, 2008; Farmer, Klauer, McClafferty, & Guo, 2015; Fitch et al., 2013; Strayer, Drews, & Johnston, 2003) or may be related to accident or near-accident frequency (Klauer et al., 2013; National Center for Statistics and Analysis, 2016). Instead of an experimental design, we could ask participants how frequently they text while driving and how many accidents or near-accidents they have had over the past 6 months. (There are other appropriate designs, but correlation is one obvious possibility.)

There are many variables that it would be unethical for us as researchers to study experimentally, even if information about the impact of a variable would be beneficial in helping others or in furthering our knowledge about people and their behavior. You can probably think of several unethical experiments such as the effect of divorce on children's academic performance, domestic violence on women's self-esteem, nutritional deprivation on cognitive agility, death of a pet on aged people's loneliness, and on and on. These are all important variables to study, and correlational designs provide an ethical method to examine relationships among them.

Examining Stable Traits or Characteristics

There are some variables that we are not able to manipulate or control—such as personality, weather, natural disasters, or the outcome of an election. As in the case of variables that we should not manipulate because of ethics, we also want to study many of the variables that we cannot control. Correlational designs provide us with a legitimate method to examine the relationships of these uncontrollable variables with other variables. The study by Williams et al. (2010) (described at the beginning of the chapter), which examined the relationship between personality and academic dishonesty, provides an example of a situation where it is not possible to manipulate a stable personality trait. However, because the researchers were interested in its relationship to a behavior (academic dishonesty), they employed a correlational design.

Pilot Studies

Correlational designs are also employed as pilot studies to see whether an experiment should be conducted. The controls and planning required for an experiment may discourage researchers from testing a hunch or idea without some empirical evidence that their idea has some merit. The results of a correlational study that demonstrates that a relationship exists can then assist the researchers in designing a study that manipulates one of the variables in order to see its impact on the second variable. For instance, researchers may wonder if there are ways to increase grit, or persistence toward goals, and what effects that might have. Before embarking on an experiment, the researchers should first determine what factors correlate with grit. In doing so, they would find some evidence that a low level of grit is correlated with excessive Internet use and spending (Maddi et al., 2013). Conducting additional correlational research to validate these correlations would be a reasonable step before conducting an experiment.

Supplementing Another Design

Correlations are not always the main analysis or purpose of a study. They are used in descriptive studies to see how variables of interest are related. Such studies may include observations, questionnaires, or interviews where the researcher is collecting data about a large number of variables. In addition to examining descriptive statistics, the researcher may also want to analyze the data for relationships among the different variables. For instance, a researcher might survey participants about their views toward political issues (economy, environment, international affairs, etc.) as well as collect information about the participants' age, income, education level, and voting likelihood. In addition to describing the participants' views about specific political issues, the researcher can examine whether the views of the sample are correlated with age, income, education level, or voting likelihood. Correlation can also be a component of an experiment that is examining a causal relationship.

Increased External Validity

Although at first it may seem counterintuitive, an advantage of correlational studies is related to the lack of control in assessing relationships. We do not control the situation or variables but measure behaviors (or attitudes, affect, etc.) as they "naturally" occur. Our findings are more easily generalized to everyday life and thus may have greater external validity than findings from experimental studies in an artificial laboratory environment. For example, although we could ethically study the relationship between texting while driving and accidents by using a simulation in the laboratory, we may not be confident that a simulation of driving and cell phone use represents the reality of driving on roads with other vehicles and distractions or the reality of making or answering a text on the spur of the moment. It would be difficult to mimic the combination of traffic patterns, weather conditions, other distractions on the road (animals, pedestrians, children), or the behaviors of the other drivers. Collecting data about actual texting and accidents is a more feasible study and provides data that is more easily generalized to the reality of daily driving experience.

Assessment of Measurement Reliability and Validity

Finally, correlation is the statistic that we use to assess reliability and validity. Remember the various measures of reliability—test-retest, split-half, interrater/interobserver. In each of these types of reliability, we are comparing the scores on two measures for evidence that they are closely related or show evidence of reliability. The same is true when we are assessing certain types of validity—we are hoping to find that our measure is related to an already established measure (congruent), current behavior (concurrent), or a future behavior (predictive). Or we might hope to find that our measure is not related to a scale assessing a different variable (discriminant). We hope you are able to see from this brief discussion why correlational designs are important in social science research. As you can see in Figure 8.1, correlational studies provide valuable information about relationships between variables, allow us to examine relationships with variables that we cannot or should not study experimentally, and assist in the development or interpretation of experiments. Thus, correlational designs contribute to our understanding of social science concepts and theories and supplement the understanding we gain from other designs.

FIGURE 8.1

Summary of Rationale for Correlational Designs

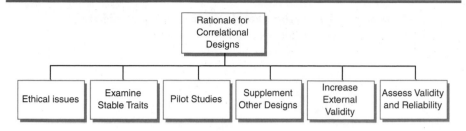

Limitation of Correlational Designs

Although correlation is a valuable design, it is not without limits. Consider the study by Williams et al. (2010) that found a significant correlation between personality and academic dishonesty. Can we conclude on the basis of the findings that personality causes academic dishonesty? Beginning in introductory courses, you have likely learned that correlation does *not* equal causation so you already know that the answer to this question is "no." When the scores on two variables, such as cheating and psychopathy, are related, or in research terminology are correlated, this tells us that the two variables move in a predictable pattern to each other but we cannot assume causality. Causality requires that we can identify which variable occurred first and created a change in a second variable. As you can see, Figure 8.2 depicts an example of the dilemma of identifying the variable that occurred first. In addition, a third variable may be responsible for a relationship. Figure 8.3 provides an example of how a relationship between two variables (spilled milk and presence of a cat) does not equal causation. In this instance, it may be that the dog chased the cat, which then resulted in the split milk. Both of these examples demonstrate why we must always be careful in interpreting correlations between variables. We will discuss how to determine causality in Chapter 9.

Designing Powerful Correlational Designs

You learned in Chapter 6 that power is the ability to correctly reject a false null hypothesis. In a correlational design, you increase the power of your study by careful attention to the validity and reliability of your measures. If possible, it is a good idea to assess the variables in your study with scales or inventories that have already established validity. In the example above, Williams et al. (2010) used scales to measure psychopathy, Machiavellianism, and narcissism that had been validated by earlier research and have been widely used in past studies. They included information about the validity of each measure when they described them in their Method section. Remember that a measurement cannot be valid unless it is reliable. This fact is important because even if a relationship truly exists, it will be difficult to find

FIGURE 8.2

Which Came First?

Correlation does not allow us to tell the order of events and so we cannot make assumptions about what event caused another.

Source: Sandi Coon

FIGURE 8.3

Correlation But Not Causation

Although it is often easy to jump to a conclusion about causality when two events are related, as researchers we must remember that a relationship between two events or scores does not mean there is causality.

Source: Sandi Coon

the relationship between two variables if the measurement of one or both of your variables is unreliable or inconsistent. Obviously, if your measurement technique does not accurately represent a variable (or is not valid), you will have a difficult time determining whether a correlation exists between variables or whether the correlation you find reflects a stable association.

Another factor that can influence our ability to find an existing correlation is the range of scores for the measures being correlated. In order to establish a relationship between two measures, they must each show variability in their scores. When one or both of the measures have a restricted range of scores, it becomes difficult to see how the scores of the two measures move up and down in relationship to one another. Restricted range can be created when either floor or ceiling effects occur. A **ceiling effect** occurs when the highest score of a measure is set too low and the measure does not assess higher levels that exist within the sample. For example, suppose we measure frequency of texting in one hour and we arbitrarily set the highest number of texts as 10. If most of the participants send or receive more than 10 texts each hour, there is in effect a ceiling for the number of texts, which means the measure will not adequately reflect the reality of texting frequency. In contrast, a **floor effect** occurs when a measure does not assess the lowest levels that exist in a sample. In terms of a measure of texting frequency, we would see a floor effect if we began our measure of texting frequency per hour with 10 and many in our sample send fewer than 10 texts in an hour. When the outer limits of a measure (either at the high or low end) are truncated, we cannot see the true variation between two variables, and this decreases our ability to accurately establish a correlation. Either floor or ceiling effects then decrease the power of our study or our ability to see whether a relationship exits.

> **Ceiling effect:** Restricting the upper limit of a measure so that higher levels of a measure are not assessed accurately.
>
> **Floor effect:** Restricting the lower limit of a measure so that lower scores are not assessed accurately.

External validity for a correlation study is also important and is determined by the sampling procedure. Most of the time, correlational studies use a sample of convenience, as in our example at the beginning of the chapter (students taking undergraduate psychology courses). Random sampling is less important in a correlational study than in a descriptive one, such as a survey that has the primary purpose of describing attitudes or behaviors of a much larger population. The primary focus of a correlational study is to learn about consistent relationships among variables, so that measurement validity is more essential to the success of our goal. Although external validity is always a consideration, correlational studies are less concerned with generalizing the findings about a relationship among variables to a large population than

Although correlational studies do not involve the control or manipulation of variables, students of research methods (as well as experienced researchers) should still follow the ethical guidelines for research in general. The study should be carefully designed and use valid and reliable measures in order not to waste the time of participants. Potential participants should be informed about the data that will be collected and should provide their written consent. Frequently, surveys and interviews ask participants to reveal personal information about sensitive topics such as sexual activity or experiences, health status, or criminal or violent activities. Assurances about the participants' anonymity and confidentiality are particularly important in these studies. In addition, the physical and psychological state of participants should be carefully considered, and participants should not be made to feel uncomfortable in providing responses about the particular variables of interest. Although it is reassuring that at least one study (Yeater, Miller, Rinehart, & Nason, 2012) found that participants reported that responding to questions regarding trauma or sex was less troublesome than dealing with daily hassles, researchers should be alert for any signs of distress or concern among participants. In addition, participants should be guaranteed anonymity and assured that data will be reported in aggregate form so that their individual responses or behaviors will not be identified in any reports or articles.

with finding a stable relationship. When external validity is important, the researcher can examine the correlation using different groups as a way to establish the external validity of the relationship.

BASIC STATISTICS TO EVALUATE CORRELATIONAL RESEARCH

Relationships can be assessed using different statistics; the specific statistic is determined by the scale of measurement used for the variables rather than the type of research design. You learned earlier that the scale of measurement is important in determining the type of statistic you can compute—here is another application of that requirement. In this chapter, we will introduce you to correlational analyses that involve at least one interval or ratio variable, where there is no manipulation of either variable. Other correlation analyses involve two nominal or two ordinal variables, and they are described in Chapter 13.

It is important that you distinguish between correlation as a design, which we have covered thus far in this chapter, and correlation as a statistic, which we will cover in the rest of this chapter. Some correlational designs are analyzed with a correlation statistic, and other correlational designs are analyzed using different statistics that you will learn about later. In later chapters, we will discuss how to analyze correlational designs using analyses other than correlational statistics. (We know this is confusing, but try to keep designs and statistics separate.)

Name the four scales of measurement and give an example of each scale.

If you named nominal, ordinal, interval, and ratio as the scales, you are correct. Examples of the four scales might include (in the same order) type of pet, rankings of restaurants from most to least expensive, a 25-item scale assessing joyfulness, and time to complete reading this chapter. Your examples surely will vary from these, but hopefully you are reminded of the criteria for each scale.

Relationship Between Two Interval or Ratio Variables

The **Pearson product-moment correlation coefficient**, commonly referred to as a **Pearson's *r***, is the statistical test used to determine whether a **linear relationship** exists between two variables. The statistic is named after the English mathematician Karl Pearson, who developed it. The test requires that each of the two variables (referred to as *X* and *Y*) is measured using an interval or ratio scale.

A Pearson's *r* provides two pieces of information about the correlation:

- The direction (positive or negative) of the relationship
- The strength or magnitude of the relationship

> **Pearson's *r* (Pearson product-moment correlation coefficient):** Statistic used to describe a linear relationship between two interval/ratio measures; describes the direction (positive or negative) and strength (between ±1.0) of the relationship.
>
> **Linear relationship:** A relationship between two variables, defined by their moving in a single direction together.

The sign (+ or −) in front of the correlation designates the direction of the relationship. A **positive correlation** occurs when the scores for the two measures move in the same direction (increase or decrease) together, such as might happen in relating minutes of study and scores on a quiz. As students spend more time studying, their scores on a quiz increase. Or if they spend less time studying, their scores decrease. A **negative correlation** occurs when the scores for the two measures move in opposite directions and as one score increases, the other score decreases. The relationship between anxiety and happiness suggests a negative correlation. As anxiety increases, happiness would be expected to decrease (or as happiness increases, anxiety decreases).

> **Positive correlation:** A relationship where scores on two variables move in the same direction (both either increase or decrease).
>
> **Negative correlation:** A relationship where scores on two variables move in opposite directions (one increases while the other decreases).

The value of Pearson's r ranges from +1.0 to −1.0. The closer the r is to the absolute value of 1.0 (symbolized as |1.0|), the stronger the relationship. This means that the strength of the relationship is not related to its direction (positive or negative), so that $r = -.85$ is identical in magnitude to $r = .85$. Although these relationships are equally strong (both are .85), the direction of the relationships is opposite; the first correlation ($r = -.85$) implies that scores in one variable increase as the other scores decrease, and the second one ($r = .85$) implies that scores in the two variables move in the same direction. When there is no relationship between the two variables, r is zero ($r = 0.0$) or close to zero, while a perfect relationship is described by either plus or minus 1.0 ($r = \pm 1.0$). In a perfect correlation, for every unit of change in the first measure, the second measure changes a specific amount. Take the example of students studying for a quiz. If there was a perfect relationship between studying and quiz scores, for every minute that students studied, they might earn an additional 2 points on the quiz. In this case, in order to earn a score of 80, they would have to study 40 minutes. If they studied 10 more minutes (a total of 50 minutes) they could earn a perfect 100 on the quiz. Wouldn't it be nice if relationships were so predictable? However, we are working in the social sciences, where many variables are operating on a quiz score or whatever variable we are examining, so that perfect correlations do not exist. Researchers are happy to find a correlation of .50 ($r = .50$), which is considered a strong correlation.

Variables that affect the strength of the relationship can include the sample size (it is more difficult to find a correlation with smaller samples because we do not have as many scores to compare and a few outliers can dramatically reduce the correlation), a restricted range of scores (as we discussed at the beginning of the chapter), the sensitivity or validity of our measures, the environment in which data are collected, and on and on. Because we do not control the environment and we are measuring already existing variables, there is much variability in the variables not associated with their relationship to each other. In general, we consider $r = \pm .50$ to be a strong correlation, $r = \pm .30$ to be a moderate correlation, and $r = \pm .20$ or below to be a weak correlation. Table 8.1 provides a summary of these ranges. Unlike with criterion levels, where we have clear cutoff points, these numbers are meant to be guidelines, and there is some flexibility in how they are applied. For example, it is acceptable to refer to a correlation of .27 as moderate.

TABLE 8.1

Guidelines for the Approximate Strength of a Correlation

Absolute Value	Description
$r \geq .50$	Strong
$.30 \leq r < .50$	Moderate
$r \leq .20$	Weak

Before we compute Pearson's r, it is a good idea to graph the relationship between the two variables we want to correlate. Such a graph is called a

scatterplot (or **scattergram**). To graph a relationship, each participant in a sample must have a pair of scores, one for the X variable and one for the Y variable. It does not matter which of our variables is the X variable and which is the Y variable as long as the designation is consistent. Each point on our graph will then represent 2 scores, X and Y. The X variable is measured on the x-axis and the Y scores are measured on the y-axis.

> **Scatterplot (or scattergram):** A graph of the data points created by participant scores on two measures; each data point represents a score on the X variable and a score on the Y variable.

We can then examine the pattern among the points on our graph. We want to see if the scores for X and Y represent a positive or negative relationship. A positive relationship occurs when the scores of X move in the same direction (increase or decrease) as the scores of Y. A negative relationship occurs when the scores of X move in the opposite direction as the scores in Y, so as X scores increase, Y scores decrease, or vice versa. We also examine the scatterplot to see how strong the relationship between the two variables is. In general, the clearer the pattern among the data points, the stronger the relationship. The strength is shown by how closely the points lie in a straight line. However, if a horizontal line is suggested by the points, there is no relationship, as it means that the values of the Y variable do not change while the values on the X variable do. Thus, the scores do not vary in the same pattern.

Figure 8.4 depicts different types of relationships you could find in a scatterplot. Figure 8.4a shows a positive relationship where as the X scores increase, so do the Y scores—such as might happen in relating minutes of study and scores on a quiz. Although the points do not lie totally along a straight line, one can see a linear pattern and imagine a straight line dissecting the points starting at the lower left corner of the graph and moving up toward the upper right corner of the graph.

Figure 8.4b shows a negative relationship where as the X scores increase, the Y scores decrease, such as might occur when relating ratings of anxiety and happiness. In this graph, the points are more dispersed, suggesting a weaker relationship than the one depicted in 8.4a. The points show movement from the upper left corner of the graph to the lower right corner.

Figure 8.4c shows a scatterplot that occurs when there is almost no relationship between the X and Y scores. There appears to be no pattern among the points in the graph—rather, the points are scattered all over the graph.

Figure 8.4d is a scatterplot of a perfect correlation or the strongest possible relationship. Notice that all of the data points lie on a straight line. Remember that this type of correlation is theoretical in the social sciences because the variables of interest in our area are not so perfectly aligned.

Relationships can also be nonlinear or curvilinear. In these cases, the points on a scatter plot would go up and down (inverted U-shaped) or down and then up (U-shaped). The classic example of an inverted U-shaped relationship (see Figure 8.4e) is the Yerkes-Dodson Law, which describes the relationship between arousal and performance. When we are not motivated (aroused) or have very little motivation, our performance is often minimal. As our arousal/motivation increases, so does our performance until some point at which our arousal becomes debilitating and our performance drops off. More sophisticated statistics

FIGURE 8.4
Types of Relationships

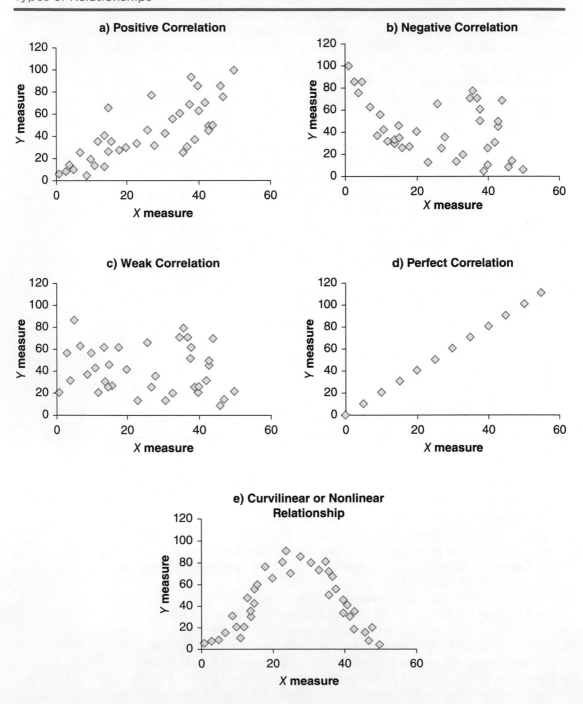

Practice 8.1

TYPES OF RELATIONSHIPS

1. Give examples of the following kinds of relationships. Do not use examples already provided in the text or by your professor.

    *   positive relationship

    *   negative relationship

    *   two variables that you think are not related (no relationship)

2. A study examined the relationship of job satisfaction to both supervisor ratings and to sick days taken. Suppose the data showed the following scatterplot for each of the relationships.

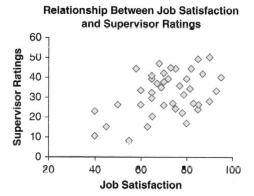

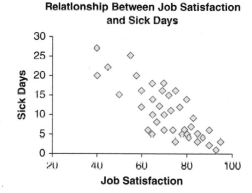

a. Which relationship is positive? Which is negative?

b. Which relationship appears to be stronger?

c. How might you interpret these findings?

See Appendix A to check your answers.

(than Pearson's r) are used to analyze curvilinear relationships. We will consider only linear relationships in this text, and that is the more common relationship examined in psychology.

FORMULAS and CALCULATIONS: Pearson's r

The computation of the Pearson's r is best understood by first considering standard scores. Remember from Chapter 5 that z scores are standard scores that allow us to compare scores from different distributions. z scores designate the number of standard deviations a score is from the mean of its distribution. The distribution is normal and described by ±3 z scores. For every z distribution, $M_z = 0$, $SD_z = 1$. A z score of +1.6 then means that its raw score equivalent is 1.6 SDs above the M of the frequency distribution it belongs to. Our definitional formula for the Pearson correlation coefficient uses z scores and is:

$$r = \frac{\Sigma(z_x z_y)}{N - 1}$$

This formula shows that we:

- translate each X score in our sample to a z_x score and each Y score to a z_y score, then

- multiply each pair of scores together $(z_x z_y)$, then

- add all of the products together $[\Sigma(z_x z_y)]$, then

- divide by the number of pairs of scores minus one $(N - 1)$. (In the case of correlation, $N =$ the number of pairs of scores rather than the frequency of individual scores [which it did for z scores].)

The product of each pair of z scores $(z_x z_y)$ may be positive or negative, depending on whether the raw score for each X or Y was greater or less than the M for its distribution. Scores below the M will have a negative z score, and scores above the M will have a positive z score. The product represents the deviation of a particular pair from the mean; we then add the deviation products for all pairs of scores and divide by the number of pairs. Thus, a correlation represents the average relationship of the pairs of scores to the mean of the distribution (which in the case of z scores is zero).

Pearson's r will vary between plus and minus 1.0 (±1.0). If you obtain a value outside of this range, you will know that you made a mistake, and you should redo your calculations. The closer the r you compute is to the absolute value of 1.0, the stronger the relationship. The sign of the correlation will tell you whether the relationship between the variables is positive or negative.

To make all of this description about relationships and computing correlation statistics more concrete and understandable, let's examine a specific study. Suppose we are interested in whether the verbal ability of students at our institution is related to willingness to cheat. Williams et al. (2010) found that verbal ability was negatively related to a behavioral measure of cheating. In other words, lower verbal ability was associated with more cheating and higher verbal ability with less cheating. Suppose we are interested in reducing cheating before it happens and want to study the willingness to cheat rather than actual cheating. Because we will measure two variables (verbal ability and willingness to cheat) as they currently exist, without manipulating any variables, we are conducting a correlational study. Suppose we believe that lower verbal ability will be negatively related to willingness to cheat or as verbal ability increases, willingness to cheat will decrease. We might express our null and alternative hypotheses as below:

H_0: Verbal ability and willingness to cheat will not be related.

H_a: Verbal ability will be negatively related to willingness to cheat.

Or we could state the formulas in numerical terms:

$$H_0: r = 0$$

$$H_a: r \neq 0$$

REVIEW OF KEY CONCEPTS: HYPOTHESIS TESTING

Can you name the steps in the hypothesis-testing process?

Can you distinguish one- and two-tailed tests in terms of what they imply about the region of rejection?

When do you reject the null hypothesis and support the alternative hypothesis?

a. In your answer, you should include stating null and alternative hypotheses (based, of course, on a review of past research that leads you to predictions for your variables), determining the type of alternative hypothesis (directional or nondirectional) and criterion level, collecting the data, computing the appropriate statistic, and deciding on the basis of your findings whether you can reject your null hypothesis and support your alternative hypothesis. If you have trouble remembering all these steps, a review of the chart in Practice 6.3 in Chapter 6 might help you.

b. You are correct if you said a one-tailed test is associated with a directional hypothesis and has all of its region of rejection on one end of the sampling distribution, while a two-tailed test is associated with a nondirectional hypothesis and has its region of rejection equally divided on both tails of the distribution. Because the region of rejection for a two-tailed test is split on each end of the distribution, it is harder to reject the null hypothesis and thus it is the more conservative test.

c. You reject the null hypothesis when your computed statistic is greater than the critical value of the statistic. Statisticians have computed the critical values that determine where $p < .05$ and $< .01$ for both one- and two-tailed tests; the critical values for various statistical tests are found in tables in Appendix C in our text.

Following the steps for hypothesis testing, we now need to collect our data. From earlier in the chapter, you know that we need to find valid measures of our variables that will demonstrate a range of scores. Assume that we find a valid measure of verbal ability that ranges from 25 to 100, with higher scores reflecting higher ability and a measure of willingness to cheat that ranges from 10 to 50, with higher scores reflecting greater willingness. We decide to designate verbal ability as our X variable and willingness to cheat as our Y variable. Each student we survey will complete two different scales, one assessing verbal ability and one assessing willingness to cheat. Suppose we survey 20 students and obtain the scores in Table 8.2.

TABLE 8.2

Example Scores for the Calculation of a Pearson Correlation

Student	Verbal Ability (X)	Willingness to Cheat (Y)
1	25	48
2	30	40
3	35	36
4	65	24
5	67	32
6	56	46
7	68	27
8	69	42
9	75	28
10	42	38
11	73	35
12	76	40
13	79	41
14	81	20
15	55	36
16	50	29
17	85	30
18	89	25
19	92	11
20	95	15

Before computing a Pearson's *r*, we should first graph the data to see if we can discern the direction and strength of the relationship between verbal ability and willingness to cheat. Using verbal ability as the *X* variable and willingness to cheat as the *Y* variable, you would plot each (*X*,*Y*) pair on a graph to get a scatterplot of the data as shown in Figure 8.5. The graph shows a clear pattern of data points moving from left top of the graph to the right bottom of the graph. This pattern shows a negative linear relationship, because as scores for verbal ability increase willingness to cheat scores decrease. In addition, the relationship between the two variables appears to be fairly strong as the pattern is fairly easy to see with the data points coalescing around a straight line.

Next we compute a Pearson's *r* for the data, using the formula:

$$r = \frac{\Sigma(z_x z_y)}{N-1}$$

FIGURE 8.5

Student Scores on Verbal Ability and Willingness to Cheat Scales

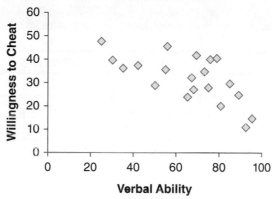
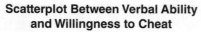

We can ease this process by adding columns to our original data table that match the different aspects of the formula as shown below. After the data, the fourth column lists the z score for each verbal ability score; the fifth column lists the z score for each willingness to cheat score; and the final column is the cross product of the z scores for the two variables $(z_x z_y)$. We have also computed the sum of the cross products $\Sigma(z_x z_y)$ at the bottom of the last column. (See Table 8.3.)

We are now ready to enter the values from the table into the Pearson's r formula. We also need N, which is equal to the number of pairs of scores, or 20 in the case of our example.

$$r = \frac{\Sigma(z_x z_y)}{N-1} = \frac{-12.50}{19} = -.6579$$

Rounding to the nearest hundredth, our Pearson's $r = -.66$, which we can interpret as a strong negative correlation between verbal ability and willingness to cheat (see Table 8.1). But we also want to know whether the correlation is significantly different from what we would obtain by chance alone for this sample size. To do this, we use a table of critical Pearson's r values from Appendix C.5, just as we used a table of critical t values for the one-sample t test in Chapter 7. An excerpt from Appendix C.5 can be found in Table 8.4.

To find the critical value, which our calculated/obtained Pearson's r must equal or exceed, we look at the df on the far left-hand column and read across the top of the chart to the criterion level and type of test (one- or two-tailed) we want to consider. Remember that generally we use a two-tailed test because it is more conservative and

TABLE 8.3

Table of Sample Values to Compute Pearson's r

Student	Verbal Ability X	Willingness to Cheat Y	z score for Verbal Ability (z_x)	z score for Willingness to Cheat (z_y)	$z_x z_y$
1	25	48	–1.9629	1.5940	–3.1289
2	30	40	–1.7197	0.7895	–1.3576
3	35	36	–1.4764	0.3872	–0.5717
4	65	24	–0.0170	–0.8196	0.0140
5	67	32	0.0803	–0.0151	–0.0012
6	56	46	–0.4549	1.3929	–0.6336
7	68	27	0.1289	–0.5179	–0.0668
8	69	42	0.1776	0.9906	0.1759
9	75	28	0.4695	–0.4174	–0.1959
10	42	38	–1.1359	0.5883	–0.6683
11	73	35	0.3722	0.2866	0.1067
12	76	40	0.5181	0.7895	0.4090
13	79	41	0.6640	0.8900	0.5910
14	81	20	0.7613	–1.2219	–0.9303
15	55	36	–0.5035	0.3872	–0.1950
16	50	29	–0.7467	–0.3168	0.2366
17	85	30	0.9559	–0.2162	–0.2067
18	89	25	1.1505	–0.7191	–0.8273
19	92	11	1.2965	–2.1270	–2.7576
20	95	15	1.4424	–1.7248	–2.4878
					$\sum(z_x z_y) = -12.50$

results in a lower chance of making a Type I error. In this case, we will use $p < .05$ and the more conservative two-tailed test.

The df for the Pearson's r is equal to $(N-2)$, so for our example we move down the far left column to 18 ($N-2 = 20 - 2 = 18$). Moving across from 18 df to the column for .05 for a two-tailed test, we find that the critical r value in this case is .4438. Our $r = -.66$, and it is greater than the critical value of r in the table. Note that in comparing the obtained r value to the critical r value in the table, we consider the absolute value of the obtained r value, which means for the time being we ignore the sign in front of our r.

TABLE 8.4

Excerpt of Table From Appendix C.5 for Critical Values for Pearson's Correlation Coefficient (*r*)

	One-tailed	.10	.05	.025	.01	.005
df	Two-tailed	.20	.10	.05	.02	.01
1		.9511	.9877	.9969	.9995	9999
2		.8000	.9000	.9500	.9800	.9900
16		.3170	.4000	.4683	.5425	.5897
17		.3077	.3887	.4555	.5285	.5751
18		.2992	.3783	.4438	.5155	.5614
19		.2914	.3687	.4329	.5034	.5487
20		.2841	.3598	.4227	.4921	.5363
21		.2774	.3515	.4132	.4815	.5256
22		.2711	.3438	.4044	.4716	.5151
23		.2653	.3365	.3961	.4622	.5052
24		.2598	.3297	.3882	.4534	.4950

Thus, we can reject our null hypothesis and support our alternative hypothesis that there is a significant negative hypothesis between verbal ability and willingness to cheat. Because we rejected the H_0 using the .05 criterion level, there is less than a 5% chance that we have made a Type I error.

Although the relationship is statistically significant and strong, it does *not* mean that having lower verbal ability *causes* people to be willing to cheat or that everyone with low verbal ability will cheat. We may stop with the descriptive information this correlation provides. However, we might decide to explore the topic further by conducting an experiment. Research has linked texting on cell phones with literacy (see Application 8.1), so we might try to temporarily decrease participants' verbal skills by having them text on a phone and then seeing if that increases their willingness to cheat. Or we may decide to explore the relationship of verbal ability to willingness to cheat by surveying people about why they cheat . . . perhaps we will find that they do not understand assignments or material and feel that cheating is the only way to get a good grade. A later experiment may then work to compare the impact of assignments that are easily understood versus those that are more difficult to understand on willingness to cheat.

Application 8.1

A STUDY EXAMINING THE RELATIONSHIP BETWEEN TEXTING AND LITERACY

Following many claims in the media that the frequent use of texting abbreviations ("textese") decreased children's and young adult's reading and writing skills, Drouin (2011) investigated whether there were negative relationships between literacy and the frequency of the texting. The participants were college students in an introductory psychology class. The students reported on their frequency of texting using a 6-point scale ranging from *never* to *very frequently*. The students also completed tests that assessed reading accuracy and speed, and spelling accuracy as measures of literacy. The relationships between all of the variables were then examined. The frequency of texting was positively correlated to spelling accuracy ($r = .29$, $p < .01$) and reading speed ($r = .24$, $p < .01$) but showed no relationship to reading accuracy ($r = .09$). In contrast to the hypothesis, two aspects of literacy (spelling accuracy and reading speed) were higher (and not lower as the hypothesis predicted) the more frequently the students reported texting. These results (which only partially summarize the scope of the study) do not support the media claims that texting is related to lower literacy levels.

Practice 8.2

EVALUATING CORRELATIONS

A researcher is interested in the relationship between the time (measured in minutes) spent exercising per week and scores on a life satisfaction scale that ranges from 10 to 70, with higher scores signifying more satisfaction. She collects data from 25 students and computes a Pearson correlation coefficient, and finds $r = .53$.

a. State a null and a directional alternative hypothesis for her study.

b. What is the *df* for this study?

c. Can the researcher reject the null hypothesis at the $p < .05$ if she uses a two-tailed test? (Use Table 8.4 to first determine the critical *r* value that the obtained *r* must exceed.) Explain your answer.

d. Can the researcher reject the null hypothesis at the $p < .01$ if she uses a two-tailed test? (Use Table 8.4 to determine the critical *r* value for this example.) Explain your answer.

See Appendix A to check your answers.

Relationship Between a Dichotomous Variable and an Interval/Ratio Variable

We often want to assess the relationship when one of the variables is a **dichotomous variable,** meaning the variable has two levels or groups, and the other variable is on an interval or ratio scale. Examples of dichotomous variables include registered to vote and not registered to vote, owns a home and does not own a home, and passed the test or did not pass the test. We can also recode an interval or ratio variable to a dichotomous one, such as when we divide students' grade point averages (a ratio scale) to 2.0 or higher ("in good academic standing") and 1.99 or lower ("not in good standing"). The statistic we employ to assess the relationship between a dichotomous variable and interval/ratio variable is called the **point-biserial correlation coefficient** (r_{pb}). It is interpreted similarly to Pearson's r in that it can tell us whether a relationship is positive or negative; the value varies between plus and minus one; and the closer the absolute value of r_{pb} is to 1.0, the stronger the relationship. Conversely, values close to zero (0.0) signify that no relationship exists between the two variables.

> **Dichotomous variable:** A nominal variable that has two levels or groups.
>
> **Point-biserial correlation coefficient (r_{pb}):** Describes the relationship between a dichotomous variable and an interval/ratio variable; interpreted similarly to a Pearson correlation coefficient.

Formulas and Calculations: Point Biserial r

When computing r_{pb}, the dichotomous variable is generally considered the X variable and the interval/ratio variable is the Y variable. Point-biserial correlation is computed using the formula:

$$r_{pb} = \frac{M_p - M_q}{SD_t} \sqrt{pq}$$

where:

the dichotomous variable is coded as 1 and 2;

the sample is divided into 2 groups based on whether $X = 1$ or $X = 2$ on the dichotomous variable;

M_p = the mean on the interval/ratio variable for the group that is coded as 1;

M_q = the mean on the interval/ratio variable for the group that is coded as 2;

SD_t = the standard deviation for the total sample on the interval/ratio variable;

p = the proportion of the sample that has a value of 1 for the dichotomous variable;

q = the proportion of the sample that has a value of 2 for the dichotomous variable;

$q = 1 - p$ because p + q includes the entire sample, which equals 100% or 1.00.

Suppose we have a sample of 25 people who provide the amount they contributed last month to their IRA (individual retirement account) and check off whether or not they have earned a college degree.

Let's assume:

a. having a college degree is coded as 1, and not having a college degree is coded as 2;

b. 15 people have a college degree, while 10 people do not;

c. the mean contribution to an IRA for those with a college degree was $100 or $M_p = 100$;

d. the mean contribution to an IRA for those who have not earned a college degree was $85 or $M_q = 85$; and

e. the standard deviation for everyone's IRA contribution was $25 or $s_t = 25$.

We translate these data into p = the proportion of the sample that was coded as 1 (have a college degree) or $15/25 = .60$, and q = the proportion that was coded as 2 (do not have a college degree home) or $10/25 = .40$.

Using our formula, we have:

$$r_{pb} = \frac{M_p - M_q}{SD_t}\sqrt{pq} = \frac{100 - 85}{25}\sqrt{.60(.40)}$$

$$\frac{15}{25}\sqrt{24} = .60(.49) = +.29$$

Application 8.2

AN EXAMPLE OF THE USE OF POINT-BISERIAL CORRELATION

Anderson and Fuller (2010) examined the use of lyrical music on the reading scores of seventh and eighth graders. Students completed parallel forms of a reading test on consecutive days while listening or not listening to music. The conditions were randomly ordered, so half of the students heard music and then no music while completing the reading tests, and the other half participated in the conditions in reverse order. The music had been previously rated as liked by this age group. Students also rated their preferences for studying while listening to music. Although females showed a greater decline ($M = -5.01$) than males ($M = -3.20$) in their reading scores while listening to music than in the no music condition, the females had a significantly higher preference than males for listening to music while studying ($r_{pb} = .28$, $p < .001$). The authors suggest that teachers should be aware that females in the seventh and eighth grades may desire to study in conditions that decrease their ability to read.

Practice 8.3

SELECTING THE APPROPRIATE STATISTIC

Should you use a Pearson's *r* or a point-biserial *r* to help answer each of the following questions?

1. Is monthly income related to time spent weekly on leisure activities?

2. Is view of global warming (human caused, not human caused) related to one's years of education?

3. Is health status (assessed on a 25-point scale) predicted by one's weight?

4. Is grit (measured by a scale ranging from 8–40) related to positive affect (measured by a PANAS subscale ranging from 10–50)?

5. Does having children versus not having children relate to health status (assessed on a 25-point scale)

See Appendix A to check your answers.

Our results show that there is a positive relationship (r_{pb} = .29) between our sample's monthly IRA contribution and education that is close to moderate strength (see Table 8.1). We use the table for critical values of Pearson correlation coefficient (see Table 8.4) to determine whether our correlation is significantly different from what we would obtain by chance. We again use *df* = (# of pairs − 2) or 25 − 2 = 23 and a two-tailed test. The critical correlation value listed in Table 8.4 is .3961. Our value of +.29 is less than that, so we did not find a significant correlation. We will then retain our null hypothesis that there is no relationship between having a college degree and the amount of one's monthly contribution to a retirement account.

USING DATA ANALYSIS PROGRAMS: PEARSON'S *r* AND POINT-BISERIAL *r*

As discussed in previous chapters, there are multiple statistical packages available to compute statistics, and researchers almost always use one of these packages to analyze their data. The example below uses SPSS. The overall data entry and output will be similar, whatever software package you use. And of course, the statistics that result for the same data will be identical, even if the output is presented in slightly different formats.

Pearson's *r*

When computing Pearson's *r* you will have pairs of scores for each participant in the sample—one score for each *X* variable and one score for each *Y* variable. When entering data, you should consider each pair of *X* and *Y* values together, and therefore should enter them in the same row. Suppose you are interested in the relationship of grit and sense of purpose. A recent study found that these traits were significantly related ($r = .44$) in a sample of undergraduates (Hill et al., 2016), but you wonder whether the same relationship would be found for employees in minimum wage jobs. A local company allows you to ask for volunteers, and 20 employees earning minimum wage agree to participate in your study. The grit scale consists of 10 items; scores can range from 0 to 40, with higher scores representing greater grit. The sense of purpose scale consists of 15 items; scores on this scale range from 15 to 105, with higher scores representing a higher sense of purpose. Table 8.5 depicts the data from this study.

In analyzing our relationship using a statistical package, we follow the same process and obtain the same information we did when we hand calculated the statistics. We first request a scatterplot of the data; in SPSS the graph would look like the graph in Figure 8.6 if we defined X as grit and Y as sense of purpose. We can see that we have a fairly strong positive correlation; and as grit scores increase, so do sense of purpose scores.

TABLE 8.5

Sample Dataset to Compute Pearson's *r*

Student	Grit *X*	Sense of Purpose *Y*
1	4	16
2	5	20
3	6	26
4	8	18
5	10	29
6	15	25
7	18	32
8	20	36
9	22	24
10	23	16
11	24	27
12	30	34
13	33	40
14	38	41
15	28	37
16	36	44
17	26	39
18	32	41
19	29	50
20	30	48

FIGURE 8.6

Scatterplot Using SPSS

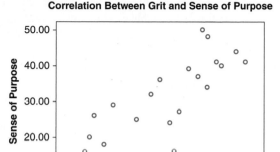

Correlation Between Grit and Sense of Purpose

After getting some of idea of the direction and strength of the relationship from viewing the graph, we then request a Pearson's *r*. The output from SPSS is shown below in Figure 8.7

The output eliminates the need to refer to the Table of Critical Pearson's *r* values. You learn that not only is your correlation significant at the .05 criterion level but you get a more exact *p* value of .000. (APA format now requires that we use the specific *p* value provided by a statistical package rather than the more general .05 or .01 levels. When *p* = .000, you cite *p* < .001 rather than the value provided by the statistical package.) The output also verifies that we have 20 pairs of scores.

FIGURE 8.7

SPSS Output for Pearson's *r*

Correlations		Grit	Sense of Purpose
Grit	Pearson Correlation	1	.776**
	Sig. (2-tailed)		.000
	N	20	20
Sense of Purpose	Pearson Correlation	.776**	1
	Sig. (2-tailed)	.000	
	N	20	20

**. Correlation is significant at the 0.01 level (2-tailed).

Looking at the Pearson's *r* Table from SPSS, you find that the correlation between grit and sense of purpose for your sample is stronger than the one found by Hill et al. (2016).

In addition to the Pearson's *r* value; the *p* value (.000) and *N*(20) are also shown in the Correlation table.

Note that the correlation information is repeated so that you need only read the first three lines of the table.

Point-Biserial *r*

The data entry for point-biserial correlation is the same as that for the Pearson's *r*. Pairs of data are entered in two columns. The primary difference is that one variable is dichotomous and each value for that variable can be only a 1 or 2 (or any other pair of scores such as 0, 1). It does not make sense to request a scatterplot, as the *X* variable will show only 2 values, and so data points will stack up on one another. In SPSS, the same correlation command is used for Pearson's *r* and r_{pb} and results in the same correlation output you just saw for the Pearson's *r*.

Suppose we are examining the correlation between relationship status (in a relationship, not in a relationship) and the amount of time (in hours) spent on Facebook yesterday. We ask the first 20 people we see on campus and find the following, as shown in Table 8.6.

The data would be entered in pairs so that each participant's response to "relationship status" and "time on Facebook" would be entered in different columns on the same row. Note that in this case, we coded 1 = in a relationship and 2 = not in a relationship

TABLE 8.6

Sample Dataset to Compute a Point-Biserial Correlation

Relationship Status*	Time on Facebook
1	0
1	1.1
1	0.6
1	0
2	2.8
2	5.0
2	2.5
2	0
2	3.0
2	1.8
1	2.2
1	0
1	1.0
1	2.4
2	0.5
2	1.6
2	1.0
2	2.1
2	0.75
2	1.5

*1 = in a relationship; 2 = not in a relationship

for responses to our dichotomous variable. The output for r_{pb} is identical to that for the Pearson's r as shown in Figure 8.8.

The output below shows that $r_{pb} = .38$, and we interpret the correlation as we would a Pearson's r. Although the findings show a low-moderate positive relationship between being in a relationship and time spent on Facebook the previous day, the relationship is not significant ($p = .10$) and we must retain the H_0 that there is no correlation between relationship status and time on Facebook. If we had predicted a positive relationship and obtained these findings, we might decide to collect data from more people since the correlation is in the direction we predicted; and even with such a small sample, the results are not so far away from achieving significance. Even if we had found a significant relationship, we would not compute a regression equation because we do not meet the assumption of having interval/ratio variables. The point-biserial correlation is usually part of a larger analysis and so would be reported in a Results section along with the primary analysis.

FIGURE 8.8

SPSS Output for Point-Biserial r

Correlations

		In a Relationship	Time on Facebook
In a Relationship	Pearson Correlation	1	.380
	Sig. (2-tailed)		.098
	N	20	20
Time on Facebook	Pearson Correlation	.380	1
	Sig. (2-tailed)	.098	
	N	20	20

Ethics Tip: Interpreting Correlations

The media often reports correlations between variables ("Children who live in poverty are more likely to fail in school" or "Children who live in wealthier homes are more likely to graduate from high school."). Sometimes the reports then discuss findings as if they are causal, such as the suggestion that children are doomed to lower performance in school if their parents do not make a lot of money. The public does not always make the distinction between correlation and causation, and it is our responsibility as social science researchers to make this distinction clear in all of our reports (verbal and in writing). You should always be careful to note the limitations of a correlation, even if it is a strong one.

REGRESSION

Linear Regression

If we find a significant relationship using Pearson's r, then we can compute a **regression equation** that allows us to predict any Y from a given X. **Linear regression** is appropriate when we have two interval or ratio measures and a significant Pearson's r. Remember that a significant relationship means that we know how X and Y scores vary together. Without a significant relationship, the best estimate of any score in a distribution is the mean (the most representative score of the distribution); but knowing there is a significant relationship between two variables (X and Y) means that we can more closely estimate a value of Y if we know the value of X. The regression equation provides the formula for the line of best fit for the data points in our scatterplot. It shows the straight line that results in the least amount of error in predicting Y from any X value. The X value we use to predict is sometimes called the **predictor variable**, and the Y value we predict is sometimes called the **criterion variable** or **Y predicted**. Y' is the symbol for the Y predicted value, given a particular X value. Each predicted Y score (Y') will fall on the **line of best fit**. Most actual Y values from our sample do not fall exactly on the line; but as the correlation between two variables (X and Y) increases, the predicted Y values (Y') come closer to the line.

Think about the scatterplot in Figure 8.4d of the perfect correlation ($r = 1.0$), where all the points lie on a straight line. If the computed r is very weak, then we will have a large amount of error in our predicted Y values; or to state it differently, there will be a large difference between actual Y values and predicted Y values. In such a case, it does not make sense to compute the regression equation or line of best fit. But if r is strong, then Y' will come close to the actual Y value associated with an X value. This is why we generally compute a regression equation only if our r is significant. Once we know that we have a significant correlation, we can determine the line of best fit for our data points and make predictions of Y from any X value.

The line of best fit described by the regression equation passes through (close to) the means of Y for any X value. For any X value, there can be several Y values unless we

Regression equation: Equation that describes the relationship between two variables and allows us to predict Y from X.

Linear regression: Process of describing a correlation with the line that best fits the data points.

Predictor variable: The X variable used to predict a Y value.

Criterion variable: Predicted variable.

Y predicted (Y'): The value that results from entering a particular X value in a regression equation.

Line of best fit: The straight line that best fits a correlation and consists of each X value in the relationship and its predicted Y value.

have perfect correlation. If $r = \pm 1.0$, then all of the predicted Y values (Y's) will fall on the line of best fit. But in reality, for each X value, we can see more than one Y value associated with it. We can use regression to predict scores from X values in our sample and from X values not in our sample, as long as they are within the range of our sample.

Let's reexamine the scatterplots presented in Figures 8.4 (a–d), which show positive, negative, very weak, and perfect relationships. Note that in Figure 8.9 we have now computed the regression equation and graphed the line of best fit for each of the relationships. Figure 8.9a depicts a strong positive relationship, and we see that the line of best fit (as defined by the regression equation) has some Y values on or very close to it while other Y values are farther away. For each value of X, there is only one Y' value so we show error between the actual Y and Y'. Take $X = 40$. The scatterplot shows that $Y = 62$ and 85 while Y' appears to be about 60. This same situation occurs for other X values; there is one Y' for each X value, but the actual Y values fall off the line. However, if we computed the difference between Y' and the actual Y values, the line of best fit is the line that would show the least amount of difference between all the Y' and all the actual Y values. Hence, the name—line of best fit.

FIGURE 8.9

Scatterplots (From Figure 8.4) With Lines of Best Fit

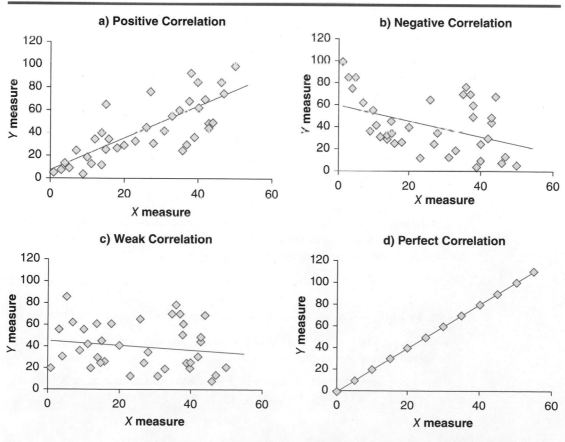

If you look at the line of best fit that the regression equation for 8.9b determined, you see that more Y values fall farther from the line than is true for the values in 8.9a. That is because the correlation for the two measures depicted in 8.9b is weaker. Thus, the error between Y' and actual Y values will be greater. In 8.9c, where there was a very weak correlation (one might say no correlation), there is even more error between Y' and actual Y. You have difficulty when you look at Figure 8.9c finding a pattern of data points around the line; instead the points seem to vary from the line without any pattern. And in Figure 8.9d, you see that for a perfect correlation, there are no differences between Y' and actual Y values. Hopefully, you can now see why it does not make sense to compute the regression equation unless you have a significant correlation. There is so much difference between Y' and Y values (or so much error in the prediction of Y values) that the equation is not of any benefit.

FORMULAS AND CALCULATIONS: SIMPLE LINEAR REGRESSION

We now move from a conceptual understanding of regression to the computation of the regression equation that defines the line of best fit. To compute this equation, we would specify which variable we are using to predict (X) and which variable we are predicting (Y) so:

$$X = \text{predictor variable}$$

$$Y = \text{criterion variable or the predicted variable}$$

The equation for a regression line is:

$$Y' = bX + a$$

where b = slope of the line; a = Y-intercept.

In computing a regression equation, we calculate a **Y-intercept** value or the value where the regression line hits the y-axis (which can be positive or negative) and the **slope** of the line. The slope tells us the direction and rate of change in Y as X changes. It is positive for a positive r and negative for a negative r.

> ($Y' = bX + a$): Formula for a linear regression equation.
>
> **Y-intercept:** The point at which a line of best fit crosses the y-axis, designated as "a" in the regression equation.
>
> **Slope:** Describes the rate of change in Y with each unit of change in X (or the incline of the line of best fit), designated by "b" in the regression equation.

The computational formulas for these two values are:

$$\text{Slope}(b): b = \frac{N(\Sigma XY) - (\Sigma X)(\Sigma Y)}{N(\Sigma X^2) - (\Sigma X)^2}$$

$$\text{Y-intercept }(a): a = M_y - bM_x$$

where N = sample size; X = X scores; Y = Y scores; M_y = mean of Y scores; b = slope; and M_x = mean of X scores.

In our example earlier in the chapter examining the correlation of verbal scores and willingness to cheat, we found a significant correlation ($r = -.66$) so we are justified in computing a regression equation. Suppose we decide to predict willingness to cheat from verbal scores. That means that X = verbal scores (predictor) and Y = willingness to cheat (criterion). In order to compute the slope, we first add all the X values (verbal scores) and then all the Y values (willingness to cheat scores), then multiply each X value by its corresponding Y value. We also square all of the X values and sum them and square all of the Y values and sum them. You can follow these computations in Table 8.7.

Using the terms from Table 8.7, we can now compute the slope. We will have the following equation:

$$\text{Slope}(b): b = \frac{N(\Sigma XY) - (\Sigma X)(\Sigma Y)}{N(\Sigma X^2) - (\Sigma X)^2}$$

$$b = \frac{20(39466) - (1307)(643)}{20(93441) - (1307)^2}$$

$$= \frac{789,320 - 840,401}{1,868,820 - 1,708,249} = \frac{-51,081}{160,571}$$

$$= -.318$$

Using the formula for the Y-intercept, we first need to find the means for verbal ability and willingness to cheat.

We plug these values into the formula:

$$M_{\text{verbal}} = \frac{1307}{20} = 65.35 \qquad M_{\text{cheat}} = \frac{643}{20} = 32.15$$

Y-intercept: $a = M_y - bM_x = 32.15 - [-.318(65.35)] = 32.15 + 20.78 = 52.94$

Note that you must keep the negative sign in front of the slope, which then changes the formula to the addition of the two terms. Always remember that a negative correlation will have a negative slope because as X increases, Y will decrease. After computing

TABLE 8.7

Computations for a Regression Equation

Student	Verbal Ability X	Willingness to Cheat Y	XY	X^2	Y^2
1	25	48	1,200	625	2,304
2	30	40	1,200	900	1,600
3	35	36	1,260	1,225	1,296
4	65	24	1,560	4,225	576
5	67	32	2,144	4,489	1,024
6	56	46	2,576	3,136	2,116
7	68	27	1,836	4,624	729
8	69	42	2,898	4,761	1,764
9	75	28	2,100	5,625	784
10	42	38	1,596	1,764	1,444
11	73	35	2,555	5,329	1,225
12	76	40	3,040	5,776	1,600
13	79	41	3,239	6,241	1,681
14	81	20	1,620	6,561	400
15	55	36	1,980	3,025	1,296
16	50	29	1,450	2,500	841
17	85	30	2,550	7,225	900
18	89	25	2,225	7,921	625
19	92	11	1,012	8,464	121
20	95	15	1,425	9,025	225
	$\Sigma X = 1307$	$\Sigma Y = 643$	$\Sigma XY = 39{,}466$	$\Sigma X^2 = 93{,}441$	$\Sigma Y^2 = 22{,}551$

the Y-intercept (a) and slope (b), we can enter these values in the regression equation and define the regression equation (line of best fit) for this particular dataset

$$Y' = bX + a = -.318(X) + 52.94$$

You can graph the line of best fit by computing Y' for any two X values and drawing a line between the two values. You should use only X values within the original range in the distribution because values which lie outside this range may not have the same relationship with Y. It is also better if you use X values that are somewhat different so that your line will be easier to draw. We could select $X = 42$ and 85 and use each of these X values to predict the Y value that will fall on the line of best fit.

For $X = 42$:

$$Y' = -.318(X) + 52.94 = -.318(42) + 52.94 = -13.36 + 52.94 = 39.58$$

For $X = 85$:

$$Y' = -.318(X) + 52.94 = -.318(85) + 52.94 = -27.03 + 52.94 = 25.91$$

We plot these two data points (42, 39.58) and (85, 25.91) on our scatterplot and connect them to show the line of best fit as shown in Figure 8.10.

Note that each of the predicted Y values (Y') falls on the regression line, while the actual Y value for the particular X is different. For example, for $X = 42$, $Y' = 39.58$, while the actual Y is slightly less than 39.58 ($Y = 38$). For $X = 85$, $Y' = 25.91$, while the actual $Y = 30$.

As discussed earlier, because we don't have a perfect relationship we know that when we use the regression equation to predict Y scores using X values within the range of our sample that our Y' will differ from somewhat to a lot from the actual Y scores for a particular X. For example, in our sample a student who scored 42 on verbal ability actually scored 38 on willingness to cheat, but when we predicted willingness to cheat for a score of 42, the regression equation predicted a score of 39.58. Thus, there was an error in the prediction of –1.58 (38–39.58). Likewise, for the student in the sample who scored 85 on verbal ability, the actual willingness to cheat score was 30, but the regression equation predicted that the willingness to cheat score would be 25.91, producing an error of 4.09. We can compute the average error in our predictions or what the average difference is between all of our predicted

FIGURE 8.10

Line of Best Fit for the Correlation Between Verbal Scores and
Willingness to Cheat

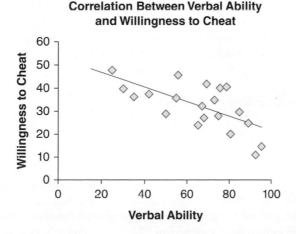

Y and the actual Y in the distribution. We do this by calculating the variance of Y', which is the deviation score (between each Y and Y' value) squared and added and then divided by N or

$$s_{y'}^2 = \frac{\Sigma(Y - Y')^2}{N}$$

Instead of using SD, we are using lowercase s here to designate variance, which is the notation used in previous years. If it helps to understand, you can substitute $SD_{y'}^2$ as a standard.

This is the error variance or residual error between the actual and predicted Y scores. The squared deviation does not tell us what we want to know, which is the average deviation between predicted Y (Y') and actual Y, so we take the square root of $s_{y'}^2$. This value or the standard deviation of predicted Y is called the **standard error of the estimate.** As its name implies $s_{y'}$ is the average deviation between predicted Y and the actual Ys in our sample. The stronger our correlation (r), the smaller $s_{y'}$ because we are able to more accurately predict Y and the smaller the difference between each of the actual and predicted Y values.

> **Standard error of the estimate ($s_{y'}$):** Average difference between the predicted Y values for each X from the actual Y values.

Knowing the relationship between two variables can help us to explain the variability in the measures and whether knowledge about the relationship is useful to us. In addition to knowing the strength and direction of a relationship, we want to know the proportion of variability accounted for in a measure by knowing its relationship with a second variable. In other words, how much better are we at predicting a score on a particular measure by knowing its relationship with another measure (think regression)? To answer this question, we compare the variance of the average error between predicted Y (Y') and actual Y (the standard error of the estimate squared—$s_{y'}^2$) and the total variance in our actual Y values. This tells us the percentage of the variability in our measure that is not accounted for. We then subtract the variance not accounted for from the total variance possible (100% or 1.0) and find what percentage of the variance we have accounted for in the measures (X and Y) by knowing their relationship with each other.

The formula describing this process is:

$$1 - \frac{s_{y'}^2}{s_y^2} = r^2$$

where 1 = the total variability; $s_{y'}^2$ = the average difference between the actual and predicted Y values squared; and s_y^2 = the variance in the actual values.

Using this formula we compute the percentage of variability that is eliminated by using X to predict Y rather than using the mean of Y (M_y) to predict Y. This term (r^2) is called the

coefficient of determination and reflects the usefulness or importance of a relationship (think effect size). The larger r^2 is, the better we can predict a measure. We interpret r^2 as the percentage of variability, in Y that is accounted for by knowing Y's relationship with X or what we gain in the prediction of a variable by knowing its relationship with another variable. This information is important to consider, because with larger samples it does not take a very large Pearson's r to obtain statistical significance; r^2 reminds us to consider the usefulness of our correlation. For example, if you have a sample of 52, a correlation of .273 is statistically significant ($p < .05$), which you would be happy with. (See the table for critical values of Pearson's r in Appendix C.5.) However, if you compute the coefficient of determination ($r^2 = .074$), you would find that you are only accounting for 7.4% of the variability in Y by knowing its relationship with X. That is not a very impressive percentage.

> **Coefficient of determination (r^2):** Proportion of variability accounted for by knowing the relationship (correlation) between two variables.

For the coefficient of determination, you may just square the correlation you compute to obtain r^2. Thus, in our example of verbal scores and willingness to cheat where $r = -.66$, $r^2 = .43$. This r^2 tells us that 43% of the variability in willingness to cheat is accounted for by knowing its relationship with verbal scores. If we had actually found these results, we would better understand one factor that is related to willingness to cheat, or something we could use to identify those who might be at risk for cheating, or even begin to study that variable (verbal scores) as a possible causal factor for cheating. We must always remember, though, that correlation does not equal causation and that having low verbal scores does not mean that a student will definitely cheat, but there is a tendency for this to happen more than when a student has higher verbal scores. In later studies, we may want to try to increase verbal scores of all students or identify the situations in which low verbal scores are associated with cheating.

For each significant correlation, we can compute two different regression equations. Each variable can thus serve as the predictor or as the predicted variable. In the example above, we correlated verbal scores and willingness to cheat. We then used verbal scores to predict willingness to cheat, but we could have used willingness to cheat to predict verbal scores. Below you can see the different regression equations that result when we specify X first as verbal scores and then as willingness to cheat scores.

Using verbal scores to predict willingness to cheat: $Y' = -.318(X) + 52.94$

Using willingness to cheat to predict verbal scores: $Y' = -1.36(X) + 109.06$

At times it makes sense to use only one variable as the predictor variable and one as the predicted variable, but often we use a variable as the predictor variable because of the past research or theory we have read. Just make sure that you are clear which variable you are using to predict (predictor) and which is your predicted variable (criterion variable). The coefficient of determination will remain the same regardless of which variable is the predictor, as there is only one r that defines the relationship between the variables and thus one r^2 or coefficient of determination that describes the percentage of variability that is accounted for by the relationship.

Multiple Regression

Sometimes we have more than two variables and we want to know the predictive ability that results from knowing the relationship among all the variables. For example, we may want to consider whether both students' verbal scores and their GPA predict willingness to cheat. In this case, we have two predictor (X) variables (verbal scores and GPA) and one predicted variable (Y' or willingness to cheat). We can compute a **multiple regression (R)**, which will tell us the relationship among each of the predictor variables with the predicted variable (verbal score and willingness to cheat, and GPA and willingness to cheat). These correlations are called B coefficients or partial correlations, and they represent the independent contribution that each predictor variable makes to the total prediction of willingness to cheat. The larger the number of variables you consider, the more B coefficients you compute in addition to the multiple regression. You can then determine whether each individual variable (in this case verbal scores and GPA) significantly adds to the prediction of willingness to cheat. You might add a fourth variable, such as the personality variable of risk taking, to see if it adds to the predictive power of your two existing measures. (Or you could have begun with all four variables since the multiple regression allows you to see how much each variable contributes to the total relationship.)

> **Multiple regression (R):** A statistical technique that computes both the individual and combined contribution of two or more variables to the prediction of another variable.

Practice 8.4

PRACTICE WITH REGRESSION EQUATIONS

Continuing with the example from Practice 8.2, suppose you find the regression equation for predicting life satisfaction from time spent exercising is $Y' = .059X + 34.5$.

a. Using this regression equation, what would the predicted life satisfaction score be if someone spends 120 minutes a week exercising?

b. What is the coefficient of determination for the study? (Refer to Practice 8.2 for the value you need to answer this question.) What does this number tell you?

c. If the life satisfaction scale ranges from 10 to 70 and you find that the standard error of the estimate $s_y = 10.27$, would you expect a large or small amount of error in your predictions of life satisfaction?

See Appendix A to check your answers.

Application 8.3

EXAMPLE OF MULTIPLE REGRESSION

Obesity is a recognized health risk in all ages, but it has been difficult to find a treatment that results in long-term weight loss. Past research has shown, however, that long-term weight loss is more successful when a program involves exercise. In a complex study examining several factors related to weight loss among obese adults, one component of the study focused on the relationship of a combination of increased exercise and increased consumption of fruits and vegetables to weight loss over six months (Annesi, 2013). The exercise program was supported by individual sessions with a wellness counselor, which focused on self-control and management of their exercise and included setting goals for their individual exercise. The nutrition program included group sessions with a wellness counselor where participants were encouraged to increase their consumption of fruits and vegetables. Each week participants completed brief scales assessing self-efficacy and regulation for exercise and eating, mood, amount of exercise, and amount of fruits and vegetables consumed. At the completion of the six-month study one analysis involved a multiple regression using the change in exercise and change in consumption of fruits and vegetables to predict weight loss. The results were significant ($F = 37.25$, $p < .001$), with the 28% of the variability in weight change accounted for by changes in exercise and consumption of fruits and vegetables. As shown in the table below, the partial correlations or B coefficients range from low to moderate strength change in exercise, and they are low strength for change in fruit and vegetable intake. The results support the hypothesis that changes in both exercise and eating contribute to long-term weight change.

	B	SE_B	R^2	F	df	p
Outcome Measure: Change in Weight			0.28	37.25	2,197	< .001
Change in Exercise	−0.40	0.02				
Change in Fruit and Vegetable Intake	−0.22	0.22				

Like r^2, we can compute R^2 as a measure of the variability accounted for in the predicted variable (in this case willingness to cheat) by knowing its relationship with the predictor variables (verbal scores, GPA, and perhaps risk taking). The B coefficients for each predictor variable tell us how much it independently contributed to R^2 and, thus, whether it adds anything more to the predictability than the other variables that are being considered. For example, perhaps verbal scores and GPA are highly correlated, and it is verbal scores that predict willingness to cheat while GPA does not add to the prediction of willingness to cheat. Multiple regression is a more complicated analysis than we will address in this text; but it is important that you understand its use and interpretation, as it is a commonly used statistical technique in many disciplines.

USING DATA ANALYSIS PROGRAMS: REGRESSION

Because the correlation between grit and sense of purpose is significant ($p < .001$—see Figure 8.7), we can then request a regression analysis. We use the same dataset that we had input for the correlation computation. Figure 8.11 shows the output obtained from SPSS. Referring to the three tables in the output, the Model Summary (first table) repeats our Pearson's r value ($-.776$) and provides the coefficient of determination (r^2 = .60) and the standard error of the estimate ($s_{y'} = 6.78$) or average error in predicting Y from X. Note that the Model Summary also reminds us of which variable (grit) we used as the predictor and which (sense of purpose) we used as the predicted.

FIGURE 8.11

SPSS Output From a Regression Analysis

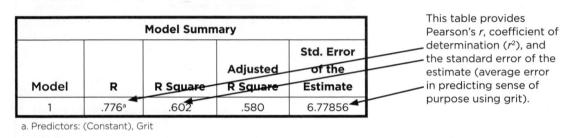

Model Summary

Model	R	R Square	Adjusted R Square	Std. Error of the Estimate
1	.776[a]	.602	.580	6.77856

a. Predictors: (Constant), Grit

This table provides Pearson's r, coefficient of determination (r^2), and the standard error of the estimate (average error in predicting sense of purpose using grit).

ANOVA[a]

Model		Sum of Squares	df	Mean Square	F	Sig.
1	Regression	1251.469	1	1251.469	27.236	.000[b]
	Residual	827.081	18	45.949		
	Total	2078.550	19			

a. Dependent Variable: Sense of Purpose

b. Predictors: (Constant), Grit

ANOVA table repeats the significance level and reminds us of the predictor (grit) and predicted (sense of purpose) variables.

Coefficients[a]

Model		Unstandardized Coefficients		Standardized Coefficients		
		B	Std. Error	Beta	t	Sig.
1	(Constant)	15.612	3.513		4.444	.000
	Grit	.757	.145	.776	5.219	.000

a. Dependent Variable: Sense of Purpose

The Coefficients Table provides in column B the Y-intercept (15.612) and slope (.757) for the regression equation.

Note: The regression output from SPSS consists of three tables, which provide statistics that you need to evaluate and report the prediction of one variable (in this case sense of purpose) from a significantly related second variable (grit).

The ANOVA table (second table) tells us that the regression is significant at the same level as our Pearson's r and again reminds us of the predictor and predicted variables. Finally, the Coefficients (third table) provides the Y-intercept (Constant under the B column, or 15.61) and the slope of .757 (associated with using grit as the predictor variable) for our regression equation. Always remember to pay attention to the sign (+ or −) of the slope as it tells us whether the relationship is a positive or negative one. We use the information from the Coefficients to write the regression equation in the standard format:

$$Y' = bX + a \text{ or } Y' = .757X + 15.61$$

We can request a scatterplot with the line of best fit (drawn according to the regression equation) as shown in Figure 8.12.

Application 8.4 provides sample Results and Discussion sections for the correlation and regression findings using APA format. Remember that these are *not* real data but are made up data that follow a pattern reported in published research (Hill et al., 2016). Thus, the interpretations and conclusions represent what we might state if we had the data presented above, and they do not represent real research findings. The sections do contain the specific format for reporting statistics and the expected information for each section.

FIGURE 8.12

Scatterplot With the Line of Best Fit for Predicting Sense of Purpose From Grit

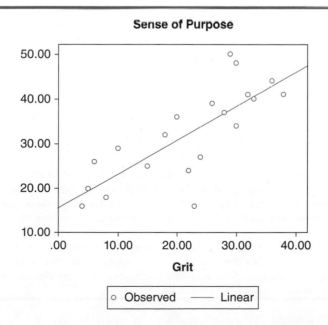

Application 8.4

SAMPLE RESULTS AND DISCUSSION FOR PEARSON'S *r* AND REGRESSION

Results

The grit scores for our sample were quite diverse, ranging from 4 to 38, with a mean at the middle of possible scores on the scale ($M = 21.85$, $SD = 10.72$). The sense of purpose scores clustered toward the lower end of possible values, ranging from 16 to 50, with a mean that was low relative to the possible purpose scores ($M = 31.50$, $SD = 10.46$).

A Pearson's *r* was computed to examine the relationship between the two variables, and a significant positive relationship was found between grit and sense of purpose, $r = .78$, $p < .001$. For this sample, 60% of the variability in sense of purpose was accounted for by its relationship to grit.

A linear regression was computed using grit to predict sense of purpose and was significant, $F(1, 18) = 27.24$, $p < .001$. The regression equation ($Y' = .757X + 15.61$) showed sense of purpose increased .757 units for each unit that grit increased and that the standard error of the estimate for predicted sense of purpose was 6.78.

Discussion

As predicted, grit was positively related to sense of purpose, with well over half of the variance in sense of purpose accounted for by its relationship to grit. The error in predicting sense of purpose from grit, however, was fairly large, given the narrow range of scores by the minimum wage employees.

These findings have obvious application for employees with minimum wage jobs. The large variability of scores on the grit scale in such a small sample suggests that these employees have very diverse perceptions regarding their perseverance. Because the scale does not assess grit in relation to a specific area of the respondent's life, we do not know whether the variability in scores is related to the employees' perception of themselves in their jobs or to their lives in general. The results imply that those supervising employees in minimum wage jobs should not make sweeping generalizations about their willingness to persist in order to achieve their goals. The restricted range of scores on the sense of purpose scale may reflect a floor effect for the scale for this particular sample, given that no one scored higher than the midpoint for the possible scale scores. Perhaps the scores reflect the employees' minimum sense of commitment to their low-paying job, even though their sense of purpose was strongly correlated to their grit level. Given the low average for sense of purpose, supervisors should pay attention to how the work environment might influence this characteristic and not just how the characteristic might influence work behavior.

Future research should explore both how those with high and low grit function at work and how different work conditions (e.g., flexible schedules, possibility to provide feedback about the structure of the work environment, opportunities to interact with other employees) can influence both characteristics. Higher wages may be one variable, but the structure of the job and working conditions may also be important.

Because these results were obtained with a small sample of employees in minimum wage jobs, future research should examine whether the findings can be replicated at different kinds of businesses where the work environment may differ and with employees at higher pay levels.

This chapter focused on correlation designs and described the rationale, benefits, and drawbacks for these designs. Although many laypersons and students think the major goal of research is to examine causal relationships among variables, correlational designs allow us to consider how variables are related when it is unethical, impossible, or too early in the research process to meet the requirements for causation. But be careful that you do not imply causation when describing correlational findings.

You also learned two types of correlational analyses that might be used to analyze a correlational design. As with all analyses, the selection depends not on the type of design but on the scale of measurement of your variables (see Figure 8.13). If your outcome is measured on an interval or ratio scale of measurement, you would use a Pearson's r when your predictor is also interval or ratio. If your predictor is nominal and dichotomous (two groups), you might use a point-biserial correlation. You might also conduct simple or multiple regression analyses. If both your variables are either ordinal or nominal, you would use other statistics that we describe in more detail Chapter 13. Spearman's rho is for ordinal data, and chi-square test of independence is for nominal data.

It would be nice and simple if correlational analyses always matched up with correlational designs. This is the case when you have interval, ratio, or ordinal data; but the situation is more complicated if you have nominal data. Nominal data can represent nonexperimental categories or experimental conditions, and therefore any statistical tests that involve nominal data can be used to analyze correlational or experimental designs

FIGURE 8.13
Decision Tree for Correlational Analyses

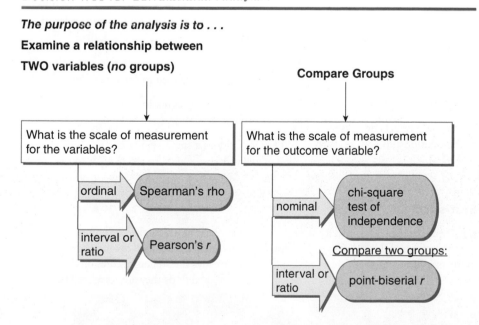

The purpose of the analysis is to . . .

Examine a relationship between

TWO variables (*no* groups)

What is the scale of measurement for the variables?

ordinal → Spearman's rho

interval or ratio → Pearson's r

Compare Groups

What is the scale of measurement for the outcome variable?

nominal → chi-square test of independence

Compare two groups:

interval or ratio → point-biserial r

CHAPTER RESOURCES

Key Terms

Define the following terms using your own words. You can check your answers by reviewing the chapter or by comparing them with the definitions in the glossary—but try to define them on your own first.

Ceiling effect 233

Coefficient of determination
(r^2) 261

Correlation 228

Correlational design 228

Criterion variable 254

Dichotomous variable 247

Floor effect 233

Line of best fit 254

Linear regression 254

Linear relationship 235

Multiple regression *(R)* 262

Negative correlation 235

Pearson's *r* (Pearson product-
moment correlation
coefficient) 235

Point-biserial correlation
coefficient (r_{pb}) 247

Positive correlation 235

Predictor variable 254

Regression equation 254

Scatterplot (or scattergram) 237

Slope 256

Standard error of the estimate 260
($Y' = bX + a$) 256

Y-intercept 256

Y predicted (Y') 254

Do You Understand the Chapter?

Answer these questions on your own, and then review the chapter to check your answers.

1. When is it appropriate to use a correlational design?

2. Explain why correlation is not equal to causation.

3. Distinguish correlational design and correlation analysis.

4. Why is measurement validity so important in correlational studies?

5. How do floor and ceiling effects decrease our ability to find a relationship between two variables?

6. What two pieces of information can we glean from any correlation coefficient?

7. Why don't we get perfect correlations in social science research?

8. Give an example of a positive and a negative relationship. What might the scatterplot of each of these relationships look like?

9. Why do we compute a regression equation, and how is it related to the line of best fit?

10. In computing regression, does it matter which variable is *X* and which is *Y*?

11. What does a small standard error of estimate tell us?

Practice With Statistics

1. An educational psychologist has developed a new 20-item test to assess risk taking among college students. In an effort to establish the validity of his new test, he has the 25 students in his first-year seminar take both his test and an already validated 50-item measure of risk taking. He correlates the students' scores on the two measures and finds they are correlated (+.78).

a. What correlation statistic should the psychologist have computed?

b. What is the critical value of the correlation (found in the table of critical values)?

c. Can the psychologist conclude that his new test is valid? Explain your answer.

d. If both tests are assessing risk taking, why didn't he get a perfect correlation?

2. A professor is interested in whether attendance on the first day of class is related to final grades. She collects information from an introductory and an advanced class for a total of 62 students and finds that first-day attendance (yes/no) is related to final course grades (+.26).

a. What correlation statistic should the psychologist have computed?

b. What is the critical value of the correlation (vs. the obtained value)?

c. What can the psychologist conclude about first-day class attendance and grades? Explain your answer.

3. A researcher explores the relationship between self-control (as a self-reported trait) and impulsive buying among 30 unemployed adults between the ages of 25 and 40. Scores on the self-control scale can range from 20 to 100, with higher scores suggesting more of the trait. Impulsive buying was assessed with 5 items, and scores can range from 5 to 25, with higher scores reflecting more impulsive buying behavior. The correlation between the variables is −.46. The researcher also computes the linear regression predicting impulsive buying from self-control and finds $Y' = -.25X + 20$.

a. State a null hypothesis.

b. State a directional alternative hypothesis.

c. Can you reject the null hypothesis? Why or why not?

d. What is the probability of a Type I error? Type II error?

e. If an adult scores 72 on self-control, what is her predicted impulsive buying score?

f. Given the information you have, can you predict a person's self-control scores from his impulsive buying score? Why or why not?

g. What percentage of the variability in impulsive buying is accounted for by knowing its relationship with self-control?

Practice With Statistical Analysis

The statistics for the following examples can be computed by hand or using a statistical package. Check with your instructor for their preference.

1. Gino and Ariely (2012) found in a series of studies that creativity was positively related to dishonest behavior, both when people are naturally creative and when they are stimulated to be creative. Suppose you want to know whether creativity is negatively related to integrity in an educational setting. You have students complete a creativity measure and report on their academic honesty (no plagiarism, completing work according to guidelines, no cheating on tests, supporting the institution's honor code, etc.). The following table presents the data for your sample:

Student ID	Creativity	Academic Honesty
1	22	21
2	45	18
3	36	15
4	40	18
5	28	21
6	32	17
7	39	10
8	18	23
9	26	19
10	22	15
11	30	16
12	34	9
13	28	13
14	17	19
15	43	7

a. After entering the data, graph the data in a scatterplot. What does the graph suggest about the relationship between creativity and academic honesty?

b. Compute the appropriate test to determine whether self-reported creativity and academic honesty are negatively related.

c. Can you reject the null hypothesis? Why or why not?

d. What is the probability of a Type I error? Type II error?

e. Compute the regression using creativity to predict academic honesty and write out the regression equation.

f. Compute the regression using academic honesty to predict creativity and write out the equation.

g. If a student scored 32 on the creativity measure, what score is predicted on the academic honesty questionnaire?

h. What percentage of variability in academic honesty is accounted for by creativity? How strong is this effect size?

i. Write a Results section for your findings. Include the descriptive statistics, statistical tests, and results of the tests.

j. Write a Discussion section for your findings. Include the findings, interpretation/explanation/implication of the findings, and possible next studies.

2. You then consider students' academic standing to better understand the creativity and academic honesty relationship. You decide to code 1 = in good standing and 2 = on probation.

Creativity	Academic Honesty	Academic Standing
22	21	1
45	18	1
36	15	1
40	18	1
28	21	1
32	17	1
39	10	2
18	23	1
26	19	2
22	15	2
30	16	2
34	9	2
28	13	2
17	19	1
43	7	1

a. Add academic standing to your dataset.

b. Compute the appropriate test to determine whether academic standing is related to academic honesty.

c. Now compute the appropriate test to determine whether academic standing is related to creativity.

d. Describe these results using APA format.

e. Discuss the meaning and implications of your findings.

3. A researcher uses a driving simulation to measure the reaction time of braking when a dog runs across the street in front of a car. His participants are newly licensed or experienced drivers, and all of the drivers are talking on a cell phone during the simulation. He finds the following data, which represent seconds to brake after a dog first appears in the street in front of a driver.

a. State the null and alternative hypothesis.

b. What statistical test should be performed to determine whether there is a relationship between the reaction times and type of driver? Explain your answer.

c. Compute the appropriate analysis.

d. Can you reject the null hypothesis? Why or why not?

e. What is the probability of a Type I error? Type II error?

f. What can you conclude about the relationship of driving experience and braking time? Support your answer.

Type of Driver	Braking Time
Newly Licensed Drivers	1
Newly Licensed Drivers	1.5
Newly Licensed Drivers	2.33
Newly Licensed Drivers	2.33
Newly Licensed Drivers	4.5
Newly Licensed Drivers	5
Newly Licensed Drivers	15
Newly Licensed Drivers	25
Experienced Drivers	.33
Experienced Drivers	.5
Experienced Drivers	.75
Experienced Drivers	1
Experienced Drivers	3
Experienced Drivers	3.5
Experienced Drivers	10
Experienced Drivers	12

Examining Causality

W hen the singer Adele won six Grammy Awards in 2012, The Wall Street Journal and National Public Radio (NPR) ran stories about why many people seem to have such a strong emotional reaction to her music, and her song "Someone Like You" in particular. One theory is that the song includes a type of note, called an appoggiatura, which begins as discordant with the melody but then changes to align with the melody. The discordance is unexpected and is believed to cause tension to the listener, which is then released when the note changes to match the melody. This tension and release is theorized to cause an emotional response, including chills running up the spine and possibly even crying (Doucleff, 2012; NPR Staff, 2012). As researchers, how might we test whether Adele's song causes an emotional reaction and, if so, whether the presence of the appoggiatura is the causative factor?

LEARNING OUTCOMES

In this chapter, you will learn

- The key components necessary to test cause and effect
- How to design an experiment
- How to manipulate an independent variable (IV)
- How to measure the dependent variable (DV)
- How to balance internal and external validity in an experiment
- Limitations to experimental designs

TESTING CAUSE AND EFFECT

Requirements for Causality

Causality implies that one action (the cause) affected another (the effect). In research, causality is a specific type of relationship in which one variable causes a change in another. Other ways to talk about causality are causation, a causal relationship, or suggesting that one variable affects another. Causality has three specific requirements.

The first requirement is correlation. If there is a causal relationship between two variables, there is also a correlational

> **Causality:** A cause-and-effect relationship.

FIGURE 9.1

A Clear Misunderstanding of Cause and Effect

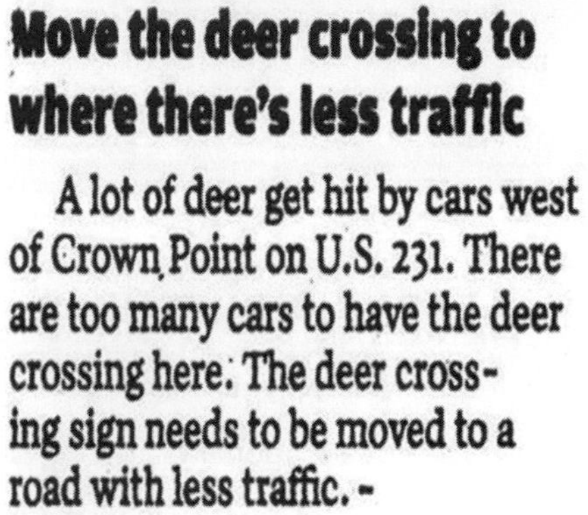

Move the deer crossing to where there's less traffic

A lot of deer get hit by cars west of Crown Point on U.S. 231. There are too many cars to have the deer crossing here. The deer cross-ing sign needs to be moved to a road with less traffic. -

Source: Letter to the Editor of *The Times of Northwest Indiana* (2011, August).

relationship. In other words, a change in one of the variables corresponds with changes in the other. If a musical note can cause an emotional response, then we would find a significant correlation between songs that have these musical notes and listeners' reports of distinct emotions. Doucleff (2012), the author of the *Wall Street Journal* article about Adele's song, cites such a study conducted by psychologist John Sloboda in the 1990s. Participants identified song passages to which they had a strong reaction, and it turned out that the majority of the passages contained the appoggiatura note. However, as we discussed in Chapter 8, finding a correlation between two variables is not enough to demonstrate the changes in one of the variables *caused* the changes in the other. Correlation is one requirement of causation but alone is insufficient (see Figure 9.1).

The second requirement of causation is sequencing. If you want to demonstrate that changes in one variable (which we will call variable *A*) caused changes in another variable (variable *B*), then the changes in variable *A* must occur before the changes in variable *B*. If we want to demonstrate that the musical note makes people have chills or cry, then exposure to the note must occur prior to any emotional response. But even with both correlation and sequencing, we do not have sufficient evidence that one variable caused a change in another.

The third and final requirement of causation is ruling out alternative explanations for why the change in variable *B* both corresponded with and came after the changes in variable *A*. It may just be a coincidence, or the change may be due to some other variable that the researcher had not tested. Although people may report feeling emotional after listening to Adele's song "Someone Like You," could it be due to a reason other than the presence of a specific type of musical note? The cowriter of "Someone Like You" gave such an alternative explanation. He suggested that the lyrics paint a vivid picture allowing listeners to imagine the experiences portrayed in the song (NPR Staff, 2012). Another explanation is that there may be differences in the people who choose to listen to that song, and those individual differences may be causing the reaction rather than the notes or the lyrics.

REVIEW OF KEY CONCEPTS: VALIDITY

Can you recall what type of validity is under examination when we wonder if one variable caused the change in the other variable? In other words, this type of validity refers to the extent to which we can rule out alternative explanations of causality.

If you answered "internal validity," you are correct! If you have forgotten about internal validity, take a minute to review Chapter 3 before reading on.

We discussed **internal validity** in Chapter 3, and this concept is very important in experimental design. You might also recall from Chapter 3 that **confounds** are variables that are not the focus of the study, and if not controlled might impact the study's results. In other words, confounds are potential alternative explanations that limit the internal validity of a study and must be addressed in order to demonstrate causality.

> **Internal validity:** The extent to which we can say that one variable caused a change in another variable.
>
> **Confound:** A variable that varies systematically with the variables of interest in a study and is a potential alternative explanation for causality.

In summary, the criteria to demonstrate that variable A caused a change in variable B are:

- *Correlation*: There must be a relationship between A and B.

- *Sequence*: The change in variable A must come before the change in variable B.

- *Ruling Out Alternative Explanations*: The researcher controlled for possible confounds so that variable A must be the only factor that could have caused the change in variable B.

Practice 9.1

TESTING CAUSE AND EFFECT

Can eating certain foods cause strange dreams or nightmares? Nielsen and Powell (2015) asked participants this question and found that 11.5% agreed that food affects their dreams. Those participants identified dairy products as the most common culprit (41%), followed by sugar (21%) and spicy foods (14%). Based on these findings, can you draw conclusions about causality?

See Appendix A to check your answer.

THREATS TO INTERNAL VALIDITY

Campbell and Stanley (1963) identified eight confounds that are **threats to internal validity**. Gliner and Morgan (2000) divided these into two categories, based on whether the threat was due to experiences or environmental factors, or whether the threat was due to participant (or subject) characteristics.

Threats to internal validity due to experiences or environmental factors:

1. History: Any event or environmental condition other than variable A caused the change in variable B.

2. Maturation: The change in variable B was due to natural changes that occur over time.

3. Testing: Observed changes in variable B were due to previous exposure to a test.

4. Instrumentation: Observed changes in variable B were due to inconsistency in the measurement instrument, administrators, or scorers.

Threats to internal validity due to participant characteristics:

1. Statistical Regression: Observed changes in variable B were due to a statistical phenomenon in which very high or low scores will regress to the mean, meaning that extreme scores will get less extreme over time.

2. Attrition (or Mortality): The change in variable B was due to participants withdrawing from the study.

3. Selection: When comparing groups, the change in variable B was due to preexisting differences.

4. Selection Interactions: The change in variable B was due to an interaction between the preexisting differences and another threat to internal validity.

> **Threats to internal validity:** Confounds that must be controlled so that a cause-effect relationship can be demonstrated. Campbell and Stanley (1963) identified the threats of (a) history, (b) maturation, (c) testing, (d) instrumentation, (e) statistical regression, (f) selection, (g) mortality, and (h) selection interactions.

Why the One-Group Pretest–Posttest Design Does Not Demonstrate Causality

In a **one-group pretest–posttest design**, the researcher gives all participants a pretest to assess variable B, then exposes them to variable A, and then gives them a posttest to assess variable B again (see Figure 9.2). The impact of variable A is determined by comparing each participant's posttest score to the pretest score and then finding the central tendency (e.g., mean) of those change scores.

For our song example, a one-group pretest–posttest design might involve first asking participants how they feel, then having them listen to Adele's song, and then again asking them how they feel. If there is a difference between the participants' mood prior to the song (pretest) and after listening to the song (posttest), can we say that Adele's song caused a change in emotion?

> **One-group pretest–posttest design:** Nonexperimental design in which all participants are tested prior to exposure to a variable of interest and again after exposure.

FIGURE 9.2

One-Group Pretest–Posttest Design

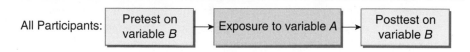

You are right if your answer was no, we have not met all the requirements for causality. Although we have satisfied the correlation and sequence criteria, we have not ruled out alternative explanations for the change in emotions. In fact, simply comparing scores from pretest to posttest among participants of one group can never satisfy that third criterion because there are many alternative explanations for why the participants would have changed between pre and posttest. Review Campbell and Stanley's (1963) threats to internal validity and see if you can identify the threats that would or might impact the one-group pretest–posttest design.

Threats to Internal Validity in One-Group Pretest–Posttest Designs Due to Experiences or Environmental Factors

1. History: Any event that occurs or environmental condition that is experienced between pretest and posttest might be the reason for the change. The threat increases the longer the time lapse between the pretest and posttest. A highly controlled laboratory setting can decrease, although not eliminate, this threat.

Example: If our participants were listening to Adele's song and the fire alarm went off, or someone in the room started crying, or the temperature changed, or a very attractive person came into the room, or some other unforeseen event occurred, it could be that the unplanned event caused the change in emotion, not the musical note under study.

2. Maturation: Any changes within the participants between the pretest and posttest might be the reason for the change. This threat is increased if the study takes place over a long period of time.

Example: Changes in emotions before and after listening to Adele's song may be due to growing tired, getting hungry, or natural changes in emotions over time.

3. Testing: Giving a pretest might impact posttest scores.

Example: Asking participants how they feel prior to Adele's song might make them think about their emotional state and consequently change it. Participants would also be clued into the purpose of the study, guess what you are expecting to find, and might provide answers based on those expectations.

4. Instrumentation: This threat would occur if a researcher uses different measures, administrators, or scores at pretest than at posttest. This threat is also

present if the same measure is used but it has poor test–retest reliability (it is inconsistent over time).

Example: For pretest, we ask participants to rate how emotionally aroused they are on a scale from 1–5, but for posttest we ask them to rate their arousal on a scale from 1–10. Or, one person administers the pretest, and a different person administers the posttest. Such changes in instrumentation may be why we observed a change in emotions.

Threats to Internal Validity in One-Group Pretest–Posttest Designs Due to Participant Characteristics

1. Statistical Regression: If a researcher recruits participants based on extreme scores, their pretest scores will regress to the mean at posttest.

Example: If we purposely recruited very lethargic individuals to determine if Adele's song could stimulate them, increased emotional arousal from pre- to posttest would likely be due to statistical regression.

The other threats to internal validity are controlled in a one-group pretest–posttest design. As long as the researcher analyzes only the data for those with both pre- and posttest data, attrition does not impact the internal validity of the study. If those who drop out are systematically different than those who stay, such attrition affects external validity but is not an issue for its internal validity. Likewise, selection and the selection interactions may impact the one-group pretest–posttest design's external validity instead of internal validity.

Group Designs

Hopefully you are now convinced that a one-group pretest–posttest design cannot demonstrate causality. If you are thinking that we might be able to improve on this design by using a **group design** in which we compare two or more groups, then you are on the right track. We might divide participants into two groups and have one group listen to Adele's "Someone Like You" and have the other group sit in silence. We could administer a pretest and posttest to both groups and compare the change scores between the groups (a *two-group pretest–posttest design*). Alternatively, we could omit the pretest and compare the posttest scores between the groups (a *two-group posttest-only design*) (see Figure 9.3).

In a group design, the researcher wants to demonstrate that the difference between the groups is due to exposure to different levels of variable *A.* To do that, the researcher must rule out that other systematic differences between the groups could have caused the groups to differ.

> **Group design:** Design in which a researcher compares two or more groups of participants who are exposed to different levels of a variable of interest.

FIGURE 9.3

Example Group Designs

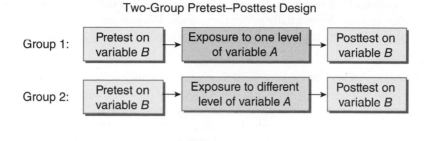

Two-Group Pretest–Posttest Design

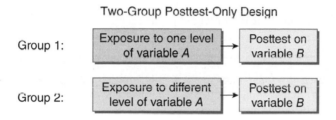

Two-Group Posttest-Only Design

Threats to Internal Validity in Group Designs Due to Experiences or Environmental Factors

The threats to internal validity due to experiences or environmental factors can be eliminated or controlled in a group design by keeping everything, except variable *A*, constant across the groups.

1. History: An event or environmental factor that occurs for only one group but not the others. This can be controlled by keeping everything except the variables of interest constant across the groups.

   Example: If we had all the participants in the song group sit in a room with windows but we had all the participants in the no-song group sit in a room without windows, it could be that the difference between the groups was due to different environments.

   We could control for this threat by having all participants be in the same room, preferably the one without windows because the room with windows would give participants access to a variety of events that could differentially affect the groups.

2. Maturation: Changes due to the passage of time are issues in group designs only if one group spends more time in the study than the other group.

   Example: If we had one group listen to Adele's song for three minutes and then complete the posttest measure, whereas the other group just completed the posttest measure.

We could control for maturation by having the other group sit in silence for three minutes before taking the posttest.

3. Testing: Pretests are an internal validity issue only if they are different across the groups or they differentially affect the groups. We can minimize the threat by giving all participants the same pretest, or completely eliminate it by omitting the pretest and just comparing our groups at posttest.

Example: Asking participants about their emotions might differentially affect the song and no-song groups, with the song group focusing their attention on sad emotions associated with the song and the no-song group having a wider variety of emotions that they focus on due to sitting in silence.

To avoid the differential impact of testing, we could conduct a posttest-only comparison.

4. Instrumentation: This threat would occur only if a researcher used different measures, interviewers, or observers for each group, or if measurement differed in some other systematic way between the groups.

Example: If we had a male interviewer for the song group and had a female interviewer for the no-song group, the difference between groups might be due to the two different interviewers.

We could eliminate this threat by having the same person interview participants from both groups.

Threats to Internal Validity in Group Designs Due to Participant Characteristics

The internal validity of group designs is particularly at risk to almost all the confounds due to participant characteristics. If the participants in each group started out being different or the group composition became different through the course of the study, we could not rule out that the participant characteristics were the causal factors.

Statistical regression alone does not impact the internal validity of a group design, but it can interact with selection.

1. Attrition: This is a threat when the groups are differentially affected by attrition, meaning that the drop-out rate is higher in one group than the other.

Example: People who drop out of the study may be more pressed for time, or they may have different emotional responses; and losing those participants differentially among your groups can bias the results. If more participants withdrew from the song group than the no-song group, when we compare those who remained in the groups we may see a difference that is due to the differential loss of certain types of participants instead of the song.

2. Selection: How the participants were selected for the groups impacted the results.

Example: If you asked participants to choose between listening to Adele's song or sitting in silence, a higher emotional response among those who listened to Adele might be due to individual characteristics such as age, gender, musical preference, and so on—rather than exposure to the song.

3. Selection Interactions: The way that participants were selected for the groups interacted with another threat, resulting in a difference between the groups.

Examples:

Selection-maturation interaction: If you had Adele fans listen to her song and non-fans sit in silence, the fans may become more emotional when listening to any music. The two groups change at different rates, and it is the difference in maturation between the groups that led to the difference in the dependent variable.

Selection-regression interaction: If all the very lethargic individuals wound up in the song group, the difference between the two groups would be due to statistical regression to the mean in the song group rather than the song itself. Note that selecting for extreme scores does not affect a group design's internal validity unless it interacts with selection, so that statistical regression alone would not impact internal validity if all the participants were very lethargic and were equally represented in the groups.

The threats due to participant characteristics are especially important to consider in a **quasi-experiment**. In a quasi-experiment, a researcher compares naturally occurring or preexisting groups that are exposed to different levels of variable *A*. For example, if we had Adele fans listen to a song and non-fans sit in silence, our study would be at risk for a selection threat (or any of the selection interaction threats) because any observed differences may have been due to the groups being different at the start. If we asked participants to volunteer to listen to the song or sit in silence, they would likely self-select based on their personal characteristics, and we would have a quasi-experiment.

> **Quasi-experiment:** A group design in which a researcher compares preexisting or naturally occurring groups that are exposed to different levels of a variable of interest.

We might instead decide to assign participants to groups in a more haphazard fashion, but even still we could bias results. For example, suppose we went into a library and saw a group of people sitting together, and we asked that group to listen to Adele's song for three minutes and then report how they feel. We then see another group of people sitting together, and we ask them to sit in silence for three minutes and then report how they feel. Most likely, the groups are made up of friends, classmates, or teammates; and, as such, they may share some participant characteristics such as musical tastes and experiences, academic background, gender, age, or other characteristics that may impact the results of the study. We would have similar issues if we recruited those in the song group from the gym and those in the non-song group from the library. These are all quasi-experiments that have limits to internal validity due to selection threats.

How then, do we assign participants to groups to avoid threats due to participant characteristics? What type of design can control threats to internal validity in order to demonstrate a causal relationship? Before reading on to find the answer to these questions, be sure you understand the threats to internal validity by completing Practice 9.2.

Practice 9.2

IDENTIFYING THREATS TO INTERNAL VALIDITY

Suppose a researcher wants to conduct a study to determine if spicy foods cause nightmares. The researcher recruits a group of university students and first has them fill out questionnaires about how often they eat spicy foods.

He then divides the groups based on their answers. Those who eat a lot of spicy foods are in one group, and those who never eat spicy foods are in another. He omits those who eat a small or moderate amount of spicy foods from the study. He asks those who eat a lot of spicy foods to eat spicy foods every day for a week. He asks those who never eat spicy foods to continue their behavior and not eat spicy foods for a week.

At the end of the week, 80% of those in the spicy food group returned and filled out a form that estimated the number of nightmares they experienced over the week. Only 45% of those in the no-spicy food group returned, and the researcher conducted face-to-face interviews about the content of their dreams over the past week.

Identify and explain the threats to internal validity in this study.

See Appendix A to check your answers.

How an Experiment Can Demonstrate Causality

Thus far we have discussed how to show that variable *A* caused a change in variable *B*. In an experiment, variable *A* is called the **independent variable (IV)** and variable *B* is called the **dependent variable (DV)**.

An experiment is designed to address the requirements of causality. The researcher defines **conditions** (also called **levels** or **groups**) that participants or subjects will experience and then actively creates those conditions. This **IV manipulation** must occur prior to measuring the DV. If change in the IV corresponds with a change in the DV, it will be clear that changes in the IV preceded any changes in the DV.

Independent variable (IV): The variable in an experiment that is manipulated.

Dependent variable (DV): The variable in an experiment that is expected to be affected by the IV.

Conditions (or levels, or groups): The values of the IV.

IV manipulation: The way the researcher creates the conditions of the IV.

REVIEW OF KEY CONCEPTS: COMPONENTS OF AN EXPERIMENT

An **experiment** is a specific type of study that includes:

- At least one independent variable (IV) that is manipulated by the researcher

- At least one dependent variable (DV) that is hypothesized to change due to the IV manipulation

- Control of as many confounds as possible by:

  ○ Keeping extraneous variables controlled across IV conditions

  ○ Using **random assignment** so that participants are assigned to IV condition based on chance.

The correlation and sequence of the IV and DV are important prerequisites for causality, but where the experimental design really shines is in ruling out alternative explanations for causality. As Cook and Campbell (1979) noted, an experiment can control for seven of the eight threats identified by Campbell and Stanley (1963). By systematically manipulating the IV and keeping as much else as possible the same across the groups, the researcher controls for threats to internal validity due to events and environmental factors. In order to control the threats due to selection or the selection interactions, the researcher assigns participants to groups randomly in order to even out any participant characteristics across the groups. Differential attrition is the one threat that the experimental design does not directly address, but random assignment to IV groups helps even out participant characteristics that might be associated with early withdrawal from the study (controlling the selection-attrition threat).

See Figure 9.4 for the steps in a simple, two-group experiment. To test if Adele's song (IV) causes an emotional reaction (DV), we could recruit participants and then randomly assign participants to two groups by flipping a coin. If the participants got heads, they would listen to Adele's song for three minutes, and if they got tails they would sit in silence for three minutes. We would test participants at the same time of day and in the same windowless room. All participants would wear headphones, even if they were not listening to the song. After the three minutes were up, we would give all participants the same measure to assess their mood. To evaluate our results, we would compare the average mood of those who listened to the song to the average mood of those who did not listen to the song.

Experiment: A design that includes manipulation of an IV, measurement of a DV, random assignment, and control of confounds.

Random assignment: Process of assigning participants to IV conditions (or order of conditions) that is based on chance.

FIGURE 9.4

Steps in a Simple Two-Group Experiment

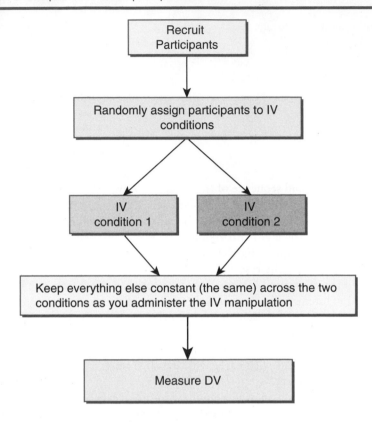

An experiment *can* demonstrate causality, but that does not mean that every experiment does so. Careful design of an experiment is critical to rule out alternative explanations for causality. Get some hands-on experience by completing Practice 9.3 so you have a better understanding of some of the decisions with which an experimenter grapples.

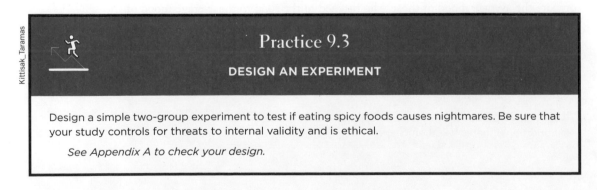

Practice 9.3

DESIGN AN EXPERIMENT

Design a simple two-group experiment to test if eating spicy foods causes nightmares. Be sure that your study controls for threats to internal validity and is ethical.

See Appendix A to check your design.

BASIC ISSUES IN DESIGNING AN EXPERIMENT

What questions and issues arose as you designed your experiment in Practice 9.3? You likely found that applying the requirements of an experiment is easier said than done; and many issues arose as you considered how to manipulate the IV, measure the DV, and control for threats to internal validity. As we have mentioned previously, there is no perfect study. Instead the researcher makes a series of decisions in order to create the best study he or she can. In designing an experiment, researchers must carefully balance the requirements of a tightly controlled study with ethical and practical considerations. Additionally, researchers balance all these issues with the need to create a powerful study.

REVIEW OF KEY CONCEPTS: POWER

Do you recall what the definition of power is (from a research perspective)? Does power avoid a Type I or Type II error? What are three factors that impact the power in a study?	Answer: Power is the ability to find statistically significant results when they exist, and having power means that you avoided a Type II error. Power increases as sample size increases, random error decreases, and the strength of the pattern or relationship increases.

Recruiting Participants

The number of participants needed to have sufficient power depends on many factors, including the number of IV conditions, the type of analysis conducted, the criterion for statistical significance (e.g., $p < .05$), how large you expect the difference between the groups to be on the DV, and how much variance you expect within each group. There are statistical formulas to determine the sample size needed based on these factors, although it is often difficult to guess the difference between the groups or the within-groups variance before conducting the study. A good rule of thumb is to aim for at least 30 participants per IV group (Wilson Van Voorhis & Morgan, 2007), but remember that is a rough estimate and there are other factors to take into account.

One of those other factors to consider is the heterogeneity, or diversity, of your sample. Recall from Chapter 6 that one way to reduce error in your study, and thus increase power, is to increase the homogeneity in your sample by limiting the population from which your sample is drawn. Depending on your topic and the research you have read, you might decide to limit your population to those who are within a certain age range, represent a specific ethnic group or gender, or have had certain life experiences. We might limit our song study to those who are not familiar with Adele's "Someone Like You" because otherwise experience with the song will vary and might alter the way our participants react to the song. **Prescreening** is the process of asking potential

Prescreening: Process of identifying those who have characteristics that the researcher wants to include or exclude in the study.

participants questions prior to the study to determine if they represent the population of interest, and we would use such a process to limit our sample to those who had not heard the song we are examining.

Once we identify our population, we will recruit a sample from that population and likely use some form of nonprobability (nonrandom) sampling. This is because randomly selecting our sample in order to increase its representativeness is not as important in an experiment as it is in a descriptive study. An experiment focuses on the differences between the IV groups within the study, and the ability to generalize the results outside of the study is typically a secondary concern that is addressed with replication rather than random sampling. However, random *assignment* is essential in an experiment (see Table 9.1).

Random Assignment

Whereas randomly selecting the sample is not essential in an experiment, randomly assigning participants once they are in the sample is essential. We want the IV groups to be as similar as possible prior to the IV manipulation so that any changes can be attributed to the DV and not to the participant characteristics. This is why many animal studies use genetically identical mice or rats and why studies of human identical twins are so important. Even being genetically identical or similar does not mean that the animal or person is exactly the same, and we know that experience shapes individuals into unique organisms. In fact, even small changes in cage environment can lead to differences in genetically identical mice (Olivia et al., 2010). It is impossible to have perfectly identical groups due to these individual differences among participants or animal subjects, so a researcher instead strives to make the groups as equal as possible by evening out the individual differences across the IV conditions.

Consider all the individual differences that might exist within our song study, even after we screened out those who had experience with Adele's song. A sample of participants would yield varying ages, genders, musical preference, musical ability, personality, temperament, and mood coming into the study. Can you imagine how difficult it would be to even out all the individual differences across our IV conditions? Even with our

TABLE 9.1

Distinguishing Between Random Selection and Random Assignment

Random Selection of Your Sample	vs.	Random Assignment to IV Condition
Most relevant for descriptive studies, but not absolutely essential for any study		Essential for an experiment, not relevant for other types of studies
Process of recruiting a sample		Occurs after the sample has been recruited
Purpose is to have a sample that represents the population		Purpose is to equally represent the participant characteristics of the sample in each IV condition
Increases external validity		Increases internal validity

Ethics Tip: Ethically Recruit Participants for an Experiment

Prescreening

Not only should you prescreen potential participants for characteristics you want to include or omit from your study, but you should also prescreen for ethical purposes. In particular:

1. Be sure that anyone who you ask to participate in your study is legally able to give consent to participate. In particular, unless you have parental consent for their participation, you should screen out any person under 18.

2. Be sure that you screen out those who would be at increased risk in your study. For example, if you will be having participants eat or drink something be sure you screen out those who might be allergic to the food or have ethical concerns with consuming the food.

Informed Consent

Most experiments require the informed consent of participants. One exception is if the DV is measured with observations in a public environment and there is no physical or emotional risk to participants. Review Chapter 1 for information about the informed consent process, and keep in mind the following when conducting an experiment:

1. Even though not all participants will experience the same conditions, you should tell all your participants what might occur (e.g., "the study might involve listening to a three-minute song" or "you may be asked to use a mobile device while walking through a situation designed to simulate traffic").

2. You do *not* need to inform participants of your hypotheses, the exact topic of study, or that participants will experience different conditions based on random assignment.

best attempts we would likely miss some important individual differences. Although a researcher might try to identify some of the most important individual variables (such as mood prior to listening to music) and balance them across conditions, doing this for all the individual differences is a daunting task indeed.

Consequently, researchers use random assignment in an experiment to help ensure that individual differences among participants are equally represented in each group. The process of random assignment depends on whether you are using an independent-groups or a dependent-groups design. In an **independent-groups experiment** (also commonly called a **between-subjects experiment**), the IV groups are independent of each other in that participants are randomly assigned to receive one level of the IV. We will discuss independent-groups designs in more detail in Chapter 10.

Independent-groups experiment (or between-subjects experiment): Experiment in which each participant experiences only one level of the IV.

Random assignment in an independent-groups design can be accomplished in one of two ways. In **simple random assignment**, each participant has an equal chance of being assigned to any of the IV levels. This can be accomplished by flipping a coin, rolling dice, drawing names or numbers out of a hat, using a random numbers table, having a computer randomize a list, or any other process that ensures that there is no distinguishable pattern to how participants came to be in the IV groups.

Any assignment process that includes a pattern is not random. It is therefore not appropriate to assign participants to a group based on what time they arrived for the study or where they are sitting in a room because arrival time and seat choice may reflect personality characteristics of the participant. Even counting participants off by twos or threes is inappropriate because that pattern might result in the IV groups being systematically different before the manipulation occurs.

Simple random assignment helps to rule out that selection, or any of the selection interaction effects, caused the change in the DV instead of the IV. However, simple random assignment does not guarantee that participant characteristics will be evened out across the IV conditions, and this procedure is often ineffective with small, heterogeneous samples. The second option in an independent-groups design is to use stratified random assignment. **Stratified random assignment** is a process by which the researcher first divides the sample into strata based on characteristics that are important to balance out across IV conditions (e.g., gender, socioeconomic status, personal experiences). The researcher then uses the same procedures in simple random assignment to assign participants from the strata to the IV conditions. You might notice that this is similar to stratified random sampling discussed in Chapter 4, but the randomization occurs after selection of the sample and is designed to even out key characteristics across IV levels.

In some cases, it is not realistic to randomly assign individuals. For example, educational interventions are often geared to entire classes or whole schools rather than individual students. In these cases, a research might use **cluster random assignment**. Such random assignment is similar to simple random assignment except that whole clusters of individuals are randomly assigned to the different IV levels rather than the individuals (see Application 9.1, p. 297, for an example).

Simple random assignment: Procedure in which each participant is assigned to one level of the IV so that every participant has an equal chance of experiencing any of the IV levels.

Stratified random assignment: Procedure in which the researcher identifies strata of participants based on key characteristics, then uses random assignment so that each member of each stratum has an equal chance of being assigned to any of the IV conditions.

Cluster random assignment: Procedure in which clusters of individuals are assigned to one level of the IV so that each cluster has an equal chance of experiencing any of the IV levels.

In a **dependent-groups experiment** the groups are related to each other. One way they may be related is through matching. **Matched random assignment** involves creating matched sets of participants who share characteristics expected to impact the DV. Each matched set will have the same number of participants as there are number of levels for the IV. The researcher then randomly assigns participants from each set to the IV levels, with one from each set in each level. As in independent-groups designs, each participant receives only one level of the IV. The difference is that participants are related due to the matched sets, and the statistical analyses used to examine the data take into account that relationship.

Another option in conducting a dependent-groups design is to have all the participants experience all the levels of the IV. If there are two levels of the IV, a participant will experience one level and then be given the DV measure. Then the participant will experience the other level and be given the DV measure again. The participants should receive the IV levels in different orders, and this is accomplished via **random assignment to order of conditions**. We will discuss dependent-groups designs in more detail in Chapter 11.

> **Dependent-groups experiment:** Experiment in which the groups are related, in that participants were matched prior to exposure to the IV or in that the participants experience all levels of the IV.
>
> **Matched random assignment:** Process in which participants are put into matched sets, and then each member of the set is assigned to one IV level so that all in the set have an equal chance of experiencing any of the levels.
>
> **Random assignment to order of conditions:** In experiments where the participants experience all levels of the IV, the participants all have an equal chance of experiencing the IV levels in a certain order.

Controlling Other Extraneous Variables and Confounds

Controlling extraneous variables and confounds means that the IV is the only variable that systematically differs between the groups. Any pretest given to one group is given to all groups so that if the pretest impacts the DV, all the groups are affected equally. History effects are controlled as much as possible by making sure that the groups experience similar environments and events.

In an ideal experiment, everything except for the IV is kept exactly the same so that when the researcher manipulates the IV, any changes in the DV can be due only to that manipulation. Laboratory studies with animals can come as close to this ideal as possible. Animal researchers can order a sample of genetically identical mice and then control the intake of food and water, amount of human contact, cage environment, lighting and temperature of the laboratory, and so on. When they measure the DV, they can be quite confident that the only thing that could have caused a difference between the IV groups was the IV manipulation.

Laboratory studies may also be conducted with humans by setting up a consistent and controlled area where participants will complete the study. Rather than the sterile animal lab with test tubes and researchers in white coats, a human lab may simply consist of a windowless, temperature-controlled classroom. The human laboratory is designed to control environmental and social variables just during the course of the experiment, as opposed to throughout the lifespan for certain animal labs. Because we cannot ethically keep humans in a controlled laboratory for a significant amount of time, most laboratory studies with humans take no more than a few hours.

Even a highly controlled laboratory may have some variations. The person administering the study may come to the study with varying moods and physical ailments that the animal subjects or human participants could pick up on, or there might be fluctuations in the building lighting or temperature due to a storm or technical problem. Once we move out of the laboratory, we introduce even more potential confounds that are compounded the longer the study lasts. The fact that a perfectly controlled study is an unrealized ideal is one of the reasons we talk about internal validity in a matter of degrees rather than as something a study has or does not have. A researcher conducting an experiment uses the ideal as something to strive for, and minimizes the threats to internal validity by controlling for as many extraneous variables as possible.

IV Manipulation

An IV is always a nominal variable because the levels represent different conditions or groups. At minimum, an IV has two levels. If we are studying the effect of Adele's song on emotional arousal, we would need at least one other condition to compare to Adele's song, such as a no-song condition or a different song condition. An IV might have more than two levels, and we could accomplish this by comparing Adele's song, sitting in silence, and one or more different songs. Assuming you can get enough participants, you can have as many IV levels as is warranted by past research and theory. Most experiments have between two and four levels per IV.

The term **experimental group** is used to describe an IV condition in which participants receive some level of the IV, and a **control group** is used to describe an IV condition where participants receive none of the IV. In our song example, the IV is Adele's music and the experimental group is the one that listened to the song under study, "Someone Like You." The control group is the one that sat in silence and therefore was at the zero level of the IV. The control group provides researchers with a baseline, or a starting point for comparison purposes.

Experiments do not always have to have a control group if a baseline comparison is not necessary (see Figure 9.5). For our song example, we may not be as interested if Adele's song causes an emotional reaction compared to sitting in silence. Plenty of research studies have demonstrated that music has an effect on mood (e.g., Pignatiello, Camp, & Rasar, 1986; Västfjäll, 2011), and our study comparing Adele's song to

---

Experimental group: The group that receives a certain amount or level of the IV.

Control group: The group that receives the zero level of the IV.

silence would not add anything to this body of research. Instead, we may wish to demonstrate that "Someone Like You" elicits a stronger emotional response compared to Adele's other songs, or we might try to tease out what parts of the song (the appoggiatura, the lyrics, the singer) might elicit emotions. In these cases, instead of having a control group that receives nothing, we would compare two or more experimental groups.

In other cases, a control group may not be feasible. Consider an experiment in which we ask participants to change the alarm sound they use to wake up in the morning. We might randomly assign one group of participants to use a particular song as their alarm, but would it be reasonable to ask participants in a control group to have no alarm? Even if participants agreed to do so, we would be introducing possible confounds because those participants who do not have an alarm may not wake up in time to get to class or meetings on time. These and other consequences of not having an alarm would be alternative explanations for any differences between the groups. Consequently, instead of a no-alarm control group, we might use an alternative alarm sound as a comparison experimental group.

FIGURE 9.5

Is a Control Group Necessary?

Contrary to popular belief, a control group that receives a zero level of the IV is not a requirement for an experiment. An experiment must compare at least two groups (conditions of the IV), but these can be two experimental groups. In this cartoon, the aliens could have chosen to compare 4 hours of sleep to 8 hours.

Source: Eva K. Lawrence

Types of Manipulations

There are many different ways to manipulate an IV. The following categories are designed to help give you some ideas, but these categories do not fully encompass the range of IV manipulations that have been used or that might be used. Moreover, these categories are not mutually exclusive so that a researcher might choose IV levels that represent two or more of these categories.

Environmental manipulations are a broad range of manipulations that change the participants' physical or social environment in a systematic way. Having participants

Environmental manipulations: Systematic changes to the physical or social environment.

listen to different types of music or use different types of alarm sounds are examples of environmental manipulations. Changing the temperature or lighting in a room, smiling or frowning at participants, or having the participants observe an interaction between other people are all environmental manipulations. Environmental manipulations may use **confederates**, who are working with the researcher but pretending to be participants or bystanders. The confederates help to stage an event that the participants observe or may interact directly with the participants.

Confederate: Someone who is working with the researcher but pretends to be a participant or bystander.

Scenario manipulations are used to elicit similar responses as environmental manipulations, but they do so by having the participant imagine or watch taped events or interactions rather than directly experiencing them. For example, instead of having a confederate smile or frown at participants based on which IV level they were assigned, a researcher might present the participant with a written scenario asking the participant to imagine meeting a person for the first time along with a picture of that person either smiling or frowning.

Crafting scenarios is easier than staging events, and a researcher can have participants in different groups participate at the same time and in large numbers. Scenarios also give the researcher more control over what participants are exposed to. At the same time, a serious limitation to scenarios is that the researcher has less control over what the participants actually experience. If you tell someone to imagine meeting someone for the first time and show them a picture of that person, all the participants will be exposed to the same exact information. However, the participants may or may not fill in the blanks for any missing information (such as what the person's voice sounds like, what the person is wearing, if the person is flirting with the participant or not). How the participants fill in the blanks and to what extent they do so will vary based on their individual personality, experiences, and expectations. Such variations can muddle the results of the study.

Instructional manipulations involve varying the instructions, information, or feedback given to participants. A researcher may tell one group of participants to take notes using paper and pencil and the other group to use a laptop, or the researcher may tell one group that the task they are about to complete is very difficult and the other that the task is very easy. A researcher might give participants different types of educational materials or vary the feedback participants receive. Like scenarios, instructional manipulations can be written or recorded to help ensure that participants within each IV group receive the

Scenario manipulations: Systematic changes to a scenario.

Instructional manipulations: Systematic changes to instructions, educational information, or feedback.

exact same instructions; but they are limited in that the participants may vary in how much they attend to or read into the written instructions.

Physiological manipulations are those that impact the participants on a physical level. These include giving human participants or animal subjects varying levels of alcohol or drugs, physical stimuli such as a shocks, or surgical procedures. There are less invasive strategies to change physiology that student researchers might consider, including reasonable levels of exercise, meditation, caffeine, cayenne pepper, or sugar.

Physiological manipulations: Systematic changes to participants' or subjects' physical functioning.

Choosing an Appropriate Manipulation

Although there are many ways to manipulate an IV, keep in mind that not all variables can, or should, be manipulated. The researcher cannot manipulate preexisting and enduring characteristics of the participants such as their gender, personality, or age. Some factors technically could be manipulated but should not be for ethical reasons, such as physical injuries to the participant or rumors about the participants that could hurt their reputations in the community.

Base Manipulation on Theory and Past Research. When deciding how to manipulate your independent variable, you will want to use both research and theory to build a case for your manipulation. In particular, you need to have some evidence prior to conducting the study that your manipulation will have the effect you expect. From an ethical standpoint, past research and theory can help you demonstrate that your manipulation is not frivolous and help you anticipate and minimize any risk to participants. From a practical standpoint, finding at least one experiment on your topic will tell you how other researchers manipulated your IV, and you can model these techniques in your own study.

If you cannot find any experiments relating to your topic, there are three possible reasons. First, you may not have been using appropriate search strategies, and you should review Chapter 2 to fine-tune your searches. Second, an experiment on your topic may be impossible because the variable you are interested in examining cannot be manipulated. In that case, you should adjust your topic using past experiments as guides. Third, you might have a new and innovative idea. If this is true, build the case for your study by using non-experimental research, but also expand your search for experiments that you might model. For example, suppose you want to manipulate Facebook status updates but have not found any experiments that have done so. Build a case for your study by using non-experimental research that focuses on Facebook, plus expand your search to experiments that manipulate similar stimuli such as online dating profiles, news stories, or e-mails.

Balance the Strength of the Manipulation With Ethical and Practical Issues. The strength of the relationship between the IV and DV is a major factor in a powerful experiment. A researcher conducting an experiment can help increase the strength of

Practice 9.4

DISTINGUISHING BETWEEN VARIABLES THAT CAN AND CANNOT BE MANIPULATED

Identify which of these variables can and cannot be independent variables in an experiment. Explain your rationale for how you categorized each one.

- The weather
- Room color
- Participant ethnicity
- Participant socioeconomic status
- Participant disability
- Confederate sexual orientation

See Appendix A to check your answers.

that relationship by having a strong manipulation. Imagine that a researcher is examining the impact of coffee on driving skills and plans to use a control group that receives no coffee. If the experimental group had one sip of coffee, it would be unlikely that that manipulation would be strong enough to result in a measurable difference on driving skills. How many cups of coffee should the researcher use for the experimental group in order to have the strongest effect? Likewise, how long and how loud must a song be in order for it to have an observable effect?

Generally speaking, a strong manipulation leads to a strong effect and, therefore, to a higher likelihood that the study will have enough power for the researcher to find a significant difference between the groups. At the same time, it is not always appropriate to expose participants to the strongest manipulation possible. Strong manipulations may be unethical, may lead to differential attrition, and may not be warranted given the current state of the research on the topic.

Consider the coffee example. If you had participants in an experimental group drink 10 cups of coffee and tested their driving skills using a driving simulator, the researcher would likely find that the experimental group is significantly more impaired than the control group. Of course, there are several problems with having participants drink 10 cups of coffee in one sitting. It is not ethical because such a high dose of coffee is hazardous to participants' health. Additionally, participants in the experimental group may decide to leave the study rather than drink all 10 cups. Even if you had participants in the control group drink 10 cups of water to control for confounds, they likely would not be as motivated to drop out; and that differential attrition is a serious threat to internal validity. Finally, there is already sufficient research on humans and animals that high doses of caffeine lead to motor skill deficits, and therefore using such a high dose of coffee does not contribute to this area of research.

Test the Manipulation. You can test your manipulation before and after you conduct your study in order to determine if your manipulation has the desired effect and is strong enough for participants to be impacted by it. Recall that a pilot study is a preliminary study undertaken prior to the actual study. In an experiment, it is often used to help ensure that the manipulation works. For example, if you are examining the impact of attractiveness on likeability, and you plan to manipulate attractiveness by using different pictures of men, a pilot study can help you choose the best pictures. You might have a small sample rate the attractiveness of a variety of men and choose those that are rated as most unattractive and most attractive to use as your IV manipulation.

Researchers may use a **manipulation check** after completion of the study to determine whether the participants noticed and attended to the manipulation. This is particularly important for scenarios and instructions because it is possible that the participants did not read carefully enough to pick up on the manipulation. A manipulation check usually appears after the DV measure and includes one or more questions about the manipulation itself.

For example, for a study examining the impact of attractiveness on likeability, we might ask participants to look at one version of a picture (IV manipulation), then rate how likeable the person depicted is (DV measurement), and then ask them to rate how attractive he is (manipulation check). When we evaluate the data, we would hope that those who were assigned to view an attractive man indeed rated him as attractive.

We could omit anyone who failed the manipulation check from further analyses, although keep in mind that sometimes the manipulation can have an effect even if the participants did not report that they attended to it. Consequently, we typically recommend that students evaluate the data with and without those who failed the manipulation check to determine if excluding those who failed leads to different results.

> **Manipulation check:** The process of verifying that the participants attended to the manipulation.

DV Measures

All the types of measures that you might use for a descriptive or correlational study are options for an experiment. That includes paper-and-pencil questionnaires, interviews, observations, and physiological tests such as heart rate. Even archives could be used if the study spans a long enough period of time for records to reflect changes in the DV, although archives are rarely used as DVs in experiments and would not be appropriate for student research that spans only one or two semesters.

Although you can use most types of measures in an experiment that you would in other types of studies, the same variables examined in other types of study may not work in an experiment. A DV must be able to vary based on the manipulation, and therefore stable traits such as intelligence and personality are not good DVs. Additionally, variables that take a lot of time to change such as income or health are not appropriate for student research that is time-limited. And of course, there are ethical issues if an experiment is expected to negatively impact someone's income or health.

As with the IV manipulation, one of the first places you will want to look for ideas about how to operationally define and measure your DV is the research literature on your topic. When choosing the actual measure for your DV, you will want to select one that is reliable, valid, and sensitive to the IV manipulation.

REVIEW OF KEY CONCEPTS: SENSITIVITY, AND FLOOR AND CEILING EFFECTS

- Sensitivity: A measure's ability to detect differences.

- Floor effect: A problem with measure sensitivity in which the majority of scores are at the lowest extreme of the scale.

- Ceiling effect: A problem with measure sensitivity in which the majority of scores are at the highest extreme of the scale.

In an experiment, a sensitive DV measure is one that can detect changes due to the IV manipulation. To avoid floor and ceiling effects in your DV measure, avoid using single-item scales with limited response options (e.g., a single yes/no question). Instead, use an item that has a range of response options, or use a measure that has multiple items that will be combined into a total score.

Even if you identify a DV that should be impacted by your IV and find a measure that is often cited in the research literature, has demonstrated reliability and validity, and is at low risk for floor and ceiling effects, it still might not be sensitive to your particular IV manipulation. For example, if we conduct a study to examine the effect of a particular musical note on mood, mood is an appropriate variable that is often used as the DV in published research about the effect of music. We do not want to choose just any measure of mood, however. If we are examining short-term mood changes, then a measure that assesses mood over the course of several weeks or months, or asks about how the person feels in general, is not appropriate. Likewise, mood questionnaires that assess sleeping and eating habits would not be appropriate because we would not expect such habits to change during our experiment. Instead, we will want to find a measure of mood that assesses how the participant feels in the present moment.

The bottom line is that it is not just a matter of finding a good measure for your DV; the measure must make sense. It must measure a variable that can in fact change, and it must be sensitive to your specific IV manipulation. Look carefully at the time frame of the measure, as well as how individual items are worded. Making slight revisions to a published measure is alright as long as you explain your revisions in your report. If you find yourself doing a major overhaul of a measure, you might be better off finding a different measure or, as a last resort, creating your own. If you do make modifications or create your own measure, it is a good idea to conduct a pilot test to check the measure's reliability and validity.

Application 9.1

RESEARCH EXAMINING THE EFFECT OF MUSIC VIDEOS

Music videos often present idealized and unrealistic body images that may have negative consequences for those who watch them. Mulgrew, Volcevski-Kostas, and Rendell (2014) examined the effects of such videos on adolescent boys, including how music videos depicting muscular versus average men impacted mood.

IV: Depiction of men in music video clips

Levels of IV: Muscular men versus average men

How the researchers chose the manipulation: The authors noted that past research has found that music videos impact adolescent girls, but little is known about the impact on boys. In selecting the video clips, the researchers followed procedures used in other published research in that they taped a large number of clips and then edited scenes and omitted clips that did not specifically focus on the physique of a male singer (attractive and muscular or average). They then conducted a pilot study to test their manipulation. A small sample of men who did not know the purpose of the study rated the body focus in the clips as well as the attractiveness and muscularity of the male singers. For the muscular IV condition, the researchers chose the clips that received the highest ratings for the muscular condition, and the clips that received middle scores for the average condition.

DV: Mood

Operational definition of DV: Participants rated their level of anger, depression, and happiness using a Visual Analogue Scale in which participants rated their current mood by placing a tick mark along a horizontal line between *not at all* and *very much.* For example:

Rate how happy you feel right now by putting a mark (/) on the line below:

*Not at All*_____*Very much*

Sample: Nonprobability convenience sampling was used to obtain a sample of early, middle, and late adolescent boys. Participants (*N* = 180) were recruited from five Catholic high schools in Melbourne, Australia.

Ethics: The video clips chosen did not include any profanity, violence, or sexually provocative scenes that would be inappropriate for adolescent boys to view in a school setting. The Institutional Review Board (IRB) at the researchers' institution approved the study, as did the Catholic Education Office that oversaw the schools in which the participants were recruited. Parents actively consented to allow their children to participate in the study, and the adolescent participants gave their assent.

How threats to internal validity were minimized:
- The researchers used cluster random assignment in which classes of students were assigned to either watch clips depicting muscular men or clips depicting average men.
- Aside from the IV manipulation, the researchers kept as much constant as possible across the IV levels:
  - The videos for both IV levels included 5 one-minute clips.
  - The videos were shown without the accompanying music.

(Continued)

(Continued)
- ○ All clips focused on a male singer who appeared to be under 30.
- ○ Segments that featured other people or scenery were removed.

Results: The videos had a statistically significant impact on happiness and depression, in that boys who viewed video clips depicting muscular singers felt less happy and more depressed than the boys who viewed clips depicting singers with an average physique. There was no significant effect on ratings of anger.

OTHER THREATS TO INTERNAL VALIDITY

Demand Characteristics

Just being in a study and having the attention of the researchers can lead to changes in behavior, which is a phenomenon known as the **Hawthorne effect**. Researchers consequently try to give participants in all conditions of the experiment the same amount of attention and have them spend the same amount of time in the research setting. By doing this, all IV conditions will hopefully be equally impacted by the Hawthorne effect so the effect does not differentially affect the groups.

Researchers must be careful to avoid **demand characteristics** of the experiment, which occur when participants respond to what they believe the study is about rather than the IV manipulation. A participant might give you responses to try to "help" you support the presumed hypothesis or might purposely try to be uncooperative (known as the "screw you effect"; Masling, 1966). Earlier in this chapter we mentioned that giving participants a pretest can clue them into the purpose of the study, and they might change their behaviors based on what they believe you expect to find. Avoiding demand characteristics is one rationale for conducting a posttest-only experiment.

Telling the participants your hypothesis or letting them know about the different IV conditions are clear demand characteristics, and this is why researchers do not disclose their hypotheses during the informed consent process and may opt not to explain that participants will be randomly assigned to different conditions. Researchers might even try to hide the fact that they are conducting an experiment with different conditions by

---

Hawthorne effect: Phenomenon in which participants change their behavior simply because they are in a study and have the attention of researchers.

Demand characteristics: Characteristics of the study that lead participants to guess at the study's hypothesis and change their behavior accordingly.

doing the random assignment procedure covertly (as opposed to having the participants draw numbers out of a hat, etc.). On the other hand, most physiological manipulations require that the participants be informed of the different conditions they could experience. If possible, in these situations, researchers conduct a **blind experiment** so that the participants do not know to which condition they were assigned. For example, participants who agree to participate will know that they may receive a drug or they may receive a **placebo** such as a sugar pill, but they will not know to which group they were assigned until after the study is complete.

Deception is sometimes employed to avoid demand characteristics. Using confederates is one such deceptive technique. Another is to tell the participants the study is about something totally different from the topic under study. In some cases, researchers might even have participants begin a fake study and then stage an event that is part of the real study but designed to look incidental. Latane and Darley's (1968) "smoke filled room study" used all these techniques. They told participants that the study was about urban life and had them sit in the waiting room filling out forms. The actual study was about how the presence and behavior of others impact behaviors in emergency situations. The researchers consequently created a mock emergency by pumping smoke into the waiting room. In one condition, the participants were alone, in another the participants were with two other participants, and in the last condition the participants were with two confederates who had been instructed to ignore the smoke. The findings revealed that those who were alone responded to the smoke much more quickly, and only a small percentage of participants in the confederate condition responded to the smoke at all. These findings would likely be impossible without the use of deception; but as we discussed in Chapter 1, deception is ethically questionable and should be used only if there is no other way to conduct the study and there is no risk to participants (see Figure 9.6). Any deception must usually be followed by a thorough debriefing before the participant leaves the study.

> **Blind experiment:** An experiment in which the participants know they have been assigned to one particular IV condition, but they do not know which one.
>
> **Placebo:** A treatment or substance that in and of itself has no therapeutic effect, such as a sugar pill.

Experimenter Expectancy Effects

If participants are impacted by what they think the researcher expects to find, it stands to reason that the researcher who knows exactly what the hypothesis is would be impacted by their expectations. This is not to say that the researcher intentionally biases the study or makes up data. That is an unfortunate possibility, but it is not the issue at hand here. An honest researcher can unintentionally bias the study

FIGURE 9.6

An Unethical Experiment

This cartoon reviews several key concepts: _Operational definitions_ are the ways in which a research measures or manipulates variables. Not telling participants to which condition (group) they've been assigned (or that there are different conditions) is one way to reduce _demand characteristics_. A _control group_ is a group that receives a zero level of the IV. Finally, this cartoon raises ethical issues of a manipulation that might harm the participants. Hopefully, no researcher would ever conduct a study that might turn the participants into vampires!

Source: Eva K. Lawrence

because of **experimenter expectancy effects**. A researcher may unconsciously treat the groups differently based on his or her expectations, and even subtle differences such as facial expressions or posture can inadvertently cause the expected differences to occur.

The first controlled study of this effect was conducted by Rosenthal and Fode (1963). They told lab assistants that one group of rats was bred to be very good at running through mazes and the other group of rats was bred to be poor maze runners. This

Experimenter expectancy effect (or Rosenthal effect): Phenomenon in which a researcher unintentionally treats the groups differently so that results support the hypothesis.

information was deceptive because the rats were randomly assigned to the groups. Even though there was no reason for one group of rats to run the maze faster, the rats identified as being better at running mazes had better times. Rosenthal conducted a similar study with humans (Rosenthal & Jacobson, 1963). He told teachers that certain students had tested as "bloomers" meaning that they had a high potential for academic success, when in fact those students had been randomly assigned to that description. Low and behold, when all the students were tested again at the completion of the study, those identified as "bloomers" showed greater improvements than the other students. Because of Rosenthal's groundbreaking research on experimenter expectancy, the effect is often referred to as the "Rosenthal effect."

A **double-blind experiment** can address the issues of demand characteristics and experimenter expectancy effects. In this type of study, neither the participants nor the researcher administering the study know which participants are in which group. These types of studies are more commonly used with drug studies where it is feasible to create a control condition such as a placebo sugar pill that looks exactly like the drug in the experimental condition. Likewise, alcohol or caffeine studies can utilize control beverages that look and taste like the experimental condition but do not contain the experimental substance.

Diffusion of Treatment

Diffusion of treatment occurs when participants assigned to different groups can impact each other and blur the differences between groups. From an educational or treatment perspective, diffusion of treatment can be good thing. A teacher or clinician who teaches participants new skills or provides educational information might hope that they intentionally share or model the newly learned information or behavior.

From a research perspective, diffusion of treatment is a serious problem because it makes it impossible to tease out the effect of the IV on the DV. To avoid this issue, experimenters must be certain to keep participants in the different groups, or experienced and naive participants in the same group from interacting with each other during the course of the study. This is relatively easy in a short-term study conducted in a laboratory, but it becomes more difficult with longer-term studies and those in natural settings. A manipulation check can be useful if the study is at risk for diffusion of treatment. If participants in one group have skills or knowledge that they could have received only through exposure to information provided to another group, there is a good chance that diffusion of treatment occurred.

Double-blind experiment: An experiment in which neither the participants nor the researcher interacting with the participants know which participants have been assigned to each condition.

Diffusion of treatment: The treatment administered to one group is shared with another group through cross-group interactions.

BALANCING INTERNAL AND EXTERNAL VALIDITY

Thus far, we have focused primarily on the internal validity of an experiment and have paid less attention to the issue of external validity, or how generalizable the results are across different settings, participants, or materials. Our strategy of focusing on internal validity more than external validity parallels how the scales are tipped for an experiment. If a researcher has reason to believe there is a causal relationship between two variables, but a controlled experiment has yet to be conducted, an experiment with strong internal validity is a logical option to move that research forward. If a causal relationship cannot be demonstrated under highly controlled conditions, it is unlikely to be found in a more natural, uncontrolled experiment.

This does not mean that external validity is not important in experimental designs; it just tends to be a concern later in the progress of science. If a causal relationship is found in a highly controlled laboratory experiment, other researchers will replicate the study to determine if the results can generalize to other laboratories, stimuli, and participants. Once a causal relationship is well established within controlled settings, researchers might begin to examine the effect within more natural settings or by using more natural stimuli. If the findings do not hold up in natural situations, it calls into question the **ecological validity**, or applicability of findings to less contrived settings. Some experimental conditions may be too artificial or controlled to reflect daily life. This does not mean the findings of an experiment are not valid, but that we can find them only in controlled settings that do not mimic real life. Thus, we cannot generalize such findings to the "real world."

Consequently, depending on what research has been done on your topic, you may opt to move the science forward by conducting a study with stronger internal or external validity. Remember that for the most part, increasing one type of validity decreases the other. No single study can do it all; but if you carefully consider how to design your study, your study can make a contribution to the larger field.

> **Ecological validity:** A type of external validity that assesses the degree to which a study's findings generalize to real-world settings.

THE BIG PICTURE: BENEFITS AND LIMITS OF EXPERIMENTAL DESIGN

Well-designed experiments can answer important questions about what causes people and animals to act in certain ways, what causes people to think and believe what they do, and how people perceive and react to different situations or variations in personal characteristics. Such findings are critical to those in the social sciences and to anyone who is interested in changing behavior or attitudes. This does not mean that the experiment is the best type of study, and there are limitations to this type of design.

We have already alluded to two limitations. First, the focus on internal validity rather than external validity might lead to results that are relevant only in very unique situations. Second, not all questions can be addressed using an experiment because some variables cannot be manipulated and some manipulations would be unethical. Many of those questions are very interesting and important, such as: How do racism and sexism develop? What is the impact of drug use on family dynamics? How does growing up poor impact one's psychosocial development? and How does personality develop and affect behavior? Correlational studies, especially those that span a long period of time, are excellent in helping to answer these types of questions.

A third limitation is that an experiment is not always feasible. In *Walden Two*, Skinner (1948) wrote about a fictional community that centered around experimental design. If members of the community wanted to see if something worked, they would test it out experimentally and base day-to-day decisions on the results. In the real world, research does not play such a central role in society, and most are not willing to give over control of their daily lives for the sake of internal validity.

In particular, someone who signs up for a class or elects a specific service will probably not take kindly to being told that a researcher will determine what class or service they receive, or that they have been assigned to the control group and will receive nothing. Some researchers use a **waitlist control** so that those assigned to the control group will eventually receive services, but it is unreasonable to expect that everyone assigned to that condition will be willing to wait for services they want or need and still complete assessment measures.

Although researchers understand that one-group pretest–posttest designs and quasi-experiments are inherently at risk for threats to internal validity, they offer decent alternatives in situations where a true experiment is not a reasonable option. One-group pretest–posttest designs are often used to evaluate programs in real-world settings where the administration or participants would be dissatisfied with adding a comparison program or control group, or when there are simply not enough participants to do so. Quasi-experiments are used in settings when a comparison or control group is possible but random assignment of participants to groups is not. We conducted a quasi-experiment of academic honesty using different classes of research methods students as our preexisting groups. See Application 9.2 for details on how we designed the study and why we chose a quasi-experiment over a true experiment.

Waitlist control: A control group in an experiment that is promised the same treatment as the experimental group after the experimental group has completed treatment and both groups have been assessed.

Application 9.2

EXAMPLE AND RATIONALE OF A QUASI-EXPERIMENT ON THE TOPIC OF ACADEMIC HONESTY

We conducted a quasi-experiment to examine an educational intervention to increase plagiarism knowledge and paraphrasing skills (Estow, Lawrence, & Adams, 2011).

We used a two-group pretest–posttest design using Research Methods classes as preexisting groups. Students in the plagiarism-education group were those who enrolled in the class during the spring 2009 semester, whereas those who were in the control group enrolled in the class during the spring 2010 semester. All students completed a plagiarism knowledge and paraphrasing skills test at the beginning and end of the semester. The plagiarism-education group used plagiarism as the class semester-long research topic, which included reading and analyzing research articles about plagiarism and conducting non-experimental and experimental studies on the topic of plagiarism. The control group completed similar assignments throughout the semester but had a different class topic.

We found that using plagiarism as the theme for our Methods course improved knowledge and skills. However, because the study was a quasi-experiment instead of a true experiment, it is limited by selection and selection–interaction threats to internal validity.

To conduct a true experiment, we would have had to randomly assign students to groups. We could not randomly assign students into the class because students expect to be able to enroll in the courses they want and need, and to have choice in class time and semester. Perhaps we could have had two class research topics and then randomly assigned all the students who signed up for the class to one or the other topic. However, there are a few problems with randomly assigning students within a class to a research topic. First, if we had two class research topics, students would prefer to choose the topic rather than be randomly assigned. Second, we discuss the class research topic in class throughout the semester. Having two class research projects would have increased the confusion in an already challenging course. Finally, we would expect diffusion of treatment to be an issue because students assigned to one condition would likely discuss their work and projects with those in the other condition. Consequently, we felt that the quasi-experiment was a good choice, given institutional and practical limitations.

CHAPTER RESOURCES

Key Terms

Define the following terms using your own words. You can check your answers by reviewing the chapter or by comparing them with the definitions in the glossary—but try to define them on your own first.

Blind experiment 299

Causality 273

Cluster random
    assignment 288

Conditions (or levels,
    or groups) 282

Confederate 292

Confound 275

Control group 290

Demand characteristics 298

Dependent variable
    (DV) 282

Do You Understand the Chapter?

Answer these questions on your own, and then review the chapter to check your answers.

1. What are the three requirements to demonstrate a causal relationship?

2. What are the eight threats to internal validity identified by Campbell and Stanley (1963)?

3. Which threats are inherent in a one-group pretest–posttest group? What threats might impact this type of design? Which threats do not apply to this design?

4. Which threats apply to a group design? What threats are inherent in a quasi-experiment?

5. How does an experiment control for these threats? Which threat is not directly controlled in an experiment?

6. What issues are most important when recruiting participants for an experiment? Include ethical issues that should be addressed.

7. What are the differences between random selection and random assignment?

8. What is an independent-groups experiment? Describe two procedures for random assignment used in an independent-groups experiment.

9. What is a dependent-groups experiment? Describe two procedures for random assignment used in a dependent-groups experiment.

10. Why is it important for the researcher to control extraneous environmental and social variables in an experiment? How does a researcher do this?

11. What is the minimum number of IV conditions in an experiment?

12. What are experimental and control groups? Do all experiments have to have a control group?

13. What are the different types of IV manipulations?

14. How can you tell if a variable can serve as an IV?

15. How might you choose a good IV for your study? How would you test your choice of manipulations?

16. How can you tell if a variable can serve as a DV? How might you choose a good DV for your study?

17. What is the difference between demand characteristics and experimenter expectancy effects? How can you address these issues?

18. What types of studies are most at risk for diffusion of treatment? How can you address this issue?

19. How do you balance internal and external validity in an experiment?

20. If a one-group pretest–posttest study or quasi-experiment cannot demonstrate causality, why would a researcher choose to conduct these types of studies?

 **edge.sagepub.com/adams2e**

Sharpen your skills with SAGE edge!
SAGE edge for students provides you with tools to help you study. You'll find mobile-friendly eFlashcards and quizzes, as well as videos, web resources, datasets, and links to SAGE journal articles related to this chapter.

Independent-Groups Designs

In the summer of 2012, researchers were surprised by the publicity given to a study by Franz Messerli, a physician who explored the relationship between the amount of chocolate annually consumed in a country and the number of Nobel Prize winners from that country (Messerli, 2012). He found a strong positive correlation, and his results were published in the *New England Journal of Medicine*. The news media picked up the story, and there were reports in multiple magazines and newspapers including *Time*, Reuters, the *Washington Post*, and *USA Today*. Many of those stories failed to make the distinction between correlation and causation, but you know from reading this text (if not from earlier social science courses) that correlation does not equal causation.

How might we follow up on this study to determine if there is a difference between individuals who eat chocolate daily and those who do not? Or, what if we wanted to examine differences between individuals who eat a lot of chocolate, a moderate amount, a little, or none? And how might we move beyond correlation to determine if eating chocolate causes a change in individuals? All of these designs require independent groups, meaning that individuals are in only one group (e.g., chocolate eaters or non-chocolate-eaters).

DESIGNS WITH INDEPENDENT GROUPS

There are three major types of independent-groups designs: correlational, quasi-experimental, and experimental. The key components of these designs are described below and summarized in Figure 10.1.

Correlational Designs

You have already learned about correlational designs that examine the relationship between two naturally occurring

LEARNING OUTCOMES

In this chapter, you will learn

- About different types of independent-groups designs with two levels

- How to analyze a two-group design with an independent-samples *t* test

- How to calculate and interpret the effect size and the confidence interval for an independent-samples *t* test

- About the characteristics and advantages of multiple-groups designs

- How to calculate and interpret data for multiple-groups designs using a one-way ANOVA

- About the purpose and interpretation of post hoc tests

FIGURE 10.1
Decision Tree for Independent-Groups Designs

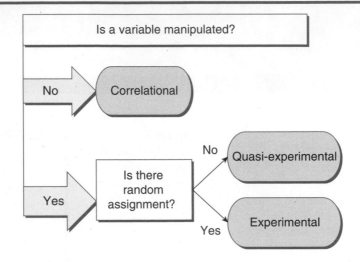

(or not manipulated) variables. In Chapter 8, we focused on correlational designs and correlational analyses in which your measures are assessed on interval or ratio scales. You can also have a correlational design that compares groups (a nominal variable) assessed on an interval or ratio scale. Such correlational studies are used because we are interested in comparing groups that we cannot or choose not to manipulate. We do not randomly assign participants to a group or control the conditions surrounding the study. We are purposely designing a study that examines relationships that already exist, rather than looking for causation. Whereas in an experiment we refer to an independent variable (IV) that is expected to cause a change in a dependent variable (DV), in a correlational design we use the more general terms *predictor* and *outcome*. A **predictor variable** is the variable that is used to predict the value of another variable (e.g., the grouping variable in a two-group design), and the **outcome** is the predicted variable that we will be measuring.

A good example is a study that examines whether males or females eat more chocolate when presented with free access to chocolate. This is a legitimate research question, particularly for marketing professionals who want to know which groups to direct their ads to or health professionals interested in teaching healthy eating habits. Obviously, we cannot manipulate or randomly assign participants to gender. In addition, each gender includes a great diversity of characteristics so there is much variability among those

Predictor variable: Variable that is used to predict the value of another variable, and a term used instead of IV in a correlational design.

Outcome: The variable that is predicted, and a term used instead of DV in a correlational design.

in the same category (say, male). Thus, we do not have control over the conditions of the study and cannot assume that differences in the variable we measure (amount of chocolate consumed) are due only to the grouping variable (gender, in this case). To be more concrete, if we find that females eat more chocolate than males, we know that the amount of chocolate eaten is related to gender but there are multiple variables that could cause the difference in addition to gender.

Another example of a correlational design is comparing those who eat chocolate daily to those who do not on the amount of time they spend reading daily or on the number of books they read each month. Our findings are then interpreted as showing that eating chocolate daily is or is not related to cognitive activities. Such studies have good external validity and if we find a significant relationship we might follow up with a study designed to determine if eating chocolate improves cognitive skills.

Quasi-Experiments

A quasi-experiment gets us one step closer to causality because it includes a manipulation but examines the manipulation among preexisting groups rather than randomly assigning participants to groups. A researcher conducting a quasi-experiment might provide a chocolate snack to students in one class and provide a non-chocolate snack to students in another class, and then compare the cognitive skills of the groups. Although the researcher manipulated the amount of chocolate, he did not randomly assign participants to the IV condition.

Like correlational studies, we are really examining the relationship in quasi-experiments between the manipulated factor—eating chocolate—and the dependent variable or variable that is measured—in this case, cognitive skills. As such, there is also the possibility that a third variable caused any differences in cognitive skills. In particular, the classes may have been different at the start of the study. This is especially relevant because classes are often assigned based on the academic skills of the students.

Experiments

Let's go back to the strong relationship that Messerli (2012) found between amount of chocolate consumed and the number of Nobel Prize winners in a country. Consider third variables that may be responsible for the relationship. In the case of chocolate and research

REVIEW OF KEY CONCEPTS: THREE REQUIREMENTS FOR AN EXPERIMENT

What are the three requirements for an experiment?
Answer:

1. An independent variable (IV) that is manipulated.

2. Participants who are randomly assigned to a level of the IV.

3. A dependent variable that is measured to test for the effect of the IV.

productivity or creativity, it may be that the level of economic stability or success in a country is what determines how much chocolate people buy and how well educated they are, which then allows them to design and carry out their research program. Or perhaps eating chocolate affects one's mood, which then allows researchers to persist in their work.

Although it would not be ethical to manipulate the socioeconomic status (SES) of participants, we could examine the effect of chocolate on mood or task persistence. Such studies could be designed as experiments where we controlled all conditions and varied only the amount or type of chocolate and measured its effect on mood or task persistence. Only then could we talk about the effect of chocolate on another variable and make assumptions about causality.

A study that manipulates a variable (the independent variable) under two conditions (no-chocolate and chocolate, for example) and examines its effect on a behavior, attitude, or status, while keeping all other conditions constant, is aptly called a **simple experiment**. To meet the requirements for an experiment, the participants also must be randomly assigned to one of the two conditions in an attempt to have equal groups when we expose them to different conditions.

To summarize, simple experiments have one independent variable with two conditions or levels that we manipulate; we assess the effect of this IV on another variable called the dependent variable. The IV is a nominal variable, and each level or condition is independent of the other—meaning there is no overlap between them, and they are distinct. If we examine the effect of type of chocolate on mood, we identify two levels or conditions of chocolate, such as bittersweet and milk, that we compare; or we could use a control group of no chocolate and compare it to one type of chocolate. In order to operationalize (explicitly define) these two types of chocolate, we could state the specific amount of chocolate and the percentage of cacao in the chocolate. For example, in our study we may use 1 ounce of bittersweet chocolate that is 60% cacao and 1 ounce of milk chocolate that contains 20% cacao. Others then will know exactly how we defined our IV and will be able to replicate our study. Although we could have more than one DV in our study, we will focus on only one DV in order to simplify our task.

> **Simple experiment:** A study investigating the effect of a manipulated IV with two conditions on a DV. The IV is nominal scale and the DV is interval or ratio.

REVIEW OF KEY CONCEPTS: DESIGNING AN EXPERIMENT

Recall that when we design an experiment, we need to (a) maximize power (our ability to reject the null hypothesis); (b) ensure that our IV manipulation is reliable and valid; (c) use a DV measure that is reliable and valid; and (d) maximize the internal validity of the study.

browndogstudios

DESIGNING A SIMPLE EXPERIMENT

Following is an example of how we might address these four issues for a simple experiment examining the effect of chocolate on mood.

1. Maximize power.

   - *Strong manipulation of the IV:* We could have participants eat an entire bar of chocolate (2 ounces), thereby ensuring that they have ingested enough of the chocolate for it to have an effect.

   - *Extreme levels of the IV:* Instead of comparing bittersweet and milk chocolate, we might decide to compare one of the chocolates to no-chocolate, such as carob; or we could compare a milk chocolate with only 20% cacao and a bittersweet chocolate with 70% cacao.

   - *Homogeneity of participants:* The more similar our participants are, especially in terms of their liking of chocolate, their hunger level, and their prestudy mood, the more likely that differences between the groups are due to the eating of chocolate. We might screen participants so that our sample is as homogeneous as possible prior to the experiment.

   - *Increase N:* We need to have a large enough sample so that we can see the pattern of different responses created by our IV. A small sample requires the effect of the IV to be very large, while a pattern is more easily identified with a larger number of participants.

2. Ensure IV manipulation is reliable and valid.

   - *Consistency of treatment:* We will want to make sure that those in the experimental condition experience the exact same treatment (amount of chocolate, percentage of cacao, brand, texture, presentation, etc.). Likewise, all those in the comparison condition should receive the same treatment.

   - *Manipulation check:* In order to check on the validity of our manipulation, we may have observers determine if the participants adhered to the condition (e.g., those asked to eat chocolate actually ate all of it). We might also have participants report about their experiences (e.g., report the amount of chocolate ingested or rate the intensity of the chocolate they ate).

3. Ensure DV measurement is reliable and valid.

   - If possible, it is best to *use an existing measure or scale* that others have already found to be valid and reliable.

   - Our measure should be *sensitive to changes in the DV.* We want to use a DV that assesses current mood and is measured on an interval or ratio scale because those scales are more sensitive to small changes in responses than a simple yes/no or positive/negative response.

- We should *consider using more than one question or item* rating mood so that participants can report their mood in several ways, and we also can check the reliability of the mood responses/scale using Cronbach's alpha.

- Anything we can do to *automate or standardize the data collection* will increase the reliability of our data. For example, we could have participants read the same directions for a mood scale rather than have us explain the scale.

- *Multiple measures:* In addition to the participants rating of their mood, we could have observers rate participants' mood based on their facial expressions (smiles, frowns, etc.). We could then check the interrater reliability of the observed mood by correlating the ratings of the two observers. We could also correlate the observed mood ratings with the participants' responses on our mood scale in order to assess the concurrent validity of our scale.

4. Maximize internal validity. By its nature, a simple experiment seeks to increase internal validity by manipulation of the IV and random assignment to IV condition. There are additional steps we could take, including:

- *Eliminate confounds:* You learned in Chapter 9 that researchers must be very aware of potential confounds or factors that can provide alternative explanations for results. As such, we will need to make sure that all participants undergo the exact same experience except for eating different types of chocolate. This means that the instructions, setting, experimenter behavior, and time spent in the experiment are the same.

- If we are using a new design and new measures we may want to *conduct a pilot study* in order to test the manipulation of our independent variable and the sensitivity, reliability, and validity of our measure. We may discover that participants do not like either of our chocolate choices (milk and bittersweet) or that many participants eat only part of the chocolate or that the participants cannot tell a difference in intensity between the two chocolates. We then may need to modify our study.

- Finally, we could try to *reduce demand characteristics by conducting a single- or double-blind experiment*. Recall from Chapter 9 that in a single-blind experiment the participants are not aware of the condition to which they have been assigned. We could accomplish this if we do not tell participants what type of chocolate they are eating. In a double-blind experiment, neither the participant nor the researcher knows the type of chocolate each participant is eating.

In order to test the effect of an IV on a DV, we employ the same hypothesis-testing process that you are familiar with from Chapter 6. Practice 10.1 provides an opportunity to test your understanding of the hypothesis-testing process and the issues that were covered in previous pages regarding the design of an experiment. Figure 10.2 depicts a simple experiment you could have outlined in Practice 10.1.

Kittisak_Taramas

Practice 10.1

SIMPLE EXPERIMENT DESIGN PRACTICE

Does the use of cell phones while driving increase aggression by other drivers?

1. Identify the IV in this study.
2. How could you manipulate your IV for a simple experiment?
3. What is the DV, and how could it be operationally defined and measured?
4. What changes would you look for in your DV?
5. State an alternative/experimental hypothesis that is specific to the IV manipulation and the DV measure that you have described above.
6. What is the null hypothesis for this experiment?
7. Outline the procedures for your proposed study.
8. What did you do in your study to increase power?
9. Did you employ single-blind or double-blind conditions? Explain.
10. What do you think will be true of the two groups after you apply the IV? (Be specific—what does the hypothesis predict about the two groups at the end of the experiment?)

Review the answers found in Appendix A.

INDEPENDENT-SAMPLES *t* TESTS

The inferential statistic that we use to analyze two-group designs is called the **independent-samples *t* test**. The *t* test compares the means of the two groups to see whether the difference between them is significantly different from what we would expect by chance alone. The *t* test is appropriate for use with experiments, correlational studies, and quasi-experiments that compare two independent groups, but the interpretation of the analysis differs for the designs, as is shown in Table 10.1.

Independent-samples *t* test: The inferential statistic used to test differences between means in a study with two independent groups.

First a brief review: You will remember from Chapter 7 that we used one-sample *t* tests to compare the mean of a sample (M) to a population mean (μ). We noted in that chapter that we did not often use a one-sample *t* test because we rarely have a population mean (μ) for comparison. It is much more common that we compare the means of two samples. The question we ask in a two-group design is: Even if we know that the means

FIGURE 10.2

Does the Use of a Cell Phone by a Driver Increase the
Aggression of Other Drivers?

Cell phone drivers are sometimes distracted! What is the impact of their distraction on other drivers?

Source: Sandi Coon

TABLE 10.1

Independent-Groups Designs

Design	Random Assignment to Groups	Manipulation of IV	Tests?
Correlational	No	No	Correlation/relationship
Quasi-experiment	No	Yes	Correlation/relationship
Simple experiment	Yes	Yes	Causality

Ethics Tip: Experiments and Ethical Concerns

We must always evaluate our and others' studies for ethical concerns. Regardless of the safeguards a researcher is taking, an Institutional Review Board (IRB) should review the proposed study and approve it.

If we design a study examining the impact of a driver's cell phone use on other drivers, a field experiment using real drivers on an actual road, such as outlined in the answer key for Practice 10.1 (as opposed to a simulated driving situation), would have a great deal of external validity. (See McGarva,

Ramsey, and Shear, 2006, for a full description.) However, there are potential risks in such a study, and safeguards must be made to minimize such risks. For example, we could conduct the study on a road that does not have very much traffic or that has a low speed limit. We would also want to make sure that the delay in moving the lead car is not more than one might sometimes experience in a daily driving experience. Even with these safeguards, do you think the benefits of a field experiment outweigh the risks?

of our two samples differ, how do we know if they are significantly different? We want to know if the difference we find is greater than what we would expect by chance alone, so just knowing the difference between means is not useful by itself.

Consider an experiment based on the cartoon in Figure 10.2 and the McGarva et al. (2006) study. Suppose we find that participants behind a driver using a cell phone honk an average of 5 seconds after the light turns green, while the participants behind the same driver with his hands on the steering wheel take an average of 10 seconds to honk. How do we interpret the 5-second difference?

When we interpreted differences with z scores and one-sample t tests, we needed to know how the difference of a *score* from a *sample mean* (for z scores) or a *mean* from a *sampling distribution of means* (for one-sample t tests) compared to the variability within a distribution. Recall that if a z score was 2 standard deviations from a sample mean, then the score was in the top or bottom 5% of the distribution. For a one-sample t test, we look at how the difference between the sample mean and population mean compares to a theoretical sampling distribution made up of the differences between a mean and mu that would result if a study was repeated an infinite number of times. So the sampling distribution is made up of thousands of difference scores when the null hypothesis is true and there is no difference between mean (M) and mu (μ).

If the null hypothesis is true, any difference between a sample mean (M) and the population mu (μ) is due to error or sampling variability. We want to see if the difference between M and μ that we obtain in a study is greater than we would expect by chance alone. We then can determine if a particular M falls at the extreme end of the sampling distribution by dividing the difference between M and μ by the standard deviation of the sampling distribution (called standard error of the mean). If our mean falls at the extreme end (upper or lower) of the sampling distribution, then we conclude that our sample mean is significantly different from mu (μ).

We use this same logic in the *independent-samples* t *test* to consider whether the means of two samples differ from one another. Instead of looking at a sampling distribution of differences between our sample M and mu (μ), though, we compare the difference we find between the means of two groups (in our case, cell phone and no–cell phone) to a sampling distribution composed of differences between the means of two groups *if the null hypothesis is true*. The null hypothesis assumes no difference between the groups so their means would not differ ($M_{cell} - M_{no-cell} = 0$). We know that if we replicate a study hundreds of times with the same sample size, we will not get exactly the same means. The t test checks to see how different our obtained mean difference is from a distribution where there was no difference in time to honk at a driver who delayed moving when he was using a cell phone versus when he was not using a cell phone. Figure 10.3 shows the theoretical sampling distribution and regions of rejection when the difference between means is zero.

The t test thus allows us to discover whether the difference between our cell phone and no–cell phone means ($M_{cell} - M_{no-cell}$) is about what we would expect because of individual differences (we then retain the H_0) or if the difference between the two groups' means is greater than what we expect by chance alone (we then reject the H_0).

Before computing a t test, we state our null (H_0) and alternative (H_a) hypotheses for our study:

H_0: There is no difference in time to honk between cell phone and no–cell phone groups.

H_a: There will be a difference in time to honk between cell phone and no–cell phone groups.

FIGURE 10.3

Sampling Distribution When $\mu_1 - \mu_2 = 0$

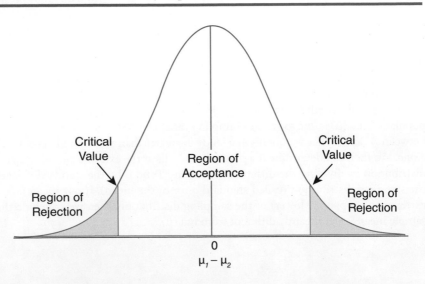

Or in numerical terms:

$$H_0: \mu_{\text{cell phone}} = \mu_{\text{no-cell phone}}$$

$$H_a: \mu_{\text{cell phone}} \neq \mu_{\text{no-cell phone}}$$

FORMULAS AND CALCULATIONS: INDEPENDENT-SAMPLES *t* TEST

Suppose the following results were obtained in our study for a sample of drivers behind a driver who did not move when a light turned green and who either used a cell phone or had his hands on the steering wheel (no cell phone). The number of seconds it took a participant driver to honk was recorded:

	Driver With Cell Phone	Driver With No Cell Phone
M	5.20	7.70
SD	2.04	3.06
SD^2	4.16	9.36
N	10	10

In order to see where the difference between our means falls on the sampling distribution, we need to know the standard deviation of the sampling distribution (or the distribution of the differences between the means). Because the distribution is theoretical, we have to estimate the standard deviation of the sampling distribution. We do that using the standard deviations (as shown above) from our samples. We use the term **standard error of the difference between the means**, symbolized as SD_{X-X}, to differentiate the standard deviation of the sampling distribution from the standard deviation (SD) of a sample. The subscript (X–X) denotes that the distribution is composed of differences between means.

Computing the standard error of the difference (SD_{X-X}) takes several steps. We first compute the variance for each of our groups, which requires you to square the standard deviation—in our case, the variance for the time to honk when participants were behind the driver using a cell phone ($SD^2_{\text{cell}} = 4.16$) and the variance for the time to honk when participants were behind a driver with his hands on the steering wheel ($SD^2_{\text{no-cell}} = 9.36$).

We then combine (or pool) the variances of the two groups so that we have a variance that represents the variability in the entire sample. The **pooled variance** squares

Standard error of the difference between the means (SD_{X-X}): The average variability in a sampling distribution of differences between means.

Pooled variance (SD^2_{pooled}): Estimate of the total variance for a sample of scores computed by combining and weighting by their respective *n* the variances of the two groups making up the sample.

the *SD* for each group in our study; it also takes into account the number in each group (in case the *N* per group is different) so that each variance is weighted according to the total *N*. The formula for the pooled variance is:

$$SD^2_{pooled} = \frac{(n_1-1)SD_1^2 + (n_2-1)SD_2^2}{(n_1-1) + (n_2-1)}$$

where n_1 = the number of participants in group 1 of the study; SD_1^2 = the variance for group 1; n_2 = the number of participants in group 2 of the study; and SD_2^2 = the variance for group 2.

Substituting the standard deviations (*SD*) and number in each group (*n*) from our study (from the table above) in the *pooled variance* formula, we find:

$$SD^2_{pooled} = \frac{(n_{cell}-1)SD_{cell}^2 + (n_{no\ cell}-1)SD_{no\ cell}^2}{(n_{cell}-1) + (n_{no\ cell}-1)}$$

$$= \frac{(10-1)(2.04)^2 + (10-1)(3.06)^2}{(10-1) + (10-1)}$$

$$= \frac{9\,(4.16) + 9\,(9.36)}{9+9} = \frac{37.44 + 84.24}{18} = \frac{121.68}{18} = 6.76$$

With the pooled variance, we can now estimate the standard error of the difference between the means (SD_{X-X}), which is the standard deviation of the sampling distribution and will tell us how much variability exists in the sampling distribution. The variability in a sampling distribution will be much smaller than the variability within a sample, which is based on raw scores. And each sampling distribution is specific to the *N* of a study so we have to take that into account. Finally, we have to take the square root of the computation because we used squared standard deviations (variances) in the pooled variance formula. The formula for the standard error of the difference is:

$$SD_{X-X} = \sqrt{SD^2_{pooled}\frac{1}{(n_1)}+\frac{1}{(n_2)}}$$

where SD^2_{pooled} = pooled variance of the two groups in the study; n_1 = number of scores in group 1; n_2 = number of scores in group 2.

We then enter the pooled variance we just computed and the number (*n*) from each group in our study into the *standard error of the difference* formula:

$$SD_{X-X} = \sqrt{SD^2_{pooled}\frac{1}{(n_{cell})}+\frac{1}{(n_{no\ cell})}}$$

$$= \sqrt{6.76\,\frac{1}{10}+\frac{1}{10}} = \sqrt{6.76\,(.2)} = \sqrt{1.352} = 1.16$$

We are now ready to compute the independent-samples t test. The formula for the independent-samples t test is:

$$t = \frac{M_1 - M_2}{SD_{X-X}}$$

The t value that results from this formula represents the number of standard deviations the mean difference of our samples is from the zero difference expected by the null hypothesis (see Appendix D.6 for the computational formula).

Using the values from our study, we find:

$$t = \frac{M_{cell} - M_{no\ cell}}{SD_{X-X}} = \frac{5.20 - 7.70}{1.16} = \frac{-2.50}{1.16} = -2.15$$

In computing the independent-samples t test, we make several assumptions:

- IV (or predictor) is dichotomous (nominal scale with two groups)
- Groups are independent
- DV (or outcome) is interval or ratio scale of measurement
- DV (or outcome) is normally distributed
- Variability (SD) in each sample is similar (*homogeneity of variance*)

Because we combine or "pool" the variances of our two groups to create an estimate of the population variance for the sampling distributions, it is important that the variances are similar. This similarity is referred to as **homogeneity of variance**, and we can check that this assumption has been met before computing independent-samples t tests using a test called **Levene's Test for Equality of Variances**.

The t value we compute is called t obtained (t_{obt}). We compare this value to the critical t value (t_{crit}), which is shown below in Table 10.2. This is the same table we used in Chapter 7 to find our critical value for a one-sample t test. (The values shown in Table 10.2 are an excerpt from the full table of critical t values in Appendix C.4.) The table lists the values of t that denote the regions of rejection for samples with specific degrees of freedom (df).

Homogeneity of variance: Assumption that the variance of populations is the same; group standard deviations serve as estimates of the population variances.

Levene's Test for Equality of Variances: A statistical test that examines whether the variability within different samples is similar.

Remember that df are computed from N or the number of participants in a study. We lose one df for each group in a simple experiment so in an independent-samples t test:

$$df = (n_1 - 1) + (n_2 - 1)$$

In our study, we had 10 participants in the cell phone and in the no–cell phone groups so:

$$df = (10 - 1) + (10 - 1) = 18$$

When we look at Table 10.2, we see that the top rows define the type of hypothesis (one- or two-tailed) and the p value we want to use to reject the null hypothesis. In our alternative hypothesis, we predicted a difference between the time to honk when behind a driver using a cell phone and a driver with his hands on the wheel (a two-tailed test). Suppose we want to reject our null hypothesis at the .05 level. We would use the second row or two-tailed test and go to the third column of t_{crit} values because it is designated as the $p = .05$ level. We then go down the third column until we match the degrees of freedom for our study ($df = 18$).

TABLE 10.2
Excerpt of Table of Critical t Values

Probability Levels					
One-tailed	**0.10**	**0.05**	**0.025**	**0.01**	**0.005**
Two-tailed		**0.10**	**0.05**	**0.02**	**0.01**
df					
1	3.078	6.314	12.706	31.821	63.657
2	1.886	2.920	4.303	6.965	9.925
15	1.341	1.753	2.131	2.602	2.947
16	1.337	1.746	2.120	2.583	2.921
17	1.333	1.740	2.110	2.567	2.898
18	1.330	1.734	2.101	2.552	2.878
19	1.328	1.729	2.093	2.539	2.861
20	1.325	1.725	2.086	2.528	2.845
21	1.323	1.721	2.080	2.518	2.831

We find $t_{crit} = 2.101$ (the value is shaded in the table). This means that the extreme 5% of the t values in a sampling distribution for a sample with 18 df falls beyond plus or minus 2.101. Our t_{obt} value of -2.15 is greater than the t_{crit} and thus falls in the region of rejection. We can then reject the null hypothesis that there is no difference in the number of seconds to honk when behind a driver using a cell phone or one not using a cell phone. We accept or support our alternative hypothesis that there is a difference in time to honk between the two groups.

If, instead, we had predicted that the drivers behind the cell phone user would honk more quickly (or in fewer seconds) than those behind a driver not using a cell phone, we would have a one-tailed hypothesis. We could then use the first row of Table 10.2 and go to the second column which represents $p = .05$ for one-tailed tests and find $t_{crit} = 1.734$. Notice that the critical t values are smaller for a one-tailed than a two-tailed test, and thus it is easier to reject the null hypothesis using a one-tailed test. This is because the entire region of rejection (5%) is contained in one tail, while the 5% rejection region is split in the two-tailed test and you must obtain a t that is outside the highest or lowest 2.5% of the distribution. Remember that because the two-tailed test is the more conservative test (because it is harder to reject your null hypothesis using it), it is better to use the two-tailed test even when you predict a direction in your hypothesis (see Practice 10.2).

In interpreting results of an independent-samples t test, we must pay careful attention to the direction of the difference in the means. In our example, we found that those behind a driver using a cell phone were quicker to honk (had a lower mean time) than those behind a driver not using a cell phone, and that result is consistent with our hypothesis. Our interpretation would be very different if we instead found that the mean time for the cell phone condition was higher than the no-cell phone condition. This is an obvious point, but we find that students sometimes get so focused on statistical significance that they forget to think about the direction of the difference.

In interpreting results from an independent-samples t test, we must also be careful to note the type of study that generated the data we analyzed. In the example above, we have an experiment and thus can make conclusions about the causal effect of the use

---

REVIEW OF KEY CONCEPTS: TYPE I AND TYPE II ERRORS

What is a Type I error? A Type II error?
Answers:

    A Type I error occurs when you reject a true null hypothesis or when you think you have found a difference; but, in reality, there is not one. It is equal to the p value when you reject the null hypothesis.

    A Type II error is when you fail to reject the null hypothesis when there is in fact a difference between groups. In this text, we do not compute the exact probability of a Type II error.

of a cell phone by one driver on other drivers' aggression. In the case of correlational designs or quasi-experiments, our conclusions will be couched in terms of the relationship or correlation between the variables being analyzed. Remember that if we have a correlational study, instead of using the terms IV and DV, we would instead refer to the predictor and outcome.

Practice 10.2

TYPE I AND TYPE II ERRORS

1. Given the results in the cell phone study discussed in the previous section, what is the probability of making a Type I error? A Type II error? How do you know?

2. What are the implications of making a Type I error in this study?

Review the answers found in Appendix A.

Confidence Intervals

Another way to look at results is to define the interval of means that we are confident that our mean difference falls within. In other words, the **confidence interval** defines the highest mean difference and the lowest mean difference (and the values in between) we would expect for a population whose mean (μ) difference equals the difference we found in our study.

For example, if we use $p < .05$, we are defining the interval of mean differences where we can expect 95% of the time the mean difference would fall. We already have all of the values we need to calculate the confidence interval:

$$(SD_{x-x})\ (-t_{crit}) + (M_1 - M_2) \leq \mu_1 - \mu_2 \leq (SD_{x-x})\ (+t_{crit}) + (M_1 - M_2)$$

For our study, we computed SD_{x-x} (in the denominator of the t test formula) = 1.16, and the mean difference ($M_{cell} - M_{no\text{-}cell}$) = 5.20 − 7.70 = −2.50. To determine the 95% confidence interval, we need to use our df, which was 18, to find the t_{crit} in Table 10.2 for $p = .05$ for a two-tailed test. Looking at the table, we find $t_{crit} = \pm\ 2.101$.

If we substitute the values for our study, we have:

> **Confidence interval:** Defines the interval that we are confident contains the population μ difference represented by our sample mean difference; typically, we compute the 95% confidence interval.

$$(1.16) \, (-2.101) + (-2.50) \leq \mu_1 - \mu_2 \leq (1.16) \, (+2.101) + (-2.50)$$

After multiplying 1.16 by 2.101, we find:

$$-2.44 + (-2.50) \leq \mu_1 - \mu_2 \leq +2.44 + (-2.50)$$

We subtract and add the quotient to our mean difference of −2.50, and we find:

$$-4.94 \leq \mu_1 - \mu_2 \leq -.06$$

The results tell us that we can be 95% confident that our mean difference of −2.50 represents a population of mean differences that fall between −4.94 and −.06. Another way to state this is that we are 95% confident that drivers behind a driver using his cell phone will honk .06 to 4.94 seconds faster than those behind a driver who is just slow to move after a light change. Using APA format, we could report 95% CI [.06, 4.94].

Effect Size

As part of the analysis of a simple experiment with independent groups, we should always compute the effect size, which describes the strength or magnitude of the effect of the IV. We then interpret that effect as size as small/weak, medium/moderate, large/strong (see Chapter 6, Table 6.3). We know from the t test analyzing our example study that the manipulation of a driver using a cell phone created a

---

REVIEW OF KEY CONCEPTS: STRENGTH OF THE EFFECT

1. Remember that since 1999 the American Psychological Association requires that researchers provide information about the strength of the effect of an IV in addition to its statistical significance. What term is used to denote the magnitude or strength of an IV?

2. How do we interpret this statistic?

Answers:

1. The effect size describes the strength of the effect of an IV (or the strength of the relationship between a predictor and outcome in a correlational study). There are a couple of effect sizes used with t tests. One is the r_{pb}^2 or the squared point-

biserial correlation coefficient and the other is Cohen's d.

2. The squared point-biserial correlation coefficient is interpreted as telling us the percentage of variability in the DV (or outcome) that is accounted for by its relationship with the IV (or predictor).

Cohen's d is interpreted as the standardized size of the difference between the two group means or the magnitude of the effect of the IV on the DV expressed in standard deviation units.

If you need to review the concept of effect size, refer back to Chapter 6 for a more detailed explanation.

browndogstudios

statistically significant difference in time to honk, but we do not know how strong this effect is. One statistic we compute for the effect size of an independent-groups simple experiment is the **squared point-biserial correlation** (r^2_{pb}). The point-biserial correlation is used with a dichotomous variable and an interval/ratio variable, which we have in an independent-groups simple experiment. We square it to obtain the percentage of variance of our DV (or outcome variable) accounted for by our IV (or predictor variable).

We can calculate the r^2_{pb} for our cell phone experiment, using the formula:

$$r^2_{pb} = \frac{t^2}{t^2 + df}$$

Plugging in the t obtained in our sample study, we find:

$$r^2_{pb} = \frac{t^2}{t^2 + df} = \frac{(-2.15)^2}{(-2.15)^2 + 18} = \frac{4.62}{4.62 + 18} = \frac{4.62}{22.62} = .204$$

The result tells us that 20.4% of the variability in the seconds to honk is accounted for by the IV or the use or no use of a cell phone by a driver in front. This suggests that the use of a cell phone by a driver who does not move has moderate strength in affecting the time it takes a driver behind to honk after a traffic light turns green.

A second statistic used to assess the effect size for an independent-samples simple experiment is **Cohen's d**. It is appropriate when the standard deviations of the two groups as well as the size (n) of the two groups are similar. The formula for Cohen's d uses the means of the two groups and the pooled standard deviation. The result is a value representing a standardized difference between the two means, expressed in standard deviation units.

We can calculate Cohen's d for our cell phone experiment, using the formula:

$$\text{Cohen's } d = \frac{M_2 - M_1}{SD_{\text{pooled}}}$$

where M_2 is the mean for group 2, M_1 is the mean for group 1, and SD_{pooled} is the average standard deviation for the two groups.

We first have to compute SD_{pooled} using the formula:

$$SD_{\text{pooled}} = \sqrt{\frac{SD_1^2 + SD_2^2}{2}}$$

Squared point-biserial correlation (r^2_{pb}): A measure of effect size for the independent-samples t test, providing the percentage of variance in the outcome (or DV) accounted for by the predictor (or IV).

Cohen's d (d): Another measure of effect size for the independent-samples t test, representing the difference between two means, expressed in standard deviation units.

Inserting the values from our driving study, we have:

$$SD_{pooled} = \sqrt{\frac{SD_1^2 + SD_2^2}{2}} = \sqrt{\frac{2.04^2 + 3.06^2}{2}} = \sqrt{\frac{4.16 + 9.36}{2}} = \sqrt{\frac{13.52}{2}} = \sqrt{6.76} = 2.60$$

Inserting the SD_{pooled} and the group means into Cohen's d formula, we find:

$$d = \frac{M_2 - M_1}{SD_{pooled}} = \frac{7.70 - 5.20}{2.60} = 0.96$$

The result tells us that the means differ by 0.96 standard deviation units, which is interpreted as a strong effect size. We conclude that being delayed in traffic by a driver using a cell phone has a strong impact on the aggression of a driver in the car behind the cell phone user (as measured by the quickness to honk).

Practical Significance

As we learned in Chapter 6, we should also consider the practical significance of our results. In other words, do our results have any implications or impact for the real world? We consider practical significance by reviewing our means and the difference between them. In our example study, the drivers behind the driver using his cell phone honked 2 seconds faster than the drivers behind the driver who had his hands on the wheel.

We found that this difference was statistically significant, but is 2 seconds *practically* significant in the overall conditions of driving a car? This brief time frame can have practical significance if we think about preventing accidents, but in this study, we are talking about how quickly a driver becomes impatient or perhaps angry about a delay. Of course, the emotions drivers felt when they honked could then affect their driving capabilities. The results do suggest that drivers are quicker to show their impatience with a driver using a cell phone than the same driver who is just slow to respond to a light turning green. Obviously, there is no one answer, but we should always consider the practical implications of our results.

USING DATA ANALYSIS PROGRAMS: INDEPENDENT-SAMPLES *t* TEST

Data Entry

Today, we rarely hand-calculate statistics and instead typically use a statistical package to compute an independent-samples *t* test. Regardless of the package you use, you will need the raw data for each of your groups. Remember that your results can only be as valid as the data you enter, so always check for data entry errors. If your results do not appear to match what you expected from entering your data, go back to make sure you did not make data entry errors. Table 10.3 provides instructions for entering data for our sample simple experiment and depicts the dataset that might result.

After entering the data, you would request an independent-samples *t* test. You would specify that the variable "Cell Phone" is the IV and "Secs to Honk" is the DV. Table 10.4 presents a sample of the output you would obtain if you used SPSS to compute an independent-samples *t* test.

The first box of the output (Group Statistics) provides you with a table of the descriptive statistics (*M, SD*) for your study. The second box (Independent Samples Test) contains the results of the *t* test. The second box also includes the results for Levene's test for homogeneity of variance. Remember that one of the assumptions of the independent-samples *t* test is that your groups have similar variances. The Levene's test checks to see if this assumption is met. *It is one of the only tests that you do not want to find significant.*

If Levene's is not significant (and it was not for our study), you will continue across the top line of the output for the independent-samples *t* test. This line lists the *df*, *t* value,

TABLE 10.3

SPSS Dataset for Example Study

	Cell Phone	Secs to Honk
To enter the data for an independent-samples *t* test in SPSS, you need to define two variables as shown in the dataset to the right.	1.00	2.00
	1.00	6.00
	1.00	8.00

The first variable is the IV and in our study is "cell phone." You specify codes for each of your groups or levels. In our example,
    1 = yes (cell phone)
    2 = no (no cell phone)
as seen in the first column.
	1.00	4.00

	1.00	5.00
	1.00	5.00
	1.00	7.00
	1.00	3.00
	1.00	8.00
	1.00	4.00
	2.00	3.00
The second variable is the DV or seconds to honk, which is entered in the second column.	2.00	9.00
	2.00	10.00
	2.00	5.00
Make sure the codes for the IV in one column match the appropriate data for the DV in a second column.	2.00	8.00
	2.00	9.00
	2.00	11.00
	2.00	4.00
	2.00	12.00
	2.00	6.00

TABLE 10.4

SPSS Output for an Independent-Samples *t* Test

Group Statistics

	Cell phone use	N	Mean	Std. Deviation	Std. Error Mean
Secs to Honk	yes	10	5.2000	2.04396	.64636
	no	10	7.7000	3.05687	.96667

Independent Samples Test

	Levene's Test for Equality of Variances		t-test for Equality of Means							
	F	Sig.	t	df	Sig. (2-tailed)	Mean Difference	Std. Error Difference	95% Confidence Interval of the Difference		
Secs to Honk								Lower	Upper	
Equal variances assumed	2.603	.124	-2.150	18	.045	-2.50000	1.16285	-4.94306	-.05694	
Equal variances not assumed			-2.150	15.707	.048	-2.50000	1.16285	-4.96888	.03112	

p value, the standard error of the difference (SD_{X-X}) and the 95% confidence interval values. Note that SPSS (and other statistical packages) report the exact *p* value instead of the standard .05, .01, and so on, values that are found in the table of critical *t* values. All of the other values match what we computed by hand earlier in the chapter, and thus we can interpret them as we did our values calculated by hand. You will need these values to write the report of your study.

If, however, the Levene's test for homogeneity is significant, you need to use a more stringent *t* test, which SPSS conveniently computes for you and displays on the second line of the *t* test output. Note that the *df* changes (from 18 to 15.707); typically the *p* value also changes from that obtained when homogeneity of variance is assumed in the upper line of the output. In our case *if* Levene's had been significant, our *p* value would have increased from .045 to .048. If Levene's is significant ($p < .05$), you must report this significance and also use the values on the lower line of the output to describe your *t* test results.

Data Analysis

Because of the importance of reporting the correct analysis, when you run a *t* test you should always *first* examine the results of Levene's test for homogeneity of variance in order to decide whether to focus on the upper or the lower line of the *t* test output.

In addition to computing a *t* test, we can obtain the effect size (or r_{pb}^2) for our study by computing the correlation between the independent variable (use of cell phone) and dependent variable (seconds to honk). In SPSS, you can use the correlation command to obtain the correlation and the output is shown in Table 10.5.

We find from the correlations output that $r = .452$. Remember that you must square this term in order to find the effect size (r_{pb}^2), which represents the percentage of variance in the dependent variable (seconds to honk) that is accounted for by its relationship with the independent variable (cell phone use). In our study, $r_{pb}^2 = (.452)^2 = .20$, just as we found earlier in our hand calculations.

TABLE 10.5

SPSS Output for the Correlation Between the IV and DV

Correlations		Cell phone use	Secs to Honk
Cell phone use	Pearson Correlation	1	.452*
	Sig. (2-tailed)		.045
	N	20	20

*Correlation is significant at the .05 level (2-tailed).

Rather than reporting r^2_{pb} as your effect size, you might report Cohen's *d*. SPSS does not compute this statistic so you will need to hand compute it (as you did above), or you can enter the formula into Excel, or you can use the online calculator www.uccs.edu/~faculty/lbecker/, which requires that you enter the *M, SD* for each of your groups. Regardless of how you compute it, in our example *d* = 0.96, reflecting that the means of the groups differ by almost one *SD*. Remember to check with your instructor about which effect size statistic should be reported in your class. We are now ready to report our findings. Application 10.1 provides sample Results and Discussion sections for this study. Notice that *statistical significance, effect size*, and *confidence intervals* are included in the Results section. An interpretation of these statistical analyses is included in the Discussion section, along with a discussion of the *practical significance* of the results.

Let's see if you can apply what you have learned about two-group designs. Practice 10.3 provides an opportunity to do this.

Practice 10.3

PRACTICE INTERPRETING A TWO-GROUP DESIGN

Suppose we have conducted a study that examines the impact of auditory distraction on test performance. The test contains 50 items, each of which counts as 2 points. Students complete the test in a classroom with a constant hum from the heating vent or in the same classroom where a cell phone rings 5 minutes and 15 minutes after the test begins.

1. What type of study (correlational, quasi-experiment, experiment) is this? How do you know?

2. Identify the IV. What are the levels of the IV?

3. What is the DV? How is it operationalized? What scale of measurement is represented?

Kittisak_Taramas

The results of the study are below

Group Statistics

Distraction		N	Mean	Std. Deviation	Std. Error Mean
Test Score	constant noise	15	82.2000	6.66762	1.72157
	phone ring	15	77.3333	5.88784	1.52023

Independent Samples Test

		Levene's Test for Equality of Variances		*t* test for Equality of Means							
									95% Confidence Interval of the Difference		
		F	Sig.	t	df	Sig. (2-tailed)	Mean Difference	Std. Error Difference	Lower	Upper
Test Score	Equal variances assumed	.120	.731	2.119	28	.043	4.86667	2.29672	.16205	9.57128
	Equal variances not assumed			2.119	27.578	.043	4.86667	2.29672	.15880	9.57453

Correlations

		Distraction	Test Score
Distraction	Pearson Correlation	1	−.372*
	Sig. (2-tailed)		.043
	N	30	30

*Correlation is significant at the 0.05 level (2-tailed).

1. Do the results show homogeneity of variance? How can you tell?
2. Based on the results, would you reject or retain the null hypothesis? What is the probability of making a Type I error? A Type II error?
3. Compute the effect size for the study and interpret its meaning.
4. Comment on the practical significance of the findings.
5. Based on the findings, what do you conclude about the study in general?

See Appendix A to check your answers.

Application 10.1

SAMPLE RESULTS AND DISCUSSION FOR A SIMPLE EXPERIMENT USING INDEPENDENT GROUPS

Results

Drivers behind a driver using a cell phone honked more quickly ($M = 5.20$, $SD = 2.04$) than those behind the driver with his hands on the steering wheel ($M = 7.70$, $SD = 3.06$). An independent-samples t test was computed to compare the groups and was significant, $t(18) = -2.15$, $p = .045$, $r_{pb}^2 = .20$ (or $d = 0.96$). Those behind the driver using his cell phone honked significantly quicker than those behind the same driver when he was not using his cell phone. We are 95% confident that the difference between the means falls between -4.94 and $-.06$ seconds or 95% CI $[-4.94, -.06]$.

Discussion

This study adds to our information about the use of cell phones while driving. When there was a delay by a driver after a light turned green, drivers behind the lead driver honked significantly more quickly when the lead driver was using his cell phone than when he had his hands on the steering wheel. The strength of this variable, use of the cell phone, was moderate (for r_{pb}^2)/strong (for d), suggesting that cell phone use by drivers should be investigated further. If honking is one way of expressing aggression, these results suggest that the use of a cell phone promotes the expression of aggression in other drivers. These feelings of aggression could be dangerous if they distract the driver from the complex task of driving. This study has implications for our daily lives because in addition to the data that demonstrate drivers using cell phones are more distracted than those not using such devices (Drews, Pasupathi, & Strayer, 2008; Strayer, Drews, & Johnston, 2003), we also now have some evidence that the use of cell phones by the driver may negatively influence drivers of other cars.

We must be careful, however, not to overinterpret these data. The participants following the driver using a cell phone honked on average only 2 seconds faster than those following the slow to start driver. Such a difference may not be not be meaningful in actual traffic conditions, as the difference in this measure of irritation (time to honk) may not be noticeable to drivers. In addition, the study did not directly test the effect that a brief irritation caused by another driver has on the driving abilities of the target driver or even how long the feelings of aggression lasted. Future studies should examine the impact of this irritation, which resulted in more aggressive (quicker) honking. Drivers could be observed to see whether they tend to pass the cell phone driver car more quickly or follow the cell phone driver more closely across the intersection. Because the use of cell phones has not yet been banned while driving, more study about their effect on both the driver using them and other drivers around that driver is merited.

DESIGNS WITH MORE THAN TWO INDEPENDENT GROUPS

Most variables in real life are not limited to two levels. For example, think back to our example of chocolate. There are multiple kinds of chocolate (milk, bittersweet, dark, white, etc.) as well as various types of chocolate eaters (daily, weekly, monthly, etc.).

Likewise, there are many ways to use a cell phone (traditional talking, speakerphone, Bluetooth, texting, etc.). There are various types of therapy (cognitive, behavioral, cognitive-behavioral, drug, psychoanalysis, group, etc.). We often want to compare these multiple levels of a variable in a study. We call the type of study where we compare the effect of three or more independent levels of an IV a **multiple independent-groups design** or just a multiple-groups design. As with the two independent-groups design, the participants in each group in the multiple-groups design are different and unrelated to one another.

> **Multiple independent-groups design:** A study examining the effect of a manipulated IV or the relationship of a variable which has three or more levels on a DV; the participants in each level of the IV are unrelated.

The same three categories of two-group designs apply to multiple groups. We may have correlational, quasi-experimental, or experimental designs with three or more independent groups. For example, in a correlational design, we may want to correlate preexisting groups of chocolate eaters (daily, weekly, monthly, never) with their frequency of cognitive activities. In a quasi-experimental study, we may manipulate the amount of chocolate eaten among three or more groups (students in three 11 a.m. classes). Finally, in a multiple groups experiment, we could manipulate the amount or type of chocolate eaten, randomly assign participants to a group, and assess the effect of chocolate on mood.

When designing a multiple independent-groups experiment, we use the same controls and address the same concerns about the internal and external validity and power that were covered in the beginning of this chapter in regard to a simple experiment. We still randomly assign participants to groups, only we have more groups to assign to in this experiment.

Advantages of the Multiple Independent-Groups Design

The multiple independent-groups design has several advantages over the two-group design. Suppose we want to examine the effect of different types of chocolate on current mood. If we decided to compare bittersweet, milk, and white chocolate using simple experiments, we would have to conduct three different studies: one would compare bittersweet versus milk, one would compare bittersweet versus white, and one would compare milk versus white. The multiple-groups design is more efficient and allows us to compare all three types of chocolate in a single study. Because we can conduct one study with all three groups, we need fewer participants than if we did multiple simple experiments. If each group has 10 participants, we would need 20 participants for each of three simple experiments (e.g., 10 in the bittersweet and 10 in the milk for the first study, then 10 in the bittersweet and 10 in the white, etc.), or a total of 60 participants. If we conducted a single multiple-groups study with 10 participants in each of the three types of chocolate groups, we would need a total of only 30 participants.

In addition, for each of the studies we conduct, there is a probability of a Type I error. So, for example, for each of the three simple experiments comparing two types of chocolate, we have a .05 probability of a Type I error, which is cumulative; and we end up with more than a .05 probability of a Type I error after three studies. For the single multiple-groups study, we have only a .05 probability of a Type I error.

Because the multiple-groups experiment allows us to consider the groups that actually exist, it is more reflective of reality and so has more external validity. With a multiple-groups design, we can examine the functional (or existing) relationship between levels. With a simple experiment, we can examine only a linear relationship because all we can see is the relationship between the two values of our IV. For example, participants may feel more positive after eating milk chocolate than eating white chocolate. Thus, we have a linear relationship (see Figure 10.4a). But if we examine mood after eating milk, bittersweet, or white chocolate, we may find that people feel most positive after eating milk chocolate, somewhat positive after eating bittersweet chocolate, and least positive after eating white chocolate (see Figure 10.4b). Or we could find that people feel equally positive after eating milk and bittersweet chocolate and much less positive after eating white chocolate. Without comparing all three types of chocolate at once, we cannot determine the functional relationship or direct comparison of the chocolates on mood.

Finally, a multiple-groups design allows us to use multiple control groups, which decreases the probability of confounding. For example, in addition to white chocolate, which looks different from other chocolates and has no cacao (and is not really chocolate regardless of its name), we could add a carob group to our study. Carob also lacks the critical chocolate ingredient of cacao, but it would look very similar to the chocolate samples. This would allow us to see if types of chocolate differ from each other as well

FIGURE 10.4

Comparison of Relationships Between Two Levels of a Variable (Linear) and Three Levels of the Same Variable (Functional)

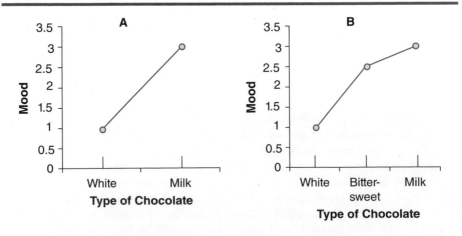

as from types of no chocolate that are similar or different in appearance from the chocolate. Using multiple control groups reduces the probability that our findings are due to confounding (see Figure 10.5).

FIGURE 10.5

Advantages of Multiple-Groups Design Over Simple Experiments

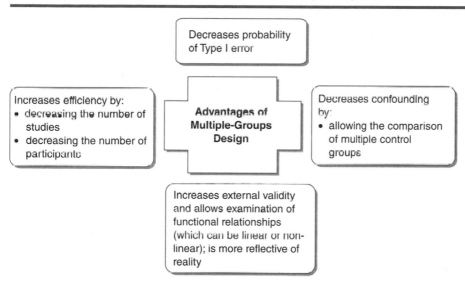

One-Way Analysis of Variance

When you have three or more conditions or groups, we use a test called the **one-way analysis of variance** or **one-way ANOVA**. This statistical test can be used with any of the three types of multiple-groups designs. In the case of an experiment, the ANOVA examines the causal effect of an IV with three or more levels on a DV. In correlational and quasi-experimental designs, the ANOVA examines the relationship between the grouping variable and the measured variable. "One-way" refers to the fact that we have only one independent variable. Designs that have more than one IV will be discussed in Chapter 12 and use a two-way or even a three-way ANOVA to analyze their results, depending on the number of IVs a study contains. The ANOVA does what its name implies—it analyzes the different kinds of variance in a study.

> **One-way analysis of variance/one-way ANOVA:** The inferential statistical test used to analyze data from a multiple-groups design.

As with a *t* test, the first step in conducting a one-way ANOVA is to state our null and alternative hypotheses. Our null (H_0) and alternative hypotheses (H_a), however, now compare more groups. In the case of our chocolate study:

H_0: There is no difference in mood ratings after eating milk, bittersweet, or white chocolate.

H_a: There will be a difference in mood ratings after eating milk, bittersweet, or white chocolate.

Or in numerical terms:

$$H_0: \mu_{milk} = \mu_{bittersweet} = \mu_{white}$$

$$H_a: \mu_{milk} \neq \mu_{bittersweet} \neq \mu_{white}$$

Figure 10.6 presents a simple question that can lead to a multiple independent-groups experiment because there are many different types of chocolate that we may want to examine.

In a one-way ANOVA, we compare the two variances identified above, **between-groups (treatment) variance** and **within-groups (error) variance**. Between-groups variance is composed of the variance from two sources: (1) treatment variance created

Between-groups (treatment) variance: Variability in scores created by the different levels of the IV; researchers attempt to maximize this variability.

Within-groups (error) variance: Variability in scores created by individual or participant differences; researchers attempt to reduce this variability.

REVIEW OF KEY CONCEPTS: WITHIN- AND BETWEEN-GROUPS VARIANCE

What types of variance have you already learned about?

Answer:

Within-groups variance (error variance) is the variability among the scores of participants. This variability is created by the individual differences of each person, which result in slight differences in scores even under the same conditions. This type of variance is also referred to as error variance, as it is not something we can control (each person is unique).

Between-groups variance (treatment variance) is the variability created by different conditions (think different levels of an IV). Although you have not used the term treatment variance before, you have learned about the variation created by different levels of an IV. We design experiments because of our belief that the conditions will affect the DV differently, and thus we attempt to create identifiable treatment variance.

FIGURE 10.6
Do Different Types of Chocolate Affect Mood?

What is the effect of the thousands of pounds of chocolate consumed around the world? Does it affect our mood?

Source: Sandi Coon

in the scores (DV or outcome variable) by the treatment, and (2) error variance created by individual differences among our participants. We can never completely delete or control the error variance so it is present in each group or condition of a study.

Another way to think about this is: In an experiment, participants in each level of the IV respond to that level of the IV (treatment variance) plus respond in their unique manner (error variance). Within each level of the IV, we control conditions to eliminate as much variability in responses as we can, but we still have each participant responding to the same level of an IV in a somewhat unique manner (error variance). Thus, between-groups variance contains both treatment and error variance:

Between-groups variance = treatment variance + error variance

Within-groups variance = error variance

The ANOVA compares these two sources of variability in order to determine if the IV creates more variability (between-groups variance) than we could expect by chance alone (within-groups variance). In other words, what is the ratio of the between-groups variance and the within-groups variance? The end point of an ANOVA is an F score, which is computed by dividing the between-groups variance by the within-groups variance or

$$F = \text{Between-groups variance/Within-groups variance}$$

Substituting what we learned above about these terms, we have

$$F = (\text{Treatment variance} + \text{Error variance})/\text{Error variance}$$

If our treatment has no effect (the null hypothesis is true), our IV does not create any effect and the treatment variability is zero (0). Then we have:

$$F = (\text{Treatment variance} + \text{Error variance})/\text{Error variance}$$

$$= 0 + \text{Error variance}/\text{Error variance}$$

$$= \text{Error variance}/\text{Error variance} = 1.0$$

Thus, if our null hypothesis is true (our IV has no effect) and there are no differences among the groups or levels in our experiment, we would expect F to be one ($F = 1.0$). In this case, the variability between our groups is the same as the variability within our groups.

The larger the effect of our treatment (IV) and the smaller the error variance, the larger we would expect F to be. As with the t test, the larger the F, the more likely it is to be statistically significant. Recall that two ways to increase power (or the likelihood of finding a statistically significant result) is to increase the magnitude of the effect (e.g., increase the between-groups variance) and increase the homogeneity of the sample (e.g., decrease the error variance). In terms of our study, we might choose to maximize the difference in the percentage of cacao in our types of chocolate in order to increase the treatment variance. We could also select a sample of homogeneous group of participants who rate chocolate as their favorite dessert in order to decrease the error variance.

After computing F, we then compare it to a sampling distribution of $F = 1.0$ (see Figure 10.7), which would result from conducting our study thousands of times if the null hypothesis is true and the between- and within-groups variances are similar. We want to see how far our calculated F is from the mean of the sampling distribution where population value (μ) of $F = 1.0$. Thus, our alternative hypothesis predicts $F > 1.0$. Because we are working with variance in the ANOVA and all terms are squared, our F can never be a negative value.

In computing the one-way independent-samples' ANOVA, we make several assumptions:

- IV (or predictor) has three or more levels (conditions)

- Groups are independent (participants belong to only one level/condition)

- DV (or outcome) is interval or ratio scale of measurement

- DV (or outcome) is normally distributed

- Homogeneity of variances is present (variability in each sample is similar)

FIGURE 10.7

Sampling Distribution of ANOVA

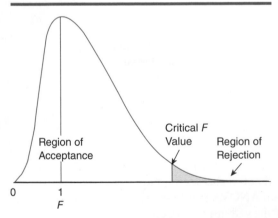

Note: Values in the sampling distribution of *Fs* will always be positive, as all values are squared. The expected value of *F* (according to the null hypothesis) is 1.0, with the alternative hypothesis always predicting larger *F* values; and thus the region of rejection always lies in the upper right-hand tail of the distribution.

FORMULAS AND CALCULATIONS: ONE-WAY INDEPENDENT-SAMPLES ANOVA

We have explained the rationale for the computation of a one-way ANOVA. Now it is time to actually compute it. We will summarize the computation here, but most researchers use a statistical package rather than hand calculations. (The detailed hand computation of the one-way ANOVA is found in Appendix D.7.) The computation involves several steps. Results for an ANOVA are displayed in a summary table (see Table 10.6 below), which contains the source of variance (treatment and error), the sums of squares, symbolized as SS (or each mean minus its raw scores squared and then summed) for each source, the df for each source, and the mean square, symbolized as MS (or the SS divided by the df), F, and p. It is a succinct way of presenting all of the steps to computing F.

Often we will substitute the name of the IV or predictor for Treatment in the summary table. In the case of our chocolate study, we may see Chocolate instead of Treatment. If you are using a statistical package such as SPSS to calculate the ANOVA, you might see Between instead of Treatment or Within instead of Error, depending on the statistical package.

In order to compute an ANOVA, you need to be familiar with the terminology and symbols used in the calculation. The sum of squares (SS) refers to the sum of deviation scores that are obtained by subtracting the mean from each score. In order to compute the treatment variance, we have to find the **sum of squares between groups (SS_B)** or treatment. Likewise, in order to compute the within group variation, we first find the **sum of squares within groups (SS_W)** or error. We also compute the sum of squared deviations around the mean of the entire sample (SS_{tot}).

Suppose for our chocolate study we compute the sums of squares between-groups (or Chocolate) and find $SS_{choc} = 17.73$. We compute the sums of squares within-groups

> **Sum of squares between groups (SS_B):** The sum of the squared deviations of treatment group means from the mean for the entire sample.
>
> **Sum of squares within groups (SS_W):** The sum of the squared deviations of each participant from the mean of their group.

TABLE 10.6

Summary Table for One-Way ANOVA

Source	SS	df	MS	F
Treatment	SS_B	$k-1$	SS/df_B	MS_B/MS_W
Error	SS_W	$N-k$	SS/df_W	
Total	SS_{tot}	$N-1$		

Note: Symbols used in the computation of ANOVA: k = number of levels; N = total number in the study; MS_B = estimate of population variance between groups; MS_W = estimate of population variance within groups.

(or error) and find $SS_{error} = 23.20$. We also find that our sums of squares total $(SS_{tot}) = 40.93$. Note that the sums of squares total is equal to the sum of the sums of squares treatment plus the sums of squares error $(SS_{tot} = SS_{choc} + SS_{error})$. We enter these values in a summary table as shown in Table 10.7a.

You can see from reading across the summary table that after computing the sums of squares for treatment (SS_B), error (SS_W), and total (SS_{tot}), our next step is to find the degrees of freedom (df) for each of these terms. Remember that we lose one degree of freedom for each value being considered. For the degrees of freedom between groups, we have the number of groups minus one or $(k - 1)$, where k = the number of levels or conditions in our study. For the degrees of freedom within groups, we use lose a degree of freedom for each group, so we have the total number of participants minus the number of groups or $(N - k)$. Finally, for the total degrees of freedom, we are working with the entire sample and lose only one degree of freedom or $(N - 1)$.

For our study we compute the degrees of freedom for between groups $(df_B$ or $df_{choc})$ and within groups $(df_W$ or $df_{error})$ according to the formulas. We have 3 types of chocolate (milk, bittersweet, and white) so $df_{choc} = k - 1 = 3 - 1 = 2$. Suppose we had a total of 15 participants in the 3 groups so our $df_{error} = N - k$ or $15 - 3 = 12$. The total degrees of freedom (df_{tot}) equals $N - 1$ or $15 - 1 = 14$. Note that, similar to the sums of squares, the total degrees of freedom is equal to the degrees of freedom between groups (chocolate) plus the degrees of freedom within (error) or $df_{tot} = df_{choc} + df_{error}$. We enter the df from our study in the summary Table 10.7a.

Continuing to read across the summary table, we use the term *mean square (MS)* for our estimate of population variance. The mean square (MS) value represents the average variance around the mean or the average squared deviation around the mean. It is obtained by dividing the sums of squares by its degrees of freedom or $MS = SS/df$.

For a one-way ANOVA we compute two mean squares, one for the **mean square within groups** (MS_W) and one for the **mean square between groups** (MS_B). The mean square within groups (MS_W) represents the average deviation within all the groups taken together or within-groups variance (think of the pooled variance you learned about for the

Mean square within groups (MS_W): The average deviation within all groups or levels of a study.

Mean square between groups (MS_B): The average deviation of group means from the total mean of a sample.

TABLE 10.7a

Summary Table for Our Sample Study

Source	SS	df	MS	F
Chocolate	17.73	2	?	?
Error	23.20	12	?	
Total	40.93	14		

independent-samples t test). We assume that the variances within each group are equal (homogeneity of variance) regardless of whether the null hypothesis is true or false, and thus pooling similar variances from the different groups will better represent our population variance. The mean square between groups (MS_B) represents the average deviation of the group means from the mean of all the participants or between-groups variance.

We have the information we need to compute the mean square values for our study because the mean square (MS) is computed by dividing the sums of squares (SS) by its degrees of freedom (df). Using the information from our summary table (Table 10.7a), we compute the mean squares for between-groups (chocolate):

$$MS_{choc} = SS_{choc}/df_{choc} = 17.73/2 = 8.86$$

and the mean squares for within-groups (error):

$$MS_{error} = SS_{error}/df_{error} = 23.20/12 = 1.93$$

We are now ready to compute F, which you should recall represents:

$$F = \text{Between-groups variance/Within-groups variance}$$

We substitute our mean squares and get:

$$F = MS_B/MS_w$$

Or for our study:

$$F = MS_{choc}/MS_{error} = 8.86/1.93 = 4.59$$

We enter all of these values in the summary table as shown in Table 10.7b.

Now we look in the Table C.6 of critical F values in Appendix C to find out whether our $F_{obt} = 4.59$ is greater than the critical F value (F_{crit}). See the excerpt of Table C.6 in Table 10.8 below. We have to use both the degrees of freedom within-groups and degrees of freedom between-groups to find our critical F value. The top row above the critical F values lists the degrees of freedom for between groups (df_B) or the treatment (df_{choc} in our study), and the far left column lists the degrees of freedom for within groups (df_W) or error (df_{error}). For our study, $df_B = 2$ and $df_W = 12$, so you go across the top of the table to 2 and then down until you match up with the row for 12 df. You find that $F_{crit} = 3.89$ for $p = .05$ and 6.93 for $p = .01$. Your value of $F_{obt} = 4.59$, so you can reject the null hypothesis at the $p = .05$ level. Your results show that there is a significant difference in mood after eating different types of chocolate.

TABLE 10.7b

Complete Summary Table for Our Sample Study

Source	SS	df	MS	F
Chocolate	17.73	2	8.86	4.59
Error	23.20	12	1.93	
Total	40.93	14		

Effect Size

Remember that in addition to statistical significance testing, we must also calculate a measure of the effect size. The statistic that measures effect size in ANOVAs is called **eta squared (η^2)**, and it is interpreted in the same way as r_{pb}^2 is for t tests. The calculation is relatively simple, as we just divide the between-groups sum of squares by the total sum of squares:

> **Eta squared (η^2):** The statistic used to assess the effect size in studies analyzed with an ANOVA.

TABLE 10.8

Excerpt of Table of Critical F Values

Critical F values for ANOVA with a particular probability level and df								
Degrees of freedom between groups (df_B) is in the numerator					$p = .05$ is in bold font			
Degrees of freedom between groups (df_w) is in the denominator					$p = .01$ is in light font			
df_B	1	2	3	4	5	6	7	8
df_w								
7	**5.59**	**4.74**	**4.35**	**4.12**	**3.97**	**3.87**	**3.79**	**3.73**
	12.25	9.55	8.45	7.85	7.46	7.19	6.99	6.84
8	**5.32**	**4.46**	**4.07**	**3.84**	**3.69**	**3.58**	**3.50**	**3.44**
	11.26	8.65	7.59	7.01	6.63	6.37	6.18	6.03
9	**5.12**	**4.26**	**3.86**	**3.63**	**3.48**	**3.37**	**3.29**	**3.23**
	10.56	8.02	6.99	6.42	6.06	5.80	5.61	5.47
10	**4.97**	**4.10**	**3.71**	**3.48**	**3.33**	**3.22**	**3.14**	**3.07**
	10.04	7.56	6.55	5.99	5.64	5.39	5.20	5.06
11	**4.84**	**3.98**	**3.59**	**3.36**	**3.20**	**3.10**	**3.01**	**2.95**
	9.65	6.93	6.22	5.67	5.32	5.07	4.89	4.74
12	**4.75**	**3.89**	**3.49**	**3.26**	**3.11**	**3.00**	**2.91**	**2.85**
	9.33	6.93	5.95	5.41	5.06	4.82	4.64	4.50
13	**4.67**	**3.81**	**3.41**	**3.18**	**3.03**	**2.92**	**2.83**	**2.77**
	9.07	6.70	5.74	5.21	4.86	4.62	4.44	4.30
14	**4.60**	**3.74**	**3.34**	**3.11**	**2.96**	**2.85**	**2.76**	**2.70**
	8.86	6.52	5.56	5.04	4.70	4.46	4.28	4.14

Practice 10.4

PRACTICE COMPLETING AND INTERPRETING A SUMMARY TABLE

1. Complete the following summary table.

   Hint: Remember the relationship between the different types of sums of squares and degrees of freedom ($SS_{tot} = SS_B + SS_W$ and $df_{tot} = df_B + df_W$).

Source	SS	df	MS	F
Treatment	??	3	??	??
Error	144	??	??	
Total	186	39		

2. How many conditions or levels does the IV have?
3. How many participants are in the study?
4. If the n is equal in each condition, how many participants are in each condition?
5. Are the results significant? How can you tell?
6. What is the effect size (η^2)?

Check your answers in Appendix A.

$$\eta^2 = SS_B/SS_{tot}$$

For our example: $\eta^2 = 17.73/40.93 = .433$

Thus, for our study 43% of the variability in mood ratings is accounted for by the type of chocolate.

We have covered a great deal of information about the one-way ANOVA. Practice 10.4 provides a chance to practice some of what you have just learned.

Post Hoc Tests

It is good to know that you can reject your null hypothesis. However, there's more to do—don't groan! Although you have found significance overall, you do not know whether the three treatment groups (milk, bittersweet, and white chocolate) differ from each other. If you find significance with your one-way ANOVA, you must then compute what is called a **post hoc test**. This test compares each group with every other group

Post hoc test: Test performed after you obtain a significant overall F with three or more groups; the results tell you which groups differ from one another.

(also called paired comparisons) so you can see where the significance in your overall F is coming from. For any study, the number of paired comparisons that are made using a post hoc test equals $k(k-1)/2$ (where k is the number of levels or groups). Remember the problem we mentioned at the beginning of this section that multiple tests of two groups results in an inflated probability of a Type I error. The post hoc tests have already taken care of this problem by employing some type of statistical correction. The type of statistical correction depends on the type of post hoc test you use, and there are many different types of post hoc tests. Some are more conservative and less likely to result in a Type I error, but then they may inflate the probability of a Type II error. Others are more liberal, allowing one to more easily find a significant difference between groups, but then the test may inflate Type I errors. Some common post hoc tests include the Bonferroni correction, Scheffé's method, Fisher's Least Significant Difference (LSD), and Tukey's Honestly Significant Difference (HSD). We will focus on Fisher's LSD in this chapter. For comparison purposes, computations for Tukey's HSD is provided in Appendix D.8.

Fisher's Least Significant Difference (LSD) test is a popular post hoc test that computes the value that groups must differ by in order to be significantly different. It is a relatively liberal test, allowing us to more easily find a significant difference than other post hoc tests such as Tukey's HSD (see Appendix D.8).

The formula for Fisher's LSD is

$$LSD = \tfrac{t_{crit}}{MS_w} \sqrt{MS_w(1/n_k + 1/n_k)}$$

where t_{crit} for MS_W = the critical value of t for $p = .05$ using df_W; MS_W = mean square within groups; n_k = number per group.

> **Fisher's Least Significant Difference (LSD) test:** A commonly used post hoc test that computes the smallest amount that group means can differ in order to be significant.

From computing our one-way ANOVA, we already know the mean square within groups (MS_W) and the number in each group (n_k) for our study. They can be obtained from the summary table for an ANOVA. (See Table 10.7b for these values in our study.) We get t_{crit} from the table of critical t values (Table C.4 in Appendix C) using $p = .05$ and the degrees of freedom for the mean square within groups or error (df_W).

The LSD formula has the flexibility of being used when you have a different number of participants in each cell. You change the n_k for each paired comparison if you have a different number of participants in groups. To make the paired comparisons, we make a matrix showing the different comparisons of each group mean with every other group mean. As noted above, the number of paired comparisons that are made using a post hoc test equals $k(k-1)/2$. For our study we have three groups, so the number of comparisons we need to make is: $3(3-1)/2$ or $3(2)/2 = 3$.

Inserting the values from our chocolate study:

$$LSD = 2.179 \sqrt{1.93 \, (1/5+1/5)} = 2.179 \sqrt{1.93 \, (.4)}$$
$$= 2.179 \sqrt{.772} = 2.179 \, (.88) = 1.92$$

The LSD results show that we need a difference between the mean mood ratings in our groups of at least 1.92. We see the mean differences between groups in our matrix:

	Milk	Bittersweet	White
Means	(6.40)	(7.20)	(4.60)
Milk	—	.80	1.80
Bittersweet		—	2.60*
White			—

*$p < .05$

After subtracting the means from one another, we find that among the three comparisons (milk with bittersweet, milk with white, bittersweet with white), only one of the three mean differences is larger than the least significant difference of 1.92. Thus, we will report that the only significant difference among the types of chocolate in producing a change in mood is between bittersweet and white. Those who ate bittersweet chocolate rated their mood significantly more positive than those who ate white chocolate. There were no differences in the ratings of those who ate milk and bittersweet chocolate or in the ratings of those who ate milk and white chocolate.

If you also want to report the confidence intervals for the individual groups, you can compute the confidence interval by hand using the formula provided in Chapter 7 or using a statistical package (e.g., SPSS, Excel).

USING DATA ANALYSIS PROGRAMS: ONE-WAY INDEPENDENT-SAMPLES ANOVA

As we have noted in regard to other statistical tests, it is most likely that you will use a statistical package to compute your analysis. In this section, we describe the one-way ANOVA and any needed post hoc tests using SPSS.

FIGURE 10.8

Data Entry for Our Sample Study to Compute a One-Way ANOVA

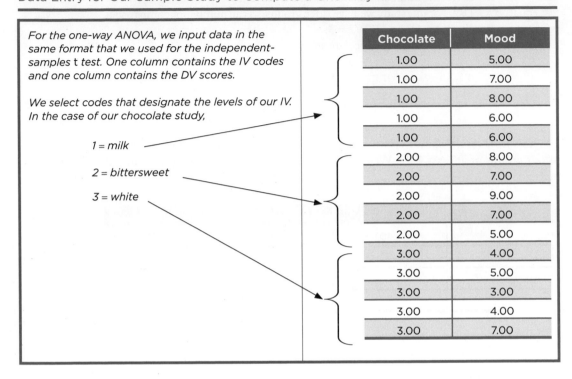

For the one-way ANOVA, we input data in the same format that we used for the independent-samples t test. One column contains the IV codes and one column contains the DV scores.

We select codes that designate the levels of our IV. In the case of our chocolate study,

1 = milk

2 = bittersweet

3 = white

Chocolate	Mood
1.00	5.00
1.00	7.00
1.00	8.00
1.00	6.00
1.00	6.00
2.00	8.00
2.00	7.00
2.00	9.00
2.00	7.00
2.00	5.00
3.00	4.00
3.00	5.00
3.00	3.00
3.00	4.00
3.00	7.00

Figure 10.8 provides instructions for entering the data for a one-way ANOVA and presents the dataset that results.

After the data are entered, we request a one-way independent-samples ANOVA. We specify the IV (chocolate) and DV (mood) for the statistical package. Table 10.9 presents the output for a one-way ANOVA using SPSS to analyze our chocolate study.

SPSS provides four boxes of output. The first box provides the descriptive statistics (*M, SD, n*) for the three groups and the total sample. The second box presents a summary table for the ANOVA results that mimics the summary table we built from hand calculations in Table 10.7b. Note that SPSS provides an exact significance value (Sig. = .033) rather than simply noting if $p < .05$ or .01.

We see that SPSS includes the test for homogeneity of variances in the third box of output. We are pleased to see that the test is not significant, so we have not violated the assumption of the ANOVA that the variability in groups is similar. Because the ANOVA is considered a robust test, it is not appreciably affected when the group variances are significantly different. Thus, we do not have to make adjustments to the analysis when

TABLE 10.9

Descriptive Statistics

Dependent Variable: Mood

Chocolate	Mean	Std. Deviation	N
milk	6.4000	1.14018	5
bittersweet	7.2000	1.48324	5
white	4.6000	1.51658	5
Total	6.0667	1.70992	15

ANOVA

Mood

	Sum of Squares	df	Mean Square	F	Sig.
Between Groups	17.733	2	8.867	4.586	.033
Within Groups	23.200	12	1.933		
Total	40.933	14			

Test of Homogeneity of Variances

Mood

Levene Statistic	df1	df2	Sig.
.117	2	12	.890

Measures of Association

	Eta	Eta Squared
Mood * Chocolate	.658	.433

Levene's is significant in a multiple-groups study. We would, however, note in the Results section of a report if Levene's is significant.

Finally, SPSS presents a box called Measures of Association as part of the ANOVA output. This box reports the effect size and includes both the eta and eta squared, but remember to report only the eta squared (η^2) in your results.

Once we determine that our one-way ANOVA has resulted in significant results, in this case $p = .033$, we should then request post hoc tests using SPSS. The output in Table 10.10 shows the results for both **Tukey's Honestly Significant Difference (HSD) test** and Fisher's LSD test. The results are presented as a matrix comparing all the means with each other. Note that the pairs are repeated (milk and bittersweet and later bittersweet and milk) so the matrix shows six paired comparisons instead of three.

> **Tukey's Honestly Significant Difference (HSD) test:** A popular post hoc test that is more conservative than most tests; it must be used with equal n and computes the least significant difference that is significant between means.

TABLE 10.10

SPSS Output for Two Commonly Used Post Hoc Tests

Tukey's HSD Output

Multiple Comparisons

Dependent Variable: Mood
Tukey HSD

(I) Chocolate	(J) Chocolate	Mean Difference (I-J)	Std. Error	Sig.	95% Confidence Interval	
					Lower Bound	Upper Bound
milk	bittersweet	-.80000	.87939	.645	-3.1461	1.5461
	white	1.80000	.87939	.143	-.5461	4.1461
bittersweet	milk	.80000	.87939	.645	-1.5461	3.1461
	white	2.60000*	.87939	.030	.2539	4.9461
white	milk	-1.80000	.87939	.143	-4.1461	.5461
	bittersweet	-2.60000*	.87939	.030	-4.9461	-.2539

* The mean difference is significant at the 0.05 level.

Fisher's LSD

Multiple Comparisons

Dependent Variable: Mood
LSD

(I) Chocolate	(J) Chocolate	Mean Difference (I-J)	Std. Error	Sig.	95% Confidence Interval	
					Lower Bound	Upper Bound
milk	bittersweet	-.80000	.87939	.381	-2.7160	1.1160
	white	1.80000	.87939	.063	-.1160	3.7160
bittersweet	milk	.80000	.87939	.381	-1.1160	2.7160
	white	2.60000*	.87939	.012	.6840	4.5160
white	milk	-1.80000	.87939	.063	-3.7160	.1160
	bittersweet	-2.60000*	.87939	.012	-4.5160	-.6840

* The mean difference is significant at the 0.05 level.

Reviewing the matrix for Tukey's HSD, you are most interested in the significance (Sig.) column, and look for values less than .05 ($p < .05$). The table shows that the paired comparison that meets this criterion is bittersweet and white chocolate ($p = .03$). The output alerts you to this significance by putting an asterisk (*) beside the mean difference (see the fourth mean difference of +2.60).

You see the same results as for Fisher's LSD or that the difference between the mean mood ratings for bittersweet and white chocolate is the only paired comparison that differs significantly ($p = .012$). The information that alerts you that Tukey's is the more conservative test is in the significance level (Sig. column). The Fisher's LSD significance level for bittersweet and white was a lower level ($p = .012$) than the significance

Application 10.2

SAMPLE WRITE-UP (OF HYPOTHETICAL RESULTS AND DISCUSSION) USING APA FORMAT

Results

The total mean score for mood ratings was 6.07 ($SD = 1.71$), indicating a moderately positive mood. Bittersweet chocolate resulted in the most positive mood scores ($M = 7.20$, $SD = 1.48$), followed by milk chocolate ($M = 6.40$, $SD = 1.14$), and then white chocolate ($M = 4.60$, $SD = 1.52$). A one-way ANOVA was computed on the mood scores and was significant, $F_{(2, 12)} = 4.59$, $p = .033$, $\eta^2 = .43$. Fisher's LSD test was computed to examine the group means. The analysis showed that bittersweet chocolate resulted in significantly higher positive mood ratings than white chocolate ($p = .012$). There were no other significant differences between the ratings of the groups.

Discussion

The results partially support our hypothesis that different types of chocolate will produce higher ratings of mood than no chocolate. While bittersweet chocolate produced higher mood ratings than white chocolate, the ratings for milk chocolate did not differ from either group. The strength of the effect was very strong, suggesting that there is something about cacao that is associated with mood. We expected that the ratings for both milk and bittersweet chocolate would differ from those for white chocolate. Although its name suggests that it belongs to the chocolate family, white chocolate does not contain any cacao and thus it served as a good control for the two types of chocolate. The bittersweet chocolate contained 60% cacao while the milk chocolate contained only 20% cacao. It may be that a certain level of cacao is required in order for mood to be significantly affected.

This pilot study does suggest that chocolate has the potential to influence mood. Future studies should examine multiple levels of cacao to see what level is sufficient to create an effect on mood. The amount of the taste sample might also be varied as the participants were given only 1 ounce in this study, which is less than the average serving size of chocolate. The sample size in this study also was quite small and does not generalize well to the populace. A larger number and more diverse group of the general public should be studied before one can make any generalizations about the effect of chocolate and mood.

level using the Tukey's HSD test ($p = .03$). In analyzing data from a study, we would use only one of these tests, depending on our stringency requirement, or equal n, or other goals. Note also that the output for both the post hoc tests provide the 95% confidence intervals for each of the paired comparisons.

We now have all the information we need to write up our results of our study. Note that the sample write-up is very simple and deals only with the analysis we have been discussing. In a study, you would often collect much more data, and the Results and Discussion sections would be longer and involve multiple analyses and more extensive discussion of theories, your hypotheses, and possible next studies.

A final reminder is that we have analyzed a multiple-groups experiment as an example in this chapter. We would use the same computations or SPSS analysis with a correlational or quasi-experiment multiple-groups design. The difference would be that, unlike our experimental design, we would be examining relationships and could not make conclusions about causation.

You now have the opportunity to practice your understanding of the analysis and interpretation of a multiple-groups study in Practice 10.5.

Practice 10.5

PRACTICE WITH THE ANALYSIS AND INTERPRETATION OF A MULTIPLE-GROUPS STUDY

A researcher conducted a study to determine if level of self-disclosure affects the trustworthiness of an individual. Participants were randomly assigned to engage in a 5-minute conversation with a stranger who disclosed a low, medium, or high level of personal information. After the conversation, the participants rated the trustworthiness of the person. The higher the score on the 25-point scale, the more trustworthy the participant rated the target.

Report

Trust			
Self-Disclosure	Mean	N	Std. Deviation
Low	15.0000	10	2.62467
Medium	20.3000	10	2.11082
High	13.7000	10	3.74314
Total	16.3333	30	4.03718

Measures of Association

	Eta	Eta Squared
Trust * Self Disclosure	.719	.517

ANOVA Table

			Sum of Squares	df	Mean Square	F	Sig.
Trust * Self-Disclosure	Between Groups	(Combined)	244.467	2	122.233	14.462	.000
	Within Groups		228.200	27	8.452		
	Total		472.667	29			

Multiple Comparisons

Dependent Variable: Trust

LSD

(I) Self-Disclosure	(J) Self-Disclosure	Mean Difference (I-J)	Std. Error	Sig.
Low	Medium	-5.30000*	1.30014	.000
	High	1.30000	1.30014	.326
Medium	Low	5.30000*	1.30014	.000
	High	6.60000*	1.30014	.000
High	Low	-1.30000	1.30014	.326
	Medium	-6.60000*	1.30014	.000

* The mean difference is significant at the 0.05 level.

a. What type of design is this study? How do you know? Identify all the characteristics that help you to identify the type of design.

b. Based on your results, would you reject or retain the null hypothesis? What is the probability of making a Type I error? A Type II error?

c. Interpret the meaning of the effect size for the study.

d. What does the post hoc test tell you about self-disclosure and trustworthiness?

e. Comment on the practical significance of the data.

See Appendix A to check your answers.

THE BIG PICTURE: IDENTIFYING AND ANALYZING INDEPENDENT-GROUPS DESIGNS

We have described several designs in this chapter. All of the designs include independent groups (i.e., the participants in different groups are not related to one another) and a DV that is on an interval or ratio scale. The designs differ on whether there is manipulation of the IV, whether there is random assignment to the IV level, and the number of groups or levels of the IV. In addition, the statistics used to analyze the designs differ as a function of whether there are two groups or more than two groups in the study. Figure 10.9 depicts the decision tree for the different types of independent-groups designs. Table 10.11 sorts the different designs by their characteristics and notes the statistical test(s) used to analyze each design. It is crucial that you are able to identify the type of design for a study as it determines the appropriate statistical analysis and the interpretation of your results.

FIGURE 10.9

Decision Tree for Independent-Groups Analyses

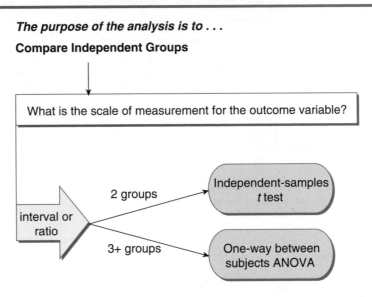

The purpose of the analysis is to . . .

Compare Independent Groups

What is the scale of measurement for the outcome variable?

interval or ratio

2 groups → Independent-samples *t* test

3+ groups → One-way between subjects ANOVA

TABLE 10.11

Overview of Independent Groups Designs and Analyses

	IV Manipulated?	Random Assignment?	Number of Groups	Statistical Analyses	Interpretation
Experiment	Yes	Yes	Two	Independent-samples *t* test, point-biserial correlation coefficient (r^2_{pb}) or Cohen's *d*, confidence interval	Causation
	Yes	Yes	Three or more	One-way ANOVA, post hoc test if significant, eta squared (η^2)	Causation

Quasi-Experiment	Yes	No	Two	Independent-samples t test, point-biserial correlation coefficient (r^2_{pb}) or Cohen's d, confidence interval	Correlation
	Yes	No	Three or more	One-way ANOVA, post hoc test if significant, eta squared (η^2)	Correlation
Correlation	No	No	Two	Independent-samples t test, point-biserial correlation coefficient (r^2_{pb}) or Cohen's d, confidence interval	Correlation
	No	No	Three or more	One-way ANOVA, post hoc test if significant, eta squared (η^2)	Correlation

CHAPTER RESOURCES

Key Terms

Define the following terms using your own words. You can check your answers by reviewing the chapter or by comparing them with the definitions in the glossary—but try to define them on your own first.

Between-groups (treatment) variance 334
Cohen's d 324
Confidence interval 322
Eta squared (η^2) 340
Fisher's Least Significant Difference (LSD) test 342
Homogeneity of variance 319
Independent-samples t test 313
Levene's Test for Equality of Variances 319

Mean square between groups (MS_B) 338
Mean square within groups (MS_W) 338
Multiple independent-groups design 331
One-way analysis of variance/ one-way ANOVA 333
Outcome 308
Pooled variance 317
Post hoc tests 341
Predictor variable 308
Simple experiment 310

Squared point-biserial correlation (r^2_{pb}) 324
Standard error of the difference between the means 317
Sum of squares between groups (SS_B) 337
Sum of squares within groups (SS_W) 337
Tukey's Honestly Significant Difference (HSD) test 346
Within-groups (error) variance 334

Do You Understand the Chapter?

Answer these questions on your own and then review the chapter to check your answers.

1. What are the characteristics of a simple experiment?

2. What are the assumptions of an independent-samples t test?

3. How does the standard error of the difference differ from the standard deviation?

4. Why is homogeneity of variance important in an experiment?

5. If Levene's test is significant, what does this mean? How does a significant Levene's test affect an independent-samples t test?

6. How are the squared point-biserial and Cohen's d similar, and how are they different?

7. How are the squared point-biserial and eta squared similar, and how are they different?

8. What information does the confidence interval provide?

9. What are the advantages of multiple-groups designs in comparison to simple experiments?

10. Distinguish between within-group and between-group variance. How are these concepts related to error variance and treatment variance?

11. What are the assumptions of a one-way analysis of variance (ANOVA)?

12. What terms make up a summary table, and how do you interpret each of them?

13. When do you compute post hoc tests, and what do these tests tell you?

Practice With Statistics

1. An independent-samples t test revealed that those participants who saw an action film ($M = 10.8$) were significantly more hostile than those participants who saw a drama film ($M = 6.78$) with the same starring actors, $t(24) = 3.54, p = .090, r_{pb}^2 = .34$. What is the flaw in this interpretation?

2. A researcher wants to know the effect of different types of music on energy level. In particular, she is interested in rap and classical music. She randomly assigns participants to each condition. Participants listen to either rap or classical music for 10 minutes and afterwards take a short quiz that assesses energy level ($1 = $ *very low energy*, $10 = $ *very high energy*). The results for the study are found below.

   a. What type of study is this? How do you know?

   b. Is there an IV? If so, identify its levels.

   c. What is the DV? How is it operationalized?

Group Statistics

	group	N	Mean	Std. Deviation	Std. Error Mean
Energy	rap	20	4.5500	1.53811	.34393
	classical	20	7.5500	.99868	.22331

Independent Samples Test

energy	Levene's Test for Equality of Variances		t-test for Equality of Means					
	F	Sig.	t	df	Sig. (2-tailed)	Mean Difference	Std. Error Difference
Equal variances assumed	5.112	.030	−7.316	38	.000	−3.00000	.41007
Equal variances not assumed			−7.316	32.602	.000	−3.00000	.41007

$r^2_{pb} = .58$

d. What assumption of the independent-samples t test has been violated?

e. What steps in reporting the results do you need to take because of this violation?

f. Write a Results section using the output.

g. What conclusions can you draw about the study?

3. A researcher wonders whether marital status is related to reported life satisfaction. She has a sample of adults provide information about their current status and respond to the five-question Satisfaction With Life Scale (SWLS). The possible range of scores is from 5 to 35, with higher scores indicating greater satisfaction with life. Demographic data are collected from the participants including marital status—single, married, separated, or divorced.

Report

Satisfaction with life scale total			
marital status	Mean	N	Std. Deviation
single	19.1667	12	7.95251
married	23.4000	45	6.12892
separated	19.0000	6	3.94968
divorced	19.5000	6	5.00999
Total	21.9420	69	6.44863

Measures of Association

	Eta	Eta Squared
Satisfaction with life scale total * marital status	.312	.098

Test of Homogeneity of Variances

Satisfaction with life scale total			
Levene Statistic	df1	df2	Sig.
2.061	3	65	.114

ANOVA

Satisfaction with life scale total					
	Sum of Squares	df	Mean Square	F	Sig.
Between Groups	275.801	3	91.934	2.342	.081
Within Groups	2551.967	65	39.261		
Total	2827.768	68			

a. State a directional alternative hypothesis.

b. Identify the type of study design and appropriate statistical analysis.

c. Report the results of the SPSS output above in APA format.

d. Do you need to compute any additional statistics? Explain.

Practice With SPSS
Trustworthiness of Politicians

1. A researcher wants to know if candidates with different levels of experience in politics are rated differently by voters on trustworthiness. She prepares a postcard with campaign information about a candidate and varies whether the candidate on the postcard is an incumbent for the office or is a first-time office seeker. She asks 20 participants (who are registered to vote) to look at the postcard for 2 minutes and rate the candidate on a variety of characteristics (e.g., experienced, attractive, knowledgeable, trustworthy) on a 7-point Likert-type scale ranging from 1 = *not at all* to 7 = *extremely*. She is interested only in the data on trustworthiness, which are shown to the right.

   a. State the null and a directional alternative hypothesis.

No Experience	Incumbent
4.00	3.00
6.00	6.00
5.00	4.00
7.00	3.00
4.00	5.00
7.00	3.00
4.00	4.00
5.00	3.00
5.00	4.00
4.00	5.00

   b. Enter the data into SPSS.

   c. Run an independent-samples *t* test to compare the two groups.

d. Compute the effect size (the proportion of variance in the DV accounted for by your IV) of political experience by running a point-biserial correlation in SPSS (which is the same way you would run a Pearson's r) or computing Cohen's d by hand. Remember that you will still need to square the correlation to get the proportion of variance accounted for to report in your Results section.

e. Write up your results as if you were going to include them in a Results section using correct APA format (i.e., double-space, italicize statistical notations, etc.).

f. Interpret your results as you would in a Discussion section. Include possible limitations to the study, recommendations for those running for political office, and a suggestion for future research.

Perceptions of Security Risk

No Hat	Knit Cap	Cowboy Hat
5	8	3
4	7	6
3	5	7
3	7	7
6	4	5
5	6	4
3	6	9
2	9	5
6	8	2
7	7	6
5	10	3
3	8	5

2. A researcher is interested in the effect that headwear has on perceptions of whether a person is a security risk at the airport. She takes pictures of a 35-year-old male with no hat, with a knit cap pulled low on his forehead, and with a cowboy hat. Security workers ($n = 36$) from the regional international airport are randomly assigned to view one of the pictures and asked to rate how much of a security risk they would consider the person in the picture. Ratings vary from 1 = *no risk* to 10 = *high risk*.

a. What is the IV? What are its levels?

b. State the null and directional alternative hypotheses.

c. Enter the data into SPSS.

d. Run the appropriate analysis(es) to compare the groups.

e. What test is required after the initial analysis? Why did you choose the test you did?

f. Write up your results as if you were going to include them in a Results section using APA format.

g. Interpret your results as you would in a Discussion section. Include possible limitations to the study, recommendations for security officials at the airport, and a suggestion for future research.

 **edge.sagepub.com/adams2e**

Sharpen your skills with SAGE edge!

SAGE edge for students provides you with tools to help you study. You'll find mobile-friendly eFlashcards and quizzes, as well as videos, web resources, datasets, and links to SAGE journal articles related to this chapter.

Dependent-Groups Designs

11

Reports of the frequency of posttraumatic stress disorder (PTSD) in soldiers returning from conflict-ridden areas around the world are fairly common in today's media; helping professionals from many different disciplines are seeking ways to reduce the symptoms of the disorder in an effort to improve the quality of life for these soldiers. Finding an appropriate therapeutic intervention that is effective for all or most soldiers is difficult as they manifest differing severities of PTSD, which then influence the type and frequency of their symptoms. In addition, the soldiers are very different individuals returning to different circumstances. How do we design studies that take into account the varied symptoms and circumstances of soldiers diagnosed with PTSD while attempting to find treatments that improve their lives?

The same three types of designs that you learned about in the last chapter—correlational, quasi-experimental, and true experiments—are relevant in this chapter. Make sure you understand the distinctions among these studies, as we will not discuss them separately in this chapter—although the examples here will be drawn from all three types of studies.

DESIGNS WITH DEPENDENT GROUPS

In group design studies, we strive to begin with participants in each of our groups who are similar in terms of their personal characteristics. We do not want all the friendly or dishonest or happy people or those high or low in verbal skills in one group; instead, we want to spread those characteristics across all of our groups, particularly if a characteristic or pattern of characteristics has the potential to influence the participants' responses that we are measuring. In the independent-groups designs that we studied in the previous chapter, we attempt to achieve equal groups (or similar characteristics across groups) through random assignment. The initial equating of

LEARNING OUTCOMES

In this chapter, you will learn

- About the two types of dependent designs—matched and repeated measures
- To identify the advantages and drawbacks of dependent designs
- How to compute and interpret dependent-groups t tests
- How to compute the confidence interval and effect size for dependent t tests
- How to compute and interpret dependent-groups one-way ANOVAs
- When and how to calculate post hoc tests for dependent one-way ANOVAs

REVIEW OF KEY CONCEPTS: TYPES OF INDEPENDENT-GROUPS DESIGNS

1. What three types of designs fall under the independent-groups designs?

2. Distinguish among these designs.

Answers:

1. Correlational, quasi-experiments, and experiments.

2. <u>Correlational designs</u> are meant to examine a relationship between variables; there is no random assignment, controlling of factors, or manipulation of a variable.

<u>Quasi-experimental designs</u> examine the relationship between previously existing groups and some other variable. There is manipulation of an independent variable (IV) but no random assignment and no causal inferences can be made.

<u>Experiments</u> involve the control of conditions within a study, random assignment to a level of the independent variable, and the measurement of a dependent variable (DV); and they allow inferences about causation.

characteristics across groups is critical because the analysis of each study compares groups to see if they are different on some variable either because they have been exposed to different levels of an IV or because they belong to a particular participant group. In experiments, we use random assignment to distribute participant characteristics so that groups are equal; this process works better with larger groups where we can be more confident that we have been able to distribute characteristics evenly across our groups. But most studies use small groups of 30 or fewer participants in each group. In correlational and quasi-experimental designs, we try to get a varied sample of each of the groups we are studying in an attempt to include different participant characteristics in each group.

The type of design that best supports our goal of beginning with similar participant characteristics in our groups is called **dependent-groups design**. This is a very powerful design, more powerful than the independent designs you learned about in the previous chapter. The power comes from the decrease in random error that is created by participant characteristics. This then decreases the chance of confounds due to participant variables and provides assurance of homogeneity of variance because the participants exhibit similar characteristics in each group. In addition, the design is more sensitive to changes in the measured variable because when you reduce the amount of error or uncontrolled variability, it is easier to see the variability created by the changes in the IV or differences related to a grouping variable. Another way to say this is: The differences due to the IV or the predictor do not have to compete for attention with

> **Dependent-groups design:** A design where the participants in different conditions are related or are the same people; the design reduces error variance and is more powerful than an independent design.

error variability. Remember that you learned in the last chapter that between-group variance includes both treatment variance (due to the level of the IV or predictor) and error variance (due to participant differences). A dependent design reduces the "noise" or variability created by participant differences that sometimes overwhelm or mask the variability created by the IV or associated with the grouping variable. There are two types of dependent designs—**matched-pairs design** and **repeated measures design (within-subjects design)**.

> **Matched-pairs design:** A design where participants in each group are matched on a characteristic relevant to the variable that is being measured (DV or outcome); in an experimental design a member of each matched pair is randomly assigned to each IV condition.
>
> **Repeated measures design (within-subjects design):** A design where participants experience every condition in a study; in an experiment, they also are randomly assigned to the order of conditions.

Matched-Pairs Design

We begin the explanation of dependent-groups designs by focusing on the matched-pairs design in which you pretest participants on some variable that is relevant to the variable you measure. In an experiment, you match the participants based on their scores, and then randomly assign them to groups. In a correlational or quasi-experiment, you are working with already defined groups so you match the participants in the existing groups. If participants do not score exactly the same on the matching variable, you can rank order all the participants by their scores and pair them by ranks (ranks 1 and 2, ranks 3 and 4, etc.). The pretest or matched variable should be highly correlated to the outcome variable you will be measuring (the DV in an experiment) and should serve to decrease the variance associated with the matching variable. We typically do not match on variables you will be analyzing but on another variable that is related to the variable of focus in your study. Once you match participants, your analysis is then focused on the effect of the IV on the DV in an experiment or the relationship of the grouping variable and the variable you measured in correlational or quasi-experimental designs. You, in effect, have multiple matched participants who replicate the effect of the IV on the DV or the relationship you are examining, and thus this design is more reliable than the independent design.

In our chocolate experiment in the previous chapter, we might match participants on their general mood, or we could match them on their liking for chocolate. If we matched on mood, we could then match the two participants who reported the most positive mood, then the next two with the most positive mood, and so on until we match the last pair who reported the least positive mood. Once we have our pairs, we would then randomly assign one participant from each pair to one of our conditions of chocolate—say bittersweet and white. When we finish this process, we will have equal groups in terms of mood; and then we conduct our study to see if eating chocolate affects mood, using the same controls as with an independent design. We also could match on both liking for chocolate and mood, which would perhaps further reduce participant (error) variability in our study so that each group would have participants who reported both the same mood and liking for chocolate. A matched design with the same variety of participant characteristics as an independent design will have the same external validity as the independent design.

Similarly, in our correlational design where we compared the amount of chocolate eaten by males and females, we might match males and females on their liking for chocolate before completing our analysis. We select the matching variable because we think it might affect how much chocolate people eat regardless of their gender. We want to be able to see the amount of chocolate eaten that is related to gender; and, by matching, we control some of the variability created by how much a person likes chocolate. This logic applies to quasi-experimental designs as well.

If the matched design reduces error variance—and thus is more sensitive to changes either created in the DV by the IV or related to a grouping variable, and thus is a more powerful design—why don't we use it all the time? You guessed it—there are some disadvantages of a matched design that we should consider when deciding what type of design to use. For one thing, we may not be able to find an *effective matching variable*. If the matching variable does not reduce the error variance, your study loses power because you decrease the *df* by half, which makes the t_{crit} larger. (Look at Table C.4 on page 575 or C.6 on page 579 to verify that as you move from larger to smaller *df,* the *t* or *F* value required to reject your null hypothesis increases.) Thus, with an ineffective matching variable, you actually may lose sensitivity to the effects of the IV or grouping variable.

Even if you find an effective matching variable, there are other potential problems. For each participant who drops out of your study (attrition), you also lose the person who was matched to him or her. You cannot generalize your results to participants who drop out after matching, so depending on how many participants you lose, you may reduce the external validity of your study. Your matching variable may *sensitize the participants* to the purpose of your study or allow the participants to guess the hypothesis and may then affect their behavior, thus affecting the construct validity of the study. Figure 11.1 demonstrates how this sensitization might affect a participant's behavior. Matching requires *more effort and time* on the part of the experimenter and also by the participants, if they have to come once to complete a measure for the matching process and return later to participate in the study. Given all the possible problems noted above, you can see why most studies use an independent groups design. Still, the increased power of a matched design makes it the preferable design if you are worried about only one or two variables confounding your results and you can match on one or both of these variables. See Figure 11.2 (p. 362) for issues to consider in matched-pairs designs.

Repeated Measures Design

In the repeated measures dependent design, participants serve as their own control and participate in every condition of the experiment. For this reason, the design is also called the within-subjects design. (Many years ago, participants were called "subjects" rather than "participants.") This design derives its power by controlling all potential confounding participant variables because the participants are the same in each condition of the IV. Be sure

One potential problem with matched-pairs designs is sensitizing participants to the purpose of the study, which can affect their behavior.

Source: Kathrynn A. Adams

you distinguish this design from a multiple trials study, where the data in each condition are collected over several trials. Multiple trials would be having half the participants eat bittersweet chocolate once a day for 5 days and assess their mood after they eat the chocolate each day, and the other half of the participants eat white chocolate once a day for 5 days and assess their mood each day. In contrast, in the repeated measures experimental design, participants would eat the bittersweet chocolate and assess their mood—and, after some time period, would eat the white chocolate and assess their mood.

A correlational design assessing flashbacks in soldiers at different time periods (1 week, 1 month, 6 months, 1 year) after a tour of duty in a war zone is an example of repeated measures. Although you could examine the number of flashbacks of different soldiers at these time periods, there are many differences among soldiers who are 6 months past their tour of duty (or at any of the time periods) that can mask the

FIGURE 11.2
Issues to Consider in Matched-Pairs Design

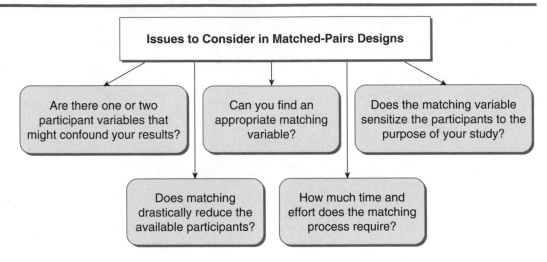

relationship of the time since the tour and the number of flashbacks. It would be better to have the same soldiers' flashbacks assessed at each of the time periods; we then could see how each individual's flashbacks differed across time and see if a pattern emerges between time and number of flashbacks.

In carrying out the repeated measures design as an experiment or quasi-experiment, you must **counterbalance** the order of the conditions of the IV. This means that in the example of the chocolate study, half of the participants will eat bittersweet chocolate first, and then eat white chocolate; the other half will eat white chocolate first and then bittersweet. Counterbalancing is done to avoid confounding order and condition (or **order effect**). If all participants experienced the conditions of the experiment in the same order (e.g., bittersweet chocolate first, then white chocolate), and you find that bittersweet chocolate increases mood, you would not be able to tell whether the change in mood was due to eating bittersweet chocolate or to the fact that mood increases as soon as any chocolate is eaten. Perhaps any chocolate that is eaten first will result in a change in mood. Thus, you must always counterbalance the order of the different conditions of the IV in a repeated measures experiment. To make your study

Counterbalancing: A procedure to eliminate order effects in a repeated measures experiment or quasi-experiment; participants are randomly assigned to different sequences of the conditions in an experiment.

Order effect: A confound that occurs when the order of each treatment condition cannot be separated from the condition.

a true experiment (instead of a quasi-experiment), the counterbalancing must be done through random assignment.

There are several advantages to a repeated measures design. Like the matched-pairs design, the repeated measures design has increased power relative to an independent design because you decrease the error variance. You do not have to worry about different participant (error) variability in each condition because the same people are in each condition. You also increase the number of observations of each participant, thereby giving you a ready-made check on consistency of responses. Finally, you reduce the number of participants needed in a study.

The repeated measures design, however, has several potential problems you need to consider or resolve in deciding whether you want to use this design. Although the design can significantly reduce error variability, it is not appropriate for studies where participants are *changed in some permanent way*. For example, if they learn something new so that they are no longer a naive participant for future conditions, you cannot use a repeated measures design. The researcher needs to address several potential problems that can possibly reduce the internal validity of a repeated measures study. For starters, in an experiment the participants may become *sensitized* to the experimental variable (IV) because they experience at least two and sometimes more levels of the IV. One way to counteract this sensitization is to keep the participant from attending to the variation in the IV, perhaps by instructing the participant to focus on another variable in the situation. For instance, participants might be instructed to focus on the color or texture of a chocolate sample in order to keep them from focusing on the different type of chocolate. If participants drop out during any part of a repeated measures study, their data are lost from all conditions (attrition); and depending on the number who drop out, you may end up with too small an N.

Carryover, practice, fatigue/boredom, and response sets can all present problems in a repeated measures design. A **carryover effect** can occur when the impact of the treatment or measurement lasts longer than the time between the different conditions. Make sure that you allow enough time between the different conditions so that the effect of one condition or measurement is not still impacting the participants when they experience the next condition. A **practice effect** can be confounded with treatment or measurement effects if the participants' improved performance is a function of repeatedly completing a measurement. Likewise, a **fatigue effect** is

Carryover effect: A confound that occurs when the effect of one condition of the treatment continues (or carries over) into the next condition.

Practice effect: A confound that occurs when participants' scores change due to repeating a task rather than because of the level of the IV.

Fatigue effect: A confound that occurs when changes in the DV occur because of participants becoming tired.

FIGURE 11.3

Potential Problems With a Repeated
Measures Design

*One of the potential problems with repeated
measures designs is fatigue/boredom.*

Source: Kathrynn A. Adams

when participants become tired or bored after participation in several different conditions or assessments. Figure 11.3 demonstrates how fatigue or boredom can be a problem. Finally, if your procedure requires that you collect data over time, you need to be aware of the potential impact of *participants' history or maturation.* You can counteract these potential problems by making your procedure interesting and brief.

All in all, a repeated measures design is a good choice when you have a situation where multiple participant variables are likely to have a strong effect on the DV because you can equalize that effect across all groups by including the same participants in each condition. For example, you may need to take into account the stress, income level, social support system, and personality of soldiers in assessing their flashbacks at different times; or the size, skill level, strength, and playing experience in testing new versus old sports equipment. Furthermore, it is a good choice for an experiment if you can address the concerns about internal validity and if your IV does not create a permanent change in the DV. See Figure 11.4 for issues to consider in repeated measures designs.

Overall, dependent-groups designs increase the power of a study because you maximize the difference between groups and minimize the error variability in scores. When we compare a larger treatment variance to a smaller error variance, this makes the overall effect stronger or more obvious; and thus the design is more powerful. As with the independent-groups designs, we have both dependent two-groups designs and dependent multiple-groups designs, which are determined by the number of groups in a study. The previous discussion about matched-pairs and repeated measures studies is relevant to both two-groups and multiple-groups designs.

Analysis of Dependent Two-Group Designs

The **dependent-samples *t* test** (also referred to as **paired-samples *t* test** and **within-subjects *t* test**) is used to analyze data from both the matched groups and repeated

> **Dependent-samples *t* test (or paired-samples *t* test/within-subjects *t* test):** The statistical test used to analyze results from a dependent two-groups design.

FIGURE 11.4

Issues to Consider in Repeated Measures Designs

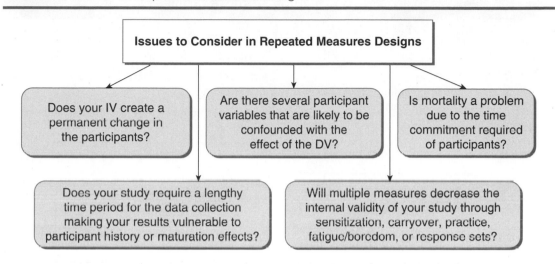

Issues to Consider in Repeated Measures Designs

Does your IV create a permanent change in the participants?

Are there several participant variables that are likely to be confounded with the effect of the DV?

Is mortality a problem due to the time commitment required of participants?

Does your study require a lengthy time period for the data collection making your results vulnerable to participant history or maturation effects?

Will multiple measures decrease the internal validity of your study through sensitization, carryover, practice, fatigue/boredom, or response sets?

Kittisak_Taramas

Practice 11.1

CONSIDERING DEPENDENT DESIGNS

In a series of studies, Strayer et al. (2003) examined the distraction of drivers in a driving simulation because of cell phone conversations. They hypothesized that driving errors would be made because of inattention to objects in the visual field while one is driving and talking on a phone. Specifically, in one of their studies, they examined memory for billboards that participants were shown during the simulation while either talking or not talking on a cell phone. They used a repeated measures design so the same participants were tested under both conditions.

1. What factors did they need to consider in the design of their study in order to counteract any potential problems with a repeated measures design?

2. What advantages does a repeated measures design offer over an independent two-group experiment in the Strayer et al. (2003) study?

3. Would a matched design have been a more effective design for Strayer et al.'s (2003) study? Explain your response.

See Appendix A to check your answers.

measures two-group designs. The logic of the analysis is the same as for the independent-samples *t* test; but instead of focusing on individual scores, we focus on the difference between the scores for each matched pair (in a matched design) or the difference between the scores for each participant in each condition (in a repeated measures design). We use the dependent-samples *t* test to analyze the data for all three types of studies (correlational, quasi-experiment, experiments) that have two dependent groups/conditions/levels.

Let's take the example from the beginning of the chapter regarding an intervention for one symptom of PTSD—flashbacks—and use a matched-pairs design. We match 20 participating soldiers on the severity of their PTSD and randomly assign one soldier of each matched pair to either a traditional intervention or the new (hopefully more effective) intervention. After a month of the intervention, the soldiers report their number of flashbacks over the last 24 hours.

The hypotheses for our study would state:

Null hypothesis (H_0): There will be no difference in the number of flashbacks in a 24-hour period between the soldiers experiencing the traditional therapy and their matched partners experiencing the new therapy.

Alternative hypothesis (H_a): There will be a greater number of flashbacks in a 24-hour period for soldiers experiencing the traditional therapy than for their matched partners experiencing the new therapy.

Or in numerical terms:

$H_0: \mu_D = 0$

$H_a: \mu_D > 0$

The assumptions of the dependent-samples *t* test are similar to those of the independent-samples *t* test, except that the groups are dependent:

- IV (or predictor) is dichotomous (nominal scale with two groups).

- Groups are dependent via matching or repeated measures.

- Because the groups are dependent, the *n* of the two groups is always equal.

- DV (or outcome) is interval or ratio scale of measurement.

- DV (or outcome) is normally distributed.

The key difference between the two types of *t* tests is that in the independent-samples *t* test, we calculate means and standard deviations using individual scores in each of the two groups in order to compare the overall differences between the means of the groups. In a dependent-samples *t* test, we focus on the differences between the matched or repeated scores in our computations and comparison of the two groups, and compute the mean and standard deviation of differences rather than scores.

FORMULAS AND CALCULATIONS: DEPENDENT-SAMPLES *t* TEST

To begin the computation of the dependent-samples *t* test for our study, we compute difference scores (*D*) for each matched pair or repeated measure by subtracting the score for each participant in one group from its matched (or repeated) score in the other group. Some differences will be positive and some will be negative. We then add up the difference scores (keeping the positive and negative signs) and divide by *N* to compute the **mean difference** (M_D). Because we focus on the difference between paired/repeated scores rather than individual scores in a dependent *t* test, *N* = number of pairs of scores (or number of difference scores).

> **Mean difference (M_D):** The average difference between the scores of matched pairs or the scores for the same participants across two conditions; computed by subtracting one score of a matched or repeated pair from the other score and dividing by N.

In our study, we compute the difference scores (*D*) by subtracting the number of flashbacks reported by each participant in the new-intervention group from the number of flashbacks reported by his or her matched soldier in the traditional-intervention group. Because we hope to reduce the number of flashbacks using the new intervention, we are expecting a positive difference (a larger number of flashbacks in the traditional-intervention group relative to their matched soldier in the new-intervention group). We add up the difference scores ($\Sigma D = 7$) and divide by the number of pairs ($N = 10$) to obtain the mean difference ($M_D = .7$).

Suppose that after completing our study, we find the following results for the number of flashbacks experienced by the soldiers:

	Flashbacks
$M_{Traditional}$	2.7
M_{New}	2.0
M_D	0.7
SD^2	0.9
N	10.0

The mean difference in the number of flashbacks for the matched pairs of soldiers experiencing the traditional and new therapies is compared to a sampling distribution for our null hypothesis, which predicts that there will be no difference between scores or that the mean difference will equal zero.

In order to find out whether the difference between our mean difference (M_D) and μ_D (of zero) is significantly different, we need to know where on the sampling distribution of $\mu_D = 0$ our mean difference falls. So we have to compute the **standard error of the mean difference (SD_D)** to find out how many standard deviations from μ_D our mean difference falls. The standard error (of the difference scores) is estimated from the standard deviation of the difference scores in our study. Because the standard deviation of a sampling distribution is smaller than that of raw scores and the sampling distribution changes as a function of N, we divide the standard deviation from our sample by N (see Figure 11.5).

$$SD_D = \sqrt{\frac{SD^2}{N}}$$

where SD^2 = variance of our sample; N = number of pairs.

Inserting the values for our study:

$$SD_D = \sqrt{\frac{.9}{10}} = \sqrt{.09} = .3$$

We can now see how many standard error of the differences our mean difference (D) is from zero by dividing the mean difference (M_D) by the standard error of the

Standard error of the mean difference (SD_D): Standard deviation of the differences for a sampling distribution of mean differences; estimated from the standard deviation of difference scores in a dependent-samples study.

mean difference (SD_D). The definitional formula for dependent-samples t test formula is shown below.

$$t_{obt} = M_D/SD_D$$

Or for our study:

$$t_{obt} = .7/.3 = 2.33$$

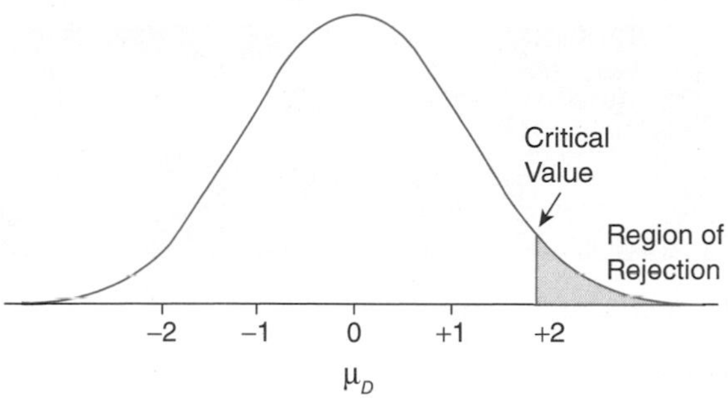

You may have noted that the last two formulas are very similar to those for the one-sample t test, as we are comparing a single sample of differences to a sampling distribution of differences. The computed t_{obt} value is then compared to t_{crit} in the same Table C.4 of critical t values we used for the independent-samples t tests in Appendix C. The degrees of freedom for a dependent-samples t test is $N-1$, where N is equal to the number of pairs of scores.

We use a one-tailed test because our alternative hypothesis predicted that the mean difference was greater than zero. The degrees of freedom for our study is $df = 10 - 1 = 9$. Table 11.1 shows an excerpt of the table of critical t values (Table C.4 in Appendix C). We find for $df = 9$ and $p < .05$, $t_{crit} = 1.833$. Our obtained value $t_{obt} = 2.33$ is greater than the $t_{crit} = 1.833$, so we can reject the null hypothesis that the mean difference was zero and conclude that the traditional intervention resulted in significantly greater flashbacks over a 24-hour period than the new intervention. We could have used a two-tailed test if we had predicted a difference in flashbacks between the new and traditional interventions without specifying which would have the smaller number of flashbacks. If we had used a two-tailed test, we would still use $df = 9$ and $p < .05$. For a two-tailed test, $t_{crit} = 2.262$. Our $t_{obt} = 2.33$ is still larger than this so we could reject the null hypothesis of H_0: $\mu_D \neq 0$. By rejecting our null hypothesis at the .05 significance level for a one-tailed or two-tailed test, we have less than a 5% probability of a Type I error and no possibility of a Type II error.

Based on our findings, we can conclude that the new treatment significantly reduced the number of flashbacks for soldiers in comparison to the traditional treatment.

Confidence Intervals

We also should compute the confidence interval for dependent-groups studies. The confidence interval describes the range of mean differences we can expect with a certain probability that the true μ_D will fall. The formula is similar to the one we used for the independent-groups design, but we use the mean difference (M_D) instead of the difference between the two group means ($M_1 - M_2$). In the formula, we substitute μ_D rather than $\mu_1 - \mu_2$ that we used for an independent-samples t test because we are looking at mean differences with dependent samples. The resulting formula is:

FIGURE 11.5

Sampling Distribution for $\mu_D = 0$

TABLE 11.1

Excerpt of Table C.4 of Critical Values for a *t* Test

Probability Levels					
One-tailed	0.10	0.05	0.025	0.01	0.005
Two-tailed		0.10	0.05	0.02	0.01
df					
1	3.078	6.314	12.706	31.821	63.657
2	1.886	2.920	4.303	6.965	9.925
3	1.638	2.353	3.182	4.541	5.841
4	1.533	2.132	2.776	3.747	4.604
5	1.476	2.015	2.571	3.365	4.032
6	1.440	1.943	2.447	3.143	3.707
7	1.415	1.895	2.365	2.998	3.499
8	1.397	1.860	2.306	2.896	3.355
9	1.383	1.833	2.262	2.821	3.250
10	1.372	1.812	2.228	2.764	3.169
11	1.363	1.796	2.201	2.718	3.106
12	1.356	1.782	2.179	2.681	3.055

$$(SD_D)(-t_{crit}) + (M_D) < \mu_D < (SD_D)(+t_{crit}) + (M_D)$$

where SD_D = standard error of the differences; t_{crit} = critical *t* value for a two-tailed test for the *df* in a study; M_D = mean difference.

We always use the t_{crit} for a two-tailed test because we are computing the upper and lower values of the confidence interval. In the case of our study, we already found that t_{crit} for $p < .05$ and 9 degrees of freedom is equal to 2.262. To compute the 95% confidence interval, we insert the values from our study of flashbacks and we have:

$$(.3)(-2.262) + .7 < \mu_D < (.3)(+2.262) + .7 = -.6786 + .7 < \mu_D < +.6786 + .7$$
$$= +.0214 < \mu_D < +1.3786$$

Thus, we are 95% confident the population mean difference that our sample mean difference represents lies between +.0214 and +1.3786.

Effect Size

We also want to determine the magnitude or strength of the effect of the new intervention. We can compute Cohen's *d*, which is the effect size typically reported for dependent-samples t tests. Cohen's d tells us the magnitude of our effect in standard deviation terms.

$$d = \frac{M_1 - M_2}{\sqrt{\left(SD_1^2 + SD_2^2\right)/2}}$$

where M_1 = mean for first group; M_2 = mean for the second group; SD_1^2 = variance for the first group; SD_2^2 = variance for the second group.

Plugging the values from our study into the formula for d, we find:

$$d = \frac{M_1 - M_2}{\sqrt{\left(SD_1^2 + SD_2^2\right)/2}} = \frac{2.7 - 2.0}{\sqrt{\left(1.41^2 + 1.57^2\right)/2}} = \frac{.7}{\sqrt{(1.99 + 2.46)/2}}$$

$$= \frac{.7}{\sqrt{4.45/2}} = \frac{.7}{\sqrt{2.23}} = \frac{.7}{1.49} = .47$$

This value of d means that the intervention approaches a moderate ($.5$ = moderate) effect on frequency of flashbacks, as it is almost half a standard deviation from μ.

Alternatively, we can then compute the squared point-biserial correlation coefficient (r_{pb}^2) to find the proportion of variability in the dependent variable that is accounted for by the independent variable. For a dependent samples design, we must first calculate Cohen's d and then use that to calculate r_{pb}^2. With our example, we find that the intervention group accounted for 5% of the variance in number of flashbacks:

$$r_{pb}^2 = \left(\frac{d}{\sqrt{d^2 + 4}}\right)^2 = \left(\frac{.47}{\sqrt{(.47)^2 + 4}}\right)^2 = \left(\frac{.47}{2.05}\right)^2 = (.23)^2 = .05$$

Practical Significance

We should also consider the usefulness of our results in everyday terms. We consider our mean difference to interpret the practical usefulness of our results. For our example study, the soldiers reported on average experiencing less than one fewer flashback over a 24-hour period with the new therapy than with the traditional therapy. You might think that this difference is so minimal that the soldiers would not notice it. However, given the severity of some flashbacks, soldiers may be very appreciative of any reduction in flashbacks. You could follow up your study by interviewing soldiers to see if they think that the difference of one fewer flashback in a 24-hour period would be noticeable to them. This additional information may help you to interpret the practical significance of your results. Remember that practical significance is an interpretation of the impact of the effect in daily life, and thus there is no precise number or critical value that you can use to judge your results. It is important, however, that you consider the everyday impact of results, and your thoughts should be included in the Discussion section of your report.

USING DATA ANALYSIS PROGRAMS: DEPENDENT-SAMPLES *t* TEST

Data Entry

As we continue to state throughout the text, most of the time we analyze data using a statistical package. In this section, we review the process for analyzing a dependent-groups or paired-samples *t* test in SPSS. Take note! You enter the data differently for dependent samples than you did for independent samples. For dependent samples, you provide a variable name for each condition of the IV and set up two columns for the raw scores. You then enter the data for each condition in one column, making sure to pair the scores for participants who are matched or for the same participant's scores. Each row in a dependent-samples *t* test represents the scores for a matched pair of participants. Table 11.2 below depicts the dataset for our experiment examining the effect of two therapies on the number of flashbacks reported by soldiers. This format is different from the independent-samples *t* test, where you entered the codes for the independent variable in one column and your raw scores in the other column.

TABLE 11.2

Data Input for Dependent-Samples *t* Test

Each row of scores represents two soldiers who were paired on their severity of PTSD, one who received the traditional treatment and one who received the new treatment.

For example, the first row presents data from two soldiers who were matched on their level of PTSD; the one who received the traditional intervention reported one flashback and the soldier who received the new intervention reported no flashbacks in the preceding 24 hours.

You must be sure to input the matched scores beside each other (in the same row) or you defeat the purpose of dependent groups, which is to decrease error variance through matching or repeated measures.

The first column lists the scores for those who had the traditional therapy.

Traditional	New
1	0
1	1
2	1
2	1
1	2
3	2
4	2
3	3
5	3
5	5

The second column lists the scores for those who had the new therapy.

Computing the Statistical Analysis

After the data are entered, you request a paired-samples t test. In SPSS, you specify the independent or grouping variable and its codes and the dependent variable. The output is shown in Table 11.3.

There are three boxes in the output that present a lot of information succinctly. Note that they all include "Paired-Samples" in their title. The first box, "Paired-Samples Statistics," presents the descriptive statistics (M, SD, N) for each group that you will need to report for your study.

The next box, "Paired-Samples Correlations," provides information about the relationship between the scores in the two groups. You want the correlation to be high and significant, which shows that the matched scores (or repeated measures) were highly related. A weaker correlation would suggest that your matching variable was not related to the DV or, in the case of repeated measures, that scores were not related across groups.

The third box, "Paired-Samples Test," presents the results from the dependent samples t test. It lists the mean difference (M_D), standard deviation of the differences (SD), the standard error of the mean differences (SD_D), the lower and upper values for the 95% confidence interval, and finally, the t_{obt}, df, and exact significance level ($p = .045$). Note that all these values (except the exact p value) match what we computed from formulas in the previous section. This information will be needed in the Results section of your report. You should list the exact p value in your report rather than $p < .05$ (.01) when you analyze your data using a statistical package.

You can use the information from the output to then compute and report either of the effect sizes, Cohen's d or the point-biserial correlation coefficient (r_{pb}^2). In this example, we report Cohen's d.

TABLE 11.3

SPSS Output for a Dependent-Groups t Test

Paired-Samples Statistics

		Mean	N	Std. Deviation	Std. Error Mean
Pair 1	New Therapy	2.0000	10	1.41421	.44721
	Trad Therapy	2.7000	10	1.56702	.49554

Paired-Samples Correlations

		N	Correlation	Sig.
Pair 1	New Therapy & Trad Therapy	10	.802	.005

Paired-Samples Test

Pair 1	Paired Differences							
				95% Confidence Interval of the Difference				Sig. (2-tailed)
	Mean	Std. Deviation	Std. Error Mean	Lower	Upper	t	df	
New Therapy- Trad Therapy	-.70000	.94868	.30000	-1.37865	-.02135	-2.333	9	.045

Application 11.1

SAMPLE RESULTS AND DISCUSSION FOR A HYPOTHETICAL EXPERIMENT USING TWO DEPENDENT GROUPS

Results

Soldiers who experienced the new therapy reported fewer flashbacks ($M = 2.00$, $SD = 1.41$) than their matched partners, who experienced traditional therapy ($M = 2.70$, $SD = 1.57$). A paired-samples t test was computed and showed that the difference in flashbacks was significant, $t(9) = 2.33$, $p = .045$, $d = 0.47$. The two groups differ by approximately half a standard deviation, and we are 95% confident that the mean difference is between .02 and 1.38.

Discussion

Soldiers who participated in the new therapy reported significantly fewer flashbacks than soldiers who participated in the traditional therapy, supporting our hypothesis. The soldiers were matched on their level of PTSD, so the level of the disorder does not explain the difference in the number of flashbacks between the two therapy groups. The strength of the effect of the type of therapy, however, was weak to moderate. This suggests that the intervention is somewhat effective, although there are other, and perhaps more potent, factors also influencing the frequency of flashbacks.

Future studies should explore the effect of more frequent therapy sessions or therapy over a longer time period in order to achieve a stronger effect due to the type of therapy. The difference in the number of flashbacks was less than 1 within a 24-hour period, which suggests that different therapies may not lead to a noticeable easing of the symptom of flashbacks in soldiers' daily lives. This study did not include a control group of soldiers who were diagnosed with PTSD and who did not participate in any therapy. If the goal is to decrease the number of flashbacks, it is important to show that whatever differences we find between therapies, we can also demonstrate that the therapies are significantly more effective than not participating in therapy.

Ethics Tip: Control Groups in Interventions

In any intervention research, we must be aware that participants in the control group are not receiving a treatment that we hope to find improves the physical or mental state of people. One ethical guideline is never to harm participants or to leave them in a worse physical or mental state than before. If we find that a technique, treatment, or intervention results in a significant improvement (in behavior, attitude, health, etc.), we have an obligation to offer that treatment to those in the control group at the end of a study. This action not only benefits the participants but also allows us the chance to replicate our findings. If we do not find a significant improvement, then we would not need to offer the new treatment to the control group.

Practice 11.2

PRACTICE WITH A DEPENDENT DESIGN

A researcher examines the impact of service learning on critical-thinking skills. The researcher uses a sample of college students enrolled in a developmental psychology course. The researcher matches the students based on their marital status and then randomly assigns one student from each pair to one of two sections of the class. The first section is the control group—they meet in a discussion section one hour each week. The second section is the service-learning group—they volunteer at a local child care center one hour each week. At the completion of the course, all the students take an exam to assess their critical-thinking skills. The critical-thinking scores can range from 1 to 15, with higher scores reflecting higher skill levels. The output from the data analysis is shown below:

T-Test

Paired-Samples Statistics		Mean	N	Std. Deviation	Std. Error Mean
Pair	control	8.2500	12	4.11483	1.18785
	Service	9.4167	12	2.90637	.83900

	Paired Differences			95% Confidence Interval of the Difference				Sig.
	Mean	Std. Deviation	Std. Error Mean	Lower	Upper	t	df	(2-tailed)
Pair 1	−1.16667	2.28963	.66096	2.62143	.28810	−1.765	11	.105

a. What type of dependent design is this (matching or repeated measures)? Explain your answer.

b. What's the IV for this study? What are its levels? What's the DV?

c. State your null and alternative hypotheses.

d. How many participants do you have?

e. Compute the effect size for the service-learning intervention.

f. Describe the results as you would in a Results section.

g. Explain what your findings mean (interpret the findings) as you would in a Discussion section.

h. Do you think the researcher chose a good matching variable, and why or why not? If you were conducting this study, what matching variable would you have chosen?

See Appendix A to check your answers.

DESIGNS WITH MORE THAN TWO DEPENDENT GROUPS

You are already familiar with the advantages and drawbacks of multiple-groups designs, so we will not cover them here. (See the Designs With More Than Two Independent Groups section in Chapter 10 if you need a review.) Remember that if there are one or two participant variables of concern, a matched design is usually best; if multiple participant variables may influence your measurement, then a repeated measures design is more appropriate.

The same procedures, advantages, and concerns are present for the dependent multiple-groups design as for the dependent two-groups design. We have an additional complication, however, for repeated measures multiple-groups designs. You learned about counterbalancing when we described the requirements for a dependent simple experiment. Each participant is randomly assigned to the order of the two conditions so that order of treatment is not confounded with treatment effects. The same concern about order exists in a repeated measures multiple-groups design.

Counterbalancing is simple when there are only two levels of the IV, but it gets more complicated as the number of conditions increases. When participants experience all the possible sequences of the conditions of an experiment, it is called **complete counterbalancing**. With a dependent design that is a simple experiment, you only have to make sure that half of the participants have each order of the two conditions. When you have three conditions, you now have six different orders that are possible. (Assume k = number of levels of your IV. You can compute the number of possible orders by the formula $k[k - 1]$. In the case of three levels, $3[3 - 1] = 3[2] = 6$.) The sequences for a three-group study are shown below:

ABC

BCA

CAB

ACB

BAC

CBA

Complete counterbalancing: Randomly assigning participants to all the possible sequences of conditions in an experiment.

Note that each condition appears an equal number of times (twice) in each order. For example, condition A appears first twice, second twice, and third twice. Each condition also occurs ahead of or behind the other conditions an equal number of times: A precedes B twice, and follows B twice. The same is true for condition B and condition C. You could randomly assign participants to the six different sequences, but the number of sequences may be a lot to keep up with while trying to maintain control over all the variables in your experiment. And if you had four conditions, you would need to keep up with $4(4 - 1)$ or 12 different sequences.

The benefit of using all possible sequences has diminishing returns as the number of conditions increases. For this reason, you can use **partial counterbalancing** or a smaller number of sequences of conditions that you then randomly assign your participants to. In **Latin Square counterbalancing**, you determine a smaller number of sequences for your number of conditions where each condition appears equally in each order. For example, you could select ABC, BCA, and CAB as the orders you will use. A matrix that lists the different combinations so that each condition occurs once in each column and once in each row is called a Latin Square. For our example, a Latin Square could appear as:

A B C

B C A

C A B

In the Latin Square, each of your three conditions occurs once in each order (1st, 2nd, 3rd). However, the conditions do not equally precede and follow each of the other conditions: A precedes B twice but does not ever follow B. Because of this limitation, the Latin Square counterbalances for order but not for sequence. We still may use this technique because of the concern that a large number of sequences will produce errors in the procedure and then increase the uncontrolled error variability that we are trying to decrease by using a dependent design.

Another option is to randomize the order for participants instead of using complete or partial counterbalancing (**randomized partial counterbalancing**). In this procedure, you randomly assign the order of conditions to each participant. It works best if you have a large number of conditions and you just want to guarantee different orders in an unsystematic way. This option misses some sequences and orders but does

Partial counterbalancing: Randomly assigning participants to different sequences of conditions so that each condition is represented in each order an equal number of times but not all sequences are represented.

Latin Square counterbalancing: A type of partial counterbalancing where each condition appears once in each sequence; participants are then randomly assigned to the different sequences.

Randomized partial counterbalancing: Randomly assigning each participant to one of the possible sequences of conditions without concern about order or sequence; used when you have a larger number of sequences than participants.

guarantee variety. Complete and partial counterbalancing are the more commonly used techniques.

Although counterbalancing controls order effects, it does not control for carryover effects, so you need to make sure that there is sufficient time in between conditions for any effect to dissipate before participants experience the next condition. For example, you might wait an hour or even a day in between the conditions of eating chocolate to make sure any effect on mood is no longer present when the participant eats the second type of chocolate. You should stick with a between-groups design if you have so many groups that counterbalancing becomes too complicated.

Matching is also more complicated for multiple-groups designs than for two-group designs. If you have four groups, you must now find four people with similar scores on the matching variable. For an experiment, you have the added step of randomly assigning each participant from a matched group to one of the experimental conditions. For correlational or quasi-experiments, you must find a match within the other groups that are already established. So if you want to match on rank and severity of PTSD in a correlational or quasi-experimental study, you would need to find the same rank and severity of PTSD among the participants in each of the services. Matching on more than one variable gets increasingly more difficult as the number of groups increases. Depending on the size of your sample pool, this may or may not present a problem. As with counterbalancing, at some point the complications and hassle of matching participants may outweigh the benefits of reduced error (participant) variance and you may decide to use an independent design.

Analysis of Dependent Multiple-Groups Designs

Similar to the independent multiple-groups design, we use a one-way ANOVA to analyze dependent multiple-groups designs—only we use a **within-subjects ANOVA** (also called a **repeated measures ANOVA** or **dependent-groups one-way ANOVA**). We use this statistical test for all of the different types of dependent multiple-groups designs (repeated measures or matched; experiments, correlational, or quasi-experiments). By definition, these designs have one manipulated or grouping variable with three or more levels of this variable, and all participants are matched either on a relevant variable or in all conditions.

> **Within-subjects ANOVA (or repeated measures ANOVA/dependent-groups one-way ANOVA):** The statistical test used to analyze dependent multiple-groups designs.

The assumptions for the within-subjects ANOVA are very similar to those for the one-way independent-groups ANOVA—except, of course, the groups are dependent. Assumptions for the one-way within-subjects ANOVA include:

- IV (or predictor) has three or more levels (conditions)
- Groups are dependent (matched or repeated measures)

Practice 11.3

PRACTICE WITH PARTICIPANT ASSIGNMENT IN DEPENDENT DESIGNS

Researchers have found that college student pedestrians are prone to accidents when using their phones in various ways while crossing the street (Byington & Schwebel, 2013; Schwebel et al., 2012; Stavrinos, Byington, & Schwebel, 2011). These studies have used both dependent and independent groups.

1. Suppose you want to examine this topic with adults in your community. You decide to use a repeated measures design and expose 24 participants to all four conditions [talking on their cell phone (T), texting on their cell phone (X), listening to music (M), and playing a game on their cell phone (G)]. How could you use complete counterbalancing to assign your participants to the order of the cell phone conditions (T, X, M, G)? Provide specifics about the possible orders and assignment to them.

2. Suppose the adults thought the repeated measures study would take too much time, and you decided to match the adults on the amount of time (in minutes) they spent daily on their cell phone. Below are the daily cell phone times for the participants. Explain in detail the matching process and assignment to different conditions.

Participant	Time	Participant	Time	Participant	Time
1	45	9	90	17	30
2	85	10	30	18	20
3	60	11	45	19	60
4	120	12	80	20	80
5	70	13	15	21	45
6	20	14	125	22	110
7	35	15	110	23	35
8	15	16	50	24	65

Check Appendix A to review your answers.

- DV (or outcome) is interval or ratio scale of measurement
- DV (or outcome) is normally distributed
- Sphericity in variances of the differences between pairs of groups

There is one new term in the assumptions for the dependent-groups ANOVA, that of sphericity, which is similar to homogeneity of variance with which you are already familiar. **Sphericity** assumes equal variances for the differences when you compare pairs of groups in a dependent design. This concept will be discussed in more detail when we cover the dependent-groups ANOVA output for SPSS.

Sphericity: The assumption that the variances of the differences between all the combinations of pairs of groups are equal.

REVIEW OF KEY CONCEPTS: ANOVA

1. What two types of variance do we compare in an analysis of variance (ANOVA), and what do these variances represent?

2. What does the F_{obt} in an ANOVA represent in terms of these different variances?

3. What terms are listed in a summary table and build toward the calculation of F_{obt}?

4. If the null hypothesis is true, what value do we expect F_{obt} to be?

Answers:

1. Between-group variance represents the variability between groups or conditions. We try to maximize this type of variance in an experiment and are looking for large between-group variance in quasi-experimental and correlational designs.

   Within-group variance represents the variability within each group or condition and is also referred to as error variance. We try to minimize this type of variance.

2. F_{obt} = between-group variance/within-group variance.

3. The summary table contains the sums of squares and degrees of freedom that are used to compute the mean squares. The mean squares are then used to compute F_{obt} so $F_{obt} = MS_B/MS_w$

4. When the null hypothesis is true we expect that there is no variability due to treatment, and thus we divide error variance by itself and get 1.0. Depicted as a formula:

   F_{obt} = between-group variance/within-group variance = (treatment variance + error variance)/error variance = (0 + error variance)/error variance = error variance/error variance = 1.0.

FORMULAS AND CALCULATIONS: WITHIN-SUBJECTS ANOVA

This section describes the rationale for calculating the within-subjects ANOVA. You will find details about the formulas and computation of raw data for hand computations in Appendix D.9.

The logic and process for the within-subjects ANOVA are similar but slightly more complicated than those for the independent-groups one-way ANOVA. We compare the between-group variance to error variance; but in the case of the within-subjects ANOVA (similar to the paired-samples t test), we are able to pull out variance associated with the participants—thanks to our matching or repeated measures.

We will discuss the within-subjects ANOVA using the following study. Many soldiers find it difficult to adjust to daily living in the United States after spending a year where there are constant stress, unpredictable conditions, a strong support system among their fellow soldiers, and the danger of violence at all times. You decide to examine what type of situation produces the most sense of calm in soldiers returning from a tour of duty in an area where there is armed conflict. Your goal is to discover ways to assist soldiers in their adjustment to life in the United States. You recognize that each soldier had a very different experience during his or her tour of duty and returned to a different situation in the United States. These differences may dramatically influence each soldier's adjustment, and so you decide to use a repeated measures design for your study.

You expose volunteers to three conditions that you think might be calming for soldiers. In one condition, the volunteers experience a session of meditation (M); in the second condition, they participate in a creative writing exercise (W); in the third condition, they take a tai chi class (T). Each session lasts one hour; and following the activity, they are asked to rate several responses, including their sense of calm. The sessions occur two days apart, and you employ partial counterbalancing using the sequences MWT, WTM, and TMW.

Although the soldiers experience the conditions in different orders, in our analysis we want to compare the conditions, not the sequences. If you look at Table 11.4, you can see in the different rows the participants who experience the three different sequences of the activities, but our analysis will focus on the columns or the scores of the participants in each condition (meditation, writing, tai chi), regardless of the order in which they experienced them.

TABLE 11.4

Matrix of the Different Orders and Conditions

	Condition		
	Meditation **(M)**	**Writing** **(W)**	**Tai chi** **(T)**
MWT	$X_1 X_2$	$X_1 X_2$	$X_1 X_2$
WTM	$X_3 X_4$	$X_3 X_4$	$X_3 X_4$
TMW	$X_5 X_6$	$X_5 X_6$	$X_5 X_6$

The analysis will focus on differences between the three conditions.

The null hypothesis (H_0) assumes no difference between our groups, whereas the alternative hypothesis (H_a) predicts a difference:

H_0: There will be no difference in soldiers' sense of calm following participation in hour-long sessions of meditation, creative writing, or tai chi.
H_a: There will be a difference in soldiers' sense of calm following participation in hour-long sessions of meditation, creative writing, or tai chi.

Or in numerical terms:

$$H_0: \mu_M = \mu_W = \mu_T$$
$$H_a: \mu_M \neq \mu_W \neq \mu_T$$

Using the information about variances reviewed above, we know that according to the null hypothesis, we do not expect any differences in our study between the conditions of meditation, writing, or tai chi. This means that treatment variability is zero, and

$$F_{obt} = \text{Between-groups variance/Within-groups variance}$$

$$= \text{(Treatment variance + error variance)/error variance}$$

$$= \text{(0 + error variance)/error variance = error variance/error variance} = 1.0$$

Like the independent-samples ANOVA, F_{obt} compares the variability between conditions or groups (MS_B) with the variability within conditions or groups (MS_w). The mean squares between (MS_B) is equal to treatment plus error variability, and in a dependent ANOVA is symbolized as MS_A. The mean squares within (MS_w) is equal to the error variability in each condition. In computing the MS_w for a dependent ANOVA, we examine the difference of each score and the mean (M) for each cell, but there is only one score per cell so the variability is always zero (0) because the score and the mean are the same value. So the MS between the conditions and participants, called the interaction mean squares and symbolized as $MS_{A \times S}$ or $MS_{Cond \times Part}$, reflects the variability between participants in the same condition.

Remember the summary table format for an ANOVA from Chapter 10. In order to obtain the end point of an ANOVA or F_{obt}, we have to compute sums of squares (SS), degrees of freedom (df), and mean squares (MS). As with the dependent-samples t test, N for a dependent-samples ANOVA equals the number of scores rather than the number of participants. So for this study where we have three calmness scores for each of six soldiers, $N = 18$.

The summary table for a dependent design (see Table 11.5) is slightly different from the one for an independent design. Instead of a single sums of squares within (SS_{error}) we divide error variability into that associated with participants in the same condition (or the interaction between the condition and subject), called the **interaction sums of squares ($SS_{A \times S}$)**, and the variability in specific participants' scores that is uniquely associated with them, called the **sum of squares of subjects (SSs)**. The more variability associated with individual participants (SS_S) that we can extract from the error term, the smaller the denominator in our F ratio. Dividing by a smaller denominator always results in a larger F, which means we are more likely to be able to see the effects of our treatment or grouping variable. Note that like the independent ANOVA, the sums of square total in the dependent ANOVA is composed of all the sources of sums of squares ($SS_{tot} = SS_A + SS_S + SS_{A \times S}$). In addition, the more effect the different conditions have on

Interaction sums of squares ($SS_{A \times S}$): The numerator of the variance created by the differences among different participants in the same condition in a dependent design; considered an interaction between condition and participants.

Sum of squares of subjects (SSs): The numerator of the variance created by adding the squared differences in the scores of individual participants across different conditions in a dependent design.

TABLE 11.5

Summary Table for Within-Subjects ANOVA

Source	SS	df	MS	F____
Condition (A)	SS_A	$k-1$	SS_A/df_A	$MS_A/MS_{A \times S}$
Subject	SS_S	$N-k$		
Interaction (A x S)	$SS_{A \times S}$	$(k-1)(k_{ps}-1)$	$SS_{A \times S}/df_{A \times S}$	
Total	SS_{tot}	$N-1$		

the measured variable (in this case, sense of calm), the larger the treatment variability (MS_A) we expect and the larger the F_{obt}. Table 11.5 lists all of the terms associated with a dependent-samples ANOVA and shows their relationship in computing F_{obt}.

We are now ready to build the summary table for our study. Suppose for our study we compute the sums of squares for each source and find the values shown in Table 11.6 (see Appendix D.9 for the complete computation). We can also compute the degrees of freedom for each source using the formulas in Table 11.5. The degrees of freedom between conditions is equal to the number of conditions (k) minus one, so for our study $df_A = k-1$ $= 3-1 = 2$. The degrees of freedom for subjects (participants) is equal to the total number of scores minus the number of conditions or $df_s = N-k = 18-3 = 15$. To compute the degrees of freedom for our condition by participants we multiply the degrees of freedom for condition ($k-1$) by the number of participants per conditions minus one or $df_{A \times S} = (k-1)$ $(k_{ps}-1) = (3-1)(6-1) = 2(5) = 10$. The degrees of freedom total is equal to the number of scores minus one or $df_{tot} = N-1 = 18-1 = 17$. Note that the total degrees of freedom is equal to the sum of the degrees of freedom for condition and for subjects ($df_{tot} = df_A + df_s$).

TABLE 11.6

Complete Sample Summary Table

Source	SS	df	MS	F
Condition (A)	14.79	2	7.395	19.06
Subject	47.61	15		
Interaction (A x S)	3.88	10	.388	
Total	66.28	17		

Once these values are entered in the summary table, we can now complete the ANOVA. The mean squares (MS) and F have the same relationships to the sums of squares (SS) and degrees of freedom (df) that they did for the independent-groups ANOVA. We divide the sums of squares for the condition by its degrees of freedom ($SS_A/df_A = MS_A$) and the sums of squares for the interaction by its degrees of freedom ($SS_{A \times S}/df_{A \times S} = MS_{A \times S}$) to get the mean square for each of these sources. As the final step, we divide the mean square for the conditions (MS_A) by the mean square for the error associated solely with the participants across conditions ($MS_{A \times S}$) to obtain F.

We now compare our computed value of $F_{obt} = 19.06$ to the F_{crit} value in Table C.6 in Appendix C. An excerpt is shown in Table 11.7. For our within-subjects ANOVA, we use the condition degrees of freedom (df_A) as the df_B in the table and the condition by participant degrees of freedom ($df_{A \times S}$) as the df_w in the table of critical values. So we go across to $df_A = 2$ and down to $df_{A \times S} = 10$ and find $F_{crit} = 4.10$ for $p = .05$ and 7.56 for $p = .01$. Our computed $F_{obt} = 19.06$, so we can reject the null hypothesis at the .01 level. In rejecting the null hypothesis that there are no differences among the sense of calm scores, we have compared our F_{obt} value to a sampling distribution where the differences between conditions was zero. (See Figure 11.6.) We conclude that there is a significant difference overall between the three conditions (meditation, writing, tai chi).

TABLE 11.7
Excerpt of Table of Critical F Values

Critical F values for ANOVA with a particular probability level and df.

Degrees of freedom between groups (df_s) is in the numerator				$p = .05$ **is in dark numbers**			
Degrees of freedom within groups (df_w) is in the denominator				$p = .01$ is in light numbers			
df_b	1	2	3	4	5	6	7
df_w							
7	**5.59**	**4.74**	**4.35**	**4.12**	**3.97**	**3.87**	**3.79**
	12.25	9.55	8.45	7.85	7.46	7.19	6.99
8	**5.32**	**4.46**	**4.07**	**3.84**	**3.69**	**3.58**	**3.50**
	11.26	8.65	7.59	7.01	6.63	6.37	6.18
9	**5.12**	**4.26**	**3.86**	**3.63**	**3.48**	**3.37**	**3.29**
	10.56	8.02	6.99	6.42	6.06	5.80	5.61
10	**4.97**	**4.10**	**3.71**	**3.48**	**3.33**	**3.22**	**3.14**
	10.04	7.56	6.55	5.99	5.64	5.39	5.20

Effect Size

The **partial eta squared ($\eta^2_{partial}$)** is used to assess the effect size of a dependent-groups ANOVA. The term *partial* is used with eta squared in dependent multiple-group designs because the variability unique to the participants (SS_s) is removed from the

Partial eta squared ($\eta^2_{partial}$): The effect size for a dependent multiple-group design that removes the variability unique to individual participants from the error term.

statistic so that only the variability associated with error ($SS_{A \times S}$) and conditions (SS_A) remains. It is interpreted in the same way as r_{pb}^2 that we used for the independent samples t test or as the percentage of variability in the DV that is accounted for by the IV or grouping variable.

$$\eta^2_{partial} = SS_A / (SS_A + SS_{A \times S})$$

For our example:

$$\eta^2_{partial} = 14.79 / (14.79 + 3.88) = .792$$

This value indicates that the type of activity had a strong effect on the soldiers' sense of calm.

Computing Post Hoc Tests

We do not yet know which conditions differ from one another. So, as we did with a significant F from an independent-samples

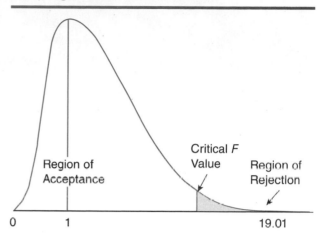

FIGURE 11.6

Sampling Distribution for ANOVA

Region of Acceptance

Critical F Value

Region of Rejection

0   1   19.01

Note: Our $F_{obt} = 19.06$ lies in the blue region of rejection and thus tells us that we would not expect to get such a large F by chance alone, if the null hypothesis of no difference between conditions is true and $F = 1.0$.

ANOVA, we must compute post hoc tests. Another way to say this is that we now need to compute paired comparisons. We can choose which test we use—you may remember from Chapter 10 that Fisher's LSD is a commonly used post hoc test that corrects for the increased probability of a Type I error, so we will use it to examine differences between the conditions in our within-subjects or dependent-samples ANOVA. (See the Post Hoc Tests section in Chapter 10 if you need to review the rationale and different kinds of tests.)

We use the same formula as we did for independent samples and compute the smallest difference (least significant difference) between the condition means that is significantly different at the $p = .05$ level. We then compare the LSD value to the differences between each of the conditions in our study to see which ones differ. There will be $k(k-1)/2$ comparisons or $3(3-1)/2 = 3(2)/2 = 3$ paired comparisons for our study.

The formula for Fisher's LSD is:

$$LSD = t_{crit \atop MS_w} \sqrt{MS_w (1/n_k + 1/n_k)}$$

where t_{crit} for MS_w = the critical value of t for $p = .05$ using df_w; MS_w = mean square within groups; n_k = number per group.

We have already computed the mean square within groups (MS_w), which is the interaction mean square ($MS_{A \times S} = .388$) for a dependent-samples ANOVA; and we

Practice 11.4

PRACTICE INTERPRETING A SUMMARY TABLE
FOR A DEPENDENT-SAMPLES ANOVA

Source	SS	df	MS	F
Condition (A)	30.00	3	???	???
Subject	66.00	??		
Interaction (A x S)	???	??	???	
Total	120.00	23		

a. Complete the summary table above. (Hint: Refer to the description of the summary table for information about what sources add up to the total sums of squares and the total degrees of freedom.)

b. What additional term is included in a dependent-samples ANOVA (in comparison to an independent-samples ANOVA)?

c. What does this additional term tell us, and why is it useful?

d. Is F significant? How can you tell?

e. What is the effect size ($\eta^2_{partial}$)?

f. Should you compute post hoc tests? Why or why not?

Review Appendix A to check your answers.

know the number in each group ($n_k = 6$) for our study. (See the summary table in Table 11.6 for these values in our study.) We get t_{crit} from the table of critical *t* values in Appendix C.4 using $p = .05$ and the degrees of freedom for the mean square within groups or interaction ($df_{A \times S} = 10$). This value is 2.228.

Substituting these values in the formula, we have:

$$LSD = t_{crit}\,_{MS_w} \sqrt{MS_w(1/n_k + 1/n_k)} = 2.228\sqrt{.388(1/6 + 1/6)}$$

$$= 2.228\sqrt{.388(.167 + .167)} = 2.228\sqrt{.388(.334)} = 2.228\sqrt{.13}$$

$$= 2.228(.36) = .80$$

This means that any difference greater than .80 between the means of our three groups will be significant. Making up a matrix of the means of our conditions and subtracting them from each other we show:

	M	W	T
Means	(5.33)	(4.67)	(6.83)
Meditation	—	.66	−1.50*
Writing	—	—	−2.16*
Tai Chi	—	—	—

*$p < .05$

The matrix shows that two of our paired comparisons meet the difference criterion of .80. We see from the means that those in the tai chi condition rated a higher sense of calm than those in either the meditation or the writing conditions, which did not differ from one another.

In interpreting our data, we would report that the within-subjects ANOVA was significant, $F(2, 10) = 19.01$, $p < .01$. The type of activity accounted for 79% of the variability in the soldiers' reported sense of calm. We also would note that we computed a Fisher's LSD post hoc test to examine differences between the activities. We would note that soldiers rated their sense of calm significantly higher ($p < .05$) in the tai chi activity ($M = 6.83$) than in either the meditation ($M = 5.33$) or writing ($M = 4.67$) conditions. The sense of calm did not differ when the soldiers participated in the creative writing or meditation activities.

USING DATA ANALYSIS PROGRAMS: WITHIN-SUBJECTS ANOVA

You enter the data for a within-subjects ANOVA in the same way that you entered your data for the dependent-samples t test; the data for each condition or level are entered in one column. You should use labels that are descriptive so that categories in the output will be clear. The dataset for our example would thus look like this in SPSS:

Meditation	Writing	Tai Chi
5	5	7
6	4	7
9	7	10
3	3	5
5	6	7
4	3	5

After entering your data, you are ready to request the "Repeated Measures ANOVA." You will specify how many factors (conditions) your study has and define them. You request descriptive statistics for your conditions and estimates of the effect size.

The output for the analysis in SPSS provides several tables, some of which you do not need. The relevant tables are shown in Table 11.8.

In the first box, you see the descriptive statistics (M, SD, n) for each condition in the study. You will need these statistics to interpret and to write up your results. Next is a box presenting Mauchly's Test of Sphericity. We assume that sphericity is met; but if this assumption is violated, then you must assume that at least some of the variances of differences between groups differ. This violation can inflate the F you obtain (F_{obt}), which then can increase the probability of a Type I error. In order to correct this problem, you can use the Greenhouse-Geisser or Huynh-Feldt as alternatives (much like you did for the independent-samples t test, when you used a more stringent test if the assumption of homogeneity of variance was violated). The alternative tests change only the degrees of freedom for your test, which then result in a larger F_{crit} that the F_{obt} value must exceed. It is recommended that you use the Greenhouse-Geisser because it is the most conservative of the tests and, thus, the least likely to result in a Type I error.

You can see from Table 11.8 that our sample study does violate the assumption of sphericity—look at the significance for the Approx. Chi-Square, and it shows $p = .031$ (shaded box). Because it is significant when you read the next table, "Tests of Within-Subjects Effects," you need to read the row for Greenhouse-Geisser to find the results for your ANOVA—SS, df, F_{obt}, sig. (p), and partial eta squared ($\eta^2_{partial}$). This row is highlighted in the summary table in Table 11.9.

If your results had not violated the assumption of sphericity, then you would have read the top line of the table labeled "Sphericity Assumed." Note that the values for

TABLE 11.8

Relevant Output From Dependent ANOVA

Descriptive Statistics

	Mean	Std. Deviation	N
Meditation	5.3333	2.06559	6
Writing	4.6667	1.63299	6
Tai Chi	6.8333	1.83485	6

Mauchly's Test of Sphericity[a]

Measure: MEASURE_1

Within Subjects Effect	Mauchly's W	Approx. Chi-Square	df	Sig.	Epsilon[b] Greenhouse-Geisser	Huynh-Feldt	Lower-bound
factor1	.176	6.942	2	.031	.548	.587	.500

Tests the null hypothesis that the error covariance matrix of the orthonormalized transformed dependent variables is proportional to an identity matrix.

a. Design: Intercept
 Within Subjects Design: factor1

b. May be used to adjust the degrees of freedom for the averaged tests of significance. Corrected tests are displayed in the Tests of Within-Subjects Effects table.

Sphericity Assumed and Greenhouse-Geisser are only slightly different, although the df for the Greenhouse-Geisser test are not whole numbers and the p value is slightly larger.

You can see from the table that F_{obt} is quite large (19.00), the results are significant ($p = .005$), and you have a very strong effect size ($\eta^2_{partial} = .79$). These figures match the results from the earlier hand-computed process. Because the ANOVA is significant, you now need to request a post hoc test to determine which conditions differ from one another. To do this, you go back to the repeated measures ANOVA and click on the Options button. You move your condition factor over to the box "Display Means for": and check the box "Compare Main Effects." Below that, click on the arrow and request "Bonferroni" adjustment. This will provide you with the post hoc results shown below in Table 11.10.

TABLE 11.9

SPSS Summary Table for Dependent-Groups ANOVA

Tests of Within-Subjects Effects

Measure: MEASURE_1

Source		Type III Sum of Squares	df	Mean Square	F	Sig.	Partial Eta Squared
factor1	Sphericity Assumed	14.778	2	7.389	19.000	.000	.792
	Greenhouse-Geisser	14.778	1.097	13.475	19.000	.005	.792
	Huynh-Feldt	14.778	1.173	12.594	19.000	.004	.792
	Lower-bound	14.778	1.000	14.778	19.000	.007	.792
Error(factor1)	Sphericity Assumed	3.889	10	.389			
	Greenhouse-Geisser	3.889	5.483	.709			
	Huynh-Feldt	3.889	5.867	.663			
	Lower bound	3.889	5.000	.778			

TABLE 11.10

Results of Post Hoc Test

Pairwise Comparisons

Measure: MEASURE_1

(I) factor1	(J) factor1	Mean Difference (I-J)	Std. Error	Sig.[b]	95% Confidence Interval for Difference[b]	
					Lower Bound	Upper Bound
1	2	.667	.494	.706	-1.081	2.414
	3	-1.500*	.224	.003	-2.290	-.710
2	1	-.667	.494	.706	-2.414	1.081
	3	-2.167*	.307	.003	-3.253	-1.081
3	1	1.500*	.224	.003	.710	2.290
	2	2.167*	.307	.003	1.081	3.253

Based on estimated marginal means
*. The mean difference is significant at the .05 level.
b. Adjustment for multiple comparisons: Bonferroni.

The table for Pairwise Comparisons is similar to the post hoc table that you saw for Tukey's HSD and Fisher's LSD for the independent-samples ANOVA. The descriptions below the table note that Bonferroni's correction was applied and that the comparisons that are significant ($p < .05$) are noted by an asterisk next to the mean difference. Assume 1 = meditation, 2 = writing, and 3 = tai chi in interpreting the output. You can see that the results are the same as we obtained with Fisher's—the sense of calm for the tai chi condition is significantly different from that for the meditation ($p = .003$) and the writing ($p = .003$) groups, which do not differ from one another ($p = .706$). You look at the means to see that the tai chi condition had the highest ratings for sense of calm, followed by meditation and then writing.

Application 11.2 contains a sample report of the Results and Discussion sections following APA format. As with previous examples of findings, you report the descriptive statistics for each of the conditions. You note that you computed a dependent-samples ANOVA and provide the results. Do not forget that for this study, you should report that the data violated the assumption of sphericity and that you used the values for the Greenhouse-Geisser test. As always, report the results of statistical analyses (including effect size) in the Results and then include the interpretation and discussion of practical significance in the Discussion. Remember that the study is hypothetical, and thus the results should not be interpreted or used as actual findings.

Application 11.2

SAMPLE RESULTS AND DISCUSSION FOR A HYPOTHETICAL EXPERIMENT USING A MULTIPLE DEPENDENT-GROUPS DESIGN

Results

Soldiers reported the highest sense of calm ($M = 6.83$, $SD = 1.83$) after practicing tai chi, the next highest sense of calm after meditation ($M = 5.33$, $SD = 2.06$), and the least sense of calm after working on a creative writing piece ($M = 4.67$, $SD = 1.63$). A within-subjects ANOVA was computed to examine whether the differences in calmness were significant. Because Mauchly's Test showed that the assumption of sphericity was violated ($p = .031$), the Greenhouse-Geisser test was used, and it showed that the soldiers' sense of calm under the three conditions was significantly different, $F(1.097, 5.483) = 19.00$, $p = .005$, $\eta^2_{partial} = .79$. Post hoc paired comparisons using Bonferroni's correction showed that soldiers reported significantly higher calmness scores after practicing tai chi than after meditating ($p = .003$) or after writing ($p = .003$). There was not a significant difference, however, in soldiers' sense of calmness after they had meditated or engaged in creative writing ($p = .706$).

Discussion

As predicted, this study found a significant difference in soldiers' sense of calm following different hour-long activities. Those who practiced tai chi reported the significantly higher sense of calm than those engaging in creative writing or meditation, which did not differ from one another. The strength of the activity was very high, accounting for about three-fourths of the variability in the calmness scores. This suggests that counselors, educators, trainers, and other helping professionals should take into account the type of activities they recommend for soldiers experiencing mental health issues upon returning from active military duty. According to these findings, the type of activity has a potent effect on the serenity of soldiers diagnosed with PTSD. In addition, the design allowed us to study differences across the three activities within each soldier, providing a powerful test of the impact of the activities.

This study is limited by the small number of participants, the specific characteristics that qualified participants for the study (in the armed services, returning from active duty in an area of conflict, volunteers), and a limited number of calming activities. Future research should expand the participant pool to include more soldiers as well as civilians who may be experiencing stressful transitions. Future studies might also explore the impact of additional activities on people's sense of calm. Many people in contemporary society who are not in the military report a high level of stress and anxiety, and this study provides evidence of one step that people can take to alleviate such feelings.

Practice 11.5

PRACTICE INTERPRETING A DEPENDENT-SAMPLES ANOVA

You want to know whether information in a syllabus truly affects whether students are likely to take a class. You prepare three syllabi for a Developmental Psychology class, which vary only in the focus of the class assignments. One syllabus uses field work to examine developmental concepts, another syllabus uses novels, and a third syllabus uses films. First-year students are randomly assigned to read a syllabus and rate the likelihood that they would take the class. They are first matched on desired major and high school GPA.

a. State the null and alternative hypotheses.

b. How many participants do you have?

c. Describe the results from the output below. Use correct APA format.

d. Explain what your findings mean (interpret the findings) and discuss the strengths and weakness of the design the researcher chose.

Review Appendix A to check your answers.

Descriptive Statistics

	Mean	Std. Deviation	N
Fieldwork	6.4000	2.59058	10
Novels	8.5000	2.12132	10
Films	10.1000	3.28126	10

(Continued)

(Continued)

Tests of Within-Subjects Effects

Measure: syllabus

Source		Type III Sum of Squares	df	Mean Square	F	Sig.	Partial Eta Squared
factor1	Sphericity Assumed	68.867	2	34.433	13.339	.000	.597
	Greenhouse-Geisser	68.867	1.731	39.782	13.339	.001	.597
	Huynh-Feldt	68.867	2.000	34.433	13.339	.000	.597
	Lower-bound	68.867	1.000	68.867	13.339	.005	.597
Error(factor1)	Sphericity Assumed	46.467	18	2.581			
	Greenhouse-Geisser	46.467	15.580	2.983			
	Huynh-Feldt	46.467	18.000	2.581			
	Lower-bound	46.467	9.000	5.163			

Pairwise Comparisons

Measure: experience

(I) factor1	(J) factor1	Mean Difference (I-J)	Std. Error	Sig.[b]	95% Confidence Interval for Difference[b]	
					Lower Bound	Upper Bound
1	2	−2.100	.767	.069	−4.349	.149
	3	−3.700*	.803	.004	−6.057	−1.343
2	1	2.100	.767	.069	−.149	4.349
	3	−1.600	.562	.057	−3.248	.048
3	1	3.700*	.803	.004	1.343	6.057
	2	1.600	.562	.057	−.048	3.248

Based on estimated marginal means
*a. The mean difference is significant at the .05 level.
b. Adjustment for multiple comparisons: Bonferroni.

THE BIG PICTURE:
SELECTING ANALYSES AND INTERPRETING
RESULTS FOR DEPENDENT-GROUPS DESIGNS

In this chapter, you learned about dependent designs that use either matched-participants or repeated measures. Like independent designs, dependent designs can be correlational, quasi-experiments, or experiments, and use either two conditions/groups or multiple conditions/groups. Because dependent designs allow the researcher to extract the variability associated with individual participants, we are better able to see the variability created by an IV or grouping variable. This characteristic makes dependent designs more powerful than comparable independent designs.

Matched designs require that we can identify an appropriate matching variable, have a sufficient number of participants to implement the match, and take care not to sensitize our participants to our hypothesis or the purpose of our study. In addition, we must randomly assign matched partners to the different conditions of our IV in experiments. Studies employing repeated measures have the advantage of needing fewer participants, but require that we avoid conditions that will fatigue or bore our participants or create a lasting effect. We also have to counterbalance the presentation of conditions to avoid an order effect. Various types of counterbalancing were discussed in the chapter, with the process becoming more complicated as the number of conditions increases.

Different statistics are used to analyze dependent two-group and multiple-group designs. Figure 11.7 depicts the decision tree for the analysis of different types of dependent-groups designs. Table 11.11 sorts the different designs by their characteristics and notes the statistical test(s) used to analyze each design. Note that the analysis and interpretation for the different types of dependent designs does not differ for matching or repeated measures. As with independent designs, it is crucial that you are able to identify the different dependent designs in order to employ appropriate statistical tests and accurately interpret the results.

FIGURE 11.7

Decision Tree for the Dependent-Design Analyses

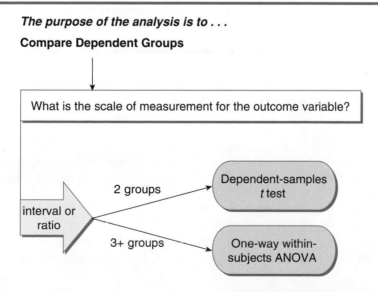

TABLE 11.11

Overview of Dependent-Groups Designs and Analyses

	IV Manipulated?	Random Assignment?	Number of Groups	Statistical Analyses	Interpretation
Experiment	Yes	Yes	Two	Dependent-samples t test, Cohen's d, confidence interval	Causation
	Yes	Yes	Three or more	One-way within-subjects ANOVA, if significant post hoc test using a correction to avoid increased Type I error, partial eta squared ($\eta^2_{partial}$)	Causation
Quasi-Experiment	Yes	No	Two	Dependent-samples t test, Cohen's d, confidence interval	Correlation
	Yes	No	Three or more	One-way within-subjects ANOVA, if significant post hoc test using a correction to avoid increased Type I error, partial eta squared ($\eta^2_{partial}$)	Correlation
Correlation	No	No	Two	Dependent-samples t test, Cohen's d, confidence interval	Correlation
	No	No	Three or more	One-way within-subjects ANOVA, if significant post hoc test using a correction to avoid increased Type I error, partial eta squared ($\eta^2_{partial}$)	Correlation

CHAPTER RESOURCES

Key Terms

Define the following terms using your own words. You can check your answers by reviewing the chapter or by comparing them with the definitions in the glossary—but try to define them on your own first.

Do You Understand the Chapter?

Answer these questions on your own and then review the chapter to check your answers.

1. What is the major advantage of dependent designs?

2. Describe the two types of dependent designs and when you might use each type.

3. What is counterbalancing, and why is it necessary in a repeated measures design?

4. What are the concerns for each type of dependent design, and how can you address them in the development of a study?

5. How does the computation of a dependent-samples t test differ from that of an independent-samples t test?

6. What are the assumptions of a dependent-groups ANOVA?

7. What additional terms are listed in the summary table for a dependent-groups one-way ANOVA? What advantages do these additional terms provide over an independent-groups one-way ANOVA in finding significance between our groups or conditions?

8. What do we do if Mauchly's Test of Sphericity is significant?

9. Why do we compute partial eta squared ($\eta^2_{partial}$) for a dependent multiple groups ANOVA rather than eta squared (η^2)?

Practice With Design and Statistics

1. A researcher does a study to see if female students have higher GPAs than male students. What type of design is this? Explain your response.

2. A researcher wants to examine the effect of caffeine on participants' ability to concentrate.

   a. How could the researcher address this question using a simple experiment?

      i. What are the pros and cons of this design choice?

      ii. What is/are the appropriate analysis/analyses?

   b. How could the researcher address this question using a matched-pairs design?

      i. What are the pros and cons of this design choice?

      ii. What is/are the appropriate analysis/analyses?

   c. How could the researcher address this question using a repeated measures design?

      i. What are the pros and cons of this design choice?

ii. What is/are the appropriate analysis/analyses?

3. A researcher wants to examine the effect of humidity on amount of hair frizz.

   a. How could the researcher address this question using a multiple-groups design?

      i. What are the pros and cons of this design choice?

      ii. What is/are the appropriate analysis/analyses?

   b. How could the researcher address this question using a dependent multiple-groups design?

      i. What are the pros and cons of this design choice? Address whatever design you select or consider both types of dependent multiple-groups designs.

      ii. What is/are the appropriate analysis/analyses?

4. Ms. Fit investigates whether children exhibit a higher number of prosocial acts after watching a 30-minute cartoon containing multiple prosocial acts in comparison to watching a 30-minute educational cartoon.

Before watching the cartoon, children were matched on empathy (as rated by one of their parents) and then one of each pair was assigned to either the prosocial cartoon or the educational cartoon. The number of prosocial acts for the children was analyzed and resulted in the output below.

a. Write a directional alternative hypothesis.

b. Identify the IV, its levels, and its scale of measurement.

c. Identify the DV and its scale of measurement.

d. Identify one limitation in the design of this specific study (not just this type of design). Explain why it is a limitation and suggest how a future study could avoid it.

e. What specific procedures should the research have followed to ensure that the study is ethical? Explain your answer.

f. Report the results of the SPSS output below in APA format.

g. Do you need to compute any additional statistics? Explain.

Paired Samples Statistics

		Mean	N	Std. Deviation	Std. Error Mean
Pair 1	Prosocial Cartoon	3.9000	10	1.79196	.56667
	Educational Cartoon	2.7000	10	2.05751	.65064

Paired Samples Correlations

		N	Correlation	Sig.
Pair 1	Prosocial Cartoon & Educational Cartoon	10	.835	.003

Paired Samples Test

		Mean	Std. Deviation	Std. Error Mean	t	df	Sig. (2-tailed)
Pair 1	Prosocial Cartoon - Educational Cartoon	1.20000	1.13529	.35901	3.343	9	.009

5. Complete the following summary table.

Source	SS	df	MS	F
Condition (A)	18	3	???	???
Subject	20	36		
Interaction (A x S)	54	???	???	
Total	92	39		

a. How many conditions are in the study?

b. How many participants are in the study?

c. How many participants are in each condition?

d. Are the results significant at the .05 level? At the .01 level? How can you tell?

e. Should you conduct post hoc tests? Why or why not?

6. A psychologist who specializes in the study of mass media wonders if the public's view of movies as R rated is impacted by content that includes sex, violence, profanity, or the combination of all these factors.

He prepares 10-minute clips from the same movie that feature one of these conditions. Participants watch each clip and rate the movie on a 10-point scale for how well the content fits an R rating (1 = not at all; 10 = definitely R-rated material). He wants to pilot his study and decides to use 8 adults from a community club who attend films together each week. Respond to the following items based on the study and the output below:

a. Identify the type of study and what must be a part of the repeated measures procedure in order to avoid confounds.

b. State a directional alternative hypothesis for the study.

c. Report the results of the analysis in APA format.

d. How would you interpret these results in terms of movie goers' views of film content?

e. Comment on the statistical and practical significance and effect size of the study.

	Descriptive Statistics		
	Mean	Std. Deviation	N
Sex	6.5000	1.85164	8
Violence	5.6250	1.76777	8
Profanity	4.1250	1.72689	8
Combination	7.1250	1.72689	8

Mauchly's Test of Sphericity[a]

Measure: Film

Within Subjects Effect	Mauchly's W	Approx. Chi-Square	df	Sig.	Epsilon[b]		
					Greenhouse-Geisser	Huynh-Feldt	Lower-bound
factor1	.523	3.714	5	.596	.769	1.000	.333

Tests the null hypothesis that the error covariance matrix of the orthonormalized transformed dependent variables is proportional to an identity matrix.

a. Design: Intercept
Within Subjects Design: factor1
b. May be used to adjust the degrees of freedom for the averaged tests of significance. Corrected tests are displayed in the Tests of Within-Subjects Effects table.

Tests of Within-Subjects Effects

Measure: Film

Source		Type III Sum of Squares	df	Mean Square	F	Sig.	Partial Eta Squared
factor1	Sphericity Assumed	40.594	3	13.531	25.471	.000	.784
	Greenhouse-Geisser	40.594	2.306	17.600	25.471	.000	.784
	Huynh-Feldt	40.594	3.000	13.531	25.471	.000	.784
	Lower-bound	40.594	1.000	40.594	25.471	.001	.784
Error(factor1)	Sphericity Assumed	11.156	21	.531			
	Greenhouse-Geisser	11.156	16.145	.691			
	Huynh-Feldt	11.156	21.000	.531			
	Lower-bound	11.156	7.000	1.594			

Pairwise Comparisons

Measure: Film

(I) factor1	(J) factor1	Mean Difference (I-J)	Std. Error	Sig.[b]	95% Confidence Interval for Difference[b]	
					Lower Bound	Upper Bound
1	2	.875	.350	.247	−.399	2.149
	3	2.375*	.324	.001	1.197	3.553
	4	−.625	.263	.295	−1.581	.331
2	1	−.875	.350	.247	−2.149	.399
	3	1.500*	.378	.032	.126	2.874
	4	−1.500*	.378	.032	−2.874	−.126

3	1	−2.375*	.324	.001	−3.553	−1.197
	2	−1.500*	.378	.032	−2.874	−.126
	4	−3.000*	.463	.002	−4.683	−1.317
4	1	.625	.263	.295	−.331	1.581
	2	1.500*	.378	.032	.126	2.874
	3	3.000*	.463	.002	1.317	4.683

Based on estimated marginal means
*. The mean difference is significant at the .05 level.
b. Adjustment for multiple comparisons: Bonferroni.

Practice With SPSS

1. Long-distance runners participated in a study of the effectiveness of a new power drink. One Saturday morning they participated in a 10k run, which simulated a road race, and half of the runners drank 12 ounces of water while the other half drank 12 ounces of a new power drink. After 30 minutes they rated their energy level and thirst. The next Saturday morning they ran another 10k simulated road race. This time each runner drank 12 ounces of whatever drink they had not had the week before. They then waited 30 minutes and rated their energy level and thirst. Results for energy-level ratings are found below; higher ratings reflect more energy.

Water	Energy Drink
35	40
40	48
45	39
25	35
19	23
20	28
25	25
32	36
35	32
38	40
21	20
40	40

a. State your null and directional alternative hypotheses.

b. Calculate the appropriate statistics.

c. Describe your findings using APA format as you would in a Results section.

d. Describe and interpret your findings as you would in a Discussion section.

e. What is the probability of a Type I error? A Type II error?

2. The Sav NerG company is interested in increasing sales of its energy-efficient small car, the LowE. Researchers modify the LowE so that the ride is smoother or the interior is more like a luxury car. Adults (25–40 years) who are considering buying a new car drive the original LowE and then the cars that have been modified (first for smoother ride and then with better interior). Drivers rate their probability of buying each version of the car immediately

after driving it. The results are presented below:

Original LowE	Smoother Ride	Improved Interior
0.55	0.60	0.65
0.60	0.70	0.65
0.70	0.70	0.75
0.65	0.65	0.65
0.50	0.55	0.60
0.45	0.70	0.70
0.70	0.70	0.75
0.65	0.60	0.65
0.55	0.65	0.60
0.50	0.65	0.70

a. State your null and alternative hypotheses.

b. Calculate all of the appropriate statistics.

c. Describe your findings in APA format as you would in a Results section.

d. Describe and interpret your findings as you would in a Discussion section.

e. What flaw do you see in the design of the study, and how could you correct it?

SAGE edge™

edge.sagepub.com/adams2e

Sharpen your skills with SAGE edge!
SAGE edge for students provides you with tools to help you study. You'll find mobile-friendly eFlashcards and quizzes, as well as videos, web resources, datasets, and links to SAGE journal articles related to this chapter.

Factorial Designs

Research has consistently demonstrated that school success depends on more than just intelligence and aptitude. Social factors including poverty, maternal depression, exposure to neighborhood violence, and other stressful life events place children at risk for academic failure. Moreover, there is a negative correlation with the number of risk factors present and academic achievement (Burchinal, Roberts, Zeisel, Hennon, & Hooper, 2006; Gutman, Sameroff, & Eccles, 2002; Herbers et al., 2011; Prelow & Loukas, 2003).

This certainly does not mean that academic success is out of reach for children who grow up in disadvantaged circumstances. Although some factors place children at risk, other factors can protect children by weakening the effect of the risk. Parenting quality is one of the most important protective factors (Herbers et al., 2011). For example, parents offset academic risk factors when they are involved in their children's academics and monitor their social activities (Prelow & Loukas, 2003), provide consistent discipline (Gutman et al., 2002; Herbers et al., 2011), and create stimulating and responsive environments (Burchinal et al., 2006; Herbers et al., 2011).

This example demonstrates that examining the relationship between any single variable and academic success provides an incomplete picture. Instead, it is important to understand how multiple factors interact to help or hinder academic achievement. Likewise, many topics in the social sciences are complex, and an examination of interactions can vastly improve our understanding. Factorial designs allow us to examine these complex relationships.

LEARNING OUTCOMES

In this chapter, you will learn

- Basic concepts in factorial designs
- Rationale for conducting factorial designs
- How to hypothesize and interpret main effects and interaction effects
- How to analyze independent-groups factorial design
- The basics of dependent-groups and mixed factorial designs

BASIC CONCEPTS IN FACTORIAL DESIGN

A **factorial design** allows you to examine how two or more variables, or factors, predict or explain an outcome. A factorial design does more than just help us understand the relationship between each variable and the outcome; rather, the factorial provides additional information about how the variables interact in influencing the outcome.

Note that we will use the terms *factor* and *variable* interchangeably throughout this chapter, and remember that:

Factor = Predictor variable in a correlational study

OR

Independent variable (IV) in a quasi-experiment or experiment

> **Factorial design:** A design used to examine how two or more variables (factors) predict or explain an outcome.
>
> **Factor:** A predictor variable in a correlational design or an IV in an experiment or quasi-experiment.

Types of Factorial Designs

A **correlational factorial design** examines how two or more preexisting characteristics predict an outcome. The research examining risk and protective factors for academic success is correlational because the researchers assessed, but did not manipulate, the presence of risk and protective factors among the children studied. For most of the risk and protective factors, a manipulation is not possible or would be unethical.

A **quasi-experimental factorial design** includes two or more quasi-experimental IVs that are manipulated, but participants are not randomly assigned to IV condition(s). An **experimental factorial design** includes two or more independent variables (IVs) that are manipulated by the researcher. To have a true experiment, participants must be randomly assigned to all the IV conditions. A **hybrid factorial design** is a mix of these

> **Correlational factorial design:** A design with two or more predictors that are not manipulated in the study.
>
> **Quasi-experimental factorial design:** A design with two or more quasi-IVs, meaning that the IVs are manipulated, but participants are not randomly assigned to IV conditions.
>
> **Experimental factorial design:** A design with two or more IVs that are manipulated and in which participants are randomly assigned to IV levels.
>
> **Hybrid factorial design:** A design with at least one experimental IV and at least one quasi-IV or predictor.

types of designs in that it includes at least one experimental independent variable (IV) and at least one quasi-IV or predictor.

Factorial Notation

Factorial notation is used to quickly communicate the number of factors and the number of levels for each factor. The most basic factorial design is the 2 × 2 ("two-by-two"), which has two factors with two levels each. You can have more complex designs that have more than two factors or more than two levels per factor, or both. In factorial notation, each number indicates how many levels or groups for that factor, and the total number of numbers indicates how many factors are in the study.

Examples:

- 2 × 3 design = Two factors, the first with two levels and the second with three levels

- 2 × 2 × 2 × 2 design = Four factors, each with two levels

- 4 × 2 × 5 design = Three factors, the first with four levels, the second with two levels, and the third with five levels

Factorial notation: A shorthand for expressing how many factors, levels, and cells are present in a factorial design.

Practice 12.1

IDENTIFY TYPES OF FACTORIAL DESIGNS

1. A study examining how gender and political affiliation impact environmental attitudes is a correlational, quasi-experimental, experimental, or hybrid factorial design?

2. A researcher randomly assigns participants to one of six groups that vary according to the type of test (math, writing, or civics) and type of environment (quiet or loud) and then measures how long it takes to complete the exam.

   a. Is this a correlational, quasi-experimental, experimental, or hybrid factorial?

   b. What is the factorial notation of this design?

   c. How many cells are there?

3. Suppose the researcher described in question 2 also examined how gender (male vs. female) impacted performance under the different conditions.

   a. Is this a correlational, quasi-experimental, experimental, or hybrid factorial?

   b. What is the factorial notation of this design?

   c. How many cells are there?

   See Appendix A to check your answers.

By multiplying the numbers in the factorial notation, we can quickly see how many cells are in the study. A single **cell** compares one level of a factor across a level of another factor. A 2 × 2 has four cells, a 2 × 3 has six cells, a 2 × 2 × 2 × 2 has 16 cells, and so on. For example, suppose we wanted to examine how gender (male vs. female) and political party (Republican vs. Democrat) predict environmental attitudes. We would have a 2 (gender) × 2 (political party) factorial and need participants who represented each of the following four cells: (a) male Republicans, (b) female Republicans, (c) male Democrats, and (d) female Democrats. If we were missing members of one cell, for example if we did not have any female Republicans in our sample, we would not have a complete 2 × 2 design.

Cell: A comparison of one level of a factor across a level of another factor.

Main Effects and Interaction Effects

A factorial design yields two distinct types of information about the relationship between the variables, the main effects and the interaction effect. A **main effect** is the impact of a single variable. In a correlational design, it is the relationship between one predictor and the outcome, and in an experiment (or quasi-experiment) it is the effect one IV has on the dependent variable (DV). You already learned about main effects in Chapters 10 and 11 as you considered how to examine the impact of a single variable. The difference is that in a factorial design, because we have more than one factor, we have more than one main effect. We have the potential of a main effect for each factor in a factorial design.

Main effects are important and interesting, but the interaction effect is usually the reason a researcher conducts a factorial design. An **interaction effect** is the effect of one variable across different levels of another variable. The presence of an interaction effect means that the impact of one variable depends on the level of another variable. For example, a child with many risk factors may have a better or worse outcome depending on the level of parental involvement. The other variable, on which the relationship depends, is called a moderator. A **moderator** impacts the strength of the relationship between the first variable and the outcome, or even changes the direction of the relationship.

Consider an example from the research on risk and protective factors for academic success. Herbers et al. (2011) examined academic achievement among homeless children.

Main effect: How one variable predicts or affects the outcome.

Interaction effect: How one variable predicts or affects the outcome based on the levels of another variable.

Moderator: In an interaction effect, the factor that changes the strength or direction of the relationship between a predictor and the outcome (or one IV and the DV in an experiment).

They found that an index of cumulative risk was negatively correlated with academic success and that quality parenting was positively correlated with academic success. Although these main effects are important, what they really wanted to know is how quality parenting might be able to offset the negative impact of risk. In other words, they wanted to know if there was an interaction between risk and parenting, and they did in fact find a significant interaction.

A graph based on Herbers et al.'s (2011) findings is presented in Figure 12.1. Take a minute to study this graph and pay attention to the interaction. First, consider the relationship between risk and academic success among those children who experienced lower quality parenting. Notice that for these children, there is a negative relationship so that children with a high level of risk are more likely to have poorer academic outcomes. But notice that this relationship is not present for those who experienced high-quality parenting. The horizontal line indicates that risk does not relate to academic success among these children. In other words, having high-quality parenting protects children from the negative consequences that are usually associated with risk.

FIGURE 12.1

Example Interaction Effect

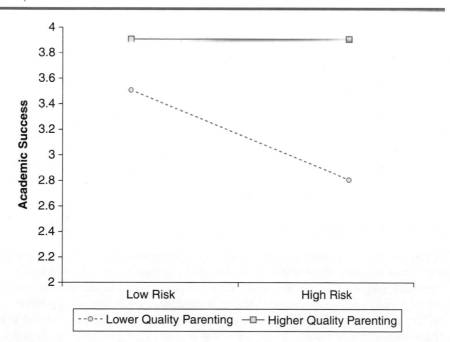

Source: Herbers, J. E., Cutuli, J. J., Lafavor, T. L., Vrieze, D., Leibel, C., Obradovic, J., & Masten, A. S. (2011). Direct and indirect effects of parenting on the academic functioning of young homeless children. *Early Education & Development, 22.*

RATIONALE FOR FACTORIAL DESIGNS

If your mind is spinning from trying to interpret the interaction effect depicted in Figure 12.1, or to grasp the concepts of factorial design in general, you are not alone. Factorial designs are complex, the results take some effort to interpret, and consequently most students find factorial designs difficult. However, we believe you will find the extra time and effort required to understand factorials well worth it because this type of design helps us to investigate some of the questions that are most interesting and relevant in the social sciences. Moreover, factorial designs allow you to systematically examine confounds or extraneous variables in a study and provide rich information without much additional time and effort in data collection.

The factorial design provides the information you would obtain from separate single-factor designs (namely, the main effect of each variable on the outcome) as well as the interaction effect. A factorial design provides all this information within a single study, often without much more effort than conducting a single-factor design. We might say that a factorial gives you a lot of "bang for the buck."

Consider our example of gender and political party affiliation as predictors of environmental attitudes. A researcher could conduct a survey of men and women about their environmental attitudes to find out if there are gender differences (a main effect). The researcher could then do a follow-up study if environmental attitudes vary based on political party (another main effect). At this point, we have two main effects but we do not know how gender and political party interact and there is no way to examine the interaction in these two separate studies. As such, we cannot determine if the relationship between gender and environmental attitudes depends on a person's political party affiliation. The researcher could have instead conducted a survey about environmental attitudes and easily assessed both gender and political affiliation without much additional time or effort. This factorial study would provide the main effects as well as the interaction effect.

Keep in mind that the bang-for-your-buck rationale should be viewed as an added benefit of a factorial, not the sole reason for designing a factorial. If you choose to conduct a factorial, you should do so because the research suggests that there is a complex relationship among your variables or because you need to control an important extraneous or confounding variable in your study. See Application 12.1 for specific examples of how to build on past research using a factorial design.

Investigate Complex Relationships

If you are like most social science students, you are not satisfied with simple explanations of complex social phenomena. Imagine you heard the following statement: "Research suggests that children who experience poverty tend to have poorer language skills." Would you be satisfied with that? Or would you ask follow-up questions such as: "Is the correlation between poverty and academics present for all children? What characteristics might place a child more or less at risk? What are ways schools, families, and communities can offset the negative impact of poverty? What types of programs can help families get out of poverty, and for whom are these programs most effective?" Those types of questions are what inspired researchers to examine protective factors;

and as that complicated graph in Figure 12.1 illustrates, we now know that risk alone is not sufficient to predict academic outcomes.

A primary reason for conducting a factorial design is to examine these complex interaction effects. It is the appropriate design choice when past research and theory give you reason to expect that the relationship between your predictor (or IV) and outcome will vary based on the levels of a third, or moderating, variable.

Systematically Examine Extraneous Variables and Confounds

REVIEW OF KEY CONCEPTS: HETEROGENEITY AND CONTROL

- Heterogeneity (diversity) of a sample increases within-groups error variance and therefore reduces power. One way to increase power is to limit the population from which your sample is drawn so as to have a homogeneous sample (see Chapter 6 for a more thorough review).

- In an experiment, our ability to say that one IV caused a change in a DV (internal validity) can be increased by keeping as many participant variables and environmental conditions constant across conditions (see Chapter 9).

Limiting the population from which your sample is drawn is one way to increase power in any study, and that strategy can also help increase internal validity in an experiment by reducing confounds due to participant variables. We might, for example, choose to study only women, or only psychology majors, or only adults over 50 years of age. By limiting the population, however, we limit the study's external validity (the ability to generalize the results). Luckily, we now have a new tool to deal with participant variables. Rather than limiting the population, we can examine these variables in a factorial design.

Application 12.1

BUILDING ON PAST RESEARCH BY DESIGNING A FACTORIAL

Investigate Complex Relationships

Most believe that grit, or determination to reach goals, is important to academic success. However, there is evidence that grit might not always be a positive trait (Lucas, Gratch, Cheng, & Marsella, 2015). Perhaps the relationship between grit and academic success is more complex than most believe? For example, the situation could moderate the efficacy of grit.

Example 1: Perhaps grit is a positive factor in academic success for both easy and challenging situations, but especially positive for the challenging tasks?

Example 2: Perhaps grit is positive for challenging situations but does not relate to academic success in easy situations?

(Continued)

Example 3: Perhaps grit is positive for challenging situations but negative for impossible situations?

Systematically Examine Extraneous Variables and Confounds

What if we wanted to rule out alternative explanations for the relationship between grit and academic success, such as overall motivation? We could conduct a factorial study to be sure that grit has a relationship with academic success that is not dependent on the person's overall motivation. In this case, we would not expect an interaction effect.

In an experiment, we would use stratified random assignment if we wanted to systematically examine participant variables. Recall from Chapter 9 that stratified random assignment is a process by which the researcher balances out participant characteristics across the IV conditions. This could ensure, for example, that there are about equal numbers of men and women in each experimental group. Those participant variables can then be used as predictors in a hybrid factorial design. Likewise, we can systematically vary environmental variables that we believe might confound the results of our experiment and create a true experimental factorial design.

The factorial design is an excellent way to examine the impact of participant variables and confounds in a study. However, you must be judicious in how many of these extraneous variables you choose to examine. Examining every single participant variable (gender, age, education, sexual orientation, political affiliation, etc.) as well as every environmental condition (lighting, noise, time of day, temperature, etc.) is impractical, if not impossible.

Remember that as you add factors to a factorial design, the number of cells increases exponentially (e.g., a 2 × 2 requires four cells, a 2 × 2 × 2 requires eight cells, a 2 × 2 × 2 × 2 requires 16 cells, and so on). This usually means that the number of participants you need will increase, and it always means that the complexity of interpreting your results will increase. As such, we recommend that beginning researchers keep their factorial designs relatively simple and select factors based on what past research suggests will have the largest impact on the results.

2 × 2 DESIGNS

In the spirit of keeping it simple, we are going to focus on 2 × 2 designs as we delve deeper into the subject of factorial designs. Once you have a handle on these types of interactions, you can start to consider more complex designs.

Let us keep with our chapter theme on factors that impact academic performance as we consider an example 2 × 2 design. Suppose we want to examine how test performance varies based on both gender and test instructions. We give all participants the same test that requires students to solve various dilemmas, and we tell all the participants that the test is designed to measure differences between men's and women's skills. We randomly assign half the students of each gender to a condition in which they are told the test measures logical intelligence; and we assign the other half to a condition in which they are told the test measures social intelligence. Thus, we have a gender (male vs. female) × instructions (logical intelligence test vs. social intelligence test) hybrid factorial design.

Main Effects in a 2 × 2 Design

We evaluate two main effects in a 2 × 2 design, one for each of the factors. Each main effect will tell us the relationship between that factor and the outcome (or DV in an experiment), without taking into consideration the other factor.

For our 2 × 2 design examining how test performance varies based on both gender and instructions, we would have a main effect hypothesis for both gender and instructions. Our main effect hypotheses, or alternative hypotheses for each of these factors, are:

Main effect hypothesis for gender (H_{a1}): There will be a difference in test performance between males and females.

Main effect hypothesis for instructions (H_{a2}): There will be a difference in test performance between those told the test measures logical intelligence and those told the test measures social intelligence.

Or in numerical terms:

$$H_{a1}: \mu_{males} \neq \mu_{females}$$
$$H_{a2}: \mu_{logical\ intelligence} \neq \mu_{social\ intelligence}$$

When we examine our first main effect hypothesis for gender (H_{a1}), we ignore the role of the test instructions. In the example dataset in Table 12.1a, we have raw scores and means for females and males in our sample. To determine if we have a main effect for gender, we would compare the mean test scores for females and males. Notice that there is less than one point separating the two means, and therefore it is unlikely that we have a main effect for gender.

When we examine the main effect hypothesis for instructions (H_{a2}), we would ignore the factor of gender and simply compare test scores for those 10 participants who received instructions that the test measured social intelligence to those 10 who were told the test measured logical intelligence. The raw scores and means are shown in Table 12.1b (notice we reordered our participants so they are now grouped by condition). As with our gender comparison, we find that the differences based on instructions alone are quite small. Therefore, if we were only examining main effects, we might conclude that neither gender nor instructions seem to be very important in student performance.

2 × 2 Tables and Graphs

Main effects ignore the possibility that the impact of two variables might depend on each other. To understand these potential interaction effects, it is useful to construct a 2 × 2 table and graph. In both, the levels of the first factor are compared across the levels of the second factor. A 2 × 2 table for the dataset of our example study is shown in Table 12.2 and provides the means for each of our four cells.

TABLE 12.1a

Dataset for Example Study Examining the Impact of Gender and Instructions on Test Scores, With Mean Scores for Gender

Participant	Gender	Told the Test Measures:	Test Score	
1	Female	Social Intelligence	88	$M_{females} = 83.30$
2	Female	Social Intelligence	83	
3	Female	Social Intelligence	85	
4	Female	Social Intelligence	86	
5	Female	Social Intelligence	90	
6	Female	Logical Intelligence	78	
7	Female	Logical Intelligence	80	
8	Female	Logical Intelligence	85	
9	Female	Logical Intelligence	82	
10	Female	Logical Intelligence	76	
11	Male	Social Intelligence	75	$M_{males} = 82.60$
12	Male	Social Intelligence	85	
13	Male	Social Intelligence	78	
14	Male	Social Intelligence	81	
15	Male	Social Intelligence	77	
16	Male	Logical Intelligence	80	
17	Male	Logical Intelligence	85	
18	Male	Logical Intelligence	93	
19	Male	Logical Intelligence	87	
20	Male	Logical Intelligence	85	

We can graph the data on either a bar graph or a line graph, and these corresponding graphs are depicted in Figure 12.2. The bar graph more accurately demonstrates that the factors are categorical rather than continuous variables. On the other hand, the line graph more clearly demonstrates the interaction effect because such an effect can be seen in the nonparallel lines. Nonparallel lines are those that intersect (or interact) on the graph or lines that would intersect if they continued off the graph. For this reason, we will use line graphs for the remainder of this chapter.

Notice in Figure 12.2 that the 2 × 2 graphs demonstrate a very clear interaction effect. Females do much worse on a test when they are told it measures logical intelligence than when they are told it measures social intelligence. Males demonstrate the opposite pattern in which they do worse when told the test measures social intelligence than when they are told it measures logical intelligence. Thus, men and women's performance on the same exact test is dependent on the instructions they were given.

TABLE 12.1b

Dataset for Example Study Examining the Impact of Gender and Instructions on Test Scores, With Mean Scores for Instruction Condition

Participant	Gender	Told the Test Measures:	Test Score	
1	Female	Social Intelligence	88	$M_{\text{social intelligence}}$ = 82.80
2	Female	Social Intelligence	83	
3	Female	Social Intelligence	85	
4	Female	Social Intelligence	86	
5	Female	Social Intelligence	90	
11	Male	Social Intelligence	75	
12	Male	Social Intelligence	85	
13	Male	Social Intelligence	78	
14	Male	Social Intelligence	81	
15	Male	Social Intelligence	77	
6	Female	Logical Intelligence	78	$M_{\text{logical intelligence}}$ = 83.10
7	Female	Logical Intelligence	80	
8	Female	Logical Intelligence	85	
9	Female	Logical Intelligence	82	
10	Female	Logical Intelligence	76	
16	Male	Logical Intelligence	80	
17	Male	Logical Intelligence	85	
18	Male	Logical Intelligence	93	
19	Male	Logical Intelligence	87	
20	Male	Logical Intelligence	85	

This example is based on an actual study conducted by Cadinu, Maass, Lombardo, and Frigerio (2006). They examined the theory of stereotype threat, in which members of a group inadvertently conform to negative stereotypes ascribed to them, especially when they are reminded of these stereotypes. The interaction between gender and instructions supports this theory of stereotype threat. Participants were told a test is designed to measure gender differences, and it appears that men conformed to the stereotype that men perform worse on social intelligence tests and women conformed to the stereotype that women perform worse on logical intelligence tests.

In case we have inadvertently activated a gender stereotype threat for you with all this talk about gender differences in test performance, remember that the tests the participants took were exactly the same and the gender differences in performance were due entirely to the instructions and not to differences in actual logic or social skills. Moreover, we hope that the stereotype that women do less well on logic tests will not affect how women perform in a research methods and statistics course. It may help to know that

TABLE 12.2

Test Scores as a Function of Gender and Instructions

Instructions

	Told Test Measures Social Intelligence	Told Test Measures Logical Intelligence
Male	M = 79.20	M = 86.00
Female	M = 86.40	M = 80.20

Gender

FIGURE 12.2

Example 2 × 2 Interaction Depicted With a Bar Graph and a Line Graph

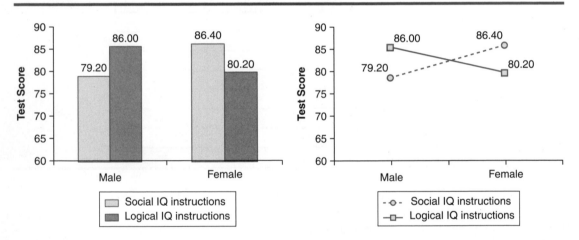

research has found no consistent differences between men and women's performance in these types of courses (Buck, 1985; Schram, 1996).

Note: It usually does not matter which factor is graphed on the X (horizontal) axis and which is graphed as separate lines.

Graphs With No Interactions

When you examine the results of a factorial design, it is possible that there will not be an interaction effect. In some cases, you might find one or two main effects with no interaction. It is also possible that the results will reveal that there are no main effects and no interactions. These variations are depicted in Figure 12.3.

Parallel lines as depicted in the graphs in Figure 12.3 suggest that there is no interaction effect between the two factors. The 2 × 2 graphs can help you understand and interpret the possible different main effects:

- The slope of the lines indicates the strength of the relationship between the factor graphed on the *x*-axis and the DV (or outcome). In Figure 12.3, graphs a. and b. demonstrate a main effect for the first factor. On the other hand, horizontal lines with no slope suggest there is no main effect for the factor on the *x*-axis. We see that pattern in graphs c. and d.

- The distance between the lines indicates the strength of the relationship between the factor graphed as separate lines and the DV (or outcome). If the lines are close or overlap, there is no main effect for the factor graphed as separate lines. Graphs a. and c. in Figure 12.3 suggest a main effect for the second factor because the lines are separate, while graphs b. and d. have lines very close to one another and suggest no main effect for the second factor.

FIGURE 12.3

Graphs Depicting No Interaction Effects

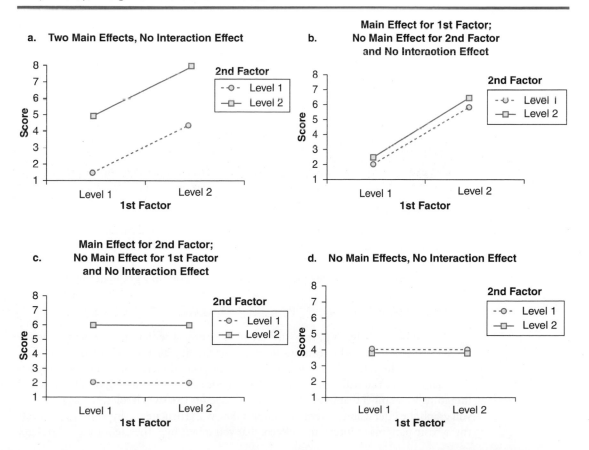

Interaction Hypotheses

You might only hypothesize main effects if you are utilizing a factorial design to control for an extraneous or confounding variable. In such cases, you might expect your results to look like one of the first three graphs depicted in Figure 12.3. You would not hypothesize the last graph, in which there are no main effects or interactions, because we would wonder why you are conducting the study at all.

However, if you are using a factorial design to examine the complex relationships between the factors, then you should have a clearly defined interaction hypothesis. On a basic level, your alternative hypothesis for the interaction ($H_{a1\times2}$) is simply that the relationship between a factor and a DV/outcome is impacted by a second factor, often referred to as a moderator. See Figure 12.4 for a conceptual representation of an interaction effect.

FIGURE 12.4

An Interaction Hypothesis Predicts the Relationship Between a Factor and the DV/Outcome Is Impacted by a 2nd Factor (the Moderator)

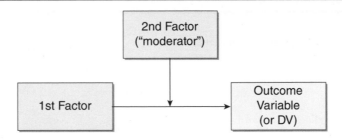

An example alternative hypothesis ($H_{a1\times2}$) for the Gender × Instructions factorial we introduced earlier in the chapter is that the relationship between gender and test performance is impacted by, or depends on, the instructions. Or, put another way:

Gender × Instructions Interaction hypothesis ($H_{a1\times2}$): The relationship between gender and test performance depends on whether the participant was told the test measures logical or social intelligence.

In numerical terms, we are predicting nonparallel lines in a graph of the cell means:

$$H_{a1\times2}: \left(\mu_{\text{females/logic IQ}} - \mu_{\text{males/logic IQ}}\right) \neq \left(\mu_{\text{females/social IQ}} - \mu_{\text{males/social IQ}}\right)$$

For hypothesis testing, it is sufficient to simply predict that a second factor/moderator will impact the relationship between the first factor and the outcome/DV. However, usually you will want to predict *how* the second factor, or moderator, impacts the relationship. You will develop such a hypothesis after a careful review of the research literature. Remember that in most cases, the two factors can switch roles; and as such, how you graph the interaction pattern may impact how you articulate the hypothesis. There are three basic patterns of interaction effects that you might hypothesize for a 2 × 2 design.

Practice 12.2

GRAPH A 2 × 2 INTERACTION

Cadinu et al. (2006) found support for the theory of stereotype threat that members of a group may underperform when they are told that a test assesses a skill their group is stereotypically poor at. They also found that the negative impact of a stereotype depends on whether students ascribe their performance to internal factors such as personal motivation and skill (internal locus of control) versus external factors such as luck or someone else's behavior (external locus of control).

Specifically, they found that "individuals with an Internal Locus of Control . . . showed a sharper decrease in the stereotype threat condition compared to individuals with External Locus of Control beliefs" (p. 183).

The researchers provided the following table (p. 193):

Locus of Control	Threat	No-Threat
Internal		
M	3.00	5.33
SD	1.63	1.30
n	13	12
External		
M	4.65	4.59
SD	1.93	1.54
n	17	17

Graph the results with threat levels on the x-axis and levels of locus of control as separate lines.

Hint: The table includes more information than is necessary for the 2 × 2 graph, although taking into consideration the standard deviations (*SD*) and sample sizes (*n*) is important for interpreting the results.

See Appendix A to check your answers.

Source: Cadinu et al. (2006) published in *European Journal of Social Psychology, 36,* 183–197.

The Second Factor (Moderator) Strengthens or Weakens the Relationship Between the First Factor and the Outcome/DV

The results described in Practice 12.2 demonstrate this pattern in that the effect of stereotype threat is stronger for those with an internal locus of control. With this type of interaction, one or both factors may also have a main effect, but any main effect is qualified by the interaction. In other words, any main effect is not sufficient to explain the relationship.

If we were designing an experiment and expected this type of interaction, we would hypothesize that the IV affects the DV, but that effect is stronger or weaker under certain conditions. In a graph, we would depict this hypothesis by having both lines slant in the same direction, with one line steeper than the other. The relationship is hypothesized to be stronger for the group represented by the steeper line, and weaker for the group represented by the less steep line.

For example, we might hypothesize that grit is a positive trait in academic success for both easy and challenging situations, but is *especially* positive for the challenging tasks. In other words, we expect the relationship between grit and academic success to be stronger in challenging situations and weaker in easy situations. If we were to find support for this hypothesis, we would expect a graph that looks something like the one in Figure 12.5a. Notice in this graph that the lines both slope to show a positive relationship between grit and academic success. However, the slope of the line for the challenging situation is steeper, indicating a stronger relationship, than the line representing the easy situation.

FIGURE 12.5
Graphs Depicting Interactions

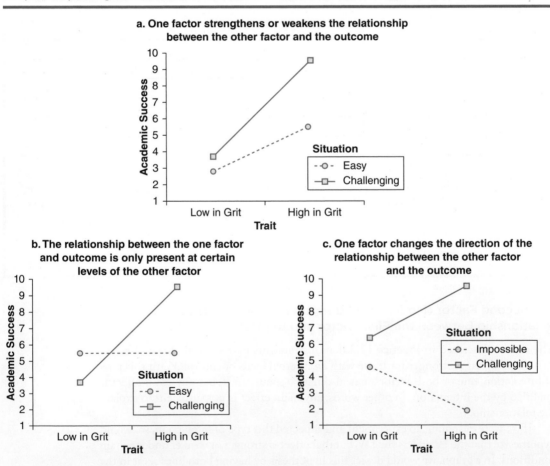

The Relationship Between the First Factor and Outcome/DV Is Present at Only One Level of the Moderator

Past research might lead you to hypothesize that one group might not be affected by your IV or that the relationship between your predictor and outcome does not apply to members of a certain group. On a graph, this type of interaction would be depicted so that there is one horizontal line and one sloped line. The horizontal line indicates that at that level of the moderator, there is no expected relationship between the predictor (or IV) and the outcome (or DV). The sloped line suggests that at the other level of the moderator, there is an expected relationship. Like the first interaction pattern, you may also see one or two main effects that are qualified by the interaction and should therefore not be interpreted alone.

The protective factor of parenting quality that we discussed early in this chapter is an example of this type of interaction (see Figure 12.1). Another example is the hypothesis that grit is a positive trait for challenging situations but does not relate to academic success in easy situations. For this example, our hypothesized interaction would look like the graph in Figure 12.5b. Notice that the line representing the challenging situation is sloped, suggesting a positive relationship between grit and academic success in a challenging situation. On the other hand, there is no slope for the line representing easy situations, suggesting that grit does not matter in an easy situation.

The Moderating Variable Changes the Direction of the Relationship Between the First Factor and Outcome/DV

When a moderating variable changes the direction of the relationship between the first factor and outcome/DV, the relationship found for one group is reversed for the other group; and, as such, the lines on the graph extend in opposite directions. When the impact of one factor is completely dependent on the other, there are no main effects and the lines on the 2 × 2 graph are fully crossed, forming an X pattern. We saw this type of interaction in our example study of gender and test instructions (see the line graph in Figure 12.2).

This type of interaction is not always fully crossed. The example shown in Figure 12.5c suggests that grit is a positive trait in challenging situations but is a negative trait in impossible situations. Notice that the lines of this graph slope in opposite directions.

ANALYZING FACTORIAL DESIGNS

Thus far, we have been describing main effects and interactions in terms of patterns. Understanding and describing these patterns is an important first step to designing a factorial design and will be useful in interpreting your results. However, as you might expect by now, you will want to determine if you have statistically significant main effects and interactions. The steepness of a line or distance between lines is insufficient evidence of a statistically significant main effect, just as the presence of nonparallel lines is insufficient evidence of a statistically significant interaction.

In order to determine if you have statistically significant main effects and interactions, you will need to conduct an inferential statistical test. The type of test you will use depends on whether you have an independent- or dependent-groups design and the scale of measurement for your outcome/DV.

Ethics Tip: Do Not Fish for Results

When you conduct any study, it is likely that you will also collect demographic information such as age, gender, and ethnicity in order to describe your sample. Any of these demographics can quite easily become predictors in a factorial design, and by exploring your data you might find some statistically significant interaction effects. Exploring your data in this way is called "data dredging" or "fishing" (see Figure 12.6) and raises ethical concerns about the appropriate use and interpretation of results. Remember that being an ethical researcher is not just about how you interact with participants or animal subjects, but it also applies to how you analyze, interpret, and share your results.

You might recall that when you run many statistical analyses, you increase your chances of making a Type I error. As such, results that you found on a fishing expedition may simply be an artifact of your particular study and not represent a pattern that truly exists in the population. Reporting potentially spurious results is misleading, and widespread use of this practice can damage the integrity of the field.

Consequently, carefully consider potential interaction effects before designing and analyzing your data. Report only results from these planned analyses. This does not mean that you cannot or should not explore your data. Some exploration can help you better understand your data and can lead to hypotheses for future research (Bem, 2003). The key is that results found through exploratory analyses should be tested with a new sample to ensure they are valid.

FIGURE 12.6
Fishing for Significant Results

This cartoon illustrates the practice of fishing for significant results. Reporting results that were fished from your data is not ethical.

Source: Eva K. Lawrence

ANALYZING INDEPENDENT-GROUPS
FACTORIAL DESIGNS

REVIEW OF KEY CONCEPTS: INDEPENDENT-GROUPS DESIGN

An independent-groups design is one in which the participants experience only one level of the predictor or IV (there are no repeated measures), and the groups are not matched. This is also referred to as a between-subjects design.

All the examples we have discussed up until this point have been independent-groups factorial designs. An **independent-groups factorial design** requires that the levels or groups of each factor are not related by repeated measures or matching. A **two-way between-subjects ANOVA** is the appropriate analysis when you have two independent factors, your DV or outcome variable is measured on an interval or ratio scale, and you have participants representing each cell. This is the appropriate analysis for an independent-groups 2 × 2 factorial. You can also use this analysis for a more complex two-factor design in which you have more than two levels per factor (e.g., 3 × 3).

Independent-groups factorial design: A factorial design in which all the factors have independent levels/groups.

Two-way between-subjects ANOVA: An analysis of variance test appropriate for designs with two independent factors and an interval or ratio outcome.

In computing the two-way between-subjects ANOVA, we make several assumptions:

- There are two factors, each with two or more conditions.
- The conditions (groups) for each factor are independent.
- DV (or outcome) is interval or ratio scale of measurement.
- DV (or outcome) is normally distributed.
- Variability (*SD*) is similar across all the conditions *(homogeneity of variance)*.

FORMULAS AND CALCULATIONS:
TWO-WAY BETWEEN-SUBJECTS ANOVA

When you conduct a two-way between-subjects ANOVA, you need to calculate several different types of means. First, you need the **grand mean**, which is the mean of

Grand mean: The mean of the DV or outcome of the entire sample.

the DV or outcome for the entire sample. You also need the **group means,** which are the means for each level or group of each factor that are used to evaluate main effects (e.g., a main effect for gender would compare the group mean of females to the group mean of males). The **cell means** are the means for each cell that compares one level of the first factor across one level of the second factor, and these help you analyze and interpret the interaction effect.

For example, consider our example study about how both gender and test instructions interact to impact test scores. The data for this study were provided earlier in the chapter, in Table 12.1. We can calculate the grand mean by averaging the test scores for all 20 participants, and earlier in the chapter we calculated the group and cell means for this dataset. It is also wise to calculate the standard deviations (*SDs*) whenever we calculate means, and this can be done using the formula in Appendix D.1 or via a statistical software program such as SPSS or Excel. A summary of these results appears in Table 12.3.

> **Group means:** The mean of each level or group of one factor that ignores the other factor.
>
> **Cell means:** The mean of each cell comparing one level of a factor across a level of another factor.

TABLE 12.3

Summary of Grand, Group, and Cell Means for Example Dataset

	Sample Size	Mean (*M*)	Standard Deviation (*SD*)
Grand Mean	*n* = 20	82.95	4.82
Group Means			
1st factor: gender			
females	*n* = 10	83.30	4.40
males	*n* = 10	82.60	5.42
2nd factor: instructions			
logical IQ	*n* = 10	83.10	4.95
social IQ	*n* = 10	82.80	4.94
Cell Means			
Gender × Instructions			
female/logical IQ	*n* = 5	80.20	3.49
female/social IQ	*n* = 5	86.40	2.70
male/logical IQ	*n* = 5	86.00	4.69
male/social IQ	*n* = 5	79.20	3.90

Similarly to calculating a one-way ANOVA, we must complete a summary table for a two-way ANOVA that contains the source of the variance (treatment and error), the sums of squares (SS) for each source, the df for each source, and the mean square (MS). See the One-Way ANOVA section in Chapter 10 for a review of these terms. However, because we now have two main effects and an interaction, we have more sources of variance (see Table 12.4). Step-by-step directions are provided after Table 12.4.

Calculate the Sum of Squares

The first step is to calculate the sum of squares (SS) for the main effects, interaction effect, error, and total. The computational formula for the sum of squares is provided in Appendix D.10. The results of the sum of squares calculations for our example dataset are shown in Table 12.5.

Calculate the Degrees of Freedom

The degrees of freedom are an estimate of sample size that we will use both to calculate the mean squares as well as use to determine the critical F value to determine if our

TABLE 12.4

Summary Table for Two-Way Between-Subjects ANOVA

Source	SS	df	MS	F
Treatment				
Factor 1	SS_{B1}	$k_{B1} - 1$	SS_{B1}/df_{B1}	MS_{B1}/MS_w
Factor 2	SS_{B2}	$k_{B2} - 1$	SS_{B2}/df_{B2}	MS_{B2}/MS_w
Interaction	$SS_{B1 \times B2}$	$(df_{B1})(df_{B2})$	$SS_{B1 \times B2}/df_{B1 \times B2}$	$MS_{B1 \times B2}/MS_w$
Error	SS_w	$C(n-1)$	SS_w/df_w	
Total	SS_{tot}	$N-1$		

TABLE 12.5

Sample Summary Table, With SS and df

Source	SS	df	MS	F
Gender	2.45	1	SS_{B1}/df_{B1}	MS_{B1}/MS_w
Instructions	0.45	1	SS_{B2}/df_{B2}	MS_{B2}/MS_w
Gender × Instructions	211.25	1	$SS_{B1 \times B2}/df_{B1 \times B2}$	$MS_{B1 \times B2}/MS_w$
Error	226.80	16	SS_w/df_w	
Total	440.95	19		

results meet the criteria for statistical significance. Just as for sum of squares, we need to calculate the degrees of freedom for each main effect, the interaction, the error, and the total.

The formula to calculate the degrees of freedom for each main effect is the same as for the one-way ANOVA ($df_B = k - 1$), where k represents the number of groups. For a 2 × 2 design, such as our example gender × instruction factorial, the degrees of freedom for each main effect will always be 1, because each factor has two groups.

The formula to calculate the degrees of freedom for the interaction is $df_{B1 \times B2} = (df_{B1})(df_{B2})$. In other words, you simply multiply the degrees of freedom of each of your main effects. For a 2 × 2 design, the degrees of freedom for the interaction is 1.

The formula to calculate the error degrees of freedom is $df_w = C(n - 1)$, where C represents the number of cells, and n is the number of participants in each cell. For our example, we have 4 cells and 5 participants in each cell, and therefore $df_w = 4(5 - 1) = 16$.

You can calculate the total degrees of freedom by adding up the degrees of freedom for each factor, the interaction, and the error. Alternatively, you can use the formula $df_{tot} = N - 1$, where N is total number of participants in the sample. For our example, we have 20 participants and 19 total degrees of freedom.

Calculate the Mean Squares

Once you have calculated the sum of squares and degrees of freedom, we use that information to calculate the mean squares (*MS*) for the main effects, interaction effect, and error. Table 12.5 provides the summary table for our example 2 (gender) × 2 (instruction) factorial, and the calculations for the mean squares for this example (*MS*) are provided below.

a. **Mean Square for the Main Effects**

For the first factor (MS_{B1}):

$$MS_{B1} = SS_{B1}/df_{B1} = 2.45/1 = 2.45$$

For the second factor (MS_{B2}):

$$MS_{B2} = SS_{B2}/df_{B2} = 0.45/1 = 0.45$$

b. **Mean Square for the Interaction ($MS_{B1 \times B2}$)**

$$MS_{B1 \times B2} = SS_{B1 \times B2}/df_{B1 \times B2} = 211.25/1 = 211.25$$

c. **Mean Square of Error (MS_w)**

$$MS_w = SS_w/df_w = 226.80/16 = 14.175$$

Calculate the F Ratios

Finally, you use the mean square (MS) calculations to calculate the F ratio. The F ratio is the between-groups variance (estimated by the mean square for the main effect or interaction) divided by the within-groups variance (estimated by the mean square of error). Calculations for our example study are provided below.

a. F Ratio for the Main Effects

For the first factor (F_{B1}):

$$F_{B1} = MS_{B1}/MS_w = 2.45/14.175 = 0.173$$

For the second factor (F_{B2}):

$$F_{B2} = MS_{B2}/MS_w = 0.45/14.175 = 0.032$$

b. F Ratio for the Interaction ($F_{B1 \times B2}$)

$$F_{B1 \times B2} = MS_{B1 \times B2}/MS_w = 211.25/14.175 = 14.903$$

Once we calculate F, we compare it against the critical values for F in Appendix C.6 to determine if we have met the criteria for statistical significance. When we do this, we find that neither main effect is statistically significant but the interaction meets the criteria for significance at the $p < .01$ level. Our complete summary table, with the statistically significant interaction noted, appears in Table 12.6.

Effect Size

We use the partial eta squared ($\eta^2_{partial}$) as a measure of the effect size, which provides the unique effect of each main effect and interaction (i.e., the formula partials out the

TABLE 12.6

Complete Sample Summary Table

Source	SS	df	MS	F
Gender	2.45	1	2.45	0.173
Instructions	0.45	1	0.45	0.032
Gender × Instructions	211.25	1	211.25	14.903*
Error	226.80	16	14.16	
Total	440.95	19		

*Statistically significant at the $p < .01$ level

impact of the other factors). We interpret each partial eta square as the percentage of variability accounted for by each effect (main effect 1, main effect 2, or interaction).

$$\text{The formula is: } \eta^2_{partial} = SS_B/(SS_B + SS_w)$$

We can apply this formula for the two-way ANOVA by calculating the eta squared for each main effect and the interaction. For our example study:

- Gender: $\eta^2_{partial} = 2.45/(2.45 + 226.80) = .010$

- Instruction condition: $\eta^2_{partial} = 0.45/(0.45 + 226.80) = .002$

- Gender $\times$ Instruction: $\eta^2_{partial} = 211.25/(211.25 + 226.80) = .482$

Practice 12.3

COMPLETE A TWO-WAY BETWEEN-SUBJECTS ANOVA SUMMARY TABLE

A researcher hypothesizes that ADHD symptoms will exacerbate the distracting impact of a cell phone ringing during a lecture. She conducts a 2 (ring vs. no-ring) × 2 (low ADHD symptoms vs. high ADHD symptoms) factorial with 100 participants, 25 in each cell.

1. Fill in the missing information in the ANOVA summary table. Look at Appendix C.6 to determine if the F meets criteria for statistical significance.

Tests of Between-Subjects Effects

Source	Sum of Squares	df	Mean Square	F	Sig.
condition	11.560	$k_{B1} - 1 =$ _____	$SS_{B1}/df_{B1} =$ _____	$MS_{B1}/MS_w =$ _____	?
ADHD	1.960	$k_{B2} - 1 =$ _____	$SS_{B2}/df_{B2} =$ _____	$MS_{B2}/MS_w =$ _____	?
condition * ADHD	1.440	$(df_{B1})(df_{B2}) =$ _____	$SS_{B1 \times B2}/df_{B1 \times B2} =$ _____	$MS_{B1 \times B2}/MS_w =$ _____	?
Error	114.000	$C(n-1) =$ _____	$SS_w/df_w =$ _____		
Total	128.960	$N - 1 =$ _____			

2. Compute the effect size ($\eta^2_{partial}$) for each main effect and the interaction.

   See Appendix A to check your answers.

Post Hoc Analyses

If you find a statistically significant interaction, you should report the pattern of that interaction. If you have a result in which both lines extend in the same direction but one is steeper, that pattern suggests that the relationship is stronger for one level of the moderator. If your lines extend in opposite directions, the pattern suggests that the moderator changed the direction of the relationship.

Without additional analyses, you cannot say that there is or is not a significant effect for one level of the moderator, nor can you say that one cell mean is significantly different from another. If you wish to make those types of statements, post hoc analyses must be conducted. For the 2 × 2, the post hoc analyses are independent-samples t tests comparing individual cell means (see Chapter 10).

Using Data Analysis Programs: Two-Way Between-Subjects ANOVA

As we have noted in regard to other statistical tests, it is most likely that you will use a statistical package for a two-way ANOVA. A data file for our Gender × Instruction factorial would look very much like Table 12.1 except that gender and instructions must be coded as numbers (e.g., females = 1 and males = 2; social IQ = 1 and logical IQ = 2). SPSS output from the two-way ANOVA of this dataset is shown in Figure 12.7.

Notice that SPSS can provide results of the Levene's test that tests our homogeneity of variance assumption. In our example (see Figure 12.9), Levene's is not statistically significant, which indicates that we have met our assumption for homogeneity of variances. As with the one-way between- and within-subjects ANOVAs, you can also use SPSS to calculate the effect size for each main effect and interaction.

REPORTING AND INTERPRETING RESULTS OF A TWO-WAY ANOVA

Results Section

The format and statistical notations for the results of a between-subjects two-way ANOVA are similar to the one-way between-subjects ANOVA described in Chapter 10. However, you must include the group means and standard deviation for each of the main effects. You also must include inferential statistics and effect sizes for each main effect and for the interaction. If your interaction is statistically significant, provide the cell means and standard deviations as well. It is also a good idea to report the confidence intervals (CI) for any means you report. You can calculate the CIs by hand (see Chapter 7) or using a statistical program such as SPSS or Excel.

Application 12.2 provides a sample APA-style Results section for our findings. As with the example write-ups in previous chapters, these are not real data but are based on a pattern reported in published research (Cadinu et al., 2006). Notice that we reported cell means, standard deviations, and the confidence intervals for the cell means in a table. Tables can be especially useful for summarizing results of a statistically significant

FIGURE 12.7

Annotated SPSS Output for the Two-Way Between-Subjects ANOVA Examining Test Scores as a Function of Gender and Instructions

Descriptive Statistics:

Dependent Variable: test score

gender	instruction condition	Mean	Std. Deviation	N
female	told test measures social IQ	86.4000	2.70185	5
	told test measures logical IQ	80.2000	3.49285	5
	Total	83.3000	4.39823	10
male	told test measures social IQ	79.2000	3.89872	5
	told test measures logical IQ	86.0000	4.69042	5
	Total	82.6000	5.42013	10
Total	told test measures social IQ	82.8000	4.93964	10
	told test measures logical IQ	83.1000	4.95424	10
	Total	82.9500	4.81746	20

cell means

group means for gender

group means for instruction condition

grand mean

Levene's Test of Homogeneity of Variance:

Dependent Variable: test score

F	df1	df2	Sig.
.273	3	16	.844

Tests the null hypothesis that the error variance of the dependent variable is equal across groups.

We met the assumption of equal variances because the Levene's test is not statistically significant.

ANOVA Summary Table:

Tests of Between-Subjects Effects

Dependent Variable: test score

Source	Type III Sum of Squares	df	Mean Square	F	Sig.	Partial Eta Squared
Corrected Model	214.150[a]	3	71.383	5.036	.012	.486
Intercept	137614.050	1	137614.050	9708.222	.000	.998
gender	2.450	1	2.450	.173	.683	.011
instructions	.450	1	.450	.032	.861	.002
gender * instructions	211.250	1	211.250	14.903	.001	.482
Error	226.800	16	14.175			
Total	138055.000	20				
Corrected Total	440.950	19				

Main effect for 1st factor

Main effect for 2nd factor

Interaction effect

Results:
-No significant main effect for gender: $F(1, 16) = 0.173$, $p = .683$
-No significant main effect for instructions: $F(1, 16) = 0.32$, $p = .861$
-A significant gender X instructions interaction: $F(1, 16) = 14.90$, $p = .001$

Application 12.2

SAMPLE RESULTS FOR A TWO-WAY BETWEEN-SUBJECTS ANOVA

Results

A 2 × 2 between-subjects ANOVA was conducted to examine test scores as a function of gender (female vs. male) and instructions (social IQ vs. logical IQ). The main effect comparing males ($M = 82.60$, $SD = 5.42$), 95% CI [78.72, 86.48] and females ($M = 83.30$, $SD = 4.40$), 95% CI [80.15, 86.45] was not statistically significant, $F(1, 16) = 0.173$, $p = .683$, $\eta^2_{partial} = .011$. Similarly, there was no significant difference between those who received instructions that the test measured social intelligence ($M = 82.80$, $SD = 4.94$), 95% CI [79.27, 86.33] and those who were told the test measured logical intelligence ($M = 83.10$, $SD = 4.95$), 95% CI [79.56, 86.64], $F(1, 16) = 0.032$, $p = .861$, $\eta^2_{partial} = .002$.

However, there was a significant interaction demonstrating that the relationship between gender and test performance was dependent on which instructions participants received, $F(1, 16) = 14.90$, $p = .001$. Forty-eight percent of the variance in test score was accounted for by this interaction. An examination of the interaction pattern suggests that female students performed better on the test if they were told the test measured social intelligence than if they were told it measured logical intelligence. The opposite pattern was found for male students, who performed better in the logical IQ condition than the social IQ condition (see Table 12.7 for cell means).

TABLE 12.7

Test Performance as a Function of Gender and Instructions

	Social IQ Instructions			Logic IQ Instructions		
	Mean (*SD*)	95% CI	*n*	Mean (*SD*)	95% CI	*n*
Females	86.40 (2.70)	83.05, 89.75	5	80.20 (3.49)	75.86, 85.54	5
Males	79.20 (3.90)	74.36, 84.04	5	86.00 (4.69)	80.18, 91.82	5

interaction. In a full APA-style research report, this table would appear on a separate page after the reference section and would be numbered (see Appendix B for an example).

Interpreting Results in the Discussion Section

You report the statistical analyses for each main effect and interaction, and you must also interpret these results in the Discussion section. Interpretation includes explaining if the results fit with your hypotheses and how the results fit with past research. Remember that if you had a significant interaction, you cannot interpret the main effects alone. Instead, you must explain how the statistically significant interaction qualifies any significant or nonsignificant main effects.

For example, in our example study, you would not want to spend too much time explaining how there was no significant main effect for gender and considering why that might be. Likewise, you should not interpret the main effect of test instructions on its own. Both of these main effects are qualified by the significant interaction, and the majority of your interpretation should be about how the relationship between gender and test scores depends on the test instructions (or vice versa).

As with other designs, the *practical significance* of the results is a critical component of the discussion section. For our example study, we would want to consider if the difference in test scores among the various cells would have real-world implications. In this case, we see that, on average, females in the logic IQ instruction condition scored about 6 percentage points lower than those in the social IQ instruction condition. Men scored an average of about 7 percentage points lower in the social IQ instructions compared to the logic IQ instructions. Those 6 to 7 percentage points translate into more than a half-letter grade; and, as such, the interaction effect has serious practical significance.

Beyond Two Ways

A two-way ANOVA is used when you have two factors and your outcome or DV is interval or ratio. Can you guess what type of ANOVA is used when you have three factors? It may come as no surprise that a three-way ANOVA would be used in this situation and that a four-way is for four factors, and so on. To calculate such ANOVAs by hand, you would build on the same formulas for the two-way ANOVA (see Table 12.4). Alternatively, you would enter additional factors into your data analysis program. Keep in mind that you will not just have additional factors, but will also need to calculate additional interactions. For a three-way ANOVA, you would have three factors, three two-way interactions (factor 1 × factor 2; factor 1 × factor 3; factor 2 × factor 3), and a three-way interaction (factor 1 × factor 2 × factor 3).

The ANOVA is used when your predictor/IV is nominal (you are comparing groups) and your outcome/DV is interval or ratio. If you have all nominal data and independent groups, you would calculate a chi-square test of independence, which is described in Chapter 13. You can even conduct factorial analyses when you do not have nominal factors, such as you might find in a correlational design; and you could conduct a regression analysis to accomplish that. We briefly introduced regression in Chapter 8.

DEPENDENT-GROUPS FACTORIAL DESIGNS

 REVIEW OF KEY CONCEPTS: DEPENDENT-GROUPS DESIGN

A dependent-groups design is one in which the groups are related in that the participants were matched or experience all levels of the IV or predictor as in a repeated measures design (also called a within-subjects design).

Factorial designs can be independent designs, as we have already discussed, dependent designs, or a mix of both these designs. In a **dependent-groups factorial design**, all the factors have levels that are related either with matching or repeated measures. In a 2 × 2 dependent-groups design, all the participants may have experienced all the levels of the two factors (both factors were repeated measures), the participants may have been matched for both factors, or one factor may be a repeated measure and the other may be matched.

For example, if we wanted to conduct a 2 × 2 dependent-groups design to examine test performance as a function of instruction (logical IQ vs. social IQ) and time of day (a.m. vs. p.m.) we could have all participants experience all four of these cells using a repeated measures design. Recall from Chapter 11 that to avoid practice and order effects in a repeated measures design, we should give different versions of the test and randomly assign the students to take the tests in a different order. A second option is to use matching instead of repeated measures so that there are different participants in each cell, but they have been matched on a key variable (such as GPA) prior to being randomly assigned to a condition. A final option is to have one of the factors be repeated and have the other be matched.

A **two-way within-subjects ANOVA** is the appropriate inferential statistic when you have two dependent factors and your DV or outcome variable is measured on an interval or ratio scale. The summary table for a two-way within-subjects ANOVA is shown in Table 12.8, and the calculations are similar to those used for the one-way within-subjects ANOVA (see Chapter 11).

> **Dependent-groups factorial design:** A factorial design in which all the levels of the factors are related via matching or repeated measures.
>
> **Two-way within-subjects ANOVA:** An analysis of variance test appropriate for designs with two dependent factors and an interval or ratio outcome.

TABLE 12.8

Summary Table for Two-Way Within-Subjects ANOVA

Source	SS	df	MS	F
Subjects	SS_S	$N-1$	SS_S/df_S	
Factor 1 Subjects × Factor 1	SS_{A1} $SS_{S \times A1}$	$k_{A1}-1$ $(df_S)(k_{A1}-1)$	SS_{A1}/df_{A1} $SS_{S \times A1}/df_{S \times A1}$	$MS_{A1}/MS_{A1 \times S}$
Factor 2 Subjects × Factor 2	SS_{A2} $SS_{S \times A2}$	$k_{A2}-1$ $(df_S)(k_{A2}-1)$	SS_{A2}/df_{A2} $SS_{S \times A2}/df_{S \times A2}$	$MS_{A2}/MS_{A2 \times S}$
Factor 1 × Factor 2 Subjects × Factor 1 × Factor 2	$SS_{A1 \times A2}$ $SS_{S \times A1 \times A2}$	$(df_{A1})(df_{A2})$ $(df_S)(df_{A1})(df_{A2})$	$SS_{A1 \times A2}/df_{A1 \times A2}$ $SS_{S \times A1 \times A2}/df_{S \times A1 \times A2}$	$MS_{A1 \times A2}/MS_{S \times A1 \times A2}$
Total	SS_{tot}	$(k_{A1})(k_{A2})(N-1)$		

The process of analyzing a two-way within-subjects ANOVA using a data analysis program is also similar to that of the one-way within-subjects ANOVA described in Chapter 11. Key differences in data entry, analysis, and interpretation follow.

- For the 2 × 2 dependent-groups design, you should have four scores for each participant (or matched pair) that represent both levels of the first factor and both levels of the second factor. All these scores should appear in one row in your dataset.

- When you run your analyses, you will request information for each of your factors.

- The output will provide results for each of your main effects and your interaction. You will interpret the results in much the same way as you would with a 2 × 2 independent-groups design, except your language should make it clear that participants either experienced all the conditions, were matched, or both.

MIXED DESIGNS

A factorial design can also be a mix between independent- and dependent-groups designs. The **mixed design** has at least one factor with independent levels and at least one factor with dependent levels. Mixed designs are commonly employed in the following designs:

1. Repeated measures experiments:

   - All participants experience all levels of the IV (dependent-groups factor).

   - The participants are randomly assigned to the order they experience each level of the IV (independent-groups factor).

   - The researcher would hypothesize that the IV had a main effect on the DV but would *not* want or expect a main effect for order or an interaction effect. A significant interaction between the IV and order would suggest that the impact of the IV levels depends on the order the levels were experienced.

2. Two-group pretest–posttest designs:

   - All participants experience the pretest and posttest (dependent-groups factor).

   - The participants are assigned to different levels of a factor (independent-groups factor).

Mixed design: A factorial design with at least one factor with independent levels and at least one factor with dependent levels.

- The researcher would hypothesize an interaction effect so that the difference between pretest and posttest scores would depend on which level the participants experienced.

A **two-way mixed ANOVA** is the appropriate inferential statistic when you have two factors, one that is dependent and one that is independent. As you might expect, the calculations are a mixture of the between-subjects ANOVA and the within-subjects ANOVA. The summary table for this design is provided in Table 12.9.

To conduct a mixed factorial ANOVA with a data analysis program, you would follow the steps for the one-way within-subjects ANOVA, with the following adjustments:

- For the 2 × 2 mixed design, you should have three scores for each participant (or matched pair). Two of these will represent each level of the within-subjects (or dependent-groups) factor, and the third will be the between-subjects (or independent-groups) factor. All these scores should appear in one row in your dataset.

- When you run your analyses, you will identify one factor as your within-subjects and the other as your between-subjects factor.

- The output will provide results for each of your main effects and your interaction. In SPSS, the within-groups main effect and interaction will appear in one table and the between-groups main effect in a separate table.

> **Two-way mixed ANOVA:** An analysis of variance test appropriate for designs with one independent factor, one dependent factor, and an interval or ratio outcome.

TABLE 12.9

Summary Table for Mixed Factorial ANOVA

Source	SS	df	MS	F
Between-subjects Factor (B1) Between-subjects Error	SS_{B1} SS_w	$k_{B1} - 1$ $k_{B1}(N - 1)$	SS_{B1}/df_{B1} SS_w/df_w	MS_{B1}/MS_w
Within-subjects Factor (A1)	SS_{A1}	$k_{A1} - 1$	SS_{A1}/df_{A1} $SS_{S \times A1}/df_{S \times A1}$	$MS_{A1}/MS_{S \times A1}$
Interaction (B1 × A1) Error	$SS_{B1 \times A1}$ $SS_{w \times B1 \times A1}$	$(df_{B1})(df_{A1})$ $k_{B1}(k_{A1} - 1)(N - 1)$	$SS_{B1 \times A1}/df_{B1 \times A1}$ $SS_{S \times B1 \times A1}/df_{S \times B1 \times A1}$	$MS_{B1 \times A1}/MS_{S \times B1 \times A1}$
Total	SS_{tot}	$(k_{B1})(k_{A1})(N - 1)$		

THE BIG PICTURE: EMBRACING COMPLEXITY

Figure 12.8 is designed to help you choose the appropriate inferential statistic based on your factorial design. This figure does not include every possible factorial analysis, but rather is meant to help you organize the options we have detailed in this chapter and earlier in the text.

In general, we have noticed that students often feel exasperated and frustrated when designing and analyzing factorials. It is difficult to conceptualize how two variables interact to impact an outcome, much less if you consider interactions of three or more variables or designs with both between- and within-groups variables. At the same time, we notice that students also seem to "get" factorials at a fundamental level. It makes sense to examine the impact of multiple variables because such examinations more closely represent the complexity of real-life situations. Regardless of whether your future career will directly involve research and analyses, we hope that learning some of the basics of factorial designs will inspire you to avoid simple explanations and encourage you instead to think about and critically question the effects of more than one factor.

FIGURE 12.8

Decision Tree for Factorial Analyses

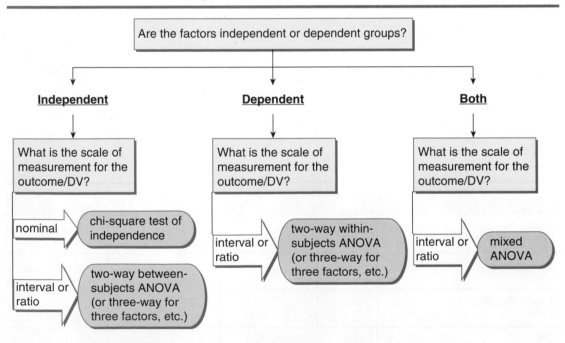

CHAPTER RESOURCES

Key Terms

Define the following terms using your own words. You can check your answers by reviewing the chapter or by comparing them with the definitions in the glossary—but try to define them on your own first.

Cell 404

Cell means 420

Correlational factorial
design 402

Dependent-groups factorial
design 429

Experimental factorial
design 402

Factor 402

Factorial design 402

Factorial notation 403

Grand mean 419

Group means 420

Hybrid factorial design 402

Independent-groups factorial
design 419

Interaction effect 404

Main effect 404

Mixed design 430

Moderator 404

Quasi-experimental factorial
design 402

Two-way between-subjects
ANOVA 419

Two-way mixed ANOVA 431

Two-way within-subjects
ANOVA 429

Do You Understand the Chapter?

Answer these questions on your own, and then review the chapter to check your answers.

1. Give an example of a correlational factorial design, quasi-experimental factorial design, experimental factorial design, and a hybrid factorial design.

2. For each example design, provide the factorial notation.

3. For each example design, identify how many main effects and how many interactions would be examined.

4. Identify the reasons for conducting a factorial design.

5. Identify and give examples of the different types of interaction hypotheses. Provide a graph of each.

6. Why is "fishing" or "data dredging" ethically questionable?

7. Explain the differences between independent-groups, dependent-groups, and mixed factorial designs.

8. When should you conduct a two-way between-subjects ANOVA?

9. When should you conduct a two-way within-subjects ANOVA?

10. When should you conduct a mixed ANOVA?

11. When should you conduct post hoc analyses for a factorial design?

Practice With Datasets and Analyses

A researcher conducts a study in which male and female participants watched one of four videos of a cell phone conversation. The researcher randomly assigned the participants to conditions where the cell phone conversation was initiated by the person in the video or not, and where the person in the video disclosed personal information or did not. The participants then rated how likeable the person in the video was on a scale from 1 to 10, with a higher score indicating higher likeability.

The data appear below:

Gender	Initiated Call	Disclosed Personal Information	Likeability Rating
female	yes	no	10.00
female	yes	no	8.00
female	yes	yes	9.00
female	yes	yes	5.00
female	yes	yes	6.00
female	no	no	8.00
female	no	no	7.00
female	no	no	8.00
female	no	yes	8.00
female	no	yes	9.00
male	yes	no	7.00
male	yes	yes	6.00
male	yes	yes	5.00
male	no	no	7.00
male	no	no	8.00
male	no	yes	10.00
female	yes	no	10.00
female	yes	no	8.00
female	yes	yes	9.00
female	yes	yes	5.00
female	yes	yes	6.00
female	no	no	8.00
female	no	no	7.00
female	no	no	8.00
male	yes	no	7.00
male	yes	yes	6.00
male	yes	yes	5.00
male	no	no	8.00
male	no	no	8.00
male	no	yes	10.00

1. The researcher wants to examine the effects of initiating the call and disclosing personal information on ratings of likeability.

    a. What specific type of research design is this? How do you know?

    b. Using a data analysis program such as SPSS, enter the data and calculate the appropriate statistics or calculate the appropriate statistics by hand.

    c. Describe the results as you would in a Results section, using proper APA format.

2. The researcher wants to examine the effects of initiating the call and participant gender on ratings of likeability.

    a. What specific type of research design is this? How do you know?

    b. Using a data analysis program such as SPSS, enter the data and calculate the appropriate statistics or calculate the appropriate statistics by hand.

    c. Describe the results as you would in a Results section, using proper APA format.

Nonparametric Statistics

13

eaver, Knox, and Zusman (2010) were interested in whether there were gender and ethnic differences among college students in their use of cell phones and in their reaction to the use of a cell phone by their romantic partner. "I use a cell phone regularly" assessed cell phone use, and "I would not be bothered if my partner talked on a cell phone when we are together" assessed if students considered the use of a cell phone detrimental to their romantic relationship. In contrast to many studies that use Likert-type scales, this study used the dichotomous response of "yes" or "no" to each of the items. Thus, although the study is an independent-groups design that compared the differences between Black and White college students, the data could not be analyzed using an independent-samples t test because the outcome measure was not an interval or ratio scale.

In another study, Oberst, Charles, and Chamarro (2005) examined the dream content of Spanish adolescents and children in an effort to determine whether gender differences existed in the overall level of aggression in participants' dreams or in the aggression expressed toward the dreamer. They ranked aggression ranging from the lowest level of "hostility expressed" to the highest level of "being killed." The researchers assumed order but did not assume equal intervals between eight levels of aggression. Thus, their scale did not meet the requirements for an interval scale but instead is an ordinal scale. This is another example of a study using one variable with two independent conditions whose data do not meet the assumptions of an independent-samples t test.

What do researchers do when their study is one of the designs you have learned about but the data in their study are not on an interval or ratio scale of measurement? Or when the data do not meet other assumptions of the statistical tests you have learned about? This chapter will describe statistical tests that are appropriate when at least one of the assumptions of parametric tests is violated.

LEARNING OUTCOMES

In this chapter, you will learn

- The differences between parametric and nonparametric tests
- When to compute different nonparametric tests
- How to compute chi-square goodness of fit and chi-square test for independence tests for nominal data
- The appropriate analyses for independent- and dependent-groups designs with nominal data
- How to compute Spearman's rank order correlation coefficient for ordinal data
- The appropriate analyses for independent- and dependent-groups designs with ordinal data

PARAMETRIC VERSUS NONPARAMETRIC STATISTICS

Consider first the requirements for the statistics you have learned about in previous chapters.

REVIEW OF KEY CONCEPTS: ASSUMPTIONS OF PARAMETRIC STATISTICS

What are the assumptions of parametric statistics?

Answer:

- Interval or ratio data

- Normally distributed variable

- Homogeneity of variance for groups

Thus far in this text, we have focused on hypothesis testing in situations that meet the assumptions for **parametric statistics**. (See Chapter 6 for a review.) Most of the time we try to collect data that are interval or ratio because parametric statistics are powerful. But what if, as in the examples at the beginning of the chapter, the data that are most appropriate for a study are nominal (categories or groups) or ordinal (ranks)? Or what if we collect both interval/ratio data and nominal or ordinal data within the same study. Or what if the interval or ratio data in our study violate other assumptions for a parametric test such as a normal distribution or homogeneity of variance? If we violate these assumptions and still use a parametric test, the probability of a Type I error is increased, and we increase the probability that we will reject the null hypothesis when it is true. In cases where a study violates the assumptions for parametric statistics, it is most appropriate to use **nonparametric statistics**. Figure 13.1 presents an amusing example of why it is not appropriate to use parametric statistics when the data are nominal.

> **Parametric statistics:** Statistics used to analyze interval and ratio data and that assume a normal distribution and homogeneity of variance between groups.
>
> **Nonparametric statistics:** Statistics used to analyze nominal and ordinal (ranked) data or used when the assumptions of parametric statistics are violated.

Parametric and nonparametric statistics differ in several ways:

- *Shape of the distribution:* Parametric statistics assume that the sample data are normally distributed while nonparametric do not. For this reason, nonparametric statistics are sometimes referred to as *distribution-free statistics*. When it is clear that the distribution of data in a study is significantly skewed, nonparametric statistics should be computed to test the hypotheses.

- *Sample size:* Parametric statistics typically have at least 10 participants in each group while nonparametric statistics can be computed with a smaller

FIGURE 13.1

Scales of Measurement and Appropriate Statistics

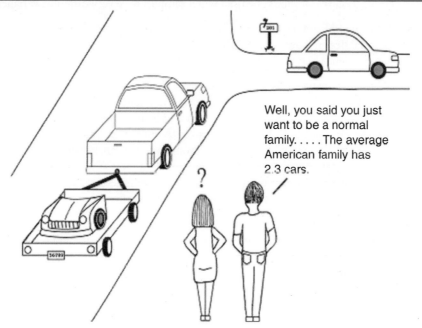

Well, you said you just want to be a normal family. . . . . The average American family has 2.3 cars.

In earlier chapters of the text, you learned about different analyses using interval or ratio data. You can see in the cartoon that sometimes it is better to use a nominal scale of measurement that assesses distinct categories (i.e., cars, in this cartoon).

Source: Sandi Coon

N where it is difficult to obtain a normal distribution. Some nonparametric tests, however, require at least 5 in a group, and some studies employing nonparametric statistics have large samples. A researcher who conducts a pilot study with a small sample may use nonparametric statistics to check for a trend before collecting a larger sample of data that will be analyzed using parametric statistics.

- *Scale of measurement:* Parametric statistics are used with interval or ratio data while nonparametric statistics are used with nominal or ordinal data. As will be discussed later, interval and ratio data can be transformed to ordinal data. This transformation is appropriate when the distribution is not normal or the sample size is too small to perform a valid test using parametric statistics.

- *Homogeneity of variance:* Parametric statistics typically assume that the variances in each group are the same. You learned in Chapter 10 that a more stringent *t* test is used when the assumption of homogeneity is violated in an independent two-group design, and that the one-way ANOVA is a more robust test and can better handle some difference in variances among the groups. Nonparametric statistics make no assumptions about the variances across groups and should be used when samples have very different variances.

- *Interactions:* Parametric statistics can test for interactions (such as in factorial designs) between variables while nonparametric statistics test for independence between variables but not for interactions.

- *Power:* Parametric tests are more powerful (have a greater probability of correctly rejecting a false null hypothesis) than nonparametric statistics. As just outlined, several assumptions should be met in order to compute parametric statistics in hypothesis testing. A study that meets all of these assumptions is somewhat "protected" from Type I errors because of the care to ensure that only in those cases where the data meet stringent requirements and show very different results for the groups, will the null hypothesis be rejected and the groups assumed to come from a different population than that of no differences between the groups.

- *Computations:* The computations for parametric statistics are much more complicated than those for nonparametric statistics. Because of the ease of computation, nonparametric statistics are sometimes used as a quick check on a trend before all the data are entered into a file or during data collection.

Although parametric statistics have some clear advantages, there are several reasons to choose nonparametric statistics (see Figure 13.2). Your study may include data that are on a nominal or ordinal scale. Sometimes the sample data are dramatically skewed so nonparametric statistics are more appropriate. Or you may have a small sample for

FIGURE 13.2

A Comparison of Parametric and Nonparametric Statistics

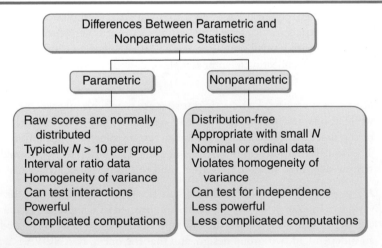

a pilot study and want to determine whether there are any trends to explore further. Finally, after collecting data, you may find that the groups have significantly different variances. As noted above, the computations are much simpler for nonparametric statistics and allow a quick check on trends in the data. Although nonparametric statistics are less powerful, they do provide useful information about differences between groups or relationships between variables and should be included in your toolbox of potential statistical tests.

Nonparametric statistics may be used for a variety of reasons: as the planned analysis for a study, as a supplement to parametric tests, or because the assumptions of the planned parametric tests could not be met. Nonparametric tests are used with a variety of types of research designs (correlation, two groups, multiple groups, and factorial designs), with the primary reason for their use being the scale of measurement for the dependent variable(s) (DV). There are nonparametric statistics that correspond to the parametric statistics you have already learned about. If you would like a preview of the tests described in this chapter, Table 13.17 at the end of the chapter summarizes the nonparametric tests and notes the corresponding parametric statistic and research design for each. As with the parametric statistics, to decide which nonparametric statistic to use, you need to identify the scale of measurement for your variables, whether a design has independent or related groups, and the number of groups or conditions for your variables. You follow the same hypothesis-testing process that you first learned about in Chapter 6.

We will cover a few of the more commonly used nonparametric tests in detail and briefly describe several others. The computational formulas for the less frequently used tests can be found in Appendix D.

NONPARAMETRIC TESTS FOR NOMINAL DATA

Independent-Groups Designs With Nominal Outcome Measures

The most commonly used type of nonparametric test, **chi-square**, is used with nominal or categorical data (e.g., gender, age groups [18–30, 31–50, 50–69, 69 plus], college year [first, sophomore, junior, senior], sport [basketball, baseball, football], etc.). Chi-square, symbolized as χ^2, is pronounced as *ki* (rhymes with *high*) square. These tests compare the expected frequencies (as predicted by the null hypothesis) with the observed or obtained frequencies in each category. There are two types of chi-square tests; the **chi-square goodness of fit** is appropriate for studies with one

Chi-square tests (χ^2): Nonparametric tests used with nominal data that compare expected versus observed frequencies.

Chi-square goodness of fit: A nonparametric test used with one nominal variable having two or more categories; tests whether the observed frequencies of the categories reflect the expected population frequencies.

nominal variable, and the **chi-square test for independence** is appropriate for studies with two nominal variables. Because chi-square is one of the most commonly used nonparametric tests, we will cover it in more detail than other nonparametric tests.

> **Chi-square test for independence:** A nonparametric test used with two nominal variables having two or more categories; tests whether the frequency distributions of two variables are independent.

Chi-Square Goodness of Fit

The chi-square (χ^2) goodness of fit is used with one variable with two or more categories. The test is called the "goodness of fit" because we want to know if our data fit what we would expect by chance or differ from an expected value. The latter use is why the chi-square goodness of fit test was referred to in Chapter 7 as a nonparametric alternative to the one-sample t test. Although there is no limit on the number of categories for a variable, the test assumes that there is an expected frequency of at least 5 in each category.

Suppose we are interested in whether there is a difference in the number of males and females who are reported for cheating. The χ^2 goodness of fit is used to test whether the frequency (number) of males who are reported for cheating is different from the frequency (number) of females who are reported. Our hypotheses would state:

H_0: The number of males and females reported for cheating will be equal.

H_a: The number of males and females reported for cheating will differ.

Or in numerical terms, where f is the symbol used to denote frequency:

$$H_0: f_{\text{males}} = f_{\text{females}}$$

$$H_a: f_{\text{males}} \neq f_{\text{females}}$$

In computing the chi-square (χ^2) goodness of fit test, we make several assumptions:

- One variable with two or more categories (or groups)

- The categories are independent (there are no matching or repeated measures)

- An expected frequency (E) of at least 5 in each category

- Every member in the analyzed dataset belongs to only one of the categories

---

FORMULAS AND CALCULATIONS: CHI-SQUARE GOODNESS OF FIT

The process of computing the χ^2 goodness of fit is very simple. You begin by counting the frequency of responses in each category, called the **observed frequency (O)**. Remember from the examples of nominal data in the section above that you can have more than two categories for a variable. We are working with only two categories in this example for simplicity's sake. In our example, assume that at a particular school 8 males and 22 females were reported for cheating. We would then have observed frequencies for each gender of:

$$O_{males} = 8 \text{ and } O_{females} = 22$$

Next we determine the **expected frequency (E)**. Because we expect the number of males and females to be the same (according to our null hypothesis), we expect that half of those reported for cheating will be male and half will be female. Thus, our expected frequency (E) is half of the total number of our sample or $N/2$. If we had three categories, then we would have an expected frequency of one-third for each category or $N/3$, and so on. The general formula for expected frequency (E) then is:

$$E = N/k$$

where k = the number of categories; N = total number in a sample.

Or for our sample with 30 students ($N = 30$) and 2 categories of gender ($k = 2$):

$$E = N/k = 30/2 = 15$$

The expected frequencies are not always a whole number, nor are the expected frequencies always equal. Suppose we have 30 students who were reported for cheating and we wanted to know whether the frequency of cheating differed by class status (first year, sophomore, junior, senior). In this case, the expected value for each category using the formula, N/k, would be $30/4 = 7.5$. Or we may hypothesize that first-year students will be twice as likely to be reported for cheating as the sophomore, junior, and senior students. In the case of our 30 students, we have $N/k + 1$ or $30/5 = 6$. We then would expect 6 students of the upper-level classes to cheat and 12 (2 times $N/k + 1$) of the first-year students to cheat. In the case where the frequencies differ and we expect twice as many in one group, we add 1 to k in the formula; if we expected three times as many in one group, we add 2 to k in the formula, and so on.

Observed frequency (O): The frequency or count we obtain in a particular category.

Expected frequency (E): The frequency or count we expect in a category according to the null hypothesis.

In computing chi-square, we compare the observed frequencies to the expected frequencies because we want to determine whether the difference is greater than one would expect by chance alone. We square the difference between each of the observed frequencies minus the expected frequencies because some differences will be positive and some will be negative, and we do not want them to cancel out each other. We then divide the squared differences by the expected frequency in order to weight them (this is important when the expected frequencies are different). For example, a difference of 2 is minimal if the expected frequency is 20, but 2 is large if the expected frequency is 4. Thus, our formula for the chi-square goodness of fit is:

$$\chi^2 = \frac{\Sigma(O-E)^2}{E}$$

where O = observed frequency; E = expected frequency.

Inserting our sample observed and expected frequencies, we would have:

$$\chi^2_{obt} = \frac{\Sigma(O-E)^2}{E} = \frac{(8-15)^2}{15} + \frac{(22-15)^2}{15}$$

$$= \frac{(-7)^2}{15} + \frac{(+7)^2}{15} = \frac{49}{15} + \frac{49}{15} = 3.27 + 3.27 = 6.54$$

Note that χ^2 will always be positive because all of the difference scores are squared. If the null hypothesis is true, we expect no difference between the observed (O) and expected (E) frequencies, or that any difference between them will be due to sampling error. The larger the difference between O and E, the less likely the difference is due to sampling error. At some point, the difference is large enough for us to conclude that it is due to a real difference in the frequencies in the categories.

To determine if the difference is large enough for this conclusion, we compare our computed χ^2 to a sampling distribution of χ^2 values obtained with the same degrees of freedom (df) as our sample when there is no difference between the frequencies. The df for a goodness of fit test are equal to the number of categories minus one or:

$$df = k - 1$$

where k = number of categories.

For our sample, where $k = 2$, we have $df = 2 - 1 = 1$.

The region of rejection, defined by χ^2_{crit}, is always in the upper-right tail of the sampling distribution because that represents the most extreme differences (those in the upper 5% or higher) when the null hypothesis is, in fact, true and there is no difference in the frequencies. The lowest possible value of χ^2_{crit} is zero (or no differences between the frequencies). Figure 13.3 depicts the chi-square sampling distribution, which is positively skewed, and its region of rejection.

FIGURE 13.3

Chi-Square Distribution With Region of Rejection

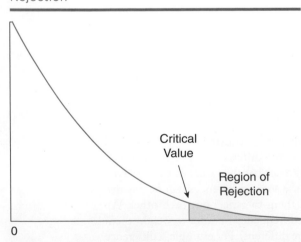

TABLE 13.1

Excerpt of Table in Appendix C.7 for Critical Values for Chi-Square (χ^2)

Levels of Significance					
p	**.05**	**.025**	**.01**	**.005**	**.001**
df					
1	3.84	5.02	6.63	7.88	10.83
2	5.99	7.38	9.21	10.60	13.82
3	7.81	9.35	11.34	12.84	16.27
4	9.49	11.14	13.28	14.86	18.47
5	11.07	12.83	15.09	16.75	20.51
6	12.59	14.45	16.81	18.55	22.46
7	14.07	16.01	18.48	20.28	24.32

The alternative hypothesis predicts a difference between the observed and expected frequencies; and our χ^2_{obt} must be greater than the χ^2_{crit}, or in the region of rejection, in order for us to reject the null hypothesis of no difference in the frequencies.

Table C.7 in Appendix C depicts the critical values which our χ^2_{obt} must exceed in order to reject the null hypothesis. A portion of the table is shown below in Table 13.1. We see that for $p < .05$ at $df = 1$, $\chi^2_{crit} = 3.84$. Our $\chi^2_{obt} = 6.54$ is greater than the critical value and thus, we reject the null hypothesis. We could also reject the null hypothesis at $p < .025$. We find support for a difference in frequency of males and females reported for cheating, with more females reported than males. We interpret these findings as showing that gender is related to being reported for cheating. We cannot assume causation from gender as it is a pre-existing group that we did not control or manipulate. We may consider how to explain the relationship of gender and cheating—perhaps females do not care as much as males about cheating, or perhaps they are less devious than males and tend to get caught more than males. Of course, we would need to see if there is support for such explanations in the research literature.

USING DATA ANALYSIS PROGRAMS: CHI-SQUARE GOODNESS OF FIT

The computation of a χ^2 goodness of fit test is very simple in SPSS. The data are entered in one column representing the single variable being analyzed (see Table 13.2). Each category of the variable is coded. In our example, comparing the frequencies of males and females, suppose 1 = *male* and 2 = *female*. We would then have a column listing eight "1s" and 22 "2s" as shown in Table 13.2.

TABLE 13.2

Example Dataset in SPSS

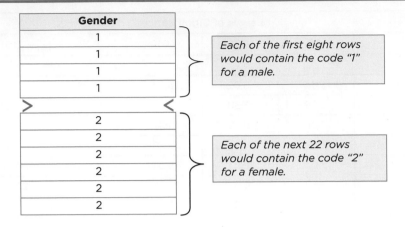

Gender
1
1
1
1

Each of the first eight rows would contain the code "1" for a male.

2
2
2
2
2
2

Each of the next 22 rows would contain the code "2" for a female.

TABLE 13.3

SPSS Output for Chi-Square Goodness of Fit

Cheating

	Observed N	Expected N	Residual
males	8	15.0	-7.0
females	22	15.0	7.0
Total	30		

Test Statistics

	Cheating
Chi-Square	6.533[a]
df	1
Asymp. Sig.	.011

a. 0 cells (.0%) have expected frequencies less than 5. The minimum expected cell frequency is 15.0.

In SPSS we click on "Analyze" and then on "Nonparametric tests," then "Legacy Dialogs," and then on "Chi-square." We move our variable (Cheating) to the "Test Variable List" box. When we click OK the output, shown in Table 13.3, is produced.

The first box lists the observed and expected frequencies for males and females, just as we had in our hand calculation of chi-square. The next box lists the values for χ^2

goodness of fit, *df* and *p* (Asymp. Sig.). Note that these values match our hand computations, although the probability is an exact value that we cannot determine from the χ^2 table in the Appendix C.7.

Distributions With Unequal Frequencies. We are not always interested in distributions where the expected values are equal. For example, in the sample problem above, we may be considering the frequency of cheating in a school where the student population is 75% female and 25% male. We may want to know if the frequency of each gender caught cheating is different from the school population. The null hypothesis would predict that the frequency of each gender caught cheating would represent the school population. Then, of the 30 students caught cheating, we would expect 75% of the sample or 22.5 to be female and 25% or 7.5 to be male. This changes the expected values (E) in our formula so that they represent the school population. The alternative hypothesis would predict that the gender of those caught cheating would differ from that of the school population. The same assumptions are made as we are still computing a χ^2 goodness of fit. So our hypotheses are:

H_0: The number of males and females reported for cheating will represent the gender division (75% female, 25% male) in the school population.

H_a: The number of males and females reported for cheating will differ from the gender division (75% female, 25% male) in the school population.

Or in numerical terms:

$$H_0: f_{females} - 3(f_{males})$$
$$H_a: f_{females} \neq 3(f_{males})$$

In this case, the observed values for males ($O = 8$) and females ($O = 22$) remain the same, but our expected frequencies for males ($E = 7.5$) and for females ($E = 22.5$) now reflect the school population. Entering these values into the chi-square formula:

$$\chi^2_{obt} = \frac{\Sigma(O-E)^2}{E} - \frac{(8-7.5)^2}{7.5} + \frac{(22-22.5)^2}{22.5}$$

$$= \frac{(+.5)^2}{7.5} + \frac{(-.5)^2}{22.5} = \frac{.25}{7.5} + \frac{.25}{22.5} = .03 + .01 = .04$$

Clearly, the computed value ($\chi^2_{obt} = .04$) is less than the $\chi^2_{crit} = 3.84$ for $p = .05$ at $df = 1$ (see Table 13.1). Thus, we do not have any evidence that the gender of those caught cheating is different from the representation of gender in the school population. Our interpretation is now that gender is not related to being reported for cheating. *It is important to remember, when you calculate a χ^2 goodness of fit, what distribution you wish to represent in your expected values.*

NOTE: Normally, we would not do both of these analyses (testing both equal and unequal distributions) on the same data; but for illustration of the different ways to approach the analysis, we have included both here.

We do not perform post hoc tests if we have more than two categories in a goodness of fit analysis. Instead, we interpret our findings as showing that all categories are different from expected or they are not. We also do not compute an effect size for goodness of fit analyses.

Computation of χ_2 Goodness of Fit Test for Unequal Frequencies Using SPSS. The data are entered the same for chi-square goodness of fit for equal and unequal frequencies, with one column representing the single variable being analyzed (see Table 13.2). As before, each category of the variable is coded. In our example, comparing the frequencies of males and females, 1 = male and 2 = female and we have one column listing eight "1s" and 22 "2s."

In the SPSS analysis for χ^2 with unequal frequencies, we request a change in the expected frequencies. Suppose we mimic our example and change the expected frequencies so that we test whether the expected frequency of females is three times that of males who are reported for cheating. To do this, we click on the Values button in the "Expected Values" box. We enter the ratio between the males and females and so enter 1 and then 3. The order of these values is important. These values tell SPSS that the first category (in our case males = 1) is to be weighted 1 while the second category in our variable (in our case females = 2) is weighted 3 times as much or expected to be 3 times as large a frequency. The following output, shown in Table 13.4, then results.

We can see in the first box of this output that our observed and expected frequencies for each gender are very similar, producing almost no residual or difference between observed and expected values. The $\chi^2 = .04$, as it did in our hand-calculated results and is not significant ($p = .833$).

Once we have completed chi-square analyses, we would report the findings in a Results section of a report following APA format. Our chi-square test may be used to supplement other results or to be the primary analysis, but we should always include:

- The test conducted and the variable analyzed

- The expected frequency (e.g., 50% females in the equal frequency example above)

- The observed frequency (e.g., in the above example, 22 females of 30 students)

- Note if the observed frequency significantly deviated from the expected frequency.

- Report the results of the chi-square goodness of fit test [e.g., testing for equal frequencies—$\chi^2(1, N = 30) = 6.53, p = .01$].

TABLE 13.4

SPSS Output for Chi-Square Goodness of Fit With Unequal Expected Values

Cheating

	Observed N	Expected N	Residual
males	8	7.5	.5
females	22	22.5	-.5
Total	30		

Test Statistics

	Cheating
Chi-Square	.044[a]
df	1
Asymp. Sig.	.833

a. 0 cells (.0%) have expected frequencies less than 5. The minimum expected cell frequency is 7.5.

In the Discussion section of the report, we state: whether we found a significant difference in the frequencies and supported or did not support our hypothesis; our interpretation of the meaning or implications of the findings; references to relevant literature; and whether the results fit or do not fit past findings. Application 13.1 provides sample results and discussion for, first, a chi-square goodness of fit with equal frequencies, and then for a chi-square goodness of fit with unequal frequencies.

Chi-Square Test for Independence

The chi-square test for independence is used when you have two nominal variables. It examines whether the distribution frequency of one variable is related to the distribution frequency of another variable. In these cases, we can represent a study using the same nomenclature that you learned about in Chapter 12 for describing factorial designs. We say we have a 2 × 2 or a 3 × 4 chi-square test for independence, with each number representing the number of categories for a variable. In the first example, we have two variables, each with two categories; in the second example, we have two variables, one with three categories and one with four categories. Unlike the factorial, however, we can have only a two-way or two-variable test for independence, never a three or four way.

Application 13.1

SAMPLE RESULTS AND DISCUSSION SECTIONS FOLLOWING APA FORMAT

Chi-Square for Equal Frequencies

Results

The frequency of reported cheating by gender was examined to see whether the frequencies were different from those expected ($n = 15$) between males and females. A chi-square goodness of fit for equal frequencies was significant, ($\chi^2[1, N = 30] = 6.53, p = .01$), showing the frequency of participants in each gender did not match the expected frequency (50% or $n = 15$). The observed frequency of males who were reported for cheating was 8 (27%), while 22 (73%) females were reported for cheating.

Discussion

As predicted, gender was related to being reported for cheating with more females than males reported. We do not, however, know why this difference occurred. Perhaps females do not care as much as males about cheating, or perhaps they are less devious than males and tend to get caught more than males. Future research should examine the reason for the observed difference by examining whether attitudes toward cheating and anonymous reports of cheating differ by gender. The number of students reported for cheating in this study is small and represents a limited time frame. Researchers should examine gender and cheating across several institutions and for longer time periods to examine whether the current findings are representative of college students in general or specific to students at a particular institution.

Chi-Square for Unequal Frequencies

Results

A chi-square goodness of fit test was computed to examine whether the frequency of reported cheating by gender was different from the population of students at the school (25% males; 75% females). The result was not significant, $\chi^2(1, N = 30) = 0.04, p = .83$. The frequency of males ($n = 8$) and females ($n = 22$) reported for cheating did not differ from the expected frequencies of 7.5 (25%) and 22.5 (75%).

Discussion

Gender was not related to being reported for cheating, which did not support our hypothesis. The frequency of males and females reported for cheating did not differ from the expected numbers based on the gender distribution of students at the school. This finding may be explained by the similar instruction and warnings that students receive about academic violations throughout their education. Future research should examine other characteristics of students and classes, or assignments that may be related to cheating by students in order to better understand and prevent cheating.

Practice 13.1

PRACTICE WITH CHI-SQUARE GOODNESS OF FIT

1. Name the minimum sample size required and the type of chi-square goodness of fit that are most appropriate for each of the following examples.

   a. Suppose you have divided your sample into three age groups (30 years or less, 31–50 years, 51 years or more). Do these age groups differ in reporting that texting is their favorite type of communication?

   b. You have data about the political affiliation of people who voted early at one voting site in your city. You want to know whether the political affiliation of your sample of early voters is different from the national percentages for voters registered as Democrat (32%), Republican (27%), and Independent (40%).

   c. You ask a sample of 50 people in the grocery store whether they prefer milk chocolate or dark chocolate. Is one type of chocolate preferred?

2. Are graduates from Prestige College more likely to work in non-profit, for-profit, or be unemployed 5 years after graduation? The alumni office collected the following data from 60 graduates:

   For-profit 29   Non-profit 19   Unemployed 12

   The following output was obtained after computing a chi-square goodness of fit.

Work

	Observed N	Expected N	Residual
for profit	29	20.0	9.0
non-profit	19	20.0	– 1.0
unemployed	12	20.0	– 8.0
Total	60		

Test Statistics

	Work
Chi-Square	7.300[a]
df	2
Asymp. Sig.	.026

[a] 0 cells (0.0%) have expected frequencies less than 5. The minimum expected cell frequency is 20.0.

(Continued)

(Continued)

a. State a null and alternative hypothesis.

b. Report the results as you would in a Results section (using proper APA format).

c. Discuss/interpret your findings as you would in a Discussion section.

See Appendix A to check your answers.

FORMULAS AND CALCULATIONS: CHI-SQUARE TEST FOR INDEPENDENCE

Similar to our calculations for the chi-square goodness of fit, we figure the observed and expected values for the test for independence. Instead of obtaining these values for each single category, however, we figure the frequencies for the combination of the two variables. Let's go back to the example we used at the beginning of the chapter from Beaver et al. (2010), who were interested the relationship between ethnicity (Black or White) and whether students considered the use of a cell phone detrimental to their romantic relationship (yes or no: "I would not be bothered if my partner talked on a cell phone when we are together"). Suppose we replicate their study with students on our campus. We count the number of students falling into each combination of the categories that are represented by a **contingency table**, as seen in Table 13.5.

For our example, we would need to count the number of Black students who answered "yes" to the statement, the number of Black students who answered "no" to the statement, the number of White students who answered "yes" to the statement, and the

TABLE 13.5

Contingency Table for a Chi-Square Test for Independence

Race	"I would not be bothered if my partner talked on a cell phone when we are together"	
	Yes	No
Black	$n = ?$	$n = ?$
White	$n = ?$	$n = ?$

Contingency table: A matrix that presents frequencies representing the combined levels of two variables.

number of White students who answered "no" to the statement; and enter four frequencies, one in each cell of the contingency table.

The chi-square test for independence has similar assumptions as those for the goodness of fit:

- Two variables with two or more categories

- Independent groups (no matching or repeated measures)

- An expected frequency (E) of at least 5 in each cell

- Every member in the analyzed dataset belongs to only one of the cells

Given that we have four cells, each of which must have an expected frequency of at least 5, the total sample in the study must be composed of at least 20 students, each of whom has reported race and responded to the statement. With the test for independence, we want to know if there is an interaction or relationship between the two variables. Another way to say this is: Are the two variables related? You might think of the chi-square test for independence as a correlation test for nominal variables, which is why it was referred to when discussing correlational techniques in Chapter 8. If the variables are independent, there is no relationship or correlation so that knowing one variable does not help to predict the other variable. The hypotheses for our sample could be stated as:

H_0: Race and views about cell phone use by a partner are independent.

H_a: Race and views about cell phone use by a partner are related.

We use the same formula to compute the χ^2 test for independence as we did to compute the χ^2 goodness of fit test.

$$\chi^2_{obt} = \frac{\Sigma(O-E)^2}{E}$$

Our first step is to get the observed frequency (O) for each of our cells. In our sample, we need the number of Blacks who agreed with the statement (said "yes"), the number of Blacks who disagreed with the statement (said "no"), the number of Whites who agreed with the statement, and the number of Whites who disagreed with the statement.

We then need to figure out the expected frequency (E) for each cell. Computing E is slightly more complicated for the test for independence, as we have to take into account the combination of the two variables for each cell. We need to know the total N and the total for each category. We then use these values to compute E for each cell. For example, if we know $N = 60$ and that the number of Blacks responding is 25, then we expect 25/60 probability for blacks or $E = 5/12$. If we also know that those who said "yes" is 45, then the probability of responding yes is 45/60 or $E = 3/4$. If the two variables are independent, the probability of both of the categories is their two probabilities multiplied together or 5/12(3/4) = .417(.75) = .313. This value represents the probability of both being Black and responding "yes." We can obtain E by multiplying this value by N, so 60(.313) = 18.76. We can repeat this process for each of the four cells to compute its expected frequency. A short form of the process is represented by the formula:

$$E = \frac{(\text{cell row total } O) \, (\text{cell column total } O)}{N}$$

For a 2 × 2 table, we have to compute four Es; for a 3 × 4 table, we have to compute 12 Es, and so on. We then enter our observed and expected values into the formula. Let's assume we obtain the data shown in Table 13.6a using the Beaver et al. (2010) question.

Using our formula and the values in the table above to compute the expected frequency (E) for each cell, we find:

$$EB_{no} = \frac{25(15)}{60} = \frac{375}{60} = 6.25 \qquad EB_{yes} = \frac{25(45)}{60} = \frac{1125}{60} = 18.75$$

$$EW_{no} = \frac{35(15)}{60} = \frac{525}{60} = 8.75 \qquad EW_{yes} = \frac{35(45)}{60} = \frac{1575}{60} = 26.25$$

Table 13.6b shows the contingency table with both the observed and expected frequencies for each cell that will be used to compute the test for independence.

Inserting these values in the chi-square formula, we have:

$$\chi^2_{obt} = \frac{\Sigma(O-E)^2}{E} = \frac{[(10-6.25)^2}{[6.25} + \frac{(15-18.75)^2}{18.75} + \frac{(5-8.75)^2}{8.75} + \frac{(30-26.25)^2]}{26.25]}$$

$$= \frac{(3.75)^2}{6.25} + \frac{(-3.75)^2}{18.75} + \frac{(-3.75)^2}{8.75} + \frac{(3.75)^2}{26.25} = \frac{14.06}{6.25} + \frac{14.06}{18.75} + \frac{14.06}{8.75} + \frac{14.06}{26.25}$$

$$= 2.25 + .75 + 1.61 + .53 = 5.14$$

Once we have computed the χ^2_{obt}, we then refer to Table C.7 in Appendix C, which lists the critical value of χ^2 needed to reject the null hypothesis for each df. It is the same

TABLE 13.6A

Observed Frequencies for Beaver et al. (2010) Study

Race	"I would not be bothered if my partner talked on a cell phone when we are together"		
	No	Yes	
Black	10	15	$N_B = 25$
White	5	30	$N_W = 35$
	$N_{no} = 15$	$N_{yes} = 45$	$N_{tot} = 60$

TABLE 13.6B

Observed and Expected Frequencies for Beaver et al. (2010) Study

Race	"I would not be bothered if my partner talked on a cell phone when we are together"		
	No	Yes	
Black			
Observed	10	15	$N_B = 25$
Expected	6.25	18.75	
White			
Observed	5	30	$N_W = 35$
Expected	8.75	26.25	
	$N_{no} = 15$	$N_{yes} = 45$	$N_{tot} = 60$

table that we used for our χ^2 goodness of fit examples. The degrees of freedom for the test for independence mimic the degrees of freedom for an interaction in a two-way factorial design:

$$df = (\text{# of rows} - 1)(\text{# of columns} - 1) \text{ or in our example, } df = (2 - 1)(2 - 1) = 1$$

Looking at Table 13.7, we see that for $df = 1$ and $p < .025$, $\chi^2_{crit} = 5.02$. Our $\chi^2_{obt} = 5.14$ is greater than χ^2_{crit} for $p < .05$ and $p < .025$, so we can reject the null hypothesis of independence between race and annoyance about a romantic partner's use of a cell phone. We support the alternative hypothesis that these variables are related. We interpret the results by reviewing the findings in our contingency table. We see that the percentage of Black students (approximately 40%) who were annoyed (responded "no" or disagreed with the statement, "I would not be bothered if my partner talked on a cell phone when we are together") was about 3 times the percentage of White students (approximately 14%) who disagreed with the statement. So more Black students were bothered than White students by the use of cell phones by their partners when they were together.

Effect Size for Chi-Square Test for Independence. If you find significance for a test for independence, you should then determine the effect size (the strength of the relationship or the degree of association between the two variables in your study). You compute one of three statistics, depending on the size of your contingency table and the relationship of rows and columns. Similar to other effect size statistics (η^2 and r^2_{pb}), the three effect size statistics range between 0 and 1. Each of them is interpreted as describing how much more accurately we can predict one variable knowing its relationship with the other variable. The formulas are very simple and use values you have already found in computing the χ^2 test for independence.

TABLE 13.7

Excerpt of Table in Appendix C.7 for Critical Values for Chi Square (χ^2)

Levels of Significance					
p	.05	.025	.01	.005	.001
df					
1	3.84	5.02	6.63	7.88	10.83
2	5.99	7.38	9.21	10.60	13.82
3	7.81	9.35	11.34	12.84	16.27
4	9.49	11.14	13.28	14.86	18.47
5	11.07	12.83	15.09	16.75	20.51

Phi Squared (ϕ^2): The appropriate effect size statistic for a 2×2 test for independence is **phi squared**, symbolized as ϕ^2. The formula for phi squared is:

$$\phi^2 = \frac{\chi^2_{obt}}{N}$$

Inserting the values from the example study above, we have:

$$\phi^2 = \frac{5.14}{60} = .086$$

We find that the effect size for the relationship is approaching moderate and that close to 9% of the variability in the frequency of reported annoyance with a partner's use of a cell phone is related to the race of the individual.

Contingency Coefficient Squared (C^2): If your study involves a test for independence that is larger than a 2×2 and the number of rows and columns is equal (3×3, 4×4, etc.), then the appropriate statistic to compute for effect size is the **contingency coefficient squared (C^2)**. The formula is:

$$C^2 = \frac{\chi^2_{obt}}{N + \chi^2_{obt}}$$

Phi squared (ϕ^2): The statistic used to assess the effect size when a 2×2 test for independence is significant; it is interpreted as the percentage of variability accounted for in the frequency of one variable by knowing its relationship with a second variable.

Contingency coefficient squared (C^2): Used to determine the effect size for a contingency table larger than 2×2 and with an equal number of rows and columns (3×3, 4×4, etc.).

Cramer's V Squared (V^2): The third statistic used to determine the effect size for a χ^2 contingency table is **Cramer's V squared**. It is used when you have a contingency table larger than a 2 × 2 and the number of rows is different from the number of columns (2 × 3, 4 × 5, etc.). The formula is:

$$\text{Cramer's } V^2 = \frac{\chi^2_{obt}}{N(k-1)}$$

where N = total number in the sample; k = the smaller number of rows or columns.

> **Cramer's V squared (V^2):** The effect size statistic used when a contingency table is larger than a 2 × 2 and the number of rows and columns are different numbers (3 × 4, 4 × 2, etc.).

USING DATA ANALYSIS PROGRAMS: CHI-SQUARE TEST FOR INDEPENDENCE

Data for a contingency table for a χ^2 test for independence are entered in two columns in a fashion similar to how data are entered for a two-way ANOVA. One column contains the data for the first variable, and a second column contains the data for the second variable. Each category of a variable is coded. So for our example data, we would have two variables, race and the statement about not being concerned about a partner using a cell phone.

Suppose for race we code Black = 1 and White = 2. For the statement, "I would not be bothered if my partner talked on a cell phone when we are together," we code no = 1 and yes = 2. We would then need to enter data so that each participant ($N = 60$) has two codes, one for race and one for the statement response. Those who are Black and responded "no" would be represented in two columns as 1/1. Those who are Black and responded "yes" would be represented by 1/2. Those who are White and responded "no" are represented by 2/1, and those who are White and responded "yes" would be coded as 2/2. The SPSS data file would look like the display shown in Table 13.8. The entire dataset is not shown because of the space it would take to display the codes for 60 participants.

The commands for the test for independence are found under Descriptive Statistics. You first click on "Analyze," then on "Descriptive Statistics," and then on "Crosstabs." You move the variable representing rows in the contingency table (Race in our contingency table) to the Row(s) box and the variable representing columns in the table (Not Bothered response in our table) to the Column(s) box.

You then click on "Statistics" and check "Chi-square" and the appropriate effect size statistic in the Nominal box. In our case, the box for "phi and Cramer's V" was checked. (Although our design requires that we use only phi, SPSS does not allow you to run these tests separately.) If we had a contingency table with more than two categories and equal numbers of categories for each variable, we would have checked "Contingency coefficient." Then click OK.

TABLE 13.8

SPSS Dataset Responses to "I Would Not Be Bothered If My Partner Talked on a Cell Phone When We Are Together"

Race	Not Bothered
1	1
1	1
1	1

Rows of "1/1" represent blacks who responded no; there would be 10 rows with this pattern.

1	2
1	2
1	2

Rows of "1/2" represent blacks who responded yes; there would be 15 rows with this pattern.

2	1
2	1
2	1

Rows of "2/1" represent whites who responded no; there would be 5 rows with this pattern.

2	2
2	2
2	2

Rows of "2/2" represent whites who responded yes; there would be 30 rows of this pattern.

We also want to display the expected values for our sample so we click on "Cells," and then check "Expected," and click OK to return to the Crosstabs box. Finally, click OK to run the analysis. The output, shown in Table 13.9, results from the data from our example:

In Table 13.9, the first box titled "Race * Phone not Bother Crosstabulation" looks like (and contains the same values as) the contingency table you are familiar with from our hand calculations. In the next box, Chi-Square Tests, you are interested only in the Pearson Chi-Square or highlighted first line. You note the value of χ^2 (the same as we computed earlier), the *df*, and *p* (called Asymp. Sig.). The final box, Symmetric Measures, displays both Phi and Cramer's *V* effect size statistics. Because our contingency table was a 2 × 2, we use phi. Do not forget that you want to report ϕ^2, so you need to square this value to get the same effect size that we hand computed or $\phi^2 = .086$.

Application 13.2 provides a sample Results section using the sample study analysis.

Dependent-Groups Designs With Nominal Outcome Measures

There are also nonparametric tests for dependent-groups designs that use nominal data for the outcome or DV measure. We briefly describe two of these tests and provide examples. The computational formulas for these tests can be found in Appendix D. The **McNemar test** is used with two dependent groups, and the **Cochran *Q* test** is used with three or more dependent groups.

> **McNemar test:** A nonparametric statistic used to analyze nominal data from a study using two dependent (matched or repeated measures) groups.
>
> **Cochran Q test:** A nonparametric statistic used to analyze nominal data from a study that includes three or more dependent groups.

TABLE 13.9

SPSS Output for Chi-Square Test for Independence

Race * Phone not Bother Crosstabulation

			Phone not Bother		Total
			No	Yes	
Race	Black	Count	10	15	25
		Expected Count	6.3	18.8	25.0
	White	Count	5	30	35
		Expected Count	8.8	26.3	35.0
Total		Count	15	45	60
		Expected Count	15.0	45.0	60.0

Chi-Square Tests

	Value	Df	Asymp. Sig. (2-sided)	Exact Sig. (2-sided)	Exact Sig. (1-sided)
Pearson Chi-Square	5.143	1	.023		
Continuity Correction	3.863	1	.049		
Likelihood Ratio	5.121	1	.024		
Fisher's Exact Test				.035	.025
Linear by Linear Association	5.057	1	.025		
N of Valid Cases	60				

a. 0 cells (.0%) have expected count less than 5. The minimum expected count is 6.25.

b. Computed only for a 2x2 table

Symmetric Measures

		Value	Approx. Sig.
Nominal by Nominal	Phi	.293	.023
	Cramer's V	.293	.023
N of Valid Cases		60	

a. Not assuming the null hypothesis.

b. Using the asymptotic standard error assuming the null hypothesis.

The McNemar Test

The McNemar test is similar to the chi-square tests that were covered in the previous sections. The McNemar test is used when you have repeated or matched measures for two categories. For example, you may ask psychology majors whether they like (yes or no)

Application 13.2

SAMPLE WRITE-UP OF THE RESULTS OF THE EXAMPLE STUDY USING CHI-SQUARE TEST FOR INDEPENDENCE

Results

A 2 × 2 chi-square test for independence was computed to examine the relationship between student race and annoyance with a partner's use of a cell phone. The interaction was significant, and the strength of the relationship was moderate, $\chi^2(1, N = 60) = 5.14$, $p = .023$, $\phi^2 = .086$. More of the Black students ($N = 10$, approximately 40%) than the White students ($N = 5$, approximately 14%) disagree with the statement, "I would not be bothered if my partner talked on a cell phone when we are together."

Practice 13.2

PRACTICE WITH DIFFERENT TYPES OF CHI-SQUARE

Name the type of contingency table (2 × 2, 4 × 6, etc.), the minimum sample size required, the chi-square statistic, and effect size statistic (if the chi-square is significant) that are most appropriate for each of the following examples.

1. a. Suppose you have divided your sample into three age groups (30 years or less, 31–50 years, 51 years or more). Do these age groups differ in reporting that texting is their favorite type of communication?

    b. Is satisfaction with one's health provider (Satisfied or Not satisfied) related to one's general health status (Good or Poor)?

    c. Wilczynski, Mandal, and Fusilier (2000) studied the relationship of type of support for educational consulting (time for consultation, inclusion in teacher assistance team, administrator support, teacher support) and levels of education (master's, specialist/equivalent, doctor). Is type of support related to education level?

    d. Do twice as many patients who exhibit depression use opioids for an extended time after hip replacement surgery than the average percentage for all patients?

2. A sample of Muslim high school students (female) were asked if they wore a hijab at school and if they had experienced bullying during the current school year. Bullying was defined as deliberate and repeated physical or verbal intimidation by a peer at school. These questions were part of a larger survey on students' experiences at school.

The following output was obtained using the students' data.

Hijab? * Bullied? Crosstabulation

			Bullied?		Total
			no	yes	
Hijab?	no	Count	11	5	16
		Expected Count	7.6	8.4	16.0
	yes	Count	8	16	24
		Expected Count	11.4	12.6	24.0
Total		Count	19	21	40
		Expected Count	19.0	21.0	40.0

Chi-Square Tests

	Value	df	Asymptotic Significance (2-sided)	Exact Sig. (2-sided)	Exact Sig. (1-sided)
Pearson Chi-Square	4.829[a]	1	.028		
Continuity Correction[b]	3.513	1	.061		
Likelihood Ratio	4.924	1	.026		
Fisher's Exact Test				.051	.030
Linear-by-Linear Association	4.708	1	.030		
N of Valid Cases	40				

[a] 0 cells (0.0%) have expected count less than 5. The minimum expected count is 7.60.
[b] Computed only for a 2 × 2 table

Symmetric Measures

		Value	Approximate Significance
Nominal by Nominal	Phi	.347	.028
	Cramer's V	.347	.028
N of Valid Cases		40	

a. What type of chi-square was computed?

b. State a null and alternative hypothesis.

c. Report the results as you would in a Results section (using proper APA format).

d. Discuss/interpret your findings as you would in a Discussion section.

See Appendix A to check your answers.

studying research at the beginning of taking a Research Methods course and again at the end of the course. We thus have nominal data in two categories (yes, no) from two time periods (before and after taking Research Methods) or repeated measures.

The data can be presented in a contingency table just as data were for the chi-square test for independence. Table 13.10 shows that we would need to enter the number of students (n) who reported that they liked studying research before and after the course (said "yes" at both time periods), students who reported that they did not like studying research before the course but reported they did like studying research after the course, and so on. The null hypothesis predicts no difference in the proportions, while the alternative hypothesis predicts differences in the proportion of students who made the different combination of responses. The statistical analysis compares the difference of Yes/No responses to No/Yes responses, and the chi-square table of critical values (Table C.7 in Appendix C) is used to determine whether the result is significant.

Remember that the McNemar test is used only for designs using matched or repeated nominal dichotomous measures, whereas the chi-square test for independence is used with designs that have two independent groups measured on a nominal scale.

TABLE 13.10

Responses to "I Like Studying Research"

Before Taking RM	After Taking RM	
	Yes	**No**
Yes	$n = ?$	$n = ?$
No	$n = ?$	$n = ?$

Cochran Q Test

The Cochran Q test is the statistical test used to analyze three or more dependent groups assessed on a nominal variable. The nominal variable is always dichotomous or has only two possible values (0 and 1, yes and no, etc.). The data are presented in blocks of the three-plus treatments, with each block representing a matched group or single participant measured three or more times.

	Treatments		
	1	**2**	**3**
Block 1	X_{11}	X_{12}	X_{13}
Block 2	X_{21}	X_{22}	X_{23}
Block 3	X_{31}	X_{32}	X_{33}

For example, a researcher may be interested in whether three 10-minute videos that discuss the signs of child abuse and the appropriate reporting process differ in their effectiveness. Suppose the researcher matched (in trios) elementary teachers on their number of years teaching and then randomly assigned one teacher in each of the trios to view one of the videos. The teachers then report (Yes or No) whether the film is effective in helping them to identify child abuse. The Cochran's Q test would determine whether there are differences in the teacher's ratings of the types of films.

Like McNemar's test, the computed Cochran's Q is compared to the chi-square table of critical values. If significance is found for the Cochran's Q comparing all groups, we then need to compute post hoc tests comparing each possible pairing of the study groups. In our example, we would compare the three film groups (film 1 vs. film 2, film 1 vs. film 3, film 2 vs. film 3).

Table 13.11 summarizes the statistical tests you may use to analyze nominal data for different types of study conditions.

TABLE 13.11

Summary of Nonparametric Tests With Nominal Data

Test	Conditions	Additional Analyses
Independent-Groups Designs		
Chi-square goodness of fit (χ^2)	One variable with two or more categories	
Chi-square test of independence (χ^2)	Two variables with two or more categories	Effect Size Statistics: 1. Phi squared with 2 × 2 table 2. Contingency coefficient squared with > 2 × 2 table with equal number of columns and rows 3. Cramer's V squared with > 2 × 2 table with unequal number of columns and rows
Dependent-Groups Designs		
McNemar's test	Two dependent categories with matched or repeated measures	
Cochran Q test	Three or more dependent groups assessed on a dichotomous variable	If significant, the post hoc test is McNemar's test using Bonferroni's correction

Practice 13.3

IDENTIFYING APPROPRIATE STATISTICS FOR NOMINAL DATA

Identify the most appropriate statistic to analyze each of the following studies and explain why you should use the statistical test you have named.

1. Is there a favorite snack among elementary school students? Students select from among three snacks (healthy, moderately healthy, junk food).

2. Researchers are interested in whether clients at a medical clinic are satisfied with their health care. Those using the clinic are asked to respond "yes," "somewhat," or "no" to whether they are satisfied before and again after they participate in a new program that includes additional follow-up calls and e-mails.

3. Is students' preference for type of snack (healthy, moderately healthy, junk food) related to their weight class (normal, overweight, obese)? Students select a snack and are also classified in terms of their weight.

4. Potential voters are asked to view the same 30-second television ad for a candidate 6 months, 1 month, and 1 week before an election. The voters note whether the ad does or does not effectively represent the candidate's views.

See Appendix A to check your answers.

NONPARAMETRIC STATISTICS FOR ORDINAL (RANKED) DATA

We also compute nonparametric statistics for ordinal or ranked data. Our variable may be on an ordinal scale because we used ranks as our measurement, such as ranking people on their time to complete a cognitive task. Or the data may violate one or more of the assumptions for parametric tests. For example, sample scores may deviate significantly from a normal distribution because of outliers or floor or ceiling effects, the variances of our groups may differ significantly from one another and violate homogeneity of variance, or the intervals of a measure may not be equal. In these later cases, we can transform interval or ratio data to an ordinal scale and analyze the data using nonparametric statistics.

Some researchers have objected to using rank-order tests if there are several ties in transforming data to ranks, so you should be aware of this issue in analyzing your data. In addition, the transformation loses preciseness in the data and may distort the original data. Still, nonparametric tests give us useful information about our data and about differences between groups.

Let's look at an example. Suppose we gather data on minutes of cell phone use from 10 people and find that although most people reported using their cell phone for 40 to 50 minutes a day, one person reported using the phone for 3 hours and another person reported using the phone for 5 hours. Table 13.12 presents such a distribution.

TABLE 13.12

Skewed Distribution of Minutes on the Phone Converted to Ranks

Participant	Minutes on the Phone	Rank
1	300	1
2	180	2
3	75	3
4	55	4
5	50	5
6	45	6
7	40	7.5
8	40	7.5
9	35	9
10	30	10

This is a skewed distribution, and we can convert the scores so that 1 = the person with the most minutes of cell phone use, 2 = the person with the next most minutes of use, and so on until 10 = the person who used the phone for the fewest number of minutes, in this case 30 minutes. The numbers 1 through 10 now represent the ranks of cell phone use rather than the actual minutes of use.

For any two people who used the phone for the same number of minutes (a tie), we would assign the average of the next two ranks to them. In our example, two people spent 40 minutes on the phone and the scores greater than 40 minutes were assigned ranks 1 through 6. The two tied scores would be considered to take up the next two ranks, say 7 and 8, and each of these scores would be assigned 7.5 as their rank, which you can see in the table below. If you had several pairs of tied scores, you would then have several pairs of scores assigned the same rank, which might further distort or reduce the sensitivity of your data. This is why some researchers advise against the use of ranked data when you have more than one or two tied ranks.

Nonparametric tests for ranks compare the sums of the ranks for those in different groups in a study instead of comparing the means (as we would in a parametric test). The null hypothesis predicts no difference in the sum of ranks for different groups because if the groups differ only by chance alone, their sums of ranks should be similar. The alternative hypothesis predicts a difference in the sums of ranks. If we find that one group has a much lower sum of ranks than the other group, we may conclude that the groups represent different populations. As usual, we expect some difference between the groups due to sampling error; but the larger the difference in the sum of ranks, the more likely it is that the groups represent different populations of ranks.

Spearman's Rho

Spearman's rho (r_s), or Spearman's rank-order correlation coefficient, is used to test for a correlation between ordinal data. Because Spearman's rho is one of the more commonly used nonparametric statistics, we will describe the test in some detail. (Note: Rho is sometimes depicted with the symbol ρ.) The value of the statistic varies from –1.0 to +1.0. The magnitude of the statistic is interpreted like the Pearson correlation coefficient, with values closer to the absolute value of 1.0 reflecting a stronger relationship between the two variables and values closer to zero (0.0) reflecting little or no relationship. The direction of the correlation is also important. A positive value $(+r_s)$ signifies that the ranks increase and decrease together, while a negative value $(-r_s)$ signifies that the ranks of the two variables move in different directions or as the ranks of one variable increase, the ranks of the other variable decrease.

> Spearman's rho (r_s): A commonly used nonparametric statistic that analyzes the relationship or correlation between two ordinal variables.

A researcher who is interested in whether the overall academic ranks of students are related to the students' ranks in her Research Methods class would use a Spearman's rho (r_s) to test whether a relationship exists between the two sets of ranks. The hypotheses are stated in terms of a relationship or correlation:

H_0: Students' overall academic rank is not related to their Research Methods course rank.

H_a: Students' overall academic rank is related to their Research Methods course rank.

The data could be depicted in two columns, where each row lists the overall rank and the Research Methods (RM) rank for each student (see Table 13.13).

TABLE 13.13
Dataset for Spearman's Rho

Overall Academic Rank (X)	RM Course Rank (Y)	Rank X – Rank Y (d)	Rank Difference Squared (d²)
1	1	0	0
2	3	–1	1
3	4	–1	1
4	2	2	4
5	6	–1	1
6	5	1	1
7	8	–1	1
8	7	1	1

$\Sigma\, d^2 = 10$

FORMULAS AND CALCULATIONS: SPEARMAN'S RHO

In the analysis, we compare the differences between the two ranks for each participant. If there are no tied ranks, we can use the formula below:

$$r_s = 1 - \frac{6 \, \Sigma \, d^2}{n \, (n^2 - 1)}$$

where d = rank for X − rank for Y; n = the number of paired ranks.

Inserting the values from our example:

$$r_s = 1 - \frac{6 \Sigma d^2}{n(n^2 - 1)} = 1 - \frac{6(10)}{8(64 - 1)} = 1 - \frac{60}{8(63)} = 1 - \frac{60}{504} = 1 - .119 = +.881$$

After computing Spearman's rho (r_s), we compare our result to the critical values of the statistic found in Appendix C.8. We use the number of pairs of scores as we did for the Pearson correlation to find the critical value. In our example, we had eight pairs of ranks and for a two-tailed test we find the critical value of r_s at $p < .05$ is .738 in Table 13.14. Our obtained value of +.881 exceeds the critical value, so we can reject the null hypothesis and support our alternative hypothesis that there is a significant positive relationship between students' overall academic rank and their rank in the Research Methods class.

TABLE 13.14

Excerpt of Table C.8 Spearman's Rho Critical Values

	Two-Tailed Test	
	Level of significance	
N (no. of pairs)	α = .05	α = .01
5	1.000	—
6	.886	1.000
7	.786	.929
8	.738	.881
9	.683	.833
10	.648	.794

USING DATA ANALYSIS PROGRAMS: SPEARMAN'S RHO

To compute Spearman's rho in SPSS, we set up the data file and use the same initial commands as we did for a Pearson correlation coefficient. We enter our data in two columns with each column representing one variable, in our case, Overall Rank and RM Rank. The dataset in SPSS would look like the first two columns of Table 13.13.

Under Analyze, we click on Correlate and Bivariate, then move our two variables of interest to the Variables box. We check the box for Spearman in the Correlation Coefficient box to get the output shown in Table 13.15.

TABLE 13.15

SPSS Output for Example Spearman's Rho

Correlations

			Overall Rank	RM Rank
Spearman's rho	Overall Rank	Correlation Coefficient	1.000	.881**
		Sig. (2-tailed)	.	.004
		N	8	8
	RM Rank	Correlation Coefficient	.881**	1.000
		Sig. (2-tailed)	.004	.
		N	8	8

**. Correlation is significant at the 0.01 level (2-tailed).

Similar to the input, the output format for Spearman's rho (r_s) is identical for that of the Pearson r. The Correlations box lists the correlation coefficient, p (Sig.) and N (number of pairs of scores), which match our hand calculations. The significance value, of course, is exact and so $p = .004$ instead of the $p < .05$ that we were able to see in the critical values table. Because the relationship is repeated, we need to read only the top half of the box.

In our Results section, we would state that we computed a Spearman's rho to examine the relationship between the Overall Ranks and the RM Ranks and that the correlation was statistically significant, $r_s = .881, p = .004$.

Two-Group Designs

Independent Groups

There are two nonparametric tests that are used to compare two independent groups when the outcome or dependent variable is measured on an ordinal scale, the **Mann-Whitney U test** and the **Rank Sums test**. We will briefly describe these tests and provide examples. The computational formulas for these tests can be found in Appendix D.

Mann-Whitney U test. The Mann-Whitney U test is used to analyze ordinal data from two independent groups when $n \leq 20$ per group. The study described at the very beginning of the chapter that examined gender differences in the aggressive content of dreams used a Mann-Whitney U test to analyze its data (Oberst et al., 2005). The researchers used an ordinal scale to rank aggression in dreams, from a low level of perceived hostility to a high level of being killed, regardless of the gender of the dreamer. The null hypothesis predicted no difference in the aggression rankings of each gender's dream content, while the alternative hypothesis predicted a difference. The Mann-Whitney U test compared the sum of aggression ranks of the two genders and found a significant difference, with young boys having more aggressive dream content than young girls.

Rank Sums test. The Rank Sums test is used to analyze ordinal data when the number in either of two independent groups is larger than 20. Thus, it could have been used to analyze the data in Oberst et al.'s (2005) study if they had included a larger number of boys and girls. In the test, we compute a z score. (See Chapter 5 if you need a review.) However, instead of comparing a sample mean (M) and a population mean (μ), we compare the observed and expected sum of ranks for our two groups, or in the case of Oberst et al. (2005) of boys and girls. The larger the difference between the sums of ranks, the larger the computed z (z_{obt}) will be and the more likely we will find significance.

The Rank Sums test is used also as part of the process of computing the effect size for the Mann-Whitney U test, but we ignore the requirement that at least one of the groups has an n greater than 20.

Assign ranks for all scores regardless of group membership or collect ordinal data in the first place.

Divide the ranks by group.

Select one group and compute the sum of ranks (ΣR).

Compute the expected sum of ranks (ΣR_{exp}) using the formula:

$$\Sigma R_{exp} = \frac{n(N+1)}{2}$$

where $n = n$ for the selected group; N = total number of ranks.

Mann-Whitney *U* test: A nonparametric test used to analyze ordinal data from two independent groups when $n \leq 20$/group.

Rank Sums test: A nonparametric test used to analyze ordinal data from two independent groups when at least one of the groups has more than 20.

Compute the rank sums statistic using the formula:

$$Z_{obt} = \frac{\Sigma R - \Sigma R_{exp}}{\sqrt{\dfrac{n_1(n_2)(N+1)}{12}}}$$

Compare the z_{obt} to the z_{crit} from the z table; for $p < .05, z_{crit} = \pm 1.96$.

Dependent Groups: Wilcoxon T Test

The **Wilcoxon T test** is used to analyze ranks of two related samples (e.g., dependent groups). Remember that related samples are produced by matching participants or through repeated measures for the participants.

> **Wilcoxon T test:** A nonparametric test used to analyze ordinal data collected from two dependent groups.

Suppose we are interested in the use of text messages to increase patient compliance with taking needed medication. The text would remind patients with chronic health conditions to take their medications at a particular time each day. For our study, we match participants who have high blood pressure on blood pressure and type of medication. We then assign them to either a group that receives the typical one-time instructions about taking medication at a regular time each morning or a group that receives a cell phone and gets a text message each morning that reminds them to take their medication at a particular time. The number of times the participants miss taking their medication on time is measured over a month. Because of the small sample (8 per group) and the widely varying scores, the data are transformed to ranks.

To compute a Wilcoxon T test, we pair the scores for the matched participants and find the difference between the number of times they missed taking their medication. The null hypothesis assumes the same number of positive and negative differences between the ranks of the two groups because any differences would be due to chance or sampling error. If, however, the conditions (typical instructions and text reminders) are different, then there should be a large difference between the two sums of ranks. Appendix D.11 contains the computational formula for the Wilcoxon T test.

Multiple-Group Designs

Independent Groups: Kruskal-Wallis H Test

The **Kruskal-Wallis H test** is used to analyze ordinal data from a study with one variable with three or more independent levels. It corresponds to the one-way independent

> **Kruskal-Wallis H test:** A nonparametric test used to analyze ordinal data from a study with one variable with at least three levels.

groups (between-subjects) ANOVA and assumes at least 5 in each condition. Kruskal-Wallis can be used even if there are uneven numbers in the groups.

As an example, suppose a researcher is interested in whether different information about diet (focus on avoiding unhealthy foods, focus on eating healthy foods, focus on losing weight) results in decreased food intake by overweight adolescents. Participants are randomly assigned to one of the instruction groups. After watching and rating four videos (one of which was related to the study), participants are offered lunch from a buffet as a way to thank them for their participation. Their food is weighed, supposedly so the researcher can pay for it. Because of the small sample size ($N = 15$), the researchers are hesitant to assume a normal distribution of the food weight so they rank order the weight of the food taken by each participant.

The Kruskal-Wallis H test involves several steps, with its focus on whether the sums of ranks for the three groups in our study differ. If the H test is significant, post hoc tests should be computed to determine which groups differ from one another. There is also an effect size computation for Kruskal-Wallis. All of these formulas can be found in Appendix D.11.

Dependent Groups: Friedman χ^2

We use the **Friedman chi-squared (Friedman χ^2)** to analyze ordinal or ranked data from a study with one variable with three or more levels/conditions that are matched or have repeated measures. The test corresponds to the dependent-samples one-way ANOVA (or within-subjects ANOVA). Friedman χ^2 requires a minimum of 10 scores per condition for three levels/conditions or 5 scores per condition for four levels.

> **Friedman chi-squared (Friedman χ^2):** A nonparametric test used to analyze ordinal or ranked data from a study with one variable with three or more dependent groups.

As an example, suppose a marketing researcher is interested in what type of chocolate is preferred. He has 1-ounce samples of four types of chocolate (white, milk, bittersweet, unsweetened), which each participant samples, drinking water in between the tastings. The eight participants then rank order the four samples in terms of what they would prefer to eat (1 = most preferred, 2 = next most preferred, etc.).

Like the chi-square tests you learned about earlier, the Friedman χ^2 computes observed and expected scores, but they are for ranks rather than frequencies. The test compares the observed and expected sums of ranks among the groups and the table of critical χ^2 values in Appendix C.7 to decide whether your computed χ^2 is significant. The larger χ^2_{obt}, the less likely that the difference between conditions is due to chance. So if we obtained a significant Friedman χ^2, we would conclude that there were significant differences in preferences for the four types of chocolate. See formula in Appendix D.11.

If the Friedman χ^2 is significant, you compute a post hoc test that corresponds to the Tukey's HSD test. You also compute a version of eta squared to assess the effect size for your data.

TABLE 13.16

Summary of Nonparametric Tests With Ordinal Data

Test	Conditions	Additional Analyses
Spearman's rank order correlation coefficient (r_s)	Examines correlation between two ordinal (ranked) variables	
Independent Groups		
Mann-Whitney U test	One variable with two independent groups and $n \leq 20$/group	For effect size compute Rank Sums test, ignoring the requirement that one group must have $n > 20$
Rank Sums test	One variable with two independent groups and $n > 20$ for at least one group	
Kruskal-Wallis H test	One variable with three or more independent groups and $n \geq 5$ for each group, allows unequal n/group	Post hoc test is rank sums test Effect size is version of eta squared (η^2)
Dependent Groups		
Wilcoxon T test	One variable with two dependent (matched or repeated) groups	
Friedman χ^2	One variable with three or more dependent groups, if three conditions requires $n \geq$ 10/group, if four conditions requires $n \geq 5$/group	Post hoc test is Nemenyi's procedure (similar to Tukey's HSD) Effect size is version of eta squared (η^2)

Kittisak_Taramas

Practice 13.4

IDENTIFYING APPROPRIATE STATISTICS FOR ORDINAL DATA

Identify the most appropriate statistic to analyze each of the following studies, and explain why you should use the statistical test you have named.

1. An instructor is interested in developing assignments that will discourage plagiarism. In an effort to accomplish her goal, she develops four different assignments and asks 20 of her students each to rank all four assignments on the likelihood of college students

plagiarizing on them (1= *most likely to plagiarize* and 4 = *least likely to plagiarize*). Are there differences in the rankings of likelihood to cheat on the four assignments?

2. Two clinical evaluators rank the effectiveness of 10 substance abuse programs (1 = *most effective*). Are their rankings related?

3. Researchers are trying to improve the reaction time of people over 75 years of age with the goal of decreasing automobile accidents in this age group. They randomly assign 20 participants to a control group or to a group that practices reaction time exercises on a computer. Both groups use a driving simulator, and their reaction time to a car unexpectedly pulling in front of them is measured. Because reaction time is usually a skewed distribution, the reaction times are converted to ranks. Do the ranks for the control and experimental groups differ?

See Appendix A to check your answers.

THE BIG PICTURE: SELECTING PARAMETRIC VERSUS NONPARAMETRIC TESTS

You can see that there are multiple nonparametric tests for analyzing data from studies that have nominal or ordinal data or from studies whose data violate the assumptions of parametric tests. And this chapter has presented only some of the more commonly used nonparametric tests! Note that there is a nonparametric statistical test corresponding to each type of parametric test. In order to decide about an appropriate test for your data, you will need to determine the scale of measurement for your measure, whether a study has independent or dependent groups, and the number of conditions or groups

TABLE 13.17

Corresponding Parametric and Nonparametric Tests

Design	Parametric Test	Nonparametric Test
Correlation/No groups	Pearson's r	Ordinal data: Spearman's rho
Two independent groups	Independent-samples t test	Nominal data: Chi-square test for independence Ordinal data: Mann-Whitney U test with Rank Sums test
Two related groups (matching or repeated measures)	Related-samples t test	Nominal data: McNemar test Ordinal data: Wilcoxon T test
Multiple independent groups	One-way ANOVA for independent groups	Ordinal data: Kruskal-Wallis H test
Multiple related groups	One-way ANOVA for related or dependent groups	Nominal data: Cochran Q test Ordinal data: Friedman χ^2

for the variable that is measured. Table 13.17 lists the different kinds of designs and the parametric and nonparametric test appropriate for each design, which may help you in deciding which one is the most appropriate statistical test for a study.

CHAPTER RESOURCES

Key Terms

Define the following terms using your own words. You can check your answers by reviewing the chapter or by comparing them with the definitions in the glossary—but try to define them on your own first.

Chi-square goodness of fit 441

Chi-square test for independence 442

Chi-square tests (χ^2) 441

Cochran Q test 458

Contingency coefficient squared (C^2) 456

Contingency table 452

Cramer's V squared (V^2) 457

Expected frequency (E) 443

Friedman chi-squared (Friedman χ^2) 471

Kruskal-Wallis H test 470

Mann-Whitney U test 468

McNemar test 458

Nonparametric statistics 438

Observed frequency (O) 442

Parametric statistics 438

Phi squared (ϕ^2) 456

Rank Sums test 468

Spearman's rho (r_s) 466

Wilcoxon T test 470

Do You Understand the Chapter?

Answer these questions on your own, and then review the chapter to check your answers.

1. What are the differences between parametric and nonparametric statistics?

2. Why are nonparametric tests less powerful than parametric tests?

3. When is it appropriate to use nonparametric statistics?

4. What are the benefits of using a nonparametric test?

5. What is the difference between the chi-square goodness of fit and the chi-square test for independence?

6. When do you use each of the three different effect size statistics for a chi-square test for independence?

7. How do you decide which nonparametric test to use to analyze ordinal data?

8. List the options for nonparametric statistics for ordinal data and the parametric test that each one corresponds to.

9. What are some of the concerns about transforming interval or ratio data to ranked data?

Practice With Statistics

1. A caterer wants to know if a particular type of cookie is preferred in the box lunches he is often asked to prepare. He asks 30 people to pick their favorite cookie from among chocolate chip, oatmeal raisin, and peanut butter. What statistic should he use to decide whether one of the cookies is preferred over the other two cookies?

2. Suppose the same caterer wants to know if children (ages 5–12) have different preferences than adults. He asks (with parents' permission) 30 children to select their favorite cookie from chocolate chip, oatmeal raisin, and peanut butter and adds these data to that of the adults. What statistic should he now use to determine whether there is an interaction (relationship) between age and cookie preference?

3. Is the race (White, person of color) of a person related to their perception (positive, negative) of the criminal justice system? You find that for a sample of 20 adults, the correlation is 5.82.

   a. What correlation statistic should you compute?

   b. What is the critical value of the correlation (found in the table of critical values)?

   c. What can you conclude about a person's race and their perception of the criminal justice system? Explain your answer.

   d. Should you compute an effect size? If yes, can you compute an effect size with the given data? Explain your answer.

4. A newly hired manager is interested in whether salaries of employees are related to their productivity. Both variables are available as rankings for the 15 employees she supervises. She finds that the correlation is .18.

   a. What correlation statistic should the manager compute?

   b. What is the critical value of the correlation (found in the table of critical values)?

   c. Can the manager conclude that employees' salaries are related to their productivity? Explain your answer.

   d. If the manager had the salary of employees in dollars and the productivity on a scale from 1-20, what type of correlation statistic could she compute? Explain your answer.

Practice With SPSS

1. Suppose the caterer in the example above finds the following data after asking people about their cookie preferences:

   Cookie Preference

Chocolate Chip	Oatmeal Raisin	Peanut Butter
17	8	5

   a. State your null and alternative hypotheses.

   b. Analyze the data using SPSS.

   c. Describe the results using APA format.

   d. What would you recommend to the caterer given the results?

2. Suppose the caterer wants to know if twice as many people prefer chocolate chip cookies as the other two types of cookie.

   a. What type of analysis should the caterer perform?

   b. State the null and alternative hypotheses.

   c. Analyze the data using SPSS.

   d. Describe the results.

   e. What would you recommend to the caterer based on the results?

3. Is age related to preferred type of exercise? You survey 60 adults in 3 age categories (18–30 years, 31–50, 50+) and ask them their preference for exercise (walking, jogging, swimming, biking). You summarize the responses in the chart below.

Age

Exercise Preference	18–30 Years	31–50 Years	50+ Years
Walking	2	5	10
Jogging	10	7	2
Swimming	1	5	3
Biking	5	4	0

   a. What statistical test is appropriate to analyze these data? Explain.

   b. Enter the data and compute the analysis.

   c. Can you reject the null hypothesis? Why or why not?

d. What effect size is appropriate for these data? Explain your answer.

e. Compute the effect size (if you haven't already). Explain the meaning of the effect size.

f. Write a brief paragraph summarizing your results (as you would in a Results section), using APA format.

4. Two clinical evaluators rank the effectiveness of 10 substance abuse programs (1 = *most effective*). Their rankings are as follows:

Evaluator 1	Evaluator 2
1	3
2	1
3	2
4	5
5	4
6	6
7	8
8	7
9	9
10	10

   a. State your null and alternative hypotheses.

   b. Analyze the data using SPSS.

   c. Describe the results using APA format.

   d. What would you recommend about the programs given the results?

 **SAGE edge**™ **edge.sagepub.com/adams2e**

Sharpen your skills with SAGE edge!
SAGE edge for students provides you with tools to help you study. You'll find mobile-friendly eFlashcards and quizzes, as well as videos, web resources, datasets, and links to SAGE journal articles related to this chapter.

Focusing on the Individual

CASE STUDIES AND SINGLE *N* DESIGNS

Throughout this book, we have referred to research on academic honesty to illustrate different concepts, designs, and analyses. We did this to demonstrate how researchers might look at the same topic in many different ways. We also have to admit that at least part of our rationale for focusing on academic honesty throughout the book was based on our own research finding that sustained attention to the topic of plagiarism in a Research Methods course improved students' skills in avoiding plagiarism (Estow et al., 2011).

Suppose that we now want to frame our research question differently. Instead of considering if, overall, students' skills improve after repeated exposure to the topic of plagiarism, we want to know if your skills have improved. This might seem like only a slight modification, but in fact the way that researchers examine individuals is very different from the research designs we have covered thus far.

SAMPLES VERSUS INDIVIDUALS

The designs we have discussed in previous chapters all involve obtaining a sample from a population. The primary goal of these designs is not to just describe the sample or examine the relationships among variables within the sample. Rather, the primary goal is to extrapolate results to the population from which the sample was drawn. Generally speaking, the larger the sample, the more likely we can make these extrapolations to the population.

Designs utilizing samples allow researchers to examine if a pattern or relationship is likely to exist in a population of interest. The results from these designs can serve as a good starting point for understanding an individual or in developing a treatment or educational plan for an individual or small group. Many of us would hope that our physicians are considering the latest research when making decisions for our individual

- The goal of a descriptive study is to describe characteristics of a population. In order to do so, a representative sample must be obtained from the population. Using probability (random) sampling and having a large sample increases the likelihood that the sample will be representative.

- The goal of both correlational and experimental studies is to examine relationships. These designs rely on inferential statistics in order to infer that a relationship found within the sample represents a relationship that exists within the population. A larger sample increases the researcher's ability to find a statistically significant result in the sample when that result exists in the population (i.e., power).

health care needs, and that teachers and counselors are likewise considering research as they interact with individuals.

There is no guarantee, however, that the results found for a sample-based study will be relevant or helpful to a specific individual. Even multiple studies may not be applicable to an individual. Thus, we may be able to extrapolate results from a sample to a population, but we cannot necessarily extrapolate results from a sample to an individual.

For example, consider a repeated measures experiment to test the effectiveness of a new drug for treating depression. The researchers would conclude the drug was effective if, on average, participants in the drug-treatment group had lower levels of depression than those in the control group and if this difference was greater than what would be expected by chance alone (i.e., the difference was statistically significant). Assuming there were no major side effects, it would be reasonable for a physician to apply the results from the study and prescribe the drug to a patient suffering with depression. Even so, there is no guarantee that the drug will work for that individual for several reasons.

First, the results suggest that on average the drug led to improvements, but this does not mean that it worked for everyone in the study. We would likely see a range of results if we examined each participant in the study, with some doing much better after taking the drug, some doing just a little better, and some staying the same or even getting worse. Second, it is possible that the study excluded certain types of participants in order to increase power or for logistical or ethical reasons. The question about a specific individual would remain whether or not the drug helps those who did not meet the inclusion criteria of the study. Finally, even if everyone in the drug-treatment group improved and the study included a large and diverse sample, the results will not necessarily generalize to every single person suffering from depression. Recall that this is one of the reasons why we never say that a study "proves" something. There is always a chance of error.

Likewise, relying on average scores and statistical significance testing might mask important individual results. Suppose that the results of drug-treatment experiment suggested that a new drug did not improve depressive symptoms at a statistically significant level. This result may be erroneous due to lack of power in the study. Some of the participants in the drug-treatment group may have gotten better, but these individual differences would be considered error variance in inferential statistics. Moreover, the results of the study will likely not generalize to every individual in the population. Consequently, a drug that might be useful to some individuals could be dismissed as ineffective.

REVIEW OF KEY CONCEPTS: TYPE I AND TYPE II ERRORS

In each of the last two paragraphs we mention a type of error possible in statistical significance testing. Take a minute to see if you can recall which example refers to Type I error and which is a Type II error.

Answers: If a researcher erroneously concludes that the drug is effective when it is not, this is Type I error. If a researcher erroneously concludes that the drug is not effective when it is, this is Type II error.

We do not want to leave you with the impression that results based on samples and inferential statistics are not useful to individuals. On the contrary, these types of designs are the cornerstones of scientific inquiry and have been used to make improvements in the fields of health care, human services, law enforcement, and education (see Zimbardo [2004] for a review). It is important, however, that you realize that these designs have limitations and consider alternative research methods that can help augment and expand our understanding of social and individual phenomena. Two of these alternatives are the case study and single *N* designs.

THE CASE STUDY

A **case study** is an in-depth examination of a single individual, group, event, or organization. The case study has a long history in the social sciences, dating back to the mid-1800s in France. In the United States, this methodology was made popular in the early 1900s by the Department of Sociology at the University of Chicago. It was a dominant research strategy until about 1935, when social scientists questioned the validity of the methods of the "Chicago school" and turned toward the experimental approach supported by Columbia University (Tellis, 1997). Since that time, the case study method has gone in and out of favor within the different social science disciplines (David, 2007; George & Bennett, 2005; Tellis, 1997). In psychology, the case study is now used primarily by clinicians as a way to evaluate client progress and is used less frequently in other areas of psychology (Kazdin, 2002). On the other hand, it is a relatively popular design in political science, anthropology, sociology, and education (Verschuren, 2003).

Case study: Detailed investigation of a single individual, group, organization, or event.

Conducting a Case Study

One of the best reasons to conduct a case study is when your goal is to gain in-depth knowledge about a particular case or set of cases (David, 2007). A case should be selected because you believe it is prototypical of a certain phenomenon, because it represents an extreme example, or because it is unique and there are few cases available.

Examining rare phenomena is an excellent reason to conduct a case study. This is illustrated by neurologist Oliver Sacks, who wrote a popular book titled *The Man Who Mistook His Wife for a Hat and Other Clinical Tales* (Sacks, 1998). The title of the book comes from an actual patient who suffered from a rare disorder called visual agnosia, and as such could not correctly recognize people or objects. He thus literally mistook his wife's head for his own hat.

Sacks (1998) chronicles a number of other rare neurological disorders in his book. With collections such as this, each case can be examined singly in order to better understand a particular case. Additionally, a series of cases can be examined collectively in order to identify potential similarities and patterns. Likewise, a researcher may set out to conduct multiple case studies in order to compare patterns across cases. Choosing multiple cases representing extremes can be particularly useful in understanding what commonalities and differences exist between the contrasting cases (Verschuren, 2003).

Additionally, Yin (2009) suggests that multiple cases can also be used to better understand a single group or organization. In this **embedded case study**, individuals and subgroups within the larger whole are studied and compared in order to gain an understanding of the group or organization to which they belong. Examples of two embedded case studies are provided in Application 14.1.

The case study is often viewed as a purely descriptive or exploratory technique, but Yin (2009) notes that data from a case study can also be used to explain phenomena. He suggests that the case study is best used to help answer "how" and "why" questions when the researcher cannot control or manipulate events. For example, a case study might be used to examine how a community responded to a natural disaster or why an individual chose not to comply with a mandatory evacuation during a natural disaster.

The goal of a case study is to capture the unique character of the individual case within a real-life context. As such, almost all case study researchers agree that it is important to include multiple measures from different sources. The methods of data collection and analysis focus on qualitative approaches such as in-depth interviews, observations, and narratives. These allow for a holistic view of the individual that can be lost with quantitative approaches. Some case study researchers supplement the qualitative methods with quantitative measures and analyses (Verschuren, 2003). The analysis of a case involves identifying discrepancies and determining how the multiple measures and sources converge.

Embedded case study: Investigation of single cases that comprise a group or organization in order to understand that group or organization as a whole.

Application 14.1

TWO EXAMPLES OF EMBEDDED CASE STUDIES FROM THE LITERATURE ON ACADEMIC HONESTY

Nagel (2001) conducted a case study of an organization. Specifically, she studied how Western Michigan University created its academic honesty policy. She focused on the process for creating the policy and examined how faculty, students, and administrators collaborated in this process. She noted that collaborative effort helped to ensure that the policy was efficient and fair, and would improve student learning and development at the institution.

Nsiah (2011) conducted and compared three case studies of U.S. high school distance education programs. His goal was to identify effective and ineffective practices that might be applied to distance education in Ghana. For each case, he conducted field observations of the site and interviews with program directors, administrators, and distance educators. Plagiarism and other academic honesty issues were a common issue that emerged across all three cases, and all sites recommended that special care be taken to help students avoid academic honesty violations, including interviewing students about their work and using online programs that compare student work to papers available online.

Strengths and Limitations of the Case Study

The holistic nature of the case study is one of its greatest strengths. Rather than reducing information into data that can be quantified and analyzed, the case study utilizes primarily qualitative methods to capture the wholeness of a case. However, this holistic nature leads to several criticisms of the case study. First, the case study often relies on anecdotal information that is difficult to verify and is subject to the interpretation of the researcher. Second, the case study lacks control and therefore has limited ability to determine causal relationships. Finally, the details of a case study can be so persuasive that it might bias the public, and even researchers, to weigh results from a single case more heavily than results from other research.

The ability of the results of a case study to generalize beyond the single case is perhaps the most controversial issue for the case study. Some suggest that the results of a case study can be generalized via replication with other cases. Instead of generalizing to the population via sampling strategies or inferential statistics, the external validity is tested on a case-by-case basis (e.g., Yin, 2009). Others argue that even a comparison of multiple cases falls short compared to sample-based studies that utilize standardized measures and methods (e.g., Kazdin, 2002).

There is also some debate as to whether a case can generalize to a theory. There appears to be consensus that a case study can be used to falsify an existing theory. If a theory suggests that something is universal, it takes only one case in which the theory does not apply to falsify that theory. The case can then serve as an important qualifier or encourage modification of the existing theory (David, 2007; Kazdin, 2002).

David (2007) also suggests that a case study that supports an already well-validated theory can be used as an exemplar to that theory. What researchers do not agree on is whether case studies can be used to validate or build a theory. Some argue that the links found between multiple case studies can be used to build, expand, and generalize theories (e.g., Yin, 2009).

Those who promote and apply **grounded theory** are firmly on the side of using cases to build theory. Grounded theory was developed by Glaser and Strauss in 1967 as an alternative to the quantitative and theory-driven research that predominated the social science fields at that time. They argued that the researchers were getting too far away from the original cases, and grounded theory was designed to firmly "ground" theory in data. Thus, Glaser and Strauss not only believed that one *could* use cases to develop theory, they strongly advocated that this is what researchers *should* do (Glaser, 2012). A researcher applying grounded theory would start with a single case and attempt to understand the case in its entirety, identifying categories and concepts that emerge from the case and making connections between them. Additional cases are collected based on the concepts that emerge, and the concepts are fine-tuned by constantly comparing them across cases until a theory emerges that captures all the cases (Egan, 2002).

Grounded theory: A method to build theory from data.

On the other side of the continuum are those who believe that the anecdotal nature of case studies precludes their usefulness in theory development and validation (e.g., David, 2007). However, few can deny that case studies have served as an important first step in the development of several influential concepts and theories. A case study can serve as an inspiration for larger scale, sample-based studies that in turn lead to the development, refinement, or validation of a theory.

Take expectancy effects as an example. An expectancy effect occurs when a researcher unintentionally biases a study. Rosenthal and Fode conducted the first controlled experiment of this effect in 1963, and the effect has been tested and verified by countless other studies since then. However, the idea for expectancy effects came much earlier, from a case study of a horse named Clever Hans that was conducted by Pfungst in the early 1900s (Pfungst, 1911). Hans's owner claimed that the horse could perform math and other intellectual tasks, and would answer by tapping his hoof. Pfungst discovered that Hans stopped tapping his hoof when his owner (or another questioner) gave subtle body cues that the right number of taps had been made. If Hans could not see the questioner, or if the questioner did not know the answer to the question, Hans was unable to provide the correct number of taps. Thus, Hans's performance was due to the expectations of the questioner, even if the questioner did not intend to influence the answers.

Another, more tragic, example of how a single case might inspire larger scale research is the case of Kitty Genovese. In 1964, she was attacked and stabbed repeatedly outside her apartment building. The attack was reportedly witnessed by 38 bystanders and lasted for 35 minutes before one person called the police. Unfortunately, Kitty died before the police arrived. The case was described in a book published by a *New York*

Times reporter (Rosenthal, 1964, as cited in Darley & Latané, 1968). That case study in turn motivated social psychologists Darley and Latané to conduct an experiment examining factors that impact a bystander's likelihood to help in a (simulated) emergency. They found that participants were less likely to help if they believed there were many other bystanders present. Thus, it appeared that the lack of helping was due to a diffusion of responsibility, rather than emotional detachment (Darley & Latané, 1968). They termed this phenomenon the "bystander effect," and many later sample-based research studies have verified and expanded this bystander effect (Hock, 2012). But it all started with a single case.

SINGLE *N* DESIGNS

Whereas a case study is primarily qualitative and is used to understand the whole of a single case, a **single *N* design** is a quantitative design used to examine a cause-and-effect relationship within a single case. A **small *N* design** utilizes a series of single *N* studies that examine the same cause-and-effect relationship. Like multiple case studies, a small *N* design is used to determine if results from one single *N* study generalize to other subjects or participants.

Single *N* designs are more prevalent in the field of psychology compared to other social science disciplines. The beginning of psychology as a science is dated to 1879 when Wilhelm Wundt used small *N* designs in his psychophysics research. Shortly thereafter, Hermann Ebbinghaus did his groundbreaking research on memory by conducting multiple single *N* studies using only himself as a research subject (Schultz & Schultz, 2008). Even after inferential statistics gained widespread use in the 1920s, single *N* designs were still the choice for many behavioral psychologists. B. F. Skinner, a pioneer in the study of operant conditioning, favored this design because he believed the ability to examine patterns of behavior within an individual organism and to compare these patterns across organisms was far superior to examining large group averages or testing general theories (Skinner, 1950).

Today, the design remains popular with experimental behaviorists and clinical psychologists. For example, researchers have lauded the benefits of single *N* designs in studying animal behavior in zoos (Saudargas & Drummer, 1996) and have advocated for more single *N* designs in the field of cognitive psychology (J. P. McCullough, 1984). Moreover, researchers generally agree that single *N* studies have many benefits for evaluating the effectiveness of psychotherapy and other interventions (e.g., Kazdin, 2002; Lundervold & Belwood, 2000; Ray & Schottelkorb, 2010).

The single *N* design is best grouped with quasi-experiments because they involve careful observation of the effect of a manipulation without random assignment to

Single *N* design: Quantitative investigation of a cause-and-effect relationship within a single case.

Small *N* designs: A series of single *N* designs.

condition. Random assignment would of course be impossible with a single subject or participant. Just as with any experiment or quasi-experiment, the extent to which a single *N* design or small *N* design can demonstrate a causal relationship depends on the extent to which the researcher can rule out threats to internal validity (see Chapter 9 for a review of these threats).

Conducting a Single *N* Study

Repeated assessments of the dependent variable is one way that a researcher conducting a single *N* study attempts to rule out alternative explanations for causality. Rather than looking at any single assessment, the researcher examines patterns formed by the repeated assessments and determines if any changes in the pattern correspond with the manipulation. The assessment occurs over two primary phases, one in which there is no manipulation present and one in which the manipulation is added.

A **baseline (phase A)** always occurs first and is used to establish the pattern of the dependent variable prior to any manipulation. Ideally, the pattern found in the baseline allows the researcher to predict what the level of the dependent variable will be for future assessments. The manipulation is added during the **manipulation (phase B)**, which is typically labeled according to the particular type of manipulation that took place (e.g., "treatment" for a therapy outcome study). The pattern found during this manipulation phase is compared to the predicted pattern based on the baseline. The simplest single *N* design is called the **AB design** and involves comparing the pattern of data from a single phase A (baseline) to the pattern in a single phase B.

Baseline (phase A): In a single *N* design, repeated assessment of the dependent variable in the absence of any manipulation.

Manipulation (phase B): In a single *N* design, repeated assessment of the dependent variable during the implementation of a manipulation (e.g., treatment).

AB design: A simple comparison of the baseline (A) and manipulation (B) phases.

Although there are inferential statistics available that can be used to examine a single *N* study, most single *N* researchers prefer the nonstatistical technique of visual inspection (Kazdin, 2002). In **visual inspection**, the researcher thoroughly examines the individual patterns and set criteria based on practical rather than statistical significance. Because visual inspection is the evaluation of choice, it is important to clearly depict the repeated assessments on a graph. The typical single *N* study is represented with a line graph in which the dependent variable is graphed on the (vertical) *y*-axis, time is graphed on the (horizontal) *x*-axis, and different phases of the study are clearly delineated (see Figure 14.1).

Visual inspection: A nonstatistical technique in which patterns of the A and B phases are compared.

FIGURE 14.1

Example AB Design

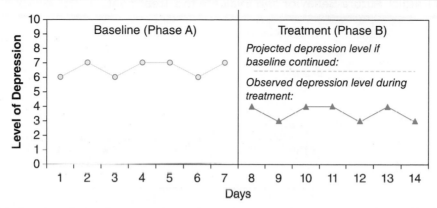

Note: Data from the baseline are used to predict the future level of depression. The observed level of depression is much lower than this projected level, suggesting that depression improved during treatment.

Figure 14.1 depicts an example AB design examining the impact of a particular treatment on an individual's level of depression. Notice that the baseline phase allows the researcher to predict what the future depression level would be without intervention. Evaluation of the manipulation involves comparing the predicted pattern to what was actually observed. In this example, the pattern found during the treatment phase suggests that treatment was associated with lower levels of depression for this individual.

Stability of the Baseline

A baseline must be stable in order for it to be a useful predictor of future behavior. A **stable baseline** has two criteria: the absence of an upward or downward trend in the data and a small amount of variability (Kazdin, 2002). The baseline depicted in Figure 14.1 meets both these criteria. The level of depression does not appear to be getting better or worse during the baseline, and the level varies only between a 6 and a 7. As such, we can predict that without intervention, the level of depression would continue to fall within this range.

In Figure 14.2, there are three examples of baselines that do not meet the criteria of stability. In the first example, the baseline shows a trend that is the opposite of what we would expect from the manipulation. In general, this is the least problematic type of unstable baselines because evidence for the effect of the manipulation can be found if the phase B data demonstrates a reversal or clear disruption of the trend.

> **Stable baseline:** A baseline that displays no trend (or slope) and little variability and therefore allows for prediction of future behavior.

FIGURE 14.2

Examples of AB Designs With Unstable Baselines That Make It Difficult to Predict Future Behavior and Evaluate the Treatment

Example 1: Baseline showing an upward trend in depression that is opposite to what treatment is designed to achieve

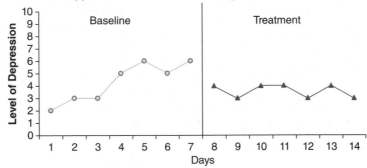

Example 2: Baseline showing a downward trend in depression that is in the same direction as what treatment is designed to achieve

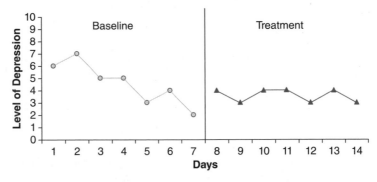

Example 3: Baseline showing large variability in depression

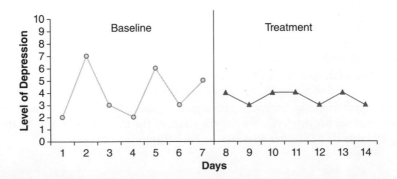

A phase B trend that is in the opposite direction of the baseline trend demonstrates the strongest evidence for a manipulation effect. A disrupted trend is trickier to assess, as we see in the first example in Figure 14.2. Notice that the depression level increased

during baseline and then was stable during treatment. It is possible that the change in pattern represents a disruption, and that treatment is associated with the leveling off of the individual's depression. On the other hand, perhaps the treatment pattern is simply the natural leveling off of the person's mood. A stronger case for disruption of the baseline trend would be found if the level of depression was much lower than what was seen during the course of the baseline (e.g., if the levels of depression varied between 1 and 2 instead of 3 and 4).

The other two examples in Figure 14.2 are even more troublesome. In the second example, the baseline shows a trend in the same direction as what would be expected during treatment. In such situations, it is possible that any evidence of improvement during phase B is not due to the manipulation but rather is a continuation of improvements that began during the baseline.

Large variations during baseline make it difficult to both predict future behavior and evaluate improvements. We see this in the third example in Figure 14.2. In this particular example, the pattern changes during the treatment phase so that the individual's mood is more stable. As with the first example, it is not clear if this change in pattern is due to the treatment or to the natural leveling of someone's mood over time. Moreover, it is not clear if the level of depression found during treatment represents an improvement because there were several days during the baseline where the individual experienced a level of depression at or lower than what was experienced in the treatment phase.

More Advanced Single *N* Designs

Even with a stable baseline, the simple AB design is limited. If the observed behavior during phase B is different from the predicted behavior, we can conclude only that the manipulation was associated with changes in the dependent variable. We cannot conclude that the manipulation caused the changes. It is possible that some other event occurred at the start of phase B and it is that event that caused the change.

In our example depicted in Figure 14.1, it is possible that the start of treatment corresponded with a new job, greater social support, an upturn in the economy, or better weather. It is also possible that the simple passage of time improved the individual's depression level, and this improvement would have taken place with or without treatment. In order to better understand the impact of a manipulation, researchers can implement a reversal, multiple-baseline, or multiple-manipulation design.

Reversal Designs

A **reversal** is a return to baseline after a manipulation has been implemented. The **ABA reversal design** begins with a baseline phase (A), then a manipulation phase (B), and ends

Reversal: The manipulation is removed and the individual returns to a baseline phase.

ABA reversal design: The simplest type of reversal design that involves an initial baseline (A), manipulation (B), and a return to baseline (A).

with another baseline phase (A). If the behavior changes between the initial baseline and the manipulation phase, and then reverts back to the first baseline levels after the manipulation is removed, we have good evidence that the manipulation caused the change. It is unlikely that some other event corresponded exactly with the beginning and end of the manipulation. The first example in Figure 14.3 depicts an ABA study in which it seems clear that the manipulation had an effect. In this example, depression levels improved after the treatment was introduced and declined when the treatment was taken away.

On the other hand, if the dependent variable does not revert back to levels comparable to the first baseline after removal of the manipulation, the ABA design offers no real advantage over the simple AB design. It may be that it was something other than the manipulation that caused the initial change, or it may be that the manipulation was effective but the effects carried over into the second baseline. This is particularly problematic with manipulations that we expect to have lasting effects. For example, psychological

FIGURE 14.3

Examples of ABA Reversal Designs

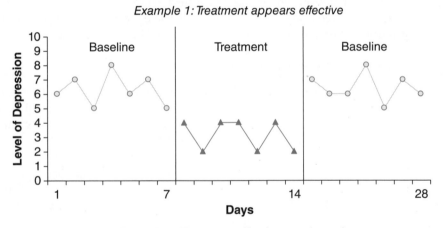

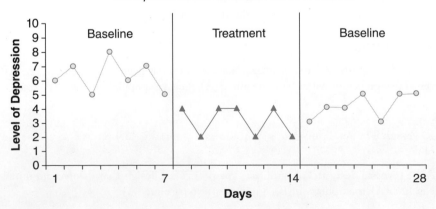

interventions are usually designed so that the client learns new skills or ways of thinking that should continue even after treatment has ended. We would not think much of a psychological approach that required the person to stay in treatment forever.

We see this problem in the second example of Figure 14.3. The individual depression levels decrease during treatment and then seem to increase slightly when the treatment is removed for the second baseline phase. The behavior does not completely revert to the original baseline levels, and we are left to wonder if some of the treatment effect may have carried over into the second baseline or if the treatment was ever effective in the first place.

One way to address the problem of an ABA reversal design is to add a second manipulation phase (ABAB). Adding additional phases helps to clarify the relationship between the manipulation and the dependent variable. We see this in the first example in Figure 14.4. The initial treatment was associated with improved mood, but mood declined only slightly at the second baseline and did not return to original baseline levels. Adding a second treatment phase helped to clarify the pattern because depression decreased again, and to an even stronger degree, during this second treatment phase.

Little or no change during the second treatment phase of an ABAB reversal design leaves us back where we started, wondering if it was the manipulation or some other factor that caused the initial change in the dependent variable. We see this in the second example in Figure 14.4. We could add more phases to help clarify whether the manipulation had an effect, but there are downsides to this approach in terms of time and effort.

Ethics Tip: Return to Baseline Only When It Is Ethically Appropriate

The reversal designs are methodological improvements over the simple AB comparison because they allow for a clearer understanding of why the behavior changed.

However, if improvement occurs in a treatment setting, it may not be ethical to remove the treatment by returning to baseline. Reverting back to the original baseline level can be especially problematic if the original baseline level was severely impacting the individual's quality of life or jeopardizing his or her health.

Multiple-Baseline Designs

Multiple-baseline designs introduce the manipulation at different points in time across multiple persons, settings, or behaviors. An example of a **multiple-baseline across persons** is depicted in Figure 14.5. In this example, we examine the impact

> **Multiple-baseline design:** The manipulation is introduced at different times across two or more persons, settings, or behaviors.
>
> **Multiple-baseline across persons:** The manipulation is introduced at different times across two or more persons.

FIGURE 14.4

Example ABAB Reversal Designs

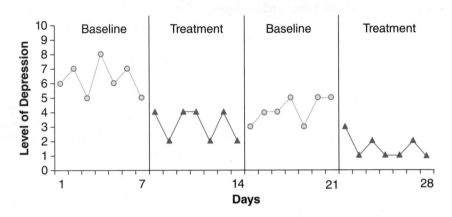

Example 1: Treatment appears effective

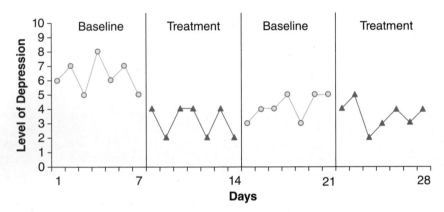

Example 2: Treatment effectiveness is unclear

of a treatment across three clients instead of a single individual. The AB design is used for all the clients, but we introduce the treatment at different points in time. The first week is the baseline phase for all three clients. During the second week, we implement the treatment for the first client while the other two clients continue their baseline. During the third week, the second client begins treatment while the third continues the baseline phase. Treatment is then introduced to the third client in the final week.

When we compare the baseline and treatment phases across the three clients depicted in Figure 14.5, we notice that treatment corresponds to improved moods regardless of the client or when treatment was introduced. When such a clear pattern emerges, this type of design rules out that history (such as changes in the weather or the economy) was the cause of the change rather than the manipulation. It also helps to demonstrate the generalizability of results across multiple individuals.

Suppose that instead of the pattern depicted in Figure 14.5 we found that the treatment was associated with improvements for only one or two of the clients. It could be that the treatment caused the effect but did not generalize across all three clients. Or, it might mean that some other event occurred in those clients' lives that caused the change. In a circumstance such as this, we might try adding a reversal (ABA or ABAB) to better tease out the results, as long as it is ethically appropriate to do so.

In a **multiple-baseline across settings**, a single individual is examined, but the assessment is spread across different settings and the manipulation begins at different times for each setting. For example, we might examine how a treatment impacts depression levels and ask that person to start a baseline for two different settings: at home and at work. At the end of the first week, we would ask the person to begin a treatment program at home while he continued to collect baseline data at work. Then at the end of the second week, we would have him begin the treatment at work.

In a **multiple-baseline across behaviors**, treatment would also focus on a single individual, but we would focus on multiple behaviors. For example, instead of just focusing on level of depression, we might also assess the number of cigarettes smoked per day, the level of anxiety, and the hours of sleep each night. As with the other multiple-baseline designs, we would implement treatment for each of these behaviors at different points in time.

As with the multiple-baseline-across-persons design, changes that clearly correspond with the addition of the manipulation across the different settings or behaviors provide evidence of a cause-effect relationship. However, if a clear pattern does not emerge, it does not rule out that the manipulation had an effect. It is possible that the manipulation might be limited to certain settings or behaviors. The opposite may also be the case in that when the manipulation is applied in one setting or for one behavior, the effect might generalize to others. For example, if the treatment seems to be reducing depression at home, the person's improved mood might carry over into the work setting before the treatment is even started at work. Again, incorporating an ABA or ABAB reversal into the multiple-baseline design might help to clarify the impact of the manipulation.

Multiple-baseline across settings: The manipulation is introduced at different times across two or more settings.

Multiple-baseline across behaviors: The manipulation is introduced at different times across two or more behaviors.

FIGURE 14.5

Example Multiple-Baseline-Across-Persons Design

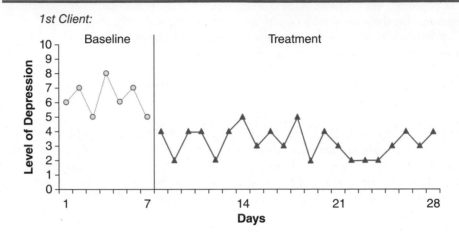

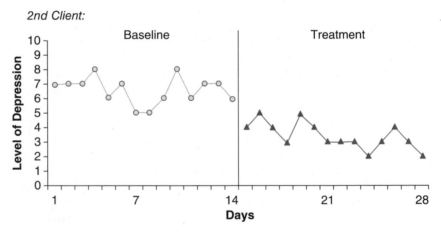

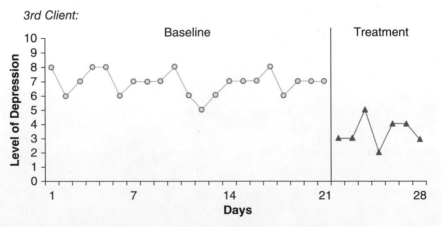

Multiple-Manipulation Designs

In a **multiple-manipulation design**, a researcher evaluates two or more manipulations. The first manipulation is designated B_1, the second as B_2, the third as B_3, and so on. A reversal might be included so that there is a return to baseline following both manipulations (AB_1B_2A) or after the first manipulation (AB_1AB_2), or after both (AB_1AB_2A). These combinations allow the researcher to assess not only the success of each manipulation but also if one manipulation appears to be more effective.

An example of an AB_1AB_2 design appears in Figure 14.6. Notice that in this example both treatments seem to have a positive effect on the individual's level of depression. The first treatment (B_1) seems to be slightly more effective than the second one (B_2). To further verify this pattern, the researcher might add additional phases of the treatments alternating with a return to baseline.

Multiple-manipulation design: A single N design in which the researcher introduces two or more manipulations over the course of the study.

FIGURE 14.6

Example Multiple-Manipulation Design (AB_1AB_2)

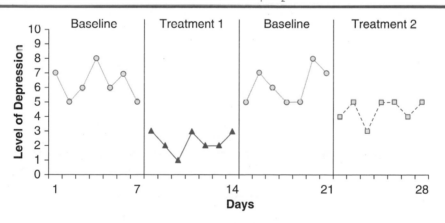

Strengths and Limitations of Single N Designs

The potential to identify a cause-and-effect relationship within a single case is the greatest strength of the single N design (although its ability to live up to that potential depends on how well controlled the design is). This is particularly important when your primary interest is to understand how one or more factors impact an individual or you want to help change an individual's behavior. As such, the single N design is a good choice for clinicians working with individuals or small groups.

Single N designs can also be valuable supplements to randomized-group experiments. Such experiments may identify a treatment that worked for only a subset of individuals within the sample, and a single *N* study can then be used to follow up on these findings. Moreover, single *N* studies provide rich auxiliary information because they track progress on a day-to-day or week-by-week basis, rather than at only a few broad assessment points (Kazdin, as cited in Clay, 2010).

The repeated assessment also allows for a lot of flexibility. We have used examples with phases spanning seven days, but phases can easily be shorter or longer than that. You do not even need to preplan the length of each phase. The original baseline can take as long as necessary for a stable pattern to emerge, and future baseline or manipulation phases can be extended or shortened. In a treatment study, the baseline can be shortened if the levels are severe enough to warrant immediate intervention and any return to baseline phases can be omitted. Likewise, the specific design of the study can be based on the patterns that emerge during the study. For example, if it is not clear that the manipulation had an effect, the researcher can add another manipulation or baseline phase or switch to a totally new manipulation.

At the same time, the repeated assessment requires a considerable amount of time and effort. The researcher must choose an assessment technique that yields reliable data,

---

Practice 14.1

SINGLE *N* DESIGNS

A student wonders if the Research Methods class he took actually improved his ability to cite and paraphrase sources. He had all of his writing assignments from the semester prior to taking Research Methods as well as his assignments from the semester during which he took Research Methods. He had a professor rate the citation and paraphrasing skill demonstrated in each assignment on a scale from 1 to 10. He gave the professor the work in a random order to avoid any potential biases, and then grouped them by semester and sequenced the ratings by due date:

Pre-Research-Methods semester	Research Methods semester
2, 2, 3, 3, 4, 3, 4, 4, 5, 5, 6	4, 5, 5, 4, 5, 5, 7, 8, 8, 9, 9, 8, 9, 9, 8, 9

1. What type of design is this?

2. Graph the results.

3. Is there evidence that the Research Methods class improved the student's citation and paraphrasing skills? Explain.

4. What are the limitations of this study?

5. Do you think the student should conduct an ABA, ABAB reversal design, or a multiple-baseline-across-persons design? Explain.

   See Appendix A to check your answers.

and the assessment must be followed consistently throughout the course of the study. The manipulation must also be administered consistently, while avoiding other systematic variations during the study. These are relatively minor issues with a highly controlled animal study; but human participants tend to be less compliant, and their compliance may decrease as the study spans weeks or even months.

As with the case study, a key advantage of the single *N* design is the ability to examine a rare phenomenon that would be impossible to study with a large sample. The single *N* design also shares a limitation with the case study, in that its ability to generalize to other individuals or to support or develop a theory is questionable. The single *N* study has some advantages over the case study in this regard because the assessments are standardized and therefore more easily compared across cases. Generalizability can be examined with a multiple-baseline-across-persons design or a small *N* design. At the same time, it is difficult to determine if variations in patterns across persons or cases are due to the manipulation, individual differences, or the interaction of both. An examination of such interactions is better examined with a factorial design.

THE BIG PICTURE: CHOOSING BETWEEN A SAMPLE, CASE STUDY, OR SINGLE *N* DESIGN

If your goal is to study a unique phenomenon, or if you are interested in just one or a handful of cases, the case study and single *N* design are far superior to sample-based studies. Use the following guidelines to choose between these designs:

A case study should be chosen when you:

- Want to gain a holistic sense of a case

- Have questions about how or why a phenomenon occurred but do not have the ability to control variables

- Are using primarily qualitative measures that primarily assess past occurrences

A single N study should be chosen when you:

- Want to examine a specific cause-effect relationship

- Have questions about how a manipulation impacts an individual

- Are using quantitative measures that can be repeated on a daily or weekly basis

If, on the other hand, your primary goal is to generalize your results to the population or to find support for a theory, you should instead use one of the many sample-based designs discussed in previous chapters. In the final chapter, we will discuss how to choose the most appropriate of these designs based on your particular study. We will also provide an overview of how to select the appropriate inferential statistics.

CHAPTER RESOURCES

Key Terms

Define the following terms using your own words. You can check your answers by reviewing the chapter or by comparing them with the definitions in the glossary—but try to define them on your own first.

ABA reversal design 487

AB design 484

Baseline (phase A) 484

Case study 479

Embedded case study 480

Grounded theory 482

Manipulation (phase B) 484

Multiple-baseline across behaviors 491

Multiple-baseline across persons 489

Multiple-baseline across settings 491

Multiple-baseline design 489

Multiple-manipulation design 493

Reversal 487

Single *N* design 483

Small *N* designs 483

Stable baseline 485

Visual inspection 484

Do You Understand the Chapter?

Answer these questions on your own, and then review the chapter to check your answers.

1. What are the limitations of sample-based designs?

2. What is a case study?

3. When would a researcher conduct multiple case studies?

4. What are the strengths and limitations of a case study?

5. What are a single *N* design and a small *N* design?

6. How is a single *N* design different from a case study?

7. Explain how you would choose between an AB design, reversal design, multiple-baseline design, and multiple-manipulation design.

8. What are the strengths and limitations of the single *N* design?

9. Explain when you should choose a case study, when you should choose a single *N* design, and when you should choose a sample-based design.

 **edge.sagepub.com/adams2e**

How to Decide?

CHOOSING A RESEARCH DESIGN AND SELECTING THE CORRECT ANALYSIS

15

In the first chapter of this book, we suggested that learning about research methods and statistics would change the way you think about the world. We hope that by this point in the semester you have indeed come to think like a researcher. In other words, you find that you are unable to take information at face value, you evaluate information based on what you know of the past research in the area, you carefully evaluate the process by which any information was obtained, and any answers you get inspire more questions.

To test how far along you are, consider a scenario in which your class is discussing a research study that suggests that female students have more concerns than male students about interacting with a professor on social media (Teclehaimanot & Hickman, 2011). Imagine that one of your classmates says, *"I just don't believe that."* The professor tries to engage your classmate in a deeper discussion about the strengths and limitations of the study and asks for evidence for your classmate's statement. Regardless of the professor's efforts, the classmate keeps repeating: *"I just don't believe it"*—and the only evidence the classmate produces is that he or she does not have personal experiences that support the research findings. How do you react to your classmate's total disregard for the research?

Now, consider the same scenario, except this time the classmate says something like, *"I just believe what the research says."* The classmate repeats, *"I just believe it"* every time the professor elicits questions or points out limitations; and the only evidence he or she offers in support of the research are personal anecdotes. Now how do you respond to your classmate's unquestioning agreement with the research?

If both situations might make you furrow your brow and wonder why your classmate is not thinking critically,

LEARNING OUTCOMES

In this chapter, you will review

- How to choose a research design
- How to select the appropriate statistical analysis based on your data
- How to be a critical consumer and producer of research

then congratulations—you are thinking like a researcher! Thinking like a researcher means that you are a critical consumer of research and rely primarily on critical thinking rather than personal beliefs or experiences. Plus, if you are really thinking like a researcher, then you are able to design ways to investigate questions, test theories, or verify or refute results of past research. This does not mean that you conduct a study every time you raise a question, learn about a theory, or read past research. That would be exhausting! However, it does mean that such situations prompt you to *think* about the different ways you might conduct a study.

FIRST AND THROUGHOUT: BASE YOUR STUDY ON PAST RESEARCH

As you likely know by now, the first steps in conducting a study are to choose a topic and then refine it based on past research. We probably sound like a broken record, but we cannot overemphasize the importance of finding and reading past research as you develop your own research study, and referring to past research throughout the entire research process.

As you narrow and reformulate your topic in this way, you will be able to determine what questions most warrant further investigation. Generating questions in this way helps you feel confident that your research study will contribute to the broader knowledge base in the area. It is also an essential step in helping you both to determine the purpose of the study and then to choose the best research design.

CHOOSING A RESEARCH DESIGN

Descriptive, Correlational, Quasi-Experimental, or Experimental Design?

As you learned throughout this book, there is no one "perfect" research design. Rather, your design decision should be based on what is warranted based on past research, what questions particularly intrigue you, and what is feasible for you to do. Each design also has advantages and disadvantages for you to consider.

Balancing Internal and External Validity

When choosing a research design, one important consideration is the balance between internal validity (i.e., the ability to determine causality) and external validity (i.e., generalizability). Descriptive and correlational designs have the advantage of better external validity because the researcher is not trying to systematically control participants' (or animal subjects') environments. Quasi-experiments and experiments include a manipulation of an independent variable (IV). Therefore, these have the advantage of better internal validity. Experiments utilize random assignment, and therefore have greater internal validity than quasi-experiments. Quasi-experiments utilize already existing groups, and therefore have greater external validity than experiments.

Both quasi-experiments and experiments can have more or less internal validity based on how well controlled the study is (or how well the researcher minimizes the threats to internal validity, described in Chapter 9). A researcher conducting one of these types of designs might purposely decrease the internal validity in order to increase external validity, or vice versa. That decision is often based on past research (of course!). If past research has consistently found a causal relationship in a highly controlled lab setting, then a less controlled, more externally valid, study is warranted. Conversely, if past research has been limited by lack of control, then a researcher might tip the balance toward internal validity.

Describe, Predict, or Explain?

Descriptive designs, not surprisingly, have the advantage if description is your goal. This is the best choice if your goal is to understand prevalence or trends or to gain in-depth information about a particular phenomenon. Thus, you might take a snapshot of some phenomenon such as the number of new members to a social media site in order to describe the prevalence, and then examine the prevalence over time to identify membership trends. An in-depth study might examine the age, ethnic group, and socioeconomic status of the social media site's members; frequency of use; and perceived strengths and limitations of being a member of that site. You might also choose a descriptive design to see if a pattern that occurs in one population generalizes to another population. For example, if most of the descriptive research about your chosen social media site has been done in the United States, you might conduct a descriptive study in Germany. Or, your descriptive study might include all of these components.

A correlational design examines a noncausal relationship. It is a useful design when your goal is to predict, but not explain, a phenomenon. For example, you might want to examine how personality predicts social media use. A correlational design might also be useful if you are testing a relationship that has not been well researched and you want to establish correlation prior to examining causation. Additionally, it is the design of choice when you are testing the reliability or validity of a measurement (such as new attitudes toward social media questionnaires). Finally, correlational designs are often the only way to examine a relationship. Even when you might prefer to explain rather than simply predict a phenomenon, it might not be feasible or ethical for you to do so. For example, you cannot manipulate stable traits (such as personality) and characteristics (such as ethnicity). It is also not ethical for you to manipulate certain variables. For example, it would not be ethical to manipulate parental monitoring of online activity by requiring one group of parents to ignore their child's online activity.

Quasi-experiments and experiments focus on explaining phenomena. They are the designs of choice when you want to examine causality and it is ethical and feasible for you to manipulate an IV. As we discussed earlier, quasi-experiments are limited in their ability to determine causality because they do not involve random assignment to an IV condition. It is the design of choice when such random assignment is not ethical or feasible, or when your goal is to maximize external validity instead of internal validity.

FIGURE 15.1
Questions to Guide Your Choice of a Research Design

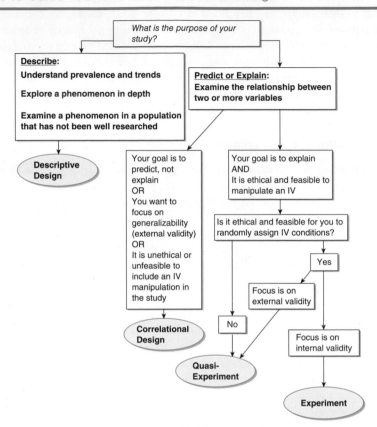

In Figure 15.1, we guide you through different decision points to help you decide between descriptive, correlational, quasi-experimental, or experimental designs. In Practice 15.1, you can practice applying these decision points with a topic of our choosing and then with your own topic. Keep in mind that almost all topics can be examined with any of these designs, and the guidelines we provide should be used to help you in the decision-making process but are not meant to be clear-cut answers. Also keep in mind that if you have multiple questions, then you may have multiple designs within the same study. (See Application 15.1, p. 507, for examples of studies that include multiple designs.)

Additional Decisions for Correlational Designs, Quasi-Experiments, and Experiments

If you have a correlational design, you next need to consider if you will be examining the relationship between two or more groups. These might be naturally occurring groups such as gender or ethnicity or groups with predetermined delineations such as academic

Practice 15.1

CHOOSING A RESEARCH DESIGN

1. We wonder how professors' use of technology impacts the classroom climate and student motivation to learn. After reading past research on this topic, we develop the following research questions:

   a. How common is it for students and professors to communicate outside of class using social media sites?

   b. What are the codes of conduct that professors and students follow when communicating in this way?

   c. Is there a relationship between professors' personalities and the frequency with which they use social media sites and how often (if ever) they interact with students on these sites?

   d. Does the use of social media have an effect on the classroom climate and student motivation to learn?

   Use Figure 15.1 to help determine what type of research design might be used to help answer each of these research questions.

   See Appendix A to check your answers.

major or discipline. For example, we might wonder if use of social media is related to a professor's gender, or if use varies based on full-time or part-time status or by discipline (social sciences, natural sciences, art, business, etc.).

For some correlational designs, you have the choice as to whether or not you want to examine your constructs as groups. For example, you could examine age as a ratio variable; or you could decide to split age into groups by categorizing your participants into younger adults, middle-aged adults, and older adults. Or, you might use a measure that asks participants to rate their level of extraversion on an interval scale. You can then examine extraversion scores using that interval scale, or you might decide to group participants into those who are high in extraversion and those who are low in extraversion. Whether or not you have naturally occurring or preset groups in your study or if you decide to define and create groups, any correlational design examining groups requires additional decisions.

By their nature, quasi-experiments and experiments examine groups. The IV is always a nominal (grouping) variable with two or more conditions (groups). For example, if we wanted to examine the effect of a professor's use of social media on classroom climate, we would need to have an IV (social media) that was defined with two or more groups (e.g., using social media vs. not using social media). Therefore, when you have a quasi-experiment or experiment, you will always have to make additional decisions about groups.

How Many Groups?

If your correlational study will compare groups or if you have a quasi-experiment or experimental design, you will next need to decide how many groups you should have. Do you know the best way to make this decision? If you said "past research," then you are on the right track!

Some reasons to choose the two-group design:

- The variable you are examining is typically divided into two groups (e.g., gender), or two groups fit with your operational definition (e.g., employment status defined as full or part time).

- You are operationally defining variables in a way that is warranted by the research but has not been tested in the research.

- The research area you are investigating is relatively new, so that a simple comparison of two groups is warranted.

- Past research has established the relationship or effect but has been limited to certain populations. You intend to study the relationship or effect in a different population.

Some reasons to choose a multilevel design:

- The variable you are examining is typically divided into multiple groups, or multiple groups fit with your operational definition.

- Research suggests there may be a nonlinear relationship between your variables.

- Past research has established a difference between two groups and adding additional levels to the IV or predictor is warranted.

Independent or Dependent Groups?

Once you have determined how many groups you will have, you need to decide if your groups will be independent or dependent. Figure 15.2 provides some guidance on deciding when to use an independent-groups design or when to use a dependent-groups design (matching or repeated measures). We will give you some opportunities to practice applying these decision points in Practice 15.2.

Should You Use a Factorial Design?

The final decision you need to make when examining groups is whether or not you should conduct a factorial study. There are two primary reasons for conducting a factorial study. One is that you have reason to expect that the relationship between your variables will depend on a third, moderating variable. The other reason is when you want to systematically control confounds or extraneous variables. If you choose the factorial design, you will have an independent-groups factorial if all of the IVs or predictors (called factors) are independent groups, a dependent-groups factorial if all of the IVs or predictors are dependent groups, and a mixed design if you have at least one independent-groups factor and one dependent-groups factor (see Figure 15.3).

SELECTING YOUR STATISTICAL ANALYSES

It would be simpler if descriptive designs involved only descriptive statistics, and correlational designs involved only correlational statistics. But it is not that simple! You will conduct descriptive statistics in all of your studies so that you better understand your sample (such as the number of men and women in the sample, and how age was distributed in your sample). It is also wise to run descriptive statistics on the key variables you are studying in order to better understand how they are distributed in your sample and check any assumptions you have about your variables (e.g., normal distribution). Likewise, you may need to use more than a correlation statistic in order to evaluate a correlational design.

We have two points in telling you this. First, you will likely run several statistical analyses in a single study. This is demonstrated in the two examples we describe in Application 15.1, p. 507. Second, the appropriate statistical analysis is *not* simply linked with the type of design you chose for your study. The analysis is based on how many variables you are examining and the type of data you have (nominal [or groups], ordinal, interval, or ratio) within the design. Figure 15.4 provides some guidelines for selecting the appropriate statistical test, and you can practice these skills in Practice 15.3.

Keep in mind that there are other statistical tests that are not included in Figure 15.4. We tried to keep this table as simple as possible by omitting more advanced statistical tests. We introduced regression analyses in Chapter 8 but did not include them in the table, primarily because they are quite flexible and can be used to analyze multiple variables that can be nominal or interval/ratio. There are also many other types of statistical analyses that we did not include in this book, but that you may have read about in research articles and that some of you who go on to research careers may learn to master.

Recall that some of these analyses require additional steps such as calculating an effect size or conducting post hoc analyses. Table 15.1 is a review of the inferential statistics covered in Figure 15.4 with information about effect size and post hoc tests.

FIGURE 15.2

Deciding Between Independent- and Dependent-Groups Designs

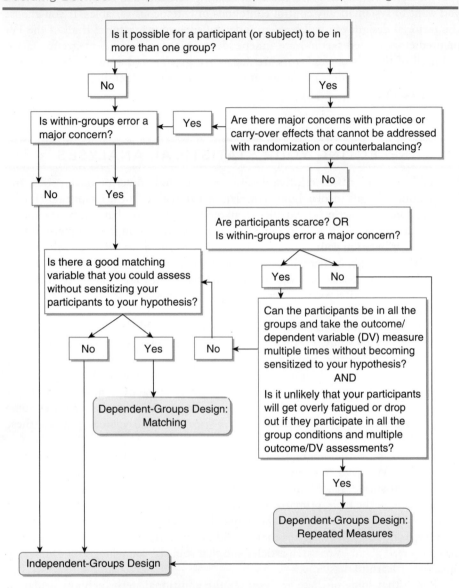

Practice 15.2

DECIDING BETWEEN THE INDEPENDENT- AND DEPENDENT-GROUPS DESIGNS

1. We want to examine the relationship between professors' personality and the frequency in which they use social media sites.

    Recall from Practice 15.1 that because personality is a stable trait that cannot be manipulated, the correlational design is most appropriate. We still need to decide how we will operationally define personality and if we will evaluate it on a nominal (grouping) scale or not.

    Suppose we decide to operationally define personality with a rating scale that assesses extraversion. We also decide to use these ratings to group professors as high or low in extraversion.

    Use Figure 15.2 to help answer the following questions:

    a. Is it possible for a professor (the participant) to be in more than one of the groups as we defined them (e.g., to be both in the high extraversion group and the low extraversion group)?

    b. If within-groups error *is not* a major concern, which design might be the best choice for our study?

    c. If within-groups error *is* a major concern, what else must we consider before choosing a design?

2. We want to conduct an experiment to examine the effect of social media on student motivation to learn. We operationalize the IV (social media) using a scenario in which we manipulate a fictional professor's use of social media to communicate with students. In one condition, the professor is described as having a policy against both initiating and accepting "friend requests" from students. In another condition, the professor accepts "friend requests" from students but does not initiate them. In the final condition, the professor both accepts and initiates "friend requests."

    Using Figure 15.2 as a guide, do you think it would be best to conduct an independent-groups design, a matched-groups design, or a repeated-measures design? Explain your answer.

    See Appendix A to check your answers.

FIGURE 15.3

Factorial Designs

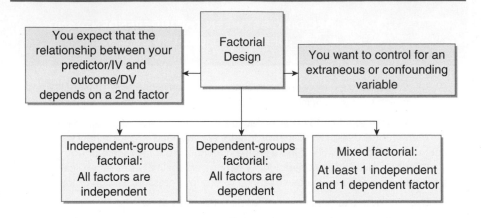

Practice 15.3

SELECTING APPROPRIATE STATISTICAL ANALYSES

Based on the information provided, identify the appropriate statistical analysis for each situation. When appropriate, identify the effect size you should calculate and any post hoc tests you might conduct. Use Figure 15.4 on pp. 508–509 as a guide.

1. We ask students how many social media sites they use, and we want to compare our results to the average reported by past research.

2. We want to test if students who interact with their professors via a social media site spend more time on social media than those who do not interact with their professors using social media.

3. We want to test if men are more likely than women to have ever contacted a professor on a social media site.

4. We have all participants read three different scenarios, each describing a professor with varying policies about interacting with students on social media. The participants rate each of the professors on their credibility (7-point scale).

5. We randomly assign participants to read one of the three scenarios described in question 4 and then rate the professor on a 7-point credibility scale.

6. In addition to the procedures described in question 5, we also ask participants' about whether they have ever interacted with a professor on social media. We wonder if this real-life personal experience moderates the impact of the fictional scenario.

See Appendix A to check your answers.

Kittisak_Taramas

Application 15.1

TWO EXAMPLES FROM THE RESEARCH LITERATURE

Example 1

Mazer, Murphy, and Simonds (2007) conducted a study with two primary goals: (1) to examine if teacher self-disclosure on the social media site Facebook had an effect on student ratings of motivation, affective learning, and classroom climate and (2) to explore student perceptions of what is and is not appropriate for their teachers to do on Facebook.

Designs

The researchers used an experimental design to address their first goal. They used the multilevel design with independent groups. They created three teacher Facebook profiles with varying levels of self-disclosure (manipulation of the IV) and randomly assigned participants to read and rate one of the three profiles.

The researchers also incorporated the descriptive design to address their second goal. They asked participants both to rate on a 5-point Likert-type scale the appropriateness of teachers using Facebook and to answer three open-ended questions about what they perceive to be appropriate or inappropriate self-disclosure.

Analyses

The researchers used descriptive statistics to describe their sample. They also used descriptive statistics to evaluate the ratings on the appropriateness of teacher use of Facebook. They coded the open-ended responses and used descriptive statistics to summarize the key themes from the responses.

To test their experimental hypothesis, the researchers used one-way ANOVAs for each of their three dependent variables that were measured on an interval scale (motivation, affective learning, and classroom climate). They reported η^2 and post hoc results when appropriate.

Example 2

Teclehaimanot and Hickman (2011) conducted a study with two goals: (1) identify what types of teacher-student interaction on Facebook is considered appropriate by students and (2) compare if perceptions vary based on general perceptions of teachers being on Facebook, graduate vs. undergraduate status, gender, and age.

Designs

The study is a combination of the descriptive and correlational designs. The first goal is a descriptive one whereas the second one compares naturally occurring groups that cannot be manipulated.

Analyses

The researchers had students rate the appropriateness of student-teacher interactions on Facebook based on behaviors by the student and behaviors by the teacher. They then created four groups based on types of interactions: student/active, student/passive, teacher/active, and teacher/

(Continued)

(*Continued*)

passive. The researchers used a one-way within-subjects ANOVA to compare these categories. They also used descriptive statistics to determine what behaviors were considered most inappropriate.

For the rest of the analyses, appropriateness was left as an interval scale. The researchers used a nominal variable to measure student status (graduate vs. undergraduate) and gender (male vs. female). They used an independent-samples *t* test to compare appropriateness ratings by student status and another independent-samples *t* test to examine gender differences in ratings.

Participant age was measured on a ratio scale. The researchers used a Pearson's *r* to determine if age was significantly related to appropriateness ratings.

FIGURE 15.4

Selecting Analyses

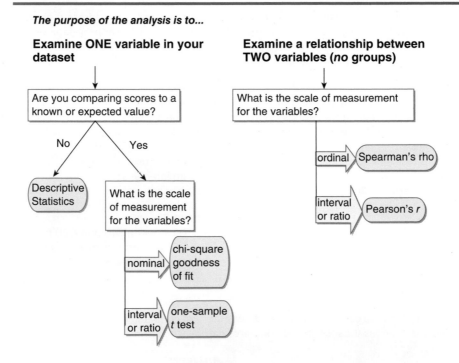

FIGURE 15.4
(Continued)

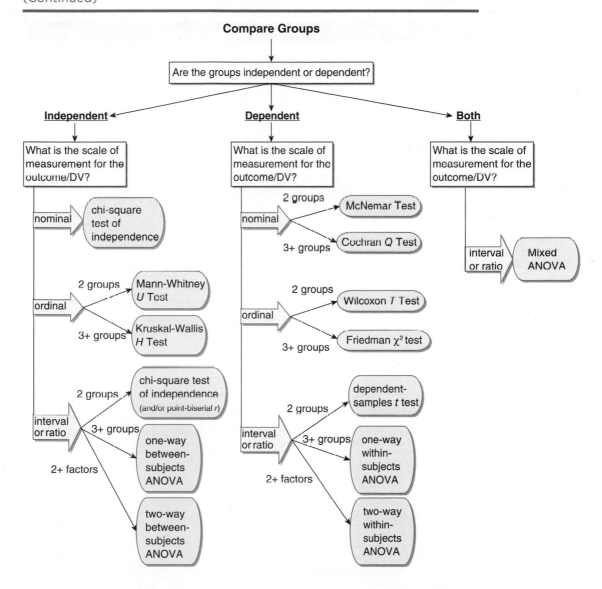

TABLE 15.1

Summary of Key Statistics

Inferential Statistic	When to Use	Effect Size?	Post Hoc?
Inferential Statistics detailed in Chapter 7:			
One-sample *t* test	Compare 1 interval or ratio variable to a known or expected value	Cohen's *d*	—
Inferential Statistics detailed in Chapter 8:			
Pearson's *r*	Examine relationship between 2 interval/ratio variables	r is an effect size, r^2 = proportion of variance accounted for	—
Point-biserial *r*	Examine 2 independent groups when the outcome/DV is interval or ratio (*although an independent-samples* t *test is often preferred as the primary inferential statistic*)	r_{pb} is an effect size, r_{pb}^2 = proportion of variance accounted for	
Inferential Statistics detailed in Chapter 10:			
Independent-samples *t* test	Compare 2 independent groups when the outcome/DV is interval or ratio	r_{pb}^2 or Cohen's *d*	—
One-way between-subjects ANOVA	Compare 3+ independent groups when outcome/DV is interval or ratio	η^2	Yes, if *F* is statistically significant use Fisher's LSD (or other options listed in Chapter 10)
Inferential Statistics detailed in Chapter 11:			
Dependent-samples *t* test	Compare 2 dependent groups when outcome/DV is interval/ratio	r_{pb}^2 or Cohen's *d*	—
One-way within-subjects ANOVA	Compare 3+ dependent groups when outcome/DV is interval/ratio	η^2	Yes, if *F* is statistically significant use Fisher's LSD (or other options listed in Chapter 10)
Inferential Statistics detailed in Chapter 12:			
Two-way between-subjects ANOVA	Examine 2 independent-groups factors when outcome/DV is interval or ratio	$\eta^2_{partial}$	Optional if interaction is significant
Two-way within-subjects ANOVA	Examine 2 dependent-groups factors when outcome/DV is interval/ratio	$\eta^2_{partial}$	Optional, if interaction is statistically significant
Mixed ANOVA	Factorial design with at least 1 independent-groups factor and 1 dependent-groups factor; outcome/DV is interval/ratio	$\eta^2_{partial}$	Optional, if interaction is statistically significant

Inferential Statistic	When to Use	Effect Size?	Post Hoc?
Nonparametric Inferential Statistics explained in Chapter 13			
Chi-square goodness of fit	Compare 1 nominal variable to a known or expected value	—	—
Chi-square test of independence	Compare 2+ independent groups when outcome/DV is nominal	ϕ^2, C^2, or V^2 (See Chapter 12 for when to use each)	—
Spearman's rho (r_s)	Examine relationship between 2 ordinal variables	r_s is an effect size r_s^2 = proportion of variance accounted for	—
Mann-Whitney U test	Compare 2 independent groups when the outcome/DV is ordinal	rank sums test	—
Kruskal-Wallis H test	Compare 3+ independent groups when outcome/DV is ordinal	Use a form of η^2	Yes, if H is statistically significant run Rank Sums test
McNemar Test	Examine 2 dependent groups when outcome/DV is nominal	—	—
Cochran Q test	Examine 3+ dependent groups when outcome/DV is nominal	—	Yes, if statistically significant— McNemar's with Bonferroni's correction
Wilcoxon T test	Compare 2 dependent groups when the outcome/DV is ordinal	r_s	—
Friedman χ^2	Compare 3+ dependent groups when outcome DV is ordinal	Use a form of η^2 as a measure of effect	Yes, if χ^2 is statistically significant Nemenyi's procedure

FIGURE 15.5

Source: Eva K. Lawrence

THE BIG PICTURE: BEYOND THIS CLASS

We have covered a lot of ground in this book, and we hope that you can appreciate how much you have learned since your first day of class. As you go forward in your academic coursework and future career, it is possible that some of you will continue to use and apply the specific skills you have learned, whereas others of you may never conduct a study or analyze data again. Regardless if you ever do research again, your ability to think like a researcher is something that we expect you will find useful in both your professional and personal life. You have honed your skills in critically evaluating all sorts of information. And although it was a lofty goal for us to set at the start, we hope that your worldview has changed and expanded. We encourage you to nurture your curiosity, to stare up in the sky and wonder about how and why different phenomena occur, and to know that you now have some basic tools to actually investigate some of the questions you have about the world.

CHAPTER RESOURCES

Do You Understand the Chapter?

Answer these questions on your own, and then review the chapter to check your answers.

Choosing a research design:

1. Explain some of the decision points you need to consider when deciding if your study will include a descriptive design, a correlational design, and/or an experimental design.

2. When you plan to compare groups, explain the additional decisions you need to make.

3. How would you choose between a two-group or multiple-group design?

4. How would you decide between an independent-groups, matched-groups, or repeated measures design?

5. What are some reasons why you might choose to do a factorial design?

Selecting statistical analyses:

1. In general, what are the key factors in selecting the appropriate statistical analyses for your study?

2. If the analysis you plan to conduct involves only one variable from your study (i.e., for that analysis, you are not examining a relationship or effect), what additional questions do you need to answer before selecting the analysis?

3. If you plan to examine the difference between two groups, what additional questions do you need to answer before selecting the analysis?

4. If you plan to examine the difference between three or more groups, what additional questions do you need to answer before selecting the analysis?

5. If you are examining the relationship between variables but are not comparing groups, what are the options for statistical analyses? How would you decide between these options?

6. Explain when you should include effect sizes and what effect sizes correspond to which analyses.

7. Explain when you should run post hoc tests.

SAGE edge™

edge.sagepub.com/adams2e

Sharpen your skills with SAGE edge!

SAGE edge for students provides you with tools to help you study. You'll find mobile-friendly eFlashcards and quizzes, as well as videos, web resources, datasets, and links to SAGE journal articles related to this chapter.

Appendix A

Answers to Practice Questions

CHAPTER 1

Practice 1.1

Thinking Critically About Ethics

1. The researchers point out that early initiation of sex is a risk factor for many other problems. Therefore, understanding the prevalence of this behavior in a specific population may help to determine the need for prevention and intervention programs.

2. One potential risk is that the participants might experience emotional pain or discomfort from being asked to remember specifics of sexual encounters, especially if the student regrets the action or worse, the sexual activity was not consensual.

   The researcher should make it very clear to the potential participants about the topic of study and tell students that they can decline to participate altogether, they can withdraw at any time, and they can leave any questions blank that they do not wish to answer.

   The participants should be debriefed in an attempt to address any negative effects of the study. Because the survey is anonymous and the researchers will not know if the student reported any sexual activity, the debriefing must be broad and general. Researchers might explain that some students may experience distress from answering the questions and provide contact information for a counselor.

3. The problem with the consent process is that it is not clear that the parents have actually been informed and have consented to their child's participation. The child's participation should require that the parents actively give their consent and are fully aware of what the study is about and that the child's responses will be anonymous.

Practice 1.2

Identifying Different Types of Research Designs

1. You cannot manipulate or randomly assign either of the variables, and it would be unethical to manipulate someone's health. A correlational study would be a more appropriate research design.

2. A researcher might conduct a descriptive study to determine how beautiful the students found the campus and ask them to rate how important the appearance of the university was in deciding to attend.

3. An experiment would be most appropriate to examine the effect of Facebook on mood. The details of the experiment can vary, but they must include randomly assigning participants to IV condition (by flipping a coin or drawing numbers out of a hat), manipulation of the IV (by having one group of participants do something differently with Facebook than the other group or groups), and then measuring the DV (by giving participants a mood questionnaire, for example).

Practice 1.3

Identifying and Avoiding Plagiarism

a. This is plagiarism. To avoid plagiarism, the phrases that were taken directly from Schuetze (2004) must be in quotations.

b. This is plagiarism. To avoid plagiarism, Schuetze (2004) must be cited to give her credit for the idea.

c. This is not plagiarism.

d. This is plagiarism. To avoid plagiarism, the author needs to state the ideas in his or her own words rather than simply substituting out a few of Schuetze's words.

CHAPTER 2

Practice 2.1

Article Comparison

1. Primary vs. Secondary Source?

   Article 1 (Datu, Yuen, & Chen, 2016) is a secondary source. The clues are that the title and excerpt refer to a "review of literature" and there is no mention that the authors conducted an original research study.

   Article 2 (Hill, Burrow, & Bronk, 2016) is the only primary source. The excerpt from this article used the phrase "the current studies" and "using college student samples," indicating that the authors conducted original research.

   Article 3 (Dahl, 2015) is a secondary source. The excerpt refers to research done by others and there is no mention that the author conducted a study.

2. Scholarly vs. Popular Source?
   - Articles 1 and 2 are scholarly sources. They are both published in academic journals that are geared toward experts in the field.
   - Article 3 is a popular source. It is published in a magazine and uses much more informal language geared at the general public.

3. Utility of the Source
   - Following are our comments for each study—how do they compare with your assessment of the articles based on the small amount of information provided in the excerpt?

     Datu et al. (2016) could provide a broad overview of research done in this area. We would want to read the full article to evaluate the research reviewed and their conclusions. After doing so, we might decide to use and cite their conclusions in a research paper. However, we would not want to rely too heavily on Datu et al.'s assessment of past research. Instead, we should find and read some of the articles that served as the basis for their review. Many of these articles may then serve as the foundation for our own study on the topic.

     Hill et al. (2016) conducted an original research study. We would want to read the full article to find out more about their method and results. By doing so, we could develop ideas of how to build on their research. Most of the articles you cite and build upon should be primary sources such as this.

     The Dahl (2015) article is a popular source, and reading the article might give us ideas about our own research. However, we would not want to rely too much on such sources. Instead, we might find and read the original research to which Dahl refers.

Practice 2.2

Write a Reference Using APA Format

Harackiewicz, J. M., Canning, E. A., Tibbetts, Y., Giffen, C. J., Blair, S. S., Rouse, D. I., & Hyde, J. S. (2014). Closing the social class achievement gap for first-generation students in undergraduate biology. *Journal of Educational Psychology*, *106*, 375–389. doi:10.1037/a0034679

CHAPTER 3

Practice 3.1

Identifying Scales of Measurement

1. Interval
2. Nominal

3. Ordinal

4. Ratio

5. Nominal, Ratio, Nominal

6. Nominal or Ordinal

Practice 3.2

Examples From the Literature

It is important that you are able to interpret the operational definition and psycho-metric qualities of scales and measures as they are described in the Method section of journal articles. See how closely your responses to the questions above match the explanations below.

Purpose of the Scale/Questionnaire

The Academic Dishonesty Scale that was used by Levett-Hooper et al. (2007) assessed exactly what its name implies: academic dishonesty.

The Self Compassion Scale – Long Form (SCS-LF) in Castilho et al.'s (2015) study assessed awareness of one's feelings and humanity as well as care and concern for oneself. .

Development of the Scale and Format

The Academic Dishonesty Scale used by Levett-Hooper et al. was a revision of the Academic Dishonesty Scale developed by McCabe (1992). As is appropriate, the authors of the current study credited the researcher who first came up with the scale. You should follow this practice even if you first become aware of a scale in a later publication. In the more recent study, the Academic Dishonesty Scale contained 20 behaviors that students rated on a 4-point scale in terms of the frequency (1 = *never*, 2 = *once*, 3 = *more than once*) of engaging in that behavior. A rating of "4," or not relevant, was also a possible response and was treated in the analysis as missing data. High scores on the scale signify more dishonesty.

Castilho et al. (2015) report that the SCS-LF was developed by Neff (2003a, b) based on Buddhist philosophy. The authors discussing this philosophy are cited so you could read their work and consider whether the SCS-LF follows from it. The scale assesses several components of self-compassion and consists of 26 items that are rated on frequency using a 5-point scale (1 = *almost never*, 5 = *almost always*). High scores denote more self-compassion.

Reliability of Scales

The internal consistency of the Academic Dishonesty Scale was high in both the origi-nal study (McCabe, 1992) (alpha = .87) and the current study (alpha = .93), suggesting that responses to the items on the scale are very consistent and that the reliability of the total score is very high.

The internal consistency of the items assessing self-compassion was also assessed using Cronbach's alpha. Both past research by Neff (2003a) and Castilho et al.'s (2015) studies with clinical and non-clinical samples found good internal consistency for the total scale (alphas = .92 to .94) and the subscales (alphas = .70 to .88). The test-retest reliability was also good (Neff, 2003a).

Validity of Scales

The validity of the Academic Dishonesty Scale was assessed by correlating the scale scores with scores from a Norm/Rule Violation Scale. A significant positive correlation was found, suggesting that students who are high in academic dishonesty are more likely in the future to violate norms and rules in the workplace. These results support the congruent validity of the Academic Dishonesty Scale.

Castilho et al. (2015) cite Neff (2003a) had found the SCS-LF showed concurrent, convergent, and divergent validity. No information was provided on how validity was tested but you could refer to Neff's (2003a) study to learn more about these procedures.

Practice 3.3

Distinguishing Between External Validity, Internal Validity, and Reliability at the Study Level

Cobb et al., 2010: *External validity* in terms of seeing whether the results of a study apply or generalize to a different sample.

Vredeveldt et al., 2015: The *internal validity* of the study is called into question, because witnesses differed in whether they closed their eyes <u>and</u> where they were interviewed. We are not sure which factor has caused the difference in the DV (amount of relevant information).

Estow et al., 2011: The example above with two classes demonstrates the *reliability* or consistency of the finding that multiple hands-on experiences with the topic of plagiarism results in increases in understanding and skills related to avoiding plagiarism.

CHAPTER 4

Practice 4.1

These questions might be examined with a descriptive study:

  a. How have the rates of peanut allergies changed over time?

  b. Where is most desirable vacation spot?

  d. What is the most popular type of social media site among older adults?

Practice 4.2

Evaluate Methods for a Descriptive Study on Academic Honesty

Surveys

  a. Pros about interviewing students about academic honesty: Interviews provide rich, detailed responses. If the interview is semi-structured, you could ask follow-up questions and you might discover something new that you might not have considered asking about. The participants might be more likely to pay attention and carefully consider each of your questions if it is a one-on-one interview. You can also record behavioral observations about not only what the participant said, but how they said it.

Cons are that interviews are time-consuming and are prone to interviewer bias. Social desirability bias might be especially high with this topic. The participants might want to answer as they think you expect, perhaps saying that they value academic honesty and have never cheated.

b. Pros of the questionnaire are that participants responses can be anonymous and confidential, and that might help to reduce the social desirability bias. Questionnaires are easy to administer, allowing you to obtain more participants.

Cons of the questionnaire are that social desirability bias might still be an issue. Additionally, participants might misinterpret questions or might be careless in responding.

Observations

It would be challenging to conduct naturalistic observations on this topic. You might be able to observe students taking an exam to try to determine if anyone seems to be cheating; but you would need the professor's permission, your presence might impact the students' behaviors, and it can be challenging to discern what behaviors indicate cheating.

You could perhaps set up a contrived observation in which a confederate attempts to cheat on an exam. This would work only if it was not a real exam (otherwise the confederate could get into a lot of trouble, and it would not be ethical to distract students taking a real exam).

Archival Research

a. Likely, your college/university keeps records of academic honesty violations.

b. It might be difficult for a student to obtain these records, although you might be able to obtain summary information about how many violations occurred each year. That could be interesting if you wanted to determine if academic honesty seems to be steady over time or if there are notable upward or downward trends.

CHAPTER 5

Practice 5.1

Numerical Coding

1. Answers will vary based on how you grouped the beverages. Some example groupings: soda or non-soda; sugary beverage, juice, or water, carbonated or non-carbonated.

2. Answers will vary depending on how you defined healthy and unhealthy. One way to categorize the beverages is to code the water and juice (orange and apple) as healthy. Then code all the sodas (Pepsi, Sprite, Coke, 7-Up) and the Kool-Aid as unhealthy.

Practice 5.2

Describe How Often Scores Appear in the Sample

1. $f_{\text{sugary drinks}} = 5, f_{\text{water}} = 3, f_{\text{juice}} = 2$

2. 30%

3. Frequency table for glasses of water drank per day:

Glasses of Water	f
0	1
1	2
2	0
3	4
4	2
5	2
6	1
7	1
8	1
9	0
10	0
11	0
12	1

4. Cumulative frequency of 5 to 8 glasses of water per day: $cf_{[5,8]} = 5$

5. Cumulative percentage of 5 to 8 glasses of water per day: $(cf_{[5,8]}/N)100$
   $(5/15)100 = 33.33\%$

Practice 5.3

Calculate the Central Tendency

1. Mode = sugary drinks

2. $Mdn = 7$

3. $M = 4.33$

Practice 5.4

Calculating Variability

1. The observed minimum is 0 and the observed maximum is 12. The possible minimum is the same as the observed minimum because the least amount of

water a person can drink is zero glasses. However, we do not know the exact possible maximum score. We might imagine that there is a limit to how many glasses of water a person can drink per day, but that number is not a known and fixed amount.

2. The range is 12.

3. $SD = 3.06$

Practice 5.5

Identifying the Type of Distribution and Choosing the Appropriate Descriptive Statistics

1. a.

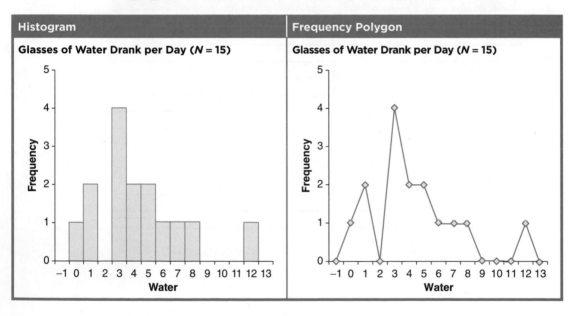

Histogram	Frequency Polygon

b. The graphs indicate a slight positive skew. The skewness statistic is 1.03 and the standard error of the skewness is 0.63. Determining if the skew is extreme enough that the mean and standard deviation are inappropriate depends on the criteria you use. This would be considered skewed under the stricter guidelines of Bulmer (1979) because it is slightly higher than 1. Most researchers, however, would likely not be that strict and might either use the greater than +/– 2 criterion or determine the distribution is not skewed because G_1 is less than twice its *SES*.

c. Answers will vary based on your assessment of the distribution in 1b. If you decided that it met criteria for normality, the best measures of central tendency and variability are the mean and standard deviation, respectively. If you decided that there was an extreme skew, report the median and minimum and maximum or range.

2. a. Because this distribution is skewed (based on all the different interpretations we have discussed), the median is the best measure of central tendency. The range or observed minimum and maximum should be reported as the measure of variability.

   b. Answers will vary, but at minimum they should include the median, either the range or observed min and max, and mention that the data were skewed. You should *not* have reported the actual skewness statistic or *SES*, or other measures of central tendency or variability.

Practice 5.6

Calculating a *z* Score and Percentile

z score:

$$z = \frac{X - M}{SD} = \frac{4 - 5.47}{1.46} = -1.01$$

Percentile:

Based on Appendix C.3, we find that the percentage of the area under the curve between this *z* score and the mean is .3438.

We have to subtract this number from .50 because the *z* score is negative.

$$.50 \quad .3458 = .1542$$

The person scored at the 15.42nd percentile.

CHAPTER 6

Practice 6.1

Null and Alternative Hypotheses

1. H_0 (null): There will be no difference in the detail included in student notes for students who listen to a lecture and students who text/post frequently.

   H_a (alternative): Students who text/post frequently and students who listen to a lecture will include different amounts of detail in their notes.

2. H_0 (null): Students who sit in the front half and back half of a classroom will not differ in the amount of detail in their notes.

   H_a (alternative): Students who sit in the front half and the back half of a classroom will include a different amount of detail in their notes.

Practice 6.2

One-Tailed and Two-Tailed Hypotheses

1. a. directional/one-tailed

   b. directional/one-tailed

c. nondirectional/two-tailed

d. directional/one-tailed

2. Only *c* or "Single adults who use online dating services will differ in a measure of shyness than single adults who do not use online dating services" is a nondirectional or two-tailed hypothesis. This sets up two smaller regions of rejection on either extreme of the sampling distribution (the lowest and highest 2.5%) and so is a more stringent test than the other three hypotheses that place the entire region of rejection (5%) on the same end of the distribution.

Practice 6.3

Understanding the Hypothesis-Testing Process

Answer:

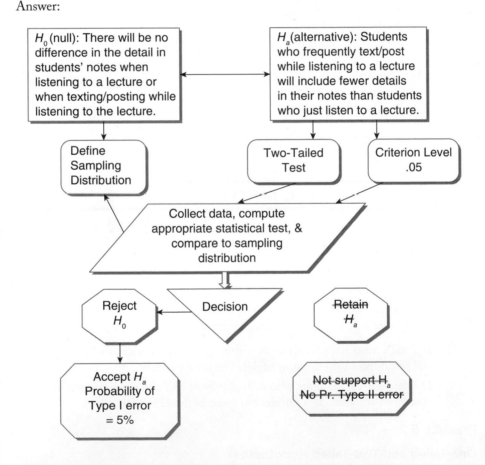

Practice 6.4

Interpreting Results

1. b. $p = .005$; (d) $p = .001$, and (f) $p = .009$ are statistically significant.

2. a. (i) Results are not significant.

(ii) You would retain the null hypothesis.

(iii) You might be making a Type II error. Ways to reduce this error in future research include increasing sample size, reducing error, and if possible, increasing the strength of the effect.

   b. (i) Results are significant.

(ii) You would reject the null hypothesis.

(iii) You might be making a Type I error (there is a 3% chance). If we wanted to eliminate the Type I error we could set a more stringent criterion. Any criterion < .03 would result in nonsignificant results, retention of the null hypothesis, and therefore a zero chance of making a Type I error. The consequence is that you now may be making a Type II error.

3.

		Decision Based on Observed Results	
		Reject	Retain
Reality	H_0 is True	Type I Error	Correct
	H_0 is False	Correct = Power	Type II Error

Practice 6.5

Interpreting Effect Size, Confidence Intervals, and Practical Significance

1. a. $p = .08$, Cohen's $d = 0.30$: These results do not show statistical significance ($p > .05$) so you must state that although the mean percentage of texting for the drivers in your sample is lower than the national mean, there is **not** a difference larger than one would expect by chance alone. In addition, the strength of the effect size is weak. The two results together suggest that the texting behavior of your sample of drivers does not differ from the national frequency. Given the large standard deviation of texting for your sample ($SD = 20$), you may want to consider a way to measure texting behavior that reflects a more consistent pattern of behavior.

   b. $p = .03$, with 10% of the variance in texting accounted for: These results are significant ($p < .05$). and show that the texting behavior for your driver sample is significantly less frequent than that of drivers nationally.

The strength of the effect is weak to moderate, so the findings do not support that education is an influential factor in this difference.

c. $M = .52$, 95% CI [.45, .59]: The small confidence interval suggests that you can be confident that your measure of texting is representative of the population mean for educated drivers and somewhat lower than the national value. You have not computed statistical significance here and cannot comment on whether your mean is significantly different for the national mean.

d. Both the sample and national texting means suggest that drivers are texting while driving at least half of the time. It is positive that the sample texts less frequently, but texting is quite frequent for all drivers suggesting that we would not notice a difference between the two groups on the road.

2. a. At a minimum, you would want to know the standard deviation for the ounces of chocolate your sample ate and the effect size. You could compute the percentage of variability accounted for or Cohen's d (not both) as a measure of the effect size. The standard deviation describes the variability around the mean and tells you whether the scores cluster tightly or spread out widely around the mean of 18 oz. The effect size helps you to better understand the magnitude of the effect and to interpret whether it is meaningful or not.

b. You found statistical significance, so the mean of chocolate consumed in a month by your sample is significantly more than the national average, and the difference would occur by chance alone only 2.5% of the time if there was no actual difference in the two means. You need additional information in order to say more about the findings.

CHAPTER 7

Practice 7.1

Determining Whether a *t* Test Result Is Significant

a. Critical t value = 2.145, which is less than the value you obtained, so the result is significant.

b. Critical t value = 2.977, which is greater than value you obtained (2.20), so the result is not significant.

c. Critical t value = 1.761, which is less than the value you obtained, so the result is significant.

d. Critical t value = 2.624, which is greater than value you obtained (2.20), so the result is not significant.

Practice 7.2

Writing Results and Discussion Sections

1. Content that should be in Results (check with your professor to see which of the results below are required in your class):

    ___Type of test used and why
    ___Mean and standard deviation for sample (italicize the statistical notations: $M = .17$, $SD = .06$)
    ___Mean of the population ($\mu = .209$)
    ___Results of one-sample t test [$t(19) = -2.82$, $p = .011$]
    ___Effect size $\eta^2 = .29$ or Cohen's $d = 0.63$
    ___Confidence interval (CI = [$-.06, -.01$])

2. Content that should be in Discussion:

    ___Explanation of results without statistics (significant difference and direction, close to 1/3 of variability accounted for or moderate effect size, very small confidence interval)
    ___Interpretation of how the results fit or do not fit with Kuznekoff and Titsworth's study (described in Application 6.1)
    ___Discussion of the practical significance/implications of the results
    ___Limitation(s) and/or alternative explanations for results
    ___Suggestion for future research based on the limitation(s) or alternative explanations

3. Overall:

    ___Did you write clearly and concisely?
    ___Did you use correct grammar, punctuation, and spelling?
    ___Did you format your Results and Discussion correctly?

CHAPTER 8

Practice 8.1

Types of Relationships

1. Your examples for positive, negative, and no relationship will vary. Compare your answers with classmates and evaluate each other's examples. Check with your professor if you do not agree that any of the examples are appropriate.

2. a. The relationship between job satisfaction and supervisor ratings is positive, while the relationship between job satisfaction and days missed is negative. Note that the data points for the positive relationship (job satisfaction and supervisor ratings) move from the lower left to the upper right of the graph, while the data points for the negative relationship (job satisfaction and sick days taken) move from the upper left to the lower right of the graph.

b. The negative relationship is stronger than the positive one. Note that the data points for the positive relationship are somewhat more dispersed than those for the negative relationship. The more definite pattern of data points results in a stronger relationship.

c. The relationships suggest that for the sample of employees, job satisfaction is related to important factors in employment (days absent and supervisor ratings). The employer should consider exploring whether there are other factors that are responsible for the relationships, such as employee morale or cooperation among employees. Future studies could also explore whether job satisfaction actually causes changes in days missed from work or supervisor ratings.

Practice 8.2

Evaluating Correlations

a. H_0: Time spent exercising is not related to life satisfaction.
H_a: Time spent exercising is positively related to life satisfaction.

b. $df = N - 2 = 25 - 2 = 23$

c. Using 23 df and $p < .05$, we see in Table 8.4 that $r_{crit} = .3961$. Our $r_{obt} = .53$ exceeds this critical value so we can reject the null hypothesis. Our results fall in the extreme tail of the sampling distribution for no relationship between the two variables.

d. For $p < .01$ the $r_{crit} = .5052$, which is still less than our computed Pearson r of .53, so we can still reject the null hypothesis.

Practice 8.3

Selecting the Appropriate Statistic

1. Pearson's r is appropriate to compute the correlation between 2 ratio variables.

2. Point-biserial correlation coefficient (r_{pb}^2) is appropriate for one dichotomous variable (view of global warming) and one ratio variable (years of education).

3. Pearson's r is appropriate when examining the relationship between an interval variable (health status) and a ratio scale (weight).

4. Pearson's r is appropriate to compute the correlation between 2 interval variables.

5. Point-biserial correlation (r_{pb}^2) is appropriate for one dichotomous variable (having children or not) and one interval variable (health status).

Practice 8.4

Practice With Regression Equations

a. Inserting 120 into the regression equation to predict life satisfaction we find:

$$Y' = .059X + 34.5 = .059(120) + 34.5 = 7.08 + 34.5 = 41.58$$

So we predict that a person who exercises 120 minutes each week will score 41.58 (or 42 if you round the value) on the life satisfaction scale.

b. The coefficient of determination is equal to r^2 or $(.53)^2 = .28$ for this study. This tells us that 28% of the variability in life satisfaction scores (or about one-fourth) is accounted for by minutes spent exercising.

c. You would expect a large amount of error in your predictions of life satisfaction because, on average, the predicted score will vary by 10 points (higher or lower) from the actual score, given a particular number of minutes spent exercising.

CHAPTER 9

Practice 9.1

Testing Cause and Effect

The information presented is not sufficient to suggest that eating spicy foods does or does not cause strange dreams or nightmares. To demonstrate causality, we would need to show that there is a correlation between eating spicy foods and types of dreams, that eating spicy foods came before the dreams, and that we ruled out alternative explanations.

Practice 9.2

Identifying Threats to Internal Validity

Threats to internal validity inherent in this study:

Instrumentation: The follow-up tests were different for the two groups, and therefore we do not know if the difference was due to the type of food or to how dreams were measured.

Selection: Groups were created based on their preexisting behaviors. Personality, attention, age, or other characteristics associated with preference for spicy foods might be the reason for any differences between the groups.

Mortality/attrition: The no-spicy food group had a higher attrition rate than the spicy food group. Results may be due to this differential attrition.

Possible threats to internal validity:

History: If one group experienced an event that the other did not (beyond the conditions to which they were assigned), history would be a threat. There is a high likelihood for this threat because the researcher did not control what exactly the participants ate or when and how they slept.

Selection-history interaction: In addition to the possibility that the groups would experience different events over the course of the study, the groups may be differentially affected by an event that all experienced.

Selection-maturation interaction: Maturation alone is not an issue because the groups spent the same amount of time in the study, but a selection-maturation interaction would be a threat if the groups mature at different rates.

Selection-testing threat: The pretests were identical, and therefore testing alone is not a threat; but it would be if the groups were differentially impacted by the pretest.

Selection-regression: The groups were assigned based on extreme scores that may regress to the mean during the course of the study. This is not a problem if statistical regression occurs about equally across the groups, but it is an issue if regression interacts with selection so that one group has a higher rate of regression than the other.

Practice 9.3

Design an Experiment

Experimental designs will vary, and as you will see in the next three chapters, there are many different types of experiments. At minimum, you should have:

- Type of food eaten as the IV (spicy vs. not spicy, at minimum)

- Random assignment to IV condition.

- Attempts to keep everything except the level of the IV constant across IV groups. In an ideal situation, you might have participants stay in a sleep lab and eat the same exact food during the course of the experiment, except that your experimental group would have cayenne pepper added to all their meals. In this setting, you would also monitor the participants' sleep so that they all went to bed at the same time, slept in similar environments, were woken up at the same time, and asked about any dreams they remember.

- It would also be a good idea to screen out any participants who have food allergies or sensitivities to cayenne pepper. You would want your manipulation to be strong enough, but not so strong that you might burn the tongues of those in your experimental group.

- Note that one serious challenge for an experiment on this topic is that people dream at multiple times throughout the night, and it is possible that the participants had a nightmare or bizarre dream that they do not remember upon waking.

Practice 9.4

Distinguishing Between Variables That Can and Cannot Be Manipulated

- *The weather:* Although you cannot manipulate actual weather, you could simulate certain weather conditions. For example, you could play a recording of rain and thunder.

- *Room color:* You can manipulate this variable if you had access to the space and resources to change the color. Barring finding different rooms that are almost identical and painting them different colors, you could use poster boards or fabric to change the color of a room.

- *Participant ethnicity:* You cannot manipulate this variable.

- *Participant socioeconomic status:* You cannot ethically manipulate this variable.

- *Participant disability:* You could temporarily manipulate certain characteristics of a disability. For example, you could assign some participants to be blindfolded.

- *Confederate sexual orientation:* You could not manipulate the confederate's actual orientation, but you could manipulate how the participants' perceive the confederate's sexual orientation by having the confederate self-disclose as a homosexual to one group and a heterosexual in another group. Likewise, you could use a scenario to describe a fictional individual and manipulate that fictional person's demographic and personal information.

CHAPTER 10

Practice 10.1

Simple Experiment Design Practice

Answers may vary but sample answers follow.

1. Cell phone use

2. A confederate driver will either obviously use or keep his hands on the steering wheel while stopped at a red light and then continue to talk on the phone and not move when the light turns green.

3. Aggression by the participant driver stopped at the light behind the IV car is the DV. Aggression could be defined as honking the horn. It could be measured by the number of times a participant driver honks the horn or by the time it takes for the participant driver to honk after the light turns green or with any other measure that suggests aggression.

4. The number of times the participant driver honks or the time it takes to honk changes.

5. We predict that participant drivers behind a confederate driver using a cell phone will honk more times and/or more quickly (fewer seconds) after the light turns green than those behind a driver not using a cell phone.

6. There will be no difference in the number of times or the speed with which participant drivers honk their horn when a driver in front of them uses or does not use a cell phone.

7. If the proposed study is a field study where participants are not aware of the study, and no identifying information about them is recorded, you do not have to obtain informed consent. If your procedure involves a driving simulation in the laboratory, you will need to have participants sign an informed consent.

   All details about the study need to be consistent: the same confederate car and placement of car at the light; same confederate, same obvious use of cell phone (experimental condition) or holding hands on the steering wheel (control condition); the street needs to be two lanes so cars could not pass the confederate car when the light turns green, and so on. The confederate would not move for 30 seconds after the light changes from red to green and then begin to drive away. An observer (could be a passenger in the confederate car or on the side of the road) would record the amount of time before the participant honks and the number of honks (if any) or other DV defined in #3.

8. Include a large number of participants (25/group); pilot the procedure to ensure that a 30-second delay after the light turns green is noticeable and annoying to drivers; and ensure consistency in the procedure (less random error).

9. Single-blind as described. You could have a double-blind experiment if the person recording the number and time to honks could not see whether the confederate was using a cell phone. This could only happen if the observer was not in the car with the confederate.

10. Drivers who are behind a slow-moving car will honk more quickly and more times when the driver is using a cell phone than when he or she does not use a cell phone (has his or her hands on the steering wheel). Or your hypothesis could match the IV/DV you specified in earlier items.

Practice 10.2

Type I and Type II Errors

1. We rejected the null hypothesis at the .05 level ($p < .05$) because our $t_{obt} > t_{crit}$ so the probability of making a Type I error = .05 or 5%. Because there

can be a probability of a Type II error only if we do not reject the null hypothesis, there is no or zero probability of making a Type II error in this case.

2. The implications of a Type I error are that we conclude that drivers behind a slow driver using a cell phone are much more irritated than when behind a slow driver not using a cell phone, when in fact there is no difference. Based on the findings, we might make changes to laws such as restricting the use of cell phones that are needless. However, in this case, such laws will not be harmful, only inconvenient. Remember that we never know for sure whether we have made a Type I or II error—we can only design our studies to try to avoid them.

Practice 10.3

Practice Interpreting a Two-Group Design

1. Because we do not have any information that students were randomly assigned to the condition (low-auditory distraction or high-auditory distraction), this study is a quasi-experiment where the auditory distraction is manipulated but not randomly assigned.

2. The IV is auditory distraction with 2 levels: low distraction and high distraction.

3. The DV is test performance, which is operationalized as a 50-item test with each item counting 2 points or a total possible score of 100. The test is on a ratio scale of measurement.

Results

1. The results show that there is homogeneity of variance for the study because Levene's test (the first two columns of results in the output box labeled "Independent Samples Test") shows that the significance level is .731, which is above .05.

2. We can reject the null hypothesis because $p = .043$. The probability of making a Type I error $= .043$ or 4.3%, and the probability of making a Type II error is zero.

3. The effect size or r_{pb}^2 is equal to the correlation squared or $(-.372)^2 = .138$. Auditory distraction accounted for 13.8% of the variability in students' test performance. This is a moderate effect. If you computed Cohen's d as the effect size, then $d = 0.80$, which is a moderate to strong effect.

4. Looking at the means of the two groups to interpret the practical significance, we see that students exposed to constant noise ($M = 82.20$) scored on average 5 points higher than students who were exposed to cell phone rings ($M = 77.33$) during a test. Students are likely to notice such a

point difference and interpret their performance as better if they earned 5 more points. This suggests that the study does have practical significance.

5. The results of the test show a statistically significant decrease in test performance when students are exposed to cell phone rings versus constant noise during a test. The effect of noise type was moderate, and the results have practical significance for students in testing situations. Teachers may want to ban cell phones from class during test time, or at least remind all students to turn off their cell phones during a test.

Practice 10.4

Practice Completing and Interpreting a Summary Table

1.

Source	SS	df	MS	F
Treatment	42	3	14	3.50
Error	144	36	4	
Total	186	39		

2. 4

3. 40

4. 10

5. The summary table shows that $F_{obt} = 3.50$. Looking at the table of critical values in Appendix C.6 for the study's degrees of freedom ($df = 3, 36$), we see that for $p < .05$ that $F_{crit} = 2.87$. Our obtained F is greater than the critical value, so we can reject the null hypothesis and conclude that our results are significant.

6. Using the formula for eta squared, we find:

$$\eta^2 = SS_B/SS_{tot} = 42/186 = .226$$

meaning that the treatment (chocolate) accounted for 22.6% of the variability in the dependent variable (mood).

Practice 10.5

Practice With the Analysis and Interpretation of a Multiple-Groups Study

a. The study is a multiple-groups design with three independent groups of self-disclosure (low, medium, high)—we can tell they are independent because participants were randomly assigned to one condition. The study is an experiment because there is an IV (self-disclosure) that was manipulated and the effect on the DV (trustworthiness) was assessed. The scale of measurement of the DV is interval.

b. The one-way ANOVA results is $p < .001$ so we can reject the null hypothesis. The probability of a Type I error is less than .1%, and there is no probability of a Type II error. (Note: Remember when $p = .000$, APA format requires that you cite $p < .001$.)

c. $\eta^2 = .517$, which tells us that the level of self-disclosure by a stranger accounts for 51.7% of the variability of trustworthiness ratings. Thus, self-disclosure accounts for about half of the variability in ratings of trustworthiness of a stranger and is a strong effect.

d. The post hoc analysis shows that those in the medium self-disclosure group differed significantly from both the high and low self-disclosure groups, who did not differ from one another. When we look at the means, we see that medium self-disclosure ($M = 20.30$) by a stranger resulted in much higher ratings of trustworthiness than low ($M = 15.00$) or high self-disclosure ($M = 13.70$).

e. Looking at the means for the three groups, we see that on a 25-point scale of trustworthiness, the medium level of self-disclosure was rated approximately 5–7 points higher than the low and high levels of self-disclosure. This suggests that there is about a 20% difference in the ratings, which means that people would have noticeably different reactions to strangers depending on how much they self-disclose. It suggests that people should be aware that too high or too low levels of self-disclosure may negatively affect new acquaintances' first impressions of them.

CHAPTER 11

Practice 11.1

Considering Dependent Designs

1. Strayer et al. (2003) considered the following factors. (You may think of others to consider):

   Use of a hands-free phone was used so that physical manipulation of a phone was not confounded with the phone conversation as a distractor. Driving conditions during the conversation versus no conversation conditions were similar (all city streets, same number of turns required, same number of billboards shown in each condition, etc.).

Practice was done on the simulation task so the participants were equally skilled on the apparatus throughout the study.

The simulation driving task was made interesting (multiple tasks, traffic, stop lights, scenery, billboards, etc.) to decrease boredom; but it was not too complicated, in order to avoid fatigue.

Because the participants were focused on the driving task and were not aware they would be asked to recall what they saw while driving, they were unlikely to be sensitized to the dependent measure (memory of the billboards they saw when driving).

The researchers needed to counterbalance the order of the conditions (conversation vs. no conversation) among the participants so that half had the conversation condition first and half had the no-conversation condition first.

2. Because participants were the same in both conditions, the researchers did not have to worry about possible confounds due to participant variables such as different driving skills, driving experience, distractibility, or attention spans.

   The error variability due to different participant characteristics in different conditions has been equalized, allowing differences due to the IV (conversation vs. no conversations) to be more easily seen.

3. You could support either a matched or repeated measures design using the advantages of either design (e.g., matched design would mean participants experience only one driving simulation and so a matched design may be less vulnerable to fatigue, practice, boredom, or sensitization effects; on the other hand, you may not be able to find an adequate matching variable that creates equal drivers because so many factors contribute to one's driving skill).

Practice 11.2

Practice With a Dependent Design

a. Matching. Each person is in only one condition but has a matched (on the basis of marital status) "equivalent" in the other group.

b. IV: Service learning (service learning or no service learning). DV: score on critical-thinking exam

c. H_0: Service learning will have no effect on critical-thinking skills relative to group discussion.
   H_1: Service learning will improve critical-thinking skills relative to group discussion.

d. 24

e. $d = -0.33$

f. A paired-samples t test was run to examine the effect of service learning on critical-thinking skills. Twenty-four participants were matched on marital status. Results reveal that there was not a statistically significant difference between those who participated in service learning ($M = 9.42$, $SD = 2.91$) and those who merely met for discussion ($M = 8.25$, $SD = 4.11$), $t(11) = -1.77$, $p = .105$, $d = 0.33$. For a mean difference of -1.17, 95% CI $[-2.62, .29]$.

g. It appears that critical-thinking skills are not improved after students take part in service learning when compared with a control group that met only for group discussion—although the results were in the expected direction, with service-learning group showing a higher mean on critical thinking. The effect size is weak and the 95% confidence interval is large, suggesting we cannot be very confident that our mean difference is reflective of the true difference.

h. The groups may not have been appropriately equivalent before taking part in the study since they were matched on the basis of marital status. Marital status is not likely to be related to critical-thinking skills. GPA or something else related to critical-thinking skills would be a better matching variable.

Practice 11.3

Practice With Participant Assignment in Dependent Designs

1. There are 4 conditions (k) in the study: First, we find out how many different orders are possible using the formula $k(k - 1)$ or $4(4 - 1) = 4(3) = 12$. We determine all of the 12 orders so that each condition appears in each order of presentation an equal number of times, and it precedes and follows each of the other conditions an equal number of times:

TXMG	XMGT	MGTX
GTXM	TMGX	TGXM
XGTM	XTMG	MTXG
MXGT	GXMT	GMTX

There are 24 participants, so we would randomly assign 2 participants to each of the 12 different condition orders.

2. First, order the times from most to least time on the phone, as shown below, and then pair the four highest scores, then next four highest, and so on.

The four participants (quads) who are matched are shown in color shading below:

Participant	Time	Participant	Time	Participant	Time
14	125	5	70	7	35
4	120	24	65	23	35
22	115	3	60	10	30
15	110	19	55	17	25
9	90	16	50	6	20
2	85	1	45	18	20
12	80	11	40	8	15
20	80	21	40	13	15

After matching the participants, you would then randomly assign one of each quad to one of the four conditions of the study. For example, participants 14, 4, 22, and 15 are matched and each one of them would be randomly assigned to talking on their cell phone (T), texting on their cell phone (X), listening to music (M), or playing a game on their cell phone (G) while walking. This process would be repeated for each of the matched quads.

Practice 11.4

Practice Interpreting a Summary Table for a Dependent-Samples ANOVA

a.   See below in bold.

Source	SS	df	MS	F
Condition (A)	30.00	3	**10.00**	**6.25**
Subject	66.00	**20**		
Interaction (A × S)	**24.00**	15	**1.60**	
Total	120.00	23		

b.   Subject source of error

c.   Subject source of error is associated with specific participants (in repeated measures) or with a specific matched group (in matched design). We can then pull out this source of variability from the overall error variance and divide treatment variance only by the error variance within each condition of the study.

d. F is significant because it ($F_{obt} = 6.25$) is greater than the critical F value ($F_{crit} = 5.42$) in the Table C.6 using $p < .01$ and $df = 3,15$.

e. Using the formula for partial eta squared, we find:

$\eta^2_{partial} = SS_A/(SS_A + SS_{A \times S}) = 30/(30 + 24) = 30/54 = .56$, which is a strong effect.

f. Yes, post hoc tests should be computed because a significant F tells us that there is an overall difference among our groups, but we do not know how the groups differ from one another.

Practice 11.5

Practice Interpreting a Dependent-Samples ANOVA

a. H_0: The focus of a syllabus (films, novels, field works) will not affect how likely students are to take a developmental course.
H_a: Students will be more likely to want to take a course that focuses on films than on novels or field work, which students will select equally.

b. 30

c. Results:

A one-way ANOVA was used to analyze the impact of a syllabus that focused on field work, novels, or films on students' likelihood of taking the class. There was a significant difference between the types of syllabi, $F(2, 18) = 13.34$, $p < .001$, $\eta^2 = .60$. Paired-samples t tests were computed to examine the differences between syllabi using Bonferroni's correction. The results showed that students were significantly more likely ($p = .004$) to take a course that focused on films ($M = 10.10$, $SD = 3.28$) than one that focused on field work ($M = 6.40$, $SD = 2.59$). Students did not differ in their likelihood of taking a course that focused on novels ($M = 8.50$, $SD = 2.12$) versus field work ($p = .069$) or novels versus films ($p = .057$).

d. The focus of a course as presented in a syllabus overall affected students' likelihood of taking the course, supporting the hypothesis. Paired comparisons showed a difference only between the likelihood of taking a course focusing on film versus a course focusing on field work. Students did not distinguish between courses focusing on novels and the other two types of courses, although the likelihood for the film course was highest, followed by the novel, with the field work course least attractive to students. This suggests that although films may be attractive to students, they are no more so than novels. Perhaps the field work course was avoided because it would require students to participate in an activity off campus and students may consider that this would take more time or require a specific time, while watching films or reading novels might be done whenever the students chose. The study should have good power as the effect size was strong and the matching variables should have decreased the error variability. However, the matching variables may not be relevant to first-year students' choice of courses. The focus of a course syllabus is worth exploring in other psychology courses and other disciplines.

CHAPTER 12

Practice 12.1

Identify Types of Factorial Designs

1. Correlational

2. a. Experimental

   b. 3(test) × 2(environment)

   c. 6 cells

3. a. Hybrid

   b. 3(test) × 2(environment) × 2(gender)

   c. 12 cells

Practice 12.2

Graph a 2 × 2 Interaction

Locus of Control (LOC) as a Moderator of the Effect of Stereotype Threat on Test Performance

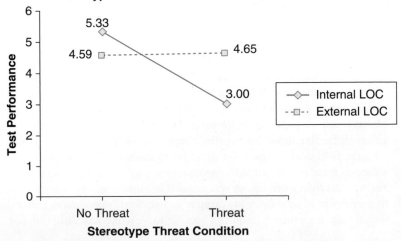

Practice 12.3

Complete a Two-Way Between-Subjects ANOVA Summary Table

1. Tests of Between-Subjects Effects

Source	Sum of Squares	df	Mean Square	F	Sig.
condition	11.560	1	11.560	9.739	Significant at $p < .01$
ADHD	1.960	1	1.960	1.651	Not significant
condition * ADHD	1.440	1	1.440	1.213	Not significant
Error	114.000	96	1.187		
Total	128.960	99			

2. Condition $\eta^2_{partial} = .092$; ADHD $\eta^2_{partial} = .017$;
   Condition × ADHD $\eta^2_{partial} = .012$

CHAPTER 13

Practice 13.1

Practice With Chi-Square Goodness of Fit

1. a. minimum size = 15; chi-square goodness of fit for equal frequencies

   b. minimum size = 15; chi-square goodness of fit for unequal frequencies

   c. minimum size = 10; chi-square goodness of fit for equal frequencies

2. A chi-square goodness of fit for equal frequencies was computed.

   a. Null: The number of graduates working in for-profit, non-profit, or unemployed will not be different from expected (33.3% in each area).

   Alternative: The number of graduates working in the three areas will be different from expected. OR The number of graduates working in for-profit will be greater than expected.

   b. State the test (chi-square goodness of fit with equal frequencies, the result $\chi^2(2, N = 60) = 7.30$, $p = .03$. Note that the frequencies deviated from expected (33.3% or 20), and state the expected and observed frequencies for each of the 3 categories (e.g., 29 graduates worked in for-profit which was greater than the 20 expected, etc.).

   c. State that the number of graduates working in the three areas deviated from the expected number, with more than expected working in for-profit and fewer than expected were unemployed. The number working in non-profit matched the expected number. Think of a reason why this finding may have occurred. Compare your findings to the literature on employment status of college graduates. Note any weakness in the study and future research that would add to your findings.

Practice 13.2

Practice With Different Types of Chi-Square

1. a. There is no contingency table as there is only one variable—age with three categories.

    The minimum sample size is 15 (3 categories × 5).

    The appropriate test is χ^2 goodness of fit.

    No effect size is computed with χ^2 goodness of fit.

    b. This is a 2 × 2 contingency table.

    The minimum sample size is 20 because there are 4 cells × 5.

    The appropriate test is χ^2 test for independence.

    The phi squared (ϕ^2) is the appropriate test for effect size in a 2 × 2 contingency table.

    c. This is a 4 × 3 contingency table.

    The minimum sample size is 60 because there are 12 cells.

    The appropriate test is χ^2 test for independence.

    The Cramer's V^2 is the appropriate test for the effect size when the number of rows and columns are not equal in a contingency table.

    d. There is no contingency table as there is only one variable—use of opioids with two categories (extended time or no extended time).

    The minimum sample size is 10.

    The appropriate test is χ^2 goodness of fit.

    No effect size is computed for a χ^2 goodness of fit test.

2. a. Chi-square test for independence.

    b. H_0: There is no relationship between wearing a hijab and being bullied.

    H_a: There is a relationship between wearing a hijab and being bullied.

    c. Your results should include:

    the variables being analyzed—wearing a hijab, being bullied

    the type of analysis—chi-square test for independence and phi squared for effect size the results of the analysis and whether they were signficant—the results are significant, $\chi^2(1, N = 40) = 4.83, p < .028, \phi^2 = .12$

if results are significant, a description of the relationship that was found including the frequencies—more students wearing a hijab ($N = 16$, approximately 76%) were bullied than students not wearing a hijab ($N = 5$, approximately 24%).

all results reported in APA format

d. The Discussion should include:

review of the main finding(s) and whether your results support or do not support the alternative hypothesis

note of whether the results are consistent with past research

interpretation of the effect size and its implications

the practical significance of your findings

discussion of possible flaws in your study and/or next steps in the research topic

Practice 13.3

Identifying Appropriate Statistics for Nominal Data

1. Chi-square goodness of fit—one variable with independent three levels; measure is nominal.

2. McNemar test—two dependent variables with repeated measures.

3. Chi-square test for independence—two variables each with independent levels measured on nominal scale; study is assessing the relationship between the variables.

4. Cochran Q test—one variable with three dependent groups (repeated measures); measure is dichotomous.

Practice 13.4

Identifying Appropriate Statistics for Ordinal Data

1. Friedman χ^2—there is one variable with four dependent groups (repeated measures), and the data are ordinal. We meet the criteria for $n > 10/\text{group}$.

2. Spearman's rho—we want to know the correlation between two sets of rankings.

3. Mann-Whitney U test—there is one variable with two independent groups, and we have fewer than 20 participants per group.

CHAPTER 14

Practice 14.1

Single N Designs

1. This is an AB design.

2. Graphed results:

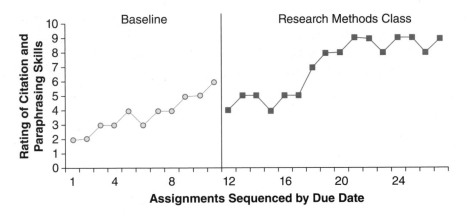

3. The Research Methods class is associated with improvements in the student's skill level. During the semester in which the student took the research class, his skill level first stabilized between a level 4 and 5 but then increased steadily and then stabilized between the 8 and 9 level.

4. There are two major limitations that keep us from concluding that the Research Methods class caused the improvements. First, the baseline was not stable prior to intervention, and the trend was in the same direction as the expected results of the class. The improvement may have simply been a continuation of the baseline trend. Second, alternative explanations for causality cannot be ruled out with an AB design. Something else may have changed in the student's life that caused the observed improvement in citation and paraphrasing skills.

5. The student may consider an ABA reversal design by analyzing the semester after the Research Methods class. There are a few problems with this, however. We would expect, and hope, that if the research class did cause improvements in citation and paraphrasing skills, there would be long-lasting results that would carry over into the next semester.

   An ABAB reversal design would be problematic because it would require taking the Research Methods class again (something most students would probably not want to do if they successfully passed the class the first time). Additionally, the ceiling effect would be a problem because the student had already leveled off at a level of 8 or 9 out of 10.

A multiple-baseline-across-persons design may work. A researcher could collect data for several students entering the college at the same time, but taking Research Methods at different semesters. Comparing the patterns across these different students may help demonstrate that the class, rather than some other factor, caused improvements.

CHAPTER 15

Practice 15.1

Choosing a Research Design

1. a. This is a question to assess prevalence, and therefore the descriptive design would be the best choice.

   b. This requires in-depth examination of a single phenomenon (code of conduct), and therefore a descriptive design would be the best choice. If we also wanted to know if professors and students differed in their codes of conduct, or if there are gender differences in attitudes and behaviors, we would add a correlational design to our study.

   c. Because we would be examining stable traits (personality), the correlational design would be best to answer these questions.

   d. This question requires examining the relationship between use of social media, climate, and motivation. We might choose a correlational design because this research area is relatively new and we want to establish a correlation prior to examining causality, or we might choose a correlational design if we believe external validity should be a primary goal. On the other hand, if we wanted to test a cause-and-effect relationship and we had a good way to manipulate the IV (use of social media) and randomly assign participants to conditions, we would choose an experiment. If we could manipulate the IV but not randomly assign, we would do a quasi-experiment instead.

Practice 15.2

Deciding Between the Independent- and Dependent-Groups Designs

1. a. No. We plan to group professors into either the high extraversion group or the low extraversion group based on their responses to an extraversion scale.

   b. Independent-groups design

   c. We must consider if we have a good matching variable, and if we could assess the variable without biasing the study. If so, a matched-groups design would be the best choice.

2. It is possible for participants to read all three scenarios, but we need to consider if it would be wise to have them do so. We might have some concerns about carry-over effects, but we could address those with counterbalancing. We could make an argument for any of the three choices from Table 15.1. Repeated measures would be the best choice if participants were scarce or we had concerns about within-groups error, and if we did not believe sensitization or fatigue would be an issue. Matching would be the best choice if power were an issue (due to sample size or within-groups error), we had concerns about sensitization or fatigue, and we had a good matching variable that we could assess without biasing our participants. If matching would not work, we could do an independent-groups design.

Practice 15.3

Selecting Appropriate Statistical Analyses

1. One-sample t test with Cohen's d for the effect size

2. Independent-samples t test, with either a point-biserial correlation or Cohen's d for the effect size.

3. Chi-square test of independence, with phi-squared as a measure of effect size.

4. One-way dependent-samples ANOVA, with η^2 or partial η^2 as a measure of effect. Run post hoc tests if ANOVA result (F) is statistically significant.

5. One-way independent-samples ANOVA, with η^2 or partial η^2 as a measure of effect. Run post hoc tests if ANOVA result (F) is statistically significant.

6. Two-way ANOVA, with η^2 or partial η^2 as a measure of effect. If the interaction is statistically significant, we may run planned post hoc analyses to determine if simple relationships are statistically significant.

Appendix B

APA Style and Format Guidelines

These guidelines are based on the 6th edition of the *Publication Manual of the American Psychological Association* (APA, 2010b).

WRITING AN APA-STYLE RESEARCH REPORT

In Chapter 2, we discussed how to read an APA-style primary research article and introduced you to the major sections of a research article and their purposes. Following is a brief review:

- Title—A concise description of the study, including key variables examined

- Abstract—A concise summary of the entire report, including purpose, method, and results

- Introduction—A review of past research that builds a rationale for the current study, describes how the study will address limitations or fill gaps of past research, and lists the questions or hypotheses that are the focus of the study

- Method—A summary of the participants (or subjects), procedures, and materials

- Results—Detailed results of the study, including results of any statistical significance and effect size analyses

- Discussion—An overview of key results, how they fit with past research, implications and practical significance of the results, limitations, and directions for future research

- References—A list of all the sources cited in the report

All of these sections will be present when you write your own research report. You will want to follow the same guidelines for organizing the report so that the introduction, method, results, and discussion flow into the hourglass shape we discussed in Chapter 2 (see Figure A2.1). The key difference is that the order you write your report will be different from the order in which you read primary research articles. Additionally, you will likely first write a proposal prior to carrying out your study.

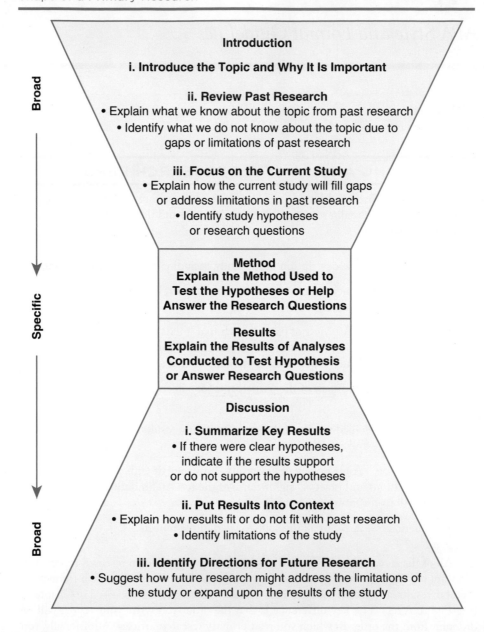

STEPS IN WRITING A RESEARCH PROPOSAL AND REPORT

These steps should serve as guidelines for writing your report, and like the steps in the scientific method, they are not purely linear. You may revisit previous steps many times throughout the writing process in order to develop a cohesive research report.

1. Prepare to write:

   a. Read past research on your topic.

   b. Decide how you can design a study to fill a gap or address a limitation of past research.

   c. Formulate your hypothesis(es).

2. Write a proposal that includes a title, introduction, and proposed Method and data analysis (see Figure A2.1). Include a reference section that includes all the sources you cited.

3. Submit your proposal for review and IRB approval, revising and resubmitting as necessary. Carry out your study after receiving approval, and analyze your data.

4. Write the Results and Discussion section (see Figure A2.1).

5. Revise the Introduction and Method section so that the paper flows from broad to narrow. Be sure the Method is updated to reflect what you actually did, not just what you expected to do.

6. Write the Abstract.

7. Update the references and title as necessary.

10 COMMON MISTAKES AND HOW TO FIX THEM

1. Mistake: Assuming you are writing the paper to your professor and he or she knows exactly what you did

   The Fix: Write the report so that a student or professor from a college across the country could understand what you did. At the same time, avoid including details that are not useful in understanding your study (such as the specific ways you named your variables in a data analysis program).

2. Mistake: Suggesting that you or past researchers "proved" something

   The Fix: Remember that we do not prove anything in science so instead use words like "suggests," "indicates," or "supports."

3. Mistake: Relying on a computer program to find spelling or grammatical errors or to format your references

The Fix: You should definitely run spell-check and grammar-check, but you should also read over the paper to check for typos, and catch spelling and grammatical errors that the computer program missed.

You can use a program to help you format your citations and references in APA format, but there is a high likelihood there will be mistakes (such as incorrect capitalization). Review the citations and references and correct errors.

4. Mistake: Writing long, awkward, vague, or redundant sentences

The Fix: Be clear, concise, and precise. Edit to remove words or phrases that are not necessary to understanding your report. One experienced writer has suggested that you delete about one-third of what you have written in order to achieve this goal (Bem, 2003).

5. Mistake: Using the wrong verb tense for proposals and research reports

The Fix: Use future tense in the Method section of a research proposal (e.g., *We will recruit participants*).

Use past tense when referring to specific research that has already been completed, such as in the introduction of a proposal or report (e.g., *These researchers found that . . .*) or in the Method, Results, and Discussion of your own research report (e.g., *We recruited participants . . .; We found that . . .*).

Use present tense when referring to events that have no clear end point (e.g., *past researchers have used this method . . .; future studies might examine . . .*).

6. Mistake: Overuse of the passive voice (e.g., *The study was conducted . . .*)

The Fix: Use the active voice (e.g., *We conducted the study . . .*), unless doing so changes the meaning or focus of the sentence.

7. Mistake: Confusing "effect" and "affect"

The Fix: Use "effect" as a noun (e.g., *Television may have an effect on aggression*); use "affect" as a verb (e.g., *Television may affect aggression*). Affect is a noun only when referring to emotional expression (e.g., *He had a flat affect*).

8. Mistake: Incorrect presentation of numbers

The Fix: Use words for numbers that start a sentence (e.g., *Seventy participants took surveys*) or are less than 10 (e.g., *There were three groups*). When the number doesn't start the sentence, use digits for statistics, number of participants, numbers 10 and over, or numbers in a series in which at least one number is 10 or above (e.g., *There were 47 children who ranged in age from 7 to 15 [*M = 10.60*, SD = 2.56]*).

9. Mistake: Incorrect spacing and paragraph indentations

The Fix: Double space throughout the proposal or report, including the reference section. Do not add extra spaces between paragraphs.

Include a space after punctuation marks such as commas, colons, semicolons, and periods (unless it is part of an abbreviation, or after "doi:" in references).

Indent each paragraph five to seven spaces (with the exception of the abstract, which is not indented).

10. Mistake: Omitting a comma before the "and" in a list of three or more (e.g., *We included pictures of the animals, Brad Pitt and Angelina Jolie.*).

The Fix: Always include a comma before the "and" in a list of three or more (e.g., *We included pictures of the animals, Brad Pitt, and Angelina Jolie.*). As in this example, not doing so can greatly change the meaning of the sentence.

And . . . one *big* but hopefully uncommon, mistake: Plagiarizing.

The Fix: Avoid plagiarism. This goes without saying, but people sometimes inadvertently plagiarize material (particularly when they are writing papers at the last minute!). Give yourself plenty of time to read and process the material before writing about it. When taking notes, summarize the material in your own words rather than copying directly.

Make sure you give credit to any sources you used.

If you copy anything directly from a source, you must put the words within quotation marks and include the page numbers from the source. However, direct quotes are *very* rare in research reports.

APA FORMAT FOR CITATIONS WITHIN YOUR PAPER

First Time Cited

One author:

- Schuetze (2004) examined . . .
- Citation knowledge can be improved with a brief homework assignment (Schuetze, 2004).

Two to five authors: Use the ampersand (&) within parentheses; use "and" outside parentheses.

- Belter and du Pré (2009) found similar results.
- Exercises requiring students to paraphrase work might reduce plagiarism (Landau, Druen, & Arcuri, 2002).

Six or more authors: Cite only the last name of the first author, followed by "et al." (or "et al.,") and the year of publication.

- Gilbert et al. (2004) examined . . .
- . . . (Gilbert et al., 2004).

To cite multiple references, cite authors in alphabetical order, separate with a semicolon (;):

Researchers have found that hands-on experience is more effective than providing explanations or resources about academic dishonesty (Belter & du Pré, 2009; Culwin, 2006; Estow, Lawrence, & Adams, 2011; Schuetze, 2004).

Citing the Same Article Later in the Paper

One or two authors: Use the same format as for the first citation.

Three or more authors: Include only the first author's last name followed by "et al." (or "et al.,") and the year of publication:

- Estow et al. (2011) suggested . . .

- Examining plagiarism as an academic topic may improve students' ability to avoid plagiarism (Estow et al., 2011).

What About Secondary Sources?

Use sparingly and only when necessary.

Suppose that you want to use a 1989 study by Nguyen and Lee, which you read about in a 1996 study by Becker and Seligman. Use one of the following citations:

- Nguyen and Lee (as cited in Becker & Seligman, 1996) found the opposite effect in two-year-olds.

- The opposite effect was observed in two-year-olds (Nguyen & Lee, as cited in Becker & Seligman, 1996).

In the References, list only Becker and Seligman (the source that you read).

APA FORMAT FOR REFERENCES

Journal Article

- What to include:
  - Author(s) names [last name followed by comma, initial(s) followed by a period]
  - Date of publication, in parentheses
  - Article title
  - Journal title and volume
  - Do not include issue number unless the journal begins numbering each issue with page 1.
  - Page numbers of article
  - doi number, if available

- Formatting the reference:
  - Do not indent the first line of the reference, but indent all subsequent lines of that reference (this is called a "hanging indent").
  - For articles with multiple authors: Keep the order of authors the same as it appears in the article, separate the authors by commas, and use both a comma and an ampersand (&) before the last author.
  - For the article title, capitalize only the first letter of the first word, the first word after a colon or other punctuation, or proper names.
  - For the journal title, capitalize the first letter of all the main words (e.g., not "of" or "and").
  - Italicize the journal title and the volume number.
  - Put a period after the parenthesized date, after the article title, and after the page numbers, but not after the doi number or URL addresses.
  - Use an en dash (–) in page number ranges.
  - Use a comma to separate the journal title, volume, and page numbers.
  - Put a space after any punctuation, with the exception of the colon after "doi."

One author:

Schuetze, P. (2004). Evaluation of a brief homework assignment designed to reduce citation

problems. *Teaching of Psychology, 31,* 257–259. doi:10.1207/s15328023top31046

Two authors:

Belter, R. W., & du Pré, A. (2009). A strategy to reduce plagiarism in an undergraduate course.

Teaching of Psychology, 36, 257–261. doi:10.1080/00986280903173165

Three to seven authors:

Landau, J. D., Druen, P. B., & Arcuri, J. A. (2002). Methods for helping students avoid plagiarism.

Teaching of Psychology, 29, 112–115. doi:10.1207/S15328023TOP2902_06

More than seven authors:

Gilbert, D. G., McClernon, J. F., Rabinovich, N. E., Sugai, C., Plath, L. C., Asgaard, G., . . .

Botros, N. (2004). Effects of quitting smoking on EEG activation and attention last for more

than 31 days and are more severe with stress, dependence, DRD2 A1 allele, and depressive

traits. *Nicotine and Tobacco Research, 6,* 249–267. doi:10.1080/14622200410001676304

The majority of the references for your research proposal or report should be primary research articles published in academic journals. However, you may use a book, chapter, or website to supplement the primary research you cite.

Book or Book Chapter

Book by one author:

Pollan, M. (1998). *A place of my own: The education of an amateur builder.* New York, NY: Delta.

Book by two or more authors:

Meyer, A. L., Farrell, A. D., Northup, W., Kung, E., & Plybon, L. (2000). *Promoting non-violence in middle schools: Responding in peaceful and positive ways.* New York, NY: Plenum Press.

Chapter in an edited book:

Hook, M. (2006). The family Simpson. In A. Brown & C. Logan (Eds.), *The psychology of the Simpsons* (pp. 1–20). Dallas, TX: Benbella.

Website

Author and date are available:

Lawrence, E. K. (2007). *Analyzing data using SPSS: A guide for psychology students.* Retrieved from http://www.guilford.edu/classes/psy/elawrenc/research.html

If there is no author available, use the name of the organization as the author:

American Psychological Association. (2001). *APA style: Frequently asked questions.* Retrieved from http://www.apastyle.org/faqs.html#10

If there is no date available, use "(n.d.)":

Pew Research Center. (n.d.). *Random digit dialing: Our standard method.* Retrieved from http://www.people-press.org/methodology/sampling/random-digit-dialing-our-standard-method/

Conference Presentation

Adams, K. A., Lawrence, E. K., & Estow, S. (2012, October). *A successful model: Combining a research methods and analysis course with a practicum.* Symposium presented at the National Best Practices in the Teaching of Psychology, Atlanta, GA.

APA Format for the Reference Section

When listing multiple sources in the reference section, you should

- Start the reference section on a new page, titled References (centered, not bolded).

- Alphabetize the list by the last name of the first author.

- Double space evenly throughout the references.

- See the reference section of the following manuscript for an example.

On the following pages is an example APA-style research report in manuscript form with some comments about formatting and style. This is what your research report should look like.

EXAMPLE OF AN APA-STYLE MANUSCRIPT

Running head: PRACTICE MAKES PERFECT   1

> Include a page number in the right corner of the header on all pages.

> In the heading, type the words –
> Running head: and then include a shortened version of your title, all in capital letters. The running head is limited to 50 characters, including spaces.
>
> On subsequent pages, the running head will appear *without the words "Running head." To set this up, you will need to indicate "different first page" for the design of the header*

Practice Makes Perfect:

Improving Students' Skills in Understanding and Avoiding Plagiarism

Sarah Estow, Eva K. Lawrence, and Kathrynn A. Adams

Guilford College

> The title is centered in the middle of the title page. It should be concise and descriptive.

> The author(s) appear on the next line.

> The name of the college/university/institution appears on the next line.

Authors' Note

Sarah Estow, Department of Psychology, Guilford College; Eva Kung Lawrence, Department of Psychology, Guilford College; Kathrynn Adams, Department of Psychology, Guilford College.

   Correspondence concerning this article should be addressed to Sarah Estow, Department of Psychology, Guilford College, 5800 W. Friendly Avenue, Greensboro, NC 27410. E-mail: sestow@guilford.edu

> The Author Note is required for articles submitted for publication.
>
> *Students typically do not need to include an Author Note on research reports turned in for course credit.*

Abstract

Plagiarism is a growing problem on college campuses, despite instructors'
best efforts. To address this issue, students in two undergraduate Research
Methods and Analysis courses investigated the topic of plagiarism for
a semester. They wrote literature reviews and conducted, analyzed, and
wrote up original research on plagiarism. At the start and end of the
semester, students ($N = 27$) completed a homework assignment to assess
plagiarism knowledge and paraphrasing skills. Results showed that
students' ability to paraphrase correctly and to recognize faulty
paraphrasing improved. At posttest, students often indicated education is
important in reducing plagiarism and noted ethical reasons for avoiding
plagiarism, suggesting that repeated hands-on exposure to the topic
of plagiarism improves plagiarism avoidance and understanding.

Keywords: college students, ethics, plagiarism, teaching

Unlike other paragraphs in the report, the beginning of the abstract is *not* indented.

The abstract is a concise and accurate description of your paper in about 150 words.

The abstract should include the number of participants, the basic procedures, and the key results.

Indent the keywords line. Italicize the word *Keywords*, and after the colon type 3–5 words that others might use to find your article in electronic searches.

Practice Makes Perfect:

Improving Students' Skills in Understanding and Avoiding Plagiarism ◄———

We in academia are currently "at war" with academically dishonest acts, including plagiarism (Leask, 2006). By many accounts, plagiarism is a pervasive problem that is becoming only more prevalent on college campuses (Lim & See, 2001; Macdonald & Carroll, 2006; Roig, 1997; Schuetze, 2004). While few students would argue that it is dishonest to copy an entire paper and pass it off as one's own work, many students do not recognize that citation and proper paraphrasing are key components of researching with integrity (Roig, 1997). One study revealed that 90% of the college student participants reported having failed to acknowledge the original source material in written work (Lim & See, 2001). While one might interpret the lack of citation as a sign that students knowingly flout the rules of good academic work, it is quite likely that this behavior is driven by a lack of understanding that omitting sources is improper practice (Culwin, 2006; Landau, Druen, & Arcuri, 2002). Although many institutions have official and accessible academic codes of conduct, these codes often lack sufficient detail and clarity about what exactly constitutes academic dishonesty (Leask, 2006; Roig, 2001). As a result, students are often left, for better or worse, to figure out the implications and consequences of such codes on their own.

If it is a lack of knowledge about proper paraphrasing and citation that drives many students to commit plagiarism, one obvious solution would be educating them on the topic (Culwin, 2006; Lim & See, 2001; Schuetze, 2004). However, research shows that merely lecturing to students and/or providing resources explaining what academic dishonesty is and how to avoid it are not as effective as hands-on experience (Culwin, 2006; Macdonald & Carroll, 2006; Schuetze, 2004).

While there is evidence that even a brief homework assignment on plagiarism can reduce its occurrence (Schuetze, 2004), we were interested in the possible added benefit of a semester-long investigation of plagiarism as a base topic for a set of varied assignments in a Research Methods and Analysis course. This represents a more immersive approach than previous research that examined how lectures and student exercises explicitly geared toward instructing on the topic of plagiarism affect plagiarism-detection skills (Landau et al., 2002; Schuetze, 2004).

The Introduction starts on a new page.

The title of the paper appears, centered, at the beginning of the Introduction.

The Introduction starts out with a broad problem or observation.

This is followed by a review of past research on the topic.

Notice that the Introduction is organized around key concepts—studies are *not* simply listed one after the next.

Sources are cited within the text using APA format.

When citing multiple sources within parentheses, list the citations in alphabetical order and separate them with a semicolon.

As the Introduction continues, notice that the authors demonstrate how their study will build on and expand past research. In other words, they lay out their rationale for their study.

Using a common theme in a research methods course can provide course continuity, a shared, and therefore larger, participant pool, and quality control in the use of primary research articles (Marek, Christopher, & Walker, 2004). Marek et al. (2004) used academic ethics as a theme and found that it was an effective way to teach students research concepts, statistical analyses, communication of research findings, and critical thinking skills. They did not, however, examine whether students' understanding and application of ethics was impacted by studying the topic throughout the semester. We expected that using plagiarism as a common theme in our research methods and analysis course would change the way that students viewed plagiarism as well as improve their skills in avoiding plagiarism.

Method

Participants

Forty-three undergraduate psychology majors at a small liberal arts college in the Southeast took part in this study. They were all enrolled in one of two sections of a Research Methods and Analysis course, which covers basic research methods and statistical techniques. This is considered an upper-level course, and most students (79%) were juniors or first semester seniors.

Procedure

The students who participated in this study complete their work under a college-wide academic honor code that is described in an online student handbook. Included in the syllabus for this course is a reminder that all work should be done according to the principles in the honor code, and students are referred to the Student Handbook should they have any questions.

Early in the semester, the students completed a homework assignment that asked them to list strategies for avoiding plagiarism and reasons why it is important to do so. Students were also presented with a sentence taken from Schuetze (2004) about plagiarism. They were asked both to paraphrase the sentence themselves and to identify which of three versions of the same sentence were examples of plagiarism. We provided prompt feedback on this assignment and led a class discussion on common misperceptions of plagiarism.

At the end of the Introduction, the authors state their hypotheses.

Method

Method is singular, centered, and bolded. This section follows right after the Introduction.

Do not start a new page.

The Method includes a description of the participants, procedures, and measures (or materials).

Notice that here the measures are described within the procedure subsection, although you may choose to have a separate subsection called Measures or Materials.

Notice also the format of the subheadings: bold and left-justified.

As we covered various study designs and statistical analyses during the semester, the students were required to use plagiarism as their topic. First, they analyzed an article on plagiarism (Schuetze, 2004) to learn more about reading primary research articles. Next, students conducted interviews with four participants regarding their knowledge of plagiarism and wrote up a report, including a literature review, in APA format. The class then helped develop a survey to further examine knowledge and attitudes about intentional and unintentional plagiarism. Students distributed four surveys each and the data were combined into a shared file. They then analyzed the dataset and wrote a full research report. Finally, students conducted experimental research on the topic, analyzed their data as both a simple and factorial design, and wrote up their findings.

At the completion of each assignment, we discussed our findings and identified new questions that helped us to segue into the next research project. For example, the results of the interviews helped to form some of the questions for the survey. We provided several primary research articles on plagiarism, and students also were required to find additional primary sources on their own. Several variables were included in the studies to allow students to choose a focus based on the research they read. At the end of the semester, students completed a homework assignment that once again included questions about how and why to avoid plagiarism. They were given a sentence taken from an article on plagiarism (Bennett, 2005) and both paraphrased the sentence themselves as well as identified which of three versions of the same sentence represented plagiarism.

Results

> **Results**
> Results are plural, centered, and bolded. This section follows the Method. Do not start a new page.

From the 43 participants, both pre- and posttest data were available for 27 participants (15 provided only pre-test data and 1 provided only posttest data). The majority of this attrition was due to students' withdrawing from the class ($n = 13$), although three students simply failed to turn in the homework assignment.

We counted the number of sentences correctly identified as plagiarism on both homework assignments. Results of a paired-samples t test indicated that the number of correctly-identified paraphrasing errors significantly increased from the first homework ($M = 1.52$, $SD = .98$) to the second ($M = 2.59$, $SD = .75$), $t(26) = -4.63$, $p < .001$.

To ensure that those students for whom only pre-test data are available did not differ significantly from those who completed both measures, an independent-samples t test was run comparing the initial scores for those that continued on with the class ($M = 1.52$, $SD = .98$) to those who dropped the course or did not turn in the second assignment ($M = 1.67$, $SD = .90$), $t(40) = -.48$, $p = .09$. Those who completed both homework assignments did not differ from those who did not in their initial ability to identify faulty paraphrasing.

We rated the students' own paraphrasing of the source sentence on a 4-point scale (1 = *direct copying of a significant portion of the original without quotation marks*; 2 = *no direct copying but missing citation*; 3 = *technically correct but poorly written*; 4 = *good paraphrasing*). One student did not answer this question on the pre-test. A paired-samples t test on the remaining 26 students indicated significant improvement from the first homework ($M = 2.54$, $SD = .86$) to the second ($M = 3.23$, $SD = .86$), $t(25) = -3.99$, $p < .01$. The pre-test paraphrasing for these students did not vary significantly from those who did not have post-test scores available ($M = 2.67$, $SD = .64$), $t(36) = -.46$, $p = .65$.

McNemar's nonparametric tests were used to compare the strategies to avoid plagiarism listed by our students on the first and second homework assignments. Students were significantly more likely to suggest in the post-test that education (i.e., practice, seeking help from instructors, or formal instruction) was important to help avoid plagiarism. Of the 27 students who turned in both assignments, only three listed this as a strategy on the first homework whereas 15 listed this on the second, $\chi^2(1) = 8.64$, $p = .003$.

The majority of students indicated that avoiding punishment was a major reason to avoid plagiarism on both the first assignment (67%) and second (56%), and McNemar's test indicated that there was no significant change across time, $\chi^2(1) = .11$, $p = .58$. However, students were more likely to add that plagiarism should be avoided because it is unethical (i.e., it hurts the original author, the college, or the field of psychology) on the second homework assignment. Seventeen out of 27 listed this additional reason on the first assignment, and 26 out of 27 listed it on the second, $\chi^2(1) = 7.11$, $p = .004$.

Discussion

Our results indicate that giving students hands-on experience and repeated exposure to the topic of plagiarism can improve their ability to identify faulty paraphrasing when presented with examples, to improve their own paraphrasing, and to deepen their understanding of why one should avoid plagiarism.

The Results section includes an explanation of what statistical analyses were used and provides the specific results.

Notice the specific statistical notation and formatting used. For example, statistical abbreviations and symbols such as M, SD, t, p, and χ^2 are always italicized and there is a space before and after an equal sign ($=$).

Write out numbers when they start a sentence.

Discussion begins the next section and is centered and bolded. Do not start on a new page.

Our findings are encouraging in that immersing students in the topic of plagiarism had clear benefits and improved their skills significantly. Moreover, this immersion appears to have changed the way that students conceptualize plagiarism. It is not surprising that at the end of the semester more students noted the importance of education as a way to avoid plagiarism, given that our first article (Schuetze, 2004) focused on this subject and the class studies examined intentional versus unintentional plagiarism. However, students were never explicitly told that education or practice was the "correct" strategy to avoid plagiarism, nor were they aware that they would be completing the homework assignment at the end of the semester. The students' inclusion of educational strategies on the homework assignment at the end of the semester may therefore represent their internalization of the subject studied. Although we had several discussions on the ethical issues surrounding plagiarism during the semester, ethics were not a focus of study. On the first assignment, students were more likely to focus exclusively on punishment, and their responses often mirrored the college handbook. The fact that all but one student raised the ethical problem with plagiarism at the end of the semester suggests a deeper consideration of this subject.

One limitation of this study is that there was no control group that spent the semester researching a different topic. While it is possible that merely completing a semester of college improved plagiarism identification scores from pre- to post-test independent of the topic covered, it seems unlikely that that alone would have resulted in the improvement we saw. Barry (2006) examined the effects of several homework assignments on plagiarism knowledge with a control group, and found the control group showed little incidental learning over the course of the semester relative to the experimental group who received the practice. We are therefore fairly certain that our course's central theme was responsible for the improved performance and recommend this method to others teaching students about methodological and/or statistical issues in psychology.

Because plagiarism is a widespread issue on college campuses (e.g., Macdonald & Carroll, 2006; Schuetze, 2004) it is important that pedagogical research focus on ways to educate students about plagiarism and teach specific strategies to avoid this ethical violation. Using plagiarism as a theme in a research-focused course is one strategy that may help to curb plagiarism and help students understand the importance of paraphrasing and accurately citing others' work.

The Discussion starts out narrow and gets broad.

Then the Discussion explains how these results fit (or don't fit) with past research. Notice that the authors refer back to specific studies and cite their sources using APA format.

In other words, it starts by explaining the results of the study (without using statistics).

Toward the end of the Discussion, the authors note limitations and suggest ideas for future research.

Discussions typically end with a few, brief comments about the importance of the study and the findings.

References

Barry, E. S. (2006). Can paraphrasing practice help students define plagiarism? *College Student Journal, 40,* 377–384.

Bennett, R. (2005). Factors associated with student plagiarism in a post-1992 university. *Assessment & Evaluation in Higher Education, 30,* 137–162. doi:10.1080/0260293042000264244

Landau, J. D., Druen, P. B., & Arcuri, J. A. (2002). Methods for helping students avoid plagiarism. *Teaching of Psychology, 29,* 112–115. doi:10.1207/S15328023TOP2902_06

Leask, B. (2006). Plagiarism, cultural diversity and metaphor— implications for academic staff development. *Assessment & Evaluation in Higher Education, 31,* 183–199. doi:10. 1080/02602930500262486

Lim, V. K. G., & See, S. K. B. (2001). Attitudes toward, and intentions to report, academic cheating among students in Singapore. *Ethics & Behavior, 11,* 261–274. doi:10.1207/S15327019EB1103_5

Macdonald, R., & Carroll, J. (2006). Plagiarism: A complex issue requiring a holistic institutional approach. *Assessment & Evaluation in Higher Education, 31,* 233–245. doi:10.1080/02602930500262536

Marek, P., Christopher, A., & Walker, B. (2004). Learning by doing: Research methods with a theme. *Teaching of Psychology, 31,* 128–131.

Roig, M. (1997). Can undergraduate students determine whether text has been plagiarized? *Psychological Record, 47,* 113–122.

Roig, M. (2001). Plagiarism and paraphrasing criteria of college and university professors. *Ethics & Behavior, 11,* 307–323. doi:10.1207/ S15327019EB1103_8

Schuetze, P. (2004). Evaluation of a brief homework assignment designed to reduce citation problems. *Teaching of Psychology, 31,* 257–259. doi:10.1207/s15328023top31046

References start on a new page, and is centered and *not* bolded.

Notice the format of the references, for example:

- The first line of each reference hangs over the rest (this is called the hanging indent).
- The list is evenly double-spaced (there are no extra spaces between references).
- The list is alphabetized by the last name of the 1st author.

Table 1

Comparisons Between Student Scores on First and Second Homework Assignments

	First Assignment (Pre-Test)	*Second Assignment (Post-Test)*
Paraphrasing Errors Identified***	$M = 1.52$, $SD = 0.98$	$M = 2.59$, $SD = 0.75$
Ratings of Student's Paraphrasing**	$M = 2.54$, $SD = .86$	$M = 3.23$, $SD = .86$
Number of Students Who Listed Ethical Reasons for Not Plagiarizing**	$n = 3$	$n = 15$

Note. **Difference is significant at $p < .01$; ***Difference is significant at $p < .001$.

Additional material, such as the measures used in your study, may be included in an appendix (or appendices).

An appendix should start on a new page, after the References and any tables or figures.

If you have one appendix, simply label it as: **Appendix**.
If you have multiple appendices, start each on a new page and use labels **Appendix A, Appendix B,** etc. Note that tables and figures are labeled with numbers and appendices are labeled with letters.

Tables and figures are presented after the References section, and each should appear on a separate page.

A table or a figure is a very useful way to summarize important information in your study.

Following is the final, published version of the manuscript. Notice that not only is the look of the paper quite different, the content has changed as well. This is because the paper went through the peer-review process, and we made changes to the original manuscript based on the reviewers' feedback.

SOCIETY FOR THE TEACHING
OF PSYCHOLOGY

Practice Makes Perfect: Improving Students' Skills in Understanding and Avoiding Plagiarism With a Themed Methods Course

Teaching of Psychology
38(4) 255-258
© The Author(s) 2011
Reprints and permission:
sagepub.com/journalsPermissions.nav
DOI: 10.1177/0098628311421323
http://top.sagepub.com

SSAGE

Sarah Estow[1], Eva K. Lawrence[1], and Kathrynn A. Adams[1]

Abstract

To address the issue of plagiarism, students in two undergraduate Research Methods and Analysis courses conducted, analyzed, and wrote up original research on the topic of plagiarism. Students in an otherwise identical course completed the same assignments but examined a different research topic. At the start and end of the semester, all students ($n = 44$) completed a homework assignment assessing plagiarism knowledge and paraphrasing skills. Students in the plagiarism-themed courses showed improvement in both knowledge and skills, and the strategies they suggested for avoiding plagiarism became more sophisticated as did the reasons for avoiding plagiarism. The control group did not show the same improvements. Results suggest repeated hands-on exposure to the topic of plagiarism improves plagiarism avoidance and understanding.

Keywords

academic integrity, plagiarism reduction, paraphrasing

Educators are currently "at war" with academically dishonest acts, including plagiarism (Leask, 2006). By many accounts, plagiarism is a pervasive problem that is only becoming more prevalent on college campuses (Lim & See, 2001; Macdonald & Carroll, 2006; Pickard, 2006; Roig, 1997; Roig & Caso, 2005; Schuetze, 2004). Although most students would agree that it is dishonest to copy an entire paper and submit it as one's own work, many students do not recognize that citation and proper paraphrasing are key components of researching with integrity (Roig, 1997). For example, students in Singapore considered paraphrasing without a citation as the least serious type of academic cheating with 90% admitting that they had done so (Lim & See, 2001). One might interpret the lack of citation as a sign that students knowingly flout the rules of good academic work, but some evidence suggests that citation problems emanate from a lack of understanding (Belter & du Pré, 2009; Culwin, 2006; Landau, Druen, & Arcuri, 2002). Moreover, academic codes of conduct may lack sufficient detail and clarity about academic dishonesty (Leask, 2006; Roig, 2001). Faculty may disagree about whether specific behaviors (e.g., self-plagiarism) constitute plagiarism (K. K. Bennett, Behrendt, & Boothby, 2011). Thus, students may be unsure about the guidelines for avoiding academic dishonesty and about its consequences.

If a lack of knowledge about proper paraphrasing and citation drives students to commit plagiarism, one obvious solution would be educating them on the topic (Belter & du Pré, 2009;

K. K. Bennett et al., 2011; Culwin, 2006; Lim & See, 2001; Schuetze, 2004). However, research shows that merely lecturing to students or providing resources explaining what academic dishonesty is and how to avoid it are not as effective as hands-on experience (Culwin, 2006; Macdonald & Carroll, 2006; Schuetze, 2004). For example, even a brief homework assignment on plagiarism can reduce its occurrence (Belter & du Pré, 2009; Schuetze, 2004).

Using a more immersive approach, we developed and implemented a semester-long plagiarism theme with multiple assignments in a methods and statistics course. Using a common theme in a research methods course provides course continuity, a larger, shared participant pool, and quality control in the use of primary research articles (Marek, Christopher, & Walker, 2004). We expected that using plagiarism as a common theme in our methods and statistics course would change the way that students viewed plagiarism as well as improve their skills in avoiding plagiarism.

---

[1] Guilford College, Greensboro, North Carolina, USA

Corresponding Author:
Sarah Estow, Psychology Department, Guilford College, 5800 W. Friendly Ave., Greensboro, NC 27410
Email: sestow@guilford.edu

Table 1. Course Assignments for Plagiarism Themed Course

Student Activity Related to Plagiarism	Details of Activity
Analyzed article (Schuetze, 2004)	Identified rationale, hypothesis, IV, DV, operational definition of plagiarism knowledge, findings, and future directions.
Conducted interviews	Questioned four participants regarding definition of plagiarism, confusion about plagiarism, reasons for plagiarism, and ways to reduce plagiarism.
Wrote APA-style report about interviews	Required citation to Schuetze (2004) and minimum of one additional source.
Developed survey and collected data	Surveyed four participants about their knowledge of, and attitudes toward, intentional and unintentional plagiarism.
Formulated descriptive hypotheses	One hypothesis pertained to the entire sample, and one compared subgroups of the sample.
Conducted descriptive analyses using SPSS	Selected appropriate variables and descriptive statistics based on hypotheses.
Wrote APA-style research report	Required information from at least two primary research articles.
Conducted experimental research	Used scenario to manipulate type of plagiarism (serious or minor) and intent (intentional or unintentional); DVs were perceived mood of student and professor and severity of punishment, with each student questioning four participants.
Analyzed data using SPSS and prepared experimental report	Selected one experimental IV, analyzed results using an independent-samples t test, wrote research report incorporating at least three primary research articles.
Analyzed data using SPSS and prepared second report	Selected two IVs (one possibly non-experimental), analyzed results using a two-way ANOVA, and wrote a research report incorporating at least four primary research articles

Note: The control group did the same assignments but focused on a different research topic.

Method

Participants

Forty-four undergraduate psychology majors in research methods courses at a small Southeastern liberal arts college completed the study by submitting both pre- and posttest data, 27 in the plagiarism theme condition (Spring 2007), and 17 in the nonplagiarism theme condition (Spring 2008). The cumulative GPAs for students in the plagiarism theme condition ($M = 2.85$, $SD = .53$) and in the nonplagiarism theme condition ($M = 3.09$, $SD = .43$) were similar, $t(42) = 1.61$, $p = .12$, $d = .51$. An additional 18 students provided only pretest data primarily because of withdrawals. The withdrawal rate was not atypical for this particular course.

Materials and Design

Students completed homework assignments at the beginning (pretest) and end (posttest) of both sections to assess knowledge of plagiarism. On both the pretest and posttest, students listed strategies for avoiding plagiarism and reasons why it was important to do so. Students also paraphrased a sentence about plagiarism and identified which of three versions listed below the original sentence illustrated plagiarism. For the pretest, the sentence to be paraphrased was taken from Schuetze (2004); for the posttest, it was taken from R. Bennett (2005). Appendix A illustrates the pre- and posttest materials.

Design and Procedure

The quasi-experimental study used a 2 (Time of Test: Pretest and Posttest) × 2 (Course Topic: Plagiarism or Nonplagiarism) mixed design. The syllabi included a statement that all work should be done according to the principles in the college-wide academic honor code and referred students to the student handbook for further information. Students in both conditions completed the identical pretest homework early in each semester. After the students turned in the pretest assignment, we discussed the importance of plagiarism avoidance in both conditions. In the plagiarism condition, as we covered various study designs and statistics during the semester, a variety of assignments were related to the plagiarism theme (see Table 1). In the nonplagiarism condition, the course structure and required assignments were the same. However, the assignments related to the effects of gender and ethnicity on teaching evaluations rather than to plagiarism. Students in both conditions completed the identical posttest homework at the end of the semester.

Results

We counted the number of sentences correctly identified as plagiarism on both homework assignments. Results of a 2 (Time) × 2 (Topic) mixed ANOVA revealed a significant interaction, $F(1, 42) = 9.19$, $p = .004$, $\eta^2 = .18$. Students in the plagiarism group had higher variance during pretest, although the mean scores between the classes on pretest were not significantly different, $t(38.51) = -1.97$, $p = .056$. At posttest, the plagiarism-themed class had higher scores than the control class, $t(42) = 2.42$, $p = .020$ (see Table 2).

One of the researchers rated the students' own paraphrasing of the source sentence on a 4-point scale from 1 (direct copying of a significant portion of the original without quotation marks) to 4 (good paraphrasing). The 2 × 2 mixed ANOVA results

Table 2. Assessment of Student Learning in Plagiarism-Themed Course Compared to a Control Course

	Pretest		Posttest	
Outcome:	Plagiarism Theme M *(SD)*	Control M *(SD)*	Plagiarism Theme M *(SD)*	Control M *(SD)*
Plagiarism identification	1.52 (0.98)	1.94 (0.43)	2.59 (0.75)	2.06 (0.66)
Quality of paraphrasing	2.54 (0.86)	3.12 (0.78)	3.23 (0.86)	2.82 (0.81)
Number of strategies	2.44 (0.93)	2.69 (0.60)	2.63 (1.18)	2.00 (0.73)

indicated a significant interaction between time and class topic, $F(1, 41) = 14.11$, $p = .001$, $\eta^2 = .26$. Students in the control course had significantly better paraphrasing scores than the plagiarism-themed course at pretest, $t(41) = -2.24$, $p = .03$. The plagiarism-themed course had higher scores at posttest, but this was not a statistically significant difference, $t(41) = 1.55$, $p = .13$ (see Table 2).

Students listed a variety of strategies for avoiding plagiarism, including citing sources and using quotation marks, improving time management, and seeking assistance. The 2 × 2 mixed ANOVA revealed a significant interaction, $F(1, 41) = 5.86$, $p = .02$, $\eta^2 = .13$. The plagiarism-themed class had a comparable number of strategies listed at pretest to the control class, $t(41) = -0.93$, $p = .36$, and had more variance and a higher mean number of strategies listed than the control at posttest, $t(40.88) = 2.16$, $p = .04$ (see Table 2).

McNemar's nonparametric tests were used to examine the specific strategies and reasons listed to avoid plagiarism. In the plagiarism-themed course, three (11%) listed education as a strategy on the first homework, whereas 15 (56%) listed this on the second homework, $\chi^2(1) = 8.64$, $p = .002$. On the other hand, only two (13%) in the control group listed educational strategies on both pre- and posttest, $\chi^2(1) = .50$, $p = 1.00$. On both the first and second assignment, the majority of students in the plagiarism-themed course (66% and 56%) and the control (69% and 88%) indicated that avoiding punishment was a major reason not to plagiarize. There was no significant change from pre- to posttest for the plagiarism-themed course, $\chi^2(1) = .11$, $p = .58$, or the control, $\chi^2(1) = 2.01$, $p = .25$. However, students in the plagiarism-themed course were more likely to add that plagiarism should be avoided because it is unethical (i.e., it hurts the original author, the college, or the field of psychology) from pretest ($n = 17$, 63%) to posttest ($n = 26$, 97%), $\chi^2(1) = 7.11$, $p = .004$. The control class did not demonstrate this increase (pre-: $n = 7$, 43%; post-: $n = 4$, 25%), $\chi^2(1) = .57$, $p = .45$.

Discussion

Results indicate that giving students hands-on experience and repeated exposure to the topic of plagiarism improves their ability to identify faulty paraphrasing, enhances their own paraphrasing, and deepens their understanding of why one should avoid plagiarism. These students were primarily juniors and seniors who had taken at least two other psychology courses before methods and statistics. Thus, it is

somewhat disheartening that initial paraphrasing and plagiarism identification scores were so low despite the institutional honor code and strict plagiarism policy. For many of our students, paraphrasing and appropriate citation appeared to be relatively new skills consistent with Macdonald and Carroll's (2006) research on plagiarism. Regardless, our findings are encouraging; immersing students in the topic of plagiarism had clear benefits and improved their skills significantly. Both groups received explicit plagiarism education at the beginning of the semester, and both improved their ability to identify plagiarism. However, the control group's quality of paraphrasing and number of strategies listed to avoid plagiarism actually decreased slightly from beginning to end of the course when plagiarism was not an explicit focus (see Table 2). These findings underscore the importance of a continued focus on plagiarism throughout the semester.

Moreover, the immersion approach appeared to deepen how students conceptualized plagiarism and its reduction. Because the first article the students analyzed (Schuetze, 2004) focused on plagiarism and students explored intentional versus unintentional plagiarism, it is not surprising that, by the end of the semester, many more students noted the importance of education as a way to avoid plagiarism. However, we never explicitly told students that education or practice was the "correct" strategy to avoid plagiarism, nor were they aware that they would be completing the homework assignment at the end of the semester. Thus, the fact that 56% of students mentioned educational strategies on the posttest may represent internalization of important concepts. We would expect this number to be even higher had we addressed this topic explicitly. Posttest responses also revealed expanded appreciation of the ethical issues surrounding plagiarism, another topic that we did not discuss explicitly.

One limitation of this study is that we required students to paraphrase only a single sentence at a time. However, it seems reasonable to consider that a plagiarism-themed course would also enhance students' ability to paraphrase more comprehensive text. An additional limitation is that we only had a single rater coding the open-ended responses. Despite these limitations, both of which may be addressed by future research, we recommend that instructors consider incorporating a plagiarism theme in methods courses. Such a theme advances multiple objectives: enhancing knowledge of plagiarism, illustrating how researchers build research programs, and highlighting multiple perspectives on the same topic.

Teaching of Psychology 38(4)

Appendix A

Sentences Used in the Pretest and Posttest to Assess Paraphrasing and Plagiarism Identification Skills

Pretest	Posttest
Sentence students paraphrased:	
Increased student confidence in their ability to avoid plagiarism would hypothetically result in an inaccurate perception that they are fully knowledgeable about the complexities involved in proper citations in scientific papers (Schuetze, 2004, p. 259).	There is a need for university staff to address forcefully the issue of academic integrity during introductory programs and to explain clearly and sympathetically the objective need for honesty in academic life (R. Bennett, 2005, p. 156).
Sentences students assessed for plagiarism:	
Increased student confidence in their ability to avoid plagiarism would hypothetically result in an inaccurate perception that they are fully knowledgeable about the complexities involved in proper citations in scientific papers.	There is a need for university staff to address forcefully the issue of academic integrity during introductory programs and to explain clearly and sympathetically the objective need for honesty in academic life (R. Bennett, 2005).
Increased student confidence in their ability to avoid plagiarism would hypothetically result in an inaccurate perception that they are fully knowledgeable about the complexities involved in proper citations in scientific papers (Schuetze, 2004).	University staff should be very clear and sympathetic about the importance of academic integrity, and they should do this early in a student's academic career.
One danger of increasing students' confidence in their ability to avoid plagiarism is that this overconfidence could leave them unaware that they do not understand the complexities of proper citation (Schuetze, 2004).	There is a need for staff of universities and colleges to forcefully address the issue of academic honesty during beginning programs and to explain clearly and sympathetically the objective desire for integrity in college life (R. Bennett, 2005).

Declaration of Conflicting Interests

The authors declared no potential conflicts of interest with respect to the research, authorship, and/or publication of this article.

Funding

The authors received no financial support for the research, authorship, and/or publication of this article.

References

Belter, R. W., & du Pré, A. (2009). A strategy to reduce plagiarism in an undergraduate course. *Teaching of Psychology, 36*, 257-261.

Bennett, K. K., Behrendt, L. S., & Boothby, J. L. (2011). Instructor perceptions of plagiarism: Are we finding common ground? *Teaching of Psychology, 38*, 29-35.

Bennett, R. (2005). Factors associated with student plagiarism in a post-1992 university. *Assessment & Evaluation in Higher Education, 30*, 137-162.

Culwin, F. (2006). An active introduction to academic misconduct and the measured demographics of misconduct. *Assessment & Evaluation in Higher Education, 31*, 167-182.

Landau, J. D., Druen, P. B., & Arcuri, J. A. (2002). Methods for helping students avoid plagiarism. *Teaching of Psychology, 29*, 112-115.

Leask, B. (2006). Plagiarism, cultural diversity and metaphor—Implications for academic staff development. *Assessment & Evaluation in Higher Education, 31*, 183-199.

Lim, V. K. G., & See, S. K. B. (2001). Attitudes toward, and intentions to report, academic cheating among students in Singapore. *Ethics & Behavior, 11*, 261-274.

Macdonald, R., & Carroll, J. (2006). Plagiarism—A complex issue requiring a holistic institutional approach. *Assessment & Evaluation in Higher Education, 31*, 233-245.

Marek, P., Christopher, A., & Walker, B. (2004). Learning by doing: Research methods with a theme. *Teaching of Psychology, 31*, 128-131.

Pickard, J. (2006). Staff and student attitudes to plagiarism at University College Northampton. *Assessment & Evaluation in Higher Education, 31*, 215-232.

Roig, M. (1997). Can undergraduate students determine whether text has been plagiarized? *Psychological Record, 47*, 113-122.

Roig, M. (2001). Plagiarism and paraphrasing criteria of college and university professors. *Ethics & Behavior, 11*, 307-323.

Roig, M., & Caso, M. (2005). Lying and cheating: Fraudulent excuse making, cheating, and plagiarism. *The Journal of Psychology, 139*, 485-494.

Schuetze, P. (2004). Evaluation of a brief homework assignment designed to reduce citation problems. *Teaching of Psychology, 31*, 257-259.

Appendix C

Statistical Tables

C.1 Table of Random Numbers

	1	2	3	4	5	6	7	8	9	10	11	12
1	212	432	400	120	217	90	292	199	305	330	377	250
2	472	345	499	125	24	415	430	359	168	181	498	23
3	126	421	60	394	236	262	268	270	246	79	26	125
4	152	154	193	330	275	103	357	341	478	306	276	400
5	447	447	192	155	181	195	186	459	253	16	27	116
6	276	366	10	82	151	140	10	483	336	176	127	9
7	375	50	296	136	163	243	1	481	32	138	99	482
8	362	196	432	440	411	349	500	294	414	327	48	398
9	7	385	16	57	237	164	145	438	146	423	342	36
10	262	110	224	82	408	38	219	135	152	68	191	259
11	99	72	237	18	331	84	230	445	392	209	427	261
12	6	356	245	185	412	49	293	322	209	115	319	42
13	174	173	201	332	252	181	445	195	75	383	396	180
14	207	310	186	419	11	360	337	461	402	365	342	323
15	320	450	478	202	180	187	414	322	200	108	145	404
16	405	286	150	183	463	367	94	47	324	38	493	229
17	435	423	441	98	350	461	389	157	300	77	420	228
18	171	213	459	444	197	56	434	79	63	99	470	249
19	332	69	72	226	311	100	129	70	163	43	270	420
20	294	185	299	16	206	209	23	415	326	389	293	112

C.2 Estimated Sample Size Needed Based on Population Size, Confidence Level, and Confidence Interval

Population Size	95% Confidence Level Confidence Interval (Margin of Error)			99% Confidence Level Confidence Interval (Margin of Error)		
	5%	2.5%	1%	5%	2.5%	1%
50	44	48	50	47	49	50
100	80	94	99	87	96	99
200	132	177	196	154	186	198
300	169	251	291	207	270	295
400	196	318	384	250	348	391
500	217	377	475	286	421	485
600	234	432	565	316	490	579
800	260	526	739	364	615	763
1000	278	606	906	400	727	943
1500	306	759	1297	461	960	1376
2500	333	952	1984	526	1290	2174
5000	357	1176	3288	588	1738	3845
10,000	370	1332	4899	624	2103	6247
25,000	378	1448	6939	648	2406	9991
50,000	381	1491	8057	657	2528	12,486
75,000	382	1506	8514	660	2571	13,619
100,000	383	1513	8763	661	2594	14,267
250,000	384	1527	9249	664	2635	15,602
500,000	384	1532	9423	665	2648	16,105
1,000,000	384	1534	9513	665	2655	16,369

C.3 Percentage of Area Under the Normal Curve Between the Mean and a z Score

z score to one decimal place	z score carried to two decimal places									
	0	0.01	0.02	0.03	0.04	0.05	0.06	0.07	0.08	0.09
0	0	0.0040	0.0080	0.0120	0.0160	0.0199	0.0239	0.0279	0.0319	0.0359
0.1	0.0398	0.0438	0.0478	0.0517	0.0557	0.0596	0.0636	0.0675	0.0714	0.0753
0.2	0.0793	0.0832	0.0871	0.0910	0.0948	0.0987	0.1026	0.1064	0.1103	0.1141
0.3	0.1179	0.1217	0.1255	0.1293	0.1331	0.1368	0.1406	0.1443	0.1480	0.1517
0.4	0.1554	0.1591	0.1620	0.1654	0.1700	0.1736	0.1772	0.1808	0.1844	0.1879
0.5	0.1915	0.195	0.1985	0.2019	0.2054	0.2038	0.2123	0.2157	0.2190	0.2224
0.6	0.2257	0.2291	0.2324	0.2357	0.2389	0.2422	0.2454	0.2486	0.2517	0.2549
0.7	0.258	0.2611	0.2642	0.2673	0.2704	0.2734	0.2764	0.2794	0.2823	0.2852
0.8	0.2881	0.291	0.2939	0.2967	0.2994	0.3023	0.3051	0.3078	0.3106	0.3133
0.9	0.3159	0.3186	0.3212	0.3238	0.3264	0.3289	0.3315	0.3340	0.3365	0.3389
1	0.3413	0.3438	0.3461	0.3485	0.3508	0.3531	0.3554	0.3577	0.3599	0.3621
1.1	0.3643	0.3665	0.3686	0.3708	0.3729	0.3749	0.3770	0.3790	0.3810	0.3830
1.2	0.3849	0.3869	0.3888	0.3907	0.3925	0.3944	0.3962	0.3980	0.3997	0.4015
1.3	0.4032	0.4049	0.4066	0.4082	0.4099	0.4115	0.413	0.4147	0.4162	0.4177
1.4	0.4192	0.4207	0.4222	0.4236	0.4251	0.4265	0.4279	0.4292	0.4306	0.4319
1.5	0.4332	0.4345	0.4357	0.4370	0.4382	0.4394	0.4406	0.4418	0.4429	0.4441
1.6	0.4452	0.4463	0.4474	0.4484	0.4495	0.4505	0.4515	0.4525	0.4535	0.4545
1.7	0.4554	0.4564	0.4357	0.4582	0.4591	0.4599	0.4608	0.4616	0.4625	0.4633

(Continued)

C.3 (Continued)

z score to one decimal place	z score carried to two decimal places									
	0	0.01	0.02	0.03	0.04	0.05	0.06	0.07	0.08	0.09
1.8	0.4641	0.4649	0.4656	0.4664	0.4671	0.4678	0.4686	0.4693	0.4699	0.4706
1.9	0.4713	0.4719	0.4726	0.4732	0.4738	0.4744	0.4750	0.4756	0.4761	0.4767
2	0.4772	0.4778	0.4783	0.4788	0.4793	0.4798	0.4803	0.4808	0.4812	0.4817
2.1	0.4821	0.4826	0.4830	0.4834	0.4838	0.4842	0.4846	0.4850	0.4854	0.4857
2.2	0.4861	0.4864	0.4868	0.4871	0.4875	0.4878	0.4881	0.4884	0.4887	0.4890
2.3	0.4893	0.4896	0.4998	0.4901	0.4904	0.4906	0.4909	0.4911	0.4913	0.4916
2.4	0.4918	0.494	0.4922	0.4925	0.4927	0.4929	0.4931	0.4911	0.4913	0.4916
2.5	0.4938	0.494	0.4941	0.4943	0.4945	0.4946	0.4948	0.4949	0.4951	0.4952

Source: From NIST/SEMATECH e-Handbook of Statistical Methods, http://www.itl.nist.gov/div898/handbook

C.4 Critical *t* Values for a Particular Probability Level and *df*

One-Tailed Two-Tailed	Probability Levels				
	.10 .10	.05 .10	.025 .05	.01 .02	.005 .01
df					
1	3.078	6.314	12.706	31.821	63.657
2	1.886	2.920	4.303	6.965	9.925
3	1.638	2.353	3.182	4.541	5.841
4	1.533	2.132	2.776	3.747	4.604
5	1.476	2.015	2.571	3.365	4.032
6	1.440	1.943	2.447	3.143	3.707
7	1.415	1.895	2.365	2.998	3.499
8	1.397	1.860	2.306	2.896	3.355
9	1.383	1.833	2.262	2.821	3.250
10	1.372	1.812	2.228	2.764	3.169
11	1.363	1.796	2.201	2.718	3.106
12	1.356	1.782	2.179	2.681	3.055
13	1.350	1.771	2.160	2.650	3.012
14	1.345	1.761	2.145	2.624	2.977
15	1.341	1.753	2.131	2.602	2.947
16	1.337	1.746	2.120	2.583	2.921
17	1.333	1.740	2.110	2.567	2.898
18	1.330	1.734	2.101	2.552	2.878
19	1.328	1.729	2.093	2.539	2.861
20	1.325	1.725	2.086	2.528	2.845
25	1.316	1.708	2.060	2.485	2.787
30	1.310	1.697	2.042	2.457	2.750
40	1.303	1.684	2.021	2.423	2.704
60	1.296	1.671	2.000	2.390	2.660
120	1.289	1.658	1.980	2.358	2.617
∞	1.282	1.645	1.960	2.326	2.576

Source: NIST/SEMATECH e-Handbook of Statistical Methods, http://www.itl.nist.gov/div898/handbook

C.5 Critical Values for Pearson's Correlation Coefficient (*r*)

df	One-Tailed Two-Tailed	.10 .20	.05 .10	.025 .05	.01 .02	.005 .01
1		.9511	.9877	.9969	.9995	.9999
2		.8000	.9000	.9500	.9800	.9900
3		.6870	.8054	.8783	.9343	.9587
4		.6084	.7293	.8114	.8822	.9172
5		.5509	.6694	.7545	.8329	.8745
6		.5067	.6215	.7067	.7887	.8343
7		.4716	.5822	.6664	.7498	.7977
8		.4428	.5494	.6319	.7155	.7646
9		.4187	.5214	.6021	.6851	.7348
10		.3981	.4973	.5760	.6581	.7079
11		.3802	.4762	.5529	.6339	.6835
12		.3646	.4575	.5324	.6120	.6614
13		.3507	.4409	.5140	.5923	.6411
14		.3383	.4259	.4973	.5742	.6226
15		.3271	.4124	.4821	.5577	.6055
16		.3170	.4000	.4683	.5425	.5897
17		.3077	.3887	.4555	.5285	.5751
18		.2992	.3783	.4438	.5155	.5614
19		.2914	.3687	.4329	.5034	.5487
20		.2841	.3598	.4227	.4921	.5368
21		.2774	.3515	.4132	.4815	.5256
22		.2711	.3438	.4044	.4716	.5151
23		.2653	.3365	.3961	.4622	.5052
24		.2598	.3297	.3882	.4534	.4958
25		.2546	.3233	.3809	.4451	.4869
26		.2497	.3172	.3739	.4372	.4785
27		.2451	.3115	.3673	.4297	.4705
28		.2407	.3061	.3610	.4226	.4629
29		.2366	.3009	.3550	.4158	.4556
30		.2327	.2960	.3494	.4093	.4487
31		.2289	.2913	.3440	.4032	.4421
32		.2254	.2869	.3388	.3972	.4357
33		.2220	.2826	.3338	.3916	.4296

df	One-Tailed Two-Tailed	.10 .20	.05 .10	.025 .05	.01 .02	.005 .01
34		.2187	.2785	.3291	.3862	.4238
35		.2156	.2746	.3246	.3810	.4182
36		.2126	.2709	.3202	.3760	.4128
37		.2097	.2673	.3160	.3712	.4076
38		.2070	.2638	.3120	.3665	.4026
39		.2043	.2605	.3081	.3621	.3978
40		.2018	.2573	.3044	.3578	.3932
41		.1993	.2542	.3008	.3536	.3887
42		.1970	.2512	.2973	.3496	.3843
43		.1947	.2483	.2940	.3457	.3801
44		.1925	.2455	.2907	.3420	.3761
45		.1903	.2429	.2876	.3384	.3721
46		.1883	.2403	.2845	.3348	.3683
47		.1863	.2377	.2816	.3314	.3646
48		.1843	.2353	.2787	.3281	.3610
49		.1825	.2329	.2759	.3249	.3575
50		.1806	.2306	.2732	.3218	.3542
51		.1789	.2284	.2706	.3188	.3509
52		.1772	.2262	.2681	.3158	.3477
53		.1755	.2241	.2656	.3129	.3445
54		.1739	.2221	.2632	.3102	.3415
55		.1723	.2201	.2609	.3074	.3385
56		.1708	.2181	.2586	.3048	.3357
57		.1693	.2162	.2564	.3022	.3328
58		.1678	.2144	.2542	.2997	.3301
59		.1664	.2126	.2521	.2972	.3274
60		.1650	.2108	.2500	.2948	.3248
61		.1636	.2091	.2480	.2925	.3223
62		.1623	.2075	.2461	.2902	.3198
63		.1610	.2058	.2441	.2880	.3173
64		.1598	.2042	.2423	.2858	.3150
65		.1586	.2027	.2404	.2837	.3126
66		.1574	.2012	.2387	.2816	.3104
67		.1562	.1997	.2369	.2796	.3081

(Continued)

C.5 (Continued)

df	One-Tailed / Two-Tailed	.10 / .20	.05 / .10	.025 / .05	.01 / .02	.005 / .01
68		.1550	.1982	.2352	.2776	.3060
69		.1539	.1968	.2335	.2756	.3038
70		.1528	.1954	.2319	.2737	.3017
71		.1517	.1940	.2303	.2718	.2997
72		.1507	.1927	.2287	.2700	.2977
73		.1497	.1914	.2272	.2682	.2957
74		.1486	.1901	.2257	.2664	.2938
75		.1477	.1888	.2242	.2647	.2919
76		.1467	.1876	.2227	.2630	.2900
77		.1457	.1864	.2213	.2613	.2882
78		.1448	.1852	.2199	.2597	.2864
79		.1439	.1841	.2185	.2581	.2847
80		.1430	.1829	.2172	.2565	.2830
81		.1421	.1818	.2159	.2550	.2813
82		.1412	.1807	.2146	.2535	.2796
83		.1404	.1796	.2133	.2520	.2780
84		.1396	.1786	.2120	.2505	.2764
85		.1387	.1775	.2108	.2491	.2748
86		.1379	.1765	.2096	.2477	.2732
87		.1371	.1755	.2084	.2463	.2717
88		.1364	.1745	.2072	.2449	.2702
89		.1356	.1735	.2061	.2435	.2687
90		.1348	.1726	.2050	.2422	.2673
91		.1341	.1716	.2039	.2409	.2659
92		.1334	.1707	.2028	.2396	.2645
93		.1327	.1698	.2017	.2384	.2631
94		.1320	.1689	.2006	.2371	.2617
95		.1313	.1680	.1996	.2359	.2604
96		.1306	.1671	.1986	.2347	.2591
97		.1299	.1663	.1975	.2335	.2578
98		.1292	.1654	.1966	.2324	.2565
99		.1286	.1646	.1956	.2312	.2552
100		.1279	.1638	.1946	.2301	.2540

C.6 Critical F Values for ANOVA With a Particular Probability Level and *df*

*df*_b	1	2	3	4	5	6	7	8	9	10
*df*_w										
1	**161**	**200**	**216**	**225**	**230**	**234**	**237**	**239**	**241**	**242**
	4052	4999	5403	5625	5764	5859	5928	5981	22	6056
2	**18.51**	**19.00**	**19.16**	**19.25**	**19.30**	**19.33**	**19.35**	**19.37**	**19.39**	**19.40**
	98.50	99.00	99.17	99.25	99.30	99.33	99.36	99.37	99.39	99.40
3	**10.13**	**9.55**	**9.28**	**9.12**	**9.01**	**8.94**	**8.89**	**8.85**	**8.81**	**8.79**
	34.12	30.82	29.46	28.71	28.24	27.91	27.67	27.49	27.35	27.23
4	**7.71**	**6.94**	**6.59**	**6.39**	**6.26**	**6.16**	**6.09**	**6.04**	**6.00**	**5.96**
	21.20	18.00	16.69	15.98	15.52	15.21	14.98	14.80	14.66	14.55
5	**6.61**	**5.79**	**5.41**	**5.19**	**5.05**	**4.95**	**4.88**	**4.82**	**4.77**	**4.74**
	16.26	13.27	12.06	11.39	10.97	10.67	10.46	10.29	10.16	10.05
6	**5.99**	**5.14**	**4.76**	**4.53**	**4.39**	**4.28**	**4.21**	**4.15**	**4.10**	**4.06**
	13.75	10.93	9.78	9.15	8.75	8.47	8.26	8.10	7.98	7.87
7	**5.59**	**4.74**	**4.35**	**4.12**	**3.97**	**3.87**	**3.79**	**3.73**	**3.68**	**3.64**
	12.25	9.55	8.45	7.85	7.46	7.19	6.99	6.84	6.72	6.62
8	**5.32**	**4.46**	**4.07**	**3.84**	**3.69**	**3.58**	**3.50**	**3.44**	**3.39**	**3.35**
	11.26	8.65	7.59	7.01	6.63	6.37	6.18	6.03	5.91	5.81
9	**5.12**	**4.26**	**3.86**	**3.63**	**3.48**	**3.37**	**3.29**	**3.23**	**3.18**	**3.14**
	10.56	8.02	6.99	6.42	6.06	5.80	5.61	5.47	5.35	5.26
10	**4.97**	**4.10**	**3.71**	**3.48**	**3.33**	**3.22**	**3.14**	**3.07**	**3.02**	**2.98**
	10.04	7.56	6.55	5.99	5.64	5.39	5.20	5.06	4.94	4.85
11	**4.84**	**3.98**	**3.59**	**3.36**	**3.20**	**3.10**	**3.01**	**2.95**	**2.90**	**2.85**
	9.65	7.21	6.22	5.67	5.32	5.07	4.89	4.74	4.63	4.54
12	**4.75**	**3.89**	**3.49**	**3.26**	**3.11**	**3.00**	**2.91**	**2.85**	**2.80**	**2.75**
	9.33	6.93	5.95	5.41	5.06	4.82	4.64	4.50	4.39	4.30
13	**4.67**	**3.81**	**3.41**	**3.18**	**3.03**	**2.92**	**2.83**	**2.77**	**2.71**	**2.67**
	9.07	6.70	5.74	5.21	4.86	4.62	4.44	4.30	4.19	4.10
14	**4.60**	**3.74**	**3.34**	**3.11**	**2.96**	**2.85**	**2.76**	**2.70**	**2.65**	**2.60**
	8.86	6.52	5.56	5.04	4.70	4.46	4.28	4.14	4.03	3.94
15	**4.54**	**3.68**	**3.29**	**3.06**	**2.90**	**2.79**	**2.71**	**2.64**	**2.59**	**2.54**
	8.68	6.36	5.42	4.89	4.56	4.32	4.14	4.00	3.90	3.81

(Continued)

C.6 (Continued)

df_b df_w	1	2	3	4	5	6	7	8	9	10
16	**4.49**	**3.63**	**3.24**	**3.01**	**2.85**	**2.74**	**2.66**	**2.59**	**2.54**	**2.49**
	8.53	6.23	5.29	4.77	4.44	4.20	4.03	3.89	3.78	3.69
17	**4.45**	**3.59**	**3.20**	**2.97**	**2.81**	**2.70**	**2.61**	**2.55**	**2.49**	**2.45**
	8.40	6.11	5.19	4.67	4.34	4.10	3.93	3.79	3.68	3.59
18	**4.41**	**3.56**	**3.16**	**2.93**	**2.77**	**2.66**	**2.58**	**2.51**	**2.46**	**2.41**
	8.29	6.01	5.09	4.58	4.25	4.02	3.84	3.71	3.60	3.51
19	**4.38**	**3.52**	**3.13**	**2.90**	**2.74**	**2.63**	**2.54**	**2.48**	**2.42**	**2.38**
	8.19	5.93	5.01	4.50	4.17	3.94	3.77	3.63	3.52	3.43
20	**4.35**	**3.49**	**3.10**	**2.87**	**2.71**	**2.60**	**2.51**	**2.45**	**2.39**	**2.35**
	8.10	5.85	4.94	4.43	4.10	3.87	3.70	3.56	3.46	3.37
21	**4.33**	**3.47**	**3.07**	**2.84**	**2.69**	**2.57**	**2.49**	**2.42**	**2.37**	**2.32**
	8.02	5.78	4.87	4.37	4.04	3.81	3.64	3.51	3.40	3.31
22	**4.30**	**3.44**	**3.05**	**2.82**	**2.66**	**2.55**	**2.46**	**2.40**	**2.34**	**2.30**
	7.95	5.72	4.82	4.31	3.99	3.76	3.59	3.45	3.35	3.26
23	**4.28**	**3.42**	**3.03**	**2.80**	**2.64**	**2.53**	**2.44**	**2.38**	**2.32**	**2.28**
	7.88	5.66	4.77	4.26	3.94	3.71	3.54	3.41	3.30	3.21
24	**4.26**	**3.40**	**3.01**	**2.78**	**2.62**	**2.51**	**2.42**	**2.36**	**2.30**	**2.26**
	7.82	5.61	4.72	4.22	3.90	3.67	3.50	3.36	3.26	3.17
25	**4.24**	**3.39**	**2.99**	**2.76**	**2.60**	**2.49**	**2.41**	**2.34**	**2.28**	**2.24**
	7.77	5.57	4.68	4.18	3.86	3.63	3.46	3.32	3.22	3.13
26	**4.23**	**3.37**	**2.98**	**2.74**	**2.59**	**2.47**	**2.39**	**2.32**	**2.27**	**2.22**
	7.72	5.53	4.64	4.14	3.82	3.59	3.42	3.29	3.18	3.09
27	**4.21**	**3.35**	**2.96**	**2.73**	**2.57**	**2.46**	**2.37**	**2.31**	**2.25**	**2.20**
	7.68	5.49	4.60	4.11	3.79	3.56	3.39	3.26	3.15	3.06
28	**4.20**	**3.34**	**2.95**	**2.71**	**2.56**	**2.45**	**2.36**	**2.29**	**2.24**	**2.19**
	7.64	5.45	4.57	4.07	3.75	3.53	3.36	3.23	3.12	3.03
29	**4.18**	**3.33**	**2.93**	**2.70**	**2.55**	**2.43**	**2.35**	**2.28**	**2.22**	**2.18**
	7.60	5.42	4.54	4.05	3.73	3.50	3.33	3.20	3.09	3.01
30	**4.17**	**3.32**	**2.92**	**2.69**	**2.53**	**2.42**	**2.33**	**2.27**	**2.21**	**2.17**
	7.56	5.39	4.51	4.02	3.70	3.47	3.31	3.17	3.07	2.98

df_b	1	2	3	4	5	6	7	8	9	10
df_w										
31	4.16	3.31	2.91	2.68	2.52	2.41	2.32	2.26	2.20	2.15
	7.53	5.36	4.48	3.99	3.68	3.45	3.28	3.15	3.04	2.96
32	4.15	3.30	2.90	2.67	2.51	2.40	2.31	2.24	2.19	2.14
	7.50	5.34	4.46	3.97	3.65	3.43	3.26	3.13	3.02	2.93
33	4.14	3.29	2.89	2.66	2.50	2.39	2.30	2.24	2.18	2.13
	7.17	5.31	4.44	3.95	3.63	3.41	3.24	3.11	3.00	2.91
34	4.13	3.28	2.88	2.65	2.49	2.38	2.29	2.23	2.17	2.12
	7.44	5.29	4.42	3.93	3.61	3.39	3.23	3.09	2.98	2.89
35	4.12	3.27	2.87	2.64	2.49	2.37	2.29	2.22	2.16	2.11
	7.42	5.27	4.40	3.91	3.59	3.37	3.20	3.07	2.96	2.88
36	4.11	3.26	2.87	2.63	2.48	2.36	2.28	2.21	2.15	2.11
	7.40	5.25	4.38	3.89	3.57	3.35	3.18	3.05	2.95	2.86
37	4.11	3.25	2.86	2.63	2.47	2.36	2.27	2.20	2.15	2.10
	7.37	5.23	4.36	3.87	3.56	3.33	3.17	3.04	2.93	2.84
38	4.10	3.25	2.85	2.62	2.46	2.35	2.26	2.19	2.14	2.09
	7.35	5.21	4.34	3.86	3.54	3.32	3.15	3.02	2.92	2.83
39	4.09	3.24	2.85	2.61	2.46	2.34	2.26	2.19	2.13	2.08
	7.33	5.19	4.33	3.84	3.53	3.31	3.14	3.01	2.90	2.81
40	4.09	3.23	2.84	2.61	2.45	2.34	2.25	2.18	2.12	2.08
	7.31	5.18	4.31	3.83	3.51	3.29	3.12	2.99	2.89	2.80
41	4.08	3.23	2.83	2.60	2.44	2.33	2.24	2.17	2.12	2.07
	7.30	5.16	4.30	3.82	3.50	3.28	3.11	2.98	2.88	2.79
42	4.07	3.22	2.83	2.59	2.44	2.32	2.24	2.17	2.11	2.07
	7.28	5.15	4.29	3.80	3.49	3.27	3.10	2.97	2.86	2.78
43	4.07	3.21	2.82	2.59	2.43	2.32	2.23	2.16	2.11	2.06
	7.26	5.14	4.27	3.79	3.48	3.25	3.09	2.96	2.85	2.76
44	4.06	3.21	2.82	2.58	2.43	2.31	2.23	2.16	2.10	2.05
	7.25	5.12	4.26	3.78	3.47	3.24	3.08	2.95	2.84	2.75
45	4.06	3.20	2.81	2.58	2.42	2.31	2.22	2.15	2.10	2.05
	7.23	5.11	4.25	3.77	3.45	3.23	3.07	2.94	2.83	2.74
46	4.05	3.20	2.81	2.57	2.42	2.30	2.22	2.15	2.09	2.04
	7.22	5.10	4.24	3.76	3.44	3.22	3.06	2.93	2.82	2.73

(Continued)

C.6 (Continued)

df_b	1	2	3	4	5	6	7	8	9	10
df_w										
47	**4.05**	**3.20**	**2.80**	**2.57**	**2.41**	**2.30**	**2.21**	**2.14**	**2.09**	**2.04**
	7.21	5.09	4.23	3.75	3.43	3.21	3.05	2.92	2.81	2.72
48	**4.04**	**3.19**	**2.80**	**2.57**	**2.41**	**2.30**	**2.21**	**2.14**	**2.08**	**2.04**
	7.19	5.08	4.22	3.74	3.43	3.20	3.04	2.91	2.80	2.72
49	**4.04**	**3.19**	**2.79**	**2.56**	**2.40**	**2.29**	**2.20**	**2.13**	**2.08**	**2.03**
	7.18	5.07	4.21	3.73	3.42	3.20	3.03	2.90	2.79	2.71
50	**4.03**	**3.18**	**2.79**	**2.56**	**2.40**	**2.29**	**2.20**	**2.13**	**2.07**	**2.03**
	7.17	5.06	4.20	3.72	3.41	3.19	3.02	2.89	2.79	2.70
51	**4.03**	**3.18**	**2.79**	**2.55**	**2.40**	**2.28**	**2.20**	**2.13**	**2.07**	**2.02**
	7.16	5.05	4.19	3.71	3.40	3.18	3.01	2.88	2.78	2.69
52	**4.03**	**3.18**	**2.78**	**2.55**	**2.39**	**2.28**	**2.19**	**2.12**	**2.07**	**2.02**
	7.15	5.04	4.18	3.70	3.39	3.17	3.01	2.87	2.77	2.68
53	**4.02**	**3.17**	**2.78**	**2.55**	**2.39**	**2.28**	**2.19**	**2.12**	**2.06**	**2.02**
	7.14	5.03	4.17	3.70	3.38	3.16	3.00	2.87	2.76	2.68
54	**4.02**	**3.17**	**2.78**	**2.54**	**2.39**	**2.27**	**2.19**	**2.12**	**2.06**	**2.01**
	7.13	5.02	4.17	3.69	3.38	3.16	2.99	2.86	2.76	2.67
55	**4.02**	**3.17**	**2.77**	**2.54**	**2.38**	**2.27**	**2.18**	**2.11**	**2.06**	**2.01**
	7.12	5.01	4.16	3.68	3.37	3.15	2.98	2.85	2.75	2.66
56	**4.01**	**3.16**	**2.77**	**2.54**	**2.38**	**2.27**	**2.18**	**2.11**	**2.05**	**2.01**
	7.11	5.01	4.15	3.67	3.36	3.14	2.98	2.85	2.74	2.66
57	**4.01**	**3.16**	**2.77**	**2.53**	**2.38**	**2.26**	**2.18**	**2.11**	**2.05**	**2.00**
	7.10	5.00	4.15	3.67	3.36	3.14	2.97	2.84	2.74	2.65
58	**4.01**	**3.16**	**2.76**	**2.53**	**2.37**	**2.26**	**2.17**	**2.10**	**2.05**	**2.00**
	7.09	4.99	4.14	3.66	3.35	3.13	2.97	2.84	2.73	2.64
59	**4.00**	**3.15**	**2.76**	**2.53**	**2.37**	**2.26**	**2.17**	**2.10**	**2.04**	**2.00**
	7.09	4.98	4.13	3.66	3.35	3.12	2.96	2.83	2.72	2.64
60	**4.00**	**3.15**	**2.76**	**2.53**	**2.37**	**2.25**	**2.17**	**2.10**	**2.04**	**1.99**
	7.08	4.98	4.13	3.65	3.34	3.12	2.95	2.82	2.72	2.63
61	**4.00**	**3.15**	**2.76**	**2.52**	**2.37**	**2.25**	**2.16**	**2.09**	**2.04**	**1.99**
	7.07	4.97	4.12	3.64	3.33	3.11	2.95	2.82	2.71	2.63

df_b	1	2	3	4	5	6	7	8	9	10
df_w										
62	**4.00**	**3.15**	**2.75**	**2.52**	**2.36**	**2.25**	**2.16**	**2.09**	**2.04**	**1.99**
	7.06	4.97	4.11	3.64	3.33	3.11	2.94	2.81	2.71	2.62
63	**3.99**	**3.14**	**2.75**	**2.52**	**2.36**	**2.25**	**2.16**	**2.09**	**2.03**	**1.99**
	7.06	4.96	4.11	3.63	3.32	3.10	2.94	2.81	2.70	2.62
64	**3.99**	**3.14**	**2.75**	**2.52**	**2.36**	**2.24**	**2.16**	**2.09**	**2.03**	**1.98**
	7.05	4.95	4.10	3.63	3.32	3.10	2.93	2.80	2.70	2.61
65	**3.99**	**3.14**	**2.75**	**2.51**	**2.36**	**2.24**	**2.15**	**2.08**	**2.03**	**1.98**
	7.04	4.95	4.10	3.62	3.31	3.09	2.93	2.80	2.69	2.61
66	**3.99**	**3.14**	**2.74**	**2.51**	**2.35**	**2.24**	**2.15**	**2.08**	**2.03**	**1.98**
	7.04	4.94	4.09	3.62	3.31	3.09	2.92	2.79	2.69	2.60
67	**3.98**	**3.13**	**2.74**	**2.51**	**2.35**	**2.24**	**2.15**	**2.08**	**2.02**	**1.98**
	7.03	4.94	4.09	3.61	3.30	3.08	2.92	2.79	2.68	2.60
68	**3.98**	**3.13**	**2.74**	**2.51**	**2.35**	**2.24**	**2.15**	**2.08**	**2.02**	**1.97**
	7.02	4.93	4.08	3.61	3.30	3.08	2.91	2.79	2.68	2.59
69	**3.98**	**3.13**	**2.74**	**2.51**	**2.35**	**2.23**	**2.15**	**2.08**	**2.02**	**1.97**
	7.02	4.93	4.08	3.60	3.30	3.08	2.91	2.78	2.68	2.59
70	**3.98**	**3.13**	**2.74**	**2.50**	**2.35**	**2.23**	**2.14**	**2.07**	**2.02**	**1.97**
	7.01	4.92	4.07	3.60	3.29	3.07	2.91	2.78	2.67	2.59
71	**3.98**	**3.13**	**2.73**	**2.50**	**2.34**	**2.23**	**2.14**	**2.07**	**2.02**	**1.97**
	7.01	4.92	4.07	3.60	3.29	3.07	2.90	2.77	2.67	2.58
72	**3.97**	**3.12**	**2.73**	**2.50**	**2.34**	**2.23**	**2.14**	**2.07**	**2.01**	**1.97**
	7.00	4.91	4.07	3.59	3.28	3.06	2.90	2.77	2.66	2.58
73	**3.97**	**3.12**	**2.73**	**2.50**	**2.34**	**2.23**	**2.14**	**2.07**	**2.01**	**1.96**
	7.00	4.91	4.06	3.59	3.28	3.06	2.90	2.77	2.66	2.57
74	**3.97**	**3.12**	**2.73**	**2.50**	**2.34**	**2.22**	**2.14**	**2.07**	**2.01**	**1.96**
	6.99	4.90	4.06	3.58	3.28	3.06	2.89	2.76	2.66	2.57
75	**3.97**	**3.12**	**2.73**	**2.49**	**2.34**	**2.22**	**2.13**	**2.06**	**2.01**	**1.96**
	6.99	4.90	4.05	3.58	3.27	3.05	2.89	2.76	2.65	2.57
76	**3.97**	**3.12**	**2.73**	**2.49**	**2.34**	**2.22**	**2.13**	**2.06**	**2.01**	**1.96**
	6.98	4.90	4.05	3.58	3.27	3.05	2.88	2.76	2.65	2.56
77	**3.97**	**3.12**	**2.72**	**2.49**	**2.33**	**2.22**	**2.13**	**2.06**	**2.00**	**1.96**
	6.98	4.89	4.05	3.57	3.27	3.05	2.88	2.75	2.65	2.56

(Continued)

df_b	1	2	3	4	5	6	7	8	9	10
df_w										
78	**3.96**	**3.11**	**2.72**	**2.49**	**2.33**	**2.22**	**2.13**	**2.06**	**2.00**	**1.95**
	6.97	4.89	4.04	3.57	3.26	3.04	2.88	2.75	2.64	2.56
79	**3.96**	**3.11**	**2.72**	**2.49**	**2.33**	**2.22**	**2.13**	**2.06**	**2.00**	**1.95**
	6.97	4.88	4.04	3.57	3.26	3.04	2.87	2.75	2.64	2.55
80	**3.96**	**3.11**	**2.72**	**2.49**	**2.33**	**2.21**	**2.13**	**2.06**	**2.00**	**1.95**
	6.96	4.88	4.04	3.56	3.26	3.04	2.87	2.74	2.64	2.55
81	**3.96**	**3.11**	**2.72**	**2.48**	**2.33**	**2.21**	**2.13**	**2.06**	**2.00**	**1.95**
	6.96	4.88	4.03	3.56	3.25	3.03	2.87	2.74	2.63	2.55
82	**3.96**	**3.11**	**2.72**	**2.48**	**2.33**	**2.21**	**2.12**	**2.05**	**2.00**	**1.95**
	6.95	4.87	4.03	3.56	3.25	3.03	2.87	2.74	2.63	2.55
83	**3.96**	**3.11**	**2.72**	**2.48**	**2.32**	**2.21**	**2.12**	**2.05**	**2.00**	**1.95**
	6.95	4.87	4.03	3.55	3.25	3.03	2.86	2.73	2.63	2.54
84	**3.96**	**3.11**	**2.71**	**2.48**	**2.32**	**2.21**	**2.12**	**2.05**	**1.99**	**1.95**
	6.95	4.87	4.02	3.55	3.24	3.03	2.86	2.73	2.63	2.54
85	**3.95**	**3.10**	**2.71**	**2.48**	**2.32**	**2.21**	**2.12**	**2.05**	**1.99**	**1.94**
	6.94	4.86	4.02	3.55	3.24	3.02	2.86	2.73	2.62	2.54
86	**3.95**	**3.10**	**2.71**	**2.48**	**2.32**	**2.21**	**2.12**	**2.05**	**1.99**	**1.94**
	6.94	4.86	4.02	3.55	3.24	3.02	2.85	2.73	2.62	2.53
87	**3.95**	**3.10**	**2.71**	**2.48**	**2.32**	**2.21**	**2.12**	**2.05**	**1.99**	**1.94**
	6.94	4.86	4.02	3.54	3.24	3.02	2.85	2.72	2.62	2.53
88	**3.95**	**3.10**	**2.71**	**2.48**	**2.32**	**2.20**	**2.12**	**2.05**	**1.99**	**1.94**
	6.93	4.86	4.01	3.54	3.23	3.01	2.85	2.72	2.62	2.53
89	**3.95**	**3.10**	**2.71**	**2.47**	**2.32**	**2.20**	**2.11**	**2.04**	**1.99**	**1.94**
	6.93	4.85	4.01	3.54	3.23	3.01	2.85	2.72	2.61	2.53
90	**3.95**	**3.10**	**2.71**	**2.47**	**2.32**	**2.20**	**2.11**	**2.04**	**1.99**	**1.94**
	6.93	4.85	4.01	3.54	3.23	3.01	2.85	2.72	2.61	2.52
91	**3.95**	**3.10**	**2.71**	**2.47**	**2.32**	**2.20**	**2.11**	**2.04**	**1.98**	**1.94**
	6.92	4.85	4.00	3.53	3.23	3.01	2.84	2.71	2.61	2.52
92	**3.95**	**3.10**	**2.70**	**2.47**	**2.31**	**2.20**	**2.11**	**2.04**	**1.98**	**1.94**
	6.92	4.84	4.00	3.53	3.22	3.00	2.84	2.71	2.61	2.52

df_b	1	2	3	4	5	6	7	8	9	10
df_w										
93	**3.94**	**3.09**	**2.70**	**2.47**	**2.31**	**2.20**	**2.11**	**2.04**	**1.98**	**1.93**
	6.92	4.84	4.00	3.53	3.22	3.00	2.84	2.71	2.60	2.52
94	**3.94**	**3.09**	**2.70**	**2.47**	**2.31**	**2.20**	**2.11**	**2.04**	**1.98**	**1.93**
	6.91	4.84	4.00	3.53	3.22	3.00	2.84	2.71	2.60	2.52
95	**3.94**	**3.09**	**2.70**	**2.47**	**2.31**	**2.20**	**2.11**	**2.04**	**1.98**	**1.93**
	6.91	4.84	4.00	3.52	3.22	3.00	2.83	2.70	2.60	2.51
96	**3.94**	**3.09**	**2.70**	**2.47**	**2.31**	**2.20**	**2.11**	**2.04**	**1.98**	**1.93**
	6.91	4.83	3.99	3.52	3.21	3.00	2.83	2.70	2.60	2.51
97	**3.94**	**3.09**	**2.70**	**2.47**	**2.31**	**2.19**	**2.11**	**2.04**	**1.98**	**1.93**
	6.90	4.83	3.99	3.52	3.21	2.99	2.83	2.70	2.60	2.51
98	**3.94**	**3.09**	**2.70**	**2.47**	**2.31**	**2.19**	**2.10**	**2.03**	**1.98**	**1.93**
	6.90	4.83	3.99	3.52	3.21	2.99	2.83	2.70	2.59	2.51
99	**3.94**	**3.09**	**2.70**	**2.46**	**2.31**	**2.19**	**2.10**	**2.03**	**1.98**	**1.93**
	6.90	4.83	3.99	3.52	3.21	2.99	2.83	2.70	2.59	2.51
100	**3.94**	**3.09**	**2.70**	**2.46**	**2.31**	**2.19**	**2.10**	**2.03**	**1.98**	**1.93**
	6.90	4.82	3.98	3.51	3.21	2.99	2.82	2.69	2.59	2.50

Note: Degrees of freedom between groups (df_b) is in the numerator. Degrees of freedom within groups (df_w) is in the denominator. $p = .05$ is in bold font; $p = .01$ is in lighter font.

C.7 Critical Values for Chi-Square (χ^2)

df	p	.05	.025	.01	.005	.001
1		3.84	5.02	6.63	7.88	10.83
2		5.99	7.38	9.21	10.60	13.82
3		7.81	9.35	11.34	12.84	16.27
4		9.49	11.14	13.28	14.86	18.47
5		11.07	12.83	15.09	16.75	20.51
6		12.59	14.45	16.81	18.55	22.46
7		14.07	16.01	18.48	20.28	24.32
8		15.51	17.53	20.09	21.95	26.12
9		16.92	19.02	21.67	23.59	27.88
10		18.31	20.48	23.21	25.19	29.59
11		19.68	21.92	24.73	26.76	31.26
12		21.03	23.34	26.22	28.30	32.91
13		22.36	24.74	27.69	29.82	34.53
14		23.68	26.12	29.14	31.32	36.12
15		25.00	27.49	30.58	32.80	37.70
16		26.30	28.85	32.00	34.27	39.25
17		27.59	30.19	33.41	35.72	40.79
18		28.87	31.53	34.81	37.16	42.31
19		30.14	32.85	36.19	38.58	43.82
20		31.41	34.17	37.57	40.00	45.31
21		32.67	35.48	38.93	41.40	46.80
22		33.92	36.78	40.29	42.80	48.27
23		35.17	38.08	41.64	44.18	49.73
24		36.42	39.36	42.98	45.56	51.18
25		37.65	40.65	44.31	46.93	52.62

Source: NIST/SEMATECH e-Handbook of Statistical Methods, http://www.itl.nist.gov/div898/handbook

C.8 Critical Values for Spearman's Rho (r_s)

	Two-Tailed Test			One-Tailed Test	
N	**Level of Significance**		**N**	**Level of Significance**	
(# of pairs)	**p = .05**	**p = .01**	**(# of pairs)**	**p = .05**	**p = .01**
5	1.000	—	5	.900	1.000
6	.886	1.000	6	.829	.943
7	.786	.929	7	.714	.893
8	.738	.881	8	.643	.833
9	.683	.833	9	.600	.783
10	.648	.794	10	.564	.746
12	.591	.777	12	.506	.712
14	.544	.715	14	.456	.645
16	.506	.665	16	.425	.601
18	.475	.625	18	.399	.564
20	.450	.591	20	.377	.534
22	.428	.562	22	.359	.508
24	.409	.537	24	.343	.485
26	.392	.515	26	.329	.465
28	.377	.496	28	.317	.448
30	.364	.478	30	.306	.432

Appendix D

Statistical Formulas

D.1 COMPUTATIONAL FORMULA FOR STANDARD DEVIATION

The computational formula for the standard deviation is:

$$SD = \sqrt{\frac{\sum X^2 - \frac{(\sum X^2)}{N}}{N-1}}$$

where Σ = sum; X = score; N = sample size.

D.2 CALCULATING A SKEWNESS STATISTIC

The formula to calculate skewness of the sample (G_1) is:

$$G_1 = \frac{N}{(N-1)(N-2)} \times \Sigma(\frac{X-M}{SD})^3$$

where N = sample size; Σ = sum; X = score; M = mean; SD = standard deviation.

D.3 COMPUTATIONAL FORMULA FOR ONE-SAMPLE *t* TEST

The computational formula for the one-sample t test is:

$$t = \frac{M-\mu}{\sqrt{\frac{SD^2}{N}}}$$

where M = mean (of the sample); μ = population mean; SD = standard deviation; N = sample size.

D.4 COMPUTATIONAL FORMULA FOR PEARSON'S r

$$r = \frac{N(\Sigma XY)-(\Sigma X)(\Sigma Y)}{[N(\Sigma X^2)-(\Sigma X)^2]\ [N(\Sigma Y^2)-(\Sigma Y)^2]}$$

where X = one variable; Y = second variable; N = number of pairs of scores; Σ = sum

D.5 COMPUTATIONAL FORMULA FOR SPEARMAN'S RHO TIED RANKS

When there are tied ranks, the following formula is used:

$$r_s = \frac{\Sigma(x_i - M_x)(y_i - M_y)}{\sqrt{\Sigma(x_i - M_x)^2(y_i - M_y)^2}}$$

where x_i = rank of X score; y_i = rank of Y score; M_x = mean of X ranks; M_y = mean of Y ranks.

D.6 COMPUTATIONAL FORMULA FOR INDEPENDENT-SAMPLES t TEST

$$t = \frac{M_1 M_2}{\sqrt{\frac{(n_1-1)SD_1^2+(n_2-1)SD_2^2}{(n_1-1)+(n_2-1)}\left[\frac{1+1}{n_1\,n_2}\right]}}$$

where M_1 = mean of group one; n_1 = number in group one; SD_1 = standard deviation squared of group one; M_2 = mean of group two; n_2 = number in group two; SD_2 = standard deviation squared of group two.

D.7 COMPUTATIONAL FORMULAS FOR SUM OF SQUARES (SS) FOR ONE-WAY INDEPENDENT-SAMPLES ANOVA

Computational formula for total sums of squares (SS_{tot})

$$SS_{tot} = \Sigma X^2 - (\Sigma X)^2/N$$

where Σ = sum; X = score; N = total sample size.

Computational formula for between-groups (treatment) sums of squares (SS_B)

$$SS_B = \Sigma \left[\frac{(\Sigma X_k)^2}{n_k} \right] - \frac{(\Sigma X)^2}{N}$$

where Σ = sum; X_k = group; k scores; X = score; n_k = sample size in group k; N = total sample size.

Computational formula for within (error) sums of squares (SS_w)

$$SS_w = SS_{tot} - SS_B$$

where SS_W = within (error) sum of squares; SS_{tot} = total sum of squares; SS_B – between groups (treatment) sum of squares.

The degrees of freedom (df), mean square (MS), and F formulas are found in Chapter 10 in Summary Table 10.6.

D.8 COMPUTATIONAL FORMULA FOR TUKEY'S HSD POST HOC TEST

$$HSD = (q_k)\,(MS_w/n)$$

where q = studentized range; k = number of groups; MS_w = mean square within groups; n = number of participants per group.

D.9 COMPUTATIONAL FORMULAS FOR SUM OF SQUARES (SS) FOR DEPENDENT-SAMPLES ANOVA

Computational formula for total sums of squares (SS_{tot})

$$SS_{tot} = \Sigma X^2 - (\Sigma X)^2/N$$

where Σ = sum; X = score; N = total sample size.

Computational formula for between-groups (treatment) sums of squares (SS_A)

$$SS_A = \Sigma \left[\frac{(\text{Sum of scores in a condition})^2}{n \text{ of scores in a condition}} \right] - \frac{(\Sigma X)^2}{N} = \frac{(\Sigma X_k)^2}{n_k} - \frac{(\Sigma X)^2}{N}$$

where Σ = sum; ΣX = sum of all scores; ΣX_k = sum of scores in group k; n_k = sample size in group k; N = total sample size.

Computational formula for subject (participant) sums of squares (SS_s)

$$SS_s = \frac{(\Sigma X_{subj1})^2 + (\Sigma X_{subj2})^2 + (\Sigma X_{subj3})^2 + (\Sigma X_p)^2}{k} - \frac{(\Sigma X)^2}{N}$$

where ΣX = sum of all scores; $\Sigma X_{subj1 \dots p}$ = score for participant or matched participants; k = number of levels/conditions; N = total sample size.

Computational formula for interaction sums of squares

$$SS_{A \times S} = SS_{tot} - SS_A - SS_S$$

where $SS_{A \times S}$ = interaction sum of squares; SS_{tot} = total sum of squares; SS_A = between groups (treatment) sum of squares; SS_S = subject sum of squares.

The degrees of freedom (df), mean square (MS) and F formulas are found in Chapter 11 in Summary Table 11.5.

D.10 COMPUTATIONAL FORMULAS FOR SUM OF SQUARES (SS) FOR A TWO-WAY ANOVA

Computational formula for total sum of squares (SS_{tot})

$$SS_{tot} = \Sigma X^2 - \left[\frac{(\Sigma X)^2}{N} \right]$$

where Σ = sum; X = score; N = total sample size.

Computational formula for factor 1 sum of squares (SS_{B1})

$$SS_{B1} = \Sigma \left[\frac{(\Sigma X_{B1})^2}{n_{B1}} \right] - \frac{(\Sigma X)^2}{N}$$

where Σ = sum; ΣX_{B1} = sum of factor 1 scores; n_{B1} = sample size for factor 1; ΣX = sum of all scores; N = total sample size.

Computational formula for factor 2 sum of squares (SS_{B2})

$$SS_{B2} = \Sigma \left[\frac{(\Sigma X_{B2})^2}{n_{B2}} \right] - \frac{(\Sigma X)^2}{N}$$

where Σ = sum; ΣX_{B2} = sum of factor 2 scores; n_{B2} = sample size for factor 2; ΣX = sum of all scores; N = total sample size.

Computational formula for interaction sum of squares ($SS_{B1 \times B2}$)

$$SS_{B1 \, X \, B2} = \sum \left[\frac{(\Sigma X_{Cell})^2}{n_{Cell}} \right] - \frac{(\Sigma X)^2}{N} - SS_{B1} - SS_{B2}$$

where Σ = sum; ΣX_{cell} = sum of cell scores; n_{cell} = sample size for the cell; ΣX = sum of all scores; N = total sample size; SS_{B1} = sum of squares for factor 1; SS_{B2} = sum of squares for factor 2.

Computational formula for within-subjects (error) sum of squares (SS_w)

$$SS_w = SS_{tot} - SS_{B1} - SS_{B2} - SS_{B1 \times B2}$$

where SS_{tot} = total sum of squares; SS_{B1} = factor 1 sum of squares; SS_{B2} = factor 2 sum of squares; $SS_{B1 \times B2}$ = interaction sum of squares.

The degrees of freedom (df), mean square (MS), and F formulas are found in Chapter 12 in Summary Table 12.4.

D.11 COMPUTATIONAL FORMULAS FOR ADDITIONAL NONPARAMETRIC STATISTICS

Computational formula for McNemar's test

$$X^2 = \frac{(c - b)^2}{(c + b)}$$

where the contingency table contains frequencies and cells are labeled as below:

		Variable 1	
		R_1	R_2
Variable 2	R_1	a	b
	R_2	c	d

Computational formula for cochran Q test

$$Q = k(k-1) \frac{\Sigma(\Sigma col_k - N/k)^2}{\Sigma row_b (k - \Sigma row_b)}$$

where k = # of treatments; b = # of blocks (each matched or repeated group); col_k = total for each column; row_b = total for each row; N = total number of participants.

Computational formula for Mann-Whitney *U* test

$$Group\,1 \quad U_1 = (n_1)(n_2) + \frac{n_1(n_1+1)}{2} - \Sigma R_1$$

$$Group\,2 \quad U_2 = (n_1)(n_2) + \frac{n_2(n_2+1)}{2} - \Sigma R_2$$

where n_1 = number in Group 1; n_2 = number in Group 2; R_1 = ranks in Group 1; R_2 = ranks in Group 2.

For a two-tailed test, you determine which U_{obt} is smaller—U_1 or U_2?

For a one-tailed test, you predict that one group will have a larger U_{obt}.

In comparing U_{obt} and U_{crit}, you want U_{obt} to be equal to or less than U_{crit}.

Computational formula for Rank Sums test

Assign ranks for all scores regardless of group membership or collect ordinal data in the first place.

Divide the ranks by group.

Select one group and compute the sum of ranks (ΣR).

Compute the expected sum of ranks (ΣR_{exp}) using the formula:

$$\Sigma R_{exp} = \frac{n(N+1)}{2}$$

Where $n = n$ for the selected group; N = total number of ranks.

Compute the rank sums statistic using the formula:

$$z_{obt} = \frac{\Sigma R - \Sigma R_{exp}}{\sqrt{\dfrac{n_1(n_2)(N+1)}{12}}}$$

Compare the z_{obt} to the z_{crit} from the z table; for $p < .05$, $z_{crit} = +/-1.96$.

Computational formula for Wilcoxon *T* test

Pair scores for matched participants and find the difference between the scores.

Assign ranks to the difference scores with 1 = the smallest difference while ignoring the sign of the difference; also ignore any zero differences.

Divide the ranks into positive and negative difference scores and compute the sum of ranks for the positive and for the negative difference scores.

Determine T_{obt}.

T_{obt} is significant if it is smaller than T_{crit}.

Computational formula for Kruskal-Wallis *H* test

Rank all of the scores in the study regardless of group membership. Rank of $1 =$ lowest score.

Sum the ranks in each group/condition.

Square the sum of ranks for each group.

Add the squared ranks for each group, symbolized by SS_{BR}.

Compute H_{obt} using the formula:

$$H_{obt} = \frac{12}{N(N+1)}(SS_{BR}) - 3(N+1)$$

where $SS_{BR} =$ sum of squared sum of ranks for all groups; $N =$ number of scores.

Computational formula for Friedman χ^2 test

$$\chi^2 = \frac{12}{nk(k+1)}\Sigma\left[\left(\Sigma R_g\right)\right]^2 - 3n(k+1)$$

where $n =$ number of scores per group; $k =$ number of groups; $\Sigma R_g =$ sum of ranks in each group.

If Friedman χ^2 is significant, compute Nemenyi's procedure as a post hoc test.

Compute the mean (*M*) of ranks in each condition.

Find the difference between the means of ranks.

Make a matrix as you do with Tukey's post hoc test.

The matrix will show the difference between the means of each pair of conditions/groups.

Any difference between the means greater than the critical difference (as determined by the formula below) is significant.

$$\text{Critical difference} = \sqrt{\frac{k(k+1)\chi^2_{crit}}{6N}}$$

where $k =$ number of conditions; $N =$ total number in sample.

Glossary

A

ABA reversal design: The simplest type of reversal design that involves an initial baseline (A), manipulation (B), and a return to baseline (A).

AB design: A simple comparison of the baseline (A) and manipulation (B) phases.

Absolute zero: See True zero.

Alternate forms reliability: The relationship between scores on two different forms of a scale.

Alternative hypothesis (H_a): A prediction of what the researcher expects to find in a study. Often called an "experimental hypothesis" in experimental research and stated in terms of differences between groups.

Anonymity: No one other than the participant can link the participant to his or her responses.

Archival research: Analysis of existing data or records.

B

Bar graph: Graph used to display nominal or ordinal data in which the frequency of scores is depicted on the y-axis and the categories for nominal data or ranks for ordinal data are depicted on the x-axis. Nonadjacent bars represent the frequency of each category or rank.

Baseline (phase A): In a single N design, repeated assessment of the dependent variable in the absence of any manipulation.

Between-groups (treatment) variance: Variability in scores created by the different levels of the IV; researchers attempt to maximize this variability.

Bimodal distribution: A non-normal distribution that has two peaks.

Blind experiment: An experiment in which the participants know they have been assigned to one particular IV condition but they do not know which one.

Blind observer: Observers are not informed of the hypotheses in order to reduce observer bias.

C

Carryover effect: A confound that occurs when the effect of one condition of the treatment continues (or carries over) into the next condition.

Case study: Detailed investigation of a single individual, group, organization, or event.

Causation (or causality): Relationship between cause and effect, in that one variable is shown to have caused the observed change in another variable.

Ceiling effect: Restricting the upper limit of a measure so that higher levels of a measure are not assessed accurately.

Cell: A comparison of one level of a factor across a level of another factor.

Cell means: The mean of each cell comparing one level of a factor across a level of another factor.

Central tendency: A single score that summarizes the center of the distribution.

Checklist: A list of qualities or behaviors that are checked if present.

Chi-square goodness of fit: A nonparametric test used with one nominal variable having two or more categories; tests whether the observed frequencies of the categories reflect the expected population frequencies.

Chi-square test for independence: A nonparametric test used with two nominal variables having two or more categories; tests whether the frequency distributions of two variables are independent.

Chi-square tests (χ^2): Nonparametric tests used with nominal data that compare expected versus observed frequencies.

Closed-ended response format: Item that provides a limited number of choices from which respondents must select.

Cluster random assignment: Procedure in which clusters of individuals are assigned to one level of the IV so that each cluster has an equal chance of experiencing any of the IV levels.

Cluster sampling: A type of probability sampling in which groups, or clusters, are randomly selected instead of individuals.

Cochran *Q* test: A nonparametric statistic used to analyze nominal data from a study that includes three or more dependent groups.

Coding: The process of categorizing information.

Coefficient of determination (r^2): proportion of variability accounted for by knowing the relationship (correlation) between two variables.

Cohen's *d*: A measure of effect size; describes the magnitude of the effect of our IV (or predictor) on the DV (or outcome) in standard deviation units.

Commentaries: Critique or comments about a published research article.

Complete counterbalancing: Randomly assigning participants to all the possible sequences of conditions in an experiment.

Concurrent validity: Positive correlation between scale scores and a current behavior that is related to the construct assessed by the scale.

Conditions (or levels, or groups): The values of the IV.

Confederate: Someone who is working with the researcher but pretends to be a participant or bystander.

Confidence interval: An estimation of the range of values within which the scores will fall (margin of error).

Confidence level: A measure of how likely the scores will fall within a stated confidence interval.

Confidentiality: A participant's responses are kept private although the researcher may be able to link the participant with his or her responses.

Confound (or confounding variable): A variable that varies systematically with the variables of interest in a study and is a potential alternative explanation for causality.

Construct: A concept that cannot be directly observed or measured.

Construct validity: Whether a measure mirrors the characteristics of a hypothetical construct; can be assessed in multiple ways.

Content validity: Inclusion of all aspects of a construct by items on a scale or measure.

Contingency coefficient squared (C^2): Used to determine the effect size for a contingency table larger than 2×2 and with an equal number of rows and columns (3×3, 4×4, etc.).

Contingency table: A matrix that presents frequencies representing the combined levels of two variables.

Contrived observation: The researcher sets up the situation and observes how participants or subjects respond.

Control group: The group that receives the zero level of the IV.

Convenience sampling: A type of nonprobability sample made up of those volunteers or others who are readily available and willing to participate.

Convergent validity: Positive relationship between two scales measuring the same or similar constructs.

Correlation: A relationship between variables.

Correlational design: See Correlational research.

Correlational factorial design: A design with two or more predictors that are not manipulated in the study.

Correlational research (or correlational design): Research design in which the relationship among two or more variables is examined, but causality cannot be determined.

Counterbalancing: A procedure to eliminate order effects in a repeated measures experiment; participants are randomly assigned to different sequences of the conditions in an experiment.

Covert observation: Observations are made without the participants' awareness.

Cramer's *V* squared (*V*²): The effect size statistic used when a contingency table is larger than a 2 × 2 and the number of rows and columns are different numbers (3 × 4, 4 × 2, etc.).

Criterion level (*p*): The percentage of a sampling distribution that the researcher selects for the region of rejection; typically researchers use 5% ($p < .05$).

Criterion validity: Positive correlation between scale scores and a behavioral measure.

Criterion variable: Predicted variable in a regression equation.

Critical value: The value of a statistic that defines the extreme 5% of a distribution for a one-tailed hypothesis or the extreme 2.5% of the distribution for a two-tailed test.

Cronbach's alpha (α): Test used to assess the internal consistency of a scale by computing the intercorrelations among responses to scale items; values of .70 or higher are interpreted as acceptable internal consistency.

Cumulative percentage: The proportion of a score that falls within a specified interval.

D

Debriefing: Clearing up any misconceptions that the participant might have and addressing any negative effects of the study.

Degrees of freedom (*df*): Determined by the sample size; number of scores free to vary in a sample.

Demand characteristics: Characteristics of the study that lead a participant to guess at the study's hypothesis and change their behavior accordingly.

Dependent-groups design: A design where the participants in different conditions are related or are the same people; the design reduces error variance and is more powerful than an independent design.

Dependent-groups experiment: Experiment in which the groups are related, in that participants were matched prior to exposure to the IV or in that the participants experience all levels of the IV.

Dependent-groups factorial design: A factorial design in which all the levels of the factors are related via matching or repeated measures.

Dependent-groups one-way ANOVA: See **Within-subjects ANOVA.**

Dependent-samples *t* test (or paired-samples *t* test/within-subjects *t* test): The statistical test used to analyze results from a dependent two-groups design.

Dependent variable (DV): The variable that is measured in an experiment and is expected to vary or change based on the IV manipulation.

Descriptive research: Research design in which the primary goal is to describe the variables, but not examine relationships among variables.

Descriptive statistics: A type of quantitative (numerical) analysis used to summarize the characteristics of a sample.

Dichotomous variable: A nominal variable that has two levels or groups.

Diffusion of treatment: The treatment administered to one group is shared with another group through cross-group interactions.

Divergent validity: Negative or no relationship between two scales measuring different constructs.

Double-blind experiment: An experiment in which neither the participants nor the researcher interacting with the participants know which participants have been assigned to each condition.

Duration: How long a behavior lasts.

E

Ecological validity: A type of external validity that assesses the degree to which a study's findings generalize to real-world settings.

Effect size: Strength or magnitude of the effect of a variable, or the strength of the relationship between two variables.

Embedded case study: Investigation of single cases that comprise a group or organization in order to understand that group or organization as a whole.

Environmental manipulations: Systematic changes to the physical or social environment.

Equal intervals: The distance between numbers on a scale is equal.

Error variance: See Within-groups variance.

Estimated standard error of the means (SD_x): Estimated standard deviation of the sampling distribution of means that is used to calculate the t test.

Eta squared (η^2): The percentage of variability in a measured variable which is accounted for by the grouping variable. It is used as a measure of effect size in studies analyzed with an ANOVA.

Expected frequency (E): The frequency or count we expect in a category according to the null hypothesis.

Experiment: See Experimental research

Experimental factorial design: A design with two or more IVs that are manipulated and in which participants are randomly assigned to IV levels.

Experimental group: The group that receives a certain amount or level of the IV.

Experimental hypothesis (H_a): An alternative hypothesis used in experiments and stated in terms of differences between groups.

Experimental research (or experimental design, or experiment): Research design that attempts to determine a causal relationship by randomly assigning participants or subjects to groups, manipulating one variable (the IV), and measuring the effect of that manipulation on another variable (the DV).

Experimenter expectancy effects (or Rosenthal effect): Phenomenon in which a researcher unintentionally treats the groups differently so that results support the hypothesis.

External validity: The degree to which we can say that the results of a study are accurate for different types of people in different settings assessed with different procedures.

F

Face validity: Whether a particular measure seems to be appropriate as a way to assess a construct.

Factor: A predictor variable in a correlational design or an IV in an experiment or quasi-experiment.

Factorial design: A design used to examine how two or more variables (factors) predict or explain an outcome.

Factorial notation: A shorthand for expressing how many factors, levels, and cells are present in a factorial design.

Fatigue effect: A confound that occurs when changes in the DV occur because of participants becoming tired.

Fisher's Least Significant Difference (LSD) test: A commonly used post hoc test that computes the smallest amount that group means can differ in order to be significant.

Floor effect: Restricting the lower limit of a measure so that lower scores are not assessed accurately.

Forced-choice response format: Response format in which there is no neutral, or middle, option.

Frequency (f): A count of how many times a score appears in the sample.

Frequency polygon: Graph used to display interval or ratio data in which the frequency of scores is depicted on the y-axis and the scores are depicted on the x-axis. Points represent the frequency of each score. The points are connected with straight lines that begin and end on the x-axis.

Friedman chi-squared (Friedman χ^2): A nonparametric test used to analyze ordinal or ranked data from a study with one variable with three or more dependent groups.

G

Grand mean: The mean of the DV or outcome of the entire sample.

Grounded theory: A method to build theory from data.

Group design: Design in which a researcher compares two or more groups of participants who are exposed to different levels of a variable of interest.

Group means: The mean of each level or group that ignores the other factor.

H

Hawthorne effect: Phenomenon in which participants change their behavior simply because they are in a study and have the attention of researchers.

Histogram: Graph used to display interval or ratio data in which the frequency of scores is depicted on the y-axis and the interval ratings or ratio scores are depicted on the x-axis. Adjacent bars represent the frequency of each rating or score.

Homogeneity of the sample: The degree to which the members of a sample have similar characteristics.

Homogeneity of variance: Assumption that the variance of populations is the same; group standard deviations serve as estimates of the population variances.

Hybrid factorial design: A design with at least one experimental IV and at least one quasi-IV or predictor.

Hypothesis testing: The process of determining the probability of obtaining a particular result or set of results.

I

Identity: Each number has a unique meaning.

Independent-groups experiment (or between-subjects experiment): Experiment in which each participant experiences only one level of the IV.

Independent-groups factorial design: A factorial design in which all the factors have independent levels/groups.

Independent-samples t test: The inferential statistic used to test differences between means in a study with two independent groups.

Independent variable (IV): The variable that is manipulated in an experiment.

Inferential statistics: Statistical analysis of data gathered from a sample to draw conclusions about a population from which the sample is drawn.

Informed consent: An ethical standard by which potential participants are informed of the topic, procedures, risks, and benefits of participation prior to consenting to participate.

Institutional Review Board (IRB): An established group that evaluates research proposals to ensure that ethical standards are being followed in research that involves human participants.

Instructional manipulations: Systematic changes to instructions, educational information, or feedback.

Interaction effect: How one variable predicts or affects the outcome based on the levels of another variable.

Interaction sums of squares ($SS_{A \times S}$): The numerator of the variance created by the differences among different participants in the same condition in a dependent design; considered an interaction between condition and participants.

Internal consistency: The consistency of participant responses to all the items in a scale.

Internal validity: The degree to which we can say that we found an accurate relationship among variables, in that changes in one variable (the DV) are caused by changes in another variable (the IV). Relevant only to studies examining causation.

Interrater reliability: Consistency of observations or ratings of a behavior made by two different people.

Interval scale: A scale of measurement that has both order and equal intervals between values on the scale.

Interviewer bias: The interviewer may provide verbal or nonverbal cues that impact how the participant responds.

IV manipulation: The way the researcher creates the conditions of the IV.

K

Kruskal-Wallis H test: A nonparametric test used to analyze ordinal data from a study with one variable with at least three levels.

Kurtosis: The degree of the peak of a normal distribution.

L

Latency: The time between stopping one task and beginning a new task.

Latin Square counterbalancing: A type of partial counterbalancing where each condition appears once in each sequence; participants are then randomly assigned to the different sequences.

Leptokurtic curve: A normal distribution with most of the scores in the middle and a sharp peak.

Levene's Test for Equality of Variances: A statistical test that examines whether the variability within different samples is similar.

Likert-type scale: A commonly used type of interval scale response in which items are rated on a range of numbers (usually between 5 and 7 response options) that are assumed to have equal intervals.

Linear regression: Process of describing a correlation with the line that best fits the data points.

Linear relationship: A relationship between two variables, defined by their moving in a single direction together.

Line of best fit: The straight line that best fits a correlation and consists of each X value in the relationship and its predicted Y value.

Literature review: Review of past research without a report of original research.

M

Main effect: How one variable predicts or affects the outcome.

Manipulation (phase B): In a single N design, repeated assessment of the dependent variable during the implementation of a manipulation (e.g., treatment).

Manipulation check: The process of verifying that the participants attended to the manipulation.

Mann-Whitney U test: A nonparametric test used to analyze ordinal data from two independent groups when $n \leq 20$/group.

Matched-pairs design: A design where participants in each group are matched on a characteristic relevant to the variable that is being measured; in an experimental design a member of each matched pair is randomly assigned to each IV condition.

Matched random assignment: Process in which participants are put into matched sets and then each member of the set is assigned to one IV level so that all in the set have an equal chance of experiencing any of the levels.

Maximum variation sampling: A nonprobability sampling strategy in which the researcher seeks out the full range of extremes in the population.

McNemar test: A nonparametric statistic used to analyze nominal data from a study using two dependent (matched or repeated measures) groups.

Mean (M): The arithmetic average.

Mean difference (M_D): The average difference between the scores of matched pairs or the scores for the same participants across two conditions; computed by subtracting one score of a matched or repeated pair from the other score.

Mean square between groups (MS_B): The average deviation of group means from the total mean of a sample; used in computing an ANOVA.

Mean square within groups (MS_W): The average deviation within all groups or levels of a study; used in computing an ANOVA.

Measurement reliability: Consistency of a measure.

Measurement validity: Measurement is accurate in that it measures what it purports to measure.

Median (Mdn): The score that cuts a distribution in half.

Mesokurtic curve: A normal distribution with a moderate or middle peak.

Meta-analysis: A type of review in which the statistical results of past research are synthesized but no original data were collected or analyzed.

Mixed design: A factorial design with at least one factor with independent levels and at least one factor with dependent levels.

Mode: The most frequent score in a distribution.

Moderator: In an interaction effect, the factor that changes the strength or direction of the relationship between a predictor and the outcome (or one IV and the DV in an experiment).

Mu (μ): Population mean.

Multiple-baseline across behaviors: The manipulation is introduced at different times across two or more behaviors.

Multiple-baseline across persons: The manipulation is introduced at different times across two or more persons.

Multiple-baseline across settings: The manipulation is introduced at different times across two or more settings.

Multiple-baseline design: The manipulation is introduced at different times across two or more persons, settings, or behaviors.

Multiple independent-groups design: A study examining the effect of a manipulated IV or the relationship of a variable that has three or more levels on a DV; the participants in each level of the IV are unrelated.

Multiple-manipulation design: A single N design in which the researcher introduces two or more manipulations over the course of the study.

Multiple regression (R): A statistical technique that computes both the individual and combined contribution of two or more variables to the prediction of another variable.

N

Narrative: A detailed account of behaviors or responses.

Naturalistic observations: Observations that occur in natural environments or situations and do not involve interference by anyone involved in the research.

Negative correlation: A relationship where scores on two variables move in opposite directions (one increases while the other decreases).

Negative skew: One or a few negative scores skew the distribution in the negative direction, but most of the scores cluster on the positive end of the scale.

Nominal scale: A scale of measurement where numbers represent categories and have no numerical value.

Nonparametric statistics: Statistics used to analyze nominal and ordinal (ranked) data or used when the assumptions of parametric statistics are violated.

Nonparticipant observation: The researcher or observer is not directly involved in the situation.

Nonprobability sampling (or nonrandom sampling): Process of obtaining a study sample without using random selection.

Nonresponse bias: The extent to which those who were selected and participated in the study differ from those who were selected but did not participate.

Normal distribution: Symmetrical distribution in which scores cluster around the middle and then taper off at the ends.

Null hypothesis (H_0): A prediction of no difference between groups; the hypothesis the researcher expects to reject.

Numerical coding: The process of categorizing and numbering information for quantitative analyses.

O

Observational measure: A measure that is rated by observers and sometimes made without the awareness of the person performing the behavior.

Observed frequency (O): The frequency or count we obtain in a particular category.

Observed minimum and maximum scores: The lowest and highest scores on a measure that are obtained in the sample.

Observer bias: The observers pay closer attention to behaviors that support their expectations or interpret behaviors in ways that support their expectations or lose their focus on the target behavior.

One-group pretest–posttest design: Nonexperimental design in which all participants are tested prior to exposure to a variable of interest and again after exposure.

One-sample t test: An inferential statistic that compares a sample mean to a known population mean.

One-tailed hypothesis: A hypothesis stating the direction (higher or lower) in which a sample statistic will differ from the population or another group.

One-way analysis of variance/one-way ANOVA: The inferential statistical test used to analyze data from a multiple-groups design.

Open-ended response format: Item on a scale that required the respondents to generate their own answers.

Operational definition: The explicit explanation of a variable in terms of how it is measured or manipulated.

Order: Numbers on a scale are ordered in sequence.

Order effect: A confound that occurs when the order of each treatment condition cannot be separated from the condition.

Ordinal scale: A scale of measurement with numbers that have order so that each number is greater or less than other numbers but the interval between the numbers is not equal; also called rankings.

Outcome: The variable that is predicted, and a term used instead of DV in a correlational design.

Outliers: Responses or observations that deviate greatly from the rest of the data.

Overt observation: No attempts are made to hide the observation.

P

Paired-samples *t* test: See Dependent-samples *t* test.

Parameters: Statistics from a population.

Parametric statistics: Statistics used to analyze interval and ratio data and that assume a normal distribution and homogeneity of variance between groups.

Partial counterbalancing: Randomly assigning participants to different sequences of conditions so that each condition is represented in each order an equal number of times but not all sequences are represented.

Partial eta squared ($\eta^2_{partial}$): The effect size for a dependent multiple-group design that removes the variability unique to individual participants from the error term.

Participant observation: The researcher or observer becomes actively involved in the situation.

Pearson's *r* (or Pearson's product-moment correlation coefficient): Statistic used to describe a linear relationship between two interval/ratio measures; describes the direction (positive or negative) and strength (between +/− 1.0) of the relationship.

Peer review: Process in which scholarly works are reviewed by other experts in the field.

Percentage: The proportion of a score within the sample.

Percentile: The percentage of the distribution that scored below a specific score.

Phi squared (ϕ^2): The statistic used to assess the effect size when a 2×2 test for independence is significant; it is interpreted as the percentage of variability accounted for in the frequency of one variable by knowing its relationship with a second variable.

Physiological manipulations: Systematic changes to participants' or subjects' physical functioning.

Pilot study: A preliminary study with a small sample to test measures and procedures.

Placebo: A treatment or substance that in and of itself has no therapeutic effect, such as a sugar pill.

Platykurtic curve: A normal distribution that is relatively spread out and flat.

Point-biserial correlation coefficient (r_{pb}): Describes the relationship between a dichotomous variable and an interval/ratio variable; interpreted similarly to a Pearson correlation coefficient.

Pooled variance: Estimate of the total variance for a sample of scores computed by combining and weighting by their respective *n* the variances of the two groups making up the sample.

Popular works: Works designed to entertain or educate and that were written for those who do not necessarily have any expertise in the topic area.

Population: The group that a researcher is interested in examining defined by specific characteristics such as residency, occupation, gender, or age.

Positive correlation: A relationship where scores on two variables move in the same direction (both either increase or decrease).

Positive skew: One or a few positive scores skew the distribution in the positive direction, but most of the scores cluster on the negative end of the scale.

Possible minimum and maximum scores: The lowest and highest scores possible for the measurement instrument.

Post hoc test: Additional analysis when you find statistically significant results when comparing 3 or more groups (sometimes also performed when you find a statistically significant interaction).

Power: The ability to reject the null hypothesis when it is, in fact, false.

Practical significance: The usefulness or everyday impact of results.

Practice effect: A confound that occurs when participants' scores change due to repeating a task rather than because of the level of the IV.

Predictive validity: Positive relationship between scale scores and a future behavior that is related to the construct assessed by the scale.

Predictor variable: The variable that is used to predict the value of another variable, and a term used instead of IV in a correlational design.

Prescreening: Process of identifying those who have characteristics that the researcher wants to include or exclude in the study.

Prevalence: How common or widespread a behavior, attitude, characteristic, or condition is within a specific time period.

Primary research article (or empirical journal article): Report of the method and results of an original research study (i.e., a primary research source) that is published in an academic journal.

Primary research source: The authors report the results of an original research study that they conducted.

Probability sampling (or random sampling): Process of obtaining a study sample using random selection.

Q

Qualitative measure: Nonnumerical assessment.

Quantitative measure: Numerical measure.

Quasi-experimental factorial design: A design with two or more quasi-IVs, meaning that the IVs are manipulated but participants are not randomly assigned to IV conditions.

Quasi-experimental research (or quasi-experimental design, or quasi-experiment): Research design that includes a key characteristic of an experiment, namely, manipulation of a variable. However, it does not have all the requirements for an experiment in that there is no random assignment to the levels of the manipulated variable. Because there is no random assignment, a quasi-experiment cannot demonstrate causation.

Questionnaire: A document, presented in hard copy or on the computer, consisting of items that assess one or more constructs.

Quota sampling: A type of nonprobability sampling that results in the sample representing key subpopulations based on characteristics such as age, gender, and ethnicity.

R

Random assignment: Process of assigning participants to IV conditions (or order of conditions) that is based on chance.

Random assignment to order of conditions: In experiments where the participants experience all levels of the IV, the participants all have an equal chance of experiencing the IV levels in a certain order.

Randomized partial counterbalancing: Randomly assigning each participant to one of the possible sequences of conditions without concern about order or sequence; used when you have a larger number of sequences than participants.

Random selection: A process of selecting a sample in which all members of a population or a subpopulation have an equal chance of being selected.

Random selection without replacement: A selected member of the population is removed from the pool of possible participants so that any member may be selected into the sample only once.

Random selection with replacement: A selected member of the population is returned to the pool of possible participants so that any member may be selected into the sample more than once.

Range: The distance between the observed maximum and minimum scores.

Rank Sums test: A nonparametric test used to analyze ordinal data from two independent groups when at least one of the groups has more than 20.

Rating scale: A numerical rating of a particular quality.

Ratio scale: A scale of measurement where values measure quantity and have order, equal intervals, and a true zero.

Reaction time: How long it takes a participant to respond to a stimulus.

Region of acceptance: Area of sampling distribution generally defined by the mean +/–2 SD or 95% of the distribution; results falling in this region imply that our sample belongs to the sampling distribution defined by the H_0 and result in the researcher retaining the H_o.

Region of rejection: The extreme 5% (generally) of a sampling distribution; results falling in this area imply that our sample does not belong to the sampling distribution defined by the H_0 and result in the researcher rejecting the H_0 and accepting the H_a.

Regression equation: Equation that describes the relationship between two variables and allows us to predict Y from X.

Reliability: Consistency of findings or measures.

Reliability of a study: How consistent the results are across similar studies.

Repeated-measures ANOVA: See Within-subjects ANOVA.

Repeated measures design (or within-subjects design): A design where participants experience every condition in a study; in an experiment they also are randomly assigned to the order of conditions.

Replication: Conducting the same study with new participants (literal replication) or conducting a study examining the same patterns or relationships but with different methods (conceptual replication).

Response format: The type of response, either participant generated or choice from among listed options, required by items on a questionnaire.

Reversal: The manipulation is removed and the individual returns to a baseline phase.

S

Sample: A subset of the population from which data are collected.

Sampling: The process by which a sample is selected.

Sampling bias: When some members of a population are overrepresented in the sample.

Sampling distribution: A distribution of some statistic obtained from multiple samples of the same size drawn from the same population.

Scale score: The score that is computed from items assessing a particular construct, most commonly a sum or average of the numbers representing responses to individual items in the document.

Scatterplot (or scattergram): A graph of the data points created by participant scores on two measures; each data point represents a score on the X variable and a score on the Y variable.

Scenario manipulations: Systematic changes to a scenario.

Scholarly works: Works designed to advance knowledge in a field, written by someone with expertise in that field for others with knowledge of the field, that cite and build upon other scholarly sources.

Secondary data: Research data that were collected by one researcher or group but analyzed by a different researcher or group.

Secondary research source: The authors review research but do not report results of an original study.

Semi-structured interviews: There is a set of core questions or topics that the interviewer will follow, but the interviewer may prompt for more information, ask follow-up questions, or clarify questions as the interviewer deems necessary.

Sensitivity: The ability of a measurement instrument to detect differences.

Sigma (σ): Population standard deviation.

Simple experiment: A study investigating the effect of a manipulated IV with two conditions on a DV. The IV is nominal scale and the DV is interval or ratio.

Simple random assignment: Procedure in which each participant is assigned to one level of the IV so that every participant has an equal chance of experiencing any of the IV levels.

Simple random sampling: A type of probability sampling in which every single member of the population has an equal chance of being selected for the sample.

Single *N* design: Quantitative investigation of a cause-and-effect relationship within a single case.

Skewed distribution: A non-normal distribution that is asymmetrical, with scores clustering on one side of the distribution and a long tail on the other side.

Skewness statistic (G_1): A number that indicates the degree of skewness in a distribution.

Slope: Describes the rate of change in *Y* with each unit of change in *X* (or the incline of the line of best fit), designated by "*b*" in the regression equation.

Small *N* designs: A series of single *N* designs.

Snowball sampling: A nonprobability sampling strategy in which participants recruit others into the sample.

Social desirability bias: Participants may respond based on how they want to be perceived or what is socially acceptable.

Spearman's rho (r_s): A commonly used nonparametric statistic that analyzes the relationship or correlation between two ordinal variables.

Sphericity: In a dependent design, the assumption that the variances of the differences between all the combinations of pairs of groups are equal.

Split-half reliability: Correlations between the responses to half the items on a scale to the other half (usually even-numbered items correlated with odd-numbered items); values of .70 or higher are considered to denote acceptable reliability.

Squared point-biserial correlation (r_{pb}^2): A measure of effect size for the independent-samples *t* test, providing the percentage of variance in the outcome (or DV) accounted for by the predictor (or IV).

Stable baseline: A baseline that displays no trend (or slope) and little variability and therefore allows for prediction of future behavior.

Standard deviation (*SD*): A single number that summarizes the degree to which scores differ from the mean.

Standard error of the difference between the means (SD_{X-X}): The average variability in a sampling distribution of differences between means.

Standard error of the estimate (s_y): Average difference between the predicted Y values for each X from the actual Y values.

Standard error of the mean differences (SD_D): Standard deviation of the differences for a sampling distribution of mean differences; estimated from the standard deviation of difference scores in a dependent-samples study.

Standard error of the means (σ_x): Standard deviation of the sampling distribution of means.

Statistical significance: When the results of a study fall in the extreme 5% (or 1% if you use a more stringent criterion) of the sampling distribution, suggesting that the obtained findings are not due to chance alone and do not belong to the sampling distribution defined by the H_0.

Statistical significance testing: A process to reduce the likelihood that the results were obtained by chance alone.

Stratified random assignment: Procedure in which the researcher identifies strata of participants based on key characteristics, then uses random assignment so that each member of each stratum has an equal chance of being assigned to any of the IV conditions.

Stratified random sampling: A type of probability sampling that results in the sample representing key subpopulations based on characteristics such as age, gender, and ethnicity.

Structured interviews: All questions, follow-up questions, and responses by the interviewer are determined beforehand to ensure that all the participants have a very similar experience.

Subpopulation: A portion or subgroup of the population.

Sum of squares between groups (SS_B): The sum of the squared deviations of treatment group means from the mean for the entire sample.

Sum of squares of subjects (SS_s): The numerator of the variance created by adding the squared differences in the scores of individual participants across different conditions in a dependent design.

Sum of squares within groups (SS_w): The sum of the squared deviations of each participant from the mean of their group.

Survey research: Interviews or questionnaires in which participants report on their attitudes and behaviors.

T

Task completion time: How long it takes to complete a task.

Testable hypothesis: An educated prediction that can be disproven.

Test-retest reliability: A measure of the stability of scores on a scale over time.

Threats to internal validity: Confounds that must be controlled so that a cause–effect relationship can be demonstrated; Campbell and Stanley (1963) identified the threats of (a) history, (b) maturation, (c) testing, (d) instrumentation, (e) statistical regression, (f) selection, (g) mortality, and (h) selection interactions.

Treatment variance: See Between-groups variance.

Trend: Pattern of change in prevalence over time.

True zero (or absolute zero): The score of zero on a scale is a fixed point.

Tukey's Honestly Significant Difference (HSD) test: A popular post hoc test that is more conservative than most tests; it must be used with equal n and computes the least significant difference that is significant between means.

Two-tailed hypothesis: A hypothesis stating that results from a sample will differ from the population or another group but without stating how the results will differ.

Two-way between-subjects ANOVA: An analysis of variance test appropriate for designs with two independent factors and an interval or ratio outcome.

Two-way mixed ANOVA: An analysis of variance test appropriate for designs with one independent factor, one dependent factor, and an interval or ratio outcome.

Two-way within-subjects ANOVA: An analysis of variance test appropriate for designs with two dependent factors and an interval or ratio outcome.

Type I error: The probability of rejecting a true H_o; defined by the probability of the significance level of your findings.

Type II error: The probability of incorrectly retaining a false H_0.

U

Uniform distribution: A non-normal distribution in which all scores or ratings have the same frequency.

Unobtrusive measure: Measure that is made of behaviors or situations without disturbing the naturally occurring behavior or situation in order to reduce changes that might occur if there was awareness of measurement.

V

Validity: Accuracy of findings or measures.

Variability: The degree to which scores differ from each other in the sample.

Variable: A factor in a research study that has two or more possible values.

Variance (SD^2): The average of the squared difference between the mean and scores in a distribution, or the standard deviation squared.

Visual inspection: A nonstatistical technique in which patterns of the A and B phases are compared.

W

Waitlist control: A control group in an experiment that is promised the same treatment as the experimental group after the experimental group has completed treatment and both groups have been assessed.

Wilcoxon *T* test: A nonparametric test used to analyze ordinal data collected from two dependent groups.

Within-groups (error) variance: The variability among the scores of participants created by individual or participant differences even under the same conditions. Researchers attempt to reduce this type of variability.

Within-subjects ANOVA (or repeated measures ANOVA/dependent-groups one-way ANOVA): The statistical test used to analyze dependent multiple-groups designs.

Within-subjects *t* test: See **Dependent-samples *t* test**.

Y

$Y' = bX + a$: formula for a linear regression equation.

Y-intercept: The point at which a line of best fit crosses the *y*-axis, designated as "a" in the regression equation.

Y predicted (Y'): The value that results from entering a particular *X* value in a regression equation.

Z

z score: A standardized score based on the standard deviation of the distribution.

References

Aldao, A., & De Los Reyes, A. (2016). Introduction to the Special Section: Toward implementing physiological measures in clinical assessments of adult mental health. *Journal of Psychopathology and Behavioral Assessments, 38,* 1–4. doi:10.1007/s10862-015-9521-y

American Anthropological Association (AAA). (2009). *Code of ethics of the American Anthropological Association.* Retrieved from http://www.aaanet.org/_cs_upload/issues/policy-advocacy/27668_1.pdf

American Educational Research Association. (2011). Code of ethics. *Educational Researcher, 40,* 145–156. doi:10.3102/0013189X1140403

American Political Science Association. (2008). *A guide to professional ethics in political science* (2nd ed.). Retrieved from http://www.apsanet.org/media/PDFs/ethics-guideweb.pdf

American Psychological Association (APA). (2001). *Publication manual of the American Psychological Association* (5th ed.). Washington, DC: Author.

American Psychological Association (APA). (2010a). *Ethical principles of psychologists and code of conduct.* Retrieved from http://www.apa.org/ethics/code/index.aspx

American Psychological Association (2010b). *Publication manual of the American Psychological Association* (6th ed.). Washington, DC: Author.

American Sociological Association (ASA). (1999). *Code of ethics and policies and procedures of the ASA Committee on Professional Ethics.* Retrieved from http://www.asanet.org/images/asa/docs/pdf/CodeofEthics.pdf

Anderson, S., & Fuller, G. (2010). Effect of music on reading comprehension of junior high school students. *School Psychology Quarterly, 25,* 178–187. doi:10.1037/a0021213

Annesi, J. (2013). Effects of treatment differences on psychosocial predictors of exercise and improved eating in obese middle-age adults. *Journal of Physical Activity and Health, 10,* 1024–1031.

Ariely, D. (2009). *Predictably irrational: The hidden forces that shape our decisions.* New York, NY: HarperCollins.

Baumrind, D. (1985). Research using intentional deception: Ethical issues revisited. *American Psychologist, 40,* 165–174. doi:10.1037/0003-66X.40.2.165

Beaver, T., Knox, D., & Zusman, M. (2010). "Hold the phone!": Cell phone use and partner reaction among university students. *College Student Journal, 44,* 629–632.

Belter, R. W., & du Pré, A. (2009). A strategy to reduce plagiarism in an undergraduate course. *Teaching of Psychology, 36,* 257–261. doi:10.1080/00986280903173165

Bem, D. J. (2003). Writing the empirical journal article. In J. M. Darley, M. P. Zanna, & H. L. Roediger III (Eds.), *The complete academic.* Washington, DC: American Psychological Association.

Birnbaum, M. H. (2004). Human research and data collection via the Internet. *Annual Review of Psychology, 55,* 803–832.

Buchanan, T. (2002). Online assessment: Desirable or dangerous? *Professional Psychology: Research and Practice, 33,* 148–154.

Buck, J. L. (1985). A failure to find gender differences in statistics achievement. *Teaching of Psychology, 12,* 100. doi:10.1207/s15328023top1202_13

Bulmer, M. G. (1979). *Principles of statistics.* New York, NY: Dover.

Burchinal, M., Roberts, J. E., Zeisel, S. A., Hennon, E. A., & Hooper, S. (2006). Social risk and protective child, parenting, and child care factors in early elementary school years. *Parenting: Science and Practice, 6,* 79–113.

Byington, K., & Schwebel, D. C. (2013). Effects of mobile Internet use on college student pedestrian injury risk. *Accident Analysis and Prevention, 51,* 78–83. doi:10.1016/j.aap.2012.11.001

Cadinu, M., Maass, A., Lombardo, M., & Frigerio, S. (2006). Stereotype threat: The moderating role of Locus of Control beliefs. *European Journal of Social Psychology, 36,* 183–197. doi:10.1002/ejsp.303

Caird, J. K., Johnston, K. A., Willness, C. R., Asbridge, M., & Steel, P. (2014). A meta-analysis of the effects of texting on driving. *Accident Analysis And Prevention, 71,* 311–318. doi:10.1016/j.aap.2014.06.005

Caird, J. K., Willness, C. R., Steel, P., & Scialfa, C. (2008). A meta-analysis of the effects of cell phones on driver performance. *Accident Analysis and Prevention, 40,* 1282–1293. doi:10.1016/j.aap.2008.01.009

Campbell, D. T., & Stanley, J. C. (1963). *Experimental and quasi-experimental designs for research.* Chicago, IL: Rand-McNally.

Castilho, P., Pinto-Gouveia, J., & Duarte, J. (2015). Evaluating the multifactor structure of the long and short versions of the Self-Compassion Scale in a clinical sample. *Journal of Clinical Psychology, 71,* 856–870. doi:10.1002/jclp.22187

Clapp, J., Reed, M., Martel, B., Gonzalez, M., & Ruderman, D. (2014). Drinking behavior among low-income older adults: A multimethod approach to estimating alcohol use. *Alcoholism: Clinical and Experimental Research, 38,* 2862–2868. doi:10.1111/acer.12550

Clay, R. (2010). More than one way to measure. *Monitor on Psychology, 41*(8). Retrieved from http://www.apa.org/monitor

Cobb, S., Heaney, R., Corcoran, O., & Henderson-Begg, S. (2010). Using mobile phones to increase classroom interaction. *Journal of Educational Multimedia and Hypermedia, 19*(2), 147–157.

Cohen, J. (1988). *Statistical power analysis for the behavioral sciences* (2nd ed.). Hillsdale, NJ: Erlbaum.

Cook, T. D., & Campbell, D. T. (1979). *Quasi-experimentation: Design and analysis issues for field settings.* Boston, MA: Houghton Mifflin.

Cramer, S., Mayer, J., & Ryan, S. (2007). College students use cell phones while driving more frequently than found in government study. *Journal of American College Health, 56,* 181–184.

Culwin, F. (2006). An active introduction to academic misconduct and the measured demographics of misconduct. *Assessment & Evaluation in Higher Education, 31,* 167–182. doi:10.1080/0260293050 0262478

Cumming, G., Fidler, F., Kalinowski, P., & Lai, J. (2012). The statistical recommendations of the American Psychological Association Publication Manual: Effect sizes, confidence intervals, and meta-analysis. *Australian Journal of Psychology, 64,* 138–146. doi:10.1111/j.1742-9536.2011.00037.x

Dahl, M. (2015, October 15). In defense of (sometimes) giving up. *New York Magazine.* Retrieved from http:\\nymag.com

Darley, J. M., & Latané, B. (1968). Bystander intervention in emergencies: Diffusion of responsibility. *Journal of Personality and Social Psychology, 8,* 377–383.

Datu, J. A. D., Yuen, M., & Chen, G. (2016). Grit and determination: A review of literature with implications for theory and research. *Journal of Psychologists and Counsellors in Schools.* doi:10.1017/jgc.2016.2

David, D. (2007). Case study methodology: Fundamentals and critical analysis. *Cognition, Brain, & Behavior, 7,* 299–317.

Doucleff, M. (2012, February). Anatomy of a tear-jerker. *The Wall Street Journal.* Retrieved from http://online.wsj.com/article/SB10001424052970203646004577213010291701378.html

Drews, F., Pasupathi, M., & Strayer, D. (2008). Passenger and cell phone conversations in simulated driving. *Journal of Experimental Psychology: Applied, 14,* 392–400. doi:10.1037/a0013119

Drouin, M. A. (2011). College students' text messaging, use of textese and literacy skills. *Journal of Computer Assisted Learning, 27,* 67–75. doi:10.1111/j.1365-2729.2010.00399.x

Duckworth, A. L., & Quinn, P. D. (2009). Development and validation of the Short Grit Scale (Grit-S). *Journal of Personality Assessment, 91,* 166–174. doi:10.1080/00223890802634290

Duggan, M. (2015). *Mobile messaging and social media—2015.* Retrieved from Pew Research Center: http://www.pewinternet.org/2015/08/19/mobile-messaging-and-social-media-2015/

Egan, M. T. (2002). Grounded theory research and theory building. *Advances in Developing Human Resources, 4,* 277–295. doi:10.1177/1523422302043004

Estow, S., Lawrence, E., & Adams, K. (2011). Practice makes perfect: Improving students' skills in understanding and avoiding plagiarism with a themed methods course. *Teaching of Psychology, 38,* 259–261. doi:10.1177/0098628311421325

Farmer, C., Klauer, S., McClafferty, J., & Guo, F. (2015, November). Relationship of near-crash risk to time spent on cell phone while driving. *Traffic Injury Prevention, 16,* 792–800.

Ferguson, C. (2009). An effect size primer: A guide for clinicians and researchers. *Professional Psychology: Research and Practice, 40,* 532–538. doi:10.1037/a0015808

Ferlazzo, F., DiNocera, F., & Sdoia, S. (2008). Shifting attention across near and far spaces: Implications for the use of hands-free cell phones while driving. *Accident Analysis and Prevention, 40,* 1859–1864. doi:10.1016/j.aap.2008.07.003

Fisher, C. B., & Fryberg, D. (1994). Participant partners: College students weigh the costs and benefits of deceptive research. *American Psychologist, 49,* 417–427.

Fitch, G., Soccolich, S., Guo, F., McClafferty, J., Fang, Y., Olson, R., . . . Dingus, T. (2013, April). The impact of hand-held and hands-free cell phone use on driving performance and safety-critical event risk. (Report No. DOT HS 811 757). Washington, DC: National Highway Traffic Safety Administration.

Fritz, C., Morris, P., & Richler, J. (2012). Effect size estimates: Current use, calculations, and interpretation. *Journal of Experimental Psychology: General, 141,* 2–18. doi:10.1037/a0024338

Fritz, C. O. (2011). Testing, generation, and spacing applied to education: Past, present, and future. In A. S. Benjamin (Ed.), *Successful remembering and successful forgetting: A Festschrift in honor of Robert A. Bjork* (pp. 199–216). New York, NY: Taylor and Francis.

Froese, A., Carpenter, C., Inman, D., Schooley, J., Barnes, R., Brecht, P., & Jasmin, D. (2012). Effects of classroom cell phone use on expected and actual learning. *College Student Journal, 46,* 323–332.

George, A. L., & Bennett, A. (2005). *Case studies and theory development in the social sciences.* Cambridge, MA: MIT Press.

Gibson, B., King, G., Kushki, A., Mistry, B., Thompson, L., Teachman, G., Batorowicz, B., & McMain-Klein, M. (2014). A multi-method approach to studying activity setting participation: Integrating standardized questionnaires, qualitative methods and physiological measures. *Disability and Rehabilitation, 36,* 1652–1660. doi:10.3109/09638288.2013.863393

Gino, F., & Ariely, D. (2012). The dark side of creativity: Original thinkers can be more dishonest. *Journal of Personality and Social Psychology, 102,* 445–459. doi:10.1037/a0026406

Glaser, B. (2012). No preconception: The dictum. *Grounded Theory Review: An International Journal, 11*(2). Retrieved from http://groundedtheoryreview.com

Gliner, J. A., & Morgan, G. A. (2000). *Research methods in applied settings: An integrated approach to design and analysis.* Mahwah, NJ: Erlbaum.

Governors Highway Safety Association. (2016). Distracted driving laws. Retrieved from http://www.ghsa.org/html/stateinfo/laws/cellphone_laws.html

Grieve, R., Witteveen, K., & Tolan, G. A. (2014). Social media as a tool for data collection: Examining equivalence of socially value-laden constructs. *Current Psychology: A Journal for Diverse Perspectives on Diverse Psychological Issues, 33,* 532–544. doi:10.1007/s12144-014-9227-4

Griffiths, M. D. (2005). A "components" model of addiction within a biopsychosocial framework. *Journal of Substance Use, 10,* 191–197. doi:10.1080/14659890500114359

Grodin, M. A., & Annas, G. J. (1996). Legacies of Nuremberg: Medical ethics and human rights. *Journal of the American Medical Association, 276,* 1682–1683.

Gutman, L. M., Sameroff, A. J., & Eccles, J. (2002). The academic achievement of African American students during early adolescence: An examination of multiple risk, promotive, and protective factors. *American Journal of Community Psychology, 30,* 367–399.

Hamilton, J. (2008, October). Think you're multitasking? Think again. *NPR*. Retrieved from http://www.npr .org/templates/story/story.php?storyId=95256794

Harackiewicz, J. M., Canning, E. A., Tibbetts, Y., Giffen, C. J., Blair, S. S., Rouse, D. I., & Hyde, J. S. (2014). Closing the social class achievement gap for first-generation students in undergraduate biology. *Journal of Educational Psychology, 106*, 375–389. doi:10.1037/ a0034679

Helsdingen, A. S., van den Bosch, K., van Gog, T., & van Merriënboer, J. G. (2010). The effects of critical thinking instruction on training complex decision making. *Human Factors, 52*, 537–545. doi:10.1177/0018720810377069

Herbers, J. E., Cutuli, J. J., Lafavor, T. L., Vrieze, D., Leibel, C., Obradovic, J., & Masten, A. S. (2011). Direct and indirect effects of parenting on the academic functioning of young homeless children. *Early Education & Development, 22*, 77–104. doi:10.1080/10409280903507261

Hertwig, R., & Ortmann, A. (2008). Deception in experiments: Revisiting the arguments in its defense. *Ethics and Behavior, 18*, 59–92. doi:10.1080/10508420701712990

Hill, P. L., Burrow, A. L., & Bronk, K. C. (2016). Persevering with positivity and purpose: An examination of purpose commitment and positive affect as predictors of grit. *Journal of Happiness Studies, 17*, 257–269. doi:10.1007/s10902-014-9593-5

Hitsch, G. J., Hortacsu, A., & Ariely, D. (2010). What makes you click? Mate preferences in online dating. *Quantitative Marketing and Economics, 8*, 393–427. doi:10.1007/s11129-010-9088-6

Hock, R. R. (2012). *Forty studies that changed psychology* (7th ed.). Upper Saddle River, NJ: Prentice Hall.

Hockenberry, M. J., & Wilson, D. (2009). *Wong's essentials of pediatric nursing* (8th ed.). St. Louis, MO: Mosby.

Iyenger, S. S., & Lepper, M. R. (2000). When choice is demotivating: Can one desire too much of a good thing? *Journal of Personality and Social Psychology, 79*, 995–1006. doi:10.1037//0022-3514.79.6.995

Joinson, A. N. (1999). Anonymity, disinhibition and social desirability on the Internet. *Behavior Research Methods, Instruments, and Computers, 31*, 433–438.

Karigan, M. (2001). Ethics in clinical research: The nursing perspective. *American Journal of Nursing, 101*, 26–31.

Kazdin, A. E. (2002). *Research design in clinical psychology* (4th ed.). Needham Heights, MA: Allyn & Bacon.

Kelman, H. C. (1967). Human use of human subjects: The problem of deception in social psychological experiments. *Psychological Bulletin, 67*, 1–11.

Kiesler, D. J. (1971). Experimental design in psychotherapy research. In A. E. Bergin & S. L. Garfield (Eds.), *Handbook of psychotherapy and behavior change: An empirical analysis* (pp. 36–74). New York, NY: Wiley.

Kimmel, A. J. (1998). In defense of deception. *American Psychologist, 53*, 803–805.

Kimmel, H. (1957). Three criteria for the use of one-tailed tests. *Psychological Bulletin, 54*, 351–353.

Klauer, S., Guo, F., Simons-Morton, B., Ouimet, M., Lee, S. & Dingus, T. (2013). Distracted driving and risk of road crashes among novice and experienced drivers. *The New England Journal of Medicine, 370*, 54–59. doi:10.1056/NEJMsa1204142

Krantz, J. H. (2011). Can the World Wide Web be used for research? In M. Gernsbacher, R. Pew, & J. Pomerantz (Eds.), *Psychology in the real world: Essays illustrating fundamental contributions to society* (pp. 10–16). New York, NY: Worth.

Kuznekoff, J., & Titsworth, S. (2013). The impact of mobile phone usage on student learning. *Communication Education, 62*, 233–252. http://dx.doi.org/10.1080/03634523.2013.767917

Landau, J. D., Druen, P. B., & Arcuri, J. A. (2002). Methods for helping students avoid plagiarism. *Teaching of Psychology, 29*, 112–115. doi:10.1207/S15328023TOP2902_06

Latane, B., & Darley, J. M. (1968). Group inhibition of bystander intervention in emergencies. *Journal of Personality and Social Psychology, 10*, 215–221. doi:10.1037/h0026570

Levett-Hooper, G., Komarraju, M., Weston, R., & Dollinger, S. (2007). Is plagiarism a forerunner of other deviance? Imagined futures of academically dishonest students. *Ethics and Behavior, 17*, 323–336.

Lewis, M. (2012, September). Obama's way. *Vanity Fair*. Retrieved from http://www.vanityfair.com

Lim, V. K. G., & See, S. K. B. (2001). Attitudes toward, and intentions to report, academic cheating among students in Singapore. *Ethics & Behavior, 11*, 261–274. doi:10.1207/S15327019EB1103_5

Loftus, E. F. (1975). Leading questions and the eyewitness report. *Cognitive Psychology, 7*, 560–772.

Loftus, E. F. (1992). When a lie becomes memory's truth: Memory distortion after exposure to misinformation. *Current Direction in Psychological Science, 1*, 121–123.

Lucas, G. M., Gratch, J., Cheng, L., & Marsella, S. (2015). When the going gets tough. Grit predicts costly perseverance. *Journal of Research in Personality, 59*, 15–22. doi:10.1016/j.jrp.2015.08.004

Lundervold, D. A., & Belwood, M. F. (2000). The best kept secret in counseling: Single-case (*N* – 1) experimental designs. *Journal of Counseling & Development, 78*, 92–102. doi:10.1002/j.1556-6676.2000.tb02565.x

Maddi, S., Erwin, L., Carmody, C., Villarreal, B., White, M., & Gundersen, K. (2013). Relationship of hardiness, grit, and emotional intelligence to internet addiction, excessive consumer spending, and gambling. *The Journal of Positive Psychology, 8*, 128–134. doi:10.1080/17439760.2012.758306

Makel, M., Plucker, J., & Hegarty, B. (2012). Replications in psychology research: How often do they really occur? *Perspectives on Psychological Science, 7*, 537–542. doi:10.1177/1745691612460688

Marck, P., Christopher, A., & Walker, B. (2004). Learning by doing: Research methods with a theme. *Teaching of Psychology, 31*, 128–131.

Masling, J. (1966). Role-related behavior of the subject and psychologist and its effect upon psychological data. In D. Levine (Ed.), *The Nebraska symposium on motivation* (pp. 67–103). Lincoln: University of Nebraska Press.

Mazer, J. P., Murphy, R. E., & Simonds, C. J. (2007). I'll see you on "Facebook": The effects of computer-mediated teacher self-disclosure on student motivation, affective learning, and classroom climate. *Communication Education, 56*, 1–17. doi:10.1080/03634520601009710

McCoy, B. (2016). Digital distractions in the classroom phase II: Student classroom use of digital devices for non-class related purposes. *Journal of Media Education, 7*, 5–32.

McCullough, J. P. (1984). The need for new single-case design structure in applied cognitive psychology. *Psychotherapy: Theory, Research, Practice, Training, 21*, 389–400. doi:10.1037/h0086102

McCullough, M., & Holmberg, M. (2005). Using the Google search engine to detect word-for word plagiarism in master's theses: A preliminary study. *College Student Journal, 39*, 435–441.

McGarva, A., Ramsey, M., & Shear, S. (2006). Effects of driver cell-phone use on driver aggression. *The Journal of Social Psychology, 146*(2), 133–146. doi:10.3200/SOCP.146.2.133–146

Messerli, F. (2012). Chocolate consumption, cognitive function, and Nobel Laureates. *New England Journal of Medicine, 367*, 1562–1564. doi:10.1056/NEJMon1211064

Micceri, T. (1989). The unicorn, the normal curve, and other improbable creatures. *Psychological Bulletin, 105*, 156–166.

Milgram, S. (1963). Behavioral study of obedience. *Journal of Abnormal and Social Psychology, 67*, 371–378.

Mulgrew, K. E., Volcevski-Kostas, D., & Rendell, P. G. (2014). The effect of music video clips on adolescent boys' body image, mood, and schema activation. *Journal of Youth and Adolescence, 43*, 92–103. doi:10.1007/s10964-013-9932-6

Nagel, S. (2001). Development of an academic honesty policy: A case study in collaboration with faculty. *College Student Affairs Journal, 20*, 104–104.

National Center for Statistics and Analysis (2016, April). Distracted driving 2014 (Traffic Safety Facts Research Note. Report No. DOT HS 812 260). Washington, DC: National Highway Traffic Safety Administration. Retrieved from https://crashstats.nhtsa.dot.gov/Api/Public/ViewPublication/812260

Neff, K. D. (2003). The development and validation of a scale to measure self-compassion. *Self and Identity, 2*, 223-250.

Nielsen, T., & Powell, R. A. (2015). Dreams of the Rarebit Fiend: Food and diet as instigators of bizarre and disturbing dreams. *Frontiers in Psychology, 6,* 1–17. doi:10.3389/fpsyg.2015.00047

NORC. (n.d.). *National Longitudinal Survey of Youth NLSY97.* Retrieved from http://nlsy.norc.org/index .html

NPR Staff. (2012, February). The ballad of the tearful: Why some songs make you cry. NPR. Retrieved from http://www.npr.org/2012/02/13/146818461/the-ballad-of-the-tearful-why-some-songs-make-you-cry

Nsiah, G. K. B. (2011). Case studies in U.S. distance education: Implications for Ghana's under-served high schools. *Creative Education, 2,* 346–353.

Oberst, U., Charles, C., & Chamarro, A. (2005). Influence of gender and age in aggressive dream content of Spanish children and adolescents, *Dreaming, 15,* 170–177. doi:10.1037/1053-0797.15.3.170

Olivia, A. M., Salcedo, E., Hellier, J. L., Ly, X., Koka, K., & Tollin, D. J. (2010). Toward a mouse neuroethology in the laboratory environment. *PLoS ONE, 5*(6), e11359. doi:10.1371/journal.pone.0011359

Ornstein, R., & Ehrlich, P. (2000). *New world, new mind: Moving toward conscious evolution* (3rd ed.). Cambridge, MA: Malor Books.

Owens, C., & White, F. A. (2013). A 5-year systemic strategy to reduce plagiarism among first-year psychology university students. *Australian Journal of Psychology, 65,* 14–21. doi:10.1111/ajpy.12055

Parameswaran, A., & Devi, P. (2006). Student plagiarism and faculty responsibility in undergraduate engineering labs. *Higher Education Research & Development, 25,* 263–276. doi:10.1080.0729436060079036

Paulhus, D. L., & Williams, K. M. (2002). The Dark Triad of personality: Narcissism, Machiavellianism, and psychopathy. *Journal of Research in Personality, 36,* 556–563.

Pew Research Center. (n.d.). *Random digit dialing: Our standard method.* Retrieved from http://www .people-press.org/methodology/sampling/random-digit-dialing-our-standard-method/

Pew Research Center. (2015). *Women and leadership: Public says women are equally qualified but barriers persist.* Retrieved from http://www.pewsocialtrends .org/files/2015/01/2015-01-14_women-and-leadership.pdf

Pfungst, O. (1911). *Clever Hans (the horse of Mr. von Osten): A contribution to experimental animal and human psychology* (C. L. Rahn, Trans.). [Project Gutenberge EBook]. Retrieved from http://www .gutenberg.org/

Phillips, M. L. (2011, November). Using social media in your research. *gradPSYCH Magazine,* American Psychological Association. Retrieved from http://www .apa.org/gradpsych/2011/11/social-media.aspx

Pignatiello, M. F., Camp, C. J., & Rasar, L. A. (1986). Musical mood induction: An alternative to the Velten technique. *Journal of Abnormal Psychology, 95,* 295–297. doi:10.1037/0021-843X.95.3.295

Prelow, H. M., & Loukas, A. (2003). The role of resource, protective, and risk factors on academic achievement-related outcomes of economically disadvantaged Latino youth. *Journal of Community Psychology, 31,* 513–529.

Ray, D. C., & Schottelkorb, A. A. (2010). Single-case design: A primer for play therapists. *International Journal of Play Therapy, 19,* 39–53. doi:10.1037/a0017725

Ripley, E. B. D. (2006). A review of paying research participants: It's time to move beyond the ethical debate. *Journal of Empirical Research on Human Research Ethics, 1,* 9–20.

Roig, M. (1997). Can undergraduate students determine whether text has been plagiarized? *Psychological Record, 47,* 113–122.

Roig, M. (2001). Plagiarism and paraphrasing criteria of college and university professors. *Ethics & Behavior, 11,* 307–323. doi:10.1207/S15327019EB1103_8

Rosenthal, R. (1990). How are we doing in soft psychology? *American Psychologist, 45,* 775–777. http://dx.doi .org/10.1037/0003-066X.45.6.775

Rosenthal, R., & Fode, K. (1963). The effect of experimenter bias on performance of the albino rat. *Behavioral Science, 8,* 183–189. doi:10.1002/bs.3830080302

Rosenthal, R., & Jacobson, L. (1963). Teachers' expectancies: Determinants of pupils' IQ gains. *Psychological Reports, 19,* 115–118. doi:10.2466/pr0.1966.19.1.115

Rotter, J. (1966). Generalized expectancies for internal versus external control of reinforcement. *Psychological Monographs General and Applied, 80*, 1–28. doi:10.1037/h0092976

Rutland, J. B., Sheets, T., & Young, T. (2007). Development of a scale to measure problem use of short message service: The SMS Problem Use Diagnostic Questionnaire. *CyberPsychology & Behavior, 10*, 841–843. doi:10.1089/cpb.2007.9943

Sacks, O. (1998). *The man who mistook his wife for a hat, and other clinical tales.* New York, NY: Touchstone.

Saudargas, R. A., & Drummer, L. C. (1996). Single subject (small *N*) research designs and zoo research. *Zoo Biology, 15*, 173–181.

Scanzoni, J. (2005). *Universities as if students mattered: Social science on the creative edge.* New York: Rowman & Littlefield.

Schram, C. (1996). A meta-analysis of gender differences in applied statistics achievement. *Journal of Educational and Behavioral Statistics, 21*, 55–70. doi:10.3102/10769986021001055

Schuetze, P. (2004). Evaluation of a brief homework assignment designed to reduce citation problems. *Teaching of Psychology, 31*, 257–259. doi:10.1207/s15328023top3104_6

Schultz, D. P., & Schultz, S. E. (2008). *A history of modern psychology* (9th ed.). Belmont, CA: Wadsworth.

Schwebel, D. C., Stravinos, D., Byington, K. W., Davis, T., O'Neal, E. E., & de Jong, D. (2012). Distraction and pedestrian safety: How talking on the phone, texting, and listening to music impact crossing the street. *Accident Analysis and Prevention, 25*, 266–271. doi:10.1016/j,aap.2011.07.001

Seligman, M. E. P. (1995). The effectiveness of psychotherapy: The Consumer Reports study. *American Psychologist, 50*, 965–974.

Shapiro, D. A., & Shapiro, D. (1982). Meta-analysis of comparative therapy outcome studies: A replication and refinement. *Psychological Bulletin, 92*, 581–604. doi:10.1037/0033-2909.92.3.581

Simmons, J., Nelson, L., & Simonsohn, U. (2011, October 17). False-positive psychology: Undisclosed flexibility in data collection and analysis allows presenting anything as significant. *Psychological Science.* Online publication. doi:10.1177/0956797611417632

Singer, M. (2013). Client perception of therapy (CPT). In K. Corcoran & J. Fischer (Eds.), *Measures for clinical practice and research: A sourcebook* (5th ed., Vol. 2, p. 163–164). Oxford, England: Oxford University Press.

Skinner, B. F. (1948). *Walden two.* Indianapolis, IN: Hackett.

Skinner, B. F. (1950). Are theories of learning necessary? *Psychological Review, 57*, 193–216. doi:10.1037/h0054367

Smith, M. L., & Glass, G. V. (1977). Meta-analysis of psychotherapy outcome studies. *American Psychologist, 32*, 752–760.

Spiegel, A. (2011, September). How psychology solved a WWII shipwreck mystery. *NPR.* Retrieved from http://www.npr.org/2011/09/27/140816037/how-psychology-solved-a-wwii-shipwreck-mystery

Stavrinos, D., Byington, K. W., & Schwebel, D. C. (2011). Distracted walking: Cell phones increase injury risk for college pedestrians. *Journal of Safety Research, 42*, 101–107. doi:10.1016/j.jsr.2011.01.004

Steering Committee of the Physicians' Health Study Research Group. (1989). Final report on the aspirin component of the Ongoing Physicians' Health Study. *New England Journal of Medicine, 321*, 129–135. doi:10.1056/NEJM198907203210301

Stockett, K. (2009). *The help.* New York, NY: Penguin.

Stones, A., & Perry, D. (1997). Survey questionnaire data on panic attacks gathered using the World Wide Web. *Depression and Anxiety, 6*, 86–87.

Strayer, D., Drews, F., & Johnston, W. (2003). Cell phone-induced failures of visual attention during simulated driving. *Journal of Experimental Psychology: Applied, 9*, 23–32. doi:10.1037/1076-898X9.1.23

Sun, S., Pan, W., & Wang, L. (2010). A comprehensive review of effect size reporting and interpreting practices in academic journals in education and psychology. *Journal of Educational Psychology, 102*, 989–1004. doi:10.1037/a0019507

Tabachnick, B. G., & Fidell, L. S. (1996). *Using multivariate statistics* (3rd ed.). New York, NY: HarperCollins.

Tangney, J., Baumeister, R., & Boone, A. (2004). High self-control predicts good adjustment, less pathology, better grades, and interpersonal success. *Journal of Personality, 72,* 271–322. doi:10.1111/j.0022-3506.2004.00263.x

Teclehaimanot, B., & Hickman, T. (2011). Student-teacher interactions on Facebook: What students find appropriate. *TechTrends, 55*(3), 19–30.

TED (Producer). (2008). *Phil Zimbardo shows how people become monsters . . . or heroes.* Retrieved from http://www.ted.com/talks/lang/eng/philip_zimbardo_on_the_psychology_of_evil.html

Tellis, W. (1997). Introduction to case study. *The Qualitative Report, 3*(2). Retrieved from http://www.nova.edu/ssss/QR/QR3-2/tellis1.html

Trost, K. (2009). Psst, have you ever cheated? A study of academic dishonesty in Sweden. *Assessment & Evaluation in Higher Education, 34,* 367–376. doi:10.1080/02602930801956067

U.S. Census Bureau. (2011). *Statistical quality standards.* Retrieved from http://www.census.gov/quality/standards/

U.S. Department of Health and Human Services. (2009). *Code of federal regulations (45 CFR Part 46).* Retrieved from http://www.hhs.gov/ohrp/policy/ohrpregulations.pdf

U.S. Department of Justice. (1999). *Eyewitness evidence: A guide for law enforcement.* Retrieved from https://www.ncjrs.gov/pdffiles1/nij/178240.pdf

Västfjäll, D. (2011). Emotion induction through music: A review of the musical mood induction procedure. *Musicae Scientia, 15,* 159–173. doi:10.1177/1029864911403367

Verschuren, P. J. M. (2003). Case study as a research strategy: Some ambiguities and opportunities. *International Journal of Social Research Methodology, 6,* 121–139. doi:10.1080/12645570110106154

Vohs, K. D., Baumeister, R. F., Schmeichel, B. J., Twenge, J. M., Nelson, N. M., & Tice, D. M. (2014). Making choices impairs subsequent self-control: A limited-resource account of decision making, self-regulation, and active initiative. *Motivation Science, 1*(S), 19–42. doi:10.1037/2333-8113.1.S.19

Vowell, P. R., & Chen, J. (2004). Predicting academic misconduct: A comparative test of four sociological explanations. *Sociological Inquiry, 74,* 226–249.

Vredeveldt, A., Tredoux, C., Nortje, A., Kempen, K., Puljević, C., & Labuschagne, G. (2015). A field evaluation of the eye-closure interview with witnesses of serious crimes. *Law and Human Behavior, 39,* 189–197. doi:10.1037/lhb0000113

Webb, E., Campbell, D., Schwartz, R., & Sechrest, L. (1966). *Unobtrusive measures: Nonreactive research in the social sciences.* Chicago, IL: Rand McNally.

Wilczynski, S., Mandal, R., & Fusilier, I. (2000). Bridges and barriers in behavioral consultation. *Psychology in the Schools, 37,* 495–504. doi:10.1002/1520-6807

Williams, K., Nathanson, C., & Paulhus, D. (2010). Identifying and profiling scholastic cheaters: Their personality, cognitive ability, and motivation. *Journal of Experimental Psychology: Applied, 16,* 293–307. doi:10.1037/a0020773

Wilson Van Voorhis, C. R., & Morgan, B. L. (2007). Understanding power and rules of thumb for determining sample sizes. *Tutorials in Quantitative Methods for Psychology, 3,* 43–50.

Wood, E., Zivcakova, L., Gentile, P., Archer, K., De Pasquale, D., & Nosko, A. (2012). Examining the impact of off-task multi-tasking with technology on real-time classroom learning. *Computers & Education, 58,* 365–374.

World Medical Association. (2008). *Declaration of Helsinki: Ethical principles for medical research involving human subjects.* Retrieved from http://www.wma.net/en/30publications/10policies/b3/17c.pdf

Yeater, E., Miller, G., Rinehart, J., & Nason, E. (2012, May 22). Trauma and sex surveys meet minimal risk standards: Implications for Institutional Review Boards. *Psychological Science.* doi:10.1177/0956797611435131

Yin, R. K. (2009). *Case study research: Design and methods* (4th ed.). Thousand Oaks, CA: Sage.

Zimbardo, P. (1972). The pathology of imprisonment. *Society, 9,* 4–8.

Zimbardo, P. G. (2004). Does psychology make a significant difference in our lives? *American Psychologist, 59,* 339–351. doi:10.1037/00003-66X.59.5.339

Author Index

Fidler, F., 202
Fisher, C. B., 8
Fitch, G., 228
Fode, K., 300, 482
Frigerio, S., 411
Fritz, C., 20, 200(footnote), 201
Froese, A., 92
Fryberg, D., 8
Fuller, G., 248 (box)
Fusilier, I., 460

George, A. L., 479
Gibson, B., 78
Giffen, Cynthia J., 60 (box)
Gino, F., 269
Glaser, B., 482
Glass, G. V., 25
Gliner, J. A., 275
Gonzalez, M., 78
Governors Highway Safety Association, 13
Gratch, J., 407
Grieve, R., 104, 124
Griffiths, M. D., 84
Grodin, M. A., 3
Guo, F., 228
Gutman, L. M., 401

Hamilton, J., 13
Harackiewicz, J. M., 45–46, 47 (table), 48, 49 (box), 51, 57, 60 (box), 93 (box), 172 (box)
Heaney, R., 92 (box)
Hegarty, B., 88
Helsdingen, A. S., 17
Henderson-Begg, S., 92 (box)
Hennon, E. A., 401
Herbers, J. E., 401, 404, 405, 405 (figure)
Hertwig, R., 8, 9
Hickman, T., 497, 507 (box)
Hill, P. L., 36 (box), 47 (table), 93 (box), 250, 251 (figure), 265
Hitsch, G. J., 110
Hock, R. R., 483
Hockenberry, M. J., 71 (figure)
Holmberg, M., 122 (box), 129
Hooper, S., 401
Hortacsu, A., 110
Hyde, J. S., 60 (box)

Iyenger, S. S., 13

Jacobson, L., 301
Johnston, K. A., 13
Johnston, W., 228, 330 (box)
Joinson, A. N., 104

Kalinowski, P., 202
Karigan, M., 3
Kazdin, A. E., 479, 481, 483, 484, 485, 494
Kelman, H. C., 8
Kempen, K., 92 (box)
Kiesler, D. J., 25
Kimmel, A. J., 9, 188 (footnote)
Klauer, S., 228
Knox, D., 437
Komarraju, M., 87 (box)
Krantz, J. H., 104
Kuznekoff, J., 92, 181 (box), 183 (box), 195–196 (box), 199, 204 (box), 222 (box)

Labuschagne, G., 92 (box)
Lai, J., 202
Landau, J. D., 14, 211, 221 (box)
Latané, B., 299, 483
Lawrence, E. K., 12 (figure), 14, 41 (figure), 47 (table), 102 (figure), 114 (figure), 150 (figure), 157 (figure), 291 (figure), 300 (figure), 304 (box), 418 (figure)
Lepper, M. R., 13
Levett-Hooper, G., 87 (box)
Lewis, M., 13
Lim, V. K. G., 14
Loftus, E. F., 12
Lombardo, M., 411
Lucas, G. M., 407
Loukas, A., 401
Lundervold, D. A., 483

Maass, A., 411
Maddi, S., 229
Makel, M., 88
Mandel, R., 460
Marek, P., 26 (table)
Marsella, S., 407
Martel, B., 78
Masling, J., 298
Mayer, J., 81
Mazer, J. P., 507 (box)
McClafferty, J., 228
McCoy, B., 222 (box)
McCullough, J. P., 483

Subject Index

Constructs:
  in correlational designs, 501
  deciding how to measure, 66–72
  as multidimensional, 73
  and operational definitions, 65–66
  physiological measures, 78
  power and strength of the effect, 198
  in questionnaires, 73–74
  validity and, 83–85
Construct validity, 83, 85, 94, 100, 360
Content validity, 84
Contingency coefficient squared (C^2), 456, 463 (table)
Contingency tables:
  for chi-square test for independence, 452–453,
    452 (table), 455
  Cramer's V squared, 457
  McNemar's test, 589
Contradictions of expectations, 12 (figure)
Contrived versus naturalistic observations, 107–108
Control groups:
  benefits and limits of experimental design and, 303
  defined, 290
  in dependent designs, 375 (box)
  ethical issues with, 294, 300 (figure)
  in intervention research, 374
  multiple, 332–333
  no-alarm, 291
  in quasi-experiments, 304 (box)
  in repeated measures designs, 478
  in simple experiments, 310
  as unfeasible, 291
  as unnecessary, 291 (figure)
Control or manipulation of variables. *See* IV
    manipulation; Manipulation (phase B)
Convenience sampling:
  defined, 123
  as nonprobability sampling, 128 (table)
  questionnaires with, 128 (table)
  steps in, 124 (table)
Convergent validity, 84–85, 87 (box)
Correlation:
  alternate forms reliability and, 80
  assessing reliability using, 78–79
  as average relationship of pairs of scores, 240
  causation and, 18, 23, 230, 307
  ceiling and floor effects and, 233
  computing internal consistency and, 83
  in concurrent validity, 85

  in criterion validity, 85
  critical values for Pearson's, 245 (table)
  defined, 228
  as design versus as statistic, 234
  divergent validity and, 85
  evaluating, 246 (box)
  example scores for calculation of Pearson, 242 (table)
  interrater reliability and, 81
  line of best fit and, 259 (table)
  negative, 235
  positive, 235
  rank-order, 466
  split-half reliability and, 79–80
  strong, 236
Correlational analyses versus correlational designs, 267
Correlational design, 18, 227
  assessment of measurement reliability and validity, 230
  basic, 234–249
  basic statistics for, 234–249
  choosing to use, 498–503
  versus correlational analyses, 267
  defined, 228
  designing powerful, 231–234
  ethical issues in, 228–229
  examining stable traits or characteristics, 229
  increased external validity with, 230
  with independent groups, 307–309
  limitation of, 231
  Pearson's r in, 235–253
  pilot studies, 229
  rationale for, 228–230, 231 (figure)
  regression in, 254–263
  relationship between dichotomous variable and
    interval/ratio variable, 247–249
  relationship between two interval or ratio variables in,
    235–239
  supplementing another design, 229–230
Correlational factorial design, 402
Correlational research, definition of, 18
  See also Correlational design
Correlation coefficients. *See* Pearson's r; Point-biserial
    correlation coefficient (r_{pb}); Squared point-biserial
    correlation (r^2_{pb})
Counterbalancing, 362
  complete, 376–377
  Latin Square, 377
  partial, 377
  randomized partial, 377–378

Declaration of Helsinki, 3
Declining to participate in a study, 7
 See also Attrition/mortality
Default way of thinking, 11, 13
Defining the population. *See* Population
Definitional versus computational formulas, 144
Degrees of freedom (*df*), 215
 critical *f* values for ANOVA with particular probability
  level and, 575–581
 critical *t* values for particular probability level
  and, 571
 in factorial designs, 421–422
 within-subjects ANOVA, 384
Demand characteristics:
 cartoon example of, 300 (figure)
 defined, 298–299
 double-blind experiments and, 301, 312
 single-blind experiments and, 312
Demographic data, 68, 353
Dependent-groups design, 289, 357–367
 analysis of dependent multiple-groups designs,
  378–380
 analysis of dependent two-group designs, 364–367
 choosing to use, 502, 504 (figure), 505 (box)
 confidence intervals, 369–370
 effect size, 370–371
 factorial designs, 428–430
 matched-pairs design, 359–360
 with more than two dependent groups, 376–380
 repeated measures design, 360–364
 selecting analyses and interpreting results for, 392–393,
  394 (table)
 Spearman's rho, 470, 471
Dependent-groups experiments, definition of, 289
 See also Dependent-groups design
Dependent-groups factorial design, 428–430, 503
Dependent-groups one-way ANOVA. *See* Within-
 subjects ANOVA
Dependent multiple-groups design, 364
 analysis of, 378–380
 complete counterbalancing in, 376
Dependent-samples ANOVA, 382, 390
 computational formulas, 587–588
 interpretation, 391 (box), 536
 mean square within groups, 385–386
 post hoc tests, 385
 summary table interpretation, 386 (box)
 terms associated with, 383

Dependent-samples *t* test, 364–367
 data analysis programs for, 372–374, 375 (box)
 formulas and calculations, 367–371
Dependent two-groups design, 364
 procedures, 376
 See also Dependent multiple-groups design
Dependent variables (DV), 19, 282–284
 controlling other extraneous variables and confounds
  and, 289–290
 measures, 295–296, 297–298 (box)
 random assignment and, 283, 286–289
 within-subjects ANOVA, 378–387
Depression study examples, 478, 485
Describing your sample:
 big picture, 172–173
 choosing the appropriate descriptive statistics for,
  145–162, 163 (table)
 comparing interval/ratio scores with *z* scores and
  percentiles in, 167–171, 172 (box)
 descriptive statistics for, 133–145
 ethical issues in, 131–132
 practical issues in, 132–133
 using data analysis programs for, 163–166,
  166–167 (box)
 See also Sample(s)
Descriptive research, 18, 499–500
 archival research, 108–110
 big picture beyond, 129
 choosing to use, 498–503
 cumulative frequency in, 138 (table)
 describing how often a score appears in a sample,
  135–137
 describing samples in, 131–133
 examining a phenomenon in a different population
  using, 98–99
 exploring a phenomenon in depth using, 98
 interviews, 102–104
 measurement methods, 101–110, 111 (table), 112 (box)
 observational research, 104–108
 pilot studies, 100
 questionnaires, 104
 secondary data in, 109–110
 survey research, 101–102
 understanding prevalence and trends using, 97–98
 validity in, 100–101
 when to use, 97–99
Descriptive statistics, 133–145
 central tendency in, 137, 141–142 (table), 164–165

Error, standard. *See* Estimated standard error of the means (SD_x); Standard error of the difference between the means (SD_{x-x}); Standard error of the estimate (s_y); Standard error of the mean difference (SD_D); Standard error of the means (σ_x); Standard error of the skew (*SES*)

Error(s):
  always some probability of, 25
  in hypothesis testing, 191–199, 321–322
  margin of, 120, 202, 206, 218–219
  residual, 260
  See also Type I errors; Type II errors

Error variability:
  in dependent-groups design, 358, 364
  in matched-pairs design, 360
  mean squares and, 382
  in repeated measures design, 363
  uncontrolled, 377

Error variance, 198, 334–335

Estimated standard error of the means (SD_x), 213

Eta squared (η^2), 216–217, 340–341

Ethics:
  anonymity, 10–11
  codes of, 2–4
  confidentiality, 10–11
  of control groups in interventions, 374
  correlational design, 228–229
  critical thinking about, 2–11, 6 (box)
  debriefing, 9
  deception, 7–9
  experiments and, 315
  giving credit to sources and avoiding plagiarism, 56
  guiding the entire research process, 22 (figure)
  informed consent, 5–7, 8 (figure), 111 (box)
  of interpreting correlations, 253
  issues in describing samples, 131–132
  IV manipulation, 293–295
  participation incentives, 10
  principles of, 4–5
  of recruiting participants for an experiment, 287
  reversal designs, 489
  scientific approach and, 11–15
  of using appropriate measures to get meaningful results, 86

Events, probability of, 178–180

Excel, data analysis using, 133, 135
  See also Data analysis programs

Expectancy effects, 482

Expectations, contradictions of, 12 (figure)

Expected frequency (*E*):
  in chi-square goodness of fit, 442–445, 450 (box), 453
  computation of, 448, 454
  defined, 443

Experience or environmental factors as threats to internal validity, 275, 277–278

Experimental factorial design, 402, 408

Experimental groups, 90
  in IV manipulation, 290–291, 294, 408, 528
  waitlist control, 303

Experimental hypothesis (H_a):
  defined, 182
  examples from research literature, 507 (box)
  in rejection of null hypothesis, 186–187
  in simple experiment design practice, 313 (box)

Experimental research, definition of, 19
  See also Experiments/experimental design

Experimenter expectancy effects, 299–301

Experiments/experimental design, 19, 282–284
  basic issues in designing, 285–296, 297–298 (box)
  benefits and limits of, 302–303, 304 (box)
  blind, 299
  choosing to use, 498–503
  controlling other extraneous variables and confounds in, 289–290
  double-blind, 301, 312, 530
  independent-group, 309
  IV manipulation in, 282, 290–295
  quasi-, 19, 281, 304 (box)
  random assignment in, 283, 286–289
  recruiting of participants for, 285–286
  simple, 310–312, 313 (box)
  two-group, 283, 284 (figure), 365

Experts in peer review process, 32

Explanation, 499–500

External validity, 99
  attrition and, 278
  balancing internal and, 91–92, 93 (box), 302, 498–499
  in case studies, 481
  correlational design and, 230
  in correlation study, 233–234
  defined, 54, 89
  defining the population and, 113
  degree of, 91
  in factorial design, 407
  increased, 230, 286 (table)
  in matched-pairs design, 360

exploring a phenomenon in depth, 98

external validity and, 91

multiple dependent-groups design and, 391 (box)

Pearson's r and regression, 266 (box)

scientific investigation as foundation for, 13–14, 25

shape of research and, 55 (figure)

that addresses limitations and expands on results, 53

F values:

for ANOVA with particular probability level, 384 (table), 575–581

critical, 339

degrees of freedom and, 421–422

in matched designs, 360

sampling distribution, 321, 336, 384

See also Analysis of variance (ANOVA)

G_1. See Skewness statistic (G1)

Gaps in past research, 33, 35 (figure)

Gender:

as appropriate statistic, 145–162, 163 (table)

interrater reliability and, 81

modal, 137

population and, 112

practice datasets, 95–96

quota sampling and, 124

stratified random sampling by, 116

as variable, 18, 50

Genetically identical animals, 286, 289

Genovese, Kitty, case study, 482–483

Giving credit. See Citations, APA; Plagiarism

Goodness of fit. See Chi-square goodness of fit

Good research, cornerstones of, 63

constructs and operational definitions as, 65–66

deciding how to measure constructs and, 66–72

reliability and validity as, 64

reliability and validity of measurement as, 64–65

Google Scholar, 43

GPA (grade point average) studies, 42 (box), 85, 117–119 (table), 126 (table), 262–263

Grammatical errors, 548

Grand mean, 419–420

Graphs. See Bar graphs; Frequency polygons; Histograms; Line graphs; Scatterplots

Greenhouse-Geisser test, 388–390

Grit Scale, Short (Grit-S), 76–77, 80

Grounded theory, 482

Group designs:

defined, 278

threats to internal validity in, due to experiences or environmental factors, 279–280

threats to internal validity in, due to participant characteristics, 280–281

types of, 279 (figure)

Group means, 420

H_a. See Alternative hypothesis (H_a)

Hawthorne effect, 298

Help, The, 132

Helsinki Declaration, 3

Heterogeneity, 129, 285, 407

Histograms, 152–153

frequency table, 153 (table), 156 (table), 162 (table)

History as threat to internal validity, 527–528

H_o. See Null hypothesis (H_o)

Holocaust, the, 3

Homogeneity:

parametric statistics and, 439–440

of participants, 311

of samples, 198

of variance, 319, 439–440

Honesty, academic. See Academic honesty

HSD test. See Tukey's Honestly Significant Difference (HSD) test

H test. See Kruskal-Wallis H test

Humanities disciplines, 30, 126 (table)

Human subjects. See Common Rule (for protection of human subjects); Participants

Huynh-Feldt correction, 388

Hybrid factorial design, 402

Hypotheses:

alternative (See Alternative hypothesis (H_a))

development of, 17

directional, 188, 190, 195 (box), 241

interaction, 414

null (See Null hypothesis (H_o))

one-tailed, 187–190

testable, 17

See also Hypothesis testing

Hypothesis testing, 180–191

choosing the appropriate test for, 209–211

errors in, 191–199

null and alternative hypothesis in, 182–187

one- versus two-tailed, 187–190

setting the criterion level in, 190–191

See also Hypotheses; Inferential statistics

Matched-pairs design, 359–360
  issues to consider in, 362 (figure)
  potential problems with, 361 (figure)
Matched random assignment, 289
Maturation as threat to internal validity, 276
Maximum scores, 142, 143 (table)
McNemar's Test, 6, 463, 589
M_D (mean difference), 367–368
Mean (M), 139–140
  cell, 420
  deviation from the, 168, 184
  grand, 419–420
  group, 420
  not calculated for nominal variables, 147
  of skewed distributions, 161 (figure)
Mean, population. *See* Population mean
Mean, sample. *See* Mean (M)
Mean difference (M_D), 367–368
Mean square between groups (MS_B), 338–339
Mean squares (MS) in factorial designs, 422
Mean square within groups (MS_w), 338–339
Measurement:
  assessing reliability of, 78–81
  assessing validity of, 83–85, 86–87 (box), 86 (figure)
  of constructs, deciding on methods of, 66–72
  correlational design and assessment of reliability and
    validity of, 230
  DV, 295–296, 297–298 (box)
  and materials section in research articles, 50–51
  methods, 101–110, 111 (table), 112 (box)
  observational and unobtrusive, 77–78
  physiological, 78–79
  qualitative, 66
  quantitative, 66–67
  reliability, data analysis programs for, 81–83
  reliability and validity at the study level, 88–92,
    93 (box)
  reliability and validity of, 64–65, 100–101
  scales of, 67–72, 106 (box), 147, 235 (box)
  sensitivity, 198
  types of, 73–78
Measures, qualitative. *See* Qualitative measures
Measures, quantitative. *See* Quantitative measures
Measures of central tendency. *See* Central tendency
Median (Mdn), 163 (table)
  calculating central tendency and, 141 (box), 161
  defined, 138–139
  ordinal scale and, 150

of skewed distributions, 161 (figure)
MEDLINE database, 38, 39 (table)
Mesokurtic curve, 154
Meta-analysis, 33, 45
Method section in research articles, 50–52
Minimum scores, 142, 143 (table)
Misleading of participants. *See* Deception
Mixed designs, 430–431
MLA (Modern Language Association), 44
MMPUS (Mobile Phone Problematic Use Scale), 84
Mobile Phone Problematic Use Scale (MPPUS), 84
Modal statistic. *See* Mode
Mode:
  calculating, 164
  defined, 137
  nominal variables and, 148
  in normal distributions, 152
Moderators (factorial design), 404–405, 415–417
Modern Language Association (MLA), 44
Mortality, 276, 280, 527
MS_{AxS}. *See* Interaction mean squares (MS_{AxS})
MS_B. *See* Mean square between groups (MS_B)
MS_B (mean square between groups), 338–339
MS_w (mean square within groups), 338–339
Multiple-baseline across behaviors, 491
Multiple-baseline across persons, 489–491, 492 (figure)
Multiple-baseline across settings, 491
Multiple-baseline designs, 489–491, 492 (figure)
Multiple-group designs, 470–471
Multiple independent-groups design:
  advantages of, 331–333
  defined, 331
Multiple-manipulation designs, 493
Multiple regression (R), 262–263
Multitasking, dangers of, 13
Mu (m) (population mean), 177, 185, 202, 219, 313–315,
  370, 469

Names of authors. *See* Authors
Narrative accounts, 105
Narrowing of database searches, 39
National Archives and Records Administration, 110
National Association of Social Work (NASW), 4 (box)
National Institute of Health (NIH), 109
National Longitudinal Study of Youth, 109
National Science Foundation (NSF), 109
Naturalistic versus contrived observations, 107–108
Nazi Germany, 2–3

Q test. *See* Cochran's Q test
Qualitative measures, 66
Quantitative measures, 66–67
Quasi-experimental factorial design, 402
Quasi-experimental research, 19, 281, 304 (box)
   choosing to use, 498–503
   independent-group, 309
Questionnaires, 73–77, 104
   e-mailed, 102, 116
   examples of different response formats for, 74–75
   mailed, 104
Quota sampling, 124–125
Quotes, direct, 56, 549

r. See Pearson's *r*
R^2. *See* Multiple regression (*R*)
r^2. *See* Linear regression
Random assignment, 283, 286–289
   cluster, 288
   matched, 289
   to order of conditions, 289
   simple, 288
   stratified, 288
Random events and probability theory, 178–180
Randomized partial counterbalancing, 377–378
Random numbers, 115, 117 (table), 118 (table), 288, 567
Random sampling. *See* Cluster sampling; Probability
   sampling; Simple random sampling; Stratified
   random sampling
Random selection, 114–115
   with replacement, 115
   without replacement, 115
Range, 161
   confidence interval and, 120
   convenience sampling and, 124 (table)
   defined, 142
   in Likert-type scale, 71
   in maximum variation sampling, 124
   in nonprobability sampling, 128 (box)
   in normal distribution, 183–184
   variability of scores and, 143
Ranked data:
   Friedman chi-squared and, 471
   nonparametric statistics and, 438, 464–466
Rank-order correlation, 466
Rank Sums test, 468, 469–470, 590
Rare phenomena, 480
Rater reliability. *See* Interrater reliability

Rating scales, 106
   See also Scales of measurement
Ratio variables, 71–72
   comparing *z* scores and percentiles with, 167–171,
      172 (box)
   in correlational research, 235–239
   describing variables measured on, 150–152
   relationship between dichotomous variable and,
      247–249
Reaction time, 105
Recoding, 77, 82–83
Records and documents in archival research, 110
Recruitment of participants, 285–286
Rectangular distributions, 155
References section in research articles, 54
   APA format for, 58–59, 60 (box), 550–552
Region of acceptance, 186, 189 (figure)
Region of rejection, 186, 189 (figure)
Regression, 254–256
   formulas and calculations for simple linear, 256–263
   multiple, 262–263
   using data analysis programs for, 264–265, 266 (box)
Regression equation, 254–256, 259
Rejection regions, 186, 189 (figure)
   See also Hypothesis testing; Statistical significance
      testing
Reliability:
   alternate forms, 80
   assessing measurement, 78–81
   big picture, 94
   broad definition of, 64
   correlational design and assessment of, 230
   data analysis programs for measurement, 81–83
   interrater, 81
   measurement, 64–65, 100–101
   split-half, 79–80
   study, 88–89
   at the study level, 88–92, 93 (box)
   test-retest, 80
Repeated measures ANOVA. *See* Within-subjects
   ANOVA
Repeated measures design, 360–364
Replication, 88
Reporting, results. *See* Research reports
Research design, 97, 497–498
   and basing a study on past research, 498
   big picture beyond description, 129
   choosing a, 498–503